TARGET AGRICULTURE

Mission **Success in All India Agriculture Entrance Examinations**
Useful for **Agriculture and Plant Science Examinations**

Mohammad Mazid

MPhil, PhD (AMU)

Assistant Professor
Department of Agriculture Sciences
Asim Siddique Memorial Degree College
affiliated to MJP Rohilkhand University, Bareilly, UP
Meera Sarai, Sheikhupur Road, Budaun, UP

CBS Publishers & Distributors Pvt Ltd

New Delhi • Bengaluru • Chennai • Kochi • Kolkata • Mumbai
Hyderabad • Nagpur • Patna • Pune • Vijayawada

Target Agriculture

ISBN: 978-93-85915-58-1

Copyright © Author and Publisher

First Edition: 2016

Published by Satish Kumar Jain and produced by Varun Jain for

CBS Publishers & Distributors Pvt Ltd

4819/XI Prahlad Street, 24 Ansari Road, Daryaganj, New Delhi 110 002, India.

Ph: 23289259, 23266861, 23266867

Fax: 011-23243014

Website: www.cbspd.com

e-mail: delhi@cbspd.com; cbspubs@airtelmail.in.

Corporate Office: 204 FIE, Industrial Area, Patparganj, Delhi 110 092

Ph: 4934 4934   Fax: 4934 4935   e-mail: publishing@cbspd.com; publicity@cbspd.com

Branches

- **Bengaluru:** Seema House 2975, 17th Cross, K.R. Road, Banasankari 2nd Stage, Bengaluru 560 070, Karnataka
  Ph: +91-80-26771678/79   Fax: +91-80-26771680   e-mail: bangalore@cbspd.com
- **Chennai:** 7, Subbaraya Street, Shenoy Nagar, Chennai 600 030, Tamil Nadu
  Ph: +91-44-26680620, 26681266   Fax: +91-44-42032115   e-mail: chennai@cbspd.com
- **Kochi:** Ashana House, No. 39/1904, AM Thomas Road, Valanjambalam, Ernakulam 682 018, Kochi, Kerala
  Ph: +91-484-4059061-62-64-65   Fax: +91-484-4059065   e-mail: kochi@cbspd.com
- **Kolkata:** 6/B, Ground Floor, Rameswar Shaw Road, Kolkata-700 014, West Bengal
  Ph: +91-33-22891126, 22891127, 22891128   e-mail: kolkata@cbspd.com
- **Mumbai:** 83-C, Dr E Moses Road, Worli, Mumbai-400018, Maharashtra
  Ph: +91-22-24902340/41   Fax: +91-22-24902342   e-mail: mumbai@cbspd.com

Representatives

- **Hyderabad** 0-9885175004
- **Nagpur** 0-9021734563
- **Patna** 0-9334159340
- **Pune** 0-9623451994
- **Vijayawada** 0-9000660880

Printed at: Swastik Packagings , 506 F.I.E., Patparganj, Delhi - 92

to
my everloving
parents

Foreword

Since Independence, food economy of India has gone through an absolute cycle starting with food shortages via comfortable food self-sufficiency and back again to the possibility of food anxiety situation. Agriculture sector is witnessing a serious problem of stagnating or even declining crop productivity.

This is the first edition of the book *Target Agriculture* covering different topics of agriculture, with presentation of suitable illustrations from India. The interpretation of subject matter in each chapter of this book has also been made carefully and systematically by the author giving much more emphasis on the requirements at the university level agricultural education in India and abroad. This book is a comprehensive one and will meet the growing needs for agricultural students.

I hope and believe that this book by Dr Mohammad Mazid would be of a great value for the students of agriculture. In addition, this will also be useful to the teaching community at large.

Khalil Khan
Scientist (soil science)
KVK, Jalaun, CSAUA&T, Kanpur

Preface

After 1947, that is, in Independent India, a number of sincere attempts has been made to improve and enhance the agriculture productivity as well as the future of agriculturists. During the recent past, Indian agriculture has faced tremendous and drastic challenges in order to enhance national demand of food grains and various agriculture associates for allied sectors. To secure better agriculture productivity, Government of India (GoI) launched a number of United Nations based programs to increase agriculture productivity and alleviate poverty, especially in rural India. All of these have produced enormous opportunities for agriculture professionals in teaching, research, extension, marketing, industries and global financial institutions. The United States of America, Food and Agriculture Organiszation (FAO) of United Nations, different international organizations, institutions and agencies have jointly played a significant role in the empowerment of Indian agriculture.

During the mid-60s, the evolution of high-yielding cultivars of rice and wheat evolved a new era of agriculture as *Green Revolution* — a situation for global grain problem and thus provide the sustainability of self-sufficiency for foodgrains. Human welfare, proper nutrition, conservation of food and allied resources for global prosperity, proper maintenance and management of nature and national resources, precision farming, etc. are a few basic priority areas of work of the government. The dream of green revolution was fulfilled in the mid-60s with the advent of high yielding varieties and improved production technology, which has brought a spectacular change in the existing cropping systems in various agroclimatic zones of the country. The Indian farmers have shown a surprising dynamism, adoptability and progressiveness in accepting recent crops production technology and predominant subsistence farming is being changed into enthusiastic enterprises, however, it lacks perfection.

Council of Scientific and Industrial Research (CSIR) and Indian Council of Agricultural Research (ICAR) are two bodies which govern all these plans under the government policies. Therefore, excellent human resources have been the prime needs for aforesaid organizations like ICAR and CSIR. Both these organizations are conducting national-level examinations annually and half-yearly to provide eligibility for lecturership [National Eligibility Test (NET)] in all Indian universities, JRF (Junior Research Fellowship), SRF (Senior Research Fellowship), etc. Moreover, both these organizations also recruit agriculture experts through Agricultural Scientist Recruitment Board. Furthermore, a number of entrance examinations for ARS (Agriculture Research Scientists) at postgraduate level, PhD courses in state-based agricultural universities. Besides this, Agricultural Developmental Services (RAEO, SADO and ADA). The state boards also conduct competitive examinations for selection of suitable candidates. All these examinations are mostly based on objective questions (MCQs). MCQs constitute an important method of objective assessment of an examiner's knowledge. Students have to refer to various books, monographs and periodicals to collect the information for various courses offered in the field of all aspects of practical agriculture. The present book is written to satisfy the requirements of the candidates preparing for various entrance examinations in the field of agriculture.

The main aim of this book is to provide materials which will help the graduate and postgraduate students of agriculture to easily and quickly grasp the comprehensively.

> *... to achieve success in your mission, you must have single-minded devotion to your goal.*

Mohammad Mazid

Acknowledgments

The first and foremost I praise and acknowledge Allah, the most beneficent and the most merciful, the great artisan, the sustainer, the omnipresent, the creator of this universe, who showered His benevolence on me and provided me the strength that made this book crusade possible. Secondly, my humblest gratitude to the Holy Prophet Muhammad (peace be upon Him) whose way of life has been a continuous guidance for me.

It is a great privilege to express my profound regard and deep sense of gratitude to my generous and most sympathetic research supervisor, Chairman and Section Head of Crop Physiology and Biochemistry Division, Aligarh Muslim University (AMU), Aligarh, for his meticulous suggestions, constructive criticism, candor discussion and ebullient encouragement throughout the accomplishment of this book. I have a great pleasure in expressing my sense of gratitude to him who has been very liberal in giving me his most valuable attention. He has suggested to me many new lines of social and moral studies and gave me invaluable guidance on a large number of complex problems and helped me to overcome my weaknesses.

Thanks are due to the Chairman for his best cooperation. Thanks are also due to Assistant Professor Abdul Quadeer for encouragement that I received from him.

I shall remain indebted to all my students of BSc, especially Musabber Ali, Raof Ali, Nausad Choudhury, Sohail Choudhury.

I express my heartfelt gratitude to Dr Khalil Khan (KVK, CAUAT, Kanpur) and Prof LN Sharma (former Vice-Principal, GPG College, Bisalpur, Pilibhit) who encouraged me from time to time during the preparation of this book.

I also acknowledge with thanks the assistance given by Dr Taqi A Khan, Iftekar Ahmed, Ms Gulnaz Sabri, Shaeryar Khan, Saima Quddusi, Miss Fiza Khan, and Ms Norris Naqvi from time to time.

I also owe thanks to my uncle and my younger brothers for their motivation and encouragement during my whole academic period. They have been a source of strong moral support throughout.

I wish to express my heartfelt gratitude to all of them for their dedication and forbearance without which this work would have not existed.

Last but not the least, I am thankful to the Mr DK Saxena, Head, Division of Environmental Science, Bareilly (UP), for support, motivation and encouragement.

Mohammad Mazid

Contents

1

Fundamentals of Agricultural Meteorology

1. **Areas with highest rice production showing**
   a. **Canal irrigated land**
   b. Bright sunny days during and after anthesis
   c. High rainfall
   d. All of the above

2. **As per principle of crop rotation pulses should be included in rotation because**
   a. **They helpful in maintenance of soil fertility**
   b. They are short duration crop
   c. They enhance total pulse production
   d. They enhance the resultant yield of next crop

3. **The usual alternative crop for jute producing areas**
   a. **Rice**   b. Corn
   c. Groundnut   d. Sunflower

4. **Pulses fit well in cropping systems as they are**
   a. **Protein yielding crops**
   b. N-fixing crops
   c. Short duration crops
   d. Insect resistant crops

5. **Mixed cropping is most suitable and maximum dynamic in**
   a. Irrigated conditions
   b. Large holding conditions
   c. Maximum soil fertility conditions
   d. **Area with water scarcity**

6. **Features responsible for low quality of jute are**
   a. Low cellulose content and minimum cell wall strength
   b. **Low fibre strands and discoloration of fibres**
   c. Low fibre strands and low cellulose content
   d. Minimum cell wall strength and low cellulose content

7. **What type of culture gained priority for groundnut cultivation?**
   a. Azotobacter   b. Azospirilla
   c. Mycorrhiza   **d. Rhizobia**

8. **'GUANO' is characterized by presence of**
   a. Low sulphur content
   b. Low phosphorus content
   c. **High phosphorus content**
   d. High calcium content

9. **Addition of soluble phosphatic fertilizers affect plant growth by**
   a. **Reducing the zinc**
   b. Precipitating the Fe and Al compounds
   c. Inhibiting the development of micro-organisms
   d. Minimizing the availability of calcium

10. **Least hygroscopic fertilizer is**
    a. **DAP**
    b. NH_2CONH_2
    c. $NH_4 (SO_4)$
    d. $Ca (NH_4) .NO_3$

11. Sandy loam is best suited for cultivation of
    a. Vegetables
    b. Fibre yielding crops
    c. Oil yielding crops
    d. Pulses

12. Which one of the following micro-organisms causes highest degree of nutrient cycling in soil?
    a. Algae   b. BGA
    c. Actinomycetes **d. Bacteria**

13. In pedology soil is
    a. A medium for growth
    b. A purely synthesized body
    c. A rock powdered mass
    d. A natural mass

14. A product of cross between the wheat and rye is known as
    a. Triticale   b. Napur
    c. Coore
    d. None of the them

15. Which one of pair of pulse crop responsible for 75% pulse production in our country?
    a. Gram and pigeonpea
    b. Pigeonpea and moonbean
    c. Moongbean and Gram
    d. Pigeonpea and moongbean

16. A least hygroscopic fertilizer is
    a. DAP
    b. Ammonium sulphate
    c. Calcium ammonium nitrate
    d. Urea

17. Potassium nitrate is a strong agent for breaking of
    a. Dormancy   b. Abscission
    c. Both a and b
    d. Nitrogen use efficiency

18. 'Dee-geo-woo-gen' is another name of rice variety
    a. IR-36   **b. IR-8**
    c. Punjab-1   d. Tilak

19. The main objective of growing inter-crops with main fruit crop is
    a. To get additional income
    b. To check soil erosion
    c. To improve soil fertility
    d. To get greater productivity of fruit crop

20. Puppet show in villages as a method for transfer of technology is an example of
    a. Mass media   **b. Group media**
    c. Individual media
    d. Tribal media

21. Which one of the following group of crop is best for water scarcity areas?
    a. Sesame, maize, oats
    b. Sorghum, wheat
    c. Seasame, sorghum/pearl millet, niger
    d. Maize, upland rice, berseem

22. Mustard can be suitably grown as a mixed crop with
    a. Rice   **b. Wheat**
    c. Maize   d. Barley

23. *Imperata cylindrica*, a dicot weed is associated with
    a. Members of Poaceae
    b. Tea
    c. Sugar beet   d. Lentil

24. The aim of inter-row tillage is
    a. Improved soil granulation
    b. Improved soil aeration
    c. Improved soil conservation
    d. Improved moisture conservation by soil mulching

25. DAPOG method of crop raising is concerned with
    a. Nursery raising
    b. Intercultivation
    c. Seed bed preparation
    d. Inter culture operation

26. Ratooning is a agriculture practice applied in
    a. Sugarcane only
    b. Maize and sugarcane

c. Sugerbeet and sugarcane
d. **Sugarcane and Napier grass**

27. Groundnut preferred in areas which receiving late rains in the *Kharif* season because
   a. Seeds are bold
   b. More water needed
   c. **Need longer duration**
   d. Seeds are dormant

28. Which part of tobacco needed for extraction of drug, nicotine?
   a. **Root**
   b. Stem
   c. Leaf
   d. Branch

29. Organic manure with the lowest C/N ratio is
   a. **Ground-nut cake**
   b. FYM
   c. Biogas slurry
   d. Compost

30. Apatite is a group of minerals which mainly contains
   a. **P**
   b. S
   c. N
   d. Sn

31. The soil layer of highest leaching is indicated by the symbol
   a. A_1
   b. **A_2**
   c. B_1
   d. B_2

32. The horizons which make up the profile of a forest soil would include
   a. A, B and O
   b. B and O
   c. A, C and O
   d. **A, B, C and O**

33. Mo is important in plants because it is a co-factor for
   a. **N-fixing enzymes**
   b. Phosphatase
   c. Cytochrome oxidase
   d. Element of ETC

34. Role of zinc sulphate in rice cultivation is
   a. **Controlling the Khaira disease**
   b. Improve fertility
   c. Both a and b
   d. None

35. Maximum cropped area in India is covered by rice because
   a. Adequate rainfall
   b. Can be grown in different season
   c. Adoptable for maximum agroclimatic regions
   d. Most population is rice eating

36. National Weed Research Institute is located at
   a. **Jabalpur, MP**
   b. Bhopal
   c. New Delhi
   d. Orissa

37. The basis of classification of igneous rocks is
   a. **Silic acid**
   b. Acetic acid
   c. Sn
   d. All

38. Concept of IPNS (Integrated Plant Nutrient System) is proposed by
   a. **FAO**
   b. WHO
   c. UN
   d. NAWARD

39. In which of the following is a method of irrigation?
   a. Border strip
   b. Center pivot
   c. Check-basin and corrugation
   d. **All**

40. Lambert's law is
   a. Light absorbed by homogenous transparent media is proportional to thickness of media
   b. Light absorbed by homogenous transparent media is proportional to intensity of light
   c. **Both**
   d. Light absorbed by homogenous transparent media is proportional to wavelength of light

41. Localized placement of fertilizer is
   a. Fertilizer application to soil close to seed or plant
   b. Specifically adopted with P-fertilizers
   c. **Both**
   d. None

42. Nitrification is
a. Formation of nitrates from ammonia
b. Formation of nitrites from ammonia
c. Process occurs in soil by microorganisms
d. All

43. Organic farming is
a. Production of system avoids excludes use of artificial fertilizers, pesticides, PGRs, livestocks feed additives
b. Relay upon crop rotations, crop residues, animal manures, legumes, green manures, off-farm organic waste, mechanical cultivation, mineral bearing rocks, biological pest control
c. Both
d. None

44. Plant tissue test is
a. Qualitative   b. Quantitative
c. Both   d. Hypothetical

45. Basis of plant tissue test is
a. Colorimetric determination
b. Photometric determination
c. Spectrometric determination
d. All

46. What is salt index (SI)?
a. One of the criteria for evaluating the quality of irrigation water
b. One of the criteria for estimation the flow of water in field
c. Both
d. None

47. Secondary plant nutrients (not directly applied) are
a. Ca   b. Mg
c. S   **d. All**

48. Primary plant fertilizers (directly applied) are
a. N   b. P
c. K   **d. All**

49. SAR is
a. Sodium absorption ratio
b. Soil absorption ratio

c. Salinity absorption ratio
d. All

50. Match column A (soil type) and column B (temperature range)

Col. A	Col. B
i. Frigid soil	A. 8–15°C
ii. Mesic soil	B. More than 8°C
iii. Thermic soil	C. 15–22°C
iv. Hyperthermic soil	D. More than 22°C

a. i. B, ii. A, iii. C, iv. D
b. i. B, ii. D, iii. C, iv. A
c. i. B, ii. C, iii. A, iv. D
d. i. D, ii. A, iii. C, iv. B

51. Soil water potential is
a. Measure of difference between free energy state of soil water and that of pure water
b. Measure of difference between free energy state of pure water and that of soil water
c. Both   d. None

52. Soil water potential consists of
a. Matric potential
b. Osmotic potential
c. Gravitational potential
d. All

53. Sustainable agriculture according to CGIAR is
a. Successful management of resources to satisfy the changing needs
b. Successful management of soil and water to satisfy the changing needs
c. Successful management of man-made resources to satisfy the changing needs
d. Successful management of soil and forest to satisfy the changing needs

54. Capacity of a system to maintain interregional balance and increase the flow of its products and services through linkages with various other systems without damaging its own long-term potential is termed as
a. Sustainable system
b. Efficient system

c. Productive system

d. None

55. **Which one of the following is true about Anabaena?**

    a. Principal algal community

    b. A blue-green algae

    c. Association with coralloid roots of cycas

    d. **All**

56. **CIMMYT is**

    a. **International Crop Research Institute**

    b. National Crop Research Institute

    c. International Institute of Vegetables Yield and Training

    d. All

57. **CIMMYT in Mexico deals with two crops which are widely grown in India**

    a. **Maize and wheat**

    b. Wheat and rice

    c. Rice and maize

    d. Maize and jowar

58. **Name of the fertilizer occupies first position in India is**

    a. **Urea**   b. DAP

    c. Ammonium sulphate

    d. Calcium ammonium nitrate

59. **Which one of the following forms of potassium present in soil would one test for evaluate the fertility of soil?**

    a. Total K

    b. Water soluble K

    c. K held in the silt

    d. **Exchangeable K**

60. **Match the column A and column B**

Col. A (Classes of fertilizers)	Col. B (Example of different classes)
A. Organic fertilizer	i. Urea
B. Inorganic fertilizer	ii. Isobutylidene diurea
C. Biofertilizers	iii. Ammonium sulphate
D. S RF	iv. 2-chloro-6-pyridine

a. **A-i, B-iii, C-iv, D-ii**

b. A-i, B-ii, C-iv, D-iii

c. A-i, B-iv, C-iii, D-ii

d. A-i, B-iv, C-iv, D-ii

61. **The ill effects of submergence of roots of deciduous fruit plants in water for very long time, is due to primarily to**

    a. Deficiency of nutrients

    b. **Lack of aeration**

    c. Poor absorption

    d. Excess of moisture

62. **In relation to crop rotation which one of the following is odd one?**

    a. Heavy feeders should be followed by low feeders

    b. **Deep rooted crops should be followed by same type of crop**

    c. Legumes may be followed by non-legumes crops

    d. Vegetables area susceptible to a particular pest should be followed by resistant crops

63. **The optimum cardinal temperature points for germination of rice seeds are**

    a. **30–32°C**   b. 37–39°C

    c. 40–45°C   d. 30–45°C

64. **Match the following in both columns**

Col. A	Col. B
A. Humus	i. Insoluble in dilute acid
B. Humic acid	ii. High molecular weight
C. Fulvic acid	iii. Insoluble in dilute alkali
D. Humin	iv. Lignoprotein complex

a. **A-i, B-ii, D-iii**   b. A-ii, B-i, D-iii

c. A-iii, B-ii, C-i   d. None

65. **Match the list A (micronutrient) and list B (typical deficiency symptoms)**

List A	List B
A. Mn	i. Reclamation disease of cereals
B. Mo	ii. White bud of maize

C. Zn iii. Speckled yellow of sugar beet
D. Cu iv. Whiptail in cauliflower
   a. A-i, B-ii, C-iv, D-iii
   b. A-iii, B-ii, C-iv, D-i
   c. A-i, B-ii, C-iv, D-iii
   d. A-ii, B-i, C-iv, D-ii

66. **Contribution of Indian agriculture to livelihood**
   a. 65%   b. 49%
   c. 70%   d. 54%

67. **The growth target for agriculture in 12th Five-Year Plan**
   a. 4%   b. 36%
   c. 51%   d. 2%

68. **Share of agriculture and allied sectors to the National GDP (2011–12)**
   a. 8%   **b. 14%**
   c. 32%   d. 12%

69. **Highest exported product of india**
   a. Mango   b. Banana
   c. Grapes   d. Orange

70. **Crop having highest acreage in india**
   a. Sorghum > wheat > maize > rice
   b. Rice > wheat > maize > sorghum
   c. Wheat > maize > rice > sorghum
   d. Sorghum > maize > wheat > rice

71. **Crop having highest grass cropped irrigation area**
   a. Rice   b. Maize
   c. Sugarcane   **d. Wheat**

72. **Leading state in production of sugarcane in India**
   a. Maharashtra > Punjab > UP
   b. MP > TN > UP
   c. UP > Maharashtra > TN
   d. TN > Maharashtra > UP

73. **Leading state in fruits crop production in India**
   a. AP > MH > TN
   b. TN > MH > AP
   c. AP > TN > MH
   d. MH > TN > AP

74. **Contribution of India agriculture to livelihood**
   a. 70%   b. 80%
   c. 65%   d. 60%

75. **The growth target for agriculture in 12th Five-Year Plan**
   a. 5%   b. 6%
   c. 8%   **d. 4%**

76. **Share of agriculture and allied sectors to the National GDP (2011–12)**
   a. 15%   b. 16%
   c. 14.1%   d. 15.5

77. **Leading fruits in area in India (2009–2010)**
   a. Mango > citrus > banana
   b. Guava > sapota > mango
   c. Banana > sapota > mango
   d. Apple > sapota > mango

78. **Translocation of water and nutrients from roots to above ground parts of plants takes place through**
   a. Phloem   b. Roots
   c. Xylem   d. Shoots

79. **Proteins are made up of**
   a. Humic acids   **b. Amino acids**
   c. Mn   d. Zn

80. **Apical bud dominance is caused by which hormone?**
   a. GA3   b. ABA
   c. Auxin   d. 2,4-D

81. **Central Soil Salinity Research Institute is situated at**
   a. Karnal
   b. Haryana
   c. UP
   d. MP

82. **Agroclimate regional planning was initiated in India, the inception**
   a. First Five-Year Plan
   b. Grow more food campaign
   c. In late eighties
   d. The seventh Five-Year Plan

83. **Biofertilizer is a**
    a. Mixture of organic manure and micro-organism
    a. Decomposed compost enriched with minerals solubilising bacteria
    c. **Culture having the desired strain of microorganism**
    d. Mixture of inorganic fertilizer and microorganism

84. **Which one of the following minerals in the main source of boron in soil?**
    a. Haematite   b. Pyrolusites
    c. **Tourmaline**   d. Hemimorphite

85. **Organic matter content of 'histosols' and 'hydromorphic' soil is**
    a. 30–40%   b. 60–70%
    c. 50–57%   d. **2–18%**

86. **The phosphorus content as P in plough layer of one hectare of soil containing 0.1% P_2O_5 is**
    a. 430 kg   b. 1500 kg
    c. **860 kg**   d. 1290 kg

87. **Which of the following pairs is correctly matched?**

Fertilizer	Nutrient
a. Urea	42.0 (% N)
b. Diammonium phosphate	20.0% (% P)
c. **Ammonium sulphate**	**21.5 (% N)**
d. Muriate of potash	47.5 (% K)

88. **The nitrogenous fertilizer of choice for tea is**
    a. Calcium ammonium nitrate
    b. Urea
    c. Ammonium sulphate
    d. **Ammonium nitrate**

89. **In a compost pit the heat of combustion of organic matter raises the temperature when decay is rapidly, during decay the temperature rises by**
    a. 75–90°C   b. **60–80°C**
    c. 5–72°C   d. 40–60°C

90. **Which of the following pairs of Rhizobium spp. and the host genera on which**

the Rhizobium spp. are correctly matched?

1. *R. leguminosorum* ....Pisum
2. *R. japonicum*.....................Glycine
3. *R. meliloti*...................... Medicago

Select the correct answer using the codes given below:
    a. 1, 2 and 3   b. 1 and 2
    c. 1 and 3   d. **2 and 3**

91. **Which of the following pairs is correctly matched?**

Fertilizer	Nutrient content
a. Urea	42.0 (% N)
b. **DAP**	**20.0 (% N)**
c. Ammonium sulphate	21.5 (% K)
d. MOP	47.5 (% K)

92. **Transport of phosphate from the cytosol (Ph about 7.0) into vacuoles pH nearly (5.5) involves**
    a. (H_2SO_4) alone
    b. $(HPO_4)^{2-}$ alone
    c. $(PO\$)^{3-}$ alone
    d. **$(H_2PO_4)^-$ and $(HPO_4)^{2-}$**

93. **Diminished carbohydrate status of the plant placed under high nitrogen supply is due to**
    a. **Lower photosynthetic activity**
    b. Vigorous protein synthesis
    c. Increased transplantation ratio
    d. Increased vegetation growth

94. **Consider the following symptoms**
    1. Younger leaves show signs of deficiency first
    2. High amide and nitrogen
    3. Effect more pronounced on shoots when compared to roots and cruciferous plants develop narrow leaf lamina
    4. Blockage of the synthesis of cystine, methionine, etc. Development of the above mentioned symptoms is attributable to the deficiency of:
    a. Calcium   b. Magnesium
    c. Nitrogen   d. **Sulphur**

95. Match list 1 (symptoms) with list 2 (causes) and select the correct answer using the codes given below the lists

List 1	List 2
A. Khaira disease	1. Phosphorus deficiency
B. Browning of cauliflower	2. Molybdenum deficiency
C. Purple coloura-tion of maize	3. Leaves potassium deficiency
D. Firing of tobacco leaves	4. Zinc deficiency

Codes:
a. A-2, B-4, C-3, D-1
b. A-2, B-4, C-3, D-1
c. A-4, B-2, C-3, D-1
d. **A-4, B-2, C-1, D-3**

96. While working as an extension specialist in a village, one finds that the package of practices is not being followed despite the best communication methods, one had employed for the purpose one finds the following reasons for non-adaptability
   1. 60% are laggards.
   2. 20% innovations but orthodox
   3. 20% are old and orthodox
   The best remedial measure would be to:
   a. Adopt 1 and 3
   b. Adopt 2 alone
   c. Avoid 3
   d. **Adopt 2 and make them team leaders**

97. Consider the following institution
   1. Zila Ghaziabad
   2. Gram panchayat
   3. Village school
   4. Village co-operations
   a. 1, 2, 3   b. 2 and 4
   c. **2, 3 and 4**   d. 1, 3 and 4

98. The latest botanical name 'greengram' is
   a. *Vigna radiata* **(L) Wilezek**
   b. *Vigna munga* (L) Kepper
   c. *Phaseolus munga* (L)
   d. *Phaseolus vulgaris* (L)

99. Consider the following statement
   1. Control weeds
   2. Reduce rate of infiltration
   3. Improve soil structure
   4. Increase aeration of these statements
   a. 1, 2, 3 and 4 are correct
   b. 2 and 4 are correct
   c. 1 and 2 are correct
   d. **1, 3 and 4 are correct**

100. Match list I (crop) with list II (optimum time of sowing in North India) and select the correct answer using the codes given below the lists

List I	List II
i. Cotton	1. First fortnight of November
ii. Barley	2. Second fortnight of October
iii. Gram	3. Whole of the month of May
iv. Groundnut	4. First fortnight of July

Codes:
a. A-3, B-1, C-4, D-2
b. A-3, B-1, C-2, D-4
c. A-1, B-3, C-2, D-4
d. **A-1, B-3, C-4, D-2**

101. Which one of the following irrigation methods is best suited for an undulating topography?
   a. Flow irrigation
   b. Check basin method
   c. **Sprinkler irrigation**
   d. Furrow irrigation

102. Which one of the following minerals is least weatherable in soil?
   a. Olivine   b. Basalt
   c. **Quartz**   d. Biotit

103. A high yielding semi-dwarf variety of rice was first developed at
   a. CRRI, Cuttack
   b. IARI, New Delhi
   c. ICRISAT, Hyderabad
   d. **IRRI, Manila**

104. The fruits of research and development findings could reach the poorest of the poor through
    a. Research personnel themselves
    b. NGOs
    c. **A strong and devoted extension agency**
    d. Agricultural universities and colleges

105. For providing inputs like quality seeds, fertilizers and pesticides, the agency that is present at the village panchayat samiti level is
    a. NABARD
    b. Nationalized banks
    c. **Cooperative society**
    d. Insurance companies

106. At present, the farming system of India has become
    a. Export oriented
    b. Technology oriented
    c. **Market oriented**
    d. Domestic need oriented

107. Which one of the following species belongs to pop maize?
    a. **Everta**
    b. Amylacea
    c. Indurata
    d. Ceratina

108. Which one of the following triazines is preferred in dryland maize?
    a. Simazine
    b. **Atrazine**
    c. Metribuzin
    d. All

109. The 'India farming' is published from
    a. ICAR
    b. **IARI**
    c. CAZRI
    d. ICRISAT

110. The popular variety, Ganga Safed-2 of maize is a
    a. Single cross hybrid
    b. Double cross hybrid
    c. 3-way cross hybrid
    d. **Double top cross hybrid**

111. The main purpose of T and V programme is to
    a. Identify research problems
    b. Bring about coordination in the administration of agricultural extension

    c. Update the technical knowledge and skills of agricultural extension workers
    d. Help farmers in the adoption of latest innovation in agriculture

112. Deficiency symptoms of calcium on plants are first noticed at
    a. Lower leaves
    b. Middle
    c. **Terminal leaves**
    d. All leaves

113. Highest number of sugar mills in India is located in
    a. Maharastra
    b. Tamil Nadu
    c. **Utter Pradesh**
    d. Bihar

114. The term 'extension' was first used by
    a. **America**
    b. England
    c. India
    d. Japan

115. Cultivation of hybrid rice is most popular in
    a. Japan
    b. Korea
    c. **China**
    d. India

116. International Crop Research Institute for semi-arid tropics is situated at
    a. Jodhpur
    b. Bharatpur
    c. **Hyderabad**
    d. Colombo

117. The translocation of sugars from source to sink takes place through
    a. **Sieve tubes of the phloem**
    b. Companion cells
    c. Xylem vessels
    d. Medullary rays

118. The secondary plant element is
    a. Nitrogen
    b. **Calcium**
    c. Zinc
    d. Boron

119. Pungency in mustard oil is caused by
    a. Amino acid
    b. Erusic acid
    c. **Glucosilates**
    d. None of these

120. Seed viability is tasted by use of
    a. Bromide
    b. Iodide
    c. Chloride
    d. **None of these**

121. The weight of a half mole of water is
    a. 0.5 gram
    b. 1.0 gram
    c. **9.0 gram**
    d. 18.0 gram

122. The core metal in chlorophyll is
    a. Fe
    b. **Mg**
    c. Mn
    d. Zn

123. Phosphorus is taken by plants in the form of
    a. Phosphorus chloride
    b. **Phosphorus acid**
    c. Phosphorus sulphite
    d. Phosphorus carbonates

124. The Food Corporation of India was established in
    a. 1960
    b. **1965**
    c. 1962
    d. 1967

125. Which gas is released from paddy field?
    a. **CH_4**
    b. NH_3
    c. CO_2
    d. H_2S

126. Chemical which regulates opening and closing of stomata is
    a. **PMA**
    b. 2, 4-D
    c. Paraquat
    d. Kaoline

127. VA micorrhiza promotes mainly the plant uptake of
    a. Nitrogen
    b. **Phosphorus**
    c. Molybdenum
    d. Potassium

128. Where one buyer and large seller the market condition is
    a. **Oligopoly**
    b. Duopoly
    c. Monopoly
    d. Perfect market

129. The central Agmark lab is located at
    a. Bangalore
    b. **Nagpur**
    c. Kolkata
    d. Mumbai

130. A mixed farming the contribution of livestock to gross farm income is
    a. At last 40%
    b. **At last 10%**
    c. At last 30%
    d. More than 50%

131. Do the TC and the VC increase with increase in the output
    a. Never
    b. **Yes**
    c. With decrease in output
    d. Partially

132. The object of a subsistence farm is to produce
    a. **Essential food crop for family only**
    b. Essential food crop for family and market
    c. Vegetable crop for family only
    d. Food and fiber crops for family and market

133. In mixed farming the contribution of livestock to gross farm income is
    a. **At last 10%**
    b. At last 49%
    c. At last 50%
    d. More than 50%

134. The net capital ratio in this case would be
    a. 7.5
    b. 11.5
    c. 4.0
    d. **3.33**

135. The term 'operational holding' refers to the
    a. Land area leased in by a farmer
    b. Net land area cultivated by a farmer
    c. Land area owned by a farmer
    d. Cropped area cultivated by a farmer

136. Which one of the following formulae gives the correct measure of 'Rate of Capital Turnover'
    a. (Gross income/total farm assets) × 100
    b. **(Net income/total farm assets) × 100**
    c. (Capital investments/total farm assets) × 100
    d. (Farm business income/total farm assets) × 100

137. Nitrogen fertilizer use efficiency in rice can be increased by using
    a. Urea supergranules
    b. Blue-green algae
    c. Sulphur-coated urea
    d. **Sulphur-coated urea and urea supergranules**

138. Which one of the following nutritions plays the most effective role in controlling the rate of transpiration?
    a. Zinc
    b. **Potassium**
    c. Magnesium
    d. Phosphorus

139. Plants roots are
    a. Positively phototropic
    b. Negative geotropic
    c. Negatively hydrotropic
    d. **Positively geotropic**

140. The ratio of 'organic carbon' to 'organic matter' in soil is
    a. 1.7:1.0
    b. 20.0:1.0
    c. 1.0:2.0
    d. **1.0:1.7**

141. The bulk density of a soil with particle density of 2.65 g/cc and pore space 40% would be
    a. 1.29 g/cc
    b. 1.72 g/cc
    c. 1.45 g/cc
    d. **1.59 g/cc**

142. Which one of the following is the special scheme launched by the ICAR for transfer of technology to the farmers?
    a. Operational Research Project
    b. **Lab to land program**
    c. All India Co-ordinated Research Projects
    d. National demonstration program

143. Groundnut is not an economical crop for deep black soils because
    a. Phosphorus requirement is high
    b. Peg penetration is very poor
    c. Swelling and shrinkage affect root system
    d. **Drainage conditions are poor**

144. Which of the following agroclimatic factors lead to successful sugar beet production?
    a. **Loam or sandy loam soils**
    b. Soil salinity between 1.0 and 1.5%
    c. Average temp of 30°C and above throughout the growing period
    d. Average temperature between 19.5°C and 22°C throughout the growing period

145. Profit is maximised when
    a. Marginal cost < marginal form
    b. **Marginal cost = marginal form**
    c. Marginal cost > marginal form
    d. None of the above

146. The elasticity of production (EP) at the starting point of stage II in law of diminishing return would be
    a. >1.0
    b. **1.0**
    c. <1.0
    d. 0.0

147. Level of optimum production is available in
    a. Stage
    b. **II stage of production**
    c. III stage of production
    d. None of these

148. Which one of the following kinds of budgeting would you advise to a new farm planner?
    a. Enterprise budgeting
    b. **Complete budgeting**
    c. Partial budgeting
    d. None of these

149. The cost of production of the crop can be minimized by using economic principle
    a. Law of diminishing return
    b. Law of opportunity cost
    c. Cost principle
    d. **Principle of least cost combination**

150. Farm budget is a tool of farm management analysis
    a. **True**
    b. False
    c. Never includes cost
    d. It is a futile exercise

151. When a farm is managed by govt. official, it is called a
    a. Peasant farm
    b. Capitalistic farm
    c. Collective farm
    d. **State farm**

152. Line passing through the least cost points in the isoquants map is called
    a. Isoclines
    b. Ridge line
    c. **Expansion path**
    d. Isoquant curve

153. The ecosystem determining agroecological zones has two components, viz.

biotic and abiotic. Abiotic components comprise

a. Light water and animals
b. Minerals, plant and soil organisms
c. **Material like water, minerals, salts, atmospheric gases, energy like light, heat and stored energy**
d. Water, wind and plants

154. Ability of a system (say agriculture) to maintain inter-regional equity and enhance, if required, the flow of its products and services by way of linkages with other systems without damaging its own long-term potential is called

a. An efficient system
b. **A sustainable system**
c. A productive system
d. None of the above

155. Which one of the following pairs is not correctly matched?

a. Relay cropping: Sowing pulse in rice crop prior to harvest
b. **Inter-cropping: Wheat after rice**
c. Multi-tier cropping: Coconut–pepper–cacao–pineapple
d. Sole cropping: Potato

156. Which of the following is the principal 'N' algae community of blue-green algae?

a. Rhizobia   b. **Anabena**
c. Azotobacter   d. Azospirillum

157. Fire curing is followed in

a. **Chewing type of tobacco**
b. Bidi tobacco
c. Hookah tobacco
d. Cheroot tobacco

158. Which of the following two crops are responsible for almost 75% of pulse production in India?

a. Gram and moongbean
b. Pigeon-pea and moongbean
c. Moongbean and lentil
d. **Gram and pigeon-pea**

159. Triticale is a cross between

a. Wheat and barley
b. Barley and rye
c. **Wheat and rye**
d. Wheat and oat

160. Barseem is a fodder crop and is recommmended for sowing in the months of

a. March–April
b. **October–November**
c. January–February
d. June–July

161. Browning of cauliflower can be corrected by use of

a. Ammonium molybdate
b. Zinc sulphate
c. **Boric acid**
d. Urea

162. The objective of preparation of calendar of operation is

a. **To prepare a cropping scheme**
b. To calculate the cost of production
c. To assess the need of human and bullock power
d. To adjust farm enterprises

163. The farm plan would be based on the availability of efficiency of various factor of production

a. **True**   b. False
c. Partially true
d. Incomplete statement

164. Farm budgets are a tool of farm management analysis

a. **True**   b. False
c. Never include cost
d. It is a futile exercise

165. When a farm is managed by Govt. officials, it is called a

a. Peasant farm   b. Capitalistic farm
c. Collective farm   d. **State farm**

166. Cell theory was applied to plants is given by

a. **Schleiden**   b. Swanson
c. Schwann   d. Janssen

167. In which of the following does not show a circular DNA?
    a. Nucleus
    b. Mitochondria
    c. Chloroplast
    d. Bacterial cell

168. Mark the odd one
    a. **Ribosome**
    b. Lysosome
    c. Peroxisome
    d. Spherosome

169. Protoplasmic theory was proposed by
    a. **Max Schultaz**
    b. Sachs
    c. Mirbel
    d. Dutrochet

170. Which of the following has one envelope system?
    a. **Prokaryotic system**
    b. Eukaryotic system
    c. Both (a) and (b)
    d. None of the above

171. Which of the following is present in both plant and animal cells?
    a. Primary wall
    b. Secondary wall
    c. **Plasma membrane**
    d. Plastids

172. Chemical responsible for the flow of information with in the cell is
    a. DNA
    b. RNA
    c. Proteins
    d. Lipids

173. The smallest cell organelle is
    a. **Ribosome**
    b. Spherosome
    c. Lysosome
    d. Peroxisome

174. Quantasomes are found in
    a. **Chloroplast**
    b. Nucleus
    c. Mitochondria
    d. Lysosome

175. Hemicellulose is a polymer of
    a. **Mannose**
    b. Glucose
    c. Galactouronic acid
    d. Coniferyl acid

176. Each quantasome contains
    a. 100 chlorophyll molecules
    b. 200 chlorophyll molecules
    c. 300 chlorophyll molecules
    d. **230 chlorophyll molecules**

177. Which of the following cell organelles breaks down polysaccharides and proteins?
    a. Golgi's complex
    b. **Lysosome**
    c. Rough ER
    d. Mitochondria

178. Thicking of cell wall, lignifications and specialization for mechanical functions are characteristics of the
    a. **Sclerenchyma**
    b. Collenchyma
    c. Arenchyma
    d. Parenchyma

179. Most of the cellular enzymes functions at
    a. pH-5
    b. Basic pH
    c. **Neutral pH**
    d. Acidic pH

180. The isolation of plasma membrane from a cell is done by one of the following progresses
    a. **Exosmosis**
    b. Diffusion
    c. Endosmosis
    d. Plasmolysis

181. Protein storing plastids are known as
    a. **Amyloplast**
    b. Elaioplast
    c. Aleuroplast
    d. Leucoplast

182. Brown plastids contain brown pigment fucoxanthin and are known as
    a. **Rhodoplast**
    b. Chloroplast
    c. Cyanoplast
    d. Phaeoplasts

183. Specific stain for cellulose detection is
    a. Methylene blue
    b. Sudan-I
    c. Saffrain
    d. **Zinc chloroiodide**

184. To isolate mitochondria
    a. Cells are plasmolysed and filtered
    b. Cells are disrupted and centrifuged
    c. **Selection of cells having a large number of mitochondria is done**
    d. None of the above

185. Chemical nature of callose is
    a. Protein
    b. Polysaccharide
    c. **Lignin**
    d. Fat

186. Secondary walls in plant cells show deposition of
    a. Lignin
    b. Pectin
    c. Cellulose
    d. Suberin

187. Which is not a non-protoplasmic cell inclusion
    a. Raphides
    b. Starch grain
    c. Ribosome
    d. Cytolith

188. A cystolith is a deposit of
    a. Calcium citrate
    b. Calcium carbonate
    c. Silica
    d. Calcium oxalate

189. The technique which is used to find out the pathway of the synthesis of a substance in a cell is known as
    a. Autoradiography
    b. Chromatography
    c. Spectrophotometry
    d. Cell fractionation

190. The process by which middle lamella is removed by treating the plant cells with strong acids is known as
    a. Lignification
    b. Cutinization
    c. Maceration
    d. Suberization

191. Meristematic cells usually consist of
    a. Primary cell wall
    b. Secondary cell wall
    c. Tertiary cell wall
    d. All of the above

192. Out of proteins, lipids and carbohydrates present in a cell membrane, what is true?
    a. Carbohydrates are minimum
    b. Carbohydrates are maximum
    c. Lipids are minimum
    d. All the three are in equal proportion

193. Engulfment of solid food particle of larger size by the plasma membrane is known as
    a. Endocytosis
    b. Pinocytosis
    c. Phagocytosis
    d. Ephagy

194. Osmosis stops when
    a. Solutions become isotonic
    b. Water concentration becomes equal
    c. External solution is hypotonic
    d. External solution is hypertonic

195. Plasma membrane particularly in animal cells is elastic due to
    a. Lipids
    b. Proteins
    c. Carbohydrates
    d. None of the above

196. Which among the following has only DNA, but no histones in its chromosome?
    a. Anabena
    b. Volvox
    c. Chlamydomonas
    d. Yeast

197. The term phragmoplast is associated with
    a. Cell elongation
    b. Division of nucleus
    c. Cytokinesis
    d. Karyokinesis

198. A solution whose osmotic concentration is greater than the cell sap is known as
    a. Hypotonic
    b. Isotonic
    c. Hypertonic
    d. None

199. Active transport is affected by
    a. Cold
    b. Cyanide
    c. Absence of oxygen
    d. All of the above

200. Plasma membrane is more permeable to
    a. Polysaccharides
    b. Proteins
    c. Glycoproteins
    d. Phospholipids

2

Theories of Agronomy

1. Jalpriya is a variety of
   - a. Maize
   - b. Jowar
   - **c. Paddy**
   - d. Barley

2. Sugarcane + potato is an inter-cropping system of
   - **a. Autumn season**
   - b. Zaid season
   - c. Spring season
   - d. Rainy season

3. Seed-rate of potato per hectare is
   - a. 25 quintal/hectare
   - b. 10 quintal/hectare
   - c. 15 quintal/hectare
   - **d. 40 quintal/hectare**

4. Deficiency symptoms of calcium on plants first appear at
   - a. Lower leaves
   - b. Middle leaves
   - **c. Terminal leaves**
   - d. All leaves

5. Which weedicide is used to kill broad leaf weeds in wheat?
   - **a. 2, 4–DSS (WPSS)**
   - b. 2, 4, 5–T
   - c. 2, 4–DB
   - d. None of these

6. Maya is the variety of
   - a. Potato
   - b. Gram
   - c. Pea
   - **d. Mustard**

7. The weed that causes asthma is
   - a. Hirankhuri
   - b. Bathua
   - **c. Parthenium**
   - d. Krishna Neel

8. Which crop requires maximum amount of nitrogen?
   - a. Potato
   - b. Wheat
   - c. Barley
   - **d. Sugarcane**

9. First dwarf variety of paddy developed in India is
   - a. Jaya
   - b. Saket-4
   - **c. Govind**
   - d. Narendra-97

10. Sprinkler irrigation is suitable, where the soil has
    - a. Clayey texture
    - b. Loamy texture
    - c. Undulating topography
    - **d. All of these**

11. Endosulphan is also known as
    - a. Lindane
    - **b. Thiodan**
    - c. Aldrin
    - d. BHC

12. Which of the following is systemic poison?
    - a. Metasystox
    - b. Phosphomidan
    - **c. Phorate**
    - d. All of these

13. DDVP is known as
    - **a. Nuvan**
    - b. Malathion
    - c. Thiodan
    - d. Sulfex

14. Seed treatment with Vitavex is the main controlling method of
    - a. Loose smut
    - b. Rust
    - c. Downy mildew
    - **d. All of these**

15. **Covered smut of barley is a disease of**
    a. Externally seed-borne
    b. **Internally seed-borne**
    c. Air-borne
    d. None of these

16. **Which of the following cakes is not edible?**
    a. **Castor cake**
    b. Mustard cake
    c. Sesame cake
    d. Groundnut cake

17. **In India, about 142 million hectare land is under**
    a. **Cultivation**   b. Waste land
    c. Forest   d. Eroded land

18. **The headquarters of Indian Meteorological Department was established in 1875 at**
    a. New Delhi   b. Hyderabad
    c. Pune   d. **Calcutta**

19. **Moisture condensed in small drops upon cool surface is called**
    a. Hail   b. **Dew**
    c. Snow   d. Fog

20. **How many agroclimatic zones (ACZ) are found in India?**
    a. 16   b. 18
    c. **15**   d. 20

21. **Tilt angle of a disc plough is generally**
    a. 10°   b. 15°
    c. 20°   d. **45°**

22. **Pudding is done to**
    a. Reduce percolation of water
    b. Pulverise and levelling soil
    c. Kill weeds   d. **All of the above**

23. **The Community Development Programme (CDP) was started in India on**
    a. 2nd October, 1950
    b. **2nd October, 1952**
    c. 2nd October, 1951
    d. None of these

24. **The main unit of Integrated Rural Development Programme is**
    a. Family   b. **Village**
    c. Block   d. District

25. **Element of communication is**
    a. Message   b. Feedback
    c. Channel   d. **All of these**

26. **The first Kshetriya Gramin Bank (KGB) was opened in India is**
    a. 1972   b. 1980
    c. **1975**   d. 1969

27. **The main function of NABARD is**
    a. Farmers' loaning
    b. Agricultural research
    c. **Refinancing to agricultural financing institutions**
    d. Development of agriculture

28. **Rent theory of profit was given by**
    a. Hawley   b. CP Blacker
    c. Tanssig   d. **FA Walker**

29. **In LDR, the profit will be maximum when**
    a. MC = MP   b. MC > MP
    c. MP = TP   d. **MP > TP**

30. **The period of 11th Five-Year Plan is**
    a. 2000–2005   b. 2002–2007
    c. **2007–2012** d. 2008–2012

31. **Acid rain contains mainly**
    a. PO_4 b. **NO_2**
    c. NO_3 d. CH_4

32. **Cell organelle found only in plants are**
    a. Mitochondria b. Golgi complex
    c. Ribosomes   d. **Plastids**

33. **Proteins are synthesized in**
    a. Centrosomes   b. **Ribosomes**
    c. Mitochondria d. Golgi bodies

34. **Milk fever is caused due to the deficiency of**
    a. P   b. **Ca**
    c. Mg   d. K

35. Milk sugar is a type of
    a. Glucose   b. Sucrose
    c. Lactose   d. Fructose

36. Muriate of potash is
    a. K_2SO_4 **b. KCl**
    c. K_2HPO_4 d. KNO_3

37. Azotobacter fixes atmospheric nitrogen in the soil by
    a. Symbiotically
    b. Non-symbiotically
    c. Both a and b
    d. None of these

38. The chemical formula of iron pyrites is
    a. $FeSO_4$ b. FeS
    c. FeS_2   d. $Fe_2(SO_4)_3$

39. Rock phosphates are used in
    a. Saline soil
    b. Sodic soil
    c. Acidic soil
    d. Neutral soil

40. Intervenous chlorosis is caused due to the deficiency of
    a. N   b. Mg
    c. S   **d. Fe**

41. Kinnow is the hybrid variety of
    a. Citrus   b. Orange
    c. Mandarin   d. Lemon

42. The permanent preservative, which is used for preservation of fruit and vege-tables, is
    a. Sodium chloride
    b. Potassium metabisulphite
    c. Potassium sulphate
    d. Sugar

43. Whip tail disease of cauliflower is caused by deficiency of
    a. Nitrogen   b. Boron
    c. Molybdenum   d. Zinc

44. The word 'Agriculture' is derived from
    a. Greek   **b. Latin**
    c. Arabic   d. French

45. Motha (grass nut) belongs to the family of
    a. Cruciferae   b. Tiliaceae
    c. Cyperaceae   d. Graminaceae

46. Which of the following is short day crops?
    a. Maize, lobia, bajra
    b. Wheat, mustard, gram
    c. Moong, soybean, bajra
    d. Wheat, soybean, bajra

47. What is the sequence of C4 plants?
    a. Sudangrass–sugarcane–paddy–bajra
    b. Sugarcane–maize–sudangrass–bajra
    c. Sugarcane–cotton–paddy–maize
    d. Cotton–maize–bajra–sugarcane

48. Match list I (crops) with list II (water requirement) and select your answer from the code given below

List I	List II
a. Jowar	1. 140 mm–300 mm
b. Soybean	2. 350 mm–450 mm
c. Cotton	3. 200 mm–300 mm
d. Groundnut	4. 300 mm–350 mm

    Codes:
    a. 3, 1, 2, 4   b. 4, 2, 3, 1
    c. 1, 4, 2, 3   d. 3, 1, 4, 2

49. In which state, are there biggest area, highest production and number of sugar mills in relation to sugarcane?
    a. Maharashtra
    b. Bihar
    c. Uttar Pradesh
    d. Andhra Pradesh

50. Which is not prepared by potato?
    a. Acetic acid   **b. Paper**
    c. Wine   d. Fanina

51. Uttar Pradesh is occupying which place in India, for guava production?
    a. Second   b. First
    c. Third   d. Fifth

52. Which of the following is TPS variety of potato?
    a. JH 222   b. Chipsona-II
    c. Anand   **d. HPS-1/113**

53. What is VAM?

a. Virus   b. Bacteria

c. Algae   **d. Fungi**

54. What is the main function of zinc in the plants?

a. Synthesis of nitrogen

b. Synthesis of phosphorus

  c. Required for synthesis of tryptophos

d. To increase activity of the boron

55. What is the area in floriculture (in 000' hectare) in India?

a. 40–50   b. 60–80

c. 100–120   d. None of these

56. Which of the following factors does not affect the nitrification?

a. Air   **b. Seed**

c. Temperature   d. Moisture

57. Which is the correct sequence of soil erosion?

a. Rill–Sheet–Gulley

b. Gulley–Sheet–Rill

c. Sheet–Rill–Gulley

d. Sheet–Gulley–Rill

58. Zinc sulphate (ZnSO$_4$) should not be mixed with

a. DAP

b. Compost fertilizer

c. Ammonium chloride

d. Urea

59. Insecticides are specific inhibitors of

a. Excretory system

b. Digestive system

c. Nervous system

d. Blood circulatory system

60. The credit for the success of Krishi Vigyan Kendras (KVK) goes to

a. Dr. RS Paroda

b. Dr. Chandrika Prasad

c. Dr. Mohan Singh Mehta

d. Dr. Mangla Rai

61. Cauliflower belongs to the family

a. Cruciferae   b. Poacae

c. Malvaceae   d. Leguminaceae

62. Which type of soil is best for knolkhol?

a. Loam

b. Clayey loam

c. Silty clayey loam

d. Clay

63. Which of the following soil types is most suitable for garlic cultivation?

a. Loamy sand   **b. Sandy loam**

c. Loam   d. Clay

64. The species of Rhizobium present in the root nodules of soybean is

a. Leguminoserum

b. Japonicum

c. Trifolium   d. Phalodi

65. Which of the following soil types has the highest field capacity?

a. Loam   b. Silty loam

c. Clayey loam   **d. Clay**

66. The trade name of phorate is

a. Temic   b. Thiodan

c. Phortox   d. Metasystox

67. The sprayers are cleaned before use by

a. 1% chlorine water

b. 1% hydrochloric acid

c. 1% ammonia water

d. 1% bromine water

68. The cyanogas pump is a/an

a. Duster   b. Fumigator

c. Sprayer   **d. Emulsifier**

69. The main reason of Irish Famine in potato was

a. Late Blight disease

b. Bacterial Blight disease

c. Blast disease

d. Ear Cockle disease

70. The instrument, which is used for sowing of seed with fertilizer together at a time, is

a. Seed drill

b. Dibbler

c. Seed sowing behind plough

d. Ferti-cum seed drill

71. **Seed treatment is done to control**
    a. Soil-borne disease
    b. Air-borne disease
    c. Seed-borne disease
    d. None of these

72. **Salt tolerant crop is**
    a. Cowpea   b. Field pea
    c. Garlic   d. Longmelon

73. **Which of the following is not a dairy breed of cattle?**
    a. Sahiwal   b. Sindhi
    c. Nagore   **d. All of these**

74. **One per cent is equal to**
    a. 1000 ppm   b. 100 ppm
    c. 10 ppm   **d. 10, 000 ppm**

75. **Which of the following pesticides has been banned in India?**
    a. Rogor   **b. DDT**
    c. Metasystox   d. Dimecron

76. **Pulses fit well in cropping system as they are**
    a. Short duration crops
    b. Disease resistant crops
    c. Long duration crops
    d. Moisture stress resistant crops

77. **Wheat is a**
    a. Cash crop   **b. Cereal crop**
    c. Covered crop   d. None of these

78. **Autumn sugarcane is planted in month of**
    a. February–March
    b. July
    c. October
    d. December

79. **Seed-rate for timely sown wheat is**
    a. 75 kg/ha   b. 100 kg/ha
    c. 125 kg/ha   d. 150 kg/ha

80. **Most critical stage in wheat for irrigation is**
    a. CRI   b. Flowering
    c. Milk   d. Dough

81. **Name of most popular variety of wheat in Uttar Pradesh is**
    a. PBW-343   **b. UP-2338**
    c. K-7903   d. K-9107

82. **KPG-59 (Udai) is a variety of**
    a. Field pea   b. Vegetable pea
    c. Lentil   **d. Gram**

83. **In plain, Rajma is cultivated during**
    a. *Kharif*   b. *Rabi*
    c. *Zaid*   d. None of these

84. **Which crop is recommended for *Zaid* season cultivation in Uttar Pradesh?**
    a. Vegetable pea   **b. Groundnut**
    c. Barley   d. Lentil

85. **The most efficient use of potassium is achieved by**
    a. Broadcasting at the sowing time
    b. Top dressing after one month of sowing
    c. Basal placement at the sowing time
    d. Foliar spray

86. **The term 'Extension' was first used in**
    a. UK   **b. USA**
    c. India   d. France

87. **The first KVK (Krishi Vigyan Kendra) in India was established in**
    a. Bombay   b. Port Blair
    c. Pondicherry   d. Madras

88. **ATMA is related to**
    a. NARP   b. NAARM
    c. NREP   **d. None of these**

89. **Albert Mayer is the name associated with**
    a. Nilokheri Development Project
    b. Firka Development Project
    c. Etawah Pilot Project
    d. Shriniketan Project

90. **Co-operative Credit Societies Act was passed in India in**
    a. 1902   b. 1904
    c. 1906   **d. 1912**

91. Maximum photosynthesis takes place in
   a. Blue light
   b. Red light
   c. Violet light
   d. Green light

92. Farm planning means
   a. Farm budgetting
   b. Cropping pattern
   c. Type of enterprises
   d. None of these

93. The first product of photosynthesis in C3 plant is
   a. Pyruvic acid
   b. Phosphoglyceric acid
   c. Oxaloacetic acid
   d. Succinic acid

94. Bending of plants towards light is called
   a. Phototropism
   b. Vernalisation
   c. Photorespiration
   d. None of these

95. Germination is inhibited by
   a. Red light
   b. Blue light
   c. UV light
   d. IR light

96. The best method of milking is
   a. Knuckling method
   b. Fisting method
   c. Stripping method
   d. None of these

97. Line breeding is a type of
   a. Inbreeding
   b. Outbreeding
   c. Natural breeding
   d. None of these

98. Match list I with list II and select answer from the codes given below

List I	List II
a. White Revolution	1. Fertilizer production
b. Grey Revolution	2. Fish production
c. Blue Revolution	3. Cereal production
d. Green Revolution	4. Milk production

Codes:
   a. 4, 1, 2, 3
   b. 1, 2, 3, 4
   c. 2, 4, 3, 1
   d. 1, 3, 4, 2

99. 'Tharparkar' breed of cow is
   a. Milch breed
   b. Working breed
   c. Dual purpose breed
   d. None of these

100. Cow and buffalo belong to the family
   a. Bovidae
   b. Suidae
   c. Equidae
   d. Cammelidae

101. What is the contribution of Animal Husbandry Sector in the agricultural growth?
   a. 10%
   b. 12%–15%
   c. 7%–9%
   d. 5%

102. How many labourers are required to run a 30 cows milch herd?
   a. 8
   b. 6
   c. 4
   d. 10

103. What is the availability of per day per capita milk in India presently (2008–09)?
   a. 229 gram
   b. 239 gram
   c. 219 gram
   d. 252 gram

104. Which place is occupied by India in egg production?
   a. First
   b. Second
   c. Third
   d. Fourth

105. How much calories (cal) may be obtained from 100 gram chicken egg?
   a. 175 cal
   b. 180 cal
   c. 160 cal
   d. 130 cal

106. Main function of biofertilizer is
   a. To increase chemical process
   b. To increase physiological process
   c. To increase biological process
   d. To increase photosynthesis process

107. How much tomato average production (q.) may be yield from one hectare?
   a. 100
   b. 105–150
   c. 250
   d. 160–275

108. Which type of soil is found near the canal banks?
    a. Acidic and alkaline
    b. Acidic
    c. **Alkaline**
    d. None of these

109. Which one is not biofertilizer?
    a. **Multiflex**   b. PSB
    c. Vermicompost
    d. NADEP

110. In which form is nitrogen absorbed by paddy under waterlogged condition?
    a. NH_4 ion   b. **Nitrate ion**
    c. NO_2 ion   d. N_2

111. Which one of the following do not relate to groundnut?
    a. Brazil   b. $2n = 40$
    c. **Pink disease**   d. Tikka disease

112. Which of the following is produced highest in India?
    a. **Mango**   b. Banana
    c. Papaya   d. Grapes

113. The optimum temperature for the banana crop is
    a. 30°C   b. **23°C**
    c. 21.5°C   d. 26.5°C

114. Which one of the following varieties has been selected to develop Narendra Aonla-6 variety?
    a. Chakaiya
    b. Hathijhool
    c. Banarasi
    d. **Narendra Aonla-6**

115. Red soil is poor in which of the following nutrients?
    a. Phosphorus and sulphur
    b. Phosphorus and nitrogen
    c. Nitrogen and zinc
    d. **Nitrogen and potassium**

116. A farming system in which airable crops are grown in alleys formed by trees or shrubs, to establish soil fertility and to enhance soil productivity, is known as
    a. Relay cropping
    b. Multiple cropping
    c. **Alley cropping**
    d. Mixed cropping

117. The cropping intensity of groundnut + arhar–sugarcane is
    a. 200%   b. 300%
    c. **150%**   d. 250%

118. The scented variety of paddy is
    a. Jaya   b. Bala
    c. **Type-3**   d. Type-1

119. From which language is the word 'Agronomy' taken?
    a. Latin   b. **Greek**
    c. French   d. German

120. Tarameera is belonged to which family?
    a. **Cruciferae**   b. Linaceae
    c. Compositae   d. Graminae

121. The size of clay particles are
    a. 1.0 mm   b. 0.2–0.02 mm
    c. < 0.02 mm   d. **< 0.002 mm**

122. When one plant has both male and female flowers separately, is called
    a. Monophrodits   b. Monoecious
    c. Hermaphrodite   d. **Apomixis**

123. Aamrapali is the cross of
    a. Neelam × Dashaheri
    b. Dashaheri × Langra
    c. Langra × Dashaheri
    d. **Dashaheri × Neelam**

124. Seed-plot technique is adopted in
    a. Onion   b. **Potato**
    c. Sugarcane   d. Tomato

125. The origin of lychee is
    a. India   b. Philippines
    c. **China**   d. Burma

126. Cucumbers, squashes, and beans are
    a. Monocots   b. **Dicots**
    c. Multicots   d. Ferns

127. Rice, corn, and wheat are
    a. **Monocots**   b. Dicots
    c. Multicots   d. Ferns

128. In which of the following process comprises important mechanisms of herbicide detoxification in soil under field conditions especially surface incorporation subsequent to rainfall or irrigation?
    a. Thermodecomposition
    b. Biodecomposition
    c. Chemodecomposition
    d. **Photodecomposition**

129. The science concerned with vegetable culture is called
    a. Floriculture   b. **Olericulture**
    c. Horticulture   d. Agriculture

130. Which of the following elements is almost non-essential for plants?
    a. Ca   b. Mo
    c. Zn   d. **Na**

131. Although a deficiency of any one of the elements listed may result in chlorosis, only one of these elements is an element found in chlorophyll. Which is it?
    a. Zinc   b. Iron
    c. **Magnesium**   d. Chloride

132. Which of the following elements is not present in a nitrogenous base?
    a. Hydrogen   b. Carbon
    c. **Phosphorus**   d. Nitrogen

133. A water-fern, which is used as a green manure in rice fields, is
    a. Salvinia   b. Mucor
    c. Aspergillus   d. **Azolla**

134. Green manure plants used by farmers mainly belong to
    a. Compositae   b. **Leguminosae**
    c. Solanaceae   d. Poaceae

135. Major food crops of the world belong to
    a. Leguminosae   b. **Gramineae**
    c. Solanaceae   d. Cruciferae

136. The principal cereal crop of India is
    a. Wheat   b. **Rice**
    c. Barley   d. Sorghum

137. Which one among the following chemicals is used for causing defoliation of forest trees?
    a. Posphon D   b. Malic hydrazide
    c. **2, 4-D**   d. Amo 161

138. Mineral particles having diameter of > 0.2 cm are known as
    a. **Gravel**   b. Coarse sand
    c. Silt   d. Fine sand

139. Fractionation of silt and clay fractions of soil particles is done by using
    a. Darcy's law   b. Poiseuille's law
    c. **Stroke's law** d. Fick's law

140. Bioherbicides have been recommended
    a. **To prevent ecodegradation**
    b. Because of their ready availability
    c. Because of their cheap rates
    d. Because of their abundance

141. The most important weed against which eradication measures would be taken on war footings is
    a. Eichhornia   b. Dactylis
    c. **Parthenium**   d. Ageratum

142. Water logging of soil makes it physiologically dry because
    a. This condition does not allow the capillary force to work
    b. **This condition does not allow oxygen to enter the soil**
    c. Both a and b   d. None of these

143. Which one of the following is natural insecticide?
    a. Pyrethrum   b. Nicotine
    c. **Both a and b** d. None of these

144. The process by which nutrient chemicals or contaminants are dissolved and carried away by water, or are moved into a lower layer of soil
    a. Mulching
    b. Desertification

c. Incineration

d. **Leaching**

145. Which of the following is an example of a weed of rabi season that infest wheat crop?

  a. Chenopodium b. Motha

  c. Jangali jowar d. None of the above

146. First bioinsecticide developed commercial scale was

  a. Quinine   b. DDT

  c. Organophosphate

  d. Sporeine

147. Composted manure is produced from

  a. Farmyard manure and green manure

  b. Farm refuse and household refuse

  c. Organic remains of biogas plants

  d. Rotten vegetables and animal refuse

148. Norin-l0 gene from Japan is a

  a. Dwarf gene of wheat

  b. Dwarf gene of rice

  c. Dwarf gene of maize

  d. Disease resistant gene of rice

149. Aims of plant breeding are to produce

  a. Disease-free varieties

  b. High-yielding varieties

  c. Early-maturing varieties

  d. All of the above

150. Growing of two or more crops simultaneously on the same piece of land is called

  a. Mixed cropping

  b. Mixed farming

  c. Intercropping

  d. Fanning

151. The Mexican dwarf wheat variety was developed by

  a. Swaminathan **b. Borlaugh**

  c. Watson   d. Khush

152. The desired varieties of economically useful crops are raised by

  a. Vernalisation

  b. Mutation

c. Natural selection

d. **Hybridisation**

153. High-yielding varieties of wheat were primarily developed by Indian scientist by crossing- breeding traditional varieties with

  a. American varieties

  b. Mexican varieties

  c. European varieties

  d. African varieties

154. A Plant breeder: Waists to develop a disease resistant variety. What should he do first?

  a. Hybridisation

  b. Mutation

  c. Selection

  d. Production of crop

155. Selection of homozygous plant is

  a. Pure line selection

  b. Mass selection

  c. Mixed selection

  d. Introduction

156. What element forms the skeleton of organic molecules?

  a. Hydrogen atoms

  b. Phosphate atoms

  c. Carbon atoms

  d. Water molecules

157. How many bonds can carbon atoms form?

  a. Two   **b. Four**

  c. One   d. Three

158. What happens in a dehydration reaction?

  a. Molecules are broken apart

  b. Monomers are bonded together and a water molecule is released

  c. Atoms are joined

  d. It depends on what molecule it is

159. What reactions break apart polymers?

  a. Hydrolysis reactions

  b. Dehydration reactions

  c. Neutralization reactions

  d. Catalytic reactions

160. What is the general formula for carbohydrates?

   a. $(CH_2O)n$ b. $(C_2HO)n$
   c. (CHCHCH)   d. (COOH)

161. In what category of organic molecules are sugars placed?

   a. Proteins   b. Lipids
   c. Hormones   **d. Carbohydrates**

162. What are long chains of sugars called?

   a. Monosaccharides
   b. Disaccharides
   c. Polysaccharides
   d. Proteins

163. What is the most common monosaccharide?

   a. Cellulose   **b. Glucose**
   c. Triglycerides   d. Starches

164. Plants store energy as _____.

   a. Starch   b. Lactose
   c. RNA   d. Protein

165. Muscle cells store energy in the form of _____.

   a. Starch   **b. Glycogen**
   c. Cellulose   d. Steroids

166. Plant cell walls contain large amounts, of what polysaccharide?

   a. Carbon   b. Water
   c. Chitin   **d. Cellulose**

167. What type of organic molecule is a fat?

   a. Carbohydrate **b. Lipid**
   c. Starch   d. Protein

168. What type of bonds found between carbon atoms cause fats to form kinks?

   a. Ionic   b. Polar
   c. Double   d. Proton

169. Fats and oils are composed of what two groups of molecules?

   a. Starch and sugar
   b. Glucose and fructose
   c. Fatty acids and glycerol
   d. Water and cellulose

170. What best describes phospholipid molecules?

   a. Their chemical formula is $(CH_2O)_n$
   b. They form cell membranes
   c. They are proteins
   d. They are ionic

171. What structures are found in steroid molecules?

   a. Molecular rings b. Proteins
   c. Waxes   d. Double helixes

172. What monomers make up proteins?

   a. Starches   b. Enzymes
   c. Nucleic acids **d. Amino acids**

173. How many different amino acids are there?

   a. Ten   **b. Twenty**
   c. Four   d. Hundreds

174. What are the bonds between amino acids called?

   a. Hydrogen bonds
   b. Peptide bonds
   c. Ionic bonds   d. Covalent bonds

175. Where do substrates attach to an enzyme?

   a. Peptide bond   b. Ring binding site
   c. Active site   d. Enzymatic site

176. Which of the following types of molecules is found in genetic material?

   a. Cellulose   b. Enzymes
   c. Lipids   **d. Nucleic acids**

177. Which of the following are found in nucleotides of DNA and RNA respectively?

   a. Deoxyribose and ribose
   b. Proteins and enzymes
   c. Fats and oils
   d. Sugars and starches

178. What are the four bases in DNA?

   a. First, second, third and fourth
   b. Adenine, guanine, cytosine, uracil
   c. Nitrogen, hydrogen, carbon and phosphate
   d. Adenine, guanine, cytosine, thymine

179. Which of the following molecules function as an intracellular message carriers?
    a. **cAMP or cyclic adenosine monophosphate**
    b. Enzymes
    c. Glycogen
    d. Water

180. What is the function of ATP, adenosine triphosphate?
    a. Message carrier
    b. **Store and transport energy**
    c. Make proteins
    d. Breakdown sugars

181. In which of the following planet is close to the sun?
    a. Pluto
    b. Jupiter
    c. **Mercury**
    d. Earth

182. Which comet appear after every 76 years?
    a. Holme
    b. Alfa
    c. **Halley**
    d. None of the above

183. In rice, Khaira disease is caused by
    a. **Zn deficiency**
    b. B deficiency
    c. Mg deficiency
    d. Cu deficiency

184. Which place in India will experience sunlight for the highest time in summer season?
    a. Kolkata
    b. **Srinagar**
    c. Chennai
    d. Mumbai

185. What is measured by the sling psychyrometres?
    a. **Humidity**
    b. Sunlight
    c. Volume
    d. Pressure

186. Cirrus is refer to
    a. **A high cloud**
    b. A low cloud
    c. A rain bearing cloud
    d. A hail-bearing cloud

187. Which soil is most common in the Indo-Gangetic plains?
    a. Podzol
    b. **Alluvial**
    c. Regure
    d. Laterite

188. What is counted through the help of the Richter scale?
    a. **Earthquakes**
    b. Heat
    c. Depth
    d. Wind velocity

189. The crustal layer of the Earth is also known as
    a. **Sial**
    b. Moho
    c. Sima
    d. Nife

190. Isohalines are the isopleths of
    a. Height
    b. Transport
    c. **Salinity**
    d. Hail

191. Cotton fibres are obtained from the
    a. Leaf
    b. **Fruits**
    c. Roots
    d. Stems

192. Most of the people of the Middle East belong to
    a. Alpines
    b. Nordic
    c. **Mediterranean**
    d. Negro

193. Feldspar is a
    a. Accessory kind mineral
    b. Clay mineral
    c. Secondary mineral
    d. **Primary mineral**

194. Basalts and granite are examples of
    a. **Igneous rocks**
    b. Metamorphic rocks
    c. Sedimentary rocks
    d. All of the above

195. An example of a natural fungicide is
    a. Furalaxyl
    b. **Wyerone**
    c. Carboxin
    d. Folpet

196. The most important fungicide against potato blight is

   a. Captan   b. Thiram

   c. Maneb   d. Benomyl

197. Acid sulphate soils are found in

   a. Bihar   **b. Kerala**

   c. MP   d. Punjab

198. Chemically water is

   a. An oxide   b. A peroxide

   c. A hydride   d. An hydroxide

199. In which of the following is a PGR?

   a. IAA

   b. Amitsol

   c. Propachlore

   d. Paraquet

200. Flint gas possess

   a. Borax

   b. Excess of sodium carbonate

   c. Lead chromate

   d. Hydrofluoric acid

3

Plant Pathology

1. Cold-like symptoms are caused by which bacteria?
   a. Pseudomonas   b. *E. coli*
   c. *Haemophilus influenzae*
   d. *Haemophilus streptococcus*

2. In *Streptococcus faecalis*, the conjugation takes place at
   a. Pili   b. Cell membrane
   c. Cell wall   d. Flagella

3. The infected mad dogs may contain
   a. Nergi bodies   b. Niagri bodies
   c. Negri bodies   d. Neisser bodies

4. What disease the Nesser will produce?
   a. Mumps   b. Rubella
   c. Polio   d. Measles

5. Rancidity in spoiled foods is due to
   a. Lipolytic organisms
   b. Proteolytic organisms
   c. Toxigenic microbes
   d. Saccharolytic microbes

6. The bacterium that is most commonly used in genetic engineering is
   a. Escherichia   b. Klebsiella
   c. Proteus   d. Serratia

7. The functions of plasmid are
   a. DNA replication
   b. Protein synthesis
   c. Cell wall synthesis
   d. None of the above

8. Mycoplasmas are bacterial cells that
   a. Fail to reproduce on artificial media
   b. Have a rigid cell wall
   c. Are resistant to penicillin
   d. Stain well with Gram's stain

9. The etiologic agent of botulism is a
   a. Neurotoxin   b. Endotoxin
   c. Enterotoxin   d. All of the above

10. The bacterial cells are at their metabolic peak during
    a. Lag phase   b. Log
    c. Stationary   d. Decline

11. Protein particles which can infect are called
    a. Virons
    b. Prions
    c. Nucleoida
    d. None of these

12. In most of purple bacteria, the light harvesting centers are
    a. B-850 and FeS
    b. B-850 and B-875
    c. B-845 and B-875
    d. B-850 and B-830

13. Endotoxin produced by gram-negative bacteria is present in
    a. Peptidoglycan
    b. Lipopolysaccharide
    c. Theichoic acid
    d. Inner membrane

14. Which one of the following were gram-negative, chemolithotrophic bacteria?
    a. Siderococcus   b. *E. coli*
    c. Spirillum   d. Mycoplasma

15. The mode of reproduction which occurs in Mycoplasma is
    a. Budding   b. Bursting
    c. Binary fission   d. Binary fusion

16. Which one of the following is about herpesviruses?
    a. Icosahedra, with envelope, dsDNA
    b. Polyhedral with envelope, dsDNA
    c. RNA, helical with envelope
    d. dsDNA, brick shape

17. Which one of the following produce typical fried egg appearance colonies on solid media?
    a. Mycobacteria   b. Mycoplasts
    c. Mycoplasma   d. Bacteroides

18. An organism that is osmophilic and has specific requirements for sodium chloride resembles
    a. Halophile   b. Basophile
    c. Barophile   d. Xerophile

19. A population of cells derived from a single cell is called
    a. Monoclonal cells
    b. Clones
    c. Protoplasts
    d. Subculture

20. Hetrolactic acid bacteria produce
    a. Lactic acid only
    b. Lactic acid + H_2O + CO_2
    c. Lactic acid + CO_2
    d. Lactic acid + alcohol + CO_2

21. In which of the following micro-organism, conjunction tube was not produced during conjunction process?
    a. *Thiobacillus thiooxidans*
    b. *T. ferroxidans*
    c. *Tetrahymena thermophila*
    d. *Cryptosporidium*

22. Which of the following is most similar to Rickettsia and Chlamydia?
    a. Bdellovibrio   b. Clostridium
    c. Mycobacterium   d. Mycoldaima

23. How would you distinguish pseudo-monas species from *E. coli*?
    a. Gram staining
    b. Morphology
    c. Glucose fermentation vs respiration
    d. All of the above

24. Which of the following is pathogenic to humans?
    a. Spirogyra   b. Cephaleuros
    c. Prototheca   d. Both b and c

25. Tumor inducing plasmids are extensively used in production of
    a. Avirulent phases
    b. Single cell proteins
    c. Transgenic plants
    d. Nitrogen fixing bacteria

26. The viruses that live as parasites on bacteria are
    a. Fungi   b. Commensals
    c. Bacteriophages   d. None of these

27. The anthrax disease is most frequently infected from
    a. Cattle   b. Sheeps
    c. Rats   **d. Both a and b**

28. The colonies produced by Pseudo-monas on MacConkey's medium are
    a. Purple colored   b. Pink colored
    c. Pale colored   d. Green colored

29. Staining material of gram-positive bacterium is
    a. Fast green   b. Haematoxylin
    c. Crystal violet   d. Saffranine

30. The pigment present in red algae is
    a. Rhodochrome
    b. Fucoxanthin
    c. Chlorophyll only
    d. Chlorophyll + phycobilin

31. **During mitosis, synapsis occurs in the phase called**
    a. Telophase   b. Anaphase
    c. Prophase   d. None of the above

32. **Which of the following change is a transition?**
    a. ATGC, ATCC   b. ATGC, ATGG
    c. ATGC, AGGC   **d. None of these**

33. **Citrus canker is caused by**
    a. Phytomonas   b. Salmonella
    c. Lactobacillus   d. Hay bacillus

34. **Bacteria that are responsible for fermentation of dairy milk are**
    a. Azotobacter   b. Rhizobium
    c. Lactobacillus   d. Hay bacillus

35. **The fungal disease that affect the internal organs and spread through the body are called**
    a. Mycoses
    b. Systemic mycoses
    c. Mycotoxicosis
    d. Superficial mycoses

36. **The staining technique used to stain the metachromatic granules of Corynebacterium**
    a. Giemsa stain   **b. Albert's stain**
    c. Acid-fast staining
    d. Both a and b

37. **The orderly increase in all components of protoplasm of a cell is called**
    a. Reproduction   b. Cell division
    c. Growth   d. All of the above

38. **The causative organism of cholera, i.e. Vibrio show the movement called**
    a. Gliding movement
    b. Darting movement
    c. Pseudopodia movement
    d. None of these

39. **Erythrocytes will get its ATP energy only by**
    a. Glycolysis
    b. Krebs cycle

    c. Electron transport
    d. HMP shunt

40. **Virus will contain**
    a. Cell membrane   b. Cell wall
    c. DNA   **d. DNA or RNA**

41. **The bacterial pili mainly contain**
    a. Carbohydrates   b. Lipids
    c. Proteins   d. Minerals

42. **The wonder drug of Second World War is produced by**
    a. Algae   **b. Fungi**
    c. Bacteria   d. Plants

43. **Role of bacteria in carbon cycle is**
    a. Photosynthesis
    b. Chemosynthesis
    c. Breakdown of organic compounds
    d. Assimilation of nitrogen compounds

44. **Centromere is that part of chromosome where**
    a. Nucleoli are formed
    b. Crossing over takes place
    c. Chromatids are attached
    d. Naking occurs

45. **Somatic cells of the adult body are haploid in many *except***
    a. Vertebrates   b. Invertebrates
    c. Fungi   d. Vascular plants

46. **Congenital diseases are**
    a. Diseases present at birth
    b. Deficiency disease
    c. Occur during life
    d. Spread from one individual to another

47. **The enzyme needed in biological systems for joining two molecules is called**
    a. Lyses   b. Diastases
    c. Polymerases   d. Hydrolase

48. **Mesosomes are the part of**
    a. Plasma membrane
    b. ER
    c. Lysosome
    d. Golgi

49. All prokaryotes are surrounded by a cell wall *except*

    a. Mycoplasmas   b. Sperochetes
    c. Actinomycetes   d. Methanogena

50. Enzyme hydrolyzing bacterial cell wall

    a. Lysosome   b. Reductase
    c. Protease   **d. Lysosome**

51. Cows can digest straw because they contain

    a. Cellulose hydrolyzing microorganisms
    b. Protein hydrolyzing bacteria
    c. Lipid hydrolyzing microorganisms
    d. Amino acid degrading bacteria

52. The nucleus controls protein synthesis in the cytoplasm by sending

    a. Chromatin
    b. A DNA template
    c. mRNA molecule
    d. A specialized protein

53. The site of energy production in a cell

    a. Micro body   b. Chromosome
    c. Ribosome   **d. Mitochondria**

54. Thylakoids is present in

    a. Mitochondria   **b. Chloroplast**
    c. ER   d. Golgi apparatus

55. Which one of the following bacteria has found extensive use in genetic engineering work in plants?

    a. *Clostridum septicum*
    b. *Xanthomonas oryzae*
    c. *Bacillus coagulans*
    d. *Agrobacterium tumefaciens*

56. Maximum application of animal cell culture technology today is in the production of

    a. Insulin   b. Interferon
    c. Vaccines   d. Edible proteins

57. Bacterial ribosomes are composed of

    a. Protein and DNA
    b. Protein and mRNA
    c. Protein and rRNA
    d. Protein and tRNA

58. The photorespiration involves

    a. Calvin cycle
    b. Hatch-Slack cycle
    c. Glycolate cycle
    d. Krebs cycle

59. Bioleaching is done by

    a. Protozoa   **b. Bacteria**
    c. Algae   d. All of the above

60. Inclusion bodies diagnostic of rabies are called

    a. Elementary bodies
    b. Pascheur bodies
    c. Negri bodies
    d. Guarnieri bodies

61. Which of the following genera is most likely to contain organisms capable of surviving high temperature?

    a. Vibrio   b. Pseudomonas
    c. Torula   d. Coxiella

62. The major role of minor elements inside living organisms is to act as

    a. Co-factors of enzymes
    b. Building blocks of important amino acids
    c. Constituents of hormones
    d. Binder of cell structure

63. The apparatus used to maintain a continuous culture

    a. Chemostat   b. Autostat
    c. Thermostat   d. Both a and c

64. The test used to detect the deamination of the amino acids by bacteria

    a. Nessler's reagent test
    b. Proteolytic test
    c. Lactose test
    d. Rose a indole reagent test

65. Diphtheria is caused by

    a. Corynebacterium
    b. Staphylococcus
    c. Streptococcus
    d. None of these

66. Koplic spots observed in the mucous membrane is characteristic feature of the disease
   a. Rubella   b. Measles
   c. Mumps   d. Influenza

67. A bacterium containing prophage is called as
   a. Lytic   **b. Lysogen**
   c. Lytogen   d. None of these

68. The most infectious food-borne disease is
   a. Tetanus   b. Dysentery
   c. Gas gangrene   **d. Botulism**

69. An example for common airborne epidemic disease
   a. Influenza   b. Typhoid
   c. Encephalitis   d. Malaria

70. Viral genome can become integrated into the bacterial genomes are known as
   a. Prophage
   b. Temperate phage
   c. Bacteriophage
   d. Metaphage

71. Rancidity of stored foods is due to the activity of
   a. Toxigenic microbes
   b. Proteolytic microbes
   c. Saccharolytic microbes
   d. Lipolytic microbes

72. Virion means
   a. Infectious virus particles
   b. Non-infectious particles
   c. Incomplete particles
   d. Defective virus particles

73. Virulence of the microorganisms can be reduced by
   a. Attenuation b. Avirulence
   c. Inactivation   d. Freezing

74. The test used for detection of typhoid fever
   a. Widal test
   b. ELISA

75. Bacteriophage capable of only lytic growth is called
   a. Temperate   b. Avirulent
   c. Virulent   d. None of these

76. Diphtheria bacillus is otherwise known as
   a. Fried-Landers bacillus
   b. Klebs-Löffler bacillus
   c. Frisch bacillus
   d. Koch's bacillus

77. Acridine dyes are more effective against
   a. Gram-positive b. Gram-negative
   c. Rickettsia   d. Mycoplasma

78. In bacteria pigment bearing structures are
   a. Chloroplast
   b. Protoplast
   c. Spheroplast
   d. Chromatophores

79. The procedure of differential staining of bacteria was developed by
   a. H. Gram   **b. W. Gram**
   c. N. Gram   d. A. Gram

80. Intermediate group of pathogen between bacteria and viruses which are intracellular parasites, are called
   a. Mycoplasmas   **b. Rickettsiae**
   c. Prions   d. Virusoides

81. Bacillus is an example of
   a. Gram-positive bacteria
   b. Gram-negative bacteria
   c. Virus
   d. Viroid

82. Amoebic dysentery in humans is caused by
   a. Plasmodium
   b. Paramecium
   c. Yeast
   d. *Entamoeba histolytica*

c. Rosewaller test
d. Western blotting

83. Viral genome that can become integrated into bacterial genome is called
    a. **Prophage**
    b. Temperate phage
    c. Bacteriophage
    d. Metaphage

84. Cytochromes are
    a. Oxygen acceptors
    b. ATP acceptors
    c. **Electron acceptors**
    d. Protein acceptors

85. The cells having F plasmid in the chromosomes were termed as
    a. **Hfr**   b. F⁻
    c. Hbr   d. C⁺

86. Recombination process occurring through the mediation of phages is
    a. Conjunction   **b. Transduction**
    c. Transformation d. Transfection

87. Mordant used in grams staining is
    a. Crystal violet   **b. Iodine**
    c. Saffranine   d. All of these

88. Parasitic form must contain
    a. Capsule   b. Cell wall
    c. Endospores   d. Flagella

89. Gram staining is an example for
    a. Simple staining
    b. Differential staining
    c. Negative staining
    d. **None of these**

90. Following cocci are non-motile *except*
    a. **Staphylococcus**
    b. Meningococcus
    c. Gonococcus
    d. *Rhodococcus agilis*

91. *Aspergillus fumigatus* can infect
    a. Birds   **b. Animal**
    c. Man   d. All of them

92. Enterotoxin responsible for food poisoning is secreted by
    a. Enterococci
    b. *Entamoeba histolytica*

    c. Enterobacteriaceae
    d. **Straphylococci**

93. Autolysis is done by
    a. Mitochondria   **b. Lysosome**
    c. Golgi bodies   d. Peroxisomes

94. A facultative anaerobic is
    a. Only grow anaerobically
    b. Only grow in the presence of O_2
    c. Ordinarily an anaerobe but can grow with O_2
    d. **Ordinarily an aerobe but can grow in absence of O_2**

95. The per centage of O_2 required by moderate anaerobe is
    a. 0%   b. <0.5%
    c. **2–8%**   d. 5–10%

96. Interferon is formed by
    a. Lymphocytes   b. Lymphoblast
    c. Fibroblasts   **d. All of these**

97. Pigment bearing structure of bacteria are
    a. Mesosomes
    b. Plasmids
    c. Mitochondria
    d. **Chromospheres**

98. Spirochete is
    a. Gonococci
    b. Staphylococci
    c. *Treponema palladium*
    d. **Streptococci**

99. Histones are found in
    a. Prokaryotes   **b. Eukaryotes**
    c. Viruses   d. None of these

100. Cell wall of gram-negative bacteria is
    a. Thick
    b. Lipids are present
    c. **Teichoic acids are absent**
    d. None of these

101. Cytoplasmic streaming is present in
    a. Prokaryotes   b. Animals
    c. **Eukaryotes**   d. Both a and b

102. The motile bacteria is
    a. *S. typhi*   b. *K. pneumoniae*
    c. Anthracis   d. Shigella

103. The stain used to demonstrate fungus
    a. Albert
    b. Nigerosin
    c. **Lactophenol cotton blue**
    d. None of these

104. Exotoxins are
    a. **Heat labile**
    b. Heat stable
    c. Part of cell wall
    d. Polymerized complexes

105. The viruses that attack bacteria are
    a. Bacterial viruses
    b. Bacterial pathogens
    c. **Bacteriophages**
    d. Various

106. The size of virus particle may range
    a. 0.02–0.2 µm   b. 0.5–10 µm
    c. **0.015–0.2 µm**   d. 0.1–100 µm

107. The bacterial cell multiplication is usually by
    a. Mitosis   b. Meiosis
    c. Conjugation   d. **Binary fission**

108. Rod-shaped bacteria are known as
    a. Cocci
    b. Comma forms
    c. **Bacilli**
    d. Polymorphic forms

109. All the groups of bacteria have cell wall
    a. Mycobacteria   b. **Mycoplasma**
    c. Clostridia   d. Rickettsiae

110. Thickness of cell wall ranges from
    a. 9–10 nm   b. 12–13 nm
    c. **10–25 nm**   d. 30–40 nm

111. Teichoic acids and teichuronic acids are found in
    a. **Gram-positive bacteria**
    b. Gram-negative bacteria
    c. Fungi
    d. None of these

112. Mesosomes are
    a. Kind of ribosomes
    b. Formed during cell lysis
    c. A part of cell wall
    d. **Principal sites of respiratory enzymes**

113. The characteristic shape of the bacteria is maintained because of
    a. Capsule   b. **Cell wall**
    c. Cell membrane   d. Slime layer

114. Bacterial capsule is chemically composed of
    a. Polypeptide
    b. Polynucleotides
    c. Polysaccharides
    d. **Polypeptides or polysaccharides**

115. The cell wall deficient form of bacteria is
    a. Mycoplasma   b. **'L' form**
    c. Protoplast   d. Spheroplast

116. Mesosomes are also known as
    a. Mitochondria   b. Chloroplasts
    c. Golgi complex   d. **Chondroids**

117. The differences between gram-positive and gram-negative bacteria is shown to reside in the
    a. **Cell wall**   b. Nucleus
    c. Cell membrane   d. Mesosomes

118. Capsule formation occurs in the presence of
    a. Albumin   b. Charcoal
    c. **Serum**   d. Starch

119. The virulence determining antigens of microorganisms may be
    a. Proteins and polysaccharides
    b. Carbohydrate–protein complexes
    c. Polysaccharide–phospholipids–protein complexes
    d. **All of these**

120. Organelles with hydrolytic enzymes are
    a. Mitochondria   b. Golgi complex
    c. **Lysosome**   d. Ribosome

121. **Bacterial locomotion is accomplished by**
    a. Fimbria
    b. Flagella
    c. Cytoskeleton
    d. Both a and b

122. **Fimbriae are demonstrated by**
    a. Culture
    b. Gram stain
    c. Biochemical reactions
    d. Haemagglutination test

123. **The motile bacteria is**
    a. *Salmonella typhi*
    b. *Klebsiella pneumoniae*
    c. *Bacillus anthracis*
    d. *Shigella flexneri*

124. **Following cocci are non-motile *except***
    a. Staphylococcus
    b. Meningococcal
    c. Gonococcus
    d. *Rhodococcus agilis*

125. **Metachromatic granules are chemically composed of**
    a. Lipids
    b. Proteins
    c. Polymetaphosphates
    d. Polysaccharide

126. **Metachromatic granules can be stained with**
    a. Saffranine
    b. Methylene blue
    c. Crystal violet
    d. Sapienic acid

127. **Bacteria multiply by**
    a. Spore formation
    b. Simple binary fission
    c. Conjugation
    d. Gametes

128. **Bacterial spores are**
    a. Weakly acid fast
    b. Strongly acid fast
    c. Alcohol fast
    d. Non acid fast

129. **Endospores can be stained with**
    a. Saffranine
    b. Crystal violet
    c. Methylene blue
    d. Malachite green

130. **The following bacteria produce pigment, *except***
    a. *Pseudomonas pyocyanea*
    b. *Serratia marcescens*
    c. Pneumoniae
    d. *Staphylococcus aureus*

131. **The order of stains in Gram-staining procedure is**
    a. Crystal violet, iodine solution, alcohol, saffranine
    b. Iodine solution, crystal violet, saffranine, alcohol
    c. Alcohol, crystal violet, iodine solution, saffranine
    d. All of these

132. **The percentage of alcohol used in Gram-staining is**
    a. 75%
    b. 90%
    c. 60%
    d. 25%

133. **Gram-positive bacteria appear as**
    a. Pink
    b. Violet
    c. Both a and b
    d. None of these

134. **Gram-negative bacteria appear as**
    a. Pink
    b. Violet
    c. Both a and b
    d. None of these

135. **The action of alcohol during Gram-staining is**
    a. Allows the color
    b. It adds color
    c. Decolorizes the cells
    d. None of these

136. **Lipid contents is more in**
    a. Gram-negative bacteria
    b. Gram-positive bacteria
    c. Same in both
    d. None of these

137. **Cell wall is**
    a. Thick in gram-positive than gram-negative
    b. Thick in gram-negative than gram-positive
    c. Equal in both
    d. In gram-negative cell wall is absent

138. The lipid content present in gram positive bacterial cell wall is
    a. 1–10%   **b. 1–5%**
    c. 2–8%   d. None of these

139. Rickettsiae stained by this technique
respond as
    a. Gram-positive
    b. Gram-negative
    c. Between positive and negative
    d. None of these

140. Chlamydiae occur in
    a. Elementary bodies
    b. Reticulate bodies
    c. Complex structures
    d. Both a and b

141. Chlamydiae can be stained better with
    a. Ziehl-Neelsen staining
    b. Castaneda and Machiavello stains
    c. Giminez stains
    d. Both b and c

142. Algae means
    a. Fresh water organisms
    b. Sea weeds
    c. Fresh water weeds
    d. None of these

143. The study of algae is known as
    a. Algalogy   **b. Phycology**
    c. Mycology   d. Bacteriology

144. The free floating algae are known as
    a. Phytoplankins b. Benthons
    c. Sea weeds   d. None of these

145. Sexual reproduction of algae is carried
by
    a. Isogamy   b. Anisogamy
    c. Oogamy   **d. All the above**

146. In algae, advanced type of sexual reproduction is
    a. Isogamy
    b. Anisogamy
    c. Oogamy
    d. None of these

147. Alginic acids and its salts are obtained
from the wall of
    a. Red algae
    b. Brown algae
    c. Green algae
    d. Red and brown algae

148. The molds obtained nutrition from dead
and decaying matter which are called
    a. Saprophytes   b. Parasites
    c. Commensals   d. None of these

149. Most molds are capable of growing in
the temperature range between
    a. 0° and 25°   b. 0° and 35°C
    c. 10° and 25°C   d. 10° and 35°C

150. Examples for actinomycetes
    a. Streptomyces   b. Spirillospora
    c. Frankia   **d. Dermatophilia**

151. Pellicle is found in only
    a. Algae   b. Fungi
    c. Bacteria   **d. Protozoans**

152. The largest virus is
    a. Parvovirus   **b. Poxvirus**
    c. Rhabdovirus   d. None of these

153. The smallest virus is
    a. Parvovirus   **b. Rhabdovirus**
    c. Poxvirus   d. Adenovirus

154. The extracellular infections virus particle is called
    a. Capsid   b. Nucleocapsid
    c. Virion   d. None of these

155. Shape of bacteriophage is
    a. Brick shape
    b. Bullet shape
    c. Helical shape
    d. Tadpole shape

156. If only one stain is used for staining a
specimen
    a. Simple staining
    b. Negative staining
    c. Differential staining
    d. None of these

157. Other than the sample (specimen) the remaining portion is stained then it is called
    a. Simple staining
    b. Negative staining
    c. Differential staining
    d. None of these

158. If more than one stain is used, such staining is called
    a. Simple staining
    b. Negative staining
    c. Differential staining
    d. None of these

159. 'Fluorescence' was first observed by
    a. Kohler   b. Coons
    c. Both a and b   d. None of these

160. By using fluorescence property fluorescent antibody technique was developed by
    a. Kohler   **b. Coons**
    c. Both and b   d. None of these

161. During staining for electron microscopy, the method which improves contrast of specimen is
    a. Positive staining
    b. Negative staining
    c. Shadow staining
    d. None of these

162. The inorganic forms of nitrogen, which are accepted by bacteria are
    a. Nitrates   b. Nitrites
    c. Ammonium salts
    d. All of these

163. Archaeobacteria are known as
    a. Halophiles
    b. Red extreme halophiles
    c. Osmophiles
    d. Extreme thermophiles

164. Nitrite is converted into nitrate by the bacteria
    a. Nitrosomonas   b. Nitrosocytes
    c. Nitrobacteria
    d. Azotobacter

165. Sulphur oxidizing bacteria is
    a. Alcaligenes   b. Pseudomonas
    c. Thiobacillus d. None of these

166. Bacillus Shigella is
    a. Hydrogen-oxidizing bacteria
    b. Sulphur-oxidizing bacteria
    c. Iron-oxidizing bacteria
    d. Nitrite-oxidizing bacteria

167. The group of bacteria which depends on organic sources in nature for their energy requirements. They are said to be
    a. Chemotrophs   b. Prototrophs
    c. Heterotrophs d. Organotrophs

168. Majority of bacteria are
    a. Saprophytes   b. Symbiont
    c. Commensalisms **d. Parasites**

169. Symbiont is
    a. Bacteria in symbiotic association
    b. The group of fungi in symbiotic association
    c. The groups participating in symbiotic association
    d. All of these

170. The best example for symbiotic association is
    a. *E. coli* in intestine of man
    b. Lichens
    c. Normal flora of skin
    d. All of the above

171. The enzymes responsible for decomposition is
    a. Lipolytic   **b. Proteolytic**
    c. Lysosome   d. Both a and b

172. Urea is decomposed by the species
    a. Micrococcus spp.
    b. Nitrosomonas spp.
    c. Proteus spp.
    d. Both a and c

173. Phycobiont is
    a. The algal part in lichens
    b. The fungal part in lichens
    c. Laustoria formation
    d. None of these

174. **Parasitic form must contain**
    a. **Capsules**   b. Cell wall
    c. Endospores   d. Flagella

175. **The total number of genes in the group of same individuals is**
    a. Genome   b. Gene map
    c. **Gene pool**   d. None of these

176. **Transformation was observed mainly in**
    a. Bacteriophages
    b. **Temperate phages**
    c. -phage
    d. All of these

177. **Capsulated forms of bacteria are**
    a. Virulent   b. Avirulent
    c. **Useful**   d. Symbiotic

178. **The bacterial cells participating in conjugation are**
    a. **Conjugants**   b. Fertile cells
    c. Exconjugants   d. None of these

179. **Phagocytes are**
    a. Monocytes   b. Macrophages
    c. Basophils   d. **All of these**

180. **The microorganism engulfed by phagocyte resides in a vacuole is known as**
    a. **Phagosome**   b. Lysosome
    c. Both a and b   d. None of these

181. **Toxic products in phagolysosome are**
    a. H_2SO_4 b. Singlet O_2
    c. Superoxide radicals
    d. **All of these**

182. **During destruction of antigen particle in phagolysosome the product formed during formulation is**
    a. Acetic acid   b. **Lactic acid**
    c. Citric acid   d. None of these

183. **The coating of a bacterium with antibody or complement that leads to enhanced phagocytosis of the bacterium by phagocytes is called**
    a. **Opsonisation**
    b. Agglutination
    c. CFT   d. None of these

184. **Attenuation means**
    a. Killing of the bacteria (microorganism)
    b. **Inactivation of bacteria**
    c. More activating the bacteria
    d. Both 1 and 2

185. **Infection that results in pus formation are called**
    a. Focal infection
    b. Acute infection
    c. **Pyogenic infection**
    d. Chronic infection

186. **Presence of viable bacteria in the blood stream is called**
    a. Viraemia   b. Septicemia
    c. **Bacteraemia**   d. Bactericidal

187. **Presence of viruses in the blood stream is known as**
    a. **Viraemia**   b. Bacteraemia
    c. Septicemia   d. Pyemia

188. **Opsonin is the**
    a. Cell wall component
    b. Plasma component
    c. **Serum component**
    d. Cytoplasm component

189. **-haemolytic bacteria is**
    a. *Streptococcus pyrogenes*
    b. *Str. pneumoniae*
    c. *Str. viridans*
    d. *Str. faecalis*

190. **The natural reservoir of infection for cholera is**
    a. Flies   b. Horse
    c. **Man**   d. None of these

191. **Main cause for cholera is**
    a. **Poverty and insanitation**
    b. Mosquitoes
    c. Toxin produced by pesticides
    d. None of these

192. *Vibrio cholerae* **differs from Vibrio El Tor by**
    a. It shares some Inaba, Ogawa subtypes with El Tor

b. Resistant to polymyxin
c. El Tor is non-motile
d. **Causes less subclinical infections as compared to El Tor**

193. **Cholera vaccine gives protection for**
    a. 1–3 months   b. **3–6 months**
    c. 6–9 months   d. 9–12 months

194. **Prophylaxis of cholera is**
    a. Protected water supply
    b. Environmental sanitation
    c. Immunization with killed vaccines
    d. **All of these**

195. *Sh. dysenteriae* **is also known as**
    a. *Sh. shiga*
    b. Shschmitzi
    c. **Both a and b**
    d. *Shpara dysenteriae*

196. **Acid-fast bacteria are**
    a. Neisseria   b. Staphylococci
    c. **Mycobacteria**   d. All of the above

197. **Mycobacteria are stained with**
    a. Gram's staining
    b. Simple staining
    c. Both a and b
    d. **Ziehl-Neelsen staining**

198. **Niacin test is positive in case of**
    a. Corynebacterium
    b. *M. tuberculosis*
    c. *M. bovis*
    d. *M. avium*

199. **Lepromin test is**
    a. Negative in tubercular leprosy
    b. Positive in lepromatous type
    c. **Indicated delayed hypersensitivity test**
    d. Indicates infection

200. **Streptococcus forms causes which type of infections?**
    a. Fever   b. Zoonotic
    c. Pyogenic   d. **None of these**

4

Principles of Soil Science

1. Sequence of soil color is
   a. **Hue-value-chroma**
   b. Value-hue-chroma
   c. Hue-chroma-value
   d. Chroma-value-hue

2. Sequence of soil structure is
   a. Class-type-grade
   b. Grade-class-type
   c. **Class-grade-type**
   d. None of these

3. In soil, about _____ mg P_2O_5 per hectare is present in plough layer.
   a. **2000–3000**   b. 20,000–30,000
   c. 1000–1500   d. 15,000–20,000

4. _____ P is present in organic form.
   a. 10%–20%
   b. **70%–80%**
   c. 40%–50%
   d. None of the above

5. When C : P is 200 : 1, then
   a. **Net mineralization will take place**
   b. Net immobilization will take place
   c. Partial mineralization and partial immobilization will take place
   d. None of these

6. When C : P is more then 300 : 1, then
   a. **Net immobilization will take place**
   b. Net mineralization will take place
   c. Both of the above
   d. None of the above

7. When P in the soil is less than 0.2% then _____ will take place.
   a. Mineralization
   b. Immobilization
   c. **Both of the above**
   d. None of the above

8. When P in the soil is more than 0.02%, then _____ will take place.
   a. Immobilization
   b. **Mineralization**
   c. Partial immobilization
   d. None of these

9. If pH is high _____ complex will be found in the soil.
   a. Fe-P   b. **Ca-P**
   c. Al-P   d. None of these

10. When pH of the soil is less, than _____ complex will be found in the soil.
    a. **Fe-P**
    b. Mg-P
    c. Ca-P
    d. None of these

11. Phosphorus potential may be defined as
    a. $pH - \frac{1}{2} PCa$
    b. $\frac{1}{2} pH - PCa$
    c. $\frac{1}{2} PCa^+$
    d. $PHa + \frac{1}{2} 2PH_2 PO_4$

12. **Lime potential may be defined as**
    a. $pH - 1/2 PCa$
    b. $1/2 PCA + PH_2 PO_2$
    c. $1/2 pH - 1/2 PCa$
    d. None of these

13. **Fraction of P which can enter into the soil solution by iso ion exchange within an appropriate limit can be defined as**
    a. Non-labile -P   **b. Labile-P**
    c. A-value   d. None of these

14. **A-value was given by friend and dean in**
    a. 1964   b. 1961
    c. 1951   **d. 1952**

15. **A-value is given in kg/ha, whereas L-value and E-value is given in**
    a. Percent   **b. ppm**
    c. Ton/ha   d. All of these

16. **Denotes A-value in which a is equal to**
    a. Amount of available nutrients in soil
    b. Amount of total nutrients in soil
    c. Quantity of unavailable nutrients in soil
    d. None of these

17. **The amount of P in soil and soil solution that can exchange with orthophosphage in addition to soil as measured by plant growth in soil system, is termed**
    a. A-value   b. E-value
    c. L-value   d. None of these

18. **K in igneous rocks is about**
    a. 8.9%   **b. 3.1%**
    c. 2.5%   d. 18.5%

19. **Amount of K in plants is**
    a. 8.0 to 15.0%   b. 0.1 to 0.5%
    c. 10.0 to 18.9%   **d. 0.3 to 6.0%**

20. **Amount of K in soil plough layer is about**
    a. $1,000-10,000 \, kg/ha$
    b. $5,000-6,000 \, kg/ha$
    c. $10,000-70,000 \, kg/ha$
    d. $8,0.0-10,000 \, kg/ha$

21. **Amount of K in feldspar and mica is about**
    a. 60%   b. 90%
    c. 20%   d. 10%

22. **$NaAlSi_3O_8$ is the formula of**
    a. Anorthite   b. Mica
    c. Albite   d. Illite

23. **$CaAl_2Si_3O_8$ is the formula of**
    a. Anorthite
    b. Montmorillonite
    c. Illite-illite
    d. Albite

24. **Olsen method of P determination is more effective in**
    a. Acidic soils
    b. Normal soils
    c. Alkaline soils
    d. None of these

25. **$0.5 \, M \, NaHCO_3$ (pH 8.5) is**
    a. Bray No.1 extractant
    b. Olsen extractant
    c. Bray No. 2 extractant
    d. None of these

26. **$0.03 \, N \, NH_4 F + 0.025 \, N \, HCl$, is called**
    a. Bray No. 1 extractant
    b. Labile-P
    c. A-value
    d. None of these

27. **Available Zn in the soil can be determined by using the solution of**
    a. $1 \, N \, NH_4 OCA$
    b. $DTPA + Cl_2$ (pH 7.3)
    c. $EDTA + (NH_4)_2 CO_2$
    d. All of these

28. **In the P-determination by Olsen method, the ratio of soil and extracting should be**
    a. 1:2   b. 1:100
    c. 1:10   d. 1:50

29. **For the determination of by Bray method, the ratio of soil and solution should be**
    a. 1:20   **b. 1:10**
    c. 1:100   d. 1:25

30. Diphenyl amine is an indicator which is used in determination of
    a. Organic carbon
    b. Potassium
    c. Phosphorus
    d. Iron

31. SMP buffer is used in _____ determination.
    a. Lime
    b. Nitrogen
    c. Potassium
    d. Calcium

32. Gypsum requirements of the soil can be determined by 344 N (A-B) in which N is equal to
    a. Normality of EDTA
    b. Amount of EDTA used
    c. Morality of EDTA
    d. None of the above

33. Average annual rainfall of India is about
    a. 212 cm
    b. 52 cm
    c. 122 cm
    d. 81 cm

34. South-west monsoon contributes about _____ of total rainfall.
    a. 50%
    b. 95%
    c. 30%
    d. 80%

35. The major source of irrigation in India is/are
    a. Wells
    b. Rainfall
    c. Canal
    d. Tanks

36. About _____ per cent of total area of India is covered by medium rainfall (75–115 cm).
    a. 40
    b. 80
    c. 20
    d. 28

37. The total area of India which obtained 115–200, 115 cm rainfall in one year is _____ %.
    a. 10
    b. 40
    c. 20
    d. 28

38. Pre-monsoon contributes about _____ of total rainfall in India.
    a. 10.5%
    b. 30.0%
    c. 20.0%
    d. 15.8%

39. Maximum rainfall in whole seeds found in
    a. UP
    b. Maharashtra
    c. MP
    d. West Bengal

40. Urea contains _____% N whereas ammonium sulphate contains about 20.6% N.
    a. 46%
    b. 42%
    c. 40%
    d. 44%

41. How much per cent of P_2O_5 is found in triple superphosphate?
    a. 25
    b. 48
    c. 16
    d. 32

42. How much per cent of K_2O is present in mutilate of potash?
    a. 60
    b. 30
    c. 40
    d. 80

43. How much per cent of K_2O is found in sulphate of potash?
    a. 30
    b. 40
    c. 50
    d. 20

44. How much per cent of N is found in DAP?
    a. 12
    b. 18
    c. 45
    d. 5

45. How much per cent of P_2O_5 is present in DAP?
    a. 26
    b. 16
    c. 46
    d. 36

46. Sulphur-coated urea contains about _____ % of nitrogen.
    a. 36
    b. 16
    c. 26
    d. 46

47. Potassium metaphosphate contains about _____ per cent of K_2O.
    a. 30
    b. 20
    c. 10
    d. 40

48. Murate of potash is more effective in _____ soils.
    a. Saline
    b. Alkaline
    c. Neutral
    d. Acidic

49. KNO$_3$ is more effective in _____ soils.
    a. **Alkaline**
    b. Neutral
    c. Acidic
    d. All of the above

50. Nitrophosphate contains about _____ per cent of N and 20% of P.
    a. 10   b. **20**
    c. 40   d. 12

51. Cow-dung contains about _____ N.
    a. **2.0%**   b. 0.5%
    c. 1.0%   d. 3.5%

52. FYM contains about 0.75% N, 0.6% P and _____ K.
    a. 0.75%   b. 4.5%
    c. **1.25%**   d. 0.25%

53. The nitrogen content of groundnut cake is about.
    a. 4.5%   b. 2%
    c. 3.0%   d. **7.0%**

54. The phosphorous and potassium content of groundnut cake is
    a. 2.5%   b. 3.5%
    c. **1.5%**   d. 4.5%

55. Til cake contains about _____ N.
    a. **0.6%**   b. 10.2%
    c. 2.5%   d. 9.8%

56. Cotton-seed cake have about 4% N, 1.9% P and _____ % F.
    a. 2.8   b. 3.5
    c. **1.7**   d. 4.0

57. In India, the area under red soil is
    a. **5.1 mha**   b. 8.0 mha
    c. 7.5 mha   d. 10.5 mha

58. Red soils are found maximum in
    a. UP   b. Assam
    c. MP   d. **Tamil Nadu**

59. The area of black soils in India is
    a. **54.6 mha**   b. 28.5 mha
    c. 5.65 mha   d. 75.0 mha

60. Black soil is the _____ largest group of Indian soils.
    a. First   b. **Second**
    c. Third   d. None of these

61. Which of the following states has maximum black soils?
    a. UP   b. Haryana
    c. **Maharashtra**   d. Bihar

62. Black soils _____ in organic matter and high in bases.
    a. Poor
    b. **High**
    c. Medium
    d. None of the them

63. Black soils are _____ when wet and very hard when dry.
    a. Very hard   b. Soft
    c. **Very soft**   d. Hard

64. Black soils have _____ about of lime and P.
    a. **High**   b. Very low
    c. Low   d. Very high

65. The contribution of hill soils in India is about
    a. **4.5 mha**   b. 1.3 mha
    c. 10.0 mha   d. 2.8 mha

66. Holly soils are low in lime and are
    a. Alkaline   b. **Saline**
    c. Acidic   d. None of these

67. The head quarter of NBSS and LUP is located at
    a. Bhopal   b. Delhi
    c. **Nagpur**   d. Mumbai

68. Tara soils are high in
    a. Iron   b. Organic
    c. **Sodium**   d. Calcium

69. Peaty soils have _____ organic matter.
    a. 5–8%
    b. **50–55%**
    c. 10–40%
    d. 60–65%

70. Peaty soils have _____ in nature.
    a. Alkaline   b. Acidic
    c. Saline   d. Neutral

71. Alluvial soils are found mostly in
    a. Kerala, Karnataka and Maharashtra
    b. **AP, MP and Assam**
    c. UP, Punjab, Haryana, Bihar and West Bengal
    d. None of the above.

72. Alluvial soils are rich in
    a. KO_2, P_2O_5, and lime
    b. Fe, Al
    c. N
    d. Si, Cu

73. Desert soils are found in
    a. Arid and semi-arid region
    b. Humid and sub-humid region
    c. Arid and humid region
    d. **All of the above**

74. Desert soils are mostly found in
    a. **Rajasthan, Haryana and South Punjab**
    b. UP, MP and Bihar
    c. Assam and Nagaland
    d. Kerala, Karnataka and Tamil Nadu

75. A number of ped on together, which is similar in nature is called
    a. Soils variant   b. Soil type
    c. **Polypedon**   d. Soil association

76. Crop logging is a method of
    a. Soil fertilizing evaluation
    b. **Plant analysis for assessing required of nutrients for crop production**
    c. Assessing crop damage
    d. Testing suitability of fertilizers

77. Hidden hunger means
    a. Deficiency symptoms are seen when the nutrient is deficient
    b. **The nutrient is not deficient but apparently seems to be deficient**
    c. Severe yield reduction may occur without appearance of deficiency symptoms

    d. Visual deficiency symptoms are suppressed by other elements

78. Which of the following is an organic horizon?
    a. **O**   b. B
    c. A   d. C

79. Which of the following is not a mineral horizon?
    a. A   b. **C**
    c. B   d. O

80. Any mineral horizon contains less than 30% organic matter, if the mineral fraction contains more than 50% clay or less than _____ organic matter, if the mineral fraction do not have clay.
    a. **20%**   b. 10%
    c. 40%   d. 5%

81. Which of the following is called elucidated horizon?
    a. A1   b. A3
    c. **A4**   d. B1

82. In soil classification B denotes
    a. **Burried horizon** b. Classic horizon
    c. Organic horizon   d. None of these

83. In soil classification, B denotes
    a. Fragipan accumulation
    b. Accumulation of illuvial clay
    c. **Comentation**
    d. All of these

84. Which of the following is not a class of topography?
    a. Smooth   b. **Broken**
    c. Wavy   d. None of these

85. The moisture content in the soil at −1/3 bar pressure is called
    a. Filed capacity b. Witting point
    c. **Both of them** d. None of them

86. The moisture content in the soil at −15 bar pressure is called
    a. **Filed capacity** b. Witting point
    c. Wilting point   d. None of these

87. Residual sodium carbonate (RSC) can be defined as
    a. $CO_3^- + HCO_3^-) - (Ca^{++} + mg^{++})$
    b. $(CO_3^- - HCO_3^-) + (Ca^{++} - mg^{++})$
    c. $(CO_3^- - HCO_3^-) - (Ca^{++} + mg^{++})$
    d. None of these

88. RSC of safe water should be
    a. 1.25–2.5
    b. **More than 1.5**
    c. Less than 1.5
    d. None of these

89. If RSC of a water is more than 2.5, then the water will be
    a. **Sefe**
    b. Unsustainable
    c. Marginal
    d. None of these

90. Which of the following is not an aerobic bacterium?
    a. **Clostridium**
    b. Beijerinckia
    c. Azotobacter
    d. Dexia

91. Clostridium may be present in the soils having pH
    a. 5–9
    b. 8–10
    c. 2–4
    d. **4–5**

92. The amount of N_2 fixed by Clostridium is _____ mg N_2 per cent.
    a. **15–25**
    b. 2–7
    c. 7–15
    d. 25–50

93. Beijerinckia may be present in the soils having pH
    a. **3–9**
    b. 7–12
    c. 1–5
    d. None of these

94. Beijerinckia may fix N_2 up to _____ ha N_2/gm sugar.
    a. **50–60**
    b. 20–25
    c. 10–12
    d. 25–50

95. Azolla can fix _____ kg N_2/ha per year.
    a. **80–100**
    b. 10–15
    c. 30–40
    d. 100–120

96. Efficiency of applied fertilizers in wheat crop is
    a. 20–50%
    b. **60–80%**
    c. 35–50%
    d. 44–64%

97. Efficiency of applied fertilizers in rice crop is
    a. 5–50%
    b. **50–75%**
    c. 10–75%
    d. 60–90%

98. Efficiency of applied fertilizers in sugarcane is
    a. 60%
    b. **40%**
    c. 20%
    d. 90%

99. Which of the following is the slow release fertilizer?
    a. **Surface coated urea**
    b. Neem cake and supergrain urea
    c. N-serve
    d. All of the above

100. Under tropical condition, the volatilization losses of nitrogen is
    a. **20–50%**
    b. 40–80%
    c. 10–20%
    d. None of the above

101. About _____% of total N per cent in soil is in the form of organic N.
    a. 95–99
    b. 100
    c. **40–80**
    d. 20

102. If crop residues have more than 2% nitrogen, than _____ will take place.
    a. Net mineralization
    b. Partial immobilization
    c. Net immobilization
    d. **None of these**

103. If the C-N ratio of crop residues is more than 30, then
    a. Immobilization will take place
    b. **Mineralization will take place**
    c. Partial mineralization will take place
    d. All of these

104. If the C-N ratio of crop residues is 20 : 3 then
    a. Mineralization may not take place
    b. Immobilization may take place
    c. **Immobilization may not take place**
    d. Not known

105. If C-N ratio of crop residues is less than 22 then
   a. Immobilized will take place
   b. Mineralization will take place
   c. Both of these
   d. None of these

106. The organism which can survive at the temperature 10–15°C is termed as
   a. Psychrophylic   b. Thermoduric
   c. Mesophylic   d. Thermophylic

107. The microbes which can survive at the temperature 25–30°C is termed as
   a. Thermoduric
   b. Psychrophylic
   c. Mesophylic   d. Thermophylic

108. The microbes which can tolerate the temperature up to 60°C but no growth will be found, is called
   a. Thermoduric   b. Mesophylic
   c. Themophylic   d. None of these

109. In whole soil body, the contribution of mineral matter is
   a. 75%   b. 45%
   c. 25%   d. 5%

110. A and B horizon collectively known as
   a. Soil solum   b. Ragolith
   c. Bed rock   d. None of these

111. The uncomplicated material above the bed rock is known as
   a. Bed rock   b. Regolith
   c. Soil solum   d. A-horizon

112. If free energy of water is less, then the water movement into the soil will be
   a. Less   b. Zero
   c. More   d. None of these

113. Phenolphthalein is an inductor, which is used in titration for the determination of
   a. Organic carbon
   b. P$_2$O$_5$ content
   c. CaCO$_3$ equivalent
   d. K$_2$O content

114. If the 60–70% portion of soil is un-aggregated, then soil structure of soil will certainly called
   a. Weak   b. Strong
   c. Moderate   d. Structureless

115. If only 20–30% portion of soil is unaggregated, then soil structure is known as
   a. Structureless   b. Weak
   c. Moderate   d. Strong

116. If the scope of the land is 3–4%, then is will be called
   a. Moderately sloped land
   b. Level land
   c. Sloping land   d. None of these

117. A process in which ammonium is formed from organic compounds, is termed as
   a. Nitrification   b. Mineralization
   c. Ammonification
   d. None of these

118. Oxidation a ammonium of nitrate is called
   a. Nitrification
   b. Immobilization
   c. Ammonification
   d. None of these

119. A process in which organic form of nitrogen is changed into inorganic form is called
   a. Mineralization   b. Immobilization
   c. Ammonification
   d. Nitrification

120. A process in which the inorganic form of nitrogen is changed into organic form is called
   a. Nitrification   b. Mineralization
   c. Immobilization
   d. Ammonification

121. Which of the following is a facultative anaerobic bacterium?
   a. Azotobacter   b. Klebsiella
   c. Beijerinckia   d. Dexia

122. Which of the following is not a photo-synthetic bacterium?
   a. Rhodomicrobium
   b. Rhodospirillum
   c. Rhodopsendomonas
   d. Bacillus

123. The name of nutrient which is critical for N-fixation in leguminous plants?
   a. Mo   b. K
   c. Ca   d. K

124. By inoculation, we can _____ the nitrogen fixation in the soil.
   a. Increase
   b. Proportionate
   c. Decrease
   d. None of the above

125. The population of bacteria is _____ by inoculation process.
   a. Decrease   b. Increase
   c. Remain same   d. None of them

126. *Rhizobium meliloti* can fix the nitrogen in roots of
   a. Alfalfa   b. Lentil
   c. Pea   d. Beans

127. *Rhizobium trifolli* can fix the nitrogen in the roots of
   a. Sweet clover   b. Lupines
   c. Clover   d. Soybean

128. *Rhizobium leguminosorum* can fix the nitrogen in the roots of
   a. Alfalfa, sweet clover
   b. Pea, sweet pea, lentil
   c. Clovers
   d. Beans

129. *Rhizobium phaseoli* can fix the nitrogen in the roots of
   a. Lentil   b. Pea
   c. Soybean   d. Beans

130. *Rhizobium japonicum,* can fix the nitrogen in the roots of
   a. Soybean   b. Beans
   c. Cowpea   d. Lentil

131. The N_2 fixation in the roots of alfalfa is _____ kg N_2/ha per year
   a. 100–150   b. 50–75
   c. 125–300   d. None of these

132. The N_2 fixation in the roots of pea is _____ kg N_2/ha per year
   a. 80–150   b. 15–75
   c. 90–110   d. 50–100

133. The N_2 fixation in soybean may up to _____ kg N_2/ha per year
   a. 100–175   b. 65–115
   c. 60–100   d. 40–90

134. The N_2 fixation by the symbiosis of Rhizobium species and legume is called
   a. Symbiotic N_2 fixation
   b. Non-symbiotic N_2 fixation
   c. Both of the above
   d. None of these

135. The N_2 fixation by Azotobacter and Azospirillum in the cereals is called
   a. Symbiotic N_2 fixation
   b. Non-symbiotic N_2 fixation
   c. Both of the above
   d. None of the above

136. Non-symbiotic bacteria fixes _____ amount of N_2 than symbiotic N_2 fixers.
   a. Less   **b. Equal**
   c. More   d. Not known

137. Nutrient index is used to prepare the
   a. Soil productivity map
   b. Soil fertility map
   c. Both of the above
   d. None of the above

138. If nutrient in India is less than 1.6, it indicates that soil is _____ in nutrients.
   a. Deficient   **b. Adequate**
   c. Average   d. None of these

139. 1.6–2.3 value of nutrient index indicates
   a. Average fertility of soil
   b. Adequate fertility of soil
   c. Both of the above
   d. None of the above

140. More than 2.3 value of nutrient index indicates
     a. **Average productivity of soil**
     b. Adequate fertility of soil
     c. Adequate productivity of soil
     d. None of them

141. The acidity of H^+ in aqueous phase of soil called
     a. Reserve acidity
     b. Permanent charge
     c. **Active acidity**   d. None of these

142. The acidity of H^+ absorbed on solid phase is known as
     a. **Reserve acidity**   b. Active acidity
     c. Both of the above
     d. None of these

143. Organic matter contains about _____ per cent organic carbon.
     a. 32   b. 68
     c. 18   d. **58**

144. Per cent nitrogen is equal to
     a. Per cent organic matter × 5
     b. Per cent organic matter × 0.05
     c. **Per cent organic matter × 1.5**
     d. None of the above

145. When 2/3 portion of the octahedral position is occupied by trivalent cation, then it is called
     a. **Dioctahedral**   b. Trioctahedral
     c. Both of the above
     d. None of the above

146. When all octahedral position is occupied by divalent cations, called
     a. Dioctahedral   b. **Tetrahedral**
     c. Trioctahedral   d. None of these

147. Chlorite is _____ type mineral.
     a. 2 : 1   b. 2 : 2
     c. **1 : 1**   d. None

148. C-spacing of chlorite is
     a. 10.0A   b. **8.2 A**
     c. 14.3 A   d. 7.3 A

149. The CEC is highest in
     a. Vermicullite   b. Chlorite
     c. Montmorillonite
     d. Kaolinite

150. When two or more than two types of clay minerals are interest rate fixed along X-axis, is called
     a. **Interstratified minerals**
     b. Intergraded clay minerals
     c. Mixed minerals
     d. None of the above

151. The minerals which have not the ideal properties of a particular mineral, but they have intermediate properties, are called
     a. Interstratified minerals
     b. Intergraded clay minerals
     c. **Mixed minerals**
     d. None of the above

152. The difference between the layers of first unit and the same layers of second unit, is called
     a. Layer distance
     b. C-spacing
     c. **Interlayer distance**
     d. None of these

153. RT in K^+/Ca^{++} is known as
     a. **Potassium potential**
     b. Phosphate potential
     c. Lime potential
     d. None of these

154. A complex, which is formed when an organic compound bound with central metal in ion with the help of co-ordinated bonding, is termed as
     a. **Chelate**   b. Chemical ion
     c. Chemical complex
     d. None of these

155. By increasing one element, the availability of other element also increases, is termed as
     a. Antagonism   b. Association
     c. Synergism   d. None of these

156. The loss N_2 from the ingaseous forms is N_2O_2, NO_2, N_2, etc. is called
    a. **Volatilization**   b. Denitrification
    c. Nitrification   d. None of these

157. $C(N_2H_2)_2 + H_2O$ $(NH_4)_2$ CO_2, indicates
    a. **Urea hydrolysis**
    b. N_2 fixation
    c. Urea oxidation
    d. None of the above

158. The microbes which use inorganic compound and make self-organic food from outside, are termed
    a. Heterotrophs   b. **Anaerobes**
    c. Autotrophs   d. None of these

159. The microbes who require H_2S as energy source and CO_2 as carbon source, are termed as
    a. Photoautotrophs
    b. Photoorganotrophs
    c. **Chemoautotrophs**
    d. Chemoorganotrophs

160. The microbes which use inorganic compound and make self-organic food from outside, are termed as
    a. Heterotrophs   b. **Anaerobes**
    c. Autotrophs   d. None of these

161. The microbe who require inorganic compound as every source and carbon source, is termed as
    a. Photoautotrophs
    b. **Photoorganotrophs**
    c. Chemoautotrophs
    d. Chemoorganotrophs

162. Which of the following Rhizobium species are not fast grower?
    a. *R. meliloti*   b. ***R. trifoli***
    c. *R. phaseoli*   d. *R. japonicum*

163. If the organic carbon content of the soil is less than 0.05% than soil is in _____ organic carbon.
    a. High   b. Poor
    c. **Medium**   d. None of these

164. If the organic carbon content of the soil is between 0.05% to 0.75% than soil is _____ in inorganic carbon.
    a. High   b. Poor
    c. **Medium**   d. None of these

165. If the organic carbon content of the soil is more than 0.75%, than soil is _____ in organic carbon.
    a. **Low**   b. Very low
    c. Medium   d. Very high

166. If the available nitrogen in the soil is less than 280 kg per hectare, then soil is _____ in available nitrogen.
    a. **Low**   b. Very low
    c. Medium   d. Very high

167. If the soil contains 280 to 500 kg nitrogen per hectare, then it is called _____ in available nitrogen.
    a. Low   b. **Medium**
    c. High   d. Very high

168. If the available phosphorus in the soil is in between 10 and 25 kg per hectare, then soil is known as _____ in available phosphorus.
    a. **Medium**   b. High
    c. Low   d. Very good

169. If the soil contains 110 to 280 kg K_2O/ha, then soil will be _____ in this regard.
    a. High   b. Low
    c. Very high   d. **Medium**

170. If the EC of the soil is less than 1 mmhos /cm², then it is known as
    a. **Normal**
    b. Critical for germination
    c. Critical for growth
    d. None of these

171. If the soil EC is more than 4 mmhos/cm², then it is known as
    a. **Injurious to most of the crop**
    b. Critical for most of the crops
    c. Normal for the crop
    d. None of these

172. **Bulk density of normal soil is**
    a. 2.33 g/cc   **b. 1.8 g/cc**
    c. 1.33 g/cc   d. 2.5 g/cc

173. **Soil water will be available to the plants at**
    a. –5 to –10 bar pressure
    b. –10 to –15 bar pressure
    c. **–1/2 to –15 bar pressure**
    d. None of these

174. **Khaira disease of rice is caused due to the deficiency of**
    a. **Zn**   b. N
    c. Mn   d. Cu

175. **Which one of the following is not a soil eroding agents?**
    a. The concentration of rainfall
    b. **The slope of the ground**
    c. The nature of plant cover
    d. None of these

176. **Which of the following is the kind of water erosion?**
    a. Sheet erosion   b. Gully erosion
    c. Rill erosion   **d. All of these**

177. **Which one of the following states has the highest area of eroded soil?**
    a. **Maharashtra**   b. Gujarat
    c. AP   d. MP

178. **Which of the following is the soil conservation measures for controlling the soil erosion?**
    a. Creation of protective surface
    b. Cultivation of soil-binding crops
    c. Control on grazing of animals
    d. **All of the above**

179. **Plant takes the potassium in the form of**
    a. **K$^+$**   b. K$_2$
    c. K$_2$O   d. All of these

180. **Plant takes the nitrogen in the form of**
    a. NO   b. N$_2$
    c. NO$_3$
    d. All of these

181. **Phosphorus is taken by the plants in the form of**
    a. H$_3$PO$_4$ b. PO$_3$
    c. PO$_4^-$ **d. H$_2$PO$_4^-$**

182. **Zinc is taken by the plants in the form of**
    a. **Zn^{++}**   b. ZnO$_2$
    c. ZnO   d. All of these

183. **Sulphur is taken by the plants in the form of**
    a. H$_2$SO$_4$ b. SO$_4^-$
    c. SO$_3$ d. S

184. **_____combines with pectin in the plants to form a cell-wall constituent, known as calcium pectate.**
    a. **Ca**   b. Na
    c. Mg   d. Fe

185. **Under the deficiency of _____ the new leaves turn yellow; roots and stems become abnormally long and develop woodiness.**
    a. Fe   b. K
    c. P   **d. S**

186. **_____deficiency shows multiple bad formation.**
    a. Zn   **b. N**
    c. Cu   d. Mo

187. **The whip-tail in cauliflower is a deficiency symptom of**
    a. **Mo**   b. Na
    c. Cl   d. Fe

188. **In the deficiency of _____ the older leaves of the plants became yellowish or pale green.**
    a. **N**   b. K
    c. P   d. Mg

189. **In the deficiency of _____ the plants fail to make a quick start, do not develop a satisfactory root system and sometimes develop a tendency to show a reddish or purplish discoloration of stem.**
    a. N   b. P
    c. **K**   d. Ca

190. _____deficiency produces the characters like ringing of alfalfa leaves with rows of small white spot, interveinal chlorosis and firing along the adages of maize leaves in which the older leaves affected first.

    a. **K**   b. Ca
    c. P   d. Cu

191. Lime is used for correcting the soil

    a. **Acidity**   b. Salinity
    c. Alkalinity   d. All of the above

192. Which of the following material is used for correcting the alkalinity of the soil?

    a. Lime   **b. Phosphorus**
    c. Gypsum   d. Potassium

193. A soil with a distinctly developed profile, including A, B and C horizons, is called

    a. ABC soil   b. Developed soil
    c. Soil solum   d. All of these

194. The head quarters of India soil server and land-used organization which was established in 1956 is at

    a. **New Delhi**   b. Nagpur
    c. Hyderabad   d. Deheradun

195. A vertical section of the soil through all horizons and extending into the parent material is known as

    a. Soil horizons   **b. Soil solum**
    c. Soil profile   d. None of the above

196. Which one of the following is not soil-forming factors?

    a. Climate   b. Organisms
    c. Relief   **d. Moisture**

197. Which one of the following is an active factor of soil formations?

    a. Parent material
    b. Relief
    c. Time
    d. Climate

198. Eluviations refer to

    a. Removal of clay from above horizons to lower horizons
    b. Removal of clay and sesquioxide from above horizons to lower horizons
    c. Removal of sesquioxide from above horizons to lower horizons
    d. None of the above

199. Illuviation refers to

    a. Accumulation of clay and sesqui-oxide in lower horozons
    b. Accumulation of clay and sesquioxide in above horizons
    c. Removal of clay and sesquioxide from lower horizons
    d. None of the above

200. International Journal of Tropical Agriculture published from

    a. India   b. Sri Lanka
    c. Pakistan   d. Ethiopia

5

Principles of Agriculture Statistics and Ag. Business

1. **Activity index measures**
   a. **Availability of water insoluble N in fertilizers**
   b. Availability of water insoluble P in fertilizers
   c. Availability of water insoluble K in fertilizers
   d. Availability of water insoluble S in fertilizers

2. **Match the following**

Column A Soil type	Column B pH
A. Extremely acidic	i. 4.5–5.0
B. Very strongly acidic	ii. 5.1–5.5
C. Strongly acidic	iii. 5.6–6.0
D. Medium acidic	iv. 6.1–6.5
E. Slightly acidic	v. Below 4.5

   a. **A-v, B-i, C-iv, D-iii, E-ii**
   b. A-v, B-i, C-ii, D-iii, E-iv
   c. A-v, B-i, C-ii, D-iv, E-iii
   d. A-iii, B-i, C-ii, D-v, E-iv

3. **The species of Azolla is not**
   a. Pinnata   b. Rubra
   c. Nilotica   d. **Max**

4. **Azolla is**
   a. Weed
   b. Weed suppressor in flooded rice acting as a nutrient supplier
   c. Fodder
   d. **All of these**

5. **Azolla provides to Anabaena**
   a. Protective cavity
   b. Nutrients
   c. **Both**   d. None

6. **What is true about Azolla, small floating aquatic fern**
   a. Applied as basal dose
   b. Applied as top dressing
   c. Weed suppressor
   d. **All**

7. **Match the following**

Column A Bacterium type	Column B Function
A. Nitrosomonas	i. Oxidixe ammonium to nitrate
B. Thiobacillus	ii. Oxidize inorganic S to sulphate
C. Nitrobacters	iii. Oxidise nitrite to nitrate
D. T. ferroxides	iv. Oxidise ferrous iron to ferric form

   a. **A-i, B-ii, C-iii, D-iv**
   b. A-iv, B-i, C-ii, D-iii
   c. A-iv, B-i, C-ii, D-iv
   d. A-iii, B-i, C-ii, D-iv

8. **Autotrophs are**
   a. Organisms which obtain energy from sunlight (photoautotrophs)
   b. Organisms obtain energy from oxidation of inorganic substances (chemoautotrophs)

51

c. Organisms which obtain energy from organic substances

d. **Both a and b**

9. **Alage are**

a. **Photoautotrophs**

b. Chemoautotrophs

c. Chemoautotrophs and photoautotrophs

d. All of the above

10. **Azotobacter is**

a. Aerobic in nature

b. Free-living bacteria

c. Utilize atmospheric N

d. **All of them**

11. **Azotobacter can be recognized on the basis of**

a. Shape

b. Pigmentation

c. Mobility

d. **All**

12. **In which of the following is not a species of Azotobacter?**

a. Chroococcum

b. Beijerinckii

c. Macrocytogenes

d. **Crass**

13. **Base saturation is**

a. Expressed as %

b. Extent to which the adsorption complex of a soil is saturated with exchangeable cations than H and Al ion

c. **Both**

d. None

14. **Beer-Lambert law stated that**

a. Magnitude of light absorption is proportional to concentration of light

b. Magnitude of light absorption is proportional to both concentration of thickness and intensity of light

c. Functionality of spectrometer

d. **All**

15. **Biological tests are**

a. **Techniques for assessing the nutrient status of soil by use of biological materials**

b. Techniques for assessing the phosphorus status of soil by use of chemical materials

c. Techniques for assessing the carbon status of soil by use of dead organisms

d. Techniques for assessing the calcium status of soil by use of micro-organisms

16. **Usually BGA found in**

a. **Fresh water**   b. Cold water

c. Both   d. Standing water

17. **Range of habitat for BGA is**

a. Fresh water

b. Standing water of rice field

c. **Both**

d. Ocean water

18. **BGA belongs to which order**

a. Chroococcales and Chmaesiphonates

b. Nostocales and Stigonematoales

c. Plerocapsales

d. **All**

19. **Additional benefits of BGA are**

a. O_2 for rice culture and supply GPS (growth promoting substances)

b. Increase SOM

c. Improve soil physical structure by increasing water-stable aggregates

d. **All**

20. **According to Bray's nutrient mobility concept**

a. Amount of nutrient produce maximum yield increases from a variable net value on decreasing the mobility of that particular nutrient in soil

b. Amount of nutrient determined principally by the magnitude of the yield and composition of crop

c. **Both are correct**

d. None

21. **Catalyst in steam reforming of natural gas or naphtha**

a. **Ni**   b. Ca

c. Ma   d. Fe

22. **Catalysts are extremely used in**
    a. Metallurgy
    b. **Fertilizer industry**
    c. Both   d. Oil production

23. **C-N ration is**
    a. **Ratio of weight of total organic carbon to the weight of total N in soil or organic material**
    b. Ratio of weight of total organic carbon to the weight of total N in soil
    c. Ratio of weight of total organic carbon to the weight of total N in organic material
    d. All

24. **Exchangeable potassium is**
    a. Form of K in soil exchange complex recovered by exchange process using agent
    b. Form of K in soil exchange complex not recovered by water solution
    c. **Above both are correct**
    d. None is correct

25. **Fertilizer is**
    a. **Natural or manufactured material, dry or liquid and supply one or more plant nutrient**
    b. Natural material, dry or liquid and supply one or more plant nutrient
    c. Manufactured material, dry or liquid and supply one plant nutrient
    d. None

26. **GIS is**
    a. Geographical information system
    b. A computerized database management system for capturing, storing, validating, analyzing, displaying and managing spatially
    c. Used to generate map on erosion hazard, land suitability
    d. **All**

27. **Plant materials helpful in green manuring are**
    a. Sann hemp   b. Dhaincha
    c. Pillipesara   d. **All**

28. **Application of gypsum in agriculture is**
    a. **Reclamation of alkali soils**
    b. Source of calcium
    c. Byproduct of phosphoric acid
    d. To make POP

29. **Match the following sets given below in column A and column B**

Column A	Column B
i. Black soils of Maharashtra	A. Alfisol
ii. Gangetic alluvial soils	B. Ultisol
iii. Laterite soils of Kerala	C. Vertisol
iv. Red soils of Chhotanagpur	D. Entisol

    a. **i-C, ii-D, iii-B, iv-A**
    b. i-D, ii-B, iii-C, iv-A
    c. i-C, ii-D, iii-B, iv-A
    d. None

30. **The number of essential minerals needed by the plants for the growth and development is**
    a. 19   b. 23
    c. 28   d. **17**

31. **Name of the disease in cauliflower due to deficiency of molybdenum is**
    a. Whiptail   b. Chlorosis
    c. Necrosis   d. Both a and c

32. **Crop logging is a procedure for**
    a. Evaluation of plant productivity
    b. Assessing the need of nutrients for crop production
    c. Assessing the crop damage
    d. Testing suitability of fertilizers

33. **Match the column A and column B in below given sets**

Col. A	Col. B
i. N	A. Root growth
ii. P	B. Acceleration of vegetative growth
iii. K	C. Reduction of nitrate
iv. Mo	D. Translocation of photosynthates

a. **i-B, ii-A, iii-D, iv-C**
b. i-A, ii-B, iii-C, iv-D
c. i-D, ii-C. iii-A, iv-B
d. None

34. **An approach which has been adopted by the Planning Commission in Delineating India into agroclimatic zones**

a. Sectoral approach
b. Project approach
c. Crop production approach
d. **Holistic approach**

35. **OMC (organic matter content) of histosols and hydromorphic soil is**

a. **2–18%**   b. 50–57%
c. 30-40%   d. 60–70%

36. **Name of elements whose deficiency would prevent the completion of plant's life cycle**

a. Macroelements
b. Trace elements
c. Micronutrients
d. **Essential elements**

37. **Poor nitrification of non-edible cake derived from *Madhuca latifolia* is due to**

a. Good C-N ratio
b. Due to oil
c. **Presence of alkaloids**
d. Low N-content

38. **Match the following**

	Col. A		Col. B
i.	Orobanche	A.	Stem semi-parasite
ii.	Loranthus	B.	Semi root parasite
iii.	Cuscuta	C.	Total root parasite
iv.	Striga	D.	Total stem parasite

a. **i-C, ii-A, iii-D, iv-B**
b. i-B, ii-A, iii-D, iv-C
c. i-C, ii-A, iii-B, iv-D
d. i-C, ii-B, iii-D, iv-A

39. **Inter-cropping is most appropriate and effective in which kind of biome?**

a. **Forest**   b. Desert
c. Semi-dry land   d. All

40. **Function of seminal roots in wheat is**

a. Strength against lodging
b. **Nutrition in early stages of crops**
c. Produce in vegetative stages of the crop
d. Produce in reproductive stage of the crop

41. **Irrigation efficiency is very low in irrigated farming in India mainly because of**

a. Poor quality of irrigation water
b. Adverse climatic conditions
c. **A major part of irrigated area is under canal irrigation system**
d. Major portion of soil is not suitable for irrigation

42. **Match the column A and B**

Column A Common Name	Column B Scientific Name
i. Sugarcane shoot borer	A. *Tryporza novella*
ii. Sugarcane root borer	B. *Emmalocera depressella*
iii. White fly of sugarcane	C. *Chilo sacchariphagus*
iv. Sugarcane top borer	D. *Aleurolobus barodensis*

a. **i-C, ii-B, iii-D, iv-A**
b. i-C, ii-A, iii-D, iv-B
c. i-C, ii-D, iii-B, iv-A
d. i-D, ii-B, iii-C, iv-A

43. **Chemical name of "Celphos" is**

a. **Aluminium phosphide**
b. Aluminium carbide
c. Copper sulphate
d. Ammonium tetrachloride

44. **Zinc phosphide releases a gas name**

a. **PH_3**   b. NH_3
c. CH_4 d. All

45. **Most important nutrient required for tomato cultivation is**

a. **B and Zn**   b. Al and B
c. P and Zn   d. S and B

46. Normal seed rate of brinjal is
    a. **100 Sq.m/ha**   b. 200 Sq.m/ha
    c. 300 Sq.m/ha   d. 500 Sq.m/ha

47. Variety "Pant Samrat" is recognized for
    a. **Phomopsis blight and bacterial blight**
    b. Early blight
    c. Late blight
    d. All

48. The study of soils in relation to crop growth
    a. Pedology   **b. Edaphology**
    c. Both   d. Soil science

49. The % of soil water in soil is
    a. **40%**   b. 30%
    c. 25%   d. 20%

50. Organic matter content in Indian soil is
    a. **5%**   b. 10%
    c. 23%   d. 7%

51. The % of porosity in soil is
    a. 30   b. 40
    c. **50**   d. 60

52. Petrology is the science which defines
    a. **Rocks**   b. Water
    c. Soil water   d. Hydrosphere

53. Examples of igneous rocks are
    a. Granite   b. Basalts
    c. **Both**   d. Stone

54. Sedimentary rocks are exemplified through
    a. Lime stone, sand stone
    b. Gypsum
    c. Dolomite
    d. **All**

55. Metamorphic rocks are
    a. Gnesis
    b. Marble
    c. Quartzite and slate
    d. **All**

56. Exfoliation is process of
    a. **Breaking of rocks into pices in effect of temperature**
    b. Breaking of rocks into pices in effect of pressure
    c. Both
    d. Breaking of rocks into pices in effect of mass flow of air

57. Chlorite is
    a. **2 : 1 : 1 or 2 : 2 type clay mineral**
    b. 3 : 2 type clay mineral
    c. 4 : 2 type clay mineral
    d. 7 : 1 type clay mineral

58. Feldspar is recognized as
    a. **Most dominant mineral on earth**
    b. Least dominant mineral on earth
    c. Moderate dominant mineral on earth
    d. None of the above

59. Kaolinite is a
    a. Weathering mineral
    b. Mineral contain most stable soil structure
    c. Ore of P
    d. **Both a and b**

60. Apetite is
    a. Source of P   b. Source of B
    c. **Both a and b**   d. None

61. In which of the following hydroxide as a agent in binding the soil particle together?
    a. Iron hydroxide
    b. Aluminium hydroxide
    c. **Both**   d. None

62. In soil profile structure, horizon-A is recognized for
    a. **Fertility**
    b. More better clay minerals
    c. More abundant silica particles
    d. Least productive zone

63. Match column A and B

Col A	Col B
i. Elevation zone	A. A + B horizons
ii. Soulm	B. A + B + C horizons
iii. Regolith	C. Elevation zone
iv. Horizon	D. O horizon

a. i-D, ii-C, iii-B, iv-A
b. i-A, ii-D, iii-B, iv-C
c. i-D, ii-A, iii-C, iv-B
d. i-D, ii-C, iii-B, iv-A

64. Bulk density of normal soil is
   a. 3.33 g/cc   b. 2.33 g/cc
   c. 1.33 g/cc   d. 2.39 g/cc

65. Picnometer is applied for
   a. Particle density measurement
   b. Particle volume measurement
   c. Particle mass measurement
   d. None of the above

66. Fixed value of particle density which is widely accepted
   a. 2.65 g/cc   b. 3.45 g/cc
   c. 1.34 g/cc   d. 2.34 g/cc

67. Methods of soil contamination in greenhouse gases are
   a. Hot steam   b. Solarization
   c. Soil fumigation   **d. All**

68. Light affect the growth of chrysan-themum due to the event of photo-periodism as
   a. Quantitatively   **b. Qualitatively**
   c. Both   d. Biochemically

69. Expellation of all life forms from soil is known as
   a. Sterilization
   b. Heat and solorization
   c. Fumigation   d. All

70. Chrysanthemum cultivars require at least 16°C temperature for flowering and 27°C temperature for rapid flowering are
   a. Thermopositive
   b. Intermediate
   c. Thermonegative
   d. None

71. In which of the following is a quantitative long day plant?
   a. Carnation   b. Aloe
   c. Tomato   d. Potato

72. What is "Rose mix"?
   a. Fertilizer   b. Fungicide
   c. Insecticide   d. Sweet dish

73. Bent neck is a common disease for
   a. Carnation   **b. Rose**
   c. Gladiolus   d. Potato

74. Bird of Paradise having a very famous variety with name of
   a. Mandel's Gold b. Gold
   c. Sobit   d. Rani

75. Which one of the helpful in the maintenance of GHGs (CO_2) in greenhouse gases
   a. Charcoal   b. Ventilation
   c. Organic mulch   **d. All**

76. Cut flower which belongs to first rank in global flower trade
   a. Gladiolus   b. Carnation
   c. Gerbera   **d. Rose**

77. Most favorable greenhouse for temperate region is
   a. Saw-tooth type
   b. Gable type
   c. Ridge and furrow type
   d. Quonset type

78. Least suitable cladding material for hilly areas is
   a. Poly ethylene
   b. Poly carbonates
   c. Glass
   d. Fibre glass

79. Rose cultivation require temperature of carbon under greenhouse gases
   a. 8–10°C   b. 20–23°C
   c. 25–28°C   d. 12–16°C

80. Netting is a most common cultivation practice applied for
   a. Carnation
   b. Rose
   c. Gerbera
   d. Chrysanthemum

81. To which group do the black cotton soils of India belong?
a. Laterite　　b. Podzol
c. Chernozem　　d. Alluvial

82. The siwaliks stretch between
a. Indus and Sutlej
b. Potwar basin and Tista
c. Sutlej and Kali
d. Sutlej and Tista

83. Which state is the largest?
a. Rajasthan　　b. UP
c. MP　　d. AP

84. Vitamin C is
a. Acetic acid　　b. Citric acid
c. Lactic acid　　**d. Ascorbic acid**

85. The synthetic drug is
a. Morphine　　b. Reserpine
c. Aspirin　　d. Digitalis

86. The earliest known pesticide is
a. Permethrin　　b. DDT
c. Nicotine　　d. Zeatin

87. The acid present in nucleic acid is
a. Nitric acid　　b. Sulphuric acid
c. Phosphoric acid　d. Carbonic acid

88. The substances which cannot be further decomposed by ordinary chemical means is
a. Water　　b. Air
c. Sugar　　**d. Silver**

89. The edible part is also called as
a. Coconut　　b. Groundnut
c. Pea　　**d. Wheat**

90. The transport of organic substance in plants is through
a. Fiber　　**b. Phloem**
c. Xylem　　d. Wood

91. What is chromosome numbering in a human ovum?
a. 24　　**b. 46**
c. 52　　d. 48

92. The disease sickle cell anemia is caused by
a. Iron deficiency
b. Malarial infection
c. Poor hygiene
d. None of these

93. The diameter of silt particles in USDA system is
a. 0.02–0.002 mm　**b. 0.05–0.002 mm**
c. 0.01–0.001 mm　d. 0.05–005 mm

94. The relative distribution of primary soil particles in given soil is known as
a. Soil texture　　b. Soil structure
c. Soil plasticity　　d. Soil consistency

95. The lightest soil texture among the following soils is
a. Silty clay loam　b. Sandy loam
c. Silty loam　　**d. Loamy sandy**

96. For the some volume the smallest specific surface is in
a. Cube　　**b. Spherical**
c. Flattened　　d. Elongated

97. The structure of a normal intensively cultivated soil is degraded due to loss of
a. Plant nutrients
b. Soluble salts
c. Organic matter
d. Organic matter and soluble bases

98. The degraded structure of alkali soil is restored by application of
a. Organic matter　**b. Gypsum**
c. Dolomite　　d. Lime stone

99. Process of soil podzolization requires which one of the following climates?
a. Humid temperate
b. Subtropical
c. Arid
d. Tropical

100. The maximum area of Indian soil is covered by
a. Alluvial soil　　b. Black cotton soil
c. Forest soil　　d. Desert soil

101. Total geographical area of India
    a. **328.7 m.ha**   b. 435.6 m.ha
    c. 433.2 m.ha   d. 322.6 m.ha

102. King of the pest is/are
    a. *Meloidogyne incognita*
    b. *Meloidogyne javanica*
    c. *Meloidogyne areina*
    d. *Meloidogyne incognita and M. javanica*

103. Root-knot nematode is a most serious pest for
    a. **Tomato**   b. Brinjal
    c. Brassica   d. Mango

104. King of pulses is
    a. *Cicer arietinum L.*
    b. *Cicer reticulatum L.*
    c. *Vigna mungo L.*
    d. *Cajanus cajanus L.*

105. White brinjal is a rich source of vitamin B, preferred by
    a. **Diabetes**   b. Cancer
    c. Asthama   d. All

106. Most preferred method for extraction of tomato seed is
    a. **Alkali seed**
    b. Chemical method
    c. Lime water method
    d. All

107. Responsible components for colour and pungency of chilli are respectively
    a. **Capsanthin and capsicin**
    b. Capsicin and capsanthin
    c. Sinigrin and capsicin
    d. Capsanthin and sinigrin

108. Plant physiology is a branch of
    a. Plant anatomy
    b. Plant geography
    c. Applied botany
    d. **Pure botany**

109. Discovery of electron microscope by
    a. **E. Ruska (1931)**   b. Pasteur
    c. Newton   d. None

110. Symplast is
    a. **Continuity of protoplasm through plasmodesmata**
    b. Discontinuity of protoplasm through plasmodesmata
    c. Cyclosis of food in plant body
    d. A method of food circulation inside the plant body

111. Apoplast is
    a. **Cell wall space outside the protoplast constitute**
    b. Cell wall space inside the protoplast constitute
    c. Cell wall space outside and inside the protoplast
    d. None of the above

112. Middle lamella is mainly made up of
    a. Cellulose
    b. Calcium phosphorus
    c. **Calcium pectate**
    d. Mg pectate

113. Singer and Nicolson is refer to
    a. **Gave fluid mosaic model of cell membrane**
    b. Propose the cell theory
    c. Propose the concept of biogenesis
    d. Role in plant biotechnology

114. Unit membrane model of cell membrane was proposed by
    a. Robertson
    b. Danielli-Devson
    c. **Singer-Nicolson**
    d. Robert-Hooke

115. In which of the following is cell organelle?
    a. Plasma membrane
    b. Vacuole
    c. Microtubule
    d. **Mitochondrion**

116. One angstrom unit is equal to
    a. 10^{-6} cm   b. **10^{-8} cm**
    c. 10^{-7} cm   d. 10^{-10} cm

117. Spherosomes are rich in
   a. **Fats**   b. Protein
   c. Carbohydrates   d. Minerals

118. Conversion of lipids into sugars inside plant body occurs
   a. ER   b. **Glyoxysomes**
   c. Peroxisomes   d. Lomasomes

119. 70S ribosomes are not exist in
   a. Mitochondria   b. **Nucleus**
   c. Chloroplast   d. Vacuoles

120. RER is concerned with
   a. Mitochondria   b. Vacuoles
   c. Spherosomes   d. **Ribosomes**

121. The chief function of Golgi bodies is in plants
   a. **Cell-wall formation**
   b. Cell-membrane formation
   c. Plasma-membrane formation
   d. Tonoplast formation

122. In which of the following is not a part of cytoskeleton?
   a. **Plasmodesmata**
   b. Microtubules
   c. Intermediate filament
   d. Actin filament

123. In which of the following is not bounded by double membrane (cell organelle)?
   a. Nucleus   b. Mitochondria
   c. Chloroplast   d. **Vacuole**

124. One of the following will settle down at last during centrifugation is
   a. **Ribosome**   b. Nucleus
   c. Vacuoles   d. Chloroplast

125. Which pair is known as microbodies?
   a. **Glyoxysome–peroxisome**
   b. Ribosome–spherosome
   c. Spherosome–peroxisome
   d. Spherosome–lysosomes

126. Desmotubules are found in
   a. **Plasmodesmata** b. Lysosome
   c. Spherosome   d. Vacuole

127. Double-stranded circular DNA is found in
   a. Nucleus   b. Chloroplast
   c. Mitochondria   d. **All**

128. Angle between the covalent bonds in water molecules in between the two hydrogen atoms
   a. **105 degree**   b. 112 degree
   c. 139 degree   d. 167 degree

129. Water molecules are polar but they are
   a. Acidic
   b. **Neutral**
   c. Positively charged
   d. Negatively charged

130. Which one of the responsible for uniqueness of water
   a. **Hydrogen bonding**
   b. Covalent bonding
   c. Both
   d. None of the above

131. The correct route of water in a plant is
   a. Passage cell of endodermis, xylem, cortex, root hair
   b. Cortex, root hair, xylem, cortex, root hair
   c. Passage cell of endodermis, root hairs, xylem, passage cells of endodermis
   d. **Root hair, cortex, passage cell of endodermis, xylem**

132. Which types of water are not available to plants?
   a. Hygroscopic water
   b. Gravitational water
   c. Capillary water
   d. **Both a and b**

133. Water potential is not affected by
   a. Water surface   b. Solute
   c. Pressure   d. DPD

134. Cells put in highly concentrated solutions will display
   a. Exosmosis
   b. **Plasmolysis**

c. Endosmosis

d. Leaching out of protoplasm from the cell

135. **Water potential can be lowered by**

a. Pressure

b. Solutes

c. Temperature

d. Both a and c

136. **Water potential can be measured by**

a. Solute partial

b. Metric potential

c. Pressure potential

d. All of the above

137. **Godlewski propounded the theory is called**

a. Pulsation theory

b. Capillary action theory

c. Relay pump theory

d. Transpiration-cohesion tension theory

138. **Water vapour in woody plants are remove via**

a. Hydathodes   **b. Lenticels**

c. Stomata   d. Cuticle

139. **Accumulation of K⁺ in guard cells of stomata results in**

a. Death

b. Opening of stomata

c. Guttation

d. Closure of stomata

140. **Accumulation of K⁺ in guard cells of stomata results in**

a. Death

b. Closure

c. Guttation

d. Opening of stomata

141. **Hydathodes are the sites for**

a. Guttation   b. Transpiration

c. Evaporation   d. Respiration

142. **Stomata are exclusively present on the upper surface of a leaf in**

a. Water lily   b. Potamogeton

c. Potato   d. Alfalfa

143. **Metabolism will be disturbed if the leaves are coated with wax/oil in**

a. Lotus   b. Vallisneria

c. Hydrilla   d. Drosera

144. **Chloroplasts are present in**

a. Epidermal cells of leaf

b. Cortex of stem

c. Guard cells of stomata

d. Pith of stem

145. **If water enters the adjacent guard cells of Oak leaf stomata, then**

a. Transpiration will occur

b. Cells are damaged

c. Stomata open more widely

d. Guttation occurs

146. **An RNA molecule which can function as a catalyst is known as**

a. RNAase

b. RNA polymerase

c. Ribozyme

d. Reverse transcriptase

147. **Which term includes all the activities required to keep an organism alive?**

a. Metabolism   b. Growth

c. Excretion   d. Transport

148. **What else is found in sweat besides water?**

a. Salt   b. Sugar

c. Glycerol   d. Amino acids

149. **For proving inputs like quality seeds, fertilizers and pesticides, the agency that is present at the Village Panchayat Samiti level is**

a. NABARD

b. Nationalized bank

c. Insurance companies

d. Co-operative society

150. **Cropping intensity and gestation period of the crops grown are**

a. Inversely related

b. Exponentially related

c. Directly related

d. Not interrelated

151. At present, the farming system of India has become
    a. Export oriented
    b. **Market oriented**
    c. Technology oriented
    d. Domestic need oriented

152. The anti-quality constituent in young seedlings of forage sorghum is
    a. **Coumarins**   b. Acetic acid
    c. Terpenes
    d. Hydrocyanic acid

153. Which one of the following species belongs to pop maize?
    a. **Everta**   b. Amylacea
    c. Ceratina   d. Indurata

154. High yield of maize is obtained in regions where the atmospheric temperature during the growing season is
    a. **High during the day and low during the night**
    b. High during the day and high during the night
    c. Low during the day and high during the night
    d. Low during the day and low during the night

155. Seed potato from the hilly regions of India is preferred because
    a. It is cheaper
    b. Good varieties are grown in the regions
    c. It has better germination percentage
    d. **It is disease free**

156. Which one of the following chemicals is used to treat seed potato to break its dormancy?
    a. Ethrel   b. **Thiourea**
    c. IAA   d. NAA

157. The intercultural operation in standing broadcast rice crop is commonly known as
    a. Thinning   b. **Spudding**
    c. Rotation   d. Beushening

158. Which one of the following is the example of parallel intercropping?
    a. **Maize + soya bean**
    b. Sugarcane + mustard
    c. Sugarcane + potato
    d. Potato + mustard

159. Need-based and skill-oriented vocational training to practicing farmers and employed extension personnel is provided through
    a. Training and visit
    b. **KVK**
    c. Lab to land
    d. National demonstration

160. Albert Mayer is the name associated with
    a. **Etawah Pilot project**
    b. Nilokheri Development Project
    c. Farraka Development Project
    d. Shantiniketan

161. Cheena (Proso millet) is
    a. *Panicum milaceum*
    b. *Cicer arietinum*
    c. *Solanum nigrum*
    d. *Solanum tuberosum*

162. Kodo millet is
    a. *Paspalum scobiculatum*
    b. *Cicer arietinum*
    c. *Solanum nigrum*
    d. *Solanum tuberosum*

163. Finger millet is
    a. *Eleucine coracana*
    b. *Cicer arietinum*
    c. *Solanum nigrum*
    d. *Solanum tuberosum*

164. Which one of the following minerals is least weatherable in soil?
    a. Calcite   b. Olivine
    c. **Quartz**   d. Biotite

165. The black cotton soils of central India have been derived from
    a. Granite   b. **Granodiorites**
    c. Rhyolite   d. Basalt

166. The unconsolidated material on the underlying rock is called
    a. **Regolith**   b. Solum
    c. Soil   d. Earth

167. The nitrogenous fertilizer of choice for tea is
    a. Calcium ammonium nitrate
    b. Urea
    c. Ammonium sulphate
    d. **Ammonium nitrate**

168. Diminished carbohydrate status of the plant placed under high N supply is due to
    a. Vigorous protein synthesis
    b. **Lower photosynthetic activity**
    c. Increased transpiration ratio
    d. Increased vegetative growth

169. The Food Corporation of India was established in
    a. 1960
    b. **1965**
    c. 1962
    d. 1967

170. Solubility of rock phosphate can be improved by
    a. Nitrosomonas
    b. Nitrobacter
    c. **Bacillus polymixa**
    d. Azotobacter

6

Agricultural Biochemistry

1. The processes of exchange of heat and moisture between earth and atmosphere over a long period is known as
   a. Weather   **b. Climate**
   c. Microclimate   d. None of these

2. The word 'Metrology' is derived from
   a. Greek   b. Latin
   c. Both a and b   d. None of these

3. First Indian metrology division was started in
   a. 1934   **b. 1932**
   c. 1978   d. 1900

4. Galileo was discovered thermometer in
   a. 1956   b. 1950
   c. 1953   d. 1945

5. World Meteorological Organization (WMO) is situated at
   a. Geneva, Switzerland
   b. Pune
   c. Mexico
   d. Peru

6. Indian Metrology department was started in
   a. 1934   b. 1932
   c. 1878   d. 1900

7. Crop weather calendar is launched by
   a. ICAR   b. IARI
   c. WMO   **d. IMD**

8. Carbon dioxide concentration on volume basis in atmosphere is
   a. 78%   b. 20%
   c. 0.930%   d. 0.033%

9. Turbulence is most effective below
   a. 12–15 km   **b. 20 km**
   c. 15–17 km   d. 10–12 km

10. Oxygen concentration on volume basis in atmosphere is
    a. 78%   **b. 21%**
    c. 0.930%   d. 0.033%

11. Concentration of ozone is mainly between
    a. 40–50 km   **b. 15–35 km**
    c. 10–15 km   d. None of these

12. Water vapour presents in atmosphere by weight basis is
    a. 5%   b. 4%
    c. 3%   d. 1%

13. The atmosphere layers are divided based on
    a. Vertical temperature
    b. Horizontal temperature
    c. Both a and b
    d. None of these

14. The layers are separated by levels of demarcation called as
    a. Spheres   **b. Pauses**
    c. Layers   d. Both a and b

15. The lowest layer of atmosphere where weather phenomena and atmospheric turbulence are most marked
    a. **Troposphere**   b. Stratosphere
    c. Mesosphere   d. Thermosphere

16. The variations in the altitude of the tropopause as different latitudes at the equator is
    a. 18 km   **b. 16 km**
    c. 20 km   d. 80 km

17. The height of troposphere is
    a. **8–18 km**   b. 16–25 km
    c. 20–30 km   d. 8–10 km

18. Temperature decreases with increase in altitude, this character of
    a. Troposphere   b. Stratosphere
    c. Mesosphere   **d. Both a and c**

19. In which layer of atmosphere, temperature increases fairly, generally, with height in summer
    a. **Stratosphere**   b. Mesosphere
    c. Troposphere   d. None of these

20. Ozone layer or ozonosphere is also known as
    a. Troposphere   b. Mesosphere
    c. **Stratosphere**   d. Thermosphere

21. The thermosphere is above the
    a. Thermosphere   b. Stratosphere
    c. **Mesosphere**   d. Both a and b

22. Agro meteorology mainly deals with
    a. Atmospheric pressure, clouds
    b. Solar radiation, temperature
    c. Wind, relative humidity and precipitation
    d. All

23. Fifty per cent of total mass of air is found below
    a. 10 km   b. 16 km
    c. 5 km   d. 8 km

24. Pascal (Pa) is the SI unit of
    a. **Pressure**   b. Temperature
    c. Humidity   d. All

25. Isotherms are used to show
    a. Humidity distribution
    b. Rain distribution
    c. Temperature distribution
    d. All

26. A line of equal moisture is called as
    a. Isotach   b. Isopleths
    c. Isohels   **d. Isostere**

27. A line of equal wind speed is called as
    a. **Isotach**   b. Isopleths
    c. Isohels   d. Isonephs

28. Which instrument is used for measuring the height
    a. **Altimeter**
    b. Aneroid barometer
    c. Anemometer
    d. Atmometer

29. Wind direction is measured by
    a. Altimeter   b. Tensiometer
    c. Anemometer   **d. Wind vane**

30. Amount of rainfall is measured by
    a. **Rain gauge**
    b. Aneroid barometer
    c. Anemometer
    d. Atmometer

31. Field capacity is measured by
    a. Pulvimeter
    b. Pressure chamber
    c. Anemometer
    d. Pressure membrane apparatus

32. Leaf water potential is measured by
    a. **Psychrometer**
    b. Aneroid barometer
    c. Anemometer
    d. Atmometer

33. Depth of water is measured by
    a. Pulvimeter
    b. Pressure chamber
    c. Peizometer
    d. Pressure membrane apparatus

34. Direct solar radiation is measured by
    a. Pyradiometer
    b. Aneroid barometer
    c. **Anemometer**
    d. Pyrheliometer

35. Hydraulic conductivity is measured by
    a. **Permeameter**
    b. Aneroid barometer
    c. Anemometer
    d. Atmometer

36. Canopy temperature is measured by
    a. Permeameter
    b. **Infrared thermometer**
    c. Anemometer
    d. Atmometer

37. Dew is measured by
    a. Hygrometer   b. Psychrometer
    c. **Drosometer**   d. Atmometer

38. Mercurial barometer is used for measuring
    a. **Atmospheric pressure**
    b. Temperature
    c. wind speed
    d. Humidity

39. Sun gives energy about
    a. 5.6×1027 cal/minute
    b. 5.6×2027 cal/minute
    c. **5.6×1227 cal/minute**
    d. 6.6×1027 cal/minute

40. Methods of transfer of heat or energy are
    a. Conduction   b. Convection
    c. Radiation   **d. All**

41. The amount of energy received on a unit surface in a unit time is called as
    a. Flux density
    b. Rain density
    c. Both a and b
    d. Radiant flux density

42. The ratio of the amount of radiant energy absorbed to the amount incident upon the substance
    a. Reflectivity
    b. Transmissivity

    c. **Absorptive**
    d. None of these

43. The fraction or per cent of the reflected solar radiation from the surface to incoming solar radiation
    a. **Solar constant**   b. Radiation
    c. Conduction   d. Albedo

44. The winds therefore flow from horse latitude to the equatorial region called
    a. **Trade winds**
    b. Subtropical high
    c. Calm   d. Blow winds

45. Photosynthetically active radiations (PARs) are the real source of energy for
    a. **Photosynthesis process**
    b. Radiation
    c. **Conduction**   d. Albedo

46. Drainage type winds are called
    a. **Katabetic winds**
    b. Ferrel cell
    c. Both a and b   d. Polar cell

47. The system of close isobars with the lowest pressure at the center is called as
    a. Anticyclone   **b. Cyclone**
    c. Both a and b   d. Isobar

48. The velocity of wind in cyclone is more than
    a. 40 knots   b. 50 knots
    c. 60 knots   **d. 34 knots**

49. A system of closed isobars with highest pressure at center is known as
    a. **Anticyclone**   b. Cyclone
    c. Both a and b   d. Wind direction

50. Water vapour present in the atmosphere is known as
    a. **Humidity**   b. Water vapour
    c. Both a and b   d. Dew

51. Partial pressure exerted by vapour is known as
    a. Low pressure
    b. High pressure

c. **Vapuor pressure**
d. All

52. An interchange air between the land and oceans due to unequal heating and cooling of continents and oceans is known as
   a. **Monsoon winds**
   b. Cooling winds
   c. Hot winds   d. All

53. Rainfall associated with hail stones is called as
   a. Precipitation   b. Hail
   c. Snow   d. **Hailstorm**

54. Simultaneous precipitation of the mixture of rain and snow is called as
   a. Precipitation   b. Hail
   c. Mist   d. **Sleet**

55. The area generally of permanent dry, arid dessert regions. Crop production due to inadequate rainfall is not possible without irrigation is called as
   a. Hydrological drought
   b. Meteorological drought
   c. **Permanent drought**
   d. Seasonal drought

56. The drought which occurs in the regions with clearly defined as rainy, wet and dry climates is
   a. Agriculture drought
   b. Meteorological drought
   c. Permanent drought
   d. **Seasonal drought**

57. Which crop is known as king of cereals?
   a. Rice   b. **Wheat**
   c. Maize   d. Sorghum

58. Which crop is known as king of pulses
   a. Red gram   b. Mungo
   c. Soybean   d. **Chick pea**

59. Meteorology is the science of
   a. Lithosphere
   b. Hydrosphere
   c. **Atmosphere**
   d. None of these

60. Which crop is known as vegetable meat?
   a. Red gram   b. Chick pea
   c. **Cow pea**   d. Soybean

61. Which crop is known as golden fibre?
   a. Jute   b. Cotton
   c. Crotoloria junisa
   d. **None**

62. Which crop is known as white golden of America?
   a. Jute   b. **Cotton**
   c. Crotoloria junisa
   d. None

63. Which crop is known as backbone of America?
   a. **Maize**   b. Wheat
   c. Soybean   d. Rice

64. Meteorology is also a branch of
   a. Chemistry   b. **Physics**
   c. Botany   d. Zoology

65. Nitrogen concentration on volume basis in atmosphere is
   a. **78%**   b. 20%
   c. 0.930%   d. 0.033%

66. The layers are termed as
   a. **Spheres**   b. Pauses
   c. Both a and b   d. Layers

67. The height of troposphere is
   a. **8–18 km**   b. 16–25 km
   c. 20–30 km   d. 8–10 km

68. The atmosphere is increasingly affected by X-rays and ultraviolet radiation causes
   a. **Ionization**   b. Radiation
   c. Both a and b   d. None of these

69. Air pressure always decreases with an increase in
   a. **Altitude**   b. Latitude
   c. Both a and b   d. All

70. A line of equal wind speed is called as
   a. **Isotach**   b. Isopleths
   c. Isohels   d. Isonephs

71. **Along the equator lies a low pressure belt known as**
    a. Equatorial low   b. Doldrums
    c. Pole   **d. Both a and b**

72. **Which instrument is used for measuring the height?**
    a. Altimeter
    b. Aneroid barometer
    c. Anemometer
    d. Atmometer

73. **Evapotranspiration is measured by**
    a. Lysimeter
    b. Aneroid barometer
    c. Anemometer
    d. Atmometer

74. **Water stress and soil moisture is measured by**
    a. Permeameter
    b. Aneroid barometer
    c. Anemometer
    d. Irrometer

75. **Sunshine duration is measured by**
    a. Campbell-Stokes recorder
    b. Aneroid barometer
    c. Anemometer
    d. Atmometer

76. **The oceans are associated with low pressure in**
    a. Winter   b. Summer
    c. Both a and b   d. None of these

77. **Mercurial barometer is used for measuring**
    a. Atmospheric Pressure
    b. Temperature
    c. Wind speed
    d. Humidity

78. **The principle of altitude barometer is same as that of**
    a. Campbell-Stokes recorder
    b. Aneroid barometer
    c. Altimeter
    d. Atmometer

79. **Wind creates moist conditions on the__.**
    a. Leeward side
    b. Windward side
    c. According to wind direction
    d. All

80. **Sources of all water are**
    a. Run off
    b. Precipitation
    c. Water harvesting
    d. All

81. **Sedimentary rock is also known as**
    a. Highly weathered rock
    b. Intrusive rock
    c. Metamorphic rock
    d. Stratified rock

82. **Who was given the concept of water is the soil nutrient of plants**
    a. Francis Bacon   b. John Woodward
    c. Boyel   **d. Van Helmont**

83. **Marble formed from**
    a. Granite   b. Sandstone
    c. Limestone   d. None of these

84. **Characteristics of organic soils are**
    a. Bogs   b. Peat
    c. Swaps   **d. All**

85. **Soil consists of major components is**
    a. Minerals matter   b. Organic matter
    c. Water and air   **d. All**

86. **Mineral matter presents in soil by volume basis is**
    a. 70%   **b. 45%**
    c. 5%   d. 25%

87. **The elements which tend to form covalent bonds with sulphide are**
    a. Lithophile elements
    b. Chalcophile elements
    c. Atmosphile elements
    d. Biophile elements

88. **Who observed that non-nitrogen fixing bacteria do not require a host plant**
    a. Beijerinck   **b. Winogradsky**
    c. Both a and b   d. Butler

89. **The immediate uppermost loose of the earth consisting of organic matter and soil organisms suitable for plant growth is called as**
    a. Organic soil   **b. Surface soil**
    c. Sub soil   d. None of these

90. **In which soil cation exchange capacity is very high?**
    a. Sub soil   **b. Surface soil**
    c. Both a and b   d. None of these

91. **Due to presence of higher organic matter content, the color of surface soil is**
    a. Deep brown   b. Dark
    c. Both a and b   d. Yellowish

92. **Which soil has no hard pan**
    a. Inorganic soil   **b. Surface soil**
    c. Sub soil   d. None of these

93. **Completely weathered soil is**
    a. Inorganic soil   **b. Surface soil**
    c. Sub soil   d. None of these

94. **Heterotrophic bacteria are divided into**
    a. Nitrogen fixing bacteria
    b. Non-nitrogen fixing bacteria
    c. Both a and b
    d. Self-nutritive bacteria

95. **Partially weathered soil is**
    a. Inorganic soil   b. Surface soil
    c. Sub soil   d. None of these

96. **The vertical section through a soil is called as**
    a. Soil profile   b. B horizon
    c. Sub soil   d. None of these

97. **Soil profile is divided into**
    a. Organic horizon   b. A horizon
    c. B horizon   d. C horizon
    e. All

98. **Like some, sandstone and dolomite are which type of rocks?**
    a. Igneous rock
    b. Sedimentary rock
    c. Metamorphic rock
    d. None of these

99. **Combination of A + B horizon is called as**
    a. Solum   b. A horizon
    c. B horizon   d. None of these

100. **Hydrogen oxidised by**
    a. Hydrogenomonas
    b. Desulphovibrio
    c. Methanobacillus
    d. All

101. **Basalt is the ___ type of rocks.**
    a. Plutonic rock
    b. Volcanic rock
    c. Sedimentary rock
    d. None of these

102. **Who was used organic material for first time?**
    a. Arthur Young
    b. Sir Humphrey Devy
    c. Jethro Tull
    d. Liebig

103. **Who was given the concept of carbon uptake if plant by roots**
    a. Sir Humphrey Devy
    b. John Woodward
    c. Jethro Tull
    d. Glauber

104. **The earth crust consists mainly the_____ that are commonly found in silicates and soils.**
    a. Biophile elements
    b. Chalcophile elements
    c. Atmosphile elements
    d. Lithophile elements

105. **Rocks are generally grouped into**
    a. Igneous rock
    b. Sedimentary rock
    c. Metamorphic rock
    d. All

106. **Igneous rock is divided based on**
    a. Origin
    b. Chemical composition
    c. Both a and b
    d. Their nature

107. Inorganic sulphur compounds converted to sulphate by
    a. Nitrosomonas   b. Nitrobacter
    c. Thiobacillus   d. Ferrobacillus

108. Balance sheet for the nutrients was given by
    a. Boussingaul
    b. John Woodward
    c. Jethro Tull
    d. All

109. Broken peds are called as
    a. Clod   b. Peds
    c. Fragment   d. Aggregates

110. Which mica is more resistant to weathering?
    a. White mica   b. Black mica
    c. Both a and b   d. All

111. Most dominant mineral on earth crust is
    a. White mica   b. Black mica
    c. Both a and b   d. All

112. The basic processes of weathering is
    a. Physical   b. Chemical
    c. Mechanical   **d. All**

113. The physical and mechanical processes are designated as
    a. Decomposition   **b. Disintegration**
    c. Both a and b   d. All

114. The end product of weathering is
    a. Rocks   b. Clay minerals
    c. Parent material   d. None of these

115. Which mineral is less resistant to weathering?
    a. Olivine   b. Bitotite
    c. Both a and b   d. Quartz

116. Which property of soil is property?
    a. Soil structure   **b. Soil texture**
    c. Particle density   d. None of these

117. The transformation of original rocks into new compounds is called as
    a. Physical weathering
    b. Chemical weathering

c. Biological weathering
    d. All

118. Which weathering is not possible without water?
    a. Physical weathering
    b. Chemical weathering
    c. Biological weathering
    d. All

119. Which property of soil can't be alternated?
    a. Soil structure   **b. Soil texture**
    c. Particle density   d. None of these

120. The mass per unit volume of dry soil is called as
    a. Bulk density   **b. Particle density**
    c. Both a and b   d. None of these

121. Which soil is known as low nutrient soils?
    a. Histosols   b. Inceptiosols
    c. Mollisols   **d. Ultisols**

122. The weight per unit volume of a substance is called as
    a. Density   b. Porosity
    c. Soil texture   d. Structure

123. Particle density is also called as
    a. Bulk density   b. Gravity
    c. True density   d. None of these

124. When an increase in organic matter of the soil then
    a. Particle density decreases
    b. Particle density increases
    c. Particle density constant
    d. None of these

125. When the units are thin of the soil structure is called as
    a. Laminar   **b. Platy**
    c. Block   d. All

126. Which soil has flocculation and friability?
    a. White alkali soil
    b. Black alkali soil

c. Reclamation of alkali soils

d. All

127. The exchange of gases between the soil and atmosphere is facilitated by

a. Mass flow

b. Diffusion

c. **Both a and b**

d. Biochemical reactions

128. Carbon dioxide present in soil is

a. **0.25%**   b. 0.03%

c. 21%   d. 78%

129. Which nutrients are showing the deficiency under pore aeration

a. Cu   b. Zn

c. **Both a and b**   d. N

130. Specific heat X mass is known as

a. Specific heat   b. Total porosity

c. **Heat capacity**   d. None of these

131. The movement of heat in and out of soil is called as

a. Specific heat   b. Porosity

c. Heat capacity   d. **Heat flux**

132. The amount of heat required to raise the temperature of one gram of a substance by 1°C if called as

a. **Specific heat**   b. Total porosity

c. Temperature   d. None of these

133. The activity of microorganisms, if lowest when soil temperature is below

a. **5°C**   b. 12°C

c. 10°C   d. 2°C

134. Soil color is inherited from its material and that is referred to as

a. Lithophile   b. Chalcophile

c. Atmosphile   d. **Lithochromic**

135. White or light color is occurs in soil due to presence of

a. Organic matter

b. Iron compounds

c. **Silica, lime**

d. None of these

136. The soil colors are best determined by

a. Color graph

b. **Munsell color chart**

c. Organic matter

d. None of these

137. There presents the purity of the color by

a. Hue   b. Value

c. **Chroma**   d. None of these

138. Soil particles less than 0.001 mm size possess is called as

a. Soil peds   b. Aggregates

c. Fragments   d. **Soil colloidal**

139. Plasticity exhibits in soil when _____.

a. Less than 15% colloidal clay

b. **More than 15% colloidal clay**

c. More than 20% colloidal clay

d. None of these

140. Soil colloidal is divided into

a. Organic   b. Inorganic

c. **Both a and b**   d. Fragments

141. Which soil colloids are the most dominant and important in agriculture field?

a. Iron

b. Aluminium hydrous

c. Both a and b

d. **Silicate**

142. Surface areas of clay particles can be measured by using

a. **Cetyle pyridinium bromide**

b. Hydrous

c. Hydrogen peroxide

d. All

143. The silicate clays are made up by

a. Oxygen atoms

b. Aluminium atoms

c. Silicon atoms

d. **All**

144. White tip in cereals occurs due to defeciency of

a. P   b. Mg

c. **Cu**   d. Mn

145. Which soil is known as alluvial soil?
  a. Alfisols
  b. Andisols
  c. Ardisols
  d. Entsols

146. The cation exchange capacity of soils increases with
  a. Increase in soil pH
  b. Decrease in soil pH
  c. Decrease activity of H
  d. All

147. The most cations in soils are
  a. Ca
  b. Mg
  c. H, K
  d. All

148. Which nutrients provide electrolytic balance in plants?
  a. N, P, S
  b. Ca, Mg, K, Cl
  c. C, H, O
  d. Fe, Mn, Co

149. Soil containing high concentration of carbon dioxide, the pH value of such soil will be
  a. Low
  b. Medium
  c. High
  d. All

150. Soils are said to be saline
  a. If they contain an excess of soluble salt
  b. If they contain an excess of sodium
  c. If they contain an excess of sodium and salt
  d. None of these

151. Saline soils mostly occurs in
  a. Arid regions
  b. Semiarid regions
  c. Both a and b
  d. Humid region

152. Highly salt resistant crops are
  a. Barley
  b. Sugar beet
  c. Cotton
  d. All

153. Modified classification of irrigation waters proposed by
  a. Wilcox
  b. Better
  c. Donald
  d. None of these

154. Low salt resistant crops are
  a. Wheat
  b. Rice
  c. Maize
  d. Beans

155. Thermophile organisms are
  a. Cold lovers
  b. Heat lovers
  c. Both a and b
  d. Middle group organisms

156. Kind of fixation in soil is
  a. Cation fixation
  b. Anion fixation
  c. Both a and b
  d. None of these

157. Bacteria are
  a. Unicellular microorganism
  b. Cellular microorganisms
  c. Both a and b
  d. None of these

158. Who was discovered the carbon?
  a. Rutherford
  b. Gris
  c. Sachs
  d. Posternack

159. Psycrophiles organisms are
  a. Cold lovers
  b. Heat lovers
  c. Both a and b
  d. None of these

160. Nostoc and Anabaena both are
  a. Symbiotic bacteria
  b. Non-symbiotic bacteria
  c. Cyanobacteria
  d. Both a and b

161. The concept of humus formation as described by
  a. Flaig
  b. Koppen
  c. Wallis
  d. Liebig

162. Organic matter acts as
  a. Chelate
  b. Buffering agent
  c. Both a and b
  d. None of these

163. Nutrient mobility concept was given by
  a. Micheli
  b. Liebig
  c. NA Cob
  d. R Bray

164. The buried substance which is found in buried soil is called as
  a. Paleo humus
  b. Organic wastage
  c. Clay humus
  d. All of these

165. Growth may be expressed in term of
  a. Dry weight
  b. Length
  c. Plant height
  d. All

166. Most of agricultural crops are grown under temperature range of
    a. 5–10°C
    b. 15–40°C
    c. 40–50°C
    d. None of these

167. The components of radiant energy are
    a. Quality
    b. Intensity
    c. Duration of light
    d. All

168. Which elements are not established as essential elements for all higher plants?
    a. Na   b. Si
    c. Co   **d. All**

169. Number of essential elements in plants nutrition according to Arnon is
    a. 90   **b. 16**
    c. 56   d. 19

170. Which is macronutrient for plant growth?
    a. N   b. K
    c. K   **d. All**

171. Which is micronutrient for plant growth?
    a. Ca   b. Mg
    c. K   **d. Fe**

172. Functional nutrients are _____ in number of plants.
    a. 21   **b. 20**
    c. 16   d. 17

173. Mobile nutrients in soil are
    a. N, B   b. Cl, S
    c. Both a and b   d. None of these

174. The role of boron in plants is
    a. Nitrate reductase activity
    b. Nucleic acid
    c. Pollen formation
    d. None of these

175. The soil saturated with water for a sufficient longer period is called as
    a. Acidic soil
    b. Alkali soil
    c. Submerged soil
    d. None of these

176. Organic manures are classified into
    a. Bulky organic manures
    b. Concentrated organic manures
    c. Both a and b
    d. None of these

177. The most and widely used bulky organic manures are
    a. FYM
    b. Compost
    c. Green manure
    d. All

178. The advantage of bulky organic manures is
    a. They improve soil physical properties
    b. Supply plant nutrients, control the nematodes and fungi
    c. Increasing the availability of nutrients
    d. All

179. Nitrogen present in urine is mostly in the form of
    a. Bulky organic manures
    b. Concentrated organic manures
    c. Both a and b
    d. None of these

180. Which weed is exhibit the three kinds of dormancy
    a. Trianthema spp.
    b. *Digera arvensis*
    c. *Setaria glauca*
    d. *Avena fatua*

181. The struggle between two organisms for a limited resource that is essential for growth is called as
    a. Competition
    b. Limiting factor
    c. Essential sources
    d. All

182. Weed prevention practices are
    a. Prevent movement of weeds
    b. Keep non-crop area clean
    c. Use vigilance
    d. All

183. Burning and flaming are method of
    a. **Physical and mechanical methods**
    b. Biological method
    c. Chemical method
    d. None of these

184. Perennial weeds also known as
    a. Difficult weeds
    b. **Pernicious weeds**
    c. Both a and b
    d. Problemic weeds

185. If weeds look exactly like crops morpho-logically and complete their life cycle is called as
    a. **Mimicry**
    b. Seasonal bound weeds
    c. Both a and b
    d. Broom rape

186. Weeds which usually parasite the host crop partially or fully for their nourish-ment are called as
    a. Seasonally un-bound weeds
    b. Season bound weeds
    c. **Crop associated weeds**
    d. None of these

187. Which weeds are indigenous?
    a. *Acalypha indica*
    b. *Abutilon indicum*
    c. *Sorghum halepense*
    d. *Cynodon dactylon, Echinocola colonum*
    e. **All**

188. The herbicides which kill some plane species when applied to a mixed plant population, without causing serious injury to other species is called as
    a. **Selective herbicide**
    b. Non-selective herbicide
    c. Both a and b
    d. None of these

189. Trade name of Oxyflourfen is
    a. Machete
    b. Graminon
    c. **Persuit**
    d. Lasso

190. The process of limiting infestation of the weed plant so that crops can be grown profitably is called as
    a. **Weed control**
    b. Weed management
    c. Limiting infestation
    d. All

191. The kinds of submerged soil is
    a. Continuous submerged soils
    b. Alternative submerged soils
    c. **Both a and b**
    d. None of these

192. Mechanism of nitrogen transformation in soil is
    a. Mineralization
    b. **Immobilization**
    c. Denitrification
    d. All

193. Who was discovered the nitrogen?
    a. **Ruther Ford**   b. Gris
    c. Sachs   d. Posternak

194. Which element is moderate mobile in plants?
    a. Mn, Cu   b. Mo, Cl
    c. **Zn**   d. N, P

195. Organic matter binds soil particles into structure units called as
    a. Peds
    b. **Aggregates**
    c. Organic decomposition
    d. None of these

196. Why saline soils are occurred in arid regions?
    a. Low rainfall available to leach the salts and transports
    b. High evaporation
    c. **Low water permeability**
    d. All

197. Alkali soil is also called as
    a. **Non-saline alkali**
    b. Sodic   c. Solonetz
    d. All

198. Total soil acidity depends on
    a. Active density
    b. Exchange acidity
    c. Both a and b
    d. Passive acidity

199. Which classification system is being followed in India?
    a. USDA classification
    b. World soil classification
    c. Both a and b
    d. None of these

200. The supply and absorption of chemical compounds required for plant growth and metabolism is called as
    a. Organic matter
    b. Growth factor
    c. Plant nutrition
    d. None of these

7

Principles of Crop Physiology

1. The Term 'Ecology' was given by
   - a. G J Mendel **b. E Haeckel**
   - c. Elton d. Odum

2. The biological evolution is investigated and explained by
   - **a. Charles Darwin** b. Watson
   - c. Crick d. Whittaker

3. Molecular structure of DNA is carried out by
   - a. Crick b. Bateson
   - c. W Flemming
   - **d. Watson and Crick**

4. _____ is the basic unit of classification in the hierarchical taxonomic system.
   - a. Genus b. Family
   - **c. Species** d. Order

5. A group of cells having same origin, same structure and performing same function is called
   - a. Organ **b. Tissue**
   - c. Cell d. Coelom

6. Arrangement of body parts in geometrical design is termed as
   - a. Asymmetry **b. Symmetry**
   - c. Orientation d. Geometry

7. The term coelom was coined by
   - a. Watson b. Crick
   - **c. Hacckel** d. Whittaker

8. Preen gland is present in
   - **a. Aves** b. Animals
   - c. Insects d. Fishes

9. _____ is a process that improves the efficiency of life in organism.
   - a. Movement b. Motion
   - c. Transmission **d. Locomotion**

10. In protozoans, a longitudinal row of kinetosomes together with kinetodesmata constitute a unit called
    - a. Kidney **b. Kinety**
    - c. Tissue d. Cell

11. *Ascaris lumbricoides* is commonly known as
    - a. Bollworm **b. Roundworm**
    - c. Filarial worm d. Plasmodium

12. _____ is a large community of plants and animals that occupies a vast region.
    - a. Habitat **b. Biome**
    - c. Biosphere d. Ecosphere

13. What do you call the study of interactions of organisms of a community?
    - a. Ecology **b. Synecology**
    - c. Autecology d. Biology

14. At _____, the water becomes more denser and heavier.
    - a. 9°C b. 7°C
    - **c. 4°C** d. 1°C

15. Study of characteristic features of fresh-water ecosystems is
    - a. Ecosystems
    - **b. Limnology**
    - c. Ecology
    - d. Autecology

16. Removal of forest or cutting of trees where the land is thereafter converted to a non-forest use
    - a. Cultivation
    - b. Forestation
    - **c. Deforestation**
    - d. Reforestation

17. Chemicals used to kill insects are
    - a. Weedicides
    - b. Fungicides
    - **c. Insecticides**
    - d. Larvicides

18. The term organic evolution is coined by
    - a. Haeckel
    - b. Odum
    - **c. Herbert Spencer**
    - d. Lawmark

19. The fundamental source of energy for all biological processes is
    - a. Moon
    - b. Stars
    - **c. Sun**
    - d. Earth

20. _____is described as cellular energy.
    - a. DNA
    - b. NADP
    - **c. ATP**
    - d. RNA

21. The sum total of all the chemical reactions occurring in the body of organisms constitute _____.
    - a. Catabolism
    - **b. Metabolism**
    - c. Anabolism
    - d. Photosynthesis

22. _____stores the information and could serve as the 'chemical basis of inheritance'.
    - a. ATP
    - b. NADP
    - **c. DNA**
    - d. NADPH

23. The practice of naming the animals or organisms, in which the generic name and species name are similar as called____.
    - a. Taxanomy
    - b. Nomenclature
    - **c. Tautonomy**
    - d. Taxon

24. The study of tissues is known as
    - **a. Histology**
    - b. Ethology
    - c. Ecology
    - d. Embryology

25. The flat area that runs through any axis is
    - **a. Plane**
    - b. Flat
    - c. Vertical
    - d. Horizontal

26. _____is a temporary union between two ciliates belonging to two different mating types for the exchange and re-constitution of nuclear material.
    - a. Fission
    - **b. Conjugation**
    - c. Fusion
    - d. Syngamy

27. Due to ____ malaria is caused in humans.
    - a. Haemoglobin
    - **b. Haemozoin**
    - c. Haemocyte
    - d. Haematin

28. Tobacco contain _____, which is injurious to health.
    - a. Adenine
    - b. Guanine
    - **c. Nicotine**
    - d. Protein

29. When the units are thin of the structure is called
    - a. Laminar
    - **b. Platy**
    - c. Block
    - d. All

30. The types of pore spaces are
    - a. Macrospore
    - **b. Microspore**
    - c. a and d
    - d. None of these

31. Water present in the soil by volume basis is
    - a. 36%
    - b. 2%
    - **c. 29%**
    - d. 25%

32. Air presents in the soil by volume basis is
    - a. 25%
    - b. 30%
    - c. 0.94%
    - **d. 78%**

33. Storehouse of nutrition in soil is
    - **a. Organic matter**
    - b. Water
    - c. Air
    - d. All

34. Soil consists of major components is
    - a. Mineral matter
    - **b. Organic matter**
    - c. Water and air
    - d. All

35. Marble formed from
    - a. Granite
    - b. Sandstone
    - **c. Limestone**
    - d. None of these

36. Characteristics of organic soils are
    a. Bogs   b. Peat
    c. Swarps   **d. All**

37. The processes of exchange of heat and moisture between earth and atmosphere over a longer period is known as
    a. Weather   **b. Climate**
    c. Microclimate d. None of these

38. Meteorology is the science of
    a. Lithosphere   b. Hydrosphere
    c. Atmosphere   d. None of these

39. Galileo was discovered the thermometer in
    a. 1956   b. 1950
    c. 1953   d. 1945

40. Oxygen concentration (%) on volume basis in atmosphere is
    a. 78%   **b. 21%**
    c. 0.930%   d. 0.033%

41. Water vapour present in atmosphere by volume basis is
    a. 5%   **b. 4%**
    c. 10%   d. 1%

42. A line of equal water table is called as
    a. Isotach   b. Isopleths
    c. Isohels   **d. Isobaths**

43. Wind velocity is measured by
    a. Altimeter
    b. Aneroid barometer
    c. Anemometer   d. Atmometer

44. Growth of plant is measured by
    a. Altimeter   **b. Crescograph**
    c. Anemometer   d. Atmometer

45. Which crop is known as king of cereals?
    a. Rice   **b. Wheat**
    c. Maize   d. Sorghum

46. Which crop is known as queen of cereals?
    a. Rice   b. Wheat
    c. Maize   d. Sorghum

47. Which crop is known as king of oil-seeds?
    a. Groundnut   b. Sesame
    c. Mustard   d. Sunflower

48. The major zone of root development for crop production is
    a. Organic soil **b. Surface soil**
    c. Sub-soil   d. None of these

49. Disturbed by tillage is
    a. Top soil   b. Surface soil
    c. Sub-soil   d. Organic soil

50. Who was given the concept of principle nourishment to plant in water?
    a. Francis Bacon b. Glauber
    c. Boye   d. Helmon

51. Heterotrophic bacteria are divided into
    a. Nitrogen fixing bacteria
    b. Non-nitrogen fixing bacteria
    c. Both a and b
    d. Self-nutritive bacteria

52. Who was given the concept of earth is the principle of vegetation?
    a. Boyel
    b. John Woodward
    c. Jethro Tull   d. Glauber

53. Factor affecting anion exchange is
    a. Soil pH
    b. Type and amount of clay colloids
    c. Salt concentration
    d. All

54. Which elements are catalysers and activators?
    a. Fe, Mn, Cu   b. B, Mo, Cl
    c. Both a and b d. Zn, Mo

55. Which nutrients are energy exchange nutrients in plants?
    a. N, P, K   b. P, Cl
    c. H, O   d. Mn, Co

56. Which nutrients are skeletal nutrients in plants?
    a. N, K, O   b. K, Cl
    c. Ca, Mg, P   d. Fe, Mn, Co

57. Which nutrients are tissue building elements in plants?

    a. N, P, S
    b. C, H, O
    c. Both a and b
    d. Ca, Mg, Co

58. Low salt resistant crops are

    a. Wheat
    b. Rice
    c. Maize
    d. Beans

59. The role of nitrogen in plant is

    a. Protein formation
    b. Nucleic acid
    c. Pollen formation
    d. Co-enzyme activity

60. Nostoc and Anabaena both are

    a. Symbiotic bacteria
    b. Non-symbiotic bacteria
    c. Cynobacteria
    d. Actinomycetes

61. Which soil is suitable for rice cultivation?

    a. Continuous submerged soils
    b. Alternative submerged soils
    c. Both a and b
    d. None of these

62. Highest area under saline soil in

    a. Uttar Pradesh
    b. Haryana
    c. Gujarat
    d. Rajasthan

63. Vermicomposting is done by

    a. Decomposers
    b. Producers
    c. Consumers
    d. All the above

64. Term necrosis indicate

    a. Atrophy
    b. Curling
    c. Blightning
    d. Death of cell

65. The viroids spread from cell to cell by

    a. Movement protein
    b. Cell division
    c. Herpervirus
    d. Plasmodesmata

66. The following organisms convert ammo-nia to nitrate

    a. Nitrosomonas
    b. Nitrobacter
    c. Azospirillum
    d. Micrococcus

67. The bollworm resistant cotton varieties contains gene from which microorganism?

    a. Fungi
    b. Bacteria
    c. Protozoa
    d. Virus

68. The following is called as extrachromosomal genetic material

    a. Gene
    b. Plasmid
    c. Genotype
    d. Phenotype

69. Term plasmid was introduced by

    a. Beadle
    b. Tatum
    c. Lederberg
    d. Kornberg

70. The most of the antibiotics are produced by

    a. Actinomycetes
    b. Cyanobacteria
    c. Methanobacterium
    d. Plasmodium

71. The father of genetics

    a. Mendel
    b. Shull
    c. Kelruter
    d. None of these

72. Father of Green Revolution of India

    a. Raddy
    b. Bourloug
    c. Swaminathan
    d. Shull

73. Rainfall is measured by

    a. Pulvimeter
    b. Pressure chamber
    c. Anemometer
    d. Pressure membrane apparatus

74. Soil moisture tension is measured by

    a. Thermograph
    b. Tensiometer
    c. Barograph
    d. Anemometer

75. Long wave radiation is measured by

    a. Altimeter
    b. Aneroid barometer
    c. Pyrgeometer
    d. Atmometer

76. Geographic factors are

    a. Altitude
    b. Latitude
    c. Longitude
    d. All of above

77. Monsoon is a _____ phenomenon on a massive scale.
   a. **Land-sea breeze**
   b. Land-river breeze
   c. Both a and b
   d. None of these

78. The heat energy received from sun is known as
   a. Light
   b. **Solar insulation**
   c. Intensity
   d. All

79. Cyclones are also known as
   a. Lows ion
   b. Press ions
   c. **Both a and b**
   d. Isobar

80. Types of monsoons in India are
   a. South-West monsoons
   b. North-East monsoons
   c. **Both a and b**
   d. West-East monsoons

81. Which crop is known as king of pulses?
   a. Red gram
   b. Mung
   c. Soybean
   d. **Chick pea**

82. Which crop is known as queen of oil-seeds?
   a. Groundnut
   b. Sesame
   c. Mustard
   d. **Sunflower**

83. Which crop is known as wonder crop?
   a. Red gram
   b. Mung
   c. **Soya bean**
   d. Groundnut

84. Which crop is known as vegetable meat?
   a. Red gram
   b. **Cow pea**
   c. Soybean
   d. Chick pea

85. Which country is known as sugar bowl?
   a. China
   b. India
   c. **Cuba**
   d. America

86. The study of soil in relation to higher plants is known as
   a. Petrology
   b. Pedology
   c. Both a and b
   d. **Edaphology**

87. Mineral matter present in soil by volume is
   a. 70%
   b. **45%**
   c. 5%
   d. 25%

88. Organic matter present in soil by volume basis is
   a. 10%
   b. 20%
   c. **5%**
   d. 25%

89. Water present in soil by volume basis is
   a. 36%
   b. 2%
   c. 29%
   d. **25%**

90. In which soil, microorganism activity is very high?
   a. Organic soil
   b. **Surface soil**
   c. **Sub-soil**
   d. None of these

91. Who was given the concept of carbon uptake of plant by roots
   a. **Sir Humphrey Devy**
   b. John Woodward
   c. Jethro Tull
   d. Glauber

92. The science of rocks is known as
   a. **Petrology**
   b. Pedology
   c. Both a and b
   d. Edaphology

93. Rocks are generally grouped into
   a. Igneous rocks
   b. Sedimentary rocks
   c. Metamorphic rocks
   d. **All**

94. When the units are thick of the soil structure is called as
   a. **Laminar**
   b. Platy
   c. Block
   d. All

95. When granules are especially porous is called as
   a. Granular
   b. Less porous
   c. Both a and b
   d. **Crumb**

96. Molecular transfer of gases is
   a. Mass flow
   b. **Diffusion**
   c. Both a and b
   d. Biochemical reactions

97. Carbon dioxide presents in soil is
    a. 0.25%   b. 0.03%
    c. 21%   d. 78%

98. The movement of heat in and out of the soil is called as
    a. Specific heat   b. Porosity
    c. Heat capacity
    d. Heat flux

99. Soil color is inherited from its material and that is referred to as
    a. Lithophile   b. Chalcophile
    c. Atmosphile   d. Lithochromic

100. Which soil is known as Prairie soil?
    a. Histosols   b. Inceptiosols
    c. Mollisols   d. Oxysols

101. The major constituent of plant protoplasm is
    a. Water   b. Air
    c. Oxygen   d. None of these

102. The process of formation of flocs is known as
    a. Deflocculating
    b. Flocculation
    c. Both a and b
    d. Fragments

103. Yellow margin in maize due to deficiency of
    a. N   b. P
    c. M   d. Fe

104. Necrosis of leaves occurs due to deficiency of
    a. K   b. Mg
    c. Mn   d. Cl

105. Which soil is known as Young soil?
    a. Histosols   b. Inceptiosols
    c. Mollisols   d. Oxysols

106. The role of phosphorous in plants is
    a. Protein formation
    b. Nucleic acid
    c. Pollen formation
    d. None of these

107. Bronzing in cotton occurs due to deficiency of
    a. P   b. K
    c. N   d. Zn

108. The most cations in soil are
    a. Ca   b. Mg
    c. H   d. K
    e. All

109. The role of potassium in plants is
    a. Nucleic acid   b. Protein formation
    c. Co-enzyme activity
    d. Pollen formation

110. The role of molybdenum in plants is
    a. Nitrate reductase activity
    b. Nucleic acid   c. Pollen formation
    d. Co-enzyme

111. The chemical compounds required by an organism is known as
    a. Essential chemical
    b. Nutrients
    c. Alleviations   d. None of these

112. Which elements acts as regulators and carriers?
    a. N, S, P   b. K, Ca, Mg
    c. N, H, O   d. Zn, Mo

113. Yellowing in upper leaves and turn white is a defeciency of
    a. Potassium   b. Magnesium
    c. Copper   d. Nitrogen

114. The elements useful in energy storage, transfer and bonding are
    a. N, S, P   b. P, Cl
    c. C, H, O   d. B, Mo

115. Moderately salt resistant crops are
    a. Wheat   b. Rice
    c. Maize   d. All

116. Soil containing higher amount of organic matter shows the color variation from
    a. Black and dark brown
    b. Yellowing tinge color

c. White-out light color

d. None of these

117. White or light color in soil occurs due to presence of

a. Organic matter

b. Iron compounds

c. Silica, lime

d. None of these

118. The process of decomposition of organic matter and synthesis of new organic substance is called as

a. Humification b. Eluviation

c. Illuviation d. None of these

119. *Rhizobium phaseoli* is used for the crops

a. Alfalfa group b. Clover group

c. Pea group **d. Beans group**

120. Full form of GIS is

a. Geographical information system

b. Geological information system

c. Jhum information system

d. None of these

121. Rhizobium leguminosorum is used for the crops

a. Alfalfa group b. Clover group

c. Pea group d. Beans group

122. Which soils are formed in high rainfall area?

a. Acidic b. Alkaline

c. Both a and b d. Saline alkaline

123. Acid forming fertilizers are

a. Ammonium sulphate

b. Ammonium nitrate

c. Both a and b

d. None of these

124. Process of mixing of soils is known as

a. Pedoturbation b. Laterisation

c. Both a and b

d. Podzolization

125. Saline soil is also called as

a. Solonchak b. Sodic

c. Both a and b d. Solonetz

126. Autrophic bacteria are

a. Nitrosomonas b. Nitrobacter

c. Thiobacillus **d. All**

127. The process of leaching of calcium is called as

a. Pedoturbation **b. Laterisation**

c. Both a and b d. Podzolization

128. The conversion of inorganic form to organic form is called as

a. Mineralization **b. Immobilization**

c. Both a and b d. Neutralization

129. Nitrogen losses in waterlodged condition through

a. Leaching

b. Denitrification process

c. Both a and b d. Mineralization

130. Non-symbiotic nitrogen fixing bacteria are

a. Clostridium b. Azotobacter

c. Azospirillum **d. All**

131. Weeds that grow primarily in wild community and migrated to crop fields or cultivated environment and associating themselves closely with man's affairs is called as

a. Facultative weeds

b. Problem weeds

c. Noxious weeds

d. Objectionable weeds

132. Aerial shoots coming from axils of lower leaves are called

a. Rhizomes **b. Runners**

c. Bulbs d. None of these

133. When crown region of a plant is compressed in shape of disc, it is called as

a. Tubers **b. Bulbs**

c. Sucker d. Runners

134. A state in which a viable seed fails to germinate even under favorable conditions for plant growth is called as

a. Seed dormancy

b. Viability of seeds

c. Both a and b
d. Seed germination

135. Some plants release some toxic substances which are harmful for other plant
called as

    a. Annidation   **b. Allelopathy**
    c. Both a and b   d. Alleleopathy

136. Weeds which usually parasite the host
crop partially or completely for their
nourishment are called as

    a. Season bound weed
    b. Season bound weeds
    c. Crop associated weed
    d. None of these

137. Seed is difficult to separate from the crop
seed after contamination is called as

    a. Mimicry
    b. Objectionable weeds
    c. Noxious weeds
    d. Problem weeds

138. When a runner, instead of tailing on the
soil surface, rises in the form of arch
before hitting the soil is called as

    a. Stolon   b. Runners
    c. Suckers   d. Offset

139. Runners of floating weeds like water
hyacinth and water lettuce are called as

    a. Stolon   b. Runners
    c. Suckers   **d. Offset**

140. The relationship between climate regimes and crop regimes is called as

    a. Meteorology
    b. Agricultural meteorology
    c. Climatology   d. None of these

141. Colorless, odorless and tasteless mix-
tures of gases are called as

    a. Meteorology
    b. Agricultural meteorology
    c. Climatology   d. Atmosphere

142. The actual density of air depends upon

    a. Temperature
    b. Humidity

c. Amount of water vapour
d. Both a and b

143. Every field contains a maximum of one
or minimum of one or more nutrients,
this concept was given by

    a. Micheli
    b. Liebig
    c. NA Cob
    d. None of the above

144. Pulses

    a. 60 K   b. 600 K
    c. 660 K   **d. 6000 K**

145. Methods of transfer of heat or energy are

    a. Conduction   b. Convection
    c. Radiation   **d. All**

146. Water vapor present in atmosphere is
known as

    a. Humidity   b. humus
    c. Both a and b   d. Dew

147. North-East monsoon is active during

    a. July and November
    b. June to July
    c. March to April
    d. October and November

148. Some solid particles like dust, smoke
from fire and industry restrict visibility
are

    a. Mist   b. Rime
    c. Smog   **d. Haze**

149. Drought is classified into three types on
the basis of

    a. Water availability
    b. Monsoon
    c. Wind direction   d. All

150. The situation of deficit rainfall when the
hydrological sources like streams, rivers,
lakes, wells dry up and ground water
level depletes is

    a. Hydrological drought
    b. Meteorological drought
    c. Agricultural drought
    d. All

151. Which crop is known as king of first crops?
   a. **Berseem**   b. Lucerne
   c. Sorghum   d. Napier grass

152. The situation resulted from inadequate rainfall, when soil moisture falls to short to meet the water demands of crop during growth
   a. Meteorological drought
   b. Hydrological drought
   c. **Agricultural drought**
   d. All

153. The densest part of atmosphere is
   a. **Troposphere**   b. Stratosphere
   c. Mesosphere   d. Themosphere

154. Warmest and dust free later is
   a. **Stratosphere**   b. Mesosphere
   c. Troposphere   d. Themosphere

155. Leaf temperature is measured by
   a. Altimeter   b. Aneroidmeter
   c. Anemometer   d. **Atmometer**

156. Temperature below 0°C is measured by
   a. **Cryometer**   b. Aneroidmeter
   c. Anemometer   d. Atmometer

157. Wavelength of light is measured by
   a. Altimeter
   b. **Spectrophotometer**
   c. Barograph
   d. Atmometer

158. Total incoming solar radition is measured by
   a. Altimeter   b. **Pyranometer**
   c. Anemometer   d. Atmometer

159. Transpiration rate is measured by
   a. Pulvimeter   b. Aneroidmeter
   c. Atmometer   d. **Porometer**

160. Soil with relatively low organic content ranging from 1 to 6% in surface layer usually called as
   a. Organic soil   b. Mineral soil
   c. Inorganic soil   d. **Both b and c**

161. Solidification which takes place on the earth surface is called as
   a. Plutonic rock
   b. **Volcanic rock**
   c. Sedimentary rock
   d. All

162. Soil consists of major components is
   a. Minerals matter   b. Organic matter
   c. Water and air   d. **All**

163. Storehouse of nutrients in soil is
   a. **Organic matter**   b. Water
   c. Air   d. All

164. The elements which tend to be associated with living organisms are
   a. Lithophile elements
   b. Chalcophile elements
   c. Atmosphile elements
   d. **Biophile elements**

165. In which soil microorganism activity is very high?
   a. Organic soil   b. **Surface soil**
   c. Sub-soil   d. None of these

166. Carbon monoxide oxidised to carbondioxide by
   a. **Carboxydomonas**
   b. Gallionella
   c. Both a and b
   d. Nitrosomonas

167. Most dominant mineral on earth crust is
   a. **White mica**   b. Black mica
   c. Both a and b   d. All

168. Elements of agricultural chemistry was written by
   a. **Sir Humphrey Devy**
   b. John
   c. Pietro de Crescenzi
   d. Jethro Tull

169. Annals of agriculture was written by
   a. Posternak
   b. Jethro Tull
   c. Pietro de Crescenzi
   d. **Arthur Young**

170. Natural aggregates are called as
    a. Clod   **b. Peds**
    c. Fragment   d. Aggregates

171. Hydrolysis is
    a. Double decomposition process
    b. Single decomposition process
    c. Both a and b
    d. Triple composition process

172. Which property of soil can't be alternated or changed
    a. Soil structure   **b. Soil texture**
    c. Particle density d. None of these

173. The chemical combination of a solid substance is
    a. Hydrolysis
    b. Hydration
    c. Biological weathering
    d. None of these

174. Which chemical is used for removal of humus from the soil sample?
    a. Hydrogen peroxide
    b. Hydrogen
    c. Carbon dioxide
    d. None of these

175. The relative per centage of sand, slit and clay in a soil is called
    a. Soil structure   **b. Soil texture**
    c. Particle density d. None of these

176. Soils are said to be sodic or alkaline
    a. If they contain an excess of soil soluble salt
    b. If they contain an excess of sodium
    c. Both a and b
    d. None of these

177. Which soil is known as highly weathered soils?
    a. Histosols   b. Inceptiosols
    c. Mollisols   **d. Oxysols**

178. The essential plant nutrient concept was proposed by
    a. Arnon   b. Stout
    c. Both a and b   d. Nicholas

179. *Rhizobium japonicum* is used for the crops
    a. Alfalfa   b. Lupine group
    c. Soybean group d. Beans group

180. When an essential element or other elements are higher to inhibit plant growth to a great extent then the use a term of great
    a. Deficient   b. Insufficient
    c. Toxic   d. Excessive

181. Which nutrients are energy exchange nutrients in plants?
    a. N, P, K   b. P, Cl
    c. H, O   d. Mn, Co

182. Which aspects are include in soil acidity?
    a. Intensity   b. Quantity
    c. Both a and b d. None of these

183. Which soils are formed in low rainfall area?
    a. Acidic   **b. Alkaline**
    c. Both a and b   d. Saline alkaline

184. Cultural operations in general tend to increase
    a. Acidity   **b. Basicity**
    c. Both a and b   d. None of these

185. WHo discovered the oxygen
    a. Rutherford   b. Sachs
    c. Shimper   **d. de Sassure**

186. Physical condition of the saline soil is
    a. Deflocculated condition and permeability to water
    b. Flocculated condition and permeability to water
    c. Flocculated and deflected condition depending on pressure of salts
    d. All

187. Organic matter content in saline soil is
    a. Very low
    b. Slightly less than normal soils
    c. Variable
    d. None of these

188. The process of which the saline alkaline soils is formed?
    a. Salinization   b. Alkalization
    c. Both a and b   d. Solidification

189. Living organisms in the soil include microorganisms such as
    a. Fungi, Actinomycetes
    b. Algae
    c. Bacteria
    d. All

190. Blue-green bacteria are
    a. Heterotrophic   **b. Autotrophic**
    c. Both a and b   d. None of these

191. Which soil is suitable for rice cultivation
    a. Continuous submerged soils
    b. Alternative submerged soils
    c. Both a and b
    d. None of these

192. The conversion of organic form to inorganic or mineral form is called as
    a. Mineralization
    b. Immobilization
    c. Both a and b
    d. Neutralization

193. The buried substance which is found in buried soils is called as
    a. Paleo humus
    b. Organic wastage
    c. Clay humus
    d. None of these

194. Factors affecting growth are
    a. Genetic factor
    b. Environmental factor
    c. Both a and b
    d. Mechanical factor

195. Interveinal chlorosis is a defeciency of
    a. Nitrogen   **b. Iron**
    c. Copper   d. None of these

196. Which elements are immobile in plants?
    a. N, P   b. K, S
    c. Mn, Mo, Cl   **d. Ca, B**

197. The role of nitrogen in plants is
    a. Protein formation
    b. Nucleic acid
    c. Pollen formation
    d. Co-enzyme activity

198. Which nutrients are immobile in soil?
    a. K, Ca   **b. P, Zn**
    c. N, P   d. Zn, K

199. Which are the primary nutrients for plant growth?
    a. N, P, K   b. Ca, Mg, S
    c. Both a and b   d. Fe, Mn, Co

200. The plant that show no obvious symptoms the nutrient content is sufficient is called as
    a. Toxicity
    b. Hidden hunger
    c. Deficiency
    d. None of these

8

Animal Genetics and Breeding

1. All amino acids are glucogenic and keto-genic, *except*
   a. Iso leucine   b. Tyrosine
   c. Tryptophan   **d. Leucine**

2. Which is non-standard amino acid?
   a. Citrullin   b. Histones
   c. Histamine   **d. All**

3. Amino acid involved in thyroxin bio-synthesis is
   a. Proline   **b. Tyrosine**
   c. Arginine   d. Tryptophan

4. Among the following which indole group containing amino acid
   a. Lysine   b. Hisitidine
   c. Tryptophan d. Tyrosine

5. Edmans reagent enables the sequential degradation of amino acids in a poly-peptide chain is
   a. FDNB   **b. PITC**
   c. Ninhydrin reagent
   d. Biuret regent

6. The amino acid which does not reacts and hydrolyzed with ninhydrin
   a. Lysine   b. Lysine
   c. Histidine   **d. Proline**

7. Which amino acid function in buffer at physiological pH
   a. Proline   **b. Hitidine**
   c. Tryptophan   d. Methionine

8. Which amino acid acts as helix broker?
   a. Proline   b. Tyrosine
   c. Arginine   d. Lysine

9. Silk in made up of strong soft lustrous fiber known as
   a. Keratin   b. Collagen
   c. Myoglobin   **d. Fibrin**

10. Amino acid presents dominantly in collagen is
    a. Glycine   b. Tyrosine
    c. Arginine   d. Cysteine

11. Which of the protein is present in nails?
    a. Keratin   b. Collagen
    c. Vitelline   d. Casein

12. The cofactor of glucokinase is
    a. Zn   **b. Mg**
    c. Cu   d. Ni

13. Alpha helix is stabilized by which type of bonds?
    a. Ionic bonds
    b. Disulphide bonds
    c. Inter H bonds   **d. Intra H bonds**

14. The protein present in hair is
    a. Keratin   b. Collagen
    c. Fibrin   d. All of these

15. The example of albumin protein is
    a. Collagen   b. Elastin
    c. Serum albumin d. Keratin

16. In sickle cell hemoglobin
    a. Valine is replaced by glutamate
    b. Alanine is replaced by valine
    c. **Glutamate is replaced by valine**
    d. None of the above

17. A double-stranded DNA has 19% of cytosine find the % of adenine
    a. 19%   b. 38%
    c. 63%   **d. 31%**

18. Which of the following enzyme is involved in prokaryotic DNA replication?
    a. Polymerase   b. Prime
    c. Helicase   **d. All**

19. The nucleic acids are made up of
    a. Amino acid   b. Fatty acid
    c. **Nucleotide**   d. None

20. Replication of DNA cannot starts itself, for initiation is requires
    a. DNA polymerase
    b. DNA primerase
    c. Helicase
    d. **10–12 ntd long RNA primer**

21. One enzyme is specified for one
    a. Nucleotide   b. **Gene**
    c. Nucleoside   d. Nucleosome

22. A scientist isolates a new organism and try to analysis its genome. By the study, it is observed that it is composed of a double-stranded DNA molecule containing 24% thymine. What is the % of cystosine?
    a. 14%   **b. 26%**
    c. 16%   d. 52%

23. Which of following is purine nucleotide?
    a. **Adenine**   b. Thymine
    c. Cytosine   d. Uracil

24. Repeating unit for Z-DNA is equal to
    a. 1 bp   **b. 2 bp**
    c. 3 bp   d. 1.5 bp

25. According to Chargaff law DNA from any source having same amount of adenine is ——————.
    a. Cytosine   b. Guanine
    c. **Thymine**   d. Guanine

26. Which of the following form of DNA has left-handed helix?
    a. A-DNA   b. B-DNA
    c. T-DNA   **d. Z-DNA**

27. Which of the following form of DNA has 2 bp repeating?
    a. A-DNA   b. T-DNA
    c. B-DNA   **d. Z-DNA**

28. A DNA has base pair of tilt of
    a. **12°**   b. 6°
    c. 7°   d. 12°

29. Nucleotide contains
    a. N_2 base
    b. Phosphate group
    c. Ribose sugar
    d. All

30. The enzyme causes the unwinding of the DNA double helix
    a. DNA polymerase III
    b. DNA gyrase
    c. SSB protein
    d. **DNA helicase**

31. The enzyme having both polypeptide chain and a co-factor is
    a. Coenzyme   b. Substrate
    c. Apoenzyme   **d. Holoenzyme**

32. Enzymes are chemically
    a. Lipids   b. Carbohydrate
    c. **Proteinaceous**   d. None

33. Substrate concentration to attained half maximum velocity is
    a. **K_m**   b. V_{max}
    c. K_{cat} d. None

34. Non-essential amino acid
    a. Alanine   b. **Tyrosine**
    c. Proline   d. Valine

35. **An abnormal number of chromosome could result during meiosis because of**
    a. Recombination
    b. A carrier
    c. Non-disjunction
    d. Inversion

36. **The enzymes activity is affect by**
    a. Changes in pH
    b. Changes in temperature
    c. Changed in substrate concentration
    d. All

37. **Enzyme active site is made up of**
    a. Catalytic site
    b. Substrate binding site
    c. Both
    d. None

38. **In case of competitive inhibitors V_{max} value**
    a. Increases   b. Decreases
    c. Unchanged   d. None

39. **In case of none-competitive inhibitors V_{max} value**
    a. Increases   **b. Decreases**
    c. Unchanged   d. None

40. **In case of un-competitive inhibitors V_{max} value**
    a. Increases   **b. Decreases**
    c. Unchanged   d. None

41. **Co-enzyme TPP is derived from vitamin**
    a. Biotin   b. Riboflavin
    c. Niacin   **d. Thiamine**

42. **Enzymes work as**
    a. Substrate that decreases activation energy
    b. Bio catalysts
    c. Substrate that increases velocity of reaction
    d. All

43. **Glutamine synthetase is_____type of enzyme.**
    a. Hydrolases   b. Lyase
    c. Ligase   d. All the above

44. **The non-protein organic subunit of enzyme is**
    a. Co-factor   b. Holoenzymes
    c. Coenzymes   d. None

45. **The enzymes are classified into**
    a. Five groups   b. Seven groups
    c. Six groups   d. Two groups

46. **Mg^{+2} is a co-factor of enzyme**
    a. Amylase
    b. Carbonic anhydrase
    c. Enterokinase   **d. Phosophatase**

47. **The trade name of DDT is**
    a. Cezarex
    b. Chlorophenothane
    c. Clofenotane   **d. All**

48. **Enzymes perform addition or removal of water is**
    a. Lipase   b. Aldolase
    c. Protease   d. Dehydrogenase

49. **Lock of key model is given by**
    a. Fischer   b. Koshland
    c. Both A and B   d. None

50. **Vitamins usually functions as**
    a. Co-enzyme   b. Enzyme
    c. Prosthetic group d. Substrates

51. **An example of a water soluble vitamin is**
    a. Vit E   **b. Vit C**
    c. Vit D   d. Vit A

52. **All the fat soluble vitamins are structurally**
    a. Steroids   **b. Isoprenoids**
    c. Nucleoprotein   d. None

53. **A deficiency of vit C produces the disease known as**
    a. Cataract   b. Beriberi
    c. Anemia   **d. Scurvy**

54. **The ascorbic acid plays an important role in**
    a. Collagen formation
    b. Bone formation

c. Folic acid metabolism
d. **All of the above**

55. **Retinol deficiencies cause**
    a. Xerophthalmia b. Keratomalacia
    c. **Night blindness** d. All

56. **The anti-row egg white injury factor is**
    a. **Avidin/ Biotin** b. Betabindin
    c. Albumin   d. Ovalbumin

57. **The vitamin B_1 thiamine is consists of molecule**
    a. Pyramidine ring
    b. Methylene bridge
    c. Thiazole ring **d. All**

58. **6, 7-dimethyl-isoalloxazine attached to ribitol is present in**
    a. **Vit B_2**   b. Vit B_1
    c. Vit C   d. Vit D

59. **The active form of folic acid is**
    a. Dihydrofolate
    b. **Tetrahydrofolate**
    c. Hexahydrofolate
    d. None

60. **A hormone produced in response to 3F is**
    a. **Catecholamine** b. Dopamine
    c. Both   d. None

61. **Vitamin destroyed on heating is**
    a. Tocopherol   b. Vit A
    c. **Vit B**   d. Vit D

62. **The structure of DNA with the help of X-ray diffraction is given by**
    a. Watson and crick
    b. Hershey-Chase
    c. **Franklin**   d. Wilkins

63. **Which of the following form of DNA has left-handed helix**
    a. A-DNA   b. B-DNA
    c. **Z-DNA**   d. T-DNA

64. **The process of DNA replication requires**
    a. mRNA, tRNA and rRNA molecules
    b. Wide variety of enzymes

c. DNA strands only
d. **DNA molecules, polymerase enzyme and other enzyme and factors**

65. **Nucleotide contain**
    a. N2 base   b. Phosphate group
    c. Ribose sugar   **d. All**

66. **The enzyme cause the unwinding of the DNA double helix**
    a. DNA polymerase 111
    b. **DNA helicase**
    c. SSB protein
    d. DNA gyrase

67. **DNA strand, which is separated during replication is not undergoes rewinding due to**
    a. DNA primase
    b. **Single strand binding proteins**
    c. DNA gyrase
    d. All

68. **When cytosine undergoes spontaneous deamination which base is formed?**
    a. Thymine   b. Guanine
    c. Adenine   **d. Uracil**

69. **Oldest medicinal plant is**
    a. Senna leaves   b. **Ashwagandha**
    c. Periwinkle   d. Opium

70. **How many base pair are present in each turn of B-DNA?**
    a. 12   b. 15
    c. **10**   d. 5

71. **Clover leaf structure explain structure of**
    a. mRNA   b. snRNA
    c. rRNA   **d. tRNA**

72. **Which is called adapter RNA in translation process?**
    a. **tRNA**   b. snRNA
    c. mRNA   d. rRNA

73. **Which enzyme is involved in joining of DNA nucleotide?**
    a. Helicase
    b. DNA polymerase

c. DNA kinase

d. DNA ligase

74. Who discovered DNA polymerase?

a. Okazaki

b. Watson and Krick

c. Kornberg

d. F. Mischer

75. Which of the following is present at 3′ end of prokaryotic mRNA?

a. Poly A tail

b. Shine-Dalgarno sequence

c. Stem loop structure

d. 7-methylguanylate

76. Transcription of rRNA is performed by

a. RNA polymerase 1

b. RNA polymerase 2

c. RNA polymerase 3

d. None

77. Section of DNA within a gene that does not encode part of the protein that the gene produces is called

a. Exons   b. Transposes

c. Intein   **d. Introns**

78. RNA splicing was discovered initially by

a. Phillip Allen Sharp

b. Hergovind Khorana

c. Richard J. Roberts

d. Watson and Crick

79. Shine-Dalgarno sequence or kozak sequence is AGGAGG, is present

a. mRNA   b. rRNA

c. tRNA   d. All of these

80. Which of the following is involved in eukaryotic transcription?

a. Mature mRNA **b. Poly A tail**

c. Splicisome   d. No

81. The template strand which as template for RNA synthesis is also called as

a. Coding strand

b. Noncoding strand

c. Both

d. None

82. Which enzyme is involved in replacement of damaged DNA strand with strand from sister molecule?

a. Rec A protein

b. DNA gyrase

c. DNA exonuclease

d. DNA polymerase

83. Which of the following is able to translocate to GATC?

a. Mut L   b. Mut S

c. Mut H   d. None

84. Which of the following acts endonulease and join to GATC?

a. Mut L   b. Mut S

c. Mut H   d. None

85. The large fragment of DNA polymerase I is 6 kD, known fragment. It has

a. 3 to 5 exonuclease activity

b. 5 to 3 polymerase activity

c. Both

d. None

86. Telomerase activity was found in highest in which cell

a. Muscle cell

b. Nerve cell

c. Embryonic stem cell

d. Blood cell

87. Homologous recombination helps to produced

a. Gene knock out animal

b. Sites specific mutagenesis

c. Clones

d. Gene library

88. 5-bromouracil is base analogues of which N2 base?

a. Thymine   b. Cytosine

c. Guanine   d. Adenine

89. Which of the following antibiotics is inhibitor of DNA gyrase?

a. Nalidixic acid   b. Novobiocin

c. Ciprofloxacin   **d. All**

90. Which of the following factors is involved in DNA recombination repir?
    a. Glycosylase   **b. Rac A**
    c. Les A   d. Uvr D

91. The ability of recombinant joint to move toward duplex is known as
    a. Patch recombinants
    b. Holiday junction
    c. Nicking
    d. Branch migration

92. The segment of DNA having the same nucleotide sequence from both forward and backward sides is known as
    a. Palindrome sequence
    b. TATAAT box
    c. Promoter region
    d. None

93. Which of the following conversions is transition mutations?
    a. A- C   b. T- G
    c. A- G   d. C- G

94. Which of the following proteins is considered a DNA mutase?
    a. DNa polymerase
    b. Umu CD
    c. Rec A   d. Lex A

95. Which of the following is not involved in homologous recombination in *E. coli*?
    a. Hot spot sequence
    b. Rec BCD
    c. Ruc A
    d. Rec A

96. Which of the following enzymes hydrolyzes the bond between base and deoxyribose sugar?
    a. Lyase   b. Glycosylase
    c. APE endonuclease
    d. XRCC

97. In Rec BCD system
    a. This is also known as exonuclease V
    b. The Rec BCD enzymes have both helicase and nuclease activity

c. After recognizing a chi sequence, the Rec BCD system helps to load Rec A onto single strand DNA
    d. All

98. What is true about Copia elements?
    a. Contains active promoters
    b. Flanked by direct repeats
    c. Approx. 300 ntd in length
    d. Are site of chemical leakage

99. What is true about topoisomerase enzyme?
    a. Initiation of replication
    b. Profeading
    c. Producing nick on DNA strand
    d. None

100. What is the no. of genetic codon formed from combination of four nitrogen bases?
     a. 16   **b. 64**
     c. 160   d. 245

101. The genes that malfunction in cancer normally
     a. Control RNA transcription
     b. Are responsible for organizing DNA packaging
     c. Code for enzymes that transcribe DNA
     d. Regulate cell division

102. Which is specific for RNA?
     a. Adenine   b. Cytosine
     c. Guanine   **d. Uracil**

103. Which of the following is stop codon?
     a. 5′UAG3′   b. 5′AAA3′
     c. 5′GUA3′   d. 5′AG3′

104. tRNA is involved in which function?
     a. Carrying rRNA from the nucleolus to RER
     b. Carrying amino acid from cytoplasm to RER
     c. Involved in translation as sense strand
     d. Involved in translation as nonsense strand

105. Which of the following triplet codons is responsible for proline coding?

   a. 5′CCU 3′   b. 5′CCC3′
   c. 5′CCA 3′   **d. All**

106. Which of the following triplet codons is responsible for glycine coding?

   a. 5′GGU 3′   b. 5′AGU3′
   c. 5′CGU 3′   **d. 5′UGU 3′**

107. Which of the following codons does not have any acceptor tRNAL?

   a. AUG   b. GUG
   c. UGA   d. CUC

108. Which among them is not the nature of genetic codon?

   a. Universality   b. Degeneracy
   c. Redundancy   **d. Multiplicity**

109. Wobble hypothesis is given by

   a. Wobble hypothesis
   b. Universality of codon
   c. Triplet codon nature
   d. All

110. The cause of codon redundancy was explain by nonspecific base pairing in which hypothesis?

   a. Wobble hypothesis
   b. Universality of codon
   c. Triplet codon nature
   d. All

111. Amino acid attached _____ site of tRNA.

   a. rRNA   **b. tRNA**
   c. mRNA   d. snRNA

112. The nonsense codon always have the first base

   a. Adenine   **b. Uracil**
   c. Guanine   d. Cytosine

113. A nucleotide is made up of N2 base sugar and phosphate backbone. These three subunits are attached together by

   a. Glycosidic bonds
   b. Peptide bond
   c. Ionic bonds
   d. Covalent bond

114. Among the following which amino acid coded for valine amino acid?

   a. GUU   b. GUC
   c. GUG   **d. All**

115. Which factors are responsible for the elongation of the polypeptide chain in eukaryotic cells?

   a. EF-T and EF-T2
   b. EF-1 and EF-2
   c. EF-1 and ef-2
   d. EF-Tu and EF-Ts

116. Which determines the sequence of amino acid formed by protein synthesis?

   a. mRNA   b. tRNA
   c. rRNA   d. siRNA

117. Enucleated protoplast is known as

   a. Cytoplasm   b. Tonoplast
   c. Nucleoplast   **d. Cytoplast**

118. Which of the following regions is associated between adjacent cells?

   a. Gap junction   b. Tight junction
   c. Desmosome   d. All

119. Plant cell without cell wall is known as

   a. Tonoplast   b. Cytosol
   c. Protoplast   d. Nucleolus

120. Discovery of cell is done by

   a. AV Leeuwenhoek
   b. Schwann
   c. Schleiden
   d. Robert Hook

121. Cell theory for animal was given by

   a. A. V. Leeuwenhoek
   b. Schleiden
   c. Schwann
   d. Robert Hook

122. A cell shows presence of mitochondria, lysosome, dictysome, ribosome and rough ER, etc. Based on this information, justify the nature of cell

   a. Plant cell   b. Mouse cell
   c. Fungal cell   d. Bacterium

123. Cell fractionation is used to
    a. Isolate mitochondria only
    b. Isolate chloroplast only
    c. Isolate all type of organelles
    d. Isolate biomolecules only

124. The cells containing haploid set of chromosome is
    a. Somatic cell   **b. Gametic cells**
    c. Myloma cell   d. Neurons

125. Mitochondria is the not the site for which pathway?
    a. Betaoxidation of fatty acid
    b. Krebs cycle
    c. Pentose phosphate pathway
    d. ETC

126. What is Plasmodesmata?
    a. It is connecting link between adjacent cells
    b. It is part of middle lamella
    c. Part of cytoskeleton
    d. Component of inner membrane of mitochondria

127. Golgi complex was discovered by
    a. Leeuwenhoek   **b. Camillo-Golgi**
    c. Morgan   d. Robert Brown

128. The site of protein synthesis is
    a. Cell walls
    b. Ribosomes
    c. Nucleus
    d. Mitochondria

129. Lampbrush chromosomes are observed in which phase of cell cycle?
    a. Mitotic metaphase
    b. Meiotic anaphase
    c. Mitotic prophase
    d. Meiotic prophase

130. Which one of the following having H_2O_2 activity?
    a. Golgi complex
    b. Lysosome
    c. Endoplasmic reticulum
    d. Peroxysome

131. A which stage of cell cycle DNA replication occurs?
    a. D   b. B
    c. A   d. C

132. What is outcome at the end of meiosis I? The number of chromosomes is
    a. Number of chromosome is halved
    b. Number of chromosome is same
    c. Number of chromosome is doubled
    d. Not justified

133. A which stage of mitosis cell cycle nuclear membrane and nucleolus begin to disappear?
    a. Interphase   **b. Late prophase**
    c. Early anaphase d. Early metaphase

134. Crossing over occurs in _____ stage of meiosis.
    a. Leptotene   b. Zygotene
    c. Pachytene   d. Diplotene

135. During which stage of meiosis synaptonemal complex is observed
    a. Leptotene   **b. Zygotene**
    c. Pachytene   d. Diplotene

136. Genome is defined as
    a. Haploid set of chromosome
    b. Diploid set of chromosome
    c. Genotypic constituent of an individual
    d. Part of housekeeping gene

137. The enzyme recombinations are used for recombination of chromosome at which stage of cell cycle?
    a. Prophase I   b. Metaphase II
    c. Telophase   d. Cytokinesis

138. Homeobox polypeptide segments
    a. Serve as histones, facilitating DNA packaging
    b. Bind to DNA and activate or repress gene transcription
    c. Are vastly different in different organisms
    d. Act as enzymes, carrying out important chemical reactions

139. Which of the following acts as carrier of amino acids to the ribosomes?
    a. mRNA
    b. tRNA
    c. snRNA
    d. rRNA

140. Gene expression in animal development seems to be regulated largely by
    a. Controlling gene packing and unpacking
    b. Controlling the transcription of genes into mRNA
    c. Controlling the translation of mRNAs into protein
    d. Selectivity eliminating certain genes from the genome

141. Formation of cell plate is directed from
    a. Centre of wall
    b. Wall to centre
    c. Same in both direction
    d. None

142. Centromere is part of which of following organelles?
    a. Lysosome
    b. Nucleus
    c. Chromosome
    d. Nucleolus

143. Nucleosome organization occur by coiling DNA on
    a. Histones protein
    b. Centromeres region proteins
    c. Positively charged proteins
    d. Negatively charged proteins

144. A cell is arrested in G_2 phase of their cell cycle
    a. It has twice the amount of DNA as present in Telophase stage
    b. The enzymatic content is more and ready to undergo M phase
    c. Possesses a distinct nuclear membrane
    d. All

145. Sister chromatids contain identical DNA sequences are held together by
    a. Hydrogen bonding
    b. Kinetochores
    c. Centromeres
    d. Telomeres of chromosome

146. The chromosome constituents of an individual organizasm is known as
    a. Phenotype
    b. Genotype
    c. Karyotype
    d. Cytoplasmic inheritance

147. Mitogen derived from plant origin is
    a. PDGF
    b. Cytokinin
    c. Epidermal growth factor
    d. Cyanide

148. Mitogen derived from animal origin is
    a. PDGF
    b. Cytokinin
    c. Epidermal growth factor
    d. Cyanide

149. The term mitosis was coined by
    a. Purkinje
    b. Fleeming
    c. Haeckel
    d. Porter

150. Cell cycle was discovered by
    a. Watson and Crick
    b. Howard and Pele
    c. Watson and Porter
    d. None of them

151. In a human cell, find the number of tetrads at prophase I
    a. 46
    b. 23
    c. 23 + 23
    d. 12 + 11

152. Mitogen derived from plant origin is
    a. PDGF
    b. Cytokinin
    c. Epidermal growth factor
    d. All

153. A charged amine molecules of small size are function as
    a. Hormones
    b. Neurotransmitters
    c. Signal transducers
    d. All

154. The enzyme breaks cAMP into AMP is
    a. Phosphorylated serine residues
    b. Phosphorylated tyrosine residues

c. Adenylyl cyclase

d. Phosphodiesterase

155. What is the mode of action of paracrine signaling molecules?

a. **It effect nearby target cells**

b. It effect target cells distant from its site of synthesis

c. It effect only local target cell

d. All

156. Single molecule that interact with cell surface receptors are

a. Epinephrine and norepinephrine

b. Glucagon

c. Insulin   d. **All of these**

157. Which of the following is not a secondary messenger?

a. cAMP   b. cGMP

c. IP3   d. **ATP**

158. The hormone or ligand is

a. **Primary messenger**

b. Secondary messenger

c. Neurotransmitters

d. Surface receptor

159. Cell-mediated immune responses are

a. Enhanced by depletion of complement

b. **Suppressed by corticosteroids**

c. Enhanced by depletion of T cells

d. Enhanced by depletion of macrophages

160. The earliest stages of B cell differentiation

a. Occur in the embryonic thymus

b. Require the presence of antigen

c. Invole re-arrangement of alpha-chain gene segments

d. **Involve rearrangement of heavy chain gene segments**

161. The clonal selection theory best accounts for

a. The production of memory cells

b. The mechanism whereby antigen and antibody unite

c. **The specificity of B cells into plasma cells**

d. The maturation of B cells into plasma cells

162. Primary and secondary antibody responses differ in

a. The predominant isotype generated

b. The number of lymphocytes responding to antigen

c. The speed at which antibodies appear in the serum

d. **All is correct**

163. Which of the following is correct regarding cellular immunity?

a. **developing T cells that bind too strongly or too weekly to self MHC molecules in the thymus are detected by apoptosis**

b. CD+ helper T-lymphocytes recognized antigen bound to MHC class I molecules

c. Full activation of T-lymphocyte requires a co-stimulatory signal

d. All is correct

164. The role of antigen presenting cell in the immune response is all of the following *except*

a. The limited catabolism of polypeptide antigens

b. To allow selective association of MHC gene product and peptide

c. To supply second signals required to fully activates T cells

d. **To present non-self peptides associated with MHC class II molecules to B cells**

165. Which of the following properties is not exhibited by TH cells?

a. Stimulates division of B cells

b. Stimulate division of cytotoxic T cells

c. **Are cytotoxic for other cells**

d. Stimulate migration of macrophages

166. Histone protein is absent in

a. **Bacterial DNA**   b. Virus DNA

c. Human DNA   d. Plant DNA

167. Bacillus is
    a. **Nitrifying bacteria**
    b. Ammonifying bacteria
    c. Soil bacteria
    d. Pathogneic bacteria

168. Rickettsia is a group of
    a. Fungi
    b. Human race
    c. Viruses
    d. **Bacteria**

169. Mycoplasma lacking of which cell organelles?
    a. Nucleus
    b. **Cell wall**
    c. Ribosomes
    d. ER

170. Tetracycline and penicillin act respectively on
    a. **Metabolic pathways and cell wall**
    b. Cell wall and metabolic pathways
    c. Only cell wall
    d. Only metabolic pathways

171. Viruses are characterized by
    a. Obligate parasites
    b. Reproduce only in living cells
    c. Facultative cell
    d. **Both a and b**

172. Lycopene is chemically in
    a. Carbohydrate
    b. Enzyme
    c. **Terpenoid**
    d. Protein

173. Calmodulin is a
    a. **Binding protein**
    b. Enzyme
    c. Hormone
    d. Terpene

174. Application of isomerase is in industry during
    a. **Conversion of glucose to fructose**
    b. Conversion of lactose to maltose
    c. Isolation of milk protein
    d. All of the above

175. Before entry into TCA (Krebs cycle) pyruvic acid changed into
    a. **Acetyl CoA**
    b. Formaldehyde
    c. Acetyldehyde
    d. Citric acid

176. Inulin is a polymer of
    a. Tylin
    b. **Fructose**
    c. Glucose
    d. Levulose

177. The best application of inulin is in
    a. **Detection in glomerular filtration rate (GFR)**
    b. Enhancing the GFR
    c. Reducing the GFR
    d. Proper kidney functioning

178. The configuration of cellulose fibres is similar as
    a. **β-sheet**
    b. β-turns
    c. α-helices
    d. All

179. How many biological energies are used in gluconeogenesis?
    a. 4 ATPs and 1 GTP per glucose
    b. 9 ATPs and 4 GTPs per glucose
    c. 6 ATPs and 2 GTPs per glucose
    d. **4 ATPs and 2 GTPs per glucose**

180. Which of the following is not the constituent of saliva?
    a. **Hormones**
    b. Amylase
    c. Enzymes kills the microorganisms
    d. Mucus

181. The process of conversion of pyruvate to oxaloacetate
    a. Requires biotin
    b. Uses carbohydrate
    c. Occurs in the mitochondria
    d. **All**

182. Which sugar is predominantly present in nucleic acid?
    a. Galactose
    b. Trehalose
    c. Glucose
    d. **Ribose**

183. All are disaccharides *except*
    a. **Amylopectin**
    b. Cellobiose
    c. Maltose
    d. None

184. Hexokinase has
    a. **Low K_m value**
    b. High K_m value
    c. More affinity for glucose
    d. None

185. In glycogenesis, precursor to glycogen is
    a. Glucose-1, 6-biphosphate
    b. Glucose-1, 6-P
    c. UDP-glucose
    d. None

186. The enzymes required in glycolysis pathway of eukaryotic cells are located
    a. Plasma membrane
    b. Cytosol
    c. Mitochondrial matrix
    d. All parts of cells

187. Phosphofructokinase (GMP enzyme) is allosterically inhibited and activated by
    a. ATP and GTP respectively
    b. GDP and Pi respectively
    c. ATP and Pi respectively
    d. Mg^+ ions only

188. In which of the following enzyme/s regulates glycolysis pathway?
    a. Phosphofructokinase
    b. Pyruvate kinase
    c. Hexokinase
    d. All

189. Which type of karyotype is considered to be a relatively advanced feature?
    a. Symmetric
    b. Asymmetric
    c. Both a and b
    d. None of the above

190. Karyotype is
    a. A technique of arranging chromosomes of a cell based on their size
    b. Study of nucleus
    c. Study of human genetics
    d. None of the above

191. Amitosis is
    a. A common method of cell division in an organism
    b. Division of cell without spindle formation
    c. Equal division of nucleus and cytoplasm
    d. None of the above

192. Zygotic meiosis occurs in
    a. Gymnosperms
    b. Ferns
    c. Chlamydomonas
    d. None of the above

193. Non-disjunction of the chromosome occurs at
    a. Anaphase   b. Prophase
    c. Telophase   d. Metaphase

194. For active mitosis, we can see
    a. Onion roots   b. Garlic roots
    c. Turnip roots   d. Mango roots

195. Prokaryotic DNA is
    a. Double-stranded round
    b. Single-stranded round
    c. Double-stranded straight
    d. None of the above

196. Which type of DNA found in bacteria?
    a. Straight DNA
    b. Helical DNA
    c. Membrane bound DNA
    d. Circular free DNA

197. Polygenic genes show
    a. Different phenotypes
    b. Different genotypes
    c. Both a and b
    d. None of the above

198. How many types of polymerase are present in prokaryotic cells?
    a. 0   **b. 3**
    c. 2   d. 1

199. Which step of translation does not consume a high energy phosphate bond?
    a. Translation
    b. Amino acid activation
    c. Peptidyl transferase reaction
    d. Aminoacetyl tRNA binding to A-site

200. Which of the following has a single ring structure?
    a. Uracil   b. Adenine
    c. Thymine   d. Guanine

9

Agricultural Genetics

1. The term genetics was coined by
   a. Charles Darwin   b. Lamarck
   c. Mendel   **d. Bateson**

2. Theory of epigenesis was proposed by
   a. August Weismann
   b. Hugo de Vries
   c. Wolff   d. Lamarck

3. Theory of pangenesis was proposed by
   a. Lamarck   b. Wolff
   c. Charles Darwin
   d. August Weismann

4. Theory of acquired character was put forth by
   a. Hugo de Vries   b. Morgan
   c. Lamarck   d. Mendel

5. The germ plasm theory was advocated by
   a. August Weismann
   b. Charles Darwin
   c. Hugo de Vries
   d. Lamarck

6. Preformation theory was proposed by
   a. Wolff   b. Lamarck
   c. Swammerdam and Bonnet
   d. Bateson and Punnett

7. The one gene one enzyme hypothesis was given by
   a. TH Morgan
   b. Bateson and Punnett

c. Beadle and Tatum
   d. Hugo de Vries

8. The operon hypothesis was proposed by
   a. RA Fisher (1918)
   b. Jacob and Monad
   c. Bateson and Punnett (1901)
   d. Morgan (1910)

9. Chromosome number in endosperm of a diploid plant (2n=20) is
   a. 10   b. 20
   c. 30   d. 40

10. Eukaryote is an organism
    a. Whose cell have double nuclei
    b. Whose cells have true nuclei
    c. Whose cell do not have true nuclei
    d. Whose cell have extra nuclei

11. In mitosis longest phase is
    a. Prophase   b. Metaphase
    c. Anaphase   d. Telophase

12. Mitosis is also known as
    a. Reduction division
    b. Homotypic division
    c. Heterotypic division
    d. None of the above

13. Meiosis is also referred to as
    a. Equational division
    b. Homotypic division
    c. Reduction division
    d. All of the above

14. Mitosis gives rise to
    a. Four haploid cells
    b. Two haploid cells
    c. Two diploid cells
    d. All of the above

15. In mitosis, daughter cells are identical to mother cell in
    a. Shape
    b. Size
    c. Chromosome complement
    d. **All of the above**

16. The daughter cells produced by mitosis are different from mother cell in
    a. Shape
    b. Size
    c. **Chromosome number and composition**
    d. All of the above

17. In mitosis, synaptonemal complex develops during
    a. Laptotene   b. **Zygotene**
    c. Pachytene   d. Diplotene

18. In mitosis, chromosomes are arranged at aquatorialplant during
    a. Early prophase
    b. Late prophase
    c. **Early metaphase**
    d. Late mataphase

19. In mitosis, duplication of chromosomes occur during
    a. **Interphase**   b. Prophase
    c. Metaphase   d. Anaphase

20. In mitosis, sequence of sub-stages of prophase I is
    a. Leptotene, diplotene, zygotene, pachytene, diakinesis
    b. **L-Z-P-diplotene, diakinesis**
    c. L-P-Z-diakinesis, diplotene
    d. Z-L-P diakinesis, diplotene

21. A chromosome with several centromeres is called
    a. Acentric   b. Dicentric
    c. **Polycentric**   d. Monocentric

22. A chromosome with diffused centromere is referred to as
    a. Acrocentric
    b. Telocentric
    c. **Holokinetic**
    d. None of the above

23. At anaphase a metacentric chromosome will assume
    a. **V shape**
    b. J shape
    c. Rod shape
    d. None of the above

24. The centromere is also known as
    a. Secondary constriction
    b. **Primary constriction**
    c. Chromomere
    d. All of the above

25. The movement of chromosomes at anaphase is associated with
    a. Chromosome   b. **Centromere**
    c. Telomere   d. All of the above

26. The polytene chromosomes where first discovered in salivary glands of dipteran insects by
    a. Strausberger (1875)
    b. Waldeyer (1888)
    c. Darlington (1881)
    d. **Balbiani (1937)**

27. The term chromosome was coined by
    a. **Strausberger (1875)**
    b. Waldeyer (1888)
    c. Balbiani (1837)
    d. Balbiani (1881)

28. Puffs are found in
    a. Lampbrush chromosome
    b. **Polytene chromosomes**
    c. B-chromosome
    d. All of the above

29. Puffs are the sites of
    a. Protein synthesis
    b. **DNA synthesis**
    c. RNA synthesis
    d. All of the above

30. **Loops are found in**
    a. Polytene chromosomes
    b. Isochromosomes
    c. **Lampbrush chromosomes**
    d. All of the above

31. **B-chromosomes are also known as**
    a. Accessory chromosomes
    b. Supernumerary isochromosomes
    c. Extrachromosomes
    d. **All of these**

32. **Laws of inheritance were discovered by Mendel in 1866 who working with**
    a. Drosophila   b. Maize
    c. **Garden pea**   d. Neurospora

33. **In garden pea, Mendel studied the dominant and recessive behaviour of**
    a. Five characters
    b. Three characters
    c. **Seven characters**
    d. Fifteen characters

34. **Mendel's results were published in 1866 in the**
    a. Journal of heredity
    b. Journal of genetics
    c. **Proceedings of natural history society of Brunn**
    d. All of the above

35. **Mendel presented his the form of**
    a. One paper   b. **Two papers**
    c. Three papers   d. Four papers

36. **Mendel's research work remained overlooked after his death for**
    a. 16 years   b. 24 years
    c. **34 years**   d. 40 years

37. **Mendel failed to confirm his findings when he worked with**
    a. Maize   b. Drosophila
    c. **Hawk weed (Hiearaceam)**
    d. Cow pea

38. **Mendel's results were first published in**
    a. English   b. French
    c. **German**   d. Russian

39. **Mendel died in**
    a. 1866   b. **1884**
    c. 1874   d. 1890

40. **Mendel had good background of**
    a. **Biology**   b. History
    c. Geography   d. **Mathematics**

41. **The F2 phenotypic ratio of a co-dominant trait governed by a single gene is**
    a. 3 : 1   b. 2 : 1
    c. **1 : 2 : 1**   d. All is correct

42. **Co-dominance is the phenomenon when**
    a. One allele masks the effects of another allele
    b. **Both the alleles of a gene expresses them in the heterozygote**
    c. Two dominance genes capable of producing a character when they present together
    d. All is correct

43. **With complete dominance and equal survival of all genotypes the genes in F2 in a monohybrid cross aggregate into**
    a. **3 : 1 ratio**
    b. 1 : 2 : 1 ratio
    c. 1 : 2 ratio
    d. None of the above

44. **A cross of F1 with its homozygous parent is known as**
    a. Reciprocal cross
    b. **Test cross**
    c. Top cross
    d. None of the above

45. **A cross between two inbreds by reversing the order of male and female present is called**
    a. Test cross
    b. Back cross
    c. **Reciprocal cross**
    d. None of the above

46. **Manifold effect of a gene refer to**
    a. Penetrance   b. Expressivity
    c. **Pleiotropy**   d. Epistasis

47. With complete dominance and equal survival of all genotypes, the genes in F2 in a monohybrid cross segregate into
    a. 3 : 1 ratio
    b. 1 : 2 : 1 ratio
    c. 1 : 2 ratio
    d. None of the above

48. A cross of F1 with homozygous recessive parent is known as
    a. Reciprocal cross
    b. **Test cross**
    c. Top cross
    d. None of the above

49. A cross between two inbreeds by reversing the order of male and female present is called
    a. Test cross
    b. Back cross
    c. **Reciprocal cross**
    d. None of the above

50. 9 : 7 ratio is obtained in gene interaction of
    a. **Complementary**
    b. Supplementary
    c. Duplicate   d. Inhibitory

51. In recessive epistasis, in F2 generation, the phenotypic ratio of 9:3:3:1 is modified to
    a. **9 : 3 : 4**   b. 9 : 7
    c. 12 : 3 : 1   d. 15 : 1

52. Dominant epistasis is also known as
    a. Supplementary epistasis
    b. Complementary epistasis
    c. **Simple epistasis**
    d. Duplicate epistasis

53. In gene interaction, the gene which has masking effect is called
    a. Dominant gene
    b. Recessive gene
    c. Co-dominant gene
    d. **Epistatic gene**

54. In interlocus interaction, the gene whose effect is masked is termed as
    a. Recessive gene
    b. Epistatic gene
    c. **Hypostatic gene**
    d. Dominant gene

55. Tendency of one crossover to enhance the chance of another crossover in its adjacent region is referred to as
    a. Positive interference
    b. **Negative interference**
    c. Coincidence
    d. Coupling

56. Crossing over takes place in pachytene during
    a. Leptotene   b. Zygotene
    c. **Pachytene**   d. Diplotene

57. Chiasma was first discovered by
    a. Bateson and Punnett (1906)
    b. Morgan (1910)
    c. **Janssens (1909)**
    d. Haldane (1942)

58. The coupling and repulsion phases of linkage were given by
    a. **Bateson and Punnett (1906)**
    b. TH Morgan (2910)
    c. Hutchinson
    d. HJ Müller

59. The term interference and coincidence were coined by
    a. Haldane (1942)   b. Morgan (1933)
    c. **Muller (1916)**   d. Janssens (1909)

60. Tendency of one crossover to enhance the chance of another crossover in its adjacent region is referred to as
    a. Positive interference
    b. **Negative interference**
    c. Coincidence   d. Couping

61. Stuctural changes in chromosome cause alteration in
    a. Phenotype   b. Fertility
    c. Viability   d. Karyotype
    e. **All of the above**

62. Deletion leads to alteration in
   a. **Gene number**
   b. Sequence of gene
   c. Structure of gene
   d. All of the above

63. Intercalary deletion leads to loss of segment in a chromosome from the
   a. **Intermediate position**
   b. Terminal portion
   c. Both
   d. None of the above

64. Duplicate was first reported by
   a. **CB Bridges (1919)**
   b. Sturtevant (1926)
   c. TH Morgan (1910)
   d. None of the above

65. Translocation leads to exchange of segments between
   a. Homologous chromosomes
   b. **Non-homologous chromosomes**
   c. Sister chromatids
   d. All of the above

66. Inversion leads to alteration in
   a. Composition of genes
   b. **Sequence of genes**
   c. Number of genes
   d. All of the above

67. Translocation homogygotes lead to alteration in
   a. Gene number
   b. Sequence of genes
   c. **Linkage map**   d. Linkage groups

68. Monoploids are represented by
   a. **x**   b. 2x
   c. n   d. 2n

69. Monoploid which develop from a normal diploid species are referred to as
   a. **Monohaploids** b. Polyhaploid
   c. Dihaploids   d. Disomic haploid

70. Autopolyploid is referred to as
   a. Hybrid polyploid
   b. **Simple polyploid**

   c. Segmental polyploid
   d. None of the above

71. The change in chromosome number which involves entire set of genome is known as
   a. Aneuploidy   b. **Euploidy**
   c. Trisomy   d. All of the above

72. An individual lacking one chromosome from the diploid set is referred to as
   a. Nulliomic   b. **Monosomic**
   c. Trisomic   d. Tetrasomic

73. In primary trisomic, the extrachromosome is
   a. Isochromosome
   b. Translocated chromosome
   c. **Normal chromosome**
   d. None of the above

74. A Nulliomic individual is represented by
   a. $2n-1$ b. **$2n+1$**
   c. $2n-2$ d. $2n+2$

75. The term polygenes was first used by
   a. RA Fisher (1918)
   b. Sewall Wright (1935)
   c. **K Mather (1941)**
   d. DS Falconer (1960)

76. Genetic variance was first divided into additive dominance and epistatic components by
   a. **RA Fisher (1918)**
   b. Sewall Wright (1921)
   c. K Mather (1949)
   d. Cayman (1954)

77. Partitioning of genetic variance into additive and non-additive components was suggested by
   a. TA Fisher (1918)
   b. **Sewall Wright (1935)**
   c. Mather and Jimks (1982)
   d. DS Falconer (1960)

78. Partitioning of phenotypic variance into heritable fixable, heritable non-fixable

and non-heritable non-fixable was suggested by

a. RA Fisher (1918)
b. **K Mather (1949)**
c. Kempthorne (1957)
d. Falconer (1960)

79. **Additive genes exhibit**

a. Complete dominance
b. Incomplete dominance
c. **Lack of dominance**
d. Over dominance

80. **Additive genetic variance is**

a. Heritable non-fixable
b. **Heritable fixable**
c. Non-heritable non-fixable
d. None of the above

81. **Additive genetic variance is related**

a. **Homogygosity**
b. Narrow sense heritability
c. Transgressive segregation
d. All of the above

82. **Dominance variance results due to**

a. **Intra-allelic interaction**
b. Inter-allelic interaction
c. Cytoplasmic effects
d. All of the above

83. **Dominance variance has relationship with**

a. Hetrozygosity
b. Heterosis
c. Specific combining ability
d. **All of the above**

84. **Holendric genes are**

a. Genes responsible for determination of sex in individual
b. **Genes carried in Y chromosomes and thereby showing only male to male transmission**
c. The sex having genes in heterozygous conditions
d. None of the above

85. **Sex chromosomes were first discovered in**

a. Drosophila   b. **Grasshoppers**
c. Garden pea   d. Maize

86. **Wilson and Stevens (1905) discovered sex chromosomes in**

a. Grasshoppers   b. Protenor
c. **Melandrium**   d. Drosophila

87. **The genetics constitution of normal Drosophila female is**

a. **XX**   b. XXY
c. XY   d. XO

88. **The gene causing Haemophilia in man is inherited through**

a. Males   b. **Both**
c. Female   d. None

89. **Sex-linked genes are located on**

a. **X-chromosomes**
b. Y-chromosomes
c. Autosomes
d. All of the above

90. **Barr body was first discovered**

a. Lyon (1969)
b. Bridges (1922)
c. **Murray Barr (1949)**
d. Morgan (1933)

91. **Barr bodies are**

a. **Sex chromatin positive**
b. Sex chromatin negative
c. Sex chromatin neutral
d. All of the above

92. **The number of Barr bodies in a female cell is always**

a. **One less than X chromosomes**
b. Equal to X chromosomes
c. One more than X chromosomes
d. Two more than X chromosomes

93. **The first case of sex reversal was reported by**

a. Bridges (1922)   b. Müller (1932)
c. **Crew**   d. McClung (1902)

94. Colour blindness is governed by a recessive gene located on
   a. Y chromosome   **b. X chromosome**
   c. Autosomes   d. All of the above

95. Holendric genes are present on
   a. X chromosome
   b. Y chromosomes
   c. Autosomes
   d. All of the above

96. The first case of cytoplasmic inheritance was reported by
   a. Correns (1909)   b. Sturtevant
   c. Caspari (1936)   d. Renner

97. Correns first reported cytoplasmic inheritance in
   a. Four o'clock plant
   b. Evening primerose
   c. Water snail
   d. Flour moth

98. Cytoplasmic inheritance is also known as
   a. Extranuclear inheritance
   b. Extrachromosomal inheritance
   c. Non-mendelian inheritance
   d. Organellar inheritance
   e. Uniparental inheritance
   f. All of the above

99. The genes which govern cytoplasmic inheritance are called
   a. Plasma genes
   b. Cytogenes
   c. Cytoplasmic genes
   d. Extranuclear genes
   e. All of the above

100. Cytoplasmic genes are found in
   a. Mitochondria   b. Chloroplast
   c. Both   d. Neither

101. In maize, IOJAP (green and white stripes) leaf colour is controlled by
   a. Nuclear gene
   b. Chloroplast genes
   c. Mitochondrial genes
   d. All of the above

102. In Drosophila, inheritance of sigma particle is an example of
   a. Maternel effects
   b. Inheritance due to infective particles
   c. Cytoplasmic inheritance
   d. None of the above

103. DNA is a polymer of
   a. Amino acids
   b. Nucleotides
   c. Non-nucleotides
   d. None of the above

104. In DNA, a molecule thymine always pairs with
   a. Adenine   b. Guanine
   c. Sytosine   d. Uracil

105. The double helical structure of DNA was proposed by
   a. Avery MecLeod and McCarty (1944)
   b. Griffith (1928)
   c. Watson and Crick (1953)
   d. Beadle and Tatum (1941)

106. DNA as the genetic material was first discovered by
   a. Griffith (1928)
   b. Avery MecLeod and McCarty (1944)
   c. Hershey and Chase (1951)
   d. Benzer (1955)

107. In DNA molecule adenine and thymine bases are joined by
   a. Single hydrogen bonds
   b. Double hydrogen bonds
   c. Triple hydrogen bonds
   d. All of the above

108. In DNA guanine and cytosine bases are joined by
   a. Double phosphate bonds
   b. Triple phosphate bonds
   c. Double hydrogen bonds
   d. Triple hydrogen bonds

109. Purines are compounds with
   a. Single ring   **b. Double ring**
   c. Triple ring   d. All of the above

110. In RNA molecule, uracil is present in place of
   a. Adenine
   b. Guanine
   c. **Thymine**
   d. Cytosine

111. RNA acts as a genetic material in
   a. **Tobacco mosaic virus**
   b. Neurospora
   c. *E. coli*
   d. None of the above

112. RNA which acts as a carrier of amino acids during protein synthesis refers to
   a. rRNA
   b. mRNA
   c. **tRNA**
   d. None of the above

113. Pyrimidine bases include
   a. A and G
   b. **G and C**
   c. A and T
   d. T, C and U

114. The one gene one enzyme hypothesis was proposed by
   a. Beadle and Eprussi (1937)
   b. Beadle and Tatum (1941)
   c. **Brenner (1955)**
   d. Crick (1966)

115. Signal codon refers to
   a. UAA
   b. UAG
   c. UGA
   d. **All of the above**

116. Reverse transcription was first reported by
   a. Watson and Crick (1953)
   b. Crick (1966)
   c. **Temin and Baltimore (1970)**
   d. None of the above

117. Initiation of protein synthesis requires
   a. Ribosome subunits
   b. mRNA
   c. An energy source
   d. **All of the above**

118. Temin and Baltimore were awarded Nobel Prize for the discovery of
   a. Translation
   b. Transcription
   c. Reverse mutation
   d. **Reverse transcription**

119. Operon model of gene regulation in *E. coli* was discovered by
   a. **Jacob and Monod (1961)**
   b. Temin and Baltimore (1971)
   c. Britten and Davidson (1969)
   d. Watson and Crick (1953)

120. Nobel Prize for the discovery of operon model was awarded to
   a. Beadle and Tatum (1958)
   b. Watson and Crick (1953)
   c. **Jacob and Monod (1961)**
   d. Britten and Davidson (1969)

121. Synthesis of mRNA only from one stand of DNA is known as
   a. Symmetrical transcription
   b. **Asymmetrical transcription**
   c. Reverse transcription
   d. Translation

122. Reverse transcription is known as
   a. Asymmetrical transcription
   b. Symmetrical transcription
   c. **Teminism**
   d. None of the above

123. Reverse transcription has been reported in
   a. *E.coli*
   b. Neurospora
   c. **Certain tumour producing viruses**
   d. Drosophila

124. The term mutation was coined by
   a. **Hugo de Vries (1900)**
   b. Morgan (1910)
   c. Müller (1927)
   d. Stadler (1928)

125. The first case of mutation was discovered in
   a. Drosophila
   b. Garden pea
   c. **Male lamp**
   d. Neurospora

126. A unit of mutations in a gene is known as
    a. Hot spot   b. Citron
    c. Muton   d. Recon

127. Induced mutations useful in
    a. Development of improved varieties
    b. Induction of male sterility
    c. Production of haploids
    d. Creation of variability

128. For experimental induction of mutations in Drosophila by X-rays the Nobel Prize was awarded to
    a. TH Morgan (1910)
    b. HJ Müller (1927)
    c. Stadler (1928)
    d. Hugo de Vries (1900)

129. A mutation which kills 50% of the individuals that carry the mutation, it is referred to as
    a. Lethal mutation
    b. Sub-lethal mutation
    c. Sub-vital mutation
    d. Vital mutation

130. Gene mutation is
    a. Smallest unit of gene capable of undergoing mutation
    b. Gene, which causes another gene to undergo mutations
    c. Mutant phenotype due to presence of mutant gene
    d. All is correct

131. The cell undergoes cancer is
    a. Divide normally by mitosis
    b. Are sensitive to extracellular responses
    c. Undergoes uncontrolled division and they are immortal
    d. Very large in size

132. A cancer cell is said to be _____, if it remain clustered at a single point and cannot spread to other site
    a. Contact inhibited
    b. Transplantable
    c. Benign
    d. Maliglant

133. A neoplastic cell that progressively invade and spread is termed as
    a. Benign   b. Mutated cell
    c. Malignant   d. Mutagenic

134. Which of the following is a type of cancer causing gene that promotes cancer by activating cell division in inappropriate manner
    a. Cellular oncogene
    b. Oncofetal genes
    c. Proto-oncogene
    d. All

135. Among the following which genes normally prevent cell division
    a. Contact inhibition
    b. Angiogenesis
    c. Agonism   d. None

136. Retinoblastoma eye tumor is caused by
    a. Translation of proto-oncogenic gene
    b. Mutation of chromosome 13 sit is called RBI
    c. Due to a somatic mutation in the RB gene
    d. None

137. Which of following gene is responsible for FAP (familial adenomatous polyposis) colon cancer
    a. APC gene of chromosome 5
    b. ISF gene of chromosome 16
    c. P53
    d. P53 None

138. Which of the following is a tumor suppressor gene instead of an oncogene?
    a. TP53 (P53)   **b. BRCA1**
    c. RB   **d. All**

139. What is true regarding cancer?
    a. It is caused by mutation of proto-oncogenes to convert into oncogenes
    b. Mutations in the gene called KIT can cause hereditary gastrointestinal stromal tumors

c. Most cancers are result of genetic mutation and also it is generally inherent

d. All

140. Which of the following having anti-cancer activity

    a. **Whole wheat pasta**

    b. Cruciferous vegetables such as broccoli

    c. Spinach

    d. All

141. Which of the following is used to diagnose and manage cancer?

    a. DNA microarrays

    b. **Genome data**

    c. Both

    d. None

142. Hippocrates is the term first used for

    a. **Cancer**   b. AIDS

    c. Viral influenza   d. None

143. What is the expected cause of cancer?

    a. RT viruses

    b. UV radiation

    c. Carcinogenic foods

    d. **All of these**

144. When neoplastic cells remain clustered in a single mass and cannot metastasizes to distant sites tumor is known as

    a. Benign tumour

    b. **Malignant tumor**

    c. Carcinoma

    d. Sarcomas

145. Which of the following is the character of cancer cells?

    a. Metastatic

    b. Genetically heritable

    c. Dedifferentiated and invasive

    d. **All**

146. The substage condenser can performs

    a. Changes the wavelength of the light

    b. **Focuses light on the specimen**

    c. Reduces the amount of light approaching specimen

    d. None

147. A 10X objective and a 40X eyepiece combined create total magnification of

    a. 50   b. **400**

    c. 90   d. 140

148. Unstained cells and living organisms are observed best by

    a. TEM

    b. SEM

    c. **Phase contrast microscopy**

    d. Black field microscope

149. Scanning electron microscopy used for observation of

    a. Cellular organelles

    b. Surface morphology

    c. Small internal cell structures

    d. **All of the above**

150. Which of the following objectives would give you the best resolution of small objects?

    a. 20X air, N.A. 0.65

    b. **30X air, N.A. 0.45**

    c. 64X oil, N.A. 1.45

    d. 10X oil, N.A. 1.2

151. Which of the following statements is most correct about atomic force microscopy (AFM)?

    a. AFM can visualize protein bound to DNA molecules

    b. AFM can visualize unifixed specimens in water or buffer

    c. AFM moves a very sharp tip over the surface of the specimen to "feel" its shape

    d. **All the statements above are true**

152. Phase contrast microscopy

    a. Continuously changes the phase of the incident light from the condenser to improve contrast in the specimen

    b. **Uses circular filters in the condenser and objective to give contrast to parts of the cell with different reflective indices**

    c. Uses special lenses to distinguish between solid and liquid phases of the cell

d. Uses special lens to change the color of light passing through them

153. **"Parfocal" refers to microscops with multiple objectives where**

a. Ovjectives are used in pairs for stereo-scopic effects

b. Each objective has the same working distance above the specimen

c. **Each objective is positioned to be in focus at the same stage height**

d. Sequential objective increases in power by a factor of 10

154. **A microscope that uses antibodies that glow to reveal the location of a protein in a cell is the**

a. Immunofluorescence microscope

b. Bright field light microscope

c. **Both**

d. None

155. **Which technique used to observe cell division or cell structure?**

a. X-ray diffraction

b. Chromatography

c. Electrophores

d. **None of them**

156. **Gradient centrifugation is used for**

a. **Separation of cell organelles**

b. Isolation of mitochondria

c. Isolation of chloroplast

d. All

157. **Cell membrane is biochemically lipo-protein contain the following compo-nent *except***

a. Phosphtidyl choline

b. Phosphotidyl ethanolamine

c. Steroids

d. **Prostaglandins**

158. **A link between generations is provided precisely by**

a. Chromosomes   b. **Nucleic acid**

c. Nucleus

d. Cytoplasm

159. **Replication of DNA takes place with the help of**

a. **DNA polymerase**

b. Lyase

c. RNAase

d. DNAase

160. **The enzymes responsible for unwind-ing of DNA helix during replication is/are**

a. **Helicases**   b. Topoisomerase

c. DNA polymerase

d. Primases

161. **DNA replication is**

a. Continuous and conservative

b. **Discontinuous and semiconser-vative**

c. Semidiscontinuous and semiconser-vative

d. Conservative and semidiscontinuous

162. **Total numbers of structural genes in Trypoperon are**

a. 3   b. **5**

c. 10   d. 4

163. **Transcription is the synthesis of**

a. **mRNA**   b. rRNA

c. Protein   d. tRNA

164. **The formation of polyribosomes from ribosomes is done in the presence of**

a. Na^+ b. K^+

c. **Mg^{+2}**   d. Ca^{+2}

165. **Which of the following amino acid is coded by single codon?**

a. Leucine   b. Alanine

c. Proline   d. **Tryptophan**

166. **The ratio of DNA in bacterial cell and eukaryotic is about**

a. 1:100   b. **1:1000**

c. 1:10000   d. 1:1 lakh

167. **Genetic engineering would not have been possible, if one of these were absent**

a. DNA polymerase

b. Reverse transcriptase

c. DNA ligase

d. RNA synthetase

168. Which of the following is associated with genetic engineering?

a. Plastids   **b. Plasmids**

c. Mutations   d. Hybrid vigour

169. An environmental agent that triggers transcription from an operon is a

a. Depressor   **b. Inducer**

c. Regulator   d. Controlling agent

170. Magic bullets are the

a. Recombinant vaccines

b. Monoclonal antibodies

c. Chemotherapy drugs for cancer

d. Anabolic steroids

171. The interferons are

a. Antibacterial

b. Antiviral drugs

c. Antibiotic drug

d. Immunosuppressive

172. Highest number of antibiotics are produced by

a. Bacillus   **b. Streptomyces**

c. Penicillium   d. Cephalosporium

173. Development of embryo without fertilization is called

a. Apomixis

b. Polyembryony

c. Parthenocarpy

d. Parthenogenesis

174. The site of photosynthesis in blue green algae is

a. Chromatophore

b. Mitochondria

c. Chloroplast

d. Root hair

175. Gene exhibiting multiple effects are known as

a. Complementary genes

b. Pleiotrophic genes

c. Cistrons

d. Pseudogenes

176. The technique which is used to find out the pathway of the synthesis of a substance in a cell is known as

a. Autoradiography

b. Chromatography

c. Spectrophotometry

d. Cell fractionation

177. The process by which middle lamella is removed by treating the plant cells with strong acids is known as

a. Lignification   b. Cutinization

c. Maceration   d. Submerization

178. Helper and suppressor T lymphocytes

a. Attack invaders directly

b. Help regulate the specific immune system

c. Activate the thymosin

d. May specialize into memory and plasma cells respectively

179. Which of the following organs where activation of T and B cells is usually occurs?

a. Bone marrow   b. Lymph vessel

c. Lymph nodes   d. All is correct

180. T lymphocytes gain immunocompetence in the

a. Thymus   b. Bone marrow

c. Lymph nodes   d. Spleen

181. Cell-mediated immunity is mainly function of

a. B cells   **b. T cells**

c. Macrophages   d. Neutrophils

182. T cells may produce in which chemical that is lethal to the target cells involved by a pathogen?

a. Interleukin-2   b. Interferon

c. Interleukin-3   **d. Perforin**

183. Which of the following properties is not exhibited by TH cells?

a. Stimulate division of B cells

b. Stimulate division of cytotoxic T cells

c. These are cytotoxic for other cells

d. Stimulate migration of macrophages

184. Indicate in which statement is not correct T-helper cells?

    a. Stimulate migration of macrophages
    b. Helper B cells to produce antibodies
    c. These are cytotoxic to virus infected cells
    d. Help in the generation of cytotoxic T cells

185. T cells mediator to immunity is attributed to

    a. Interferons
    b. Protein kinase
    c. Lymphokinase
    d. Cytokines

186. TCRs are transmembrane proteins found on T cells and consisting of

    a. Four non-polypeptide chains
    b. Four polypeptide chains
    c. Two polypeptide chains
    d. Two non-polypeptide chains

187. Which of following is involved in B cell activation?

    a. Antigen
    b. T-helper cell
    c. Cytokine   **d. All of above**

188. Where are the greatest number of B cells found?

    a. Lymph nodes
    b. Circulating blood
    c. Bone marrow
    d. Lymph vessel

189. Which factor stimulate B cell proliferation?

    a. Interleukin-1
    b. Interleukin-2
    c. Gamma-interferon
    d. CSF

190. The earliest stages of B cell differentiation

    a. Occur in the embryonic thymus
    b. Require the presence of antigen
    c. Involve rearrangement of κ-chain gene segments
    d. Involve rearrangement of heavy chain gene segments

191. Antigen binding to the B cell receptor

    a. Transduces a signal through the antigen-binding chains
    b. Invariably leads to B cell activation
    c. Transduces a signal through the IgA and IgB molecules
    d. Results in macrophages activation

192. The antigen specificity of a particular B cell is

    a. Induced by interaction with antigen
    b. Determined only by the L-chain
    c. Determined by H + L chain sequence
    d. Changes after isotype switching

193. Indentify the wrong statement about B cells

    a. They can present both exogenous and endogenous antigen
    b. They can present only antigens for which they have surface immunoglobulin
    c. They can present only protein antigen
    d. They can present both protein and non-protein antigens

194. Which of the following subclass of B cells is responsible for secretion of immunoglobulins?

    a. Lymphocytes
    b. Memory cells
    c. Plasma cells
    d. Hemopoietic cells

195. B cell represents

    a. 10–20% of lymphoid pool
    b. 5–15% of lymphoid pool
    c. 20–30% of lymphoid pool
    d. 30–40% of lymphoid pool

196. Humoral immune response relies on the production of immunoglobulins by

    a. B lymphocytes
    b. Cytotoxic T lymphocytes
    c. Killer T cells
    d. Helper T cells

197. Which of the following is an autoimmune disease of thyroid glands?

    a. **Graves' disease**
    b. SLE
    c. Scleroderma
    d. Rheumatoid arthritis

198. All of the following examples of autoimmune disorder *except*

    a. Graves' disease
    b. Rheumatoid arthirtis
    c. **Sickle cell anemia**
    d. SLE

199. Agammaglobulinemia will seriously impair in which ability?

    a. CMI   b. T cell functions
    c. **Antibody production**
    d. Phagocytosis

200. SCID can occur due to the absence of an enzyme

    a. **Adenosine deaminase**
    b. Guanosine deaminase
    c. Phosphorylase
    d. Thymidine

10

Agriculture Biotechnology

1. Non-essential amino acid
   a. Alanine **b. Tyrosine**
   c. Proline d. Valine

2. The cell which is ready to fertilizer by a sperm to become an egg is
   a. Primary oocyte
   b. Secondary oocyte
   c. Both
   d. None

3. At which stage of cell cycle chromosome is more distinct and easily countable?
   a. Prophase **b. Metaphase**
   c. Anaphase d. Interphase

4. Movement of chromosome towards the poles of the spindle occurs at
   a. Prophase b. Metaphase
   c. Anaphase d. Interphase

5. The genome of vaccinia virus is
   a. Double-stranded RNA
   b. Single-stranded DNA
   c. Single-stranded RNA
   d. Double-stranded DNA

6. The prokaryotic ribosome has a sedimentation value of
   a. 80S **b. 70S**
   c. 60S d. 40S

7. The marker protein for mitochondria is
   a. Ribosomes
   b. Catalase

   c. Acid phosphatase
   d. Cytochrome-C

8. An essential amino acid is one that
   a. Cannot be synthesized in the body
   b. Cannot be reabsorbed by the renal tubules
   c. Is required for the synthesis of certain protein only
   d. Is poorly absorbed from the diet

9. Under the five kingdom systems of classification of living world eubacteria are placed under the kingdom
   a. Plantae b. Protista
   c. Fungi d. Monera

10. The scientist who proved by experiments that the theory of spontaneous generation is wrong is
    a. Joseph Lister b. Robert Koch
    c. Louis Pasteur d. Edward Jenner

11. Dipicolinic acid is present in
    a. Endospores b. Exospore
    c. Cysts d. Conidia

12. Epinephrine decreases
    a. Heart rate
    b. Cardiac contractility
    c. Basal metabolic rate
    d. Cutaneous blood flow

13. The main constituent of a blood clot is
    a. Thrombin b. Fibrin
    c. Plasminogen **d. Thromboplastin**

14. Which one is the correct hierarchical order in taxonomy?
  a. Genus < species < class < order
  b. Genus < class < order < family
  c. **Species < order < class < phylum**
  d. Genus < class < division < order

15. Systematic botany means
  a. System analysis
  b. Systematic arrangement of organ of plants
  c. Systematic study of organelles and tissues
  d. **Methodical study of plants, dealing with identification, naming and classification**

16. The kingdom of prokaryotes is
  a. Protista   b. **Monera**
  c. Fungi   d. Plantae

17. The non-living characteristic of viruses is
  a. Ability to multiply only inside the host
  b. Ability to cause diseases in the host
  c. Ability to undergo mutation
  d. **Ability to be crystallized**

18. The term bacteria was coined by
  a. Leeuwenhoek   b. Louis Pasteur
  c. Robert Koch   d. **Ehrenberg**

19. The Periyar sanctuary is located in
  a. **Kerala**   b. Tamil Nadu
  c. Karnataka   d. Andhra Pradesh

20. The photosynthetic or assimilatory roots are observed in
  a. Banyan   b. Vanda
  c. Cucuta   d. **Tinospora**

21. The bladder serving as floats and for trapping insects is found in
  a. Zizypus   b. **Utricularia**
  c. Nepenthes   d. Acacia

22. The order of opening of flower parts from the periphery towards the centre is called
  a. Acropetal   b. **Centripetal**
  c. Centrifugal d. Basipetal

23. Tobacco and Petunia belong to the family
  a. Poaceae   b. Fabaceae
  c. **Solanaceae** d. Brassicaceae

24. Simple, cluster of radial leaves, stipulate and parallel venation leaves and "Cymes" or Umbel influorescence are the characteristics of
  a. Poaceae   b. **Liliaceae**
  c. Asteraceae d. Fabaceae

25. The gene which control many character is called
  a. Co-dominant   b. Poly gene
  c. **Pleiotropic gene**
  d. Multiple genes

26. Which of the following movements is related to the auxin level?
  a. Movement of shoot towards the source of light
  b. Nyctinasty
  c. Movement of sunflower
  d. **All of the above**

27. Embryo developed from the somatic cells are called
  a. Cybrids   b. **Embryoid**
  c. Callus   d. Hybrids

28. Vegative fertilization is also called
  a. **Triple fusion**   b. True fertilization
  c. Syngamy
  d. Generative fertilization

29. Vivipary is observed in
  a. Banyan   b. Bryophyllum
  c. Ipomoea   d. **Rhizophora**

30. The scientist who performed some experiments with oat coleoptiles for the presence of a substance which could diffuse into agar blocks is
  a. Ganong   b. **Went**
  c. Boysen-Jensen d. Fujikura

31. Micropyle is useful for the entry of
  a. Pollen grain   b. Pollen tube
  c. **Water**   d. Male gamete

32. Abscissic acid is primarily synthesized in
a. Lysosome   b. Golgi complex
c. Chloroplast   d. Ribosomes

33. Which one of the following inhibits seed germination for a particular period?
a. Light   b. Water
c. Carbon dioxide   **d. Dormancy**

34. Flocculation or coagulation of proto-plasm is the
a. Interchangeability between sol and gel states
b. The ability to scatter the bean of light
c. The errati zig-zag movement if protoplasmic particles
d. The ability of protoplasm to increase in size when they lose charge

35. Plasmolysis is the result to
a. Ex-osmosis   b. Plasmolysis
c. Reverse osmosis
d. Diffusion

36. Which one is incorrect statement?
a. Movement of water is expressed in term of free energy
b. Free energy determines the direction by which physical and chemical changes should occur
c. Water potential is the sum of free energy of water molecules in pure water and in any other system
d. Water potential of pure water is zero

37. Ascent of sap in plants was demons-trated by
a. Girdling experiments
b. Ganong's experiments
c. Went experiments
d. Lever auxanometer

38. Cohesion and adhesion theory is other-wise called
a. Relay pump theory
b. Pulsation theory
c. Root pressure theory
d. Transpiration pulls theory

39. Molybdenum is the essential consti-tuent of
a. Nitrogenase   b. Respiratory chain
c. Growth regulators
d. Chlorophyll

40. Which one is true about guttation?
a. It occurs through specialized pores called hydathodes
b. It occurs in herbaceous plants when root pressure is low and transpiration
c. It only occur during the time
d. It occurs in plants growing under condition of low soil moisture and high humidity

41. Which one does not occur in cyclic pho-tophosphorylation?
a. Oxygen is not given off
b. Water is consumed
c. Only photo system I is involved
d. NADPH2 formation

42. Genetically adapted population to a particular habitat is called
a. Ecotone   **b. Ecotype**
c. Biome   d. Niche

43. Which one is the edaphic factor in bio-sphere?
a. Light   b. Temperatures
c. Water   **d. Soil**

44. CO_2, CH_4, N_2O and CFC are called green-house gases because they observe and emit
a. UV rays   **b. Heat rays**
c. X-rays   d. Gamma rays

45. In plant succession when climax commu-nity is reached, the net productivity
a. Continues to increase
b. Becomes zero   c. Becomes reduced
d. Becomes stable

45. Which one is not the renewable energy of natural resources?
a. Tidal energy   b. Wind energy
c. Fossil fuel   d. Solar energy

11

Fundamentals of Horticulture

1. Horticulture GDP to agriculture is
   - a. 30%
   - **b. 15%**
   - c. 20%
   - d. 10%

2. Most usually applied bactericide is
   - a. Mancozeb
   - b. Sulfex
   - **c. Streptomycin sulphate**
   - d. Carboxin

3. Specimen plant in garden which does not shade lawn is
   - a. Rain tree
   - **b. Christmas tree**
   - c. Banyan tree
   - d. Bougainvillea

4. Mallika is hybrid developed through cross of
   - a. Chausa × Neelum
   - **b. Deshehari × Neelum**
   - c. Neeluddin × Neelum
   - d. Vanarashi × Neelum

5. Which one of the following instruments used for measuring the leaf area?
   - **a. Planometer**
   - b. Porometer
   - c. Auxanometer
   - d. Barometer

6. In 2 × 3 factorial experiment with 3 replications then the degree of freedom will be
   - **a. 21**
   - b. 28
   - c. 26
   - d. 30

7. Which fruit has highest anti-oxidant properties (according to NIN)?
   - a. Pineapple
   - **b. Guava**
   - c. Mango
   - d. Sweet orange

8. In cushing material of fruit packaging which chemical applied
   - a. ABA
   - b. Ethylene
   - **c. Boric acid**
   - d. $KMNO_4$

9. In which of the following crops is highly tolerant to low pH?
   - **a. Potato**
   - b. Okra
   - c. Onion
   - d. Cabbage

10. In which of the following is a climatic fruit?
    - **a. Annona**
    - b. Ber
    - c. Lychee
    - d. Apple

11. Which fruit is called bathroom fruit?
    - a. Banana
    - b. Guava
    - c. Kiwi
    - **d. Mango**

12. Propagation method in cashew nut is
    - a. Seedling cutting
    - b. Seedling
    - c. Patch buding
    - **d. Softwood cutting**

13. Variety as a polinizer used in mongo is
    - a. Mallika
    - b. Desahari
    - **c. Bombay green**
    - d. Chausa

115

14. Suitable temperature for banana cultivation is
    a. 17–20°C   b. 30–40°C
    c. 10–15°C   **d. 20–30°C**

15. Enzyme presents in pineapple is
    a. Papain   **b. Bromelin**
    c. Caprine   d. Bromacil

16. Fruit cracking in pomegranate is more take place in
    a. Ambe bahar   b. Haste bahar
    c. Mrig bahar   d. All of the above

17. Which state is known as Apple Bowl?
    a. Uttarakhand   **b. HP**
    c. J & K   d. None

18. Scientific name of Japanese plum is
    a. *Pyrus serotina*   b. *P. pashia*
    c. *P. communis*   **d. *P. pyrifolia***

19. Largest producer of cashewnut in the world is
    a. USA   b. India
    c. China d. Brazil

20. Apple is divided in how much grades
    a. 6   b. 3
    c. 8   d. 10

21. Major disease of grape is
    a. Downy mildew
    b. Powdery mildew
    c. Pink berry formation
    d. Blosson drop

22. Which one is serious pest in apple
    a. Fruit fly
    b. Wooly apple aphid
    c. Sanjose scale
    d. Shoot and fruit borer

23. Chromosome no. of coconut is
    a. 42   b. 40
    c. 32   d. 36

24. Vijay and Azad are cultivars in
    a. Tomato   **b. Brinjal**
    c. Capsicum   d. Onion

25. After tomato which crop F1 hybrid has covered maximum area?
    a. Brinjal   b. Onion
    c. Peas   **d. Cabbage**

26. Seed rate of early cultivars of cauliflowers is
    a. 150–200 gm   **b. 500–600 gm**
    c. 250–400 gm   d. 700–850 gm

27. Harvesting stage of watermelon is
    a. Half slip stage   b. 1/2 maturity
    c. Full slip stage d. None

28. Onion is rich source of
    a. Vitamin A   b. Vitamin C
    c. Vitamin K   **d. Vitamin B**

29. Scientific name of Chinese potato is
    a. *Solenostemon rotundifolium*
    b. *Xanthosoma sagittifilium*
    c. *Helianthus tuberouse*
    d. *Eleocharis dulcis*

30. Family of carrot is
    a. Aliaceae   b. Araceae
    c. Compositae   **d. Apiaceae**

31. Which part of guggal is used as medicine?
    a. Leaves   b. Oleoresin gums
    c. Roots   d. None

32. Seed rate for one hectare propagation of turmeric is
    a. 6 qtl   b. 18 qtl
    c. 14 qtl   **d. 24 qtl**

33. Devana belongs to which family
    a. Geranniaceae   b. Lamiaceae
    c. Asteraceae   d. Labiateae

34. Rainy season annuals are sown in nursery during
    a. April   b. August
    c. February   **d. June**

35. Heterostyly is common in which annual plant
    a. Primula   b. Petunia
    c. Marigold   d. All of the above

36. **Mahatama Gandhi is important cultivar of**
    a. Chrysanthemum
    b. Marigold
    c. Rose   d. Gladiolus

37. **Temperature of liquid nitrogen for cryo-preservation is**
    a. –196°C   b. –430°C
    c. –140°C   d. –18000°C

38. **Central food laboratory is situated at**
    a. Nagpur   b. Delhi
    c. Mumbai   **d. Calcutta**

39. **Trade name of Alachor is**
    a. Basalin   **b. Lasso**
    c. Machet   d. Hyver-X

40. **Parthenocarpic cultivar of guava is**
    a. Lucknow-49
    b. Allahabad surkha
    c. Allahabad safeda
    d. Allahabad round

41. **Which one is man-made hybrid?**
    a. Atemoya   b. Strawberry
    c. Lemon   **d. Both A and B**

42. **What is scientific name of Rose Apple?**
    a. *Syzygium jombos*
    b. *S. uniflora*
    c. *S. densifoliya*   d. *S. cumini*

43. **Which part of kewada is use?**
    a. Leave   b. Seed
    c. Root   **d. Flower**

44. **Which one is sexually sterile diploid?**
    a. Onion   b. Leek
    c. Garlic   d. None

45. **Which one is called vegetable meat?**
    a. Pea   b. French bean
    c. Horse bean   d. Bean

46. **Custard apple is which kind of fruit botanically**
    a. Eteario of achenes
    b. Drupe
    c. Nut   d. None

47. **Rose is harvested at which stage**
    a. Tight bud stage   **b. Half open stage**
    c. Fully open stage d. None

48. **Mahua is rootstock of**
    a. Fig   **b. Sapota**
    c. Peach   d. Plum

49. **Most commonly used chemical for flowering of pineapple**
    a. Etherl or CEPA Kerala
    b. Gibberellic acid
    c. Salicylic acid
    d. Triacontanol

50. **Pusa Basanti is a open pollinated cultivar of**
    a. Zinnia   b. Chrysanthemum
    c. Marigold   d. Gladiolus

51. **Rajendra Sonia is important cultivar of**
    a. Turmeric   b. Fenugreek
    c. Coriander   d. None

52. **Which part of cinchona is used for medicinal purpose?**
    a. Leaves   b. Roots
    c. Bark   d. Fruits

53. **Potato is which type of plant on the basis of tuber formation?**
    a. Short day plant
    b. Long day plat
    c. Day neutral plant
    d. None

54. **International potato center (CIP) is situated at**
    a. Belguim   b. Brazil
    c. Peru   d. Netherland

55. **Which vegetable is monocot one from the following?**
    a. Asparagus   b. Amaranths
    c. Palak   d. None

56. **Processed and fresh market variety of tomato is**
    a. Angurlata   b. Pusa ruby
    c. Arka saurab   d. Sioux

57. Annual drumstick is propagated by
    a. Limb cutting   b. Root cutting
    c. Seed   d. None

58. Max area of pumpkin is under which state?
    a. Bihar   b. Punjab
    c. Odisha   d. West Bangal

59. Multiple disease resistant variety of watermelon is
    a. Arka maik   b. Arka jyoti
    c. Pusa bedana   d. None

60. Most devastating disease in seed production of onion is
    a. Wilting   **b. Purple blotch**
    c. Basal rot   d. None

61. Early varieties of cauliflower is harvested in months of
    a. May   b. June
    c. July   d. August

62. Fruit rot resistant variety of chilli is
    a. NP-46A   b. Pusa lal
    c. CK-2

63. Which vegetable is processed most?
    a. Potato   b. Cucumber
    c. Tomato   d. Chilli

64. Which temperate fruit require highest pruning for regular fruiting?
    a. Apricot   b. Pear
    c. Peach   d. Plum

65. Chromosome number of coffee Arabica is
    a. 22   b. 24
    c. 36   **d. 44**

66. Chromosome number of mango is
    a. 40   b. 42
    c. 38

67. Which of fruit has highest rate of ethylene production?
    a. Apple   b. Peach
    c. Pear   d. Banana

68. Pollination in mango is done by
    a. Wind   b. Honeybees
    c. House flies   d. Stone Weevil

69. National fruit of Japan is
    a. Carambola   b. Mangosteen
    c. Persimmon   d. Passion fruit

70. Pain enzyme extracted from papaya has how much protein?
    a. 22%   b. 44%
    c. 60%   **d. 72.2%**

71. Oil of mint is in
    a. Hydrocarbons   **b. Carvone**
    c. Citrinellol   d. None

72. Major source of steroids in India is
    a. Madicinal yam
    b. Medicinal solanum
    c. Rye ergot
    d. None

73. Chemical present in dill or sowa seeds is
    a. Reserpine   b. Atropine
    c. Hyoscyamine   **d. Carvone**

74. Digitalis perpurea is scientific name of
    a. Henbane   b. Datura
    c. Foxglove   d. Belladonna

75. Foxglove belongs to which family
    a. Scrophulariaciae
    b. Graminae
    c. Leguminoceae   d. Rubiaceae

76. Plant to plant distance in citrus plantation is
    a. 4–6 cm   b. 9–10 cm
    c. 12–15 cm   d. 8–12

77. Seed production of Amaranthus species is
    a. 170   **b. 1, 96, 000**
    c. 16, 000   d. 72, 000

78. Monohybrids are derived by hybridizing two individuals which differ for
    a. Multiple characters
    b. Double characters

c. Single characters

d. Quadruple characters

79. **Mendelian population refers to sharing individuals**
    a. **Same gene pool**
    b. Different gene pool
    c. Mixed gene pool
    d. Both a and b

80. **Cells without cell wall is referes to as**
    a. Cytoplasm
    b. **Protoplasm**
    c. Chromoplast
    d. Protoplast

81. **Hardening is a process in the tissue culture for**
    a. Plant regeneration
    b. Callus formation
    c. **Making plants suitable for farm conditions**
    d. Morphogenesis

82. **A serious physiological disorder of mango orchards near bricks**
    a. Spongy tissue   b. **Black tip**
    c. Fruits drop   d. Malformation

83. **While applying basal dose of DAP, it should never mixed with**
    a. **Zn**   b. Fe
    c. Cu   d. Mg

84. **Oryza sativa is**
    a. Triploid   b. Haploid
    c. **Diploid**   d. Polyploid

85. **Akra surabhi is a variety of**
    a. Gauva   b. Apple
    c. Gladiolus   d. **Jasmine**

86. **Horticultural practice of giving different shape**
    a. Training   b. **Topiary**
    c. Pruning   d. Pinching

87. **Japanese garden style is**
    a. Formal   b. Informal
    c. **Free**   d. None

88. **Mughal style of gardening in India developed by**
    a. Akbar   b. Shershah Suri
    c. **Babar**   d. Shahjahan

89. **Extra early variety of pigeon pea is**
    a. Type 7   b. Pusa Ageti
    c. UPSA-120   d. **Prabhat**

90. **Latest method of stogie**
    a. MAS   b. CAM
    c. **Hypobaric storage**
    d. Low temperature storage

91. **CRD is used when the material is**
    a. Heterogeneous   b. **Homogeneous**
    c. Both a and b   d. Specialized

92. **Regression value is always lies between**
    a. 1 to +1   b. –1 to +1
    c. + 1 to –1   d. **None**

93. **Ideal processing potato cultivar should have**
    a. High TSS and low sugars
    b. **High dry matter and low sugars**
    c. High sugars
    d. High acidity

94. **In which crop gives higher production per unit area?**
    a. Pea   b. Gherkin
    c. **Carrot**   d. Potato

95. **Kaoline used as an anti-transparent**
    a. Reduces growth of the plant
    b. **Does reflect light from plant leaf surface**
    c. Affects the closure and opening the stomata
    d. Froms thin layer on the leaf surface

96. **Cultivated strawberry is**
    a. Tetraploid   b. Hexaploid
    c. Diploid   d. **Octaploid**

97. **The serious handicap in citrus breeding is**
    a. Self incompatibility
    b. **Nucellar embryony**

c. Dichogamy
d. Protandry

98. Autoclaving is a technique in tissue culture for sterilization of

a. **Glassware**   b. Explant
c. Atmosphere   d. Callus

99. Kinnow is commercially grown in

a. Northern India   b. Southern India
c. **Western India**   d. Eastern India

100. Transgenic varieties are available in

a. Mango   b. Cherry
c. Banana   d. **Papaya**

101. Pollination and fertilization before anthesis is called

a. **Cleistogamy**   b. Chasmogamy
c. Homogamy   d. Dichogamy

102. Top worked tree grow faster due to

a. Higher trunk food reserve
b. Established root system
c. **Both a and b**
d. Polarity

103. La France was the first variety of

a. Floribunda rose b. **Hybrid tea rose**
c. Polyantha rose   d. Rambler rose

104. NAA is applied to control mango malformation in the month of

a. December   b. **October**
c. January   d. May

105. Sathgudi Malta is commercially grown in

a. Punjab   b. UP
c. AP   d. **Maharashtra**

106. Contour system of orchard layout is practiced in

a. Low slope areas b. **High slope areas**
c. Zero slope areas d. Undulated land

107. Spur bearing apple varities are

a. Early bearer
b. Erect in growth habit
c. **Dwarf in stature**
d. All of the above

108. Indian Farming is a publication of

a. IARI   b. ICRISAT
c. CAZRI   d. **ICAR**

109. Which of the following is the early variety of ber?

a. **Gola**   b. Umran
c. Banarasi   d. Goma Kitrti

110. Molecular markers are used for determining variation in plants

a. **Genetic**   b. Phenotypic
c. Cytoplasmic
d. Endoplasmic

111. Cavity spot disorder of carrot is caused due to deficiency of

a. Mg   b. S
c. Fe   d. **Ca**

112. Use of rootstock is common in

a. Cole crops
b. Cucurbits
c. Tuber crops
d. Leaf vegetable crops

113. Shade loving purple colour flowering annual is

a. Salvia   b. Saponaria
c. **Cinereria**   d. None

114. Root suckers of chrysanthemum are separated during

a. January   b. October
c. December   d. **March**

115. Mulathi (liquorice) is mainly used for curing

a. Fever   b. Carminative
c. **Cough**   d. Epilepsy

116. Carnation is commercially propagated through

a. **Tip cutting**   b. Tuberlets
c. Suckers   d. Seed

117. African Marigold is botanically known as

a. Tagetses   b. *T. erecta*
c. *T. minula*   d. None

118. Which of the following crops in rich source of lutein?
    a. Mint
    b. Jasmine
    c. **Marigold**
    d. Rose

119. Commercial varieties of rose are popularly multiplies by
    a. Air layering
    b. **Budding**
    c. Tip cutting
    d. Tissue culture

120. Sweet potato is a
    a. **SDP**
    b. LDP
    c. DNP
    d. Intermidiate

121. Which chemical used in lay peeling?
    a. K_2SO_4
    b. KOH
    c. NaOH
    d. **$Ca(NO_3)_2$**

122. Early December in the improved variety of
    a. Cabbage
    b. Pea
    c. Carrot
    d. **Cauliflower**

123. Pinching is necessary in
    a. Tuberose
    b. Jasmine
    c. **Chrysanthemum**
    d. Carnation

124. Nutritionl quality breeding deals with genetic improvement in
    a. Vitamin
    b. Protein
    c. Oil
    d. **All of the above**

125. In green vegetables the limiting amino acid is
    a. Tryptophan
    b. Arginine
    c. **Methionine**
    d. Lysine

126. Development of embryo from egg without fertilization is called
    a. Autogamy
    b. Apospory
    c. Apogamy
    d. **Parthenogensis**

127. South west monsoon contributes about ____ of total rain.
    a. **30%**
    b. 20%
    c. 50%
    d. 85%

128. Self pollination is a form of
    a. Out breeding
    b. **Inbreeding**
    c. Random mating
    d. None

129. Crossing over takes place in which stage
    a. Leptotene
    b. Diplotene
    c. **Pachytene**
    d. Zygotene

130. In genome each type of chromosome is represented
    a. Thrice
    b. **Many times**
    c. Twice
    d. One

131. Cytoplasmic genes are found in
    a. Mitochondria
    b. Chloroplast
    c. Nucleus
    d. **Both a and b**

132. Ber propagation by budding is done during
    a. July–Aug
    b. May–June
    c. March–April
    d. **June–Feb**

133. The best suited intercrop in banana in
    a. Lychee
    b. **Papaya**
    c. Ginger
    d. Guava

134. About 95–99% portion of plant tissues are made of
    a. **C, H and O**
    b. Ca, Mg, and O
    c. Cu, Zn, and Fe
    d. NP and K

135. The predominant pigment responsible for red colour of tomatoes is
    a. β-carotene
    b. Xanthophyll
    c. Anthocyanin
    d. **Lycopene**

136. In which of the following fruit crops contain highest vitamin A?
    a. **Mango**
    b. Straberry
    c. Grape
    d. Papaya

137. Nutmeg plants are
    a. **Dioecious**
    b. Monoecious
    c. Androcieous
    d. Andromonoecious

138. In mango emergence of new growth flushes, simultaneously with fruiting or immediately after harvest, is indicative of
    a. Biennial bearing
    b. Vigorous growth
    c. **Regular bearing**
    d. Poor bearing

139. As expression of skin colour is genetically controlled by

    a. **Single dominant gene**
    b. Polyegene
    c. Cytoplasmic gene
    d. Oligogene

140. Name the evergreen subtropical fruit crop belonging to Rosaceae family

    a. **Loquat**   b. Avocado
    c. Peach   d. Plum

141. Mitosis takes place in

    a. Reproductive cells
    b. Somatic cells   c. Anthers
    d. **Both a and b**

142. As per in self incompatible loquat cultivars the site of self incompatibility reaction is in

    a. Ovary organ   b. Stigmatic surface
    c. **Styler region**
    d. Pollen tube germination inhibition

143. Colour blindness gene is located on

    a. Y chromosome   b. **X chromosome**
    c. Autosome   d. All of the above

144. Regeneration of a plant from a single cell in culture medium is called

    a. Protoplast culture
    b. Meristem culture
    c. **Cell culture**   d. Organ culture

145. Building slow fire emitting smoke in the orchard to induce flowering in some fruit crops is called

    a. **Smudging**   b. Smoking
    c. Firing   d. None

146. CARI is located at

    a. **Port Blair**
    b. Thiruvananthapuram
    c. Visakhapatnam
    d. Kolkata

147. Quarantine inspection of agricultural and horticultural crops is carried out by

    a. BSI   b. FRI
    c. **NBPGR**   d. IARI

148. Rubber plant is commercially propagated through

    a. Cutting   b. Layering
    c. **Budding**   d. Seed

149. State has largest area in pineapple production is

    a. Meghalaya   b. Asssam
    c. Manipur   d. **West Bengal**

150. Pollination of mango is facilitated by

    a. Hoverfly   b. Dragonfly
    c. Butterfly   d. **Housefly**

151. Which fruit shows heterodichogamy

    a. **Peanut**   b. Cashewnut
    c. Walnut   d. Chestnut

152. Paradox is famous cultivar of

    a. Plum   b. **Walnut**
    c. Apricot   d. None

153. Chilling requirement of cherry is

    a. 400–700 hrs   b. 1000–1200 hrs
    c. **1500–1800 hrs**   d. 200–2700 hrs

154. Sharanpur prabahat important cultivar of peach cross of

    a. Sharbati × red beauty
    b. Sharbati × shan–e Punjab
    c. **Sharbati × flordasum**
    d. Sharbati × redheaven

155. Commercial cultivar of apple in USA

    a. Starling delicious
    b. **Golden delicious**
    c. Royal delicious   d. Red gold

156. Which temperate fruit introduced in India under the name of Japanese madler?

    a. Peach   b. Plum
    c. Apricot   d. **Loquat**

157. Rootstock of jamun is

    a. *Syzygium jambos* b. *S. uniflora*
    c. ***S. densifloflora*** d. None

158. Chromosome number of coffee Arabica is

    a. 22   b. 24
    c. 36   d. **44**

159. Processed green nuts of areca nut are called
    a. Kalipak   b. Kottapak
    c. Chali   d. None

160. Chromosome number of mango is
    a. 40   b. 42
    c. 38   d. 48

161. Which fruit has highest rate of ethylene production?
    a. Apple   b. Passion fruit
    c. Pear   d. Banana

162. Pollination in mango is done by
    a. Wind   b. Honeybees
    c. House flies   d. Stone weevil

163. Papain enzyme extracted from papaya has how much protein?
    a. 22%   b. 44%
    c. 60%   **d. 72.2%**

164. Typical example of parthenocarpic fruit development is
    a. Persimmon   b. Banan
    c. Mangosteen d. Grape

165. Jonathan spot of apple is due to deficiency of
    a. B   b. Ca
    c. Zn   **d. Water**

166. Mango rust is caused by
    a. Virus   b. Fungus
    c. Bacteria   **d. Algae**

167. Paradox is famous cultivar of
    a. Apricot   **b. Walnut**
    c. Plum   d. None

168. Which fruit shows heterodichogamy?
    a. Chestnut   b. Walanut
    c. Peanut d. Cashewnut

169. Mendel's third law exception is
    a. Recombination
    b. Linkage
    c. Both
    d. Epistasis

170. Oldest known spice plant is
    a. Cumin   b. Black pepper
    c. Cardamom   **d. Cinnamon**

171. Aniseed belongs to which family?
    a. Apiaeae   b. Araceae
    c. Mytaceae   d. Guttiferaceae

172. Which cucurbit has cooling effect on body?
    a. Round melon   b. Bitter gourd
    c. Pumpkin   d. Bottle gourd

173. Acidity of tomato sauce is
    a. 0.3%   b. 1.0%
    c. 1.2%   d. 1.5%

174. The best time of pruning of roses in the north plains of India is
    a. Sept–Oct   b. Oct–Nov
    c. Dec–Jan   d. June–July

175. Bluing of rose is due to
    a. Auxin   **b. Ethylene**
    c. CO_2
    d. Accumulation of ammonia

176. Botanical name of parrot flower is
    a. *Erythrina indica*
    b. *Erythrina varigeta*
    c. *Erythrina subrosa*
    d. *Erythrinacris galli*

177. Which of the following is not a woody landscape plant?
    a. Shurbs   b. Tree
    c. Annuals   **d. Climbers**

178. Blue colour cultivar of gladiolus is
    a. Suchitra   b. Friendship
    c. Blue sky   d. Har majesty

179. Fruit of coffee botanical known as
    a. Berry   b. Drup
    c. Capsule   d. Nut

180. Which one fruit is called poor man's food?
    a. Ber   b. Coconut
    c. Jackfruit   d. Date

181. Inflorescence of guava is
    a. **Fasicule**   b. Panicle
    c. Solitary   d. Spadix

182. Seedless cultivar of mango is
    a. Ratna   b. Neelam
    c. Sindhu   d. **Amrapali**

183. Dwarf cultivar of sapota is
    a. **Kirti bharti**   b. Cricket ball
    c. Pala   d. Kalipat

184. Male parent of kiwi fruit is
    a. Allison   b. Tomuri
    c. **Both a and b**   d. Bruno

185. Tautra Trellis HDP System is following in which temperature fruit?
    a. Peach   b. **Plum**
    c. Apple   d. Loquat

186. Late season cultivar of loquat
    a. **California Advance**
    b. Fireball

187. Commercial method of propagation of apple rootstock is
    a. Seed
    b. **Stooling**
    c. Air layering
    d. Tongue grafting

188. Roopa is important cultivar of
    a. **Walnut**   b. Peach
    c. Plum   d. None

189. Wich group of coconut is shows autogamy?
    a. **Dwarf**   b. Tall
    c. Both   d. None

190. Coffe rust resistant species of coffee is
    a. *C. arabica*   b. *C. robusta*
    c. *C. liberica*   d. *C. canephora*

191. Physiological disorder of cocoa is
    a. **Albinism**
    b. Multiple crown
    c. Flattening of leaves
    d. Frut cracking

192. Cluster of tomato flowers is known as
    a. Bunch   b. **Truss**
    c. Unit   d. Group

193. Cultivar of reddish grown throughout the year
    a. Arka Nishant   b. Pusha Rashmi
    c. Arka Chetaki   d. **Pusa Himani**

194. Early variety of musk melon is
    a. Punjab Sunahri   b. **Pusa Sarbati**
    c. Arka Jeet   d. Pusa Rasraj

195. Pox and scruf is physiological of
    a. High moisture
    b. Ca deficiency
    c. **Boron deficiency**
    d. Excess pH

196. Inbreeding depression is highest in which crop?
    a. **Carrot**   b. Cole crop
    c. Cucurbits   d. None

197. Family of elephant foot yam is
    a. Alliaceae   b. **Araceae**
    c. Liliaceae   d. Dioscoraceae

198. Alkaloid presents in brinjal is
    a. Solanin   b. Sinigrin
    c. Saponin   d. **Solasodin**

199. Plant part use of vanilla is
    a. Rhizome   b. Tender pods
    c. Seed   d. **Mature pods**

200. Plum is originated from which place?
    a. China   b. **Japan**
    c. Europe   d. Asia-Minor

201. Fruit having single sigmoid curve
    a. **Apple**   b. Grape
    c. Fig   d. Guava

202. Which fruit is known as butter fruit?
    a. **Avocado**   b. Coconut
    c. Cashewnut   d. Walnut

203. Largest producer of clove is
    a. India   b. Malaysia
    c. Thailand   d. **Indonesia**

204. Inflorescence of pear is
  a. Corymb   b. Catkin
  c. Cymose   d. Spadix

205. TSS of ripe banana is
  a. 16%   b. 22%
  c. 26%   d. 20%

206. CO⁻¹ cultivar banana has same characters to
  a. Hill banana
  b. Nendran
  c. Poovan
  d. Dwarf cavendish

207. HDP cultivar of mango is
  a. Ratna   b. Alphonso
  c. Amrapali   d. Sindhu

208. Which one is only triploid citrus fruit?
  a. Pummelo   b. Kagzi lime
  c. Tahti lime   d. Acid lime

209. Physiological disorder of aonla is
  a. Fruit necrosis   b. Stone fruit
  c. Cracking   d. Fruit rotting

210. One kg fully ripe dates provide how much energy?
  a. 3300   b. 2700
  c. 3150   d. 2300

211. Most commonly used rootstock for pear is
  a. Quince A   **b. Quince B**
  c. Quince C   d. Kainth

212. President is important cultivar of
  a. Pear   **b. Plum**
  c. Peach   d. Walnut

213. Harvesting of cashewnut is done in months of
  a. Feb–March   b. June–July
  c. Sept–Oct   d. Dec–Jan

214. Pomology is derived from which language?
  a. Latin   b. English
  c. French   **d. Greek**

215. Chromosome no. of papaya is
  a. 16   **b. 18**
  c. 20   d. 32

216. Serious pest of lychee is
  a. Aphid   b. White fly
  c. Mite   d. Jasside

217. Coffee is rich source of which vitamin?
  a. Thiamine   b. Riboflavin
  c. Niacin   d. None

218. Origin of lychee is from
  a. India   b. East China
  c. South China   d. Brazil

219. Variety of lychee mainly used for purpose is
  a. Kasaba   b. Rose scented
  c. Swarm roopa   **d. Shahi**

220. Late maturity cultivar of grape is
  a. Arka Shayam   b. Arka Hans
  c. Arka Kanchan   d. Arka Chitrah

221. Golden star is important variety of
  a. Persimmon   b. Grapes
  c. Carambola   d. Peach

222. Which is monocarpic and monocotyledonus fruit crop?
  a. Banana   b. Pineapple
  c. Both a and b   d. Strawberry

223. Malika is very famous cultivar of mango is cross of
  a. Neelum × Desahri
  b. Desahri × Neelum
  c. Ratna × Alphonso
  d. Neelum × Alphonso

224. Inflorescence of mango is
  a. Fasicle   **b. Panicle**
  c. Solitary   d. Spadix

225. Serious pest of okra
  a. Leaf hopper
  b. Fruit and shoot borer
  c. White fly
  d. Mite

226. **Machintose is which season cultivar of apple?**
    a. **Early**   b. Mid
    c. Late   d. Off season

227. **Which fruit is called Adam's fig?**
    a. **Banana**   b. Mango
    c. Fig   d. Sapota

228. **Which one is temperature fruit?**
    a. Mango   b. Banana
    c. Cashewnut   d. **Walnut**

229. **Aonla is botanically which kind of fruit?**
    a. Nut   b. Stone
    c. **Capsule**   d. Berry

230. **Which one is photoinsensitive crop?**
    a. Sweet potato   b. **Cassava**
    c. Yams   d. Coleus

231. **Family of coleus is**
    a. Araceae   b. Convolvulaceae
    c. Liliaceae   d. **Labiate**

232. **Seriuos pest of okra is**
    a. **Leaf hopper**   b. White fly
    c. Fruit   d. Mite

233. **Palak belongs to which family?**
    a. Convolvulaceae
    b. **Chenopodaceae**
    c. Cruciferae
    d. Compostea

234. **Deficiency of molybdenum in cauli-flower leads to**
    a. brown   b. Ricyness
    c. **Whip–tail**   d. None

235. **Largest producer of ginger is**
    a. **Karnataka**
    b. Kerala
    c. Andhara Pradesh
    d. Tamil Nadu

236. **Which part of isabagol is use for medicinal purpose**
    a. Leaves   b. **Seed**
    c. Husk   d. Both b and c

237. **Which part of Indian basil is used to extract aromatic oil?**
    a. Seed   b. **Inflorescence**
    c. Leaves   d. Both b and c

238. **Which fruit is called apple of tropics?**
    a. **Ber**   b. Guava
    c. Pomegranate   d. Sapota

239. **Which fruit has stimulative partheno-carpy?**
    a. Banana   b. Grape
    c. **Lychee**   d. Fig

240. **Edible part of ber is**
    a. Pericarp   b. **Mesocarp**
    c. Endocarp   d. Epicarp

241. **What should be sugar per centage in jam?**
    a. 65%   b. Less than 68%
    c. **More than 68%** d. None

242. **Which crop is known as king of cereals?**
    a. Rice   b. **Wheat**
    c. Maize   d. Sorghum

243. **Which crop is known as queen of cereals?**
    a. Rice   b. **Maize**
    c. Wheat   d. Sorghum

244. **Which plant is considered as king of coarse cereals?**
    a. Rice   b. Wheat
    c. Maize   d. **Sorghum**

245. **Which crop is considered as king of pulses?**
    a. Red gram   b. Soya bean
    c. Mung   d. **Chickpea**

246. **Arka abir is important variety of**
    a. Brinjal   b. Onion
    c. Capsicum   d. **Paprika**

247. **Edible part of cauliflower is**
    a. Stem
    b. Leaves
    c. Flower bud   d. **Inflorescence**

248. Inflorescence of beet root is
    a. **Cymose**   b. Spike
    c. Racemose   d. Ctkin

249. Yellow-coloured variety of onion is:
    a. Early Grano   b. Brown Spanish
    c. **Both a and b**   d. Arka pragarti

250. MDR variety of cucumber is:
    a. Himangi   **b. Poinsettia**
    c. Pusa sanyog
    d. Japanese long green

251. Which one of the following is acash crop?
    a. **Cow pea**   b. French bean
    c. Pea   d. Lima bean

252. Scientific name of Lesser Yam is
    a. ***D. alata***   b. *D. Rotundata*
    c. *D. floribunda*   d. *D. esculenta*

253. Indian spinach is native of
    a. Brazil   b. India
    c. China   **d. South Africa**

254. Richest source of carbohydrates is
    a. **Cassava**   b. Sugar beet
    c. Potato   d. Sweet potato

255. Sex form of Leek is
    a. Diploid sterile   b. Diploid fertile
    c. Autotriploid   **d. Autotetraploid**

256. The optimum temperature for germination of pea
    a. 5%   b. 10%
    c. 15%   **d. 22%**

257. Origin of black pepper is form
    a. S-E Asia   **b. Indo-Burma**
    c. Sri Lanka   d. Indonesia

258. Isabgol or psyllium has which property?
    a. Fuxative   **b. Laxative**
    c. Cardiotonic   d. Ampholingeric

259. A kitchen garden of 50 m² supply how much of fresh vegetables/day
    a. 1.0 kg   **b. 1.5 kg**
    c. 2.0 kg   d. 2.5 kg

260. Which one of fruit is not a stone fruit?
    a. Pear   b. Peach
    c. Plum   **d. Cherry**

261. Origin of sweet orange is
    a. Brazil   b. India
    c. **China**   d. Europe

262. Persimmon is national fruit of
    a. China   **b. Japan**
    c. Thailand   d. Indonesia

263. Coffee is native of which place?
    a. India   b. Brazil
    c. **Abyssinia**   d. Europe

264. Pollination in fig is by
    a. **Wasp**   b. Honybees
    c. House fly   d. Fig weevil

265. Leading commercial cultivar of banana of
    a. **Dwarf cavendish**
    b. Nendran
    c. Poovan   d. Grand naine

266. Which of the following things characterize horticulturists?
    a. They usually grow only one plant species in each field
    b. They usually live in large towns/cities
    c. **Their farming techniques are relatively unproductive and they are ignorant of soil characteristics and plant nutrients**
    d. None of the above

267. Which fruit is recommended as a high energy fruit diabetic patient?
    a. Banana   **b. Avocado**
    c. Passion fruit   d. Jackfruit

268. Most vigorous rootstock of apple is
    a. **M-27**   b. Merton-793
    c. MM-104   d. MM-111

269. Punjab Gold is famous cultivar of
    a. **Pear**   b. Peach
    c. Plum   d. None

270. Spongy tissue is main problem of mango cultivar
    a. **Alphonso**   b. Bombay green
    c. Ratna   d. Langra

271. Leaf rust of coffee
    a. Algae   b. Bacteria
    c. *Fungus*   d. Virus

272. Which cultivar of mango
    a. **Gross Michel**   b. Basrai dwarf
    c. Poovan   d. None

273. Highest productivity of nuts
    a. Indonesia   b. Malaysia
    c. Philippines   **d. India**

274. Most popular method of breeding in India is
    a. **Mass selection**
    b. Pedigree method
    c. Hybridization
    d. Introduction

275. Most of patato cultivar tuberize below temperature of
    a. **Pusa H-1**
    b. Pusa sheetal
    c. Pusa sadhabahar
    d. Pusa ruby

276. Edible part of cabbage is known as
    a. **Head**   b. Curd
    c. Bud   d. Tuber

277. Harvesting period of garlic is
    a. Jan–Feb   **b. March–Apr**
    c. June–July   d. None

278. Which cultivar of musk melon is harvesting at netting stages?
    a. Arka Jeet   b. Arka Rajhans
    c. Hara Madhu   d. Punjab Sunheri

279. Maturity of pea is measured by
    a. Pycnometer   b. Todometer
    c. Tendrometer   d. None

280. Which bean is drought tolerant?
    a. Cow pea   b. French bean
    c. Pea   d. Lima bean

281. Food product order was passed by Govt. in
    a. 1949   b. 1954
    c. 1955   d. 1963

282. Which one is post emergence herbicide?
    a. Bromacil   b. Alachlor
    c. Butachlor   d. None

283. Which one is not summer annual?
    a. Kochia   b. Portulaca
    c. Coreopsis   **d. Salvia**

284. Mahatama Gandhi is famous cultivar of
    a. Chrysanthemum
    b. Bougianvillea
    c. Marigold   d. Gladious

285. Which plants are generally propagated by spores?
    a. Ferns   b. Palms
    c. Cactus   d. Climbers

286. Seed of which annual germinate only in the light?
    a. Nicitiana   b. Nigella
    c. Balsam   d. Stock

287. Which is the long stem cut rose in India?
    a. Sidoor   b. Confetti
    c. Rakatsgandha   d. First red

288. Lotus is belong to which family?
    a. Rosaceae   b. Compositae
    c. Nymphaeceae   d. Lotaceae

289. On the basis photoperiodism papaya is
    a. SDP   b. LDP
    c. Neutral plant d. None

290. Amrapali important rootstock of mango is cross of
    a. Desahari × Neelam
    b. Neelam × Desahari
    c. Alphonso × Neelam
    d. Neelam × Alphanso

291. No. of pineapple plants under HDP
    a. 25,000   b. 45,000
    c. 53,000   **d. 64,000**

292. Blood red is important cultivar of
   a. **Sweet orange**   b. Grapefruit
   c. Pomegranate   d. Guava

293. Acid percentage in sour type carambola is
   a. 0.4%   b. **1.0%**
   c. 1.2%   d. 1.8%

294. Pruning in grape is done how many times in a year?
   a. Once–twice   b. **Twice**
   c. Thrice   d. No pruning

295. Rose scented is popular cultivar of
   a. Apple   b. Peach
   c. Pomegranate   d. **Lychee**

296. Highest vitamin C is present in which fruit?
   a. Aonla   b. Lychee
   c. **Barbados cherry**
   d. Guava

297. Seven large is very famous cultivar of
   a. Coconut   b. Peach
   c. **Beal**   d. Jackfruit

298. Scab resistance variety of apple is
   a. Prima   b. Liberty
   c. Freedom   d. **All of the Above**

299. Mehal is important rootstock of which fruit crop?
   a. Peach   b. Pear
   c. Apple   d. **Plum**

300. Ne Plus Ultra is most important cultivar of
   a. **Almond**   b. Apricot
   c. Peach   d. Plum

301. Which temperature fruit is highly perishable in nature?
   a. Cherry   b. Apricot
   c. **Peach**   d. Plum

302. Tomato is graded on how much grades?
   a. 26   b. 6
   c. **4**   d. 3

303. Scuffing is important cultural practice performed in
   a. Oil palm   b. **Coffee**
   c. Tea   d. Cocoa

304. Moko disease of banana is caused by
   a. MLO   b. Virus
   c. **Bacteria**   d. Fungus

305. Tea mosquito bug is major pest problem of
   a. Tea   b. **Cashewnut**
   c. Coconut   d. Arecanut

306. Metsubre is physiological disorder of
   a. Sweet potato   b. Yams
   c. **Calocasia**   d. None

307. White rust of cole crop is controlled by soil treatment of
   a. **Lime**   b. Gypsum
   c. Lead aresenate   d. Copper sulphate

308. Cheap source of carbohydrate is
   a. Cassava   b. **Sweet potato**
   c. Potato   d. Sugar beet

309. Pusa Alankar is important cultivar of
   a. Snake gourd   b. Winter squash
   c. Pumpkin   d. **Summer squash**

310. Chromosome no. of pea is
   a. **14**   b. 18
   c. 22   d. 24

311. Toxin presents in water melon
   a. Trypsin inhibitor
   b. **Serotonin**
   c. Choline esterase
   d. Haemagglutinin

312. Garden beet belongs to which genus?
   a. Brassica   b. Raphanus
   c. **Beta**   d. None

313. Buttenut squash is important cultivar of
   a. Snake gourd
   b. Winter squash
   c. **Pumpkin**
   d. Summer squash

314. Which one is sheophyte spice plant?
    a. **Large cardamom**
    b. Small cardamom
    c. Cinnamon
    d. Black papper

315. Which spice is dioecious in nature?
    a. All spice   b. Nutmeg
    c. Vanilla   d. **All of the above**

316. Largest producer and consumer eromatic oils
    a. Brazil   **b. USA**
    c. India   d. China

317. Senna leaves have properties of
    a. Fixative   b. Cardiotonic
    c. **Laxative**   d. Cooling agent

318. Scientific name of Sarpagandha is
    a. *Withania somnifera*
    b. *Rauwolfia serpentina*
    c. *Cassia angustifolia*
    d. None

319. Most devastating disease of calocasia is
    a. **Blight**
    b. Rust
    c. Powdery mildew
    d. None

320. Which one is semi-aquatic perennial plant?
    a. Rosemary   b. Mint
    c. **Sweet flag** d. None

321. Kiran is important cultivar of
    a. **Mint**   b. Davana
    c. Rose geranium
    d. Lemon grass

322. Atropine is chemical constituent present in
    a. Faxglove   **b. Belladora**
    c. Senna   d. Henbane

323. Which part of Datura is used as medicinal plants?
    a. Leaves   b. Seed
    c. **Whole herb** d. Fruit

324. Which part of black pepper is used as spice?
    a. **Fruit**   b. Seeds
    c. Leaves   d. None

325. Largest producer of chilli is
    a. Kerala
    b. Rajasthan
    c. **Andhra Pradesh**
    d. Gujarat

326. Purple vienna is which season cultivar of knol-khol?
    a. **Mid**   b. Late
    c. Early   d. None

327. Chromosome no. of bottle gourd is
    a. 14   b. 22
    c. **24**   d. 26

328. Endiva belongs to family of
    a. Cruciferae   **b. Compositae**
    c. Convolvulaceae d. None

329. Seed ball is present in
    a. Beet root   b. Turnip
    c. **Both a and b** d. Carrot

330. Shoot 7 fruit borer is major pest of
    a. Tomato   **b. Brinjal**
    c. Potato   d. Chilli

331. Edible part of asparagus is
    a. Leaves
    b. Flowers
    c. Fleshy peduncle
    d. **Tender shoots**

332. Crop harvesting is staggering in which crop?
    a. Sweet potato   b. Cassava
    c. Potato   **d. Yams**

333. Great lake is important cultivar of
    a. Broccoli   **b. Lettuce**
    c. Amaranthus   d. Brussels

334. Which bean is grown for whole pod?
    a. Broad bean   b. Cow pea
    c. **Dolichos bean** d. Lima bean

335. Which is called as vegetable of immense values?
    a. Water mellon   b. Musk melon
    c. Pumpkin   d. Bottle gourd

336. Yellow fleshed variety of water melon is
    a. Durgapur Kesar
    b. Durgapur Meetha
    c. Pusa Bedana
    d. Pusa Rasal

337. Egg plant or Aubergine is common name of
    a. Tomato   b. Potato
    c. Brinjal   d. Capsicum

338. Which vegetable has tap root system?
    a. Tomato   b. Brinjal
    c. Chilli   d. Onion

339. Inflorescence of onion is
    a. Spike   b. Racemose
    c. Cymose   **d. Umble**

340. Capsicum required how much irrigation?
    a. 7–8   b. 8–10
    c. 10–12   **d. 12–15**

341. Becterial wilt resistant variety of tomato is
    a. Arka Abir   b. Arka Abha
    c. Sonali
    d. All of the above

342. Late blight of potato is mainly confined to which region
    a. Northern part
    b. Southern part
    c. Centrel-Western part
    d. Eastern part

343. Guggal belongs to which family?
    a. Burseraceae   b. Solanaceae
    c. Apocynaceae   d. Papavaraceae

344. Which part of cinchon is usad in malaria treatment?
    a. Leaves   b. Roots
    c. Bark   d. Flower

345. Which plant is used a preanaesthetic in medicinal surgeries?
    a. Henbane   **b. Datura**
    c. Ipecac   d. Opium

346. Niharika is important cultivar of
    a. Medicinal yam
    b. Opium
    c. Medicinal solanum
    d. Periwinke

347. Which part of *Aloe vera* is used?
    a. Leaves   **b. Roots**
    c. Bark   d. Flower

348. Which part of Henbane is use?
    a. Leaves   b. Roots
    c. Bark   d. Flower

349. Safed Musali belongs to which family?
    a. Solanaceae
    b. Rubiaceae
    c. Liliaceae
    d. Leguminoceae

350. Scientific name of senna
    a. *Withania somnifera*
    b. *Rauwolfia serpentina*
    c. *Cassia angustifolia*
    d. None

351. Which part of Safed Musali is used?
    a. Leaves   b. Bark
    c. Roots   d. Flower

352. Kiran is important cultivar of
    a. Davana   b. Rose geranium
    c. Lemong grass   **d. Mint**

353. Propagation in turmeric is done by
    a. Stolon   **b. Rhizome**
    c. Offset   d. Runner

354. Fenugreek belongs to which family?
    a. Fabaceae   b. Apiaceae
    c. Rutaceae   d. None

355. Chemical presents in saffron
    a. Cicrocrocin   b. Acorin
    c. Carvone   d. Anithol

356. Important chemical presents in black pepper
    a. **Piperine**   b. Cineol
    c. Eugenol   d. Curcumine

357. Which part of coriander is used for spice?
    a. Leaves   b. Seed
    c. **Both a and b** d. None

358. Plastic mulches are used in horticulture because it helps in the following
    a. Weed control
    b. Moisture conservation
    c. Microbial conservation
    d. **All of the above**

359. Planting material of saffron is
    a. Bulb   b. **Corn**
    c. Offset   d. Rhizome

360. Most of capsicum is present in chilli is in which part?
    a. Seed   b. **Placenta**
    c. Paricarp   d. None

361. All spices are belong to which family?
    a. **Myrtaceae**   b. Myrsticaceae
    c. Luraceae   d. Apiaceae

362. Which cultivar of rose has been patented by the USA
    a. Sindoor   b. **Mohini**
    c. Priya   d. None

363. Rajendra Swathi is important cultivar of
    a. Turmeric   b. Fenugreek
    c. **Coriander**   d. None

364. Opium belongs to which family?
    a. Cannabinaceae   b. **Papaveraceae**
    c. Malvaceae   d. Apocynaceae

365. Origin centre of dill or sowa is
    a. S-E Asia   b. **Eurasia**
    c. Sri Lanka   d. West Indies

366. Which one of following is multiple fruit?
    a. **Fig**   b. Strawberry
    c. Aonla   d. Pomegranate

367. Which of the following plants is day neutral plant?
    a. Papaya   b. Guava
    c. **Both a and b** d. Cashewnut

368. Which one is called food of good?
    a. Coffee   b. **Cocoa**
    c. Beal   d. Banana

369. Pollination in oil palm is done by
    a. Honeybee   b. Wasp
    c. Hand pollination
    d. **Weevil**

370. Mango seed kernel has percentage of protein
    a. **9.5%**   b. 22%
    c. 24%   d. 12%

371. Who is famous grape breeder?
    a. J.H. Higgin   b. **H.D. Olmo**
    c. H.B. Frost   d. None

372. Seedless cultivar of jamun is
    a. Paras   b. Desi jamun
    c. **Narendra jamun-6**
    d. Raj jamun

373. Most popular variety of almod is
    a. Pearless   b. Ne Plus Ultra
    c. Non-pereil   d. **All of these**

374. High and low temperatures suitable cultivar of tomato is
    a. Pusa H-1   b. Arka Sauabh
    c. Pusa Sheetal   d. **Pusa Sadabahar**

375. Brinjal is good source of
    a. Vitamin A   b. **Vitamin B**
    c. Vitamin C   d. None

376. Male plantation should be in pointed gourd is
    a. 5%   b. 50%
    c. 20%   d. **10%**

377. Pea cultivar resistance to powdery mildew and rust is
    a. Bonneville   b. Harbhajan
    c. Arkel   d. **Arka Ajit**

378. Dwarf variety of cow pea
   a. **Pusa Phalguni**
   b. Pusa Komal
   c. Pusa Garima   d. Arka Suman

379. Scientific name of White Yam is
   a. *D. alata*   b. *D. esculenta*
   c. *D. rotundata*   d. *D. floribunda*

380. Cheap source of carbohydrate is
   a. Cassava   b. Potato
   c. **Sweat potato**   d. Sugar beet

381. Raddish belongs to which family?
   a. **Cruciferae**
   b. Compositae
   c. Chenopodaceae
   d. Convolvulaceae

382. Pusa Alankar is famous cultivar of
   a. Snake gourd
   b. Winter squash
   c. **Summer squash**
   d. Pumkin

383. Origin from of pumkin is
   a. Dioecious
   b. Gynodioecious
   c. **Hermaphrodite**
   d. Monoecious

384. Blossom end rot of chilli is due to
   a. Bacteria   b. Fungi
   c. Virus   d. **Non-parasitic**

385. Garlic bulb is which from bulb
   a. **Multiple bulb**
   b. Compound bulb
   c. Clove   d. All of the above

386. Which one of the following is only sub-tropical pome fruit?
   a. Pear   b. Plum
   c. **Loquat**   d. Peach

387. Which one is called pepo?
   a. **Water melon**   b. Guava
   c. Pear   d. Banana

388. Origin centre of pineapple is
   a. India   b. China
   c. Europe   d. **Brazil**

389. Storage temperature of pineapple is
   a. 0°C   b. **11–13°C**
   c. 5–6°C   d. 8–9°C

390. TSS of mango is generally
   a. 18%   b. 22%
   c. 24%   d. **20%**

391. Most banana cultivar is in nature of
   a. Diploid   b. Amphidiploid
   c. **Triploid**   d. Allotetraploid

392. No. of papaya plants under HDP is
   a. 1600   b. **6000**
   c. 6400   d. 3300

393. Propagation in jackfruit is done by
   a. Air layering   b. Seed
   c. Petch budding   d. **Inarching**

394. Foster is well-known cultivar of
   a. Grape   b. Avocado
   c. **Grapefruit**   d. Straweberry

395. Which crop is known as queen of pulses?
   a. Red gram   b. Pea
   c. **Mung**   d. Chickpea

396. Softening of dates is taken place at which stage
   a. Doka   b. **Dang**
   c. Gandora   d. Pind

397. Banana takes how many days for maturity?
   a. 70–80 days   b. **90–120 days**
   c. 120–150 days   d. 150–180 days

398. Fruit juice and TSS of barley water is
   a. 25, 30   b. 10, 10
   c. 20, 15   d. **40, 50**

399. Which fruit is rich source of calcium?
   a. **Lychee**   b. Date
   c. Beal   d. Sapota

12

Floriculture and Landscaping

1. **International Society of Horticultural Science (ISHS) is situated at**
   a. Netherland
   b. Bulgaria
   c. UK
   d. Belgium

2. **National Horticulture Board (NHB) was established in**
   a. 1984
   b. 1990
   c. 1985
   d. 1986

3. **Leading flower product importing country is**
   a. USA
   b. Italy
   c. Germany
   d. Norway

4. **The largest flower market in the world is**
   a. Aalsmeer
   b. Germany
   c. Columbia
   d. Pakistan

5. **Carnation is national flower of**
   a. Pakistan
   b. Spain
   c. China
   d. USA

6. **The main countries which exporting fresh flowers are**
   a. Netherlands, Colombia, Israel
   b. India, Japan, China
   c. Belgium, Israel, UK
   d. None of the above

7. **Madhavi lata is a common name of**
   a. *Hiptase benghalensis*
   b. *Wisteria sinesis*
   c. *Clerodendron splendens*
   d. *Clitoria ternata*

8. **International registration authority of rose (IRAR) is situated at**
   a. USA
   b. India
   c. China
   d. Netherlands

9. **In India, Agri Export Zones (AEZs) for flowers has been developed to create infrasturucture for floriculture and increase exports**
   a. 6
   b. 15
   c. 9
   d. 11

10. **Leading cut flower, grown commercially all over the world is**
    a. Rose
    b. Chrysanthemum
    c. Carnation
    d. Gladiolus

11. **"Garden Through Ages" book is written through which writer?**
    a. G.S. Randhawa
    b. K.L. Chadha
    c. M.S. Randhawa
    d. A.V. Swarup

12. **"The Indian Journal of Ornamental Horticulture" is being published from**
    a. IARI, New Dehli
    b. IIPR, Kanpur
    c. A.M.U., Aligarh
    d. B.H.U., Varanasi

13. **First Indian Horticulture Congress was held in**
    a. 2004
    b. 2001
    c. 2002
    d. 2009

14. Which is number one foliage plant at global level?
    a. **Dieffenbachia** b. Fiscus
    c. Asparagus d. Croton

15. The book "Indoor Gardening" was written by which Indian writer?
    a. H.P. Singh b. V.P. Sharma
    c. **V. Swarup** d. S.K. Mukherjee

16. The book "Gladiolus" was written by which Indian writer?
    a. **A. Mukhopadhayay**
    b. K.V. Rajpur
    c. P. Trivedi
    d. A.A. Khan

17. The book "Home Gardening" was written by
    a. **Pratibha P. Trivedi**
    b. K.L. Chadha
    c. B.P. Pal
    d. S.P. Ghosh

18. The book "The Rose in India" was written by
    a. G.S. Randhawa b. **B.P. Pal**
    c. J.S. Arora d. V. Swarup

19. Which country ranked first in export of floriculture products in the world?
    a. **Netherlands** b. Brazil
    c. China d. India

20. The book "Floriculture in India" has been written by which Indian Scientist?
    a. M.S. Randhawa
    b. V. Swurp
    c. **G.S. Randhawa**
    d. K.L. Chadha

21. India is divided into following agro-climatic zone
    a. **15** b. 20
    c. 21 d. 22

22. The book "Ornamental Horticulture in India" was written by
    a. T.R. Chadha b. V.P. Sharma
    c. **K.L. Chadaha** d. A.A. Khan

23. The book "Orchids" was written by
    a. K.L. Mukherjee
    b. T.R. Chadha
    c. **S.K. Mukherjee**
    d. V.P. Sharma

24. In India, total area under greenhouse is
    a. 300 b. 900
    c. **600** d. 1200

25. Dahlia is the national flower of
    a. **Mexico** b. USA
    c. India d. Italy

26. The book entitled "Beautiful Gardens" is written by
    a. **M.S. Randhawa**
    b. A.K. Singh
    c. R.L. Mishra d. V. Swaurup

27. In India, which state has highest area under protected cultivation?
    a. Punjab b. Tamil Nadu
    c. AP d. **MH**

28. Maximum cut flower producing state is
    a. Tamil Nadu b. Karnataka
    c. **West Bengal** d. AP

29. "Garden Flowers" book is written by
    a. **V. Swarup** b. M.S. Randhawa
    c. G.S. Randhawa d. A.A. Khan

30. The largest exporter of cut flower in the world is
    a. Japan b. **Netherlands**
    c. China d. USA

31. Indian horticulture is a semi-technical magazine published from
    a. **ICAR, New Dehli**
    b. IARI, New Dehli
    c. NBRI, New Dehli
    d. IIHR, Bengaluru

32. Division of Floriculture and Landscaping at IARI, New Delhi was established in
    a. **1983** b. 1987
    c. 1905 d. 1879

33. When Division of Floriculture and Landscape Gardening was started at IIHR, Bengaluru in
    a. 1976   b. 1979
    c. 1969   d. 1945

34. "Beatiful Garden" is written by
    a. M.S. Randhawa
    b. V.D. Singh
    c. K.L. Singh
    d. None

35. World's biggest auction of flowers is situated in
    a. USA   b. India
    c. Sri Lanka   **d. Netherlands**

36. How many agro-ecological zones present in India?
    a. 22   **b. 21**
    c. 24   d. 25

37. International Registration Authority for Bougainvillea is situated at
    a. India   b. Japan
    c. Pakistan   d. Afghanistan

38. Organization which is related to agricultural marketing is
    a. NAFED   b. NHB
    c. FCI   d. NABARD

39. Which group of plants rank first in cut greens in global flower market?
    a. Ferns   b. Bryophytes
    c. Cypress   d. Asparagus

40. Diploid chromosome number of French marigold is
    a. 2n = 21   **b. 2n = 48**
    c. 2n = 54   d. 2n = 25

41. Pusa Tara is the variety of
    a. Coreopsis   b. Gladiolus
    c. Bougainvillea   d. Jasmine

42. Leading flower seed producing state in India is
    a. Punjab   b. Haryana
    c. Tamil Nadu   d. West Bengal

43. "Mohni" is the variety of rose which is
    a. Diploid
    b. Octaploid
    c. Haploid
    d. Triploid

44. "Ornamental Crop Breeding" book is written by
    a. L.C. De and S.K. Bhattacharjee
    b. A.A. Khan
    c. M.M.R.K. Afridi
    d. J.S. Arora and B.P. Pal

45. Basic chromosome number of rose is
    a. n = 7   b. n = 9
    c. n = 6   d. n = 23

46. National Research Centre for Orchids (NRCO), as unit of ICAR was established in 1996. The centre is located at
    a. Pakyong (Sikkim)
    b. Palampur (HP)
    c. Lucknow (UP)
    d. Bangalore (Karnataka)

47. "Shoba" is the mutant variety of
    a. Gladiolus   b. Lily
    c. Tuberose   d. Crocus

48. Pelargonidin pigment is responsible for which colours in flowers?
    a. Orange   b. Yellow
    c. Blue   d. Red

49. Nugget is an interspecific hybrid of marigold
    a. Triploid   b. Hexaploid
    c. Tetraploid   d. Diploid

50. First interspecific hybrid in dianthus was produced by
    a. Andrew Thomas
    b. Thomas Fairchild
    c. Johannsen
    d. Rimpu

51. In Petunia which type male sterility is found
    a. GMS   **b. CMS**
    c. CGMS   d. None

52. Larkspur is a pollinated flower annual
   a. **Cross**   b. Self
   c. Both   d. Often cross

53. A head or capitulum is characteristic of which family?
   a. **Compositae**   b. Malvaceae
   c. Fabaceae   d. Umbelliferae

54. The National Seed Corporation was established in which year?
   a. 1964   b. **1963**
   c. 1961   d. 1966

55. Most commonly used tool for hybrid seed production in Petunia is
   a. GMS   b. Polyploidy
   c. **CMS**   d. Mutation

56. An organism having the gametic chromosome number is called
   a. **Haploid**   b. Genome
   c. Diploid   d. Gametes

57. Which is interspecific cultivar of Bougainvillea?
   a. Begum Sikander b. Wazi Ali Shah
   c. Chitra   d. **All of these**

58. Fruits of gladiolus is known as
   a. **Capsule**   b. Pod
   c. Legume   d. Siliqua

59. Which of the following cultivars of gladiolus is resistant to fusarium wild?
   a. Topez
   b. American beauty
   c. Priscilla   d. **Dhiraj**

60. A method of breeding which commonly used when desired variation is required to be induced in a vegetatively propagated crop is
   a. **Polyploidy**   b. Mutation
   c. Pedigree   d. Mass selection

61. The target of genetic engineering in Petunia is to evolve which colour
   a. **Orange**   b. Red
   c. Yellow   d. Blue

62. What is the major problem in rose breeding?
   a. Pollination   b. **Low seed setting**
   c. Both   d. None

63. ELISA application used for identification of
   a. Bacterial   b. **Viral**
   c. Fungal   d. All

64. The F_2 seeds are more common in
   a. Antirrhinum   b. Balsam
   c. Petunia   d. **All**

65. Clone is generally
   a. **Heterozygous**   b. Homozygous
   c. Both   d. None

66. The name of fruit of rose is
   a. **Hips**   b. Beery
   c. Drupe   d. All

67. Which is the first scented variety of gladiolus?
   a. Monohar   b. **Lucky star**
   c. Pink perfume   d. None

68. Shoba, a variety of gladiolus developed at
   a. NBRI   b. IARI
   c. ICAR   d. **IIHR**

69. Male sterile line is known as
   a. B-line   b. **A-line**
   c. Maintainer line   d. Restorer line

70. In plants, flower colour is a type of characteristic of
   a. **Qualitative**   b. Quantitative
   c. Both   d. None

71. The condition where a single gene control multiple characteristic is known as
   a. **Pleiotrophy**   b. Multigene
   c. Metazenia   d. Multiple allele

72. Aneuploids which used as ornamentals as generally as
   a. **Trisomoic**   b. Monosomic
   c. Tetrasomic   d. Nullisomic

73. A tetraploid cultivar name as SAMRAT is belongs to which plant?
    a. Antirrhinum   b. Gladiolus
    c. Lily   **d. Amaryllis**

74. In China rose flower is
    a. Epigynous   b. Perigynous
    c. Hypogynous   d. None

75. H. P. B. Bajrang Bahadur Singh Bhadari has developed 160 cultivars of
    a. Hibiscus   b. Bougainvillea
    c. Pepper   **d. Gladiolus**

76. The male sterility is most common in which of the following?
    a. Marigold   b. Anthurium
    c. Petunia   **d. All**

77. Dioecy is very common in
    a. Petunia   b. Narcissus
    c. Salvia   **d. Asparagus**

78. Pedigree selection is a method of
    a. Scion   b. Mutation
    c. Breeding   d. Hybridization

79. Bharat Sundari is cultivar of
    a. Rose   b. Pepper
    c. Mango   **d. Hibiscus**

80. Gene mutation is most common in
    a. Phlox   b. China aster
    c. Sweet pea   **d. All**

81. In which century, gladiolus introduced in India by
    a. American   b. Chinese
    c. Portuguse   **d. Britishers**

82. Which person is nonprofessionally gave great contribution in floriculture and landscaping in India?
    a. M.S. Randhawa
    b. G.S. Randahawa
    c. H.P. Singh   d. K.L. Chadha

83. In which century marigold was introduced in India?
    a. 16th   b. 13th
    c. 19th   d. 20th

84. The Orchid's gynoecium is known as
    a. Column   b. Peak
    c. Cheask   d. Tube

85. Queen Elizabeth cultivar of rose belongs to which category?
    a. Floribunda   b. Grandiflora
    c. Hybrid tea   d. Polyantha

86. Pigment responsible for blue coloration in rose flower is
    a. Chlorophyll-a   b. Chlorophyll-b
    c. Pelargonidin   **d. Delphinidin**

87. Priya Darshini is a main variety of which flowering plant?
    a. Hibiscus   b. Crossendra
    c. Rose   d. Bougainvillea

88. "Arka" series of varieties are released from
    a. IIHR, Bengaluru
    b. IARI, New Delhi
    c. ICAR, New Delhi
    d. NBRI, Lucknow

89. "Swarna Rekha" and "Rajat Rekha" cultivars of tuberose released by
    a. NBRI   b. IVRI
    c. IARI   d. ICAR

90. Dr. A.K. Roy Choudhury is famous for
    a. As first rose breeder in India
    b. As first taxonomist of India
    c. As first paleobotanist
    d. None of the above

91. Genetic nature of variety of Mohni of rose is
    a. Aneuploid   b. Polyploid
    c. Tetraploid   d. Triploid

92. "Nishikant" is a thornless rootstock of rose and it is developed at
    a. NBRI   **b. IIHR**
    c. IARI   d. IHBT

93. Generally triploids are of nature
    a. Male sterile   b. Male fertile
    c. Fertile   **d. Sterile**

94. "Pusa Anmol" cultivar of chrysanthemum is
    a. **Photo- and thermo-insensitive**
    b. Photo-insensitive
    c. Thermo-negative
    d. Thermo-zero

95. Most common is heterostyly in which plants?
    a. **Primula**   b. Petunia
    c. Balsam   d. Allysum

96. Vishakha (pink) with variegated leaves is a cultivar of
    a. **Bougainvillea**   b. Acalypha
    c. Croton   d. Hibiscus

97. CMS (cytoplasmic male sterility) is common in
    a. Petunia   b. Sunflower
    c. Ageratum   **d. All**

98. In which of the following is a variety of white rose?
    a. B.P. Pal   b. Arjun
    c. **Tushar**   d. Suchitra

99. In which of the following thornless variety of rose?
    a. B.P. Pal   b. Arjun
    c. Tushar   **d. Suchitra**

100. Need of seed certification is
    a. Improve variety
    b. Genetic and physical purity
    c. Prescribed germination
    d. **All**

101. "Pusa Narangi" is an often pollinated cultivar of
    a. Asparagus
    b. **Marigold**
    c. Chrysanthemum
    d. China aster

102. The progeny of breeder seed is called
    a. **Foundation seeds**
    b. Certified seeds
    c. Nucleus seed
    d. Registered seed

103. Generally male sterility is enhanced by
    a. **Outbreeding**   b. Inbreeding
    c. Homogeneity   d. None

104. The approach of germplasm conservation during the *in situ* conservation is
    a. Gene bank
    b. **Natural condition**
    c. Both
    d. None

105. Tagetus patula (French Marigold) is
    a. Aneuploid   b. **Tetraploid**
    c. Diploid   d. None

106. Cultivar name, Princes of Wells, is of
    a. **Malmaison carnation**
    b. Marguerite carnation
    c. Annual chrysanthemum
    d. None

107. Cultivar name, Delhi Princes, is of
    a. **Floribunda**   b. Bougainvillea
    c. Hibiscus   d. Gladiolus

108. Dr Homibhaba is a cultivar of
    a. **Hybrid tea rose** b. Hibiscus
    c. Floribunda   d. Bougainvillea

109. In which of the following processes is responsible for increasing the in-breeding in the crosss pollinated crop?
    a. **Homozygosity**   b. Selection
    c. Polyploidy   d. All

110. Agri-Horticultural Society of India introduced Dahlia in our country in which century?
    a. **1857**   b. 1957
    c. 2007   d. 1876

111. The Indus Valley civilization is specialized for
    a. Town planning   b. Architecture
    c. Craftsmanship   **d. All of the above**

112. Kalanchoe plant belongs to which category of plant group?
    a. **Succulents**   b. Cactus
    c. Trees   d. Shrubs

113. Zebrina pendula is propagated through which part?
    a. Cuttings   b. Runners
    c. Suckers   d. Bulbs

114. Fish tail palm is a common name of
    a. *Caryota urens*   b. *Cicer arietinum*
    c. *Cicer reticulata*   d. None of the above

115. Which indoor plant belongs to family Araceae?
    a. Acalypha   b. Alocasia
    c. Aglonema   d. Anthurium

116. Royal palm is
    a. *Oreodoxa regia*
    b. *Cicer arietinum*
    c. *Vigna radiata*
    d. *Antirrhinum robustum*

117. Dieffenbachia (Dumb cane), a indoor plant, is commonly known as
    a. Stem cutting   b. Seeds
    c. Root cuttings   d. Leaf cuttings

118. In which of the following plant is grown for his beautiful spike?
    a. *Acalypha hispida* (Euphosbiaceae)
    b. *Cicer arietinum*
    c. *Cicer reticulata*
    d. None

119. Monstera belongs to the family
    a. Araceae   b. Fabaceae
    c. Apocyanaceae   d. Cucurbitaceae

120. Usually and mostly palms can be propagated through which method?
    a. Seeds   b. Rhizome
    c. Offshoots   d. Suckers

121. Furcraea is propagated by
    a. Bulbils   b. Seeds
    c. Runners   d. Offshoots

122. Most of the indoor plants grow in which range of light intensity?
    a. 100–1000 lux
    b. 1200–2000 lux
    c. 1000–1500 lux   d. 2500–3000 lux

123. Sensevieria propagated by
    a. Leaf cutting   b. Stem cuttings
    c. Seeds   d. Gafting

124. Method of Bryophylum propagation is
    a. Cutting   b. Budding
    c. Leaf blade   d. Air layering

125. What is "Terrarium"?
    a. Plant growing in a glass enclosed container
    b. Grass growing in open land
    c. Shrubs growing in between the main crops
    d. Palms tree growing in a field side-by-side

126. Aim of root pruning is
    a. Accommodate the root system in the pot
    b. Accommodate the leafy portion out-side from the pot
    c. Both
    d. None

127. Best time of re-potting is
    a. Rainy season   b. Any season
    c. Summer season   d. Winter season

128. In cactus, best time for grafting is
    a. March–April   b. Feb–March
    c. Jan–Feb   d. April–June

129. "Lady care" is a cultivar of
    a. Dahalia   b. Euphorbia
    c. Camellia   d. Impatiens

130. Which plant (Palm) is not suitable for indoor
    a. *Phoenix roebelenii*
    b. *Chamaerops humilis*
    c. *Chamaerops erumpens*
    d. *Phoenix dactylifera*

131. The common name of Flaming Lily is
    a. *Cicer arietinum*
    b. *Cicer reticulata*
    c. *Antirrhinum alba*
    d. *Antirrhinum andreanum*

132. "Sago Palm" is common name of a gymnosperm plant
   a. *Cycas revoluta*
   b. *Rhapis excelsa*
   c. *Washingtonia filifera*
   d. *Licuala grandis*

133. Antirrhinum belongs to the family
   a. Scrophularaiaceae
   b. Asteraceae
   c. Solanaceae
   d. None

134. Globe amaranth (Gomphrena globosa) is which type of season crop
   a. Summer   b. Spring
   c. Rainy   d. Winter

135. Hollyhocks (Alcea spp.) is used for
   a. Screening
   b. Pots
   c. Hanging basket
   d. Peculiar shape

136. In which of the following is a hardest annual crop?
   a. Digitalis   b. Antirrhinum
   c. Aster   d. Carnation

137. *Calendula officinalis* is a
   a. Winter season annual
   b. Summer season annual
   c. Zaid season annual
   d. All is correct

138. In which plant, seeds require stratification and scarification?
   a. Marigold   b. Petunia
   c. Nigella   d. Clianthus

139. Seeds of which plant germinate only in dark conditions?
   a. Coleus   b. Violas
   c. Nigella   d. All of the above

140. Which is one blue colour flowering annual?
   a. Larkspur   b. Ageratum
   c. Delphinium   d. All of the above

141. Which plant bloom in the dark conditions only?
   a. Coleus   b. Violas
   c. Pansies   d. All of the above

142. In China aster, one gram of seed number is about
   a. 200–300   b. 100–200
   c. 400–500   d. 800–1000

143. Curly top virus disease is a drastic problem in
   a. China aster   b. Zinnia
   c. Petunia   d. Salvia

144. Gypsophila paniculata (baby's breath) belongs to family
   a. Caryophyllaceae
   b. Solanaceae
   c. Asteraceae   d. Poaceae

145. Plants which survive for one growing season is known as
   a. Annual   b. Perennial
   c. Biennial   d. None of the above

146. Geranium, impatiens and begonia are
   a. Day neutral plants (DNP)
   b. Long day plants (LDP)
   c. Night neutral plants
   d. Short-long day plants

147. Plant suitable for making of hanging basket is
   a. Portulaca   b. China aster
   c. Cosmos   d. Rudbeckia

148. Zinnia, a flowering annual which having a texture of which type?
   a. Coarse   b. Medium
   c. Gerbera   d. Shiny

149. Viola tricolor (Pancy) belongs to
   a. Violaceae   b. Asteraceae
   c. Caryophyllaceaed. Labiatae

150. Following plants are commercially multiplied by seeds *except*
   a. Cactus   b. Pholx
   c. Balsam   d. Marigold

151. "Amar shoal" is a cultivar of
   a. Marigold
   b. Lakspur
   c. Pholx
   d. Amaranthus

152. Kochia is which kind of annual plant?
   a. Zaid
   b. Winter
   c. Summer
   d. All

153. Annuals show which kind of colour range in the monochromatic colour scheme?
   a. Different shade
   b. Just opposite colour
   c. Same colour
   d. None

154. Petunia is a native plant of South Africa belongs to which family?
   a. Solanaceae
   b. Brassicaceae
   c. Asteraceae
   d. Poaceae

155. Colour dominant throughout the year in the garden is
   a. Green
   b. Black
   c. Blue
   d. Red

156. Amarathus is considered beautiful for their
   a. Foliage
   b. Fruits
   c. Flowers
   d. Stem

157. Sweet pea is which kind of plant?
   a. Climber
   b. Dwarf
   c. Creeping
   d. Serrate

158. A colour scheme that uses one primary colour and other colours derived from same primary is
   a. Adjacent
   b. Complementary
   c. Monochromatic
   d. All of these

159. The botanical name of Pancy is
   a. *Viola tricolor*
   b. *Cicer arietinum*
   c. *Cicer reticulatum*
   d. *Cajanus cajanus*

160. Which plant is propagated through the soft wood cuttings?
   a. Pilea
   b. Begonnia
   c. Amaranthus
   d. None

161. Lathyrus odoratus (sweet pea) is used for which purpose in society
   a. Departure
   b. Regard
   c. Luxury
   d. Success

162. Requirement of complete darkness for germination is a characteristic feature
   a. Nigella
   b. Aster
   c. Zinnia
   d. Petunia

163. Which annual is grown in shady conditions?
   a. Antirrhinum
   b. Cineraria
   c. Both
   d. Chrysanthemum

164. Nasturtium is
   a. Annuals
   b. Binnuual
   c. Climber
   d. Tree

165. Raised nursery bed is prepared during
   a. Winter season
   b. Summer season
   c. Rainy season
   d. Zaid season

166. The plants which blooms twice a year?
   a. Biennial
   b. Annuals
   c. Perrenials
   d. All

167. The famous name of Nigella Sativa is
   a. Kalonji
   b. Rye
   c. Sarsoon
   d. All

168. Planting time of tuberose is
   a. Oct–Nov
   b. July–Aug
   c. March–April
   d. Whole year

169. Clivia miniata (Amaryllidaceae) is commonly known as
   a. Natal lily
   b. Bush lily
   c. Kaffir lily
   d. All of the above

170. Which part of saffron is economic
   a. Stigma
   b. Anthers
   c. Style
   d. Calyx

171. Crop which propagated by the corm is
   a. Gladiolus
   b. Crocus
   c. Tulip
   d. Both a and b

172. Which bulb is planted at maximum depth?
  a. **Tulip**   b. Lily
  c. Tuberose   d. Gladiolus

173. In which of the following is propagated by the help of corms?
  a. *Crocus sativus*   b. Dahlia
  c. Lily   d. None

174. Plants that grow from underground organs (bulbs, corms, rhizomes) are
  a. **Bulbous plants**
  b. Underground plants
  c. Rhizomatous plants
  d. None

175. Gladiolus is commonly known as
  a. **Corn flag**   b. Mesia Haj
  c. Thorn flag   d. None

176. China aster is a
  a. **Self pollinated**
  b. Cross pollinated
  c. Often cross pollinated
  d. None of the above

177. Application of thiourea is
  a. Bud formation
  b. **Breaking dormancy**
  c. Root formation
  d. Weed removal

178. Match the correct pairs given below
  i.   Crocus   A. Nyctaginaceae
  ii. Gram   B. Iridaceae
  iii. Mirabilis jalapa C. Fabaceae
       and iris
  iv. Sunflower   D. Asteraceae
  a. i-A, ii-C, iii-D, iv-B
  b. **i-B, ii-C, iii-A, iv-D**
  c. i-A, ii-B, iii-A, iv-D
  d. i-B, ii-A, iii-C, iv-D

179. Corm should be stored at 3–4°C temperature for which months in order to break dormancy
  a. **3–4 months**   b. 2–5 months
  c. 5–8 months   d. None of the above

180. Most common method of propagation for Lilium is
  a. Rhizome   b. **Bulb**
  c. Tuber   d. Corm

181. Which plants is most sensitive for CO_2
  a. Gladiolus   b. Crocus
  c. Gloriosa   d. All of the above

182. In North Indian Plains, best time for Lilium planting is
  a. **Oct–Nov**
  b. Jan–Feb
  c. March–April
  d. None of the above

183. Best method of Lilium propagation is
  a. **Bulb**   b. Corm
  c. Rhizome   d. Tuber

184. Dahlia is best propagated by
  a. Rhizome   b. Corm
  c. Bulb   d. **Tuberous roots**

185. In North Indian Plains, best time for gladiolus planting is
  a. **Oct–Nov**   b. July–Aug
  c. Jan–Feb   d. None

186. "CORMEL" is a swollen end of
  a. Primary roots   b. **Stolon**
  c. Axillary bud   d. Fibrous root

187. The late cutting method of Dahlia propagation was developed in 1960 at
  a. Delhi   b. Bareilly
  c. Kanpur   d. **Calcutta**

188. The National flower of Italy is
  a. **Lily**   b. Iris
  c. Begonia   d. Tuberose

189. Lily is the symbol of
  a. **Purity**   b. Impurity
  c. Jealousy   d. Pride

190. In which of the following is the leading importer of bulbous plants?
  a. **USA**   b. Japan
  c. Australia   d. India

191. "Vaibhav" is a cultivar of
    a. Tuberose b. Chrysanthemum
    c. China aster d. Gladiolus

192. The common name of Nelumbo nucifera is the
    a. Sacred lotus b. Common lotus
    c. Pure lotus d. Impure lotus

193. Tiger lily is characterized by the presence of
    a. Bulbil
    b. Gamma cup formation
    c. Protonema
    d. All

194. Which of the following climb by secreting sticking substance?
    a. *Fiscus repens*
    b. *Compsis grandiflora*
    c. Bougainvillea
    d. *Pyrostegia venusta*

195. Common name of *Quisqualis indica* is
    a. Rangoon creeper
    b. Garlic creeper
    c. Railway creeper
    d. Madhumalti

196. Vines function in the landscape as
    a. Sufacing elements
    b. Softeners
    c. Wall elements
    d. All of the above

197. Crop plants which have weak stems and ability to climb up the support with the help of modified organs known as
    a. Climbers b. Shrubs
    c. Trees d. Annuals

198. Which of the following climber is suitable for pot?
    a. *Clitoria ternatea* b. *Quisqualis indica*
    c. Bougainvillea d. Both a and b

199. Aristolochia elegans is an ornamental plant which is
    a. Shrub b. Climber
    c. Tree d. Annual

200. Which one of the following is a climber?
    a. *Quisqualis indica*
    b. *Ixora cocinea*
    c. *Hibiscuses rosa chinensis*
    d. *Cassia gluaca*

201. Which of the following climbers is commonly used as hedge?
    a. Bougainvillea
    b. *Clerodendron splendens*
    c. *Ficus repens*
    d. Both a and b

202. Which of the following is suitable for indoor decoration?
    a. Philodendron species
    b. *Monstera deliciosa*
    c. *Epipremnum aureum*
    d. All of the above

203. Climber grown for scented flowers is
    a. *Hiptage benghalensis*
    b. *Jasminum grandiflora*
    c. Both a and b
    d. *Clerodendron splendiflora*

204. Parda Bel (*Vernonia ekaegnifolia*) belongs to family
    a. Asteraceae b. Bignoniaceae
    c. Apocynaceae d. Acanthaceae

205. Which climber is suitable for making topiary?
    a. *Clerodendron inerme*
    b. Tecoma species
    c. *Hiptage benghalensis*
    d. Scindapsus

206. Which of the following climbers bears blue colour flowers?
    a. *Clitorea ternatea* b. *Passiflora caerulea*
    c. *Wisteria sinensis* d. All of the above

207. Which of the following is evergreen climber?
    a. *Cissus discolour*
    b. *Clematis paniculata*
    c. *Solanum jasminoides*
    d. Antigonon

208. Bougainvillea belongs to family
   a. Oleaceae
   b. Apocynaceae
   c. Bignoniaceae
   d. Nyctaginaceae

209. Which ornament plant blooms through-out the year?
   a. Silver oak   **b. Bougainvillea**
   c. Jasminum   d. Crossendra

210. Ficus repens belongs to family
   a. Oleaceae   **b. Moraceae**
   c. Verbanaceae   d. Leguminoceae

211. Multi bract cultivar of Bougainvillea is
   a. Mahara
   b. Cherry blossom
   c. Los Banos beauty
   d. All of the above

212. When shrubs are planted at regular interval to form a thick screen is known as
   a. Topiary   **b. Hedge**
   c. Shrubbery   d. Edge

213. For making good hedge, the shrub should be
   a. Thick and dense
   b. Quick growth
   c. Tolerant to repeated triming
   d. All

214. The best budding time in Bougain-villea is
   a. Feb–Aug   b. July–Aug
   c. Feb–March   d. None

215. Blue colour flowering shrubs is/are
   a. *Plumbago auriculata*
   b. *Duranta plumeri*
   c. *Daedalcanthus nervosus*
   d. All

216. Which of the following shrubs bears flowers?
   a. *Acalypha tricolor*
   b. *Codiaeum variegatum*
   c. *Manihot variegata*
   d. Cestrum nocturnum

217. Which of the following shrubs is not originated in India?
   a. Thevetia nerifolia
   b. *Jasminum auriculatum*
   c. *Ixora acuminata*
   d. *Cassia glauca*

218. Chashmogamy found in which flowers
   a. Pansy   b. *Clitorea ternatea*
   c. Both a and b   d. None of the above

219. Protogyny found in which flower crop?
   a. Petunia   b. Antirrhinum
   c. Marigold   **d. Both a and b**

220. Protoandry observed in which flower crop?
   a. Morigold   b. Gerbera
   c. Petunia   d. All of the above

221. Male sterility is not found in____flower crops.
   a. Zinnia   b. Vinca
   c. Rose   d. Verbena

222. GMS persents in which flower crops?
   a. Ageratum   b. Vinca
   c. Pelargonium   **d. All of the above**

223. Back cross method of breeding means
   a. Polyploidy breeding
   b. Crossing back the F1 to desired parents
   c. Mutation breeding
   d. Clonal selection

224. First artificial plant was made by
   a. Thomas Fair Child (1717)
   b. Joseph Kolreuter (1760)
   c. Rudolph Jacob Camerarius (1694)
   d. Harlan and Pope (1922)

225. National Bureau of Plant Genetic Resource (NBPGR) is situated at
   a. Dehradun   b. Karnal
   c. New Delhi   d. Lucknow

226. In which clonal selection is effective?
   a. Rose
   b. Orchids

c. Chrysanthemum
d. **All of the above**

227. Jasmine cultivars "Parimullai" and "Arka Surabhi" have been developed through
    a. Introduction   b. Hybridization
    c. **Clonal selection** d. Mass selection

228. Abhisarika, Pusa Christina and Madhosh cultivar of rose are developed through
    a. Bud sports
    b. **Induced mutation**
    c. Spontaneous mutation
    d. Selection

229. Where is the Head Quarter of PPV and FR Authority in India?
    a. Lucknow   b. Chennai
    c. Calcutta   d. **New Delhi**

230. Diploid chromosome number of lily is
    a. 2n = 14   b. **2n = 24**
    c. 2n = 12   d. 2n = 18

231. A crop species whose somatic chromosome number is the exact multiple of the basic number is called
    a. Aneuploid   b. **Euploid**
    c. Monosomic   d. Coreopsis

232. Rosa bourboniana is
    a. Diploid   b. Hexaploid
    c. **Triploid**
    d. Pentaploid

233. The method through which we can able to introduce foreign gene into transformed cell or cytoplasm is
    a. **Genetic engineering**
    b. Molecular marker
    c. Tissue culture
    d. Back cross

234. Manmohan and Manhar are varieties of
    a. Chrysanthemum
    b. **Gladiolus**
    c. Gaillardia
    d. Rose

235. Peach blossom is the variety of
    a. Marigold   b. Carnation
    c. Crossandra   d. **Chrysanthemum**

236. The failure pollen to fertilize the same flower or other flower of the same plant is known as
    a. Pollen sterility
    b. Male sterility
    c. Mutation
    d. **Self incompatibility**

237. "Glory of east" is the common name of
    a. **Chrysanthemum**
    b. Gladiolus
    c. Carnation   d. Marigold

238. Commercially Gladiolus is propagated by
    a. **Corm**   b. Rhizome
    c. Seed   d. Bulb

239. "Pusa Basanti" is a variety of which flower crop
    a. **Marigold**   b. Chrysanthemum
    c. China aster   d. Gaillardia

240. Suckers of Chrysanthemum are separated during which months of year
    a. July–Aug   b. Sep–Oct
    c. **Feb–March**   d. Dec–Jan

241. Pollen free lily variety is
    a. Sphinx   b. Tiara
    c. Aphrodite   d. **All**

242. Which is growing in largest area as cut flower in our country?
    a. **Rose**   b. Gladiolus
    c. Orchid   d. Chrysanthemum

243. The late cutting method of Dahlia propagation was developed in
    a. 1857   b. **1860**
    c. 1960   d. 1974

244. Cultivation of Crossendra is done on commercially scale in
    a. North India   b. **South India**
    c. West India   d. East India

245. Leaf scorch and bud blast are disorder of
   a. Lilum   b. Gladiolus
   c. Gerbera   d. Carnation

246. Which is growing in largest area as cut flower in our country?
   a. Gladiolus   b. Orchid
   c. Rose   d. Chrysanthemum

247. The late cutting method of Dahlia propagation was developed in
   a. 1860   b. 1857
   c. 1970   d. 1976

248. Leaf scorch and bud blast are disorder of
   a. Lilum   b. Gladiolus
   c. Gerbera   d. Carnation

249. William Sim is a cultivar of
   a. Anthurium   b. Chrysanthemum
   c. Lily   d. Carnation

250. When the outer two rows of disc florets are perpendicular to the stalk is harvesting stage of
   a. China aster b. Carnation
   c. Gerbera   d. Marigold

251. The best period for rose puring in North India is
   a. February–March
   b. October–November
   c. April–May
   d. June–July

252. Which type of carnation produces one large bloom?
   a. Spray   b. Semi-spray
   c. Standard   d. All of the above

253. Cuttage-buddage is very fast method of propagating
   a. Rose   b. Jasmine
   c. Dahila   d. Bougainvillea

254. Anthurium is originate from
   a. South America
   b. West Indies
   c. India
   d. North America

255. Yellow-coloured rose sp. is
   a. *Rosa gallica*   b. *Rosa indica*
   c. *Rosa centifolia* d. *Rosa foetida*

256. The casual organism of powdery mildew of rose is
   a. *Sphaerotheca pannosa*
   b. *Diplocarpon rosae*
   c. *Diplodia rosarum*
   d. *Peronospora sparsa*

257. Which of the following is not used as a cut flower?
   a. Jasmine   b. Gladiolus
   c. Gerbera   d. Anthurium

258. Blooming period of chrysanthemum is
   a. March–April
   b. July–August
   c. September–October
   d. December–January

259. Which colour rose is most popular?
   a. Pink   b. Red
   c. White   d. Yellow

260. Chrysanthemium is a
   a. Annual plant
   b. Biennial plant
   c. Perennial plant
   d. None of the above

261. Planting time of tuberose is
   a. October–November
   b. March–April
   c. May–June
   d. July–August

262. The spectacular flower of golden rod has a _____ colour.
   a. Yellow   b. Red
   c. Blue   d. White

263. Most serious pest of rose is
   a. Jassids   b. Thrips
   c. White fly   d. Red spider mite

264. Thornless varity of rose is
   a. Mohini   b. First red
   c. Both a and b d. Suchitra

265. Which flower grown for the loose flower over the largest area in the country
    a. Marigold
    b. Tuberose
    c. Jasmine
    d. Crossendra

266. Dahlia is a national flower of
    a. Mexico
    b. Malaysia
    c. Nigeria
    d. Brazil

267. Endosperm is absent in _____ seeds.
    a. Orchids
    b. Jasmine
    c. Rose
    d. Tuberose

268. Which disease is most serious in gladiolus?
    a. Rust
    b. Fusarium wilt
    c. Damping off
    d. Botrytis

269. Tip burning in gladiolus is due to
    a. High temperature
    b. Water stress
    c. B deficiency
    d. Excessive fluorides

270. Jasmine is commercially propagated through
    a. Cutting
    b. Budding
    c. Suckers
    d. Seeds

271. Yellow color jasmine species is
    a. *Jasmonium flexile*
    b. *J. officinale*
    c. *J. grandiflora*
    d. *J. humile*

272. First variety of hybrid teas rose is
    a. Arjun
    b. Mohni
    c. La France
    d. Banjaran

273. "T" budding also reffered to as
    a. Patch budding
    b. Ring budding
    c. Shield budding
    d. Annular budding

274. Topple disorder in gladiolus is due to deficiency of
    a. P
    b. K
    c. N
    d. Ca

275. Cymbidium is a kind of
    a. Orchids
    b. Chrysanthemum
    c. Golden rod
    d. Gladiolus

276. Pinching (stopping) is generally done in
    a. Rose
    b. Gladiolus
    c. Tuberose
    d. Carnation

277. Inflorescence of anthurium is called as
    a. Spike
    b. Spadix
    c. Raceme
    d. Hypanthodium

278. Which of the following does not belong to family Iridaceae?
    a. Crocus
    b. Freesia
    c. Iris
    d. Tulip

279. Die back is a serious disease of which flower crop?
    a. Rose
    b. Gerbera
    c. Tuberose
    d. Marigold

280. Which of the following is resistant to root knot nematodes?
    a. Chrysanthemum
    b. Marigold
    c. China aster
    d. Gerbera

281. Dr B.P. Pal evolved 1st rose variety
    a. Dr S.D. Mukherjee
    b. Rosa Sherbet
    c. First Red
    d. La France

282. Breaking virus was 1st reported in
    a. Carnation
    b. Tulip
    c. Gerbera
    d. Rose

283. "First Red" kind is generally referred to in
    a. Rose
    b. Tuberose
    c. Gladiolus
    d. Carnation

284. Dr S.D. Mukherjee "I" rose cultivar developed in India by
    a. B.K. Roy Choudhury
    b. A.A. Khan
    c. Poulsen
    d. H.P. Singh

285. The genus named for honour of botanist belongs to Germany
    a. Traught Gerber
    b. E. Mayer

c. C. Lineaus

d. M.J. Schleiden

286. What is the pruning time of Rosa dama-scene?

a. December–March

b. December–February

c. December–January

d. December–June

287. What is National flower of Spain?

a. Carnation   b. Rose

c. Kamal   d. Sadabahar

288. Chrysanthemum morifolium belongs to dicotyledonous family

a. Araceae   **b. Asteraceae**

c. Agavaceae   d. Araliaceae

289. Polyanthas, ramblers and climber roses are multiplied by

a. Layering

b. Patch budding

c. Stem cutting

d. Root cutting

290. Very small-sized carmels are used for

a. Planting stock   b. Flower stock

c. Root stock   d. Leaf stock

291. Perpetual carnation is multiplied through

a. Root cutting   **b. Stem cutting**

c. Budding   d. Seeds

292. Stenting is a different method of propagation reported in

a. Rose   b. Sadabahar

c. Genda   d. Jamun

293. Which cultivar/s are of No-pinch No-stake type belong to genus Chrysanthemum?

a. Gandiji   b. Nehruji

c. Patelji

d. Appu, Mother Terasa Haldighati

294. Lilium longiflorum is commonly known as

a. Eastern lily   b. Tiger lily

c. Star lily   d. Mountain lily

295. National flower of China is

a. Rose   b. Gladiolus

c. Bougainvillea   **d. Chrysanthemum**

296. Gerbera flowers are recognized as

a. Umbel   **b. Capitulum**

c. Spadix   d. Raceme

297. Chrysanthemum is sign of royal life in which country of world?

a. India   b. Africa

c. Spain   **d. Japan**

298. If which is not a cultivar of gladiolus?

a. Tiara

b. Friendship

c. American beauty

d. Her Majesty

299. Exhibitors area not classified as in a flower show competition

a. Scientist

b. Amateur grower

c. Normal grower

d. Professional growers

300. The marigold seeds are black in colour and they counted about____seeds /g.

a. 399–650   **b. 300–350**

c. 500–650   d. 100–200

301. The optimum required spacing for African Marigold is

a. 40 × 30 cm   b. 30 × 20 cm

c. 30 × 30 cm   d. 20 × 20 cm

302. The common name of Lady Slipper orchids is

a. Paphiopedilum

b. Dendrobium

c. Phalaenopsis

d. Jewel orchids

303. Sowing seed rate of marigold is

a. 299 g/acre   b. 200 g/acre

c. 500 g/acre   d. 800 g/acre

304. Name of family in which Gaillaria placed?

a. Apocynaceae   b. Asteraceae

c. Compositae   d. Graminae

305. CO_2 concentration in greenhouse for rose cultivation should be
   a. 500–700 ppm **b. 1000–1500 ppm**
   c. 300–500 ppm d. 2500–3200 ppm

306. Hyponasty in leaves of Chrysanthemum is due to
   a. Gibberellic acid b. Cytokinin
   c. Auxins **d. Ethylene**

307. Which type of carnation grown on greenhouse on large scale?
   a. Perpetual
   b. Border and picotee
   c. Marguerite
   d. Malmaison

308. In case of quality production, which % of light interception are suitable?
   a. 40–50 b. 35–68
   c. 80–90 d. 90–100

309. Ideal location for greenhouse in plains
   a. North-East **b. North-South**
   c. South-West d. South-East

310. Most suitable cultivar of rose in greenhouses is
   a. First Red b. Konfetti
   c. Grand Galla **d. All**

311. In which of the following is not able to control the light intensity?
   a. Tarpaulin b. Black nylon
   c. White nylon
   d. Aluminium

312. In which of the following is qualitative short-day plant?
   a. Chrysanthemum
   b. Chameli
   c. Gulbahar
   d. All

313. Ajay and Pusa Anmol are Chrysanthemum cultivar which are
   a. Thermosensitive
   b. Thermosensitive and photosensitive
   c. Photoasensitive
   d. Photoinsensitive

314. In which of the following flower crops we should apply practice of bending?
   a. Gerbera
   b. Rose
   c. Chrysanthemum
   d. Lilium

315. Thickness of cladding material of greenhouse is generally
   a. 200 micron b. 1000 micron
   c. 500 micron d. 230 micron

316. Which % of water can be saved by the drip irrigation method?
   a. 20–30 b. 30–40
   c. 40–70 d. 10–15

317. Greenhouse cultivation is mostly applied for growing of
   a. Climers b. Angiosperms
   c. Lower plants **d. Cut flowers**

318. Greenhouse technology in India was firstly introduced by
   a. IAHS, Bengaluru
   b. NBPGR, New Delhi
   c. AMU, Aligarh
   d. BHU, Varanasi

319. In which the following cannot be a limiting factor?
   a. Water **b. O_2**
   c. Nutrients d. Light

319A. Which is the biological active form of phytochrome?
   a. Pfr b. Pr
   c. Both a and b d. None

320. Determination of available N in soils is done by
   a. Alkaline potassium permanganate method
   b. Lewis method
   c. Haber method d. All is correct

321. Determination of available P in soils is done by
   a. Alkaline potassium permanganate method

b. Bray's method
c. Olsen's method
d. Both b and c

322. Determination of available K in plants or soils is done by

  a. Flame photometer
  b. Bray's method
  c. Olsen's method
  d. Berger's method

323. Determination of lime requirement of acid soils is done by

  a. Shoemaker's method
  b. Bray's method
  c. Olsen's method
  d. Berger's method

324. Determination of gypsum requirement of sodic (alkali) soils is done by

  a. Schoonover's method
  b. Bray's method
  c. Olsen's method
  d. Berger's method

325. Determination of P in plant sample is done by

  a. Vanadomolybdate yellow colour method
  b. Bray's method
  c. Olsen's method
  d. Berger's method

326. The amount of total soluble salts in sample is generally expressed in terms of

  a. Sample's electrical conductivity
  b. Sample melting point
  c. Sample boiling point
  d. None

327. Quickest method of lawn making is

  a. Turfing   b. Dibbling
  c. Plastering   d. Seeding

328. In home garden total area under lawn should not be more than

  a. 30%   **b. 40%**
  c. 60%   d. 50%

329. Seed rate of lawn grass is ____ kg/ha.

  a. 10   b. 15
  c. 20   **d. 25**

330. Reclamation of acidic soil can be done by

  a. Gypsum   **b. Lime**
  c. Both a and b   d. None of the above

331. The best situation for lawn is

  a. South-East   b. West
  c. West-East   d. North-West

332. Brown patch on all the major

  a. *Gaeumannomyces graminis*
  b. *Rhizactonia solani*
  c. *Colletotrichium cereale*
  d. *Sclerotinia homoeocarpa*

333. Garden is considered incomplete without establishment of

  a. Lawn   b. Hedge
  c. Ground cover   d. Herbarium

334. Fairy rings disease in lawn is caused by which organism?

  a. *Marasmius ordeades*
  b. *Colletotrichium cereale*
  c. *Sclerotina homoeocarpa*
  d. None of the above

335. Most common weed of lawn grass is

  a. *Euphorbia thymefolia*
  b. *Cyperus rotundus*
  c. Both   d. None of the above

336. Rolling is done for

  a. Touch nodes with ground
  b. Killing of weeds
  c. Mixing of fertilizers
  d. To prevent excess growth of lawn

337. In a single mowing how much grass should be cut?

  a. 2/3   b. 1/4
  c. 1/3   d. 1/2

338. Raking is done for

  a. Mixing fertilizers
  b. Proper aeration

c. Levelling of ground
d. All of the above

339. Lawn mower is inverted by
    a. **Edwin budding** b. Edwin Aldrin
    c. Edwin Lutyens d. Edwin Abbott

340. Doob grass is a member of which family in plant kingdom?
    a. **Graminae** b. Asteraceae
    c. Apocyanaceae d. Rosaceae

341. Famous and commoneast, cheapeast method of lawn planting is
    a. **Dibbing** b. Bricking
    c. Turfing d. Plastering

342. Most widely used herbicide used for pre-emergence in lawn is
    a. **Glyphosphate B. Ronstar**
    b. Dacthal
    c. 2, 4-D
    d. All of the above

343. Establishment rate of cynodon dactylon is
    a. Medium b. Slow
    c. Fast d. **Very fast**

344. Cyanodon dactylon grass is what kind of texture?
    a. **Fine medium** b. Fine
    c. Medium coarse d. Coarse

345. Which is maximum tolerant power for shade?
    a. *Agrostis canina* b. *Axonopus affinis*
    c. *Agrostis alba* d. All of these

346. Turf grasss which is shade tolerant
    a. Festuca sp.
    b. St. Augustine grass
    c. **Both**
    d. None of the above

347. Root type in Doob grass is
    a. **Shallow rooted**
    b. Deep rooted
    c. Rootless
    d. Very highly deep rooted

348. Best irrigation method for lawn is
    a. **Over head sprinkler**
    b. Basin method
    c. Flooding
    d. Drip irrigation

349. Stem of lawn grass is known as
    a. Sheath b. **Culm**
    c. Rhizome d. Tiller

350. Flowering time of Gulmohar is
    a. Feb–March
    b. Aug–September
    c. October–November
    d. **May–June**

351. Which of the following flowering trees not bears yellow-coloured flowers?
    a. *Cassia nodosa* b. *Grevillea robusta*
    c. *Cassia fistula* d. *Cassia siamea*

352. Blue Jacaranda (*Jacaranda mimosifolia*) is a subtropical tree native to
    a. India b. **South-America**
    c. China d. South Africa

353. *Cassia nodosa* bears which colour flowers during April–May?
    a. **Pink** b. White
    c. Yellow d. Blue

354. *Grevillea robusta* bears which colour of flowers
    a. **Golden-yellow** b. Blue
    c. Pink d. Red

355. Which of the following shade trees is/are of Indian origin?
    a. *Fiscus religosa*
    b. *Terminaria arjuna*
    c. *Terminalia catappa*
    d. **All of the above**

356. The flowering time of *Cassia fistula*, *Cassia nodosa* and *Delonix regia* is
    a. **April–June**
    b. July–October
    c. January–March
    d. November–Feburary

357. *Terminalia arjuna* (tree of Arjun) is a member of which family
   a. **Combretaceae**   b. Bignoniaceae
   c. Leguminoceae   d. Moraceae

358. Dhak, Palas and flame of forest are the common names of which plant?
   a. **Butea monosperma**
   b. Bauhinia purpurea
   c. Lagerstroemia specicosa
   d. Jacaranda acutifolia

359. A particulae single tree planted in the center of garden for attraction is known as
   a. **Specimen tree**   b. Flowering tree
   c. Focal tree   d. Centre tree

360. Bombax ceiba is recognized as
   a. **Red silk cotton**   b. White silk cotton
   c. Black silk cotton d. Yellow silk cotton

361. Tree culture is a synonym of
   a. **Arboriculture**   b. Monoculture
   c. Both a and b   d. Multiculture

362. Which tree has drooping branches?
   a. *Delonix regia*
   b. *Polyalthia longifolia*
   c. *Salix babylonia*   d. **Both b and c**

363. *Polyalthia longifolia* is a plant of which family?
   a. **Annonaceae**   b. Mimosaceae
   c. Araucariaceae   d. Acearaceae

364. *Jacaranda mimosifolia* is a botanical name of
   a. Wild fire   b. **Blue Gulmohar**
   c. Amaltas   d. Red chille

365. Which of the following is a fine texture tree?
   a. Coral tree   b. Cassia
   c. Kanak champa   d. **Silver oak**

366. *Jacaranda acutifolia* belongs to which family of plant kingdom?
   a. **Bigoniaceae**   b. Leguminoceae
   c. Myrtaceae   d. None

367. *Bauhinia alba* (White Kachnar) is a symbol of
   a. Renewal of life   b. Life
   c. Immortality   d. **Youth and life**

368. *Jacaranda acutifolia* is a botanical name of
   a. Giul Mohar   b. **Nili Gulmohar**
   c. Red Gulmohar   d. Cora tree

369. Arboriculture is recognized for
   a. **Cultivation of trees for their aesthetic or recreational value**
   b. Cultivation of shrubs for fire materials
   c. Cultivation of herbs for fodder purposes
   d. All is correct

370. Which palm is planted for avenue purposes?
   a. *Licuala grandis*
   b. *Saraca indica*
   c. *Thrinax parviflora*
   d. *Phoenix rupicola*

371. Which ornamental tree act as specimen tree?
   a. *Cassia javanica*
   b. *Alstonia scholaris*
   c. *Araucaria columnaria*
   d. *Saraca indica*

372. In which of the following plants is suitable for small home garden?
   a. *Cassia nodosa*
   b. *Cassia javanica*
   c. *Casssia fistula*
   d. *Casssia siamea*

373. Which is the growth pattern of *Callistemon lanceolatus*?
   a. **Drooping**   b. Weeping
   c. Upright   d. Semi-pendulus

374. The botanical name of coral tree is
   a. *Erythrina indica*
   b. *Bauhinia varigata*
   c. *Sapium sebiferum*
   d. *Erythrina suberosa*

375. **Neem tree is a member of which family of plants kingdom?**
    a. **Meliaceae**   b. Moraceae
    c. Momoceae   d. Myrtaceae

376. **Indian Botanical Garden, Sibpur, Culcutta is famous for**
    a. **Location of oldest banyan tree**
    b. Location of Sunderban
    c. Location of oldest pepal treee
    d. Location of advanced banyan tree

377. **Mughal considered which plant as symbol of death and eternity**
    a. **Cypress**   b. Kachnar
    c. Ashok   d. Palas

378. **Name of Emperor planted avenue trees along grand trunk road from Calcutta to Lahore**
    a. **Sher Shah Suri (1540–1544 AD)**
    b. Ashok (264–227 BC)
    c. Ibrahim Lodhi (1526–AD)
    d. Feroz Shah Tuglak (1351–1388 AD)

379. **Lord Krishna is concerned with which tree?**
    a. *Bauhinia variegata*
    b. *Cicer arietinum*
    c. *Vigna radiata*
    d. *Anthocephalus cadamba*

380. **The Enlightenment of Lord Budha is concerned with which tree?**
    a. *Ficus religiosa*
    b. *Saraca indica*
    c. *Vigna radiata*
    d. *Bauhinia variegata*

381. **World Forest Day and World Environment Day is celebrated respectively**
    a. **March, 21 and June, 5**
    b. March, 5 and June, 21
    c. March, 1 and June, 7
    d. March, 2 and June, 15

382. **Which of the following has fine texture foliage?**
    a. Jacardanda   b. Silver oak
    c. Deodar   d. **All of the above**

383. **In which of the following is a summer deciduous?**
    a. **Cassia fistula**   b. Casssia siames
    c. Saraca indica   d. None of the above

384. **The biggest formal garden of India is**
    a. National Botanical garden
    b. **Brindhavan garden**
    c. Nishat Bagh
    d. Lal Bagh garden

385. **Presence of running water is feature of which style of garden?**
    a. **Formal garden**   b. Informal
    c. Free   d. Wild

386. **White flower plants are grown in which gardens?**
    a. **Night garden**   b. Water garden
    c. Publich garden   d. Bottle garden

387. **Which garden is located at Kaveri river of India**
    a. **Brindhavan garden**
    b. National Botanical garden
    c. Sibpur Botanical garden
    d. None of the above

388. **Free style of garden is exhibited by the**
    a. **Rose garden of Ludhiana**
    b. Zakir Husssain rose garden of Chandigarh
    c. Both   d. None of the above

389. **The concept of informal garden is**
    a. Rockery
    b. Path are either striaight or curved
    c. **Imitate the nature**
    d. Shrubs and tree

390. **Rock garden of Chandigarh was created by**
    a. Ranjeet Singh   b. Bhupinder Singh
    c. Sansaar Chand   d. **Nek Chand Saini**

391. **Specific feature of Mughal garden were**
    a. **Walls and gate**
    b. Pond
    c. Herbs and shrubs
    d. Parking

392. Largest banyan tree in the world is found at
    a. **Indian Botanical garden, Culcutta**
    b. NBRI, Lko
    c. Pune University
    d. Aligarh Muslim University

393. Garden of Rashtrapati Bhavan is a type of
    a. Hindu type
    b. **Mughal type**
    c. Japanese type
    d. English type

394. Asaf Khan established the
    a. Naseem Bagh
    b. **Nishat Bagh**
    c. Mughal garden, Bangalore
    d. Dal Lake

395. Budha Jayanti park is characterized by the feature of
    a. Running water
    b. Staging water
    c. Herbs and shrubs
    d. Natural flora

396. Main features of Mughal garden are
    a. Baradari
    b. Terminal building
    c. Running water
    d. **All**

397. Budhist garden originated in
    a. India
    b. Thailand
    c. **Japan**
    d. China

398. Nature is miniature is theme of which garden?
    a. **Japanese**
    b. Mughal
    c. English
    d. Italian

399. Mughal garden is a replica of which garden?
    a. **Persian garden**
    b. Italian
    c. Japanese garden
    d. English

400. For formal gardening style the site is seleceted according to
    a. **Plan**
    b. Land
    c. Environment
    d. All of the above

13

Agricultural Economics and Farm Management

1. Alternate host of *Paccinia gramaminis triticii* is
   a. **Berberis**
   b. Chickpea
   c. Zea mays
   d. Sorghum bicolor

2. Organic matter generally contains ___% organic corbon.
   a. 45
   b. **58**
   c. 87
   d. 64

3. What is the percentage of nitrogen in urea?
   a. 47
   b. 87
   c. **46**
   d. 23

4. Mousam Bhavan is located at
   a. **New Delhi**
   b. Aligarh
   c. Rampur
   d. Bareilly

5. Which is called a herbicide?
   a. Cuper-sulphate
   b. Silver nitrate
   c. **Glyphosate**
   d. Nitric oxide

6. Trysem was introduced in the year
   a. 1976
   b. 1986
   c. 1956
   d. **1979**

7. High Yieding Variety Program was launched in
   a. 1954
   b. 1965
   c. **1969**
   d. 1954

8. The chairman of national development of council in India
   a. President of country
   b. Foreign Minister
   c. Prime Minister
   d. Finance Minister

9. NARP was launched by
   a. **Govt. of India in 1979**
   b. Govt. of UP in 1979
   c. Govt. of MP in 1979
   d. Govt. of WB in 1979

10. Director General, ICAR
    a. Dr BP Pandey
    b. **Dr Mangla Ray**
    c. Dr GA Munday
    d. AA Khan

11. Largest state in India
    a. MP
    b. WB
    c. **Rajasthan**
    d. UP

12. Father of hybrid rice
    a. **Y L Ping**
    b. YL Jiang
    c. YL Teixeria
    d. AN Xeria

13. A day neutral plant is
    a. Rice
    b. Wheat
    c. **Maize**
    d. Soya bean

14. Famous Indian pathologist, extensively studied about cereal rust
    a. **KC Mehta**
    b. MC Thakur
    c. AA Khan
    d. None of the above

15. Grey speck out is due to the deficiency of
    a. Zn   **b. Mn**
    c. Pb   d. Cd

16. Prominent foul smell of karnal bunt is due to
    a. Trimethyl amine
    b. MIC
    c. Urea   d. H_2SO_4

17. Prominent foul smell of karnal is due to
    a. MIC
    b. Urea
    c. Trimethyl amine
    d. None

18. The most important process in chemical weathering
    a. Polymerization
    b. Hydrolysis
    c. Ozonization
    d. Alkalinization

19. Vector of leaf curl disease of cotton and tobacco
    a. TMV   b. CMV
    c. Bemesia tabaci   d. All

20. Vector of tomato spotted wilt
    a. TMV   **b. Thrim tabaci**
    c. CMV   d. *E coli*

21. The level to which given pest population should be reduced to achieve the point where marginal revenue just exceeds marginal cost
    a. MTL   b. CTL
    c. ETL   d. PTL

22. Reagent used for the extraction of phosphorus in alkaline soils
    a. Olesen's reagent
    b. Haber's reagent
    c. Both
    d. Hen's reagent

23. Pusat delicious is which ype of papaya
    a. Androecious   b. Bisexual
    c. Gynecious   d. Monoecious

24. The first insect resistant variety under hill is related to
    a. Wheat   **b. Rice**
    c. Mays   d. Brassica

25. Odomos is the mosquito repellent contains
    a. $CuSO_4$ **b. Pyrithrin**
    c. $MgSO_4$ d. $CaCO_3$

26. Which among the following is not a correct?
    a. Rice   **b. Wheat**
    c. Gram   d. Maize

27. India has monopoly in the production of
    a. Muga silk
    b. Pond silk
    c. Both
    d. None of the above

28. The pest which is a result feature and confined to a particular locality
    a. Epidemic   **b. Endemic**
    c. Pendemic   d. All

29. Bundle sheath chloroplast
    a. Lack stroma
    b. Lack granna
    c. Lack both
    d. Lack stromal membrane

30. High auxin and low cytokinin favours
    a. Shoot   b. Leaf
    c. Root
    d. All is above

31. Precursor of ethylene
    a. Methionine   b. Cysteine
    c. Phenylalanine   d. Tyrosine

32. Kranz anatomy is seen in
    a. Wheat   b. Rice
    c. Amaranthus   d. Brassica

33. An international pest
    a. Helicoverpa
    b. Meloidogyne incognita
    c. Meloidogyne javanica
    d. Both b and c

34. Corbohydrate factory of cell is
a. Mitochondria
b. Chloroplast
c. Endoplasmic reticulum
d. Vacuoles

35. In photorespiration NH_3 evolution take place at
a. Chloroplast
b. Endoplasmic reticulum
c. Mitochondria   d. ER

36. Organelles involved in photorespiration
a. Chloroplast, mitochondria, peroxisome
b. Chloroplast, mitochondria, ER
c. Chloroplast, ER, peroxisome
d. Chloroplast, vacuole, peroxisome

37. Which is a total root parasite?
a. Cuscutta   **b. Rafflesia**
c. Both   d. Artemisia

38. Partial size of colloids is (in microns)
a. 1–10   b. 1–1000
c. 1–100   d. 1–10000

39. Term genetics was coined by
a. Bateson   b. Mendel
c. Weisman   d. Johanssen

40. Components of prokaryotic ribosome are
a. 40s and 30s   **b. 50s and 30s**
c. 40s and 90s   d. None of the above

41. Plasma membrane is
a. Selectively permeable
b. Permanent permeable
c. Both   d. None of the above

42. ABO blood group is an example of
a. Single allele   **b. Multiple alleles**
c. Triple alleles   d. None of the above

43. In which of the following is a sex limited character?
a. Ear hair   b. Nose hair
c. Baldnees   d. Head hair

44. The most common form of DNA is
a. A-DNA   **b. B-DNA**
c. C-DNA   d. E-DNA

45. Replication of DNA is
a. Partial conservative
b. Fully conservative
c. Semi conservative
d. None of the above

46. Which is the first cotton hybrid?
a. H4   b. H1
c. H3   d. H5

47. The wheat and maize improvement centre is located at
a. USA   b. Canada
c. Mexico   d. Pakistan

48. In cereals, grain starch is consists of
a. Starch, glucose
b. Amylopectin, amylase
c. Glycogen, fructose
d. Lignin, galactose

49. The national agricultural insurance scheme was started in
a. 2000–2010
b. 2010–2015
c. 1999–2000
d. 2005–2010

50. Loose shut disease of wheat is a
a. Seed born   b. Leave born
c. Root born   d. None of the above

51. Flaver Savr is a variety of
a. Wheat   **b. Tomato**
c. Maize   d. Rice

52. Cotton leaf curl virus is transmitted by
a. Housefly   b. Viruses
c. Whitefly   d. Bacteria

53. The region in India where boron deficiency is mostly occurs
a. SW region
b. Western region
c. Eastern region
d. NW region

54. The brown box dots on food package indicates

a. **Organically produce product**
b. Inorganically produce product
c. Without organic fertilizer used product
d. Solar energy produce product

55. The first DG of ICAR was

a. Dr AA Khan
b. **Dr BP Pal**
c. Dr MS Swaminathan
d. Dr N Bourlag

56. Land resources in India as a whole world is

a. 4%   b. 3%
c. **2%**   d. 6%

57. The soil order vartisol is related to

a. Laterite soil   b. Red soil
c. Both   d. **Black soil**

58. Which transgenic crop has maximum cultivated area in the world?

a. **Soybean**   b. Corn
c. Rice   d. Wheat

59. The estimate food grain production during 2004–05 as per economic survey is

a. 312 mt   b. **212 mt**
c. 215 mt   d. 245 mt

60. Which state has a maximum area in fruit production?

a. UP   b. MP
c. **Maharashtra**   d. WB

61. The statistical test used to determine the goodness of fit is

a. **Chi-square test**
b. Student t-test
c. Student z-test
d. SD test

62. The cartigen quato protocol for agriculture product was came in the year of

a. 2009   b. **2005**
c. 2006   d. 2008

63. The citrus canker disease of lemon was introduced in India from

a. Germany   b. Canada
c. **USA**   d. India

64. The organization related to export of agricultural producessed product is

a. **APEDA**   b. AMU
c. BHU   d. AGU

65. Ultracultivation is precticed mainly in

a. Bangalore   b. **Chhattisgarh**
c. J & K   d. UP

66. In the pulse crops, which fertilizer is advised to basal application?

a. DAP   b. Urea
c. **SSP**   d. $KMNO_4$

67. Which is not a greenhouse gas?

a. **N_2**   b. O_2
c. CO_2 d. H_2SO_4

68. The agricultural and allied commodity has maximum contribution to GDP

a. Butter   b. **Milk**
c. Pulses   d. Grains

69. The contribution of agriculture in GDP is

a. 34%   b. 45%
c. **23%**   d. 68%

70. The soil amendment mainly used for reclamation of sodic (alkali) soil is

a. **Gypsum**   b. $CaCO_3$
c. $MgSO_4$ d. HNO_3

71. The political personality who got Norman Borlaug award

a. **Subramanium**   b. Tayagi
c. GP Rathore   d. None of the above

72. The biogas has major content with CO_2 is

a. N_2 b. **CH_4**
c. CO_2 d. H_2O

73. IVLP stands for

a. Institute village link process
b. Institute village link programmes

c. Institute village linkage programme

d. Institute village link principles

74. The most common method of hybridization for wheat is

a. Gogo method   b. Haber process

c. Both   d. Natural method

75. Hatch and stack pathway is pound in

a. Rice   **b. Maize**

c. Wheat   d. None

76. Alternate host of *Paccinia gramaminis triticii* is

a. Rice   b. Maize

c. Berberis   d. Tomato

77. TRYSEM was introduced in the year

a. 1979   b. 1987

c. 1980   d. 1985

78. First discovered bacterial disease plants

a. Late blight   b. Early blight

c. Both   d. Diphtheria

79. A day neutral plant is

a. Wheat   **b. Maize**

c. Chickpea   d. Brassica

80. An international pest

a. Meloidogyne   b. Cuscutta

c. Helicoverpa   d. All is correct

81. Term genetics was coined by

a. Bateson   b. Mendel

c. Johanassen   d. Weisman

82. The most common form of DNA is

a. C-DNA   **b. B-DNA**

c. A-DNA   d. All is correct

83. Whip tail of cauliflower is the deficiency of

a. Cu   b. Cd

c. Mo   d. Pb

84. NRC for orchids is at

a. Gangtok

b. Himachal Pradesh

c. Uttar Pradesh

d. Madhya Pradesh

85. Which represents Midian?

a. First quartile

b. Third quartile

c. Both

d. Second quartile

86. The relation between AM, GM , HM

a. AM > GM > HM

b. AM < GM < HM

c. AM > GM < HM

d. All is correct

87. Which is the Indian sugarcane?

a. S. Berberea   b. S. Tamilli

c. Both   d. None

88. Concentration of corbon dioxide in atmosphere

a. 370 ppm   b. 340 ppm

c. 320 ppm   d. 310 ppm

89. Which is macroni wheat?

a. T. aceticum   **b. T. Durum**

c. Both   d. None

90. In rice crop which biofertilizer is commonly used?

a. Noctoc   b. Ocillatoria

c. Azolla   d. All

91. Which is the monophagus pest?

a. Rice hispa

b. *Meloidogyne incognita*

c. *Meloidogyne javanica*

d. *Puccinia graminis*

92. Central Agmark Laboratory is located at

a. Mumbai   **b. Nagpur**

c. Bareilly   d. Kanpur

93. Silver shoot is due to

a. Brown midge

b. Gall midge

c. Both   d. None

94. Loose smut of wheat is

a. Physiologically seed born

b. Externary seed born

c. Internary seed born

d. All is correct

95. Polymer of different monosaccharides is termed as
    a. Heteropolysaccharides
    b. Homopolysaccharides
    c. Structural polysaccharides
    d. None of the above

96. Which sequence of minerals is correct as per their degree of decreasing weathering resistance?
    a. Quartz < Muscovite < Gypsum > Olyvine
    b. **Quartz < Muscovite < Gypsum < Olyvine**
    c. Quartz < Muscovite > Gypsum < Olyvine
    d. Quartz > Muscovite < Gypsum < Olyvine

97. Vitamin B_{12} contains
    a. **Co**   b. Cr
    c. Cd   d. Cu

98. KVK was started in
    a. 1990   b. 1989
    c. **1974**   d. 1987

99. Which is the only carbohydrate of animal origin in means food supply?
    a. **Glycogen**   b. Starch
    c. Lignin   d. Suberin

100. MOYLA disease is caused due to
    a. Viruses   b. **Nematode**
    c. Bacteria   d. Fungi

101. The statistical test used to determine the goodness of fit is
    a. **Chi-square test** b. F-test
    c. T-test   d. Both b and c

102. The cartigen quato protocol for agriculture product was came in the year of
    a. **1998**   b. 2000
    c. 2002   d. 20009

103. Components of prokaryotic ribosome are
    a. 40s and 70s   b. 50s and 50s
    c. **60s and 40s** d. 30s and 40s

104. Plasma membrane is
    a. Selectively permeable
    b. Partial permeable
    c. Both
    d. None of the above

105. Pahala blight of sugarcane is due to the deficiency of
    a. **Mn**   b. Zn
    c. Mg   d. Ca

106. How many member countries there in WTO from ibtail to till January 2007?
    a. 200   b. **150**
    c. 230   d. 400

107. Random or free segregation chromosomes and genes during gamete formation is known as
    a. Law of dominance
    b. Law of segregation
    c. **Low of independent assortment**
    d. None of the above

108. OBA blood group controlled by
    a. **Multiple alleles**
    b. Epistasis
    c. Criss-cross inheritance
    d. Law of segregation

109. Citrus canker is caused by
    a. Virus   b. **Bacteria**
    c. Fungi   d. protozoa

110. Which is not a monosaccharide in nature?
    a. Laevulose   b. Fructose
    c. **Lactose**   d. Glucose

111. Availability of which form of P is highest at pH 6.7?
    a. H_2PP_4 b. H_2PO_3
    c. H_2PO_5 d. H_2PO_6

112. Conservation tillage saves
    a. **Soil moisture and time**
    b. Soil moisture only
    c. Time only
    d. None of the above

113. Nobel prize for micro-credit was given to
    a. APJ Abdul Kalam
    b. Mohammad Yunus
    c. Naseem Ahmed
    d. Both a and b

114. Which is formula of leaf area index?
    a. Root area/ground area
    b. Stem area/ground area
    c. Leaf area/ground area
    d. Both a and b

115. Pure line theory was given by
    a. Johansen   b. Mendel
    c. Weismann   d. Bateson

116. Exanthema disease is caused by deficiency of
    a. Mg   **b. Cu**
    c. Ca   d. B

117. Contribution of animal husbandry in agriculture GDP is
    a. 23%   b. 12%
    c. 17%   d. 20%

118. In which type of soil low permeability is present?
    a. Alkali   b. Acidic
    c. Both   d. Neutral

119. Which is a P solubilizing bacterium?
    a. SSB   **b. PSB**
    c. Thiobacillus   d. Bacillus

120. Which is natural genetic engineer?
    a. *Agrobacterium tumefaciens*
    b. *Bacillus thuriengensis*
    c. *Pseudomonas perpurea*
    d. Nostoc

121. In maize first product formed during photosynthesis is
    a. Pyruvic acid   b. Maleic acid
    c. Oxalic acid   d. Fumeric acid

122. Which amino acid is positively charged
    a. Lysine   b. Cysteine
    c. Leucine   d. Tyrocine

123. Translocation of nutrient and water through xylem is due to
    a. Mesophyll cell
    b. Bundle sheath cell
    c. Both
    d. Parenchyma cells

124. How was the chairman of formers commission till December 2006?
    a. MS Swaminathan
    b. Sarad Pawar
    c. Mamta Banerjee
    d. Manmohan Singh

125. Which instrument used for land leveling?
    a. Khurpi   b. Patella
    c. Bhopal leveller d. Knife

126. Water held between 1/3 bar to 31 bars in the soil is classified as
    a. Capillary water
    b. Gravitational water
    c. Hygroscopic water
    d. Soil water

127. Chloropyriphos belongs to which group
    a. Super phosphate
    b. Organophosphate
    c. Diammonium phosphate
    d. Ammonium phosphate

128. Why rice grown easily under submerged condition?
    a. CO_2 transfer from root to shoot
    b. N_2 transfer from root to shoot
    c. O_2 transfer from stem to root
    d. None of the above

129. Global warming potential of methane (CH_4) in composition to CO_2 is_____ (times).
    a. 21   b. 2
    c. 3   d. 8

130. Father of hybrid rice
    a. MS Swaminathan
    b. YL Ping
    c. Both
    d. N Bouerlag

131. A day neutral plant is
   a. Wheat
   b. Rice
   c. Maize
   d. Sugarcane

132. Famous Indian pathologist extensively studied about cereal rust
   a. KC Mehta
   b. Prof KC Tripathi
   c. MMRK Afridi
   d. RD Mishra

133. Which represents median
   a. Secound quartile, 5 deciles
   b. First quartile, 4 deciles
   c. AM > GM > HM
   d. AM > GM < HM

134. Which is measure of dispersion?
   a. Mean
   b. Standard deviation
   c. Standard error
   d. All of the above

135. Ear cockle disease is due to
   a. *Puccinia graminis*
   b. *Anguina tritici*
   c. *Puccinia triticina*
   d. All of the above

136. Support price fixed on the recommendation of
   a. NAWARD
   b. ICAR
   c. CACP
   d. All of the above

137. Vitamin B_1 is also known as
   a. Thiamine
   b. Riboflavin
   c. Ascorbic acid
   d. Carotene

138. Price fixed by government recently for agricultural products
   a. Maximum support price
   b. Minimum support price
   c. Average support price
   d. Less than average price

139. If farmer has only one irrigation is available for wheat crop, at which stage it is recommended?
   a. SRI
   b. PRI
   c. CRI
   d. LRI

140. Which is not biocontrol agent?
   a. Xanthomonas
   b. Bacillus
   c. Pseudomonas
   d. Rhizobium

141. Which is complex phosphate?
   a. DAP
   b. SSP
   c. Urea ammonium phosphate
   d. $KMNO_4$

142. IVLP stands for
   a. Institute village linkage programme
   b. Institute village linkage process
   c. Institute village link programme
   d. None of the above

143. In which type of soil low permeability is present?
   a. Acid
   b. Alkali
   c. Neutral
   d. None of the above

144. Which is a P solubilizing bacterium?
   a. Thiobacillus
   b. PSB
   c. Pseudomonas
   d. Rhizobium

145. Which is natural genetic engineer?
   a. *Bacillus thuriengensis*
   b. *Rhizobium leguminoserum*
   c. *Agrobacterium tumefaciens*
   d. All of the above

146. N-fixing enzymes are
   a. NR
   b. NiR
   c. N-ase
   d. All is above

147. OBA blood group controlled by
   a. Single allele
   b. Double alleles
   c. Multiple alleles
   d. Epistasis

148. Citrus canker is caused by
   a. Bacteria
   b. Viruses
   c. Fungi
   d. Mycoplasma

149. Which is not a monosaccharide in nature?
   a. Glucose
   b. Fructose
   c. Lactose
   d. Lavulose

150. Which is macroni wheat?
   a. *T. aestivum*
   b. *T. durum*
   c. Both
   d. None of the above

151. In rice crop which biofertilizer is commonly used?
  a. Ocillatoria   b. Nostoc
  c. Azolla   d. Chara

152. Who discovered Bordeaux mixture?
  a. Millardet
  b. Haber
  c. Os-Wald and Tippo
  d. Mendel

153. Which is the monophagus pest?
  a. Helicoverpa
  b. Rice hispa
  c. Meloidogyne spp.
  d. Silver pest

154. Silver shoot is due to
  a. Meloidogyne incognita
  b. Meloidogyne javanica
  c. Gall midge
  d. Cotton bollworm

155. Loose smut of wheat is
  a. Internary seed born
  b. Externary seed born
  c. Both
  d. Physiological seed born

156. TRYSEM was introduced in the year
  a. 1987   **b. 1979**
  c. 1985   d. 1973

157. First discovered bacterial disease plants
  a. Early blight   b. Citrus canker
  c. Late blight   d. All is correct

158. In the pulse crops, which fertilizer is advised to basal application?
  a. DAP   b. AMP
  c. SSP   d. None of the above

159. Which is not a greenhouse gas?
  a. CO_2 b. H_2
  c. N_2 d. CH_4

160. The contribution of agriculture in GDP is
  a. 23%   b. 25%
  c. 12%   d. 76%

161. Which crop is known as wonder crop?
  a. Millets   b. Soya bean
  c. Mung   d. Chick pea

162. The National Agricultural Insurance Scheme was started in
  a. 1999–2000   b. 2003–2004
  c. 2008–2010   d. 2004–2015

163. Loose shut disease of wheat is a / an
  a. Leaf born   b. Root born
  c. Seed born d. All is correct

164. "Flower Savr" is a variety of
  a. Wheat   b. Rice
  c. Tomato   d. Maize

165. Highest procurement of wheat in 2009 was _____ million tonnes.
  a. 17.8   b. 20.8
  c. 21.3   d. 22.6

166. Contribution of agriculture to GDP is
  a. 45   b. 56
  c. 22   d. 20

167. IVLP stands for
  a. Institute village linkage process
  b. Institute village link programme
  c. Institute village linkage programme
  d. None of the above

168. Which is major constituent of poultry feed?
  a. Maize   b. Rice
  c. Wheat   d. Maize

169. In binomial distribution
  a. Mean < variance
  b. Mean > variance
  c. Mean = variance
  d. All is correct

170. Bordeaux mixture is
  a. Ploughing   b. Levelling
  c. Harrowing d. Mixing

171. National Bureau for the genetic resource (NBFGR) is situated at
  a. Lucknow   b. Delhi
  c. Hyderabad   d. Bareilly

172. **Which is not biocontrol agent?**
    a. Bacillus   **b. Xanthomonas**
    c. Pseudomonas   d. Rhizobium

173. **Which is complex fertilizer?**
    a. DAP
    b. SSP
    c. Urea ammonium phosphate
    d. Urea

174. **Soil having ESP (exchangeable sodium percentage) greater than 15 are**
    a. Alkali soil   b. Basic soil
    c. Acidic soil   d. None of the above

175. **Rain, moist, fog and cloud all these phenomena occurs in**
    a. Stratosphere   **b. Troposphere**
    c. Mesosphere   d. Both a and c

176. **Farming system is**
    a. Substantial   b. Partial
    c. All agril, inputs and commodities
    d. Subsidiary

177. **Which nutrient helps in biological nitrogen fixation?**
    a. Mn   b. Fe
    c. Mo   d. Pb

178. **Silt is intermediate between**
    a. Sand and clay   b. Only clay
    c. Only sand   d. None of the above

179. **First CO_2 acceptor C4 pathway**
    a. RuBP oxygenase
    b. RuBP carboxylase
    c. Aldohexose
    d. PEPcase

180. **From 1960s onword which operation is in effect for milk?**
    a. Operation drought
    b. Operation desert
    c. Operation flood
    d. Both a and b

181. **CIMMYTworks on**
    a. Maize and wheat
    b. Rice and wheat
    c. Rice and maize
    d. Maize and wheat

182. **Which is highly salt tolerant fruit crop?**
    a. Bottle palm   b. Glass palm
    c. Date palm   d. None of the above

183. **Price fixed by government recently for agricultural products**
    a. Minimum support price
    b. Maximum support price
    c. Average support price
    d. Low support price

184. **If farmer has only one irrigation is available for wheat crop, at which stage it is recommended?**
    a. FDI   **b. CRI**
    c. Both   d. None of the above

185. **Which one of the diseases occurring regularly in the same area?**
    a. Epidemic   b. Pandemic
    c. Endemic   d. All is correct

186. **Which is essential component of nucleic acid and protein?**
    a. N   b. P
    c. K   d. Mg

187. **Widely cultivated wheat species in India after *T. durum***
    a. *T. monoecius*   **b. *T. diococcum***
    c. *T. duraum*   d. All is correct

188. **Banana is**
    a. Allopolyploid   b. Heteropolyploid
    c. Autotriploid   d. Hybrid vigour

189. **Which crop in India has maximum area under irrigation?**
    a. Wheat   b. Rice
    c. Maize   d. Sorghum

190. **Which is not found in plant cell?**
    a. Starch   **b. Glycogen**
    c. Sucrose   d. Fructose

191. **Family of cotton is**
    a. Malvaceae   b. Cucurbiataceae
    c. Crucifereae   d. Asteraceae

192. Certified seed is produced from
- a. Original seeds obtained from harvested crops
- b. Seeds from mature plants
- **c. Foundation seed**
- d. Artificial seeds

193. In prophase which is correct
- a. Crossing over
- b. Synopsis
- **c. Elongated threads like chromosome**
- d. All is correct

194. Study of fish is called
- **a. Limnology**
- b. Herpetology
- c. Mineralogy
- d. Hydrology

195. The GM crops have highest area in order of preference
- a. Insecticide than herbicide resistance
- **b. Herbicide than insecticide resistance**
- c. Drought than flood resistance
- d. Pesticide than drought resistance

196. AADHAR indicates
- **a. Unique identification card**
- b. Formal identity proof
- c. Public-based identification
- d. College-based identification

197. Artificial bacteria culture is developed by
- a. C Gram
- **b. Dr Kraig Ventor**
- c. S Weisman
- d. L Pasteur

198. Blue tag in insecticide is for indication of
- a. High toxicity
- b. Low toxicity
- **c. Moderate toxicity**
- d. Neutral toxicity

199. Which is Indian origin fruit crop?
- a. Apricot
- b. Bananas
- **c. Jackruit**
- d. Apple

200. For virus free seed areas are
- a. Root tip
- b. Shoot tip
- **c. Meristems tip**
- d. All is correct

14

Agriculture Extension

1. The origin place of potato is
   a. **South America**
   b. East America
   c. North America
   d. None of these

2. In furrow method of irrigation
   a. Only 1/3 of furrow is wetted
   b. **Only 3/4 of the furrow is wetted**
   c. Only 1/4 of furrow is wetted
   d. None of these

3. Maximum yield of mustard is obtained in a plant geometry of
   a. 30 × 20 cm   b. 45 × 20 cm
   c. **45 × 40 cm**   d. None of these

4. An example of companion cropping is
   a. Sugarcane + wheat
   b. Sugarcane + rice
   c. **Sugarcane + potato**
   d. None of these

5. Intercultural operations in groundnut is avoided at
   a. **Pegging stages**
   b. Fruiting stages
   c. Flowering stages
   d. None of these

6. Agriculture Price Commission was constitute in
   a. 1960   b. 1962
   c. **1965**   d. None of these

7. The Trade Union Act was enacted in
   a. **1920**   b. 1926
   c. 1930   d. None of these

8. State having highest forest area is
   a. Uttar Pradesh   b. Rajasthan
   c. **Madhya Pradesh**
   d. None of these

9. Aruna is mutant variety of
   a. Mustard   b. Wheat
   c. **Castor**   d. None of these

10. PDM 11 is a variety of
    a. Chick pea   b. Black gram
    c. Urd   d. **Arhar**

11. For notification the optimum pH is
    a. 6.5   b. 7.5
    c. **8.5**   d. None of these

12. Pushameghali is an improved variety of
    a. Brinjal   b. **Carrot**
    c. Potato   d. Tomato

13. Varsha Upahar is a variety of
    a. **Okra**   b. Tomato
    c. Potato   d. None of these

14. Indian society of agronomy was established in
    a. 1950   b. 1952
    c. **1955**   d. None of these

15. Golden revolution is associated with
    a. **Horticulture**
    b. Wheat revolution

c. Okra revolution
d. None of these

16. Food Corporation of India was came into existence on
a. 1935   b. 1950
c. 1955   **d. 1965**

17. ADT- 45 is a popular variety of
a. Rice   b. Maize
c. Wheat   d. Soya bean

18. The agriculture produce and marketing Act was passed in
a. 1930   **b. 1937**
c. 1940   d. 1947

19. The Indian Science Congress was found in
a. 1914   b. 1917
c. 1920   d. 1922

20. Every year World Food Day is celebrate on
a. 14th October   **b. 16th October**
c. 18th October   d. None of these

21. In India, the productivity of banana is highest in
a. West Bengal   **b. Tamil Nadu**
c. Assam   d. Maharashtra

22. Irrigation efficiency of loamy soil is
a. 40%   b. 60%
c. 70%   d. None of these

23. The anti-sterility vitamin is
a. Vitamin A   b. Vitamin B
c. Vitamin E   d. Vitamin K

24. Hard fruit of citrus is due to the deficiency of
a. Ca   **b. B**
c. P   d. N

25. Seed rate of sugarcane when 3 budded sets are used
a. 80000 sets/ha
b. 120000 sets/ha
c. 35000 sets/ha
d. None of these

26. Normal sea surface temperature is
a. 20°C   b. 22°C
c. 23°C   d. None of these

27. Excess amount of sodium causes deficiency of
a. Ca   b. B
c. P   d. Cu

28. Sweetest sugar in fruit is
a. Sucrose   b. Glucose
c. Fructose   d. None of these

29. The fat content in rice plant is
a. 1–1.5%   **b. 2–2.5%**
c. 3–3.5%   d. None of these

30. The protein content in milled rice is
a. 4.5%   b. 5.0%
c. 6.7%   d. None of these

31. Pollen sterility is a serious problem in
a. Pineapple   b. Apple
c. Ber   d. None of these

32. Photos I compulsion plays an important role in loss of urea herbicides from soil surface, which is
a. Moist   **b. Dry**
c. Both a and b   d. None of these

33. The crop stages which are more prone to weed competition is
a. Germination to seedling
b. Vegetative
c. Reproductive
d. All of these

34. Pf refers to logarithm of
a. Logarithm H ion concentration
b. Logarithm of free flow water
c. Soil moisture tension
d. Logarithm of salt concentration

35. An instrument used for indirect measurement of soil moisture is
a. Electron moisture meter
b. Positron moisture meter
c. Proton moisture meter
d. Neutron moisture meter

36. The law of diminishing return was proposed by
    a. Wilcox
    b. **Mitscherliah**
    c. Blackman
    d. None of these

37. DRIS approach for recommending fertilizer schedule is based on analysis
    a. Soil sample
    b. Water sample
    c. **Plant sample**
    d. None of these

38. The crop which is more tolerant against drought is
    a. Green gram
    b. Black gram
    c. Moth gram
    d. **Cowpea**

39. Photo thermal unit is related to
    a. **Day degrees**
    b. Average 1 monthly temperature
    c. Reflected solar radiation
    d. Daily sunshine hours

40. Ammonia presents in the soil can be lost in significant quantities from
    a. Acid soils
    b. **Alkaline soil**
    c. Saline soil
    d. Both a and c

41. Drip irrigation is moist suitable for
    a. Acid soil
    b. Alkaline soil
    c. **Saline soil**
    d. Both a and b

42. The optimum plant population of sorghum for seed purpose can be obtained by using seed rate of
    a. 10–12 kg/ha
    b. **12–15 kg/ha**
    c. 15–20 kg/ha
    d. None of these

43. The practice which is not related to the crop
    a. Jute: Retting
    b. **Wheat: Picking**
    c. Groundnut: Pegging
    d. Maize: Tasseling

44. Castor belongs to the family
    a. Leguminosae
    b. Compositae
    c. **Euphorbiaceae**
    d. None of these

45. The optimum number of treatments studied in Latin square design is
    a. 2–4
    b. **5–12**
    c. 5–15
    d. 5–20

46. When the calculated F is greater than tabulated F value is 5% only, the difference in treatment is consider
    a. **Significant**
    b. Nonsignificant
    c. Highly significant
    d. None of these

47. The alternate land use system which is not suitable on cultivable waste and marginal lands is
    a. Pasture management
    b. Tree farming
    c. Timber and fiber system
    d. **Timber system**

48. Rainbow revolution refers to
    a. **Overall development of agriculture sector**
    b. Increase in food grain production
    c. Productive performance of agriculture over time
    d. None of these

49. Weed that has become an integral part of a crop ecosystem is called
    a. Noxious weed
    b. Alien weed
    c. Objectionable weed
    d. **Satellite weed**

50. Removal of weeds by cutting of below the soil surface is called
    a. Chaining
    b. Mowing
    c. **Spudding**
    d. None of these

51. SSP is a
    a. Alkali producing
    b. Acid forming
    c. **Neutral fertilizer**
    d. All of these

52. Ammonium thiosulphate is a
    a. Slow release N-fertilizer
    b. **Urease inhibitor**
    c. Nitrification inhibitor
    d. All of these

53. The fermentation process is
    a. **Aerobic**
    b. Anaerobic
    c. Facultative anaerobic
    d. Facultative aerobic

54. Micas and field spars are the native source of
    a. **K**   b. N
    c. Ca   d. B

55. PPM is equal to
    a. mg/1000 kg   b. **mg/1000 gm**
    c. kg/1000 gm   d. None of these

56. The enzyme involved in BNG is
    a. **Nitrogenase**   b. Azotobacter
    c. Rhizobium   d. Nitrosomonas

57. Ectomycorrhiza is present on the root of plants like
    a. Oak   b. Pinus
    c. Eucalyptus   d. **All**

58. Green manure crops supply mainly
    a. Nitrogen   b. Organic matter
    c. **Both a and b**   d. None of these

59. Movement of nutrient ions from soil to plant roots occurs by
    a. Diffusion
    b. Mass flow
    c. Contact exchange
    d. **All of these**

60. Irreversible increase in size and weight of plants is known as
    a. Development
    b. **Growth**
    c. Both a and b
    d. None of these

61. C : N ratio of FYM is
    a. 10 : 1   b. 20 : 1
    c. **40 : 1**   d. None

62. C : N ratio of saw dust is
    a. **225 : 1**   b. 235 : 1
    c. 245 : 1   d. None

63. The micro-organisms responsible for maximum nutrient fixation is
    a. Fungi   b. **Bacteria**
    c. Algae   d. None

64. Most micro-organism function at their best within a pH range of
    a. 5.5–6.5   b. 6.5–7.5
    c. **7.5–8.5**   d. None

65. The carbon dioxide per centage in the soil air is
    a. **0.25**   b. 0.30
    c. 0.32   d. 0.35

66. Olivine is the best source of
    a. Ca   b. **Mo**
    c. Cu   d. Mn

67. Tourmaline is the best source of
    a. P   b. K
    c. Mo   d. **Ca**

68. Dolomite is rich in
    a. Ca   b. **Mg**
    c. S   d. Mn

69. Average nitrogen concentration in plant tissue is
    a. 0.5%   b. 1.0%
    c. **1.5%**   d. None

70. Chemically the most active soil separate is
    a. **Clay**   b. Silt
    c. Sand   d. None

71. Central Soil Salinity Research Institute is situated at
    a. Bhopal   b. Kanpur
    c. New Delhi   d. **Karnal**

72. Root growth is particularly affected by
    a. **P**   b. N
    c. B   d. Mo

73. The colour of hematite is
    a. **Red**   b. White
    c. Black   d. Brown

74. The soil type which has the highest field capacity is
    a. Sand
    b. Clay
    c. Silt
    d. None

75. Ammonia is converted into nitrate by
    a. Fungi
    b. Azotobacter
    c. Bacteria
    d. None

76. Cereal straw is a particularly rich source of
    a. Potash
    b. Nitrogen
    c. Phosphorus
    d. None

77. FYM contains
    a. 0.5% N
    b. 1.5% N
    c. 2%N
    d. None

78. Kishan khad contains
    a. 20–25% N
    b. 25–28% N
    c. 28–30% N
    d. None

79. Ammonium sulphate contains
    a. 18.5% N
    b. 20.5% N
    c. 20.6% N
    d. 22.5% N

80. Specific heat is higher in
    a. Sand
    b. Clay
    c. Humus
    d. None

81. Concentration of which element is highest in soil
    a. O_2
    b. CO_2
    c. H_2O
    d. None

82. Sulphur content in ammonium sulphate is
    a. 22%
    b. 24%
    c. 26%
    d. 28%

83. Hill soils are generally
    a. Neutral
    b. Saline
    c. Acidic
    d. Alkaline

84. Mycorrhiza increases the availability of
    a. Phosphorus
    b. Boron
    c. Potassium
    d. Cupper

85. Ammonium sulphate is
    a. Straight fertilizer
    b. Complex fertilizer
    c. Combined fertilizer
    d. None of these

86. Element responsible for pollen development is
    a. P
    b. K
    c. N
    d. B

87. The per centage of soluble salt present in alkali soils
    a. 0.1–0.2%
    b. 0.2–0.5%
    c. 0.5–1%
    d. None of these

88. The CO_2 content of the cultivated soil is per cent
    a. 0.25
    b. 0.30
    c. 0.45
    d. 0.50

89. The residual effect of urea on soil reaction is
    a. Acidic
    b. Alkaline
    c. Neutral
    d. None of these

90. The zinc content in zinc sulphate is _____per cent.
    a. 18
    b. 20
    c. 21
    d. 24

91. Bulk density of normal soil is g/cc
    a. 1.20
    b. 1.30
    c. 1.33
    d. 1.35

92. CO_2 concentration in organic soil is
    a. High
    b. Low
    c. Constant
    d. None of these

93. The most deficit micronutrient in Indian soil is
    a. Cu
    b. Ca
    c. Zn
    d. B

94. Plant nutrient critical for nitrogen fixation of
    a. Ca
    b. Mo
    c. Co
    d. Zn

95. The C : N ratio in humus is
    a. 5 : 1
    b. 10 : 1
    c. 20 : 1
    d. None of these

96. In which soil rice is grown?
a. Sandy loam   **b. Clay loam**
c. Clay   d. Sandy clay loam

97. Edaphic factors are related to
a. Water   b. Air
c. Soil   d. Both b and c

98. Soil is composed of
a. Mineral + organic matter
b. Mineral + organic matter + air
c. Mineral + organic matter + air + water
d. None of these

99. Good indicator plant for N deficiency is
a. Maize   b. Rice
c. Wheat   d. Barley

100. Soil with poorest water holding capacity is
a. Clay   **b. Sandy**
c. Loam   d. None of these

101. Application of murate of potash is not suitable for
a. Rice   **b. Tobacco**
c. Potato   d. Wheat

102. Carbon : organic matter ratio is
a. 1 : 5.50   b. 1 : 1.70
c. 1 : 1.72   d. None of these

103. C : N ratio of arable soil is
a. 6 : 1 – 10 : 1   b. 8 : 1 – 10 : 1
c. 8 : 1 – 15 : 1   d. None of these

104. C : N ratio of Indian soil is
a. 5 : 1   **b. 10 : 1**
c. 20 : 1   d. 30 : 1

105. Wood is decomposed by
a. Bacteria   b. Fungi
c. Actinomycetes   d. None

106. Clay soil has total pore space is
a. 40 – 45%   **b. 50 – 60%**
c. 55 – 66%   d. None

107. Loamy soil has total pore space is
a. 20 – 40%   b. 25 – 45%
c. 30 – 50%   d. None of these

108. Sandy soil has total pore space is
a. 20 – 30%   b. 30 – 35%
c. 35 – 40%   d. 40 – 45%

109. Silt contains diameter of
a. Less than 0.002 mm
b. 0.02 – 0.05 mm
c. 0.5 – 0.002 mm
d. None

110. Clay has diameter of
a. Less than 0.002 mm
b. 0.2 – 0.02 mm
c. 0.02 – 0.05 mm
d. None

111. Azospirillium is used for
a. Sorghum   b. Soybean
c. Til   d. Wheat

112. The application of Mg increases
a. Nitrogen uptake
b. Phosphorus uptake
c. Potassium uptake
d. None of these

113. Fixation of phosphate is more in
a. Acid soil   b. Alkalie soil
c. Saline soil   d. Neutral soil

114. Ratio of NPK in India is
a. 2 : 1 : 1   b. 3 : 2 : 1
c. 4 : 2 : 1   d. 4 : 3 : 1

115. Soil compaction increases the
a. Bulk density   b. Particle density
c. Both a and b   d. None of these

116. Sulphur is essential for
a. Cereal crops   b. Pulses crops
c. Fruit crops   **d. Oil seed crops**

117. Silicon is essential for
a. Rice   b. Maize
c. Both a and b   d. None of these

118. Indicator plant of copper is
a. Rice   b. Maize
c. Wheat   d. Barley

119. Digestion mixture ratio for ashing is
    a. 5:1:1   **b. 10:1:1**
    c. 15:1:1   d. None

120. Element essential for the flocculation of soil particle is
    a. P   b. B
    c. Cu   **d. Ca**

121. Canker nodules are found mostly in
    a. Red soil   b. Black soil
    c. Brown soil   d. Yellow soil

122. Permissible soil loss by water is
    a. 8 t/ha   b. 10 t/ha
    c. 12 t/ha   d. 15 t/ha

123. Nif: gene responsible for
    a. N-fixation b. P-fixation
    c. K-fixation   d. None

124. Sterility in wheat due to deficiency of
    a. Sulphur   **b. Boron**
    c. Nitrogen   d. Potassium

125. Red soils are dominant in
    a. Uttar Pradesh
    b. West Bengal
    c. Tamil Nadu
    d. None of these

126. The soil which is suitable for most of the crop
    a. Sandy loam b. Clay loam
    c. Loam   d. None

127. Black cotton soil is deficient in
    a. Nitrogen   b. Phosphorus
    c. Potassium   d. Calcium

128. Sandy soil contains more than
    a. 70% sand   b. 80% sand
    c. 85% sand   d. 90% sand

129. Silt soil contains more than
    a. 70% silt   **b. 80% silt**
    c. 85% silt   d. None of these

130. Clay soil contains more than
    a. 25% clay   b. 30% clay
    c. 35% clay   **d. 40% clay**

131. Extension teaching is
    a. Vertical   **b. Horizontal**
    c. Both a and b   d. None of these

132. Puppet show is
    a. Audiovisul b. Visual aids
    c. Audio aids   d. None of these

133. The most influencing type of demonstration is
    a. Method demonstration
    b. Field demonstration
    c. Both a and b
    d. None of these

134. National Rural Employment Guarantee Scheme started in the year
    a. 2004   **b. 2006**
    c. 2007   d. 2008

135. The role of extension education in India is performed by
    a. Central Agriculture University
    b. State Agriculture University
    c. Both a and b
    d. None of these

136. Cooperative society is basic institution for
    a. Socioeconomic growth of family
    b. Socioeconomic growth of society
    c. Socioeconomic growth of villagers
    d. Both b and c

137. IRDP introduced in the year
    a. 1956   b. 1970
    c. 1974   **d. 1980**

138. T and B system started in the year
    a. 1966   b. 1967
    c. 1974   d. 1978

139. NSS was started in
    a. 1966   **b. 1969**
    c. 1972   d. 1974

140. The President of ICAR is
    a. Agriculture Minister
    b. Chief Minister

c. Prime Minister
d. None of these

141. The Royal Commissions report came in

    a. 1928   b. 1930
    c. 1932   d. None of these

142. Community Development Programme (CDP) was started in the year

    a. 1950   **b. 1952**
    c. 1954   d. None of these

143. HYVP was introduced in

    a. 1962   b. 1964
    c. 1966   d. 1968

144. Lab to land programme was started by

    a. ICAR   b. IARI
    c. Both a and b   d. None of these

145. Initially, the CDP was introduced in

    a. 45 Blocks   **b. 55 Blocks**
    c. 60 Blocks   d. 65 Blocks

146. Which programme is properly known as package programme?

    a. IADP   b. IRDP
    c. Both a and b   d. None of these

147. The Royle Commissions report came in

    a. 1920   b. 1922
    c. 1928   d. 1930

148. Meagan's model consists of

    a. Four elements   **b. Six elements**
    c. Five elements   d. None of these

149. The first state where the Panchayati Raj system was introduced is

    a. Rajasthan   b. Uttar Pradesh
    c. Andhra Pradesh
    d. Madhya Pradesh

150. No. of flash cards used for one talk is

    a. 8–10   **b. 10–12**
    c. 12–15   d. 15–18

151. Rural development depends on

    a. Research   b. Extension
    c. Both a and b   d. None of these

152. Examples of projected aids are

    a. Cinema
    b. Slide
    c. Overhead projector
    d. All of these

153. Methods of group communication are

    a. News paper
    b. Demonstration
    c. Symposium
    d. All of these

154. Television broadcast for rural development in India, started in

    a. 1952   b. 1955
    c. 1957   d. 1958

155. A bulletin should contain

    a. 12–24 pages   b. 24–30 pages
    c. 24–48 pages   d. 30–50 pages

156. National Agriculture Sciences Museum is located at

    a. West Bengal   **b. New Delhi**
    c. Punjab   d. None of these

157. Extension education is a

    a. Science   b. Art
    c. Both a and b   d. None of these

158. Drought Prone Area Programme was started in

    a. 1965   **b. 1970**
    c. 1975   d. None of these

159. National Adult Education Programme was launched in

    a. 1980   b. 1982
    c. 1988   d. 1990

160. Srinikethan institute was established in

    a. 1910   **b. 1914**
    c. 1918   d. 1920

161. National Service Scheme was started in

    a. 1966   **b. 1969**
    c. 1970   d. None of these

162. Operation flood was launched in

    a. 1969   b. 1970
    c. 1971   d. 1972

163. T and V programme is also known as
    a. **Basten X Benon Scheme**
    b. NES Programme
    c. NSS Scheme
    d. None of these

164. The age of rural youth in TRYSEM is
    a. 18–30 years   b. **18–38 years**
    c. 18–45 years   d. None of these

165. Family is included under
    a. **A primary group**
    b. Secondary group
    c. Both a and b
    d. None of these

166. Year of establishment of extension service in India is
    a. 1950   b. 1951
    c. 1952   d. **1953**

167. Krishi Sudhar had been started from
    a. **1914**   b. 1915
    c. 1916   d. 1920

168. Farm domestication work started in the year
    a. 1889   b. 1900
    c. **1903**   d. 1914

169. APEDA came into existence in the year
    a. 1885   b. **1986**
    c. 1987   d. None of these

170. In which year the RRB setup?
    a. 1940   b. 1970
    c. 1972   d. **1975**

171. Democracy is derived from which word?
    a. French   b. Latin
    c. **Greek**   d. **None of these**

172. 1st step of evaluation is
    a. Sampling   b. **Objective**
    c. Analysis of data
    d. None of these

173. Father of sociology is
    a. Max Weber
    b. Rogers

    c. **August Compte**
    d. None of these

174. Radio is an example of
    a. **Hot media**   b. Cold media
    c. Fiber media   d. None of these

175. The component poster is
    a. Wards   b. Picture
    c. Colour   d. **All of these**

176. Radio is a media for
    a. Mass communication
    b. Group communication
    c. **Both a and b**
    d. None of these

177. Optimum numbers of flash card are
    a. **10–12**   b. 12–15
    c. 15–18   d. 18–22

178. Poster is a
    a. Individual contact
    b. Group contact
    c. **Mass contact**
    d. None of these

179. Number of speakers in symposium is
    a. **2–5**   b. 8–10
    c. 10–15   d. 18–20

180. A good message should be
    a. Specific   b. Significant
    c. Timely   d. **All of these**

181. The pilot project for rural development was started in
    a. 1947   b. **1948**
    c. 1950   d. 1952

182. HYVP was introduced in
    a. **1966**   b. 1968
    c. 1970   d. None of these

183. 4th club was started by
    a. 1980   b. 1894
    c. 1895   d. **1896**

184. Panchayati Raj system operates at
    a. District level
    b. Block level

c. Village level
d. **All of these**

185. **Ministry of human resources development considers which age group as youth groups**

    a. 18–35 years   b. 15–30 years
    c. **15–35 years**   d. 20–30 years

186. **KVK was introduced in which Five-Year**

    a. **V**   b. VI
    c. III   d. VI

187. **Concept of KVK was introduced by**

    a. Balwant Rai   b. WH Wisher
    c. **Mohan Singh Mehta**
    d. None of these

188. **T and V system was first used in**

    a. India   b. Japan
    c. China   d. **Turkey**

189. **ATICs are set by**

    a. Minister of agriculture, GOI
    b. **Indian Council Agriculture of Agricultural Research**
    c. State Department of agriculture
    d. None of these

190. **ATICs are under the administrative control of**

    a. Director General, ICAR
    b. **Deputy Director Extension, ICAR**
    c. Minister of State of agriculture
    d. None of these

191. **The Chairman of Planning Commission**

    a. President
    b. **Prime Minister**
    c. Finance Minister
    d. None of these

192. **Which of the following is a vocational training institute?**

    a. SAU   b. **KVK**
    c. DOE   d. None of these

193. **Which of the following is a traditional and simple aid of communication?**

    a. Radio   b. Model
    c. TV   d. **Puppet**

194. **The first district in the country to launch IADP was**

    a. **Thanjavur**   b. Shahabad
    c. Ludhiana   d. None of these

195. **Which one is a non-projected aids?**

    a. Slide
    b. Cinema
    c. **Pictures**
    d. Overhead projector

196. **Which of the principal is made use in slide-cum film projector?**

    a. **Direct projector**
    b. Indirect projector
    c. Both a and b
    d. None of these

197. **Extension education process includes**

    a. Three steps
    b. Four steps
    c. **Five steps**   d. Six steps

198. **Extension is a**

    a. One way channel
    b. **Two-way channel**
    c. Three-way channel
    d. None of these

199. **The extension education was first coined in the year**

    a. 1850   b. 1852
    c. 1856   d. **1873**

200. **Gurgaon projected was started in**

    a. **Punjab**   b. West Bengal
    c. Kerla   d. Delhi

201. **Fertilizer control order issued in**

    a. **1957**   b. 1958
    c. 1959   d. 1960

15

Poultry Science and Animal Nutrition

1. A nucleoside is
- a. Purine/pyramidine + phosphate
- **b. Purine/pyramidine + sugar**
- c. Pyramidine + purine + phosphate
- d. Purine + sugar + phosphate

2. Feather stigma is present in
- a. Pea
- b. Hibiscus
- **c. Wheat**
- d. Poppy

3. In angiosperms regarding development of micro-gametophyte each microspore mother cell undergoes
- a. Mitosis to produce 4 microspores
- b. Two successive mitosis to form 4 microspores
- c. Two successive meiotic division to form 4 microspores
- **d. Meiosis to produce 4 haploid microspores**

4. Formation of diploid embryo sac from diploid vegetative structure, e.g. nuceolus or integument, etc. without meiosis is called
- **a. Apospory**
- b. Apomixes
- c. Diplospory
- d. Adventives polyembryony

5. Process of water exudation through hydathodes is known as
- a. Guttation
- b. Transpiration
- c. Evaporation
- d. Bleeding

6. Basal placentation is found in the family
- a. Malvaceae
- b. Solanaceae
- c. Fabaceae
- **d. Asteraceae**

7. Insectivorous plants grow in
- a. Nitrogen-rich soil
- **b. Nitrogen deficient soil**
- c. Potassium deficient soil
- d. Carbohydrate-rich soil

8. In a pond ecosystem, benthos mean
- a. Zooplanktons on water surface
- b. Large fishes eating small ones
- **c. Primary consumes in the bottom of a pond**
- d. All phytoplanktons

9. Eyes on potato tubers represent
- a. Rootlets
- **b. Nodes with buds**
- c. Scars
- d. Sutures

10. Fungus without mycelium is
- a. Puccinia
- b. Rhizopus
- **c. Saccharomyces**
- d. Mucor

11. The organelles involved in photorespiration are
- a. Glyoxysomes, chloroplast and mitochondria
- b. Chloroplast, peroxisome and glyoxisomes

c. Mitochondria, peroxisome and glyoxisomes

d. **Chloroplast, mitochondria and peroxisome**

12. ω, X l74 has

a. **Single-stranded DNA**
b. Single-stranded RNA
c. Double-stranded RNA
d. Double-stranded DNA

13. Floridian starch is found in

a. Chlorophyceae b. Myxophyceae
c. Phaeophyceae **d. Rhodophyceae**

14. The hormone reducing transpiration rate by inducing stomatal closure is

a. **ABA**   b. Ethylene
c. Cytokinin   d. Auxin

15. In bryophytes the female sex organ is called

a. **Archegonia** b. Antheridia
c. Carpgonium   d. Ascogonium

16. The pigment involved in photomorphogenetic movements is

a. Cytochromes   **b. Phytochrome**
c. Chromatin   d. Vernalin

17. First CO_2 receptor in C_4 plants is

a. PGA   **b. PEP**
c. RuBD   d. OAA

18. The components of an ecosystem are

a. Trees and weeds
b. Plants and animals
c. Man and plants
d. **Biotic and abiotic**

19. The two great industrial tragedies MIC and Chernobyl occurred respectively in

a. **Bhopal 1984, Ukraine 1986**
b. Madhya Pradesh 1980, Russia 1990
c. Bhopal 1980, Ukraine 1984
d. Ukraine 1990, Bhopal 1986

20. Tyloses are

a. Lactiferous channels
b. Secretory cells
c. Sieve plates
d. **Tracheal plugs plugging the lumen of vessels and tracheids**

21. The 10% energy transfer law of food chain was given by

a. Lederberg   **b. Lindeman**
c. Weismann   d. Lindley

22. Reaction centre of photo system-I in green plants is

a. P680   b. P690
c. P700   d. P780

23. Number of cotyledons in Zea mays, Cycas and Pinus respectively are

a. 1, 2, 4   **b. 1, 2, many**
c. 2, 2, many   d. 2, 1, 4

24. Double fertilization is found in

a. Bryophytes
b. **Angiosperms**
c. Gymnosperms
d. Pteridophytes

25. If a sporangium derived from a single cell is called

a. **Leptosporangiate**
b. Eusporangiate
c. Heterosporangiate
d. None of the above

26. The term water potential was proposed by

a. Godlewski
b. **Slatyer and Taylor**
c. Dixon and Jolly
d. JC Bose

27. A plant having two types of haploid structures in its life cycle is known as

a. **Haplobiontic** b. Diplobiontic
c. Haplontic   d. Diplontic

28. Ribozyme is

a. Enzyme
b. **RNA with enzymatic activity**
c. Hormone
d. Protein

29. A chain of amino acids joined by peptide bonds is called
   a. Peptide chain
   b. Polypeptide chain
   c. Polyamino acid chain
   d. Nucleotide chain

30. Root cap is not found in
   a. Mesophytes   b. Hydrophytes
   c. Xerophytes   d. Halophytes

31. The high yielding hybrid crop varieties to exploit hybrid vigor, the farmers need to purchase fresh hybrid seed every year because
   a. Hybrid vigour is not long standing due to inbreeding depression
   b. They are not allowed to grow their own seed
   c. It is always associated with increased heterozygosity
   d. Government has accepted Dunkel's proposals

32. In *Bignonia eapreolata* pollination is carried out by
   a. Bat   b. Bird
   c. Insect   d. Wind

33. Fragrant flowers with well developed nectarines are an adaptation for
   a. Anemophily
   b. Ornithophily
   c. Entamophily
   d. Hydrophily

34. Genetic engineering is related with
   a. Eugenics   **b. Euphenics**
   c. Euthenics   d. All of these

35. Floating roots are the characteristic features of
   a. Viscum   c. Vanda
   b. Cuscuta   **d. Jussiaea**

36. Various fungi are known to accumulate considerable quantities of divalent metals
   a. Cd   b. Zn
   c. Pb   d. All of these

37. Soil salinity is measured by
   a. Potometer
   b. Porometer
   c. Conductivity meter
   d. Calorimeter

38. Which one of the following is the earliest land plant?
   a. Rhynia   b. Cycas
   c. Ulothrix   d. Synchytrium

39. The scutellum of the gram embryo is a
   a. Vestigial organ
   b. Photosynthetic organ
   c. Absorptive organ
   d. Protective organ

40. The diameter of Z-DNA is
   a. 34A   b. 20A
   c. 18A   d. 45A

41. The genes which remain confined to differential region of 'Y' chromosome are
   a. Autosomal genes
   b. Holandric genes
   c. Sex-linked genes
   d. Mutant genes

42. The hormone responsible for ripening of fruits is
   a. Ethylene   b. Cytokinin
   c. Auxin   d. ABA

43. Coir is the commercial product of coconuts
   a. Mesocarp   b. Pericarp
   c. Endocarp   d. Endosperm

44. Polygenic genes show
   a. Different phenotype
   b. Different genotype
   c. Similar phenotype
   d. Similar genotype

45. Select the correct statement
   a. Legumes are incapable of fixing nitrogen
   b. Legumes fix nitrogen through bacteria living in fruits root

c. Legumes fix nitrogen only by bacteria present in nodules

d. None of the above

46. Hormogonia are the vegetative reproductive structures of

a. Chlamydomonas

b. Spirogyra

c. Occillatoria   d. Ulothrix

47. Azotobacter and Beijerinckia are the examples of

a. Symbiotic nitrogen-fixers

b. Non-symbiotic nitrogen-fixers

c. Ammonifying bacteria

d. Disease causing bacteria

48. Smilax, a climbing genus belongs to

a. Cucurbitaceous b. Solanaceae

c. Liliaceae   d. Cruciferae

49. In certain parts of India, muscular dystrophy is commonly found amongst the poor people because they eat cheap pulse from the plant

a. *Pisum sativum*

b. *Lathyrus sativus*

c. *Cicer arietinum*

d. *Phaseolus mungo*

50. If a dwarf pea plant was treated with gibberellic acid, it became as tall, as tall pea plants. If these pea plants are crossed with pure tall pea plants, what will be the phenotypic ratio in F1 generation?

a. All dwarf plants

b. 50% tall and 50% dwarf plants

c. 75% tall and 25% dwarf plants

d. 100% tall plants

51. Colchicine is obtained from *Colchicum autumnal*. It belongs to family

a. Leguminosae   b. Solanaceae

c. Asteraceae   **d. Liliaceae**

52. Moll's experiment explains that

a. Carbon dioxide is essential for photosynthesis

b. Chlorophyll and water are necessary for photosynthesis

c. Light and water are essential for photosynthesis

d. All of the above

53. Energy transfer from one trophic level to other in a food chain is

a. 10%   b. 20%

c. 1%   d. 2%

54. Stem is reduced in

a. Rhizome   b. Corm

c. Bulb   d. Tuber

55. Heterophilly of Limnophila is

a. Environmental b. Developmental

c. Habitual   **d. Adaptive**

56. Synandrous condition is the fusion of

a. Filaments only

b. Both filaments and anthers

c. Anthers only

d. Petals

57. Which one yields sunn hemp?

a. Corchorus   b. Hibiscus

c. Crotolaria   d. Cannabis

58. Rod-shaped elongated thick-walled lignified dead cells found in seed coat of pulses (legumes) are

a. Macrosclereids b. Astrosclereids

c. Brachysclereids d. Osteosclereids

59. Dicot root having more than six vascular bundles are found in

a. Pea   b. Sunflower

c. Ficus   d. Ranunculus

60. Regulator gene controls chemical synthesis (operon concept) by

a. Inhibiting transcription of mRNA

b. Inhibiting enzymes

c. Inhibiting passage of mRNA

d. Inhibiting substrate enzyme reaction

61. 'Illegitimate crossing over' is another term for

a. Transition   b. Transversion

c. Reciprocal translocation

d. None of the above

62. A substance unrelated to substrate but capable of reversibly changing activity of enzyme by binding to a site other than active site is called

a. Competitive inhibitor

b. Non-competitive inhibitor

c. Catalytic inhibitor

d. Allosteric modulator/inhibitor

63. Golgi apparatus is absent in

a. Higher plants   b. Yeast

c. Bacteria and blue-green algae

d. Liver cells

64. Which one is common amongst nucleus, chloroplast and mitochondria?

a. Cristae   b. Thylakoids

c. Nucleic acid

d. Carbohydrate metabolism

65. Sporocarp is a reproductive structure of

a. Some algae

b. Some aquatic ferns

c. Angiosperms having spores

d. Bryophytes

66. Pond ecosystem shows

a. Inverted pyramid of number

b. Inverted pyramid of biomass

c. Upright pyramid of biomass

d. Inverted pyramid of energy

67. Under anaerobic conditions, bacterium Pseudomonas changes

a. Nitrate to molecular nitrogen

b. Nitrate to ammonia

c. Nitrate to nitrite

d. Nitrite to nitrate

68. Deciduous forests have

a. Variety of grasses

b. Broad-leaved trees

c. narrow-leaved trees

d. Variety of crocodiles

69. Physiologically active form of phytochrome is

a. P730/Fr   b. P660/Pr

c. P700   d. P680

70. The archesporium of ovule is

a. Single-celled terminal

b. Single-celled central

c. Single-celled hypodermal

d. Single-celled lateral

71. Which is correct statement?

a. Seed cannot be formed after one fertilization

b. Seed is formed after one fertilization

c. Seed is formed before double fertilization

d. Fruit is produced after double fertilization

72. Hormone used in tissue culture for better growth is

a. Auxin   b. Gibberellin

c. Cytokinin   **d. Vernalin**

73. Grafting is employed for better and quicker yield of varieties of

a. Apple   b. Mango

c. Citrus   d. Tea

74. Primary root is

a. Positively geotropic

b. Positive hydrotropic

c. Negative geotropic

d. Negative hydrotropic

75. Cholodny-Went theory is connected with

a. Photomorphogenesis

b. Phototropism

c. Nastic movement

d. Geotropism

76. Photorespiration is related to

a. Chloroplast   b. Mitochondria

c. Peroxisome   d. Glyoxysomes

77. 2-4-diphenoxyacetic acid is a

a. Herbicide   **b. Weedicides**

c. Pesticide   d. Fungicide

78. Ergot is obtained from

a. Albugo   b. Yeast

c. Claviceps purpurea

d. Alternaria

79. B-DNA is

a. **Antiparallel and right-handed**
b. Antiparallel and left-handed
c. Parallel and right-handed
d. Parallel and left-handed

80. Stomata in bryophytes are present in the

a. **Capsule**   b. Leaf
c. Stem   d. Seta

81. Haploid cells belong to

a. Integument, pollen grain, endosperm
b. Embryo, endosperm and pollen grain
c. **Megaspore, pollen grain, antipodal**
d. Integument, pollen grain and antipodal

82. Rubber is commercially obtained from

a. **Euphorbia**   b. Betula
c. Hibiscus   d. Pinus

83. Endoplasmic reticulum remains in continuation with

a. **Nucleus**   b. Ribosomes
c. Mitochondria   d. Golgi bodies

84. Chondriosome is discovered by

a. **Benda**   b. Messelson
c. Dujardin   d. Taylor

85. The cell wall of both bacteria and cyanobacteria contains

a. Lipid   b. Pectin
c. Protein   d. **Muramic acid**

86. Development of saprophyte from gametophyte, is called

a. Apomixis   b. Apospory
c. **Apogamy**   d. Diplospory

87. Chiropterophily is seen in

a. **Kigelea**   b. Salvia
c. Orchid   d. Vallisneria

88. Thermal algae can live in

a. Saline soil
b. **Hot water streams of 70°C**
c. Deserts
d. Snow balls

89. Law of limiting factor was given by

a. **Blackman**   b. Hill
c. Taylor   d. Amon

90. Haploid plants can be obtained from

a. Leaf culture   b. Bud culture
c. Root culture   d. **Anther culture**

91. Embryo sac represents

a. Megaspore   b. Megagamete
c. Megasporophyll
d. **Megagametophyte**

92. Deficiency of molybdenum causes

a. Wilting   b. **Mottling**
c. Reclamation   d. Necrosis

93. The first reaction in photorespiration is

a. Decarboxylation
b. **Oxygenation**
c. Carboxylation
d. Phosphorylation

94. The specific characters of C4 plant is

a. Bulliform cells
b. **Kranz anatomy**
c. Parallel venation
d. Isobilateral leaf

95. The ovule in which embryo sac become horseshoe shaped in

a. **Amphitropous**
b. Camphylotropous
c. Orthotropous   d. Anatropous

96. Caruncle develops from

a. **Outer integument**
b. Cotyledon   c. Funiculus
d. Inner integuments

97. Aerosols having carbon and fluorine compounds are chiefly released by

a. **Refineries**   b. Automobiles
c. Industries   d. Jets

98. Coir of commerce is obtained from

a. Endocarp of coconut
b. Mesocarp of coconut
c. Stem of jute
d. **Leaves of coconut**

99. In a national park protection is provided to
   a. Entire ecosystem
   b. Flora and fauna
   c. Fauna only   d. Flora only

100. Morphine is obtained from
   a. *Aconitum nacelles*
   b. *Papaver somniferum*
   c. *Rauwolfia serpentina*
   d. *Cinchona officinalis*

101. Azides and cyanide inhibit
   a. Metaphase   **b. Prophase**
   c. Anaphase   d. Telophase

102. Cell organelle covered by single unit membrane is
   a. Glyoxisomes   b. Lysosome
   c. Peroxisomes   **d. All of these**

103. Blue-green alga that causes red blooms is
   a. Anabaena
   b. Gleacapsa
   c. Trichodesmium
   d. Nostoc

104. Gingerly oil (till) is got from
   a. *Linus usitatissimum*
   b. *Cocos nucifera*
   c. *Sesamum indicum*
   d. *Brassica napus*

105. In meiosis-I, the centromeres undergoes
   a. Division between anaphase and interphase
   b. Division between prophase and metaphase
   c. Division but the daughter chromosomes do not separate
   d. No division

106. Prokaryotic genetic material is
   a. Liner DNA + histones
   b. Circular DNA + histones
   c. Liner DNA without histones
   d. Circular DNA without histones

107. Mary's biological concept of species is mainly based on
   a. Morphological traits
   b. Reproductive isolation
   c. Modes of reproduction
   d. Morphology and reproduction

108. NADH is produced in
   a. Photosystem-II
   b. Photosystem-I
   c. Glycolysis
   d. Both a and b

109. Abscission layer developed during leaf fall is made up of
   a. Cork cells
   b. Non-sclerenchymatous cells
   c. Sclerenchymatous cells
   d. Parenchymatous cells

110. The process by which the amount of DNA, RNA and protein can be known at a time is
   a. Cell fractionation
   b. Autoradiography
   c. Phase-contrast microscopy
   d. Tissue culture

111. Retort cells are found in
   a. Funaria
   b. Pogonatum
   c. Sphagnum
   d. Porella

112. The net gain of energy from one gram mole of glucose during aerobic respiration is
   a. 2 ATP   b. 4 ATP
   c. 38 ATP   d. 40 ATP

113. Chief function of phloem is conduction of
   a. Food   b. Minerals
   c. Water   d. Air

114. Pyrenoids are the centers for formation of
   a. Proteins   b. Enzymes
   c. Fat   d. Starch

115. **Sexual reproduction in Rhizopus occurs through**
    a. Gametangial contact
    b. Gametangial copulation
    c. Planogametic copulation
    d. Spermatogamy

116. **Organelles involved in photorespiration are**
    a. Mitochondria, chloroplasts and ribosomes
    b. **Mitochondria, peroxisomes and chloroplasts**
    c. Mitochondria, nucleus and ribosomes
    d. Mitochondria, proxisomes and glyoxisomes

117. **Pith is produced by the activity of**
    a. Lateral meristems
    b. Protoderm   c. Procambium
    d. **Ground meristems**

118. **What tissue present in leaves of Pinus conducts food and water laterally?**
    a. **Transfusion tissue**
    b. Phloem   c. Xylem
    d. Medullary rays

119. **The site for light reaction of photosynthesis is**
    a. **Grana**   b. Stoma
    c. ER   d. Cytoplasm

120. **Swollen placenta, oblique septum and conniving anthers are characteristics of family**
    a. Brassicaceae   b. Asteraceae
    c. Poaceae   d. **Solanaceae**

121. **Development of shoot and root is determined by**
    a. **Cytokinin and auxin ratio**
    b. Enzymes
    c. Temperature
    d. Plant nutrients

122. **Pyramid of number in a grassland/true ecosystem is**
    a. Always inverted
    b. **Always upright**

    c. Both a and b
    d. Spindle-shaped

123. **The empirical formula for chlorophyll a is**
    a. **C35 H72 $O_5 N_4$ Mg**
    b. C65 H70 $O_6 N_4$ Mg
    c. C55 H72 $O_5 N_4$ Mg
    d. C45 H70 $O_6 N_4$ Mg

124. **Which one yields oil from seeds and orange dye from petals?**
    a. *Helianthus annus*
    b. *Calendula officinalis*
    c. *Carthamus tinctorius*
    d. *Tagetus erecta*

125. **A fern differ from a moss in processing**
    a. Swimming/flagellated anthropoids
    b. Flask-shaped archegonia
    c. **Independent sporophyte**
    d. Independent gametophyte

126. **The species of Pinus, seeds of which are edible in chilgoza comes from**
    a. *P. roxburghii*   b. *P. gerardiand*
    c. *P. monophylla*   d. *P. sylvestris*

127. **A petroleum plant is**
    a. Sugarcane   b. Maize
    c. Potato   d. **Euphorbia**

128. **Operon model of gene regulation and organization of prokaryotes was proposed by**
    a. Messelson and Stahl
    b. Wilkins and Franklin
    c. Beadle and Tatum
    d. **Jacob and Monod**

129. **Artificial ripening of fruits is accomplished by treatment with**
    a. Sodium chloride
    b. IAA
    c. **Ethylene gas**
    d. Kinetin

130. **Individuals of species which occur in a particular area constitute**
    a. Flora   b. Fauna
    c. **Population**   d. Flora and fauna

131. **Transpiration differs from evaporation in**
   a. Rate of water loss
   b. **Transpiration is a physiological process while evaporation is physical process**
   c. Transpiration is physical process while evaporation is physiological process
   d. Frequency of water loss

132. **Arrangement of leaves on a stem branch is**
   a. Venation
   b. Non-venation
   c. Ptyxis
   d. **Phyllotaxy**

133. **Water potential in leaf tissue is "positive" (near zero) during**
   a. Low transpiration
   b. Excessive absorption
   c. Excessive transpiration
   d. **Gestation**

134. **In onion, the swollen underground structure is**
   a. Root
   b. Rhizome
   c. **Bulb**
   d. Tuber

135. **Movement of leaves of sensitive plant, *Mimosa pudica* are due to**
   a. Thernonasty
   b. **Seisnonasty**
   c. Hydrothpism
   d. Chemonasty

136. **Fragrant flowers with well developed nectarines are an adaptation for**
   a. Zoophily
   b. Anemophily
   c. **Entornophily**
   d. Hydrophily

137. **Cheese and yoghurt are products of**
   a. Pasteurization
   b. **Fermentation**
   c. Dehydration
   d. Distillation

138. **Colchicines bring about**
   a. **Polyploidy**
   b. **Cell division**
   c. Cell elongation
   d. Cell differentiation

139. **Cell 'A' with OP = 10 atm and TP = 5 atm is in contact with cell 'B' having OP = 15 atm and TP = 12 atm. The flow of water will be**
   a. From A to B
   b. Equal flow
   c. **From B to A**
   d. No flow

140. **Select the one, which is pitcher plant**
   a. Drosera
   b. Utricularia
   c. **Sarracenia**
   d. Aldrovanda

141. **Nucleotide found free in the cells is**
   a. cAMP
   b. AMP
   c. ADP
   d. **ATP**

142. **Which one does not occur is Seleaginella?**
   a. Heterospory
   b. Hetrophylly
   c. **Homospory**
   d. Ligulate leaves

143. **Development of sporophyte from gametophyte tissue without fusion of gametes is**
   a. Apospory
   b. **Apogamy**
   c. Apomixis
   d. Parthenogenesis

144. **First bioinsecticide developed on commercial scale was**
   a. Quinine
   b. DDT
   c. Organophosphates
   d. **Sporeine**

145. **Cross between hybrid and recessive parent is**
   a. Back cross
   b. **Test cross**
   c. Monohybrid cross
   d. Dihybrid cross

146. **Largest egg of plant kingdom belongs to**
   a. **Cycas**
   b. Pinus
   c. Psidium
   d. Mangfera

147. **Air spaces are present in**
   a. **Hydrophytes**
   b. Xerophytes
   c. Mesophytes
   d. All of these

148. **Thick cuticle, sunken stomata are found in leaves of**
   a. Hydrophytes
   b. **Mesophytes**
   c. Xerophytes
   d. Epiphytes

149. **Cyanide resistant respiration is characteristic of**
    a. Viruses
    b. Bacteria
    c. Plants
    d. Animals

150. **Which can function as carrier in active ion absorption?**
    a. Ferredoxins
    b. Plastoquinone
    c. Cytochromes
    d. Lecithin

151. **In germinating castor seed, the RQ is**
    a. One
    b. More than one
    c. Less than one
    d. Infinite

152. **The factor influencing process of flowerings is**
    a. Amount of chlorophyll
    b. Soil water
    c. Soil pH
    d. Photoperiod

153. **The storage pathogen of rice is**
    a. *Xanthomanas oryzae*
    b. *Helminthosporium oryzae*
    c. *Pyricularia oryzae*
    d. *Calanoluca oryzae*

154. **The study of interrelationship between species and its environment of a forest is called**
    a. Autecology
    b. Syneocology
    c. Forest ecology
    d. Co-operation

155. **In moss, the middle sterile part of capsule is called**
    a. Foot
    b. Protonema
    c. Columella
    d. Spore sac

156. **In fern, vascular bundles are**
    a. Radial
    b. Hadrocentric
    c. Open
    d. Leptocentric

157. **Leptome is used for**
    a. Phloem
    b. Xylem
    c. Fibres
    d. Parenchyma

158. **In angiosperm, triple fusion is necessary for the formation of**
    a. Embryo
    b. Pollen
    c. Endosperm
    d. Leaf

159. **Colchicines prevent the spindle formation during**
    a. Prophase
    b. Metaphase
    c. Anaphase
    d. Telophase

160. **Raphides are the crystals of**
    a. Calcium oxalate
    b. Calcium
    c. Calcium phosphate
    d. Calcium carbonate

161. **The shade of a tree is cooler than the shade of a roof due to**
    a. Respiration
    b. Photosynthesis
    c. Transpiration
    d. Guttation

162. **Which of the following shows *heterothallism*?**
    a. Rhizopus
    b. Cycas
    c. Bacterium
    d. Ricinus

163. **Casparian strips are found in**
    a. Periderm
    b. Epidermis
    c. Endodermis
    d. Hypodermis

164. **The process through which the amount of DNA, RNA and protein can be known at a time is called**
    a. Autoradiography
    b. Tissue culture
    c. Cellular fractioning
    d. Phase contrast microscopy

165. ***Neisseria gonorrhoeae* was first described by**
    a. Neisser in 1879
    b. Pasteur in 1878
    c. Robert Koch
    d. None of these

166. **Rh factor of the blood was discovered by scientist**
    a. Louis Pasteur
    b. Landsteiner and Weiner
    c. Janskey
    d. Moss
    e. None of these

167. ***Trepanema pallidum* was discovered by**
    a. Schaudinn and Hoffman
    b. Louis Pasteur
    c. Burgey
    d. Laennec
    e. None of these

168. Fluorescent substance used in fluorescent microscopy is
    a. Quinine sulphate
    b. Auramine
    c. **Both of these**
    d. None of these

169. Protein part of enzyme is known as
    a. Lysozyme   b. Metalloenzyme
    c. **Apoenzyme**   d. All of the above

170. The formation of multivalent at meiosis in diploid organism is due to
    a. Monosomy
    b. Deletion
    c. Inversion
    d. **Reciprocal translocation**

171. The trees occurring in two-stories are the characteristic features of
    a. **Temperate deciduous forest**
    b. Tropical savannah
    c. Grassland
    d. Coniferous forest

172. A mature ligule, having prominent basal portion, is called
    a. **Glossopodium**   b. Rhizophore
    c. Trichome   d. None of these

173. Hormogonia are vegetative reproductive structure of
    a. Spirogyra   b. Ulothrix
    c. **Occillatoria**   d. Yeast

174. Which division of fungi includes 'club fungi'?
    a. Zygomycota   b. Ascomycota
    c. Deuteromycota   d. **Basidiomycota**

175. The hypogeal germination is found in
    a. Bean   b. **Maize**
    c. Rhizophora   d. Cucurbita

176. Which of the following matched correctly?
    a. Piper—climbing root
    b. Ficus—climbing root
    c. Buttress root—bombax
    d. **Vitis—nodulated root**

177. Select the correct statement
    a. C_4 pathway for CO_2 fixation were discovered by Hatch and Slack
    b. CO_2 is essential for photosynthesis
    c. **Addition of sodium carbonate in water retards photosynthetic rate in vallisneria**
    d. Phloem is the principal pathway for translocation of solutes

178. Select the correct statement
    a. Lenticels is the exit route for transpiration
    b. The action spectra of transpiration is blue and red
    c. **Transpiration helps the plant to remain cool**
    d. Transpiration can be measured by photometer

179. The seeds which have separate endosperm
    a. **Maize**   b. Onion
    c. Rice   d. Bean

180. Which of the following statements is correct?
    a. The causal organism for foolish seedling disease is the source of gibberellin
    b. Abscisic acid is a growth promoter
    c. The ratio of auxin: cytokinin control cell differentiation
    d. **Bolting of cabbage can be induced by treatment with IAA**

181. Principal source(s) of antibiotic is/are
    a. Streptomyces
    b. Micro-monospora
    c. **Rhizopus**   d. Nocardia

182. With reference to plant tissue culture select the matching pair
    a. **Sterile triploid—banana and seedless fruit**
    b. Somaclonal variations—differences appearing
    c. Embryoids—non-zygotic embryo produced from somatic cells
    d. Pulses—belong to Cruciferae

183. Opium alkaloids are
    a. Codeine
    b. Diethyllysergic acid
    c. Morphine   **d. Saffron**

184. In the bacteria
    a. **Mesosome is present**
    b. Nucleoid represents the genome
    c. Ribosomes are found in cytoplasm
    d. Histone proteins complexed with DNA

185. Consider the following statements
    a. Cucurbits are monoecious plant
    b. **In mango, neuter, male and female and female flowers occur together**
    c. Leguminous plants how unisexuality
    d. Oblique septa is found in Rosaceae

186. Consider the following statements
    a. **In plant cells, cytokinesis start with the formation of the phragmoplast**
    b. Phragmoplast comprises intrazonal microtubules and Golgi vesicles
    c. Primary cell wall is produced by microtubules
    d. Phragmoplast is formed by nucleus

187. Consider the following statements
    The genetic code said to be degenerate and universal which means that
    a. Amino acids may have more than one codon
    b. All amino acids have more than one codon
    c. Codons are common for higher and lower organisms
    d. **Codons are not found in bacteria**

188. Which of the following pairs is correctly matched?
    a. 700 nm—photosystem-I
    b. 650 nm—photosystem-II
    c. **690 nm—photosystem-II**
    d. 620 nm—phycocyanin

189. Consider the following statements
    a. Copper is present in cytochrome oxidase

    b. Pantothenic acid is precursor of co-enzyme-A
    c. Thiamine pyrophosphate is the prosthetic group in decarboxylases
    d. Zinc is present in RNA and DNA polymerases

190. Which of the following pairs is correctly matched?
    a. **Fertile spike—ophioglossum**
    b. Sporangiophore—equisetum
    c. Synangium—psilotum
    d. Apophysis—spirogyra

191. Consider the following statements: Marchantia polymorpha is
    a. Dioecious
    b. **Possesses antheridiophores and archegoniophores**
    c. Lacks foot and seta in its sporophyte
    d. Heterosporous

192. Which of the following is true archaeo-bacteria?
    a. **Extreme halophiles**
    b. Extreme thermophiles
    c. Methanogens
    d. Presence of peptidoglycan cell wall

193. Which of the following is endangered plants?
    a. *Saintpaulia ionantha*
    b. *Ceratozamia hildae*
    c. ***Punica granatum***
    d. *Senecio hadrasomum*

194. Consider the following statements
    The *ex situ* conservation of genetic resources can be done through
    a. Tissue culture practices
    b. Maintenance of sanctuaries
    c. **The establishment of germplasm banks**
    d. **The establishment of national parks**

195. Consider the following regions of India
    a. Eastern Himalaya
    b. Eastern Ghats

c. Western Ghats

d. **Western Himalaya**

196. Consider the following statements associated with the germination of an angiospermous seed

a. As the seed gets hydrated and germinates, enzymatic activity is increased

b. **The respiration rate of the germinating seed increases along with the increased enzymatic activity**

c. The increase in the respiratory rate continues till senescence

d. Rate of enzymatic activity decreases

197. Consider the following statements

a. The seed of pea is exalbuminous

b. **The fruit of peach is drupe**

c. The seed of tomato is albuminous

d. The fruit of coconut is berry

198. Consider the following statements

a. Cutin is a fatty acid polymer

b. **Starch is a fatty acid polymer**

c. Sucrose is monosaccharide

d. Maltose is polymer of fructose

199. Calvin cycle is

a. C_3 cycle

b. Reductive pentose-phosphate cycle

c. **Common in cereals and uncommon in cereals**

d. Uncommon in cereals

200. The empirical formula for chlorophyll b is

a. $C_{54} H_{70} O_6 N_4 Mg$

b. **$C_{55} H_{70} O_6 N_4 Mg$**

c. $C_{55} H_{22} O_5 N_4 Mg$

d. $C_{45} H_{72} O_5 N_4 Mg$

16

General Agriculture

1. **The Galapagos Islands are associated with the visit of**
   a. Jean Lamarck   **b. Charles Darwin**
   c. Gregor Mendel   d. Alfred Wallace

2. **Which of the following was most influential upon Darwin's formulation of theory of natural selection?**
   a. De Vries concept of mutation
   b. Wallace's paper on survival
   c. Malthus's essay on population
   d. Lamarck's on inheritance of acquired characters

3. **'Survival of the fittest' was used by**
   a. Charles Darwin
   b. Jean Baptiste Lamarck
   c. Hugo de Vries
   d. Herbert Spencer

4. **After observing the variations Hugo de Vries first of all described the mutation in**
   a. *Oenothera lamarkiana*
   b. *Neurospora crassa*
   c. *Pisum sativum*
   d. *Drosophila melanogaster*

5. **According to scientists, the Big Bang occurred approximately ____ years ago.**
   a. 100 million   b. 100 thousand
   c. 1 billion   **d. 15 billion**

6. **Pasteur succeeded in disproving the spontaneous generation theory because**

a. he was lucky
b. he was ingenious in drawing out the neck of glass flasks, so as to provide access to air but not to microorganisms
c. of the fact that sample of yeast taken by him was dead
d. of the clear surrounding of his laboratory

7. **The first organisms were**
   a. Primitive eukaryotes
   b. Aerobic bacteria
   c. Prokaryotic
   d. Photosynthetic

8. **Why the primitive atmosphere of Earth more beneficial to the origin of life than the modern atmosphere of Earth?**
   a. The primitive atmosphere had a layer of ozone that shielded the first delicate cells
   b. The primitive atmosphere was reducing one that facilitated the formation of complex substances from simple molecules
   c. The primitive atmosphere was an oxidizing one that facilitated the formation of complex substances from simple molecules
   d. The primitive atmosphere has less free energy than the modern atmosphere, and thus newly formed organisms were less likely to be destroyed

9. Russian scientist who proposed the theory of origin of life was

   a. Oparin   b. Miller
   c. Haldane   d. Fox

10. In their laboratory simulation of early Earth, Miller and Urey observed the abiotic synthesis

    a. Amino acids b. Coacervates
    c. DNA   d. Liposomes

11. The richest source of fossils is

    a. Basalt   b. Granite
    c. Lava
    d. Sedimentary rock

12. Biologists who study the sequences of organisms in the fossil record are

    a. Taxonomists   **b. Palaeobiologists**
    c. Misologists   d. Systematists

13. Which were dominant in Mesozoic?

    a. Dinosaurs   b. Gymnosperms
    c. Fishes   d. Mammals

14. The "Golden age of Reptiles" was

    a. Late Paleozoic   b. Cenozoic
    c. Mesozoic   d. Protozoic

15. The fossil remains of Archaeopteryx is a connecting link between

    a. Amphibians
    b. Reptiles and birds
    c. Fish and amphibians
    d. Reptiles and mammals

16. Which of the following sets is the evidence of evolution?

    a. Homologous and vestigial organs
    b. Analogous and vestigial organs
    c. Homologous and analogous organs
    d. All of the above

17. The following anatomical structures, which is homologous to the wing of a bat?

    a. The arm of a human
    b. The wing of a butterfly
    c. The tail of a fish
    d. The dorsal fin of a shark

18. Which one of the following sets of structures includes only analogous organs?

    a. Wings of butterfly, housefly and bat
    b. Hind legs of horse
    c. Hands of man, monkey and kangaroo
    d. Mandibles of cockroach, mosquito and honeybee

19. Which of the following sets represent all vestigial structures in the human body?

    a. Vermiform appendix, body hair and cochlea
    b. Wisdom teeth, coccyx and patella
    c. Coccyx, vermiform appendix and muscles of ear pinna
    d. Body hair, muscles of ear pinna and atlas vertebra

20. The earliest animals to have been domesticated by man most likely the

    a. Horse   b. Pig
    c. Dog   d. Cow

21. Presence of gill slits in the embryo of all vertebrates supports the theory of

    a. Organic evolution
    b. Recapitulation
    c. Metamorphosis
    d. Biogenesis

22. Appearance of ancestral characters in the newborn, such as tail, multiple mammae, etc. is known as

    a. Homologous   b. Analogous
    c. Atavistic   d. Vestigial

23. Evolution is defined as

    a. History of race
    b. Development of race
    c. History and development of race with variations
    d. progressive history of race

24. The book named "Philosophic Zoologique" was published in 1809 and was written by

    a. Mendel   b. Darwin
    c. de Vries   **d. Lamarck**

25. Penguin is a bird that lost the use of its wings by not flying. Such a statement would express the views of
    a. Darwin
    b. Wallace
    c. Lamarck
    d. Huxley

26. Mesophyll tissue is well differentiated into spongy tissue and palisade tissue in
    a. Dicot leaves
    b. Ophytic stem
    c. Hydrophytic stem
    d. Monocot leaves

27. Lateral meristems are responsible for
    a. Growth in parenchyma
    b. Growth in thickness
    c. Growth in cortex
    d. Growth in length

28. As a tree grows older, which increases more rapidly in thickness?
    a. Sapwood
    b. Cortex
    c. Phloem
    d. Heartwood

29. What is the other name for the cork tissue?
    a. Phellogen
    b. Phelloderm
    c. Phellem
    d. Periderm

30. Commercial cork is obtained from the species of
    a. Berberis
    b. Quercus
    c. Salix
    d. Betula

31. The cross-section of a trunk of a tree showed 50 annual rings. The age of tree is
    a. 50 years
    b. 50 months
    c. 100 years
    d. 25 years

32. Trees at seashore do not have annual rings because
    a. There is climatic variation
    b. There is no marked climatic variation
    c. There is enough moisture in the atmosphere
    d. Soil is sandy

33. Grafting is not possible in monocots because they
    a. Have scattered vascular bundles
    b. Have parallel venation
    c. Are herbaceous
    d. Lack cambium

34. A tissue is a
    a. Group of separate organs that are co-ordinate in their activities
    b. Group of similar cells that function together in a specialized activity
    c. Layer of cells surrounding an organ
    d. Sheet of cells, one layer thick

35. After complete exhalation the lungs of a healthy man contains a liter of gas, this quantity is known as
    a. Residual volume
    b. Functional residual capacity
    c. Total lung capacity
    d. Dead space

36. Generally the food chain has how many trophic levels?
    a. One
    b. Two
    c. Three
    d. Three or four

37. Correct path of energy flow in a system is
    a. Producers, herbivores, carnivores, decomposers
    b. Producers, carnivores, herbivores, decomposers
    c. Herbivores, producers, carnivores, decomposers
    d. Herbivores, carnivores, producers, decomposers

38. When man eats fish, which feeds on zooplanktons, which have eaten small plants. The producer in the chain is
    a. Zooplankton
    b. Small plants
    c. Man
    d. Fish

39. Which is the correct sequence in the food chain in grassland?
    a. Grass, wolf, deer and buffalo
    b. Grass, insect, bird and snake

c. Grass, snake, insect and deer

d. Bacteria, grass, rabbit and wolf

40. When a big fish eats a small fish, which eats water fleas supported by phyto-plankton, the water fleas are

a. **Primary consumers**

b. Secondary consumers

c. Top consumer in this food chain

d. Producers

41. In natural ecosystem, decomposers include

a. Only microscopic animals

b. **Only bacteria and fungi**

c. The above two types organisms plus microscopic animals

d. Only the above two types of organisms

42. The food chain in which microorganisms break down the energy rich compounds synthesized by producers is

a. **Detritus food chain**

b. Predator food chain

c. Consumer food chain

d. Parasitic food chain

43. An aquatic plant with floating leaves

a. have stomata on leaf surface

b. have stomata on lower surface

c. have stomata

d. **have stomata only on upper surface**

44. Which is the most stable ecosystem?

a. Desert   b. Mountain

c. **Ocean**   d. Forest

45. Which of the following is a logical sequence in carbon cycle?

a. **Producer-consumer-decomposer**

b. Decomposer-consumer-producer

c. Producer-decomposer-consumer

d. Consumer-producer-decomposer

46. Which of the following structures is thought to be exceptionally rich in hydrolytic enzymes?

a. **Lysosomes**

b. Microsome

c. Chromosomes

d. Endoplasmic reticulum

47. The selective digestion of cytoplasmic organelles by the lysosome is called

a. Osmotrophy   b. **Autophagy**

c. Heterophony   d. Autolysis

48. The arrangement of outer and central microtubules in a cilium is called the

a. 9 + 1 pattern   b. **9 + 2 pattern**

c. 8 + 2 pattern   d. 8 + 1 pattern

49. Ureotelic animals are those that eliminate the nitrogenous wastes predominantly in the form of

a. Uric acid   b. Ammonia

c. Amino acids   d. **Urea**

50. Animal species living in chronic shortage of water generally excrete uric acid as the principal nitrogenous waste product

a. **Because uric acid can be stored in the body for long periods**

b. Uric acid is highly soluble in water and can be easily eliminate

c. The kidneys are unable convert uric acid into urea

d. Enzymes for the formation of urea are absent

51. Which one of the following sets of animals produces the same substance as their chief excretory product?

a. Cockroach, camel and lizard

b. **Man, dog and camel**

c. Amoeba, ant and antelope

d. Fowl, fish and frog

52. A freshwater fish must continuously

a. Acquire water and get rid of salt

b. Get rid of both water and salt

c. Acquire both water and salt

d. **Get rid of water and acquire salt**

53. A nephridium of an earthworm drains materials directly from the

a. Gut   b. **Coelom**

c. Lymph   d. Blood

54. The basic unit of a vertebrate kidney is the
    a. Ureter
    b. Nephrons
    c. Malpighian tubule
    d. Islets of langerhans

55. Nephrons are connected with
    a. Respiratory system
    b. Nervous system
    c. Circulatory system
    d. Excretory system

56. Which of the following has no blood but respires?
    a. Earthworm   **b. Hydra**
    c. Cockroach   d. Fish

57. Which type of respiratory organs is present in spiders and scorpions?
    a. Book lungs   b. Gill books
    c. Gills   d. Lungs

58. The functional respiratory organ of a fully formed tadpole is the
    a. Skin   b. Lung
    c. Gill   d. Air bladder

59. In frog, cutaneous respiration takes place
    a. Only in water, when pulmonary respiration does not take place
    b. Only in water, but along with pulmonary respiration
    c. Only on land
    d. Always

60. At high altitude, RBCs of human blood will
    a. Increase in number
    b. Decrease in number
    c. Decrease in size
    d. Increase in size

61. Presence of large number of alveoli around alveolar ducts opening into bronchioles in mammalian lungs is
    a. Inefficient system of ventilation with a little of residual air
    b. Inefficient system of ventilation with high per centage of residual air
    c. An efficient system of ventilation with no residual air
    d. An efficient system of ventilation with a little residual air

62. The narrowest and most numerous tubes of lungs are termed as
    a. Bronchus   b. Alveoli
    c. Bronchioles   d. Hilum

63. The exchange of gases in a mammal takes place is
    a. Trachea   b. Bronchioles
    c. Bronchi   **d. Alveoli**

64. Tidal volume of air in a normal healthy man during inspiration is about
    a. 300–400 ml   **b. 500–700 ml**
    c. 900–1000 ml   d. 100–250 ml

65. 'Physical basis of living' is
    a. Cell   **b. Protoplasm**
    c. Nucleus   d. Protein

66. The study of fish culture is called
    a. Ophiology   b. Ichthyology
    c. Herpetology   **d. Pisciculture**

67. Catla and rohu are examples of
    a. Freshwater fish
    b. Marine fish
    c. Brackish water fish
    d. None of these

68. Silver Revolution is associated with the increase in the production of
    a. Meat   b. Cereals
    c. Eggs   d. Milk

69. The technique in which the developing embryo (at definite stage) from a pregnant superior breed is removed and transferred to another female with inferior characters, in whose body further development till birth takes place
    a. Embryo transfer
    b. Artificial insemination
    c. Protoplast fusion
    d. Cloning

70. Fever, inflammation of the mucous membranes, particularly the intestines, discharges from the eyes and nose, dehydration, and skin eruptions on the back and flanks; death comes after four to eight days. These are the major symptoms of
    a. **Rinderpest**
    b. Anthrax
    c. Foot and mouth disease
    d. Cholera

71. The Jersey bull used for cross breeding is exotic variety from
    a. **USA**　　b. UK
    c. Switzerland　d. Holland

72. The IPN (infectious pancreatic necrosis) and VMS (viral hemorrhagic septicemia) are well-known infectious diseases of
    a. **Fish**　　b. Cattle
    c. Poultry　d. None of the above

73. Mehsana and Jaffarabadi are examples of
    a. **Indian breeds of buffaloes**
    b. Breeds of cow
    c. Breeds of sheep
    d. Indian breeds of goat

74. The production of useful aquatic plants and animals like prawns, fish, lobsters, crabs, molluscs, etc. using various types of water resources is called
    a. **Aquaculture**　b. Pisciculture
    c. Siliviculture　d. Silver revolution

75. Human genome contains about
    a. 10, 000 nucleotides
    b. 10, 000 genes
    c. **6 billion nucleotides**
    d. 6 billion genes

76. External protective tissues of plants are
    a. Cortex and epidermis
    b. Pericycle and cortex
    c. **Epidermis and cork**
    d. Pericycle and cork

77. Bulliform cells are present
    a. In upper epidermis of dicot leaves
    b. In lower epidermis of monocot leaves
    c. **In upper epidermis of monocot leaves**
    d. In dicot stem

78. The youngest layer of secondary phloem in woody dicot stem is located
    a. **Just outside the vascular cambium**
    b. Just on the inner side of cambium
    c. Between periderm and primary cortex
    d. Just outside pith

79. The wall of cork cells is mostly impregnated with
    a. Cutin　　**b. Suberin**
    c. Lignin　d. Hemicellulose

80. Cork cells are
    a. Photosynthetic
    b. Elongated and participate in movement
    c. Meristematic
    d. **Dead**

81. Dendrochronology is the study of
    a. Height of a tree
    b. **Age of a tree by counting the number of annual rings in the main stem**
    c. Diameter of a tree
    d. Age of tree by counting the number of leaves in the main stem

82. The best method to determine the age of tree is
    a. To measure its diameter
    b. To count the number of leaves
    c. **To count the number of annual rings in the main stem at the base**
    d. To measure its height

83. If the sign was nailed to the side of a tree 5′ above the ground in 1997, how high would the sign be in 2007, if the tree grew 4″ taller each year?
    a. **5′ high**　　b. 8′ high
    c. 4′ 8″　　d. 9′4″

84. Safranin stains in which element of the tissues?
    a. Starch elements
    b. **Lignified elements**
    c. Bast
    d. Protein elements

85. Which types of tissue from the thin surface for the gas exchange in the lungs?
    a. **Epithelial**   b. Connective
    c. Nervous   d. Muscle

86. Endothelium of the inner surface of blood vessels in vertebrates is
    a. **Simple squamous epithelium**
    b. Columnar epithelium
    c. Cuboidal epithelium
    d. Ciliated cells

87. The epithelium best adapted for a body surface subject to abrasion is
    a. Simple squamous
    b. **Stratified squamous**
    c. Stratified columnar
    d. Simple cuboidal

88. In man thickest skin is found in
    a. Palm   b. Thigh
    c. **Sole**   d. Thumb

89. Which type of tissue forms glands?
    a. **Epithelial**   b. Connective
    c. Nervous   d. Muscle

90. Sebaceous glands are found in
    a. **Dermis of skin of mammals**
    b. Epithelium of stomach of frog
    c. Epithelium of intestine of frog
    d. Epidermis of skin of mammals

91. Which type of tissue forms the framework of the external ear?
    a. Epithelial   b. **Connective**
    c. Muscle   d. Nervous

92. Wrinkling in old age is due to
    a. **Collagen**   b. Myosin
    c. Keratin   d. Actin

93. Which one of the following directly helps in keeping the body warm?
    a. Sweat glands
    b. **Adipose tissue**
    c. Connective tissue
    d. Hairs

94. The fibrous tissue, which connects the two bones, is
    a. Connective tissue
    b. **Ligament**
    c. Tendon
    d. Adipose tissue

95. Tendon connects
    a. Cartilage with muscles
    b. **Bone with muscles**
    c. Ligament with muscles
    d. Bone with bone

96. Bone forming cells are
    a. Osteoblast   b. **Osteoclasts**
    c. Chondroblasts   d. Both a and c

97. A man was brought up at sea level while his brother spent all his life at an altitude of 10, 000 feet. The latter will have
    a. **More active bone marrow**
    b. Lower blood pressure
    c. Less subdermal fat
    d. More active sweat glands

98. A bone is distinguished from cartilage by the presence of
    a. Collagen   b. Lymph vessels
    c. Blood vessels   d. **Haversian canals**

99. Which one of these is a kind of tissue?
    a. Lung   b. Kidney
    c. **Blood**   d. Pancreas

100. Nissl's granules are found in cyton of nerve cells. These have affinity for basic dyes. The granules are made up of
    a. Proteins   b. DNA
    c. Amino acids   d. **RNA**

101. In camel, erythrocytes are
    a. Oval and nucleated
    b. **Circular, biconcave and nucleated**

c. Oval and non-nucleated

d. Circular, biconcave, non-nucleated

102. Iron in hemoglobin exists as

a. Unionized iron atom

b. Ferric ions only

c. Ferrous ions only

d. Ferric or ferrous ions depending upon the oxygenate state of the heme moiety

103. Red cell count is carried out by

a. Haemocytometer

b. Haemoglobinometer

c. Sphygmomanometer

d. Electrocardiogram

104. Striated muscles are found in

a. Gall bladder   b. Wall of bronchi

c. Leg muscles   d. Lungs

105. Triceps and biceps are examples of

a. Antagonistic muscles

b. Involuntary muscles

c. Sphincter muscles

d. Smooth muscles

106. Murrah is a high-yielding breed of

a. Cow   b. Hen

c. Buffalo   d. Sheep

107. White Revolution is related to the increase in production of

a. Egg   b. Wool

c. Milk   d. Meat

108. Which of the following is called the "Father of White Revolution" in India?

a. Hargobind Khorana

b. V. Kurian

c. MS Swaminathan

d. PK Sethi

109. Inland fisheries are referred to

a. Culturing fish in freshwater

b. Trapping and capturing fish

c. Deep sea fisheries

d. Extraction of oil from fish

110. Foot and mouth disease is a highly contagious disease almost exclusive to cattle, sheep, swine, goats, and other cloven-hoofed animals. It is caused by

a. Fungi   b. Bacteria

c. Protozoa   **d. Erus**

111. Anthrax is a serious disease of

a. Cattle   b. Poultry

c. Fish   d. All of these

112. High milk yielding varieties of cows are obtained by

a. Super ovulation

b. Artificial insemination

c. Use of surrogate mothers

d. All of these

113. Which of the following is the high milk yielding variety of cow?

a. Jamunapari

b. Murrah

c. Holstein

d. Kathiyabari

114. Bombay duck and hilsa are examples of

a. Freshwater fish

b. Marine fish

c. Breeds of sheep

d. Breeds of ducks

115. The surface of nerve fibers bears narrow areas called

a. Schwann cells

b. Schwann nodes

c. Nodes of Ranvier

d. Nissl's granules

116. If a couple has three daughters, what are the chances that the fourth child will be a son?

a. 100%   b. 75%

c. 50%   d. 0%

117. If a dihybrid pea plant heterozygous for flower colour (red dominant over white) and seed shape (round dominant over wrinkled) undergoes selfing, the types of gametes produced are

a. 2   **b. 4**

c. 8   d. 16

118. The crossing of a homozygous tall plant with a dwarf would yield plaits in the ratio of
    a. Two tall and two dwarf
    b. One homozygous tall, one homozygous dwarf and two heterozygous tall
    c. All homozygous dwarf
    d. All homozygous tall

119. Blue eye colour in human is recessive to brown eye colour. The expected children of a marriage between blue-eyed woman and brown-eyed male who had a blue-eyed mother are likely to be
    a. All blue-eyed
    b. Three blue-eyed and one brown-eyed
    c. All brown-eyed
    d. One blue-eyed and one brown-eyed

120. The genotype of a dominant parent is determined by crossing it with the recessive parent. This cross is called
    a. Back cross   **b. Test cross**
    c. Long cross   d. Out cross

121. Chromosome theory of heredity was postulated by
    a. Charles Darwin
    b. Gregor Mendel
    c. Sutton and Boveri
    d. Hargobind Khorana

122. Continuity of germplasm theory by Weisman was proposed in
    a. 1838   **b. 1883**
    c. 1865   d. 1859

123. Allosomes are
    a. Bead-like structure on chromosomes
    b. Sex chromosomes
    c. Rounded bodies
    d. Node-like structure on chromosomes

124. Mutation is
    a. a change that is inherited
    b. a change, which affects the parents only but never inherited

    c. a change, which affects the offspring of F2 generation only
    d. a factor responsible for plant growth

125. Recessive mutations are expressed normally
    a. has to express always since it is a mutation
    b. in heterozygous condition
    c. neither in homozygous nor in heterozygous condition
    d. in homozygous condition

126. Which of the following is not heritable?
    a. Point mutation
    b. Chromosomal mutation
    c. Somatic mutation
    d. Gene mutation

127. Which of the following is a mutagen?
    a. SO_2 b. CO_2
    c. CO   **d. HNO_2**

128. The plant that was made popular by "De Vries mutation theory"
    a. *Triticum vulgare*
    b. *Oenothera lamarkiana*
    c. *Pisum sativum*
    d. *Primula vulgaris*

129. Which of the following is an example of a point mutation?
    a. Thalassaemia
    b. Night blindness
    c. Sickle cell anaemia
    d. Down's syndrome

130. Mutations used in agriculture are
    a. Lethal and recessive
    b. Artificially induced and recessive
    c. Lethal and dominant
    d. None of the above

131. Inheritance of total colour-blindness is
    a. X-linked   b. XY-linked
    c. Y-linked   d. None of these

132. A man is hemophiliac. This indicates that he
    a. inherited the condition from his father
    b. is afraid of sight of blood

c. inherited the condition from his mother

d. is carrying parasite in his blood

133. Genes located on Y chromosome are

a. Mutant genes

b. Sex-linked genes

c. Autosomal genes

d. Holoandric genes

134. "Barr body" is derived from

a. Autosomes in males

b. Autosomes in females

c. X-chromosome in female

d. X-chromosome in males

135. Heterosis is

a. Hybrid incompatibility

b. Hybrid vigour

c. Structural hybridity

d. Hybrid sterility

136. Pure line selection results in retention of desired characters

a. for one generation

b. for two generations

c. for several generation

d. permanently

137. Which of the following has equal number of chromosomes?

a. Klinefelter's syndrome and Down's syndrome

b. Klinefelter's and Turner's syndrome

c. Turner's syndrome and Down's syndrome

d. Turner's syndrome and gynandromorphy

138. Rh factor derives its name from

a. Monkey b. Ape

c. Rhino d. Human care

139. The DNA is the genetic material was proved conclusively by

a. JD Watson

b. Hershey and Chase

c. Alfred Griffith

d. Boveri and Sutton

140. Watson and Crick composed the model of DNA structure in

a. 1953 b. 1943

c. 1955 d. 1963

141. Which one of the following is responsible for guttation?

a. Root pressure b. Transpiration

c. Photosynthesis d. Osmosis

142. Which one of the following blood vessels in mammals would normally carry the largest amount of urea?

a. Dorsal aorta

b. Hepatic portal vein

c. Renal artery

d. Hepatic artery

143. Pressure exerted in the tracheary elements of a xylem as a result of metabolic activity of roots which forces the water into xylem vessel and upwards into the stem for a certain height is

a. Osmotic pressure

b. Root pressure

c. Atmospheric pressure

d. Turgor pressure

144. In what ways do lymph capillaries differ from blood capillaries?

a. Lymph capillaries contain red blood cells

b. Lymph capillaries have a wall of only one cell layer

c. Lymph capillaries begin with blind ends throughout interstitial fluid

d. Contain plasma

145. In a closed circulatory system, blood is completely enclosed within

a. The skeleton b. Sinuses

c. Vessels d. Hearts

146. Which is the most correct statement?

a. Most of the water that filters into Bowman's capsule is reabsorbed

b. One-half of the water that filters into Bowman's capsule is reabsorbed

c. One-half of the glucose that filters into Bowman's capsule is reabsorbed

d. None of the salts that are filtered in Bowman's capsule is reabsorbed

147. In which of the following groups of animal the heart pumps only deoxygenated blood?

a. **Fishes**
b. Reptile
c. Birds
d. Amphibians

148. Which of the following parts of the nephron is least permeable to water?

a. Proximal tubule
b. Descending limb of the loop of Henle
c. **Ascending limb of the loop of Henle**
d. Collecting duct

149. The mechanism of uric acid excretion in nephron is

a. Diffusion
b. **Ultrafiltration**
c. Osmosis
d. Secretion

150. Hemoglobin is found in

a. All invertebrates
b. Only in vertebrates
c. **Earthworm and rabbit**
d. Cockroach and earthworm

151. The plasma resembles in is composition the filtrate produced in the glomerulus except for the presence of

a. Glucose
b. Amino acids
c. Proteins
d. **Chlorides**

152. Indicate correct statement for man

a. Arteries always carry oxygenated blood while veins always carry deoxygenated blood

b. Arteries are provided with valves while veins are devoid of valves

c. **Arteries always carry blood away from the heart, while veins always carry blood towards the heart**

d. Venous blood is returned to left auricle

153. Antidiuretic hormone is put into the blood by the

a. Hypothalamus
b. **Pituitary gland**
c. Liver
d. Small intestine

154. The smallest blood vessel in the body is a

a. **Capillary**
b. Artery
c. Vena cava
d. Vein

155. The reabsorption of glucose in a nephron occurs in

a. Loop of Henle
b. **First half of proximal tubule**
c. Distal convoluted tubule
d. Proximal part of collecting ducts

156. Which of the following has no muscular walls?

a. Artery
b. Arteriole
c. **Capillary**
d. Vein

157. The ultrastructure has shown that in glomerulus of a nephron, the process of filtration mainly takes place due to

a. Podocytes
b. **Pores in blood capillaries**
c. Basement membrane
d. Endothelium of the blood capillaries

158. The cells constituting walls of the blood capillaries are known as

a. Parietal cells
b. Haemocytes
c. Oxyntic cells
d. **Endothelial cells**

159. What percentage of the water that filters into the nephron is reabsorbed?

a. 25%
b. 75%
c. 85%
d. **99%**

160. Which of the following in NOT reabsorbed from the filtrate to the blood at the proximal tubule?

a. Glucose
b. Na
c. **Plasma proteins**
d. Water

161. The exchange of materials between blood and interstitial fluid occurs only at the

a. Veins
b. **Capillaries**
c. Arteries
d. Arterioles

162. About how much blood is in the circulatory system of an average person?

a. 1 liter
b. 2 liters
c. **5 liters**
d. 10 liters

163. The proteins present in blood and necessary for developing immunity to diseases are

a. Albumins and globulins
b. Globulins
c. **Globulins only**
d. Albumins

164. Lack of antidiuretic hormone (ADH) causes water loss from the body by

a. Increased water loss through expiration
b. **Excessive urination**
c. By combination of all the above factors
d. Increased sweating

165. Both erythrocytes and leukocytes are formed in the

a. **Bone marrow**
b. Thymus
c. Arterial walls
d. Lymph nodes

166. A normal man respires in a minute

a. 10–15 times
b. **14–18 times**
c. 20–25 times
d. 25–30 times

167. Osmoregulation is control over the

a. Removal of nitrogen from the body
b. **Concentrations of salt and water in the body**
c. Osmotic properties of cell membranes
d. pH of the blood

168. Lungs have a large number of alveoli for

a. Having spongy texture and proper shape
b. **More surface area for diffusion of gases**
c. More space for increasing volume of inspired air
d. More nerve supply

169. A malpighian tubule empties urine into the

a. **Gut**
b. Coelom
c. Lymph
d. Ureters

170. Which one of the following events takes place during inspiration in man?

a. The internal intercostals muscles relax
b. **Due to contraction of external intercostals muscles and flattening of diaphragm the volume of thoracic cavity increases**
c. Due to contraction of external intercostals muscles, and flattening of diaphragm the volume of thoracic cavity decreases
d. The abdominal muscles contract

171. In insects, malpighian tubules drain materials directly from the

a. Gut
b. **Haemocoel**
c. Spider
d. Jelly fish

172. Kidneys are not only organs of excretion but their work is supplemented by

a. **Liver**
b. Heart
c. Large intestine
d. Skin

173. During inspiration, as a result of contraction of muscles attached to it, the diaphragm

a. Becomes dome-shaped
b. **Flattens**
c. Rotates
d. Flattens and rotates

174. Forced deep breathing for a few minutes by a person sitting at rest may be followed by a temporary cessation of breathing. This is due to

a. Too much oxygen in blood
b. Too much carbon dioxide in blood
c. Both, too much oxygen and very little carbon dioxide in blood
d. **Little carbon dioxide in blood**

175. The conversion of protein waste, the ammonia into urea occurs mainly in

a. Kidney
b. Lungs
c. **Liver**
d. Intestine

176. In man, expired air contains oxygen about

a. 4%
b. 10%
c. **16%**
d. 20%

177. **Oxygen is transported in blood mainly by**
    a. Leucocytes
    b. **Erythrocytes**
    c. Thromobocytes
    d. Blood plasma

178. **Carbon monoxide has greater affinity for hemoglobin as compare to oxygen**
    a. 1000 times
    b. **200 times**
    c. 20 times
    d. 2 times

179. **Kidney of vertebrates resembles with contractile vacuole of protozoan in**
    a. Expelling out glucose
    b. Expelling out urea and uric acid
    c. **Expelling out excess of water**
    d. Expelling out salts

180. **In man percentage of CO_2 transported as bicarbonates is**
    a. 5 to 10%
    b. 70 to 75%
    c. 90 to 95%
    d. 50 to 65%

181. **About 30% of CO_2 is transported as**
    a. **Ha carbaminocompounds**
    b. Bicarbonates of Na and K
    c. Carboxyhemoglobin
    d. Oxyhemoglobin

182. **Which of the following is the part of kidney?**
    a. **Pelvis**
    b. Ileum
    c. Somniferous tubules
    d. Cystic duct

183. **If a respiratory surface dries out, gas exchange will**
    a. Increase
    b. Decrease
    c. **Stop**
    d. Not be affected

184. **Long loops of Henle correlate with**
    a. **More concentrated urine**
    b. More dilute urine
    c. Urine hypotonic to the blood
    d. Urine isotonic to the blood

185. **Function of glomerulus in mammalian kidney is**
    a. Reabsorption of salts
    b. **Urine formation through blood filtration**

    c. Urine collection
    d. All of the above

186. **The function of kidney in mammals is to excrete**
    a. Extra urea, extra water and extra amino acids
    b. Extra urea, extra water and carbo-hydrate
    c. **Extra urea, salts and excess water**
    d. Extra salts, urea and excess water

187. **The breathing centre in the brain responds to changes in the**
    a. Oxygen concentration of the blood
    b. **Carbon dioxide concentration of the blood**
    c. Glucose in the mitochondria
    d. Acetyl coenzyme A in the mitochondria

188. **Which is present in the kidney?**
    a. **Glomeruus**
    b. Ciliated nephron
    c. Middle kidney duct
    d. Nephridism

189. **Most of the carbon dioxide in the blood is carried in the form of**
    a. Carbonic acid
    b. **Bicarbonates**
    c. Carbaminohemoglobin
    d. Dissolved CO_2

190. **Which one of the following binds with hemoglobin irreversibly?**
    a. Carbon dioxide
    b. **Carbon monoxide**
    c. Ethane
    d. Nitrogen

191. **Mechanical tissues are very poorly developed in**
    a. Xerophytes
    b. Halophytes
    c. **Hydrophytes**
    d. Lithophytes

192. **Desert can be converted into green land by**
    a. Halophytes
    b. **Psammophytes**
    c. Tropical trees
    d. Oxylophytes

193. Mangrove plants show vivipary. This is
    a. Germination of seeds within fruits while still attached to parent plant
    b. Germination of seeds in fruits on the soil
    c. Germination of seeds within fruit on sterile artificial culture medium
    d. Germination of seeds only after dispersal of fruits

194. **Among the following, which plant is completely devoid of roots?**
    a. **Ceratophyllum** b. Hydrilla
    c. Vallisneria   d. Azolla

195. What is the name given for an association of two species where one is benefited and other remains unaffected or unharmed?
    a. Parasitism   b. Symbiosis
    c. **Commensalism** d. Predation

196. Occurrence of Zoochlorellae in the body wall of Hydra is an example of
    a. A predation
    b. A food chain involving a parasite
    c. Commensalism
    d. **Mutualism**

197. Which one of the following is a protective device?
    a. Competition   **b. Camouflage**
    c. Commensalism d. Symbiosis

198. What is the sequence of species through which the organic molecules in a community pass called?
    a. Pyramid of energy
    b. Nutrient cycle
    c. Food web
    d. **Food chain**

199. A food chain consists of
    a. Producers and primary consumers
    b. Producers, herbivores and carnivores
    c. **Producers, consumers and decomposers**
    d. Producers, carnivores and decomposers

200. Which of the following is the correct sequence in food chain?
    a. Fallen leaves, bacteria insect, larvae and birds
    b. **Phytoplankton, zooplankton, fish**
    c. Grasses, fox, rabbit
    d. Grasses, chameleon, insects, birds

Model Test Paper 1

1. Pepsin is an example for the class of enzymes, namely
   a. Oxidoreductases
   b. Tarnsferases
   c. Hydrolases
   d. Ligases

2. The coenzyme not involved in hydrogen transfer
   a. FMN   b. FAD
   c. NADP⁺   d. FH4

3. In the feedback regulations the end product binds at
   a. Active site   b. Allosteric
   c. E-S complex   d. None of these

4. Which one of the vitamin A functions as a setroid hormone?
   a. Retinal   b. Retinol
   c. Provitamin   d. Carotene

5. The functionally active form of vitamin D is
   a. Cholecalciferol
   b. Ergocalciferol
   c. Dehydrocholesterol
   d. Calcitriol

6. The functionally active form of vitamin D is
   a. Cholecalciferol
   b. Ergocalciferol
   c. Dehydrocholesterol
   d. Calcitriol

7. The metabolite ex-read in murine in thimine deficiency is
   a. Pyruvate
   b. Glucose
   c. Xanthurenic acid
   d. FIGLU

8. The one that directly concerned with the synthesis of biogenic amines
   a. Tpp
   b. NADP
   c. Biotin
   d. Pyridoxal phosphate

9. Folic acid antagonist used in the treatment of cancer
   a. Methotrexate   b. Trimethoprim
   c. Sulfonamide   d. All of these

10. The key enzyme that converts trypsinogen to trypsin is
    a. Secretin
    b. Chymotrypsin
    c. Elastase
    d. Enteropeptidase

11. Hemophilia a is due to the deficiency of clothing factor
    a. X   b. V
    c. VII   d. II

12. Plasma albumin performs the following functions
    a. Osmotic   b. Transport
    c. Nutritive   d. All of them

13. The immunoglobulin presents in most abundant quantity
    a. IgG
    b. IgA
    c. IgM
    d. IgE

14. Name the immunoglobulin involved in body allergic reaction
    a. IgA
    b. IgE
    c. IgD
    d. IgM

15. The following anticoagulants binds with Ca^2 and prevent blood cloting
    a. Heparin
    b. Oxalate
    c. Protein
    d. All of them

16. The number of heme group presents in myoglobin
    a. 1
    b. 2
    c. 3
    d. 4

17. The patients of sickle cell anemia are resistant to
    a. Filaria
    b. Malaria
    c. Diabetes
    d. Trypanosomiasis

18. Name the amino acid that directly participates in the synthesis of heme
    a. Methionine
    b. Aspartate
    c. Glycine
    d. Tryptophan

19. Name the compound with the greatest standard free energy
    a. ATP
    b. Cyclic AMP
    c. Phosphocreatine
    d. Phosphoenolpyruvate

20. One of the following components of ETC possesses isoprenoid unites
    a. Coenzyme Q
    b. Cytochrome
    c. Cytochrome b
    d. None of them

21. The P : O ratio for the oxidation of FADH2 is
    a. 1
    b. 2
    c. 3
    d. 4

22. Inner mitochondrial membrane is impermeable to
    a. H^+
    b. K^+
    c. OH^-
    d. All of them

23. ATP synthase activity is associated with the mitochondrial enzyme complex
    a. V
    b. III
    c. IV
    d. I

24. The following substance is ketogenic
    a. Fatty acid
    b. Leucine
    c. Lysine
    d. All of them

25. The lipoprotein possessing the highest quantity of phospholipid
    a. HDL
    b. LDL
    c. VLDL
    d. Chylomicrons

26. Hormones sensitive lipase activity is inhibited by the hormone
    a. Epinephrine
    b. Insulin
    c. Thyroxine
    d. Glucocorticoids

27. The synthesis of urea occurs in
    a. Kidney
    b. Liver
    c. Muscle
    d. Brain

28. The amino acid required for the formation of glutathione
    a. Glycine
    b. Cysteine
    c. Glutamate
    d. All of them

29. The amino acid that does not participate in transamination
    a. Lysine
    b. Glutamate
    c. Alanine
    d. Tryptophan

30. Orotic aciduria can be treated by a diet-rich in
    a. Adenine
    b. Guanine
    c. Uridine
    d. Any one of them

31. The end product of purine metabolism in human is
    a. Xanthine
    b. Uric acid
    c. Urea
    d. Allantoin

32. The nitrogen atoms in the purine ring are obtained from
    a. Glycine   b. Glutamine
    c. Aspartate   d. All of them

33. The following is a sulfur-containing essential amino acid
    a. Methionine   b. Cysteine
    c. Cystine   d. All of them

34. Iron in the mucosal cells binds with the protein
    a. Transferrin
    b. Ferritin
    c. Ceruloplasmin
    d. Hemosiderin

35. The following element is involved in wound healing
    a. Calcium   b. Sodium
    c. Zinc   d. Magnesium

36. The number of polypeptide chains present in collagen
    a. 1   b. 2
    c. 3   d. 4

37. The functional unit of muscle
    a. Fiber cell   b. Myofibril
    c. H-band   d. Sarcomere

38. One of the following minerals is lacking in milk
    a. Calcium   b. Sodium
    c. Iron   d. Potassium

39. The essential amino acid limiting in rice
    a. Methionine
    b. Tryptophan
    c. Lysine   d. Histidine

40. The repeat sequence of nucleotides in telomere
    a. TTGGGA   b. TTGGG
    c. GGGATT   d. TTGAGG

41. The codon that terminates protein bio-synthesis
    a. UAA   b. UAG
    c. UGA   d. All of them

42. The nitrogenous base that is never found in the genetic code
    a. Adenine   b. Guanine
    c. Thymine   d. Cytosnine

43. Western blotting is the techniques for the identification of
    a. DNA   b. RNA
    c. Carbohydrates   d. Protein

44. Genetic immunization involves the administration of
    a. Antigens   b. Antibodies
    c. DNA   d. RNA

45. The cells organelles involved primarily in the digestion process are
    a. Nucleus   b. Glyoxysome
    c. Lysosomes   d. Ribosome

46. Which one the following types of RNA is not present in larger subunit of eukaryotic ribosome?
    a. 285   b. 5.85
    c. 185   d. 235

47. Which one of the following is not present in a higher plant cell?
    a. Peroxisome   b. Basal body
    c. Vacuole   d. Lysosome

48. Raisins when soaked in a hypotonic solution
    a. Shrink   b. Remain the same
    c. Swell   d. None of these

49. Wooden doors swell in rainy season due to
    a. Cell division   b. Imbibition
    c. Osmosis   d. Diffusion

50. The pH of pure water in
    a. Acid   b. Neutral
    c. Alkaline   d. Variable

51. Isomers are compounds having
    a. Same structure
    b. Some molecular weight
    c. Same function
    d. All of these

52. **Acidity or alkalinity of a solution is**
    a. Its molecular formula
    b. Its pH
    c. Its concentrations
    d. All of these

53. **A buffer solution has**
    a. More H^+ ions
    b. No free ions
    c. More OH^+ ions
    d. Variable

54. **Brownian movement in shows by**
    a. True solutions
    b. Suspension
    c. Colloidal solutions
    d. Solids

55. **Fog is an example of**
    a. Aerosol
    b. Emulsions
    c. Gel
    d. Suspension

56. **Petal is an example of**
    a. Gas dispersed in solid
    b. Liquid
    c. Liquid dispersed in liquid
    d. Gas dispersed in liquid

57. **Roots help in**
    a. Absorption of water
    b. Assimilation of nutrient
    c. Storage of food material
    d. All of these

58. **Cohesion theory was given by**
    a. Briggs
    b. Deovins
    c. Dixon
    d. None of these

59. **Loss of sap in liquid form is**
    a. Transportation
    b. Plasmolysis
    c. Guttation
    d. None of these

60. **Mycorrhiza is a**
    a. Saprophytic association
    b. Symbiotic of association
    c. Parasites of association
    d. None of these

61. **Upward translocation of water is called**
    a. Ascent of water
    b. Transportation
    c. Ascent of sap
    d. None of these

62. **Mycorrhizal association is**
    a. Endotrophic
    b. Ectotrophic
    c. Both
    d. None of these

63. **Which plant can absorb atmospheric water?**
    a. Lemon
    b. Orchid
    c. Trapa
    d. None of these

64. **Sunken stomata are seen in**
    a. Xerophytes
    b. Hydrophytes
    c. Mesophytes
    d. All of these

65. **Translocation of water and minerals is**
    a. Apoplastic
    b. Both of these
    c. Symplastic
    d. None of these

66. **Translocation of sugar and minerals**
    a. Apoplastic
    b. Symplastic
    c. Both of these
    d. None of these

67. **The unloading of the sieve elements occurs in the**
    a. Source
    b. Leaves
    c. Sink
    d. All of these

68. **Mycorrhizal association increases**
    a. Water demand
    b. Nutrient demand
    c. Water nutrient availability
    d. None of these

69. **Essential elements are**
    a. Micronutrients only
    b. Macronutrients only
    c. Both
    d. None of these

70. **Deficincy sympotms are show by.**
    a. Micronutrients only
    b. Macronutrients only
    c. Both
    d. None

71. **Nicked RNA molecule can be ligated by**
    a. T4 RNA ligase
    b. DNA polymerase
    c. T4 DNA ligase
    d. All of these

72. Which of the following is not a disaccharide?

a. Hyaluronic acid
b. Maltose
c. Lactose
d. Sucrose

73. What is the molecular formula of glucose?

a. $CH_3 OH$
b. $C_{12} H_{22} O_{11}$
c. $C_6 H_{12} O_6$
d. $C_6 H_{12} O_5$

74. Sucrose is composed of which two sugars?

a. Glucose and glucose
b. Glucose and fructose
c. Glucose and galactose
d. Fructose and galactose

75. In which of the following forms of glucose is stored in plants?

a. Starch
b. Dextrins
c. Glycogen
d. Cellulose

76. Which out of the following is a carbohydrate with no nutritional value?

a. Glycogen
b. Starch
c. Dextrin
d. Cellulose

77. Choose a sugar out of the following that is nonreactive to Selivanoff reagent?

a. Sucrose
b. Fructose
c. Inulin
d. Ribose

78. Choose a ketotriose

a. Glyceraldehyde
b. Dihydroxyacetone
c. Erythrose
d. Arabinose

79. A pentose sugar presents in the heart muscle is

a. Xylose
b. Xylulose
c. Lyxose
d. Aldose

80. d-glucose and l-glucose are

a. Stereoisomers
b. Anomers
c. Keto-aldose isomers
d. Optical isomers

81. All the following tests are positive for lactose, *except*

a. Benedict
b. Barfoed
c. Molisch
d. Osazone

82. Glucose can have isomers due to the presence of 4 asymmetric carbon atoms

a. 4
b. 2
c. 12
d. 16

83. Fructose and ribulose are

a. Epimers
b. Anomers
c. Ketoses
d. Ketose-aldose isomers

84. The compounds having same structural formula but differing in configuration around one carbon atom are called

a. Optical isomers
b. Anomers
c. Stereoisomers
d. Epimers

85. Which among the following does not belong to welfare schemes for the farmers?

a. Kisan Credit Card Scheme
b. SHG Bank Linkage Programme
c. National Agricultural Insurance Scheme
d. Employee Referral Scheme

86. The carbohydrate of honey is

a. Fucose
b. Maltose
c. Lactose
d. Fructose

87. Which of the following is a non-reducing disaccharide?

a. Galactose
b. Maltose
c. Trehalose
d. Sucrose

88. Which of the following is a true statement about glucose?

a. It cannot be utilized by red blood cells
b. It has 4 asymmetric carbon atoms
c. It is stored as starch in animals
d. It is oxidized to form glycerol

89. Sucrose is composed of which of the following two sugars?

a. Glucose and glucose
b. Glucose and fructose

c. Glucose and galactose

d. Fructose and galactose

90. Which of the following is not a homo-polysaccharide?

a. Starch   b. Heparin

c. Glycogen   d. Cellulose

91. Which out of the following is a fructosan?

a. Glycogen   b. Agar

c. Inulin   d. Cellulose

92. Choose a sugar abundantly presents in honey

a. Maltose   b. Fructose

c. Ribulose   d. Lactose

93. Choose an aldopentose

a. Glyceraldehyde

b. Dihydroxyacetone

c. Erythrose

d. Arabinose

94. Which of the following is a ketotetrose?

a. Xylose   b. Erythrulose

c. Fructose   d. Sedoheptulose

95. α-D-glucose and β-D-glucose are

a. Stereoisomers

b. Anomers

c. Keto-aldose isomers

d. Optical isomers

96. All tests are positive for lactose *except*

a. Benedict   b. Barfoed

c. Molisch   d. Osazone

97. Which out of the following is a carbohydrate with 6 carbon atoms and a keto group as the functional group?

a. Glyceraldehyde

b. Dihydroxy acetone

c. Fructose

d. Galactose

98. Mucin acid and gluconic acid are

a. Glycosides   b. Sugar acids

c. Amino sugar acids

d. Sugar alcohols

99. Sorbitol and mannitol are

a. Optical isomers

b. Anomers

c. Stereoisomers

d. Epimers

100. Which of the following tests is not based on the reaction of carbohydrates with strong acids?

a. Molisch   b. Benedict

c. Bial   d. Selivanoff

101. Which of the following is a simple sugar or monosaccharide?

a. Galactose   b. Lactose

c. Maltose   d. Sucrose

102. What is the molecular formula for glucose?

a. CH_3OH b. $C_6H_{12}0_6$

c. $C_{12}H_{22}O_{11}$ d. $C_6H_{12}O_5$

103. Maltose is composed of which two sugars?

a. Glucose and glucose

b. Glucose and galactose

c. Glucose and fructose

d. Fructose and galactose

104. In which form is glucose stored in animals?

a. Starch   b. Glycogen

c. Dextrins   d. Cellulose

105. All are glucosans (polymers of glucose) *except*

a. Glycogen   b. Inulin

c. Starch   d. Cellulose

106. Choose the aldose sugar out of the following

a. Sucrose   b. Ribulose

c. Fructose   d. Ribose

107. Choose the ketotriose

a. Glyceraldehyde

b. Erythrose

c. Dihydroxyacetone

d. Arabinose

108. A pentose sugar presents in the heart muscle is
    a. Xylose
    b. Lyxose
    c. Xylulose
    d. Aldose

109. α-D-glucose and β-D-glucose are
    a. Epimers
    b. Keto-aldose isomers
    c. Anomers
    d. Optical isomers

110. All tests are negative for sucrose *except*
    a. Benedict
    b. Selivanoff
    c. Barfoed
    d. Osazone

111. Glucose can have ——— isomers due to the presence of 4 asymmetric carbon atoms.
    a. 4
    b. 12
    c. 8
    d. 16

112. Galactose and glucose are
    a. Epimers
    b. Isomers
    c. Anomers
    d. Ketose-aldose isomers

113. The compounds having same structural formula but differing in configuration around one carbon atom are called
    a. Optical isomers
    b. Stereoisomers
    c. Anomers
    d. Epimers

114. When did the government present Kisan Credit Card Scheme?
    a. April, 1853
    b. August, 1998
    c. July, 1991
    d. November, 1995

115. The carbohydrate of blood group substance is
    a. Fucose
    b. Xylose
    c. Lyxose
    d. Fructose

116. Dulcitol is a
    a. Sugar acid
    b. Amino sugar
    c. Deoxysugars
    d. Sugar alcohol

117. Which of the following is a non-reducing sugar
    a. Arabinose
    b. Erythrose
    c. Trehalose
    d. Ribulose

118. A polysaccharide formed by 1, 4 glycosidic linkages is
    a. Starch
    b. Dextrin
    c. Glycogen
    d. Cellulose

119. Invert sugar is
    a. Starch
    b. Glucose
    c. Fructose
    d. Hydrolytic product of sucrose

120. The polysaccharide found in the exoskeleton of insects is
    a. Hyaluronic acid
    b. Cellulose
    c. Chitin
    d. Chondrosamine

121. Which of the following is a polymer of fructose?
    a. Inulin
    b. Dextrin
    c. Cellulose
    d. Glycogen

122. A disaccharide produced on hydrolysis of starch is called
    a. Sucrose
    b. Lactose
    c. Maltose
    d. Trehalose

123. The typical cyclical structure of glucose is α- and β-D
    a. Glucopyranose
    b. Glucoside
    c. Glucofuranose
    d. Glucosamine

124. Which test can be undertaken to differentiate between glucose and fructose?
    a. Benedict
    b. Molisch
    c. Selivanoff
    d. Osazone

125. Which of the following molecules is a carbohydrate?
    a. $C_3H_7O_2N$
    b. $C_{13}H_{26}O_2$
    c. $C_6H_{12}O_6$
    d. $C_{20}H_{40}O_2$

126. Which of the following monosaccharides is not an aldose?
    a. Ribose
    b. Fructose
    c. Glucose
    d. Glyceraldehyde

127. Which of the following is an anomeric pair?
   a. D-glucose and L-glucose
   b. α-D-glucose and β-D-glucose
   c. D-glucose and D-fructose
   d. α-D-glucose and β-L-glucose

128. Which of the following monosaccharides is not a carboxylic acid?
   a. Glucuronate   b. Gluconate
   c. Glucose   d. Muramic acid

129. From the abbreviated name of the compound Gal (β1→4) Glc, we know that
   a. The glucose residue is the β anomer
   b. The galactose residue is at the non reducing end
   c. C-4 of glucose is joined to C-1 of galactose by a glycosidic bond
   d. The compound is in its furanose form

130. The compound that consists of ribose linked by an N-glycosidic bond to N-9 of adenine is
   a. A purine nucleotide
   b. A pyrimidine nucleotide
   c. Adenosine   d. AMP

131. The active coenzyme form of cobalamin is
   a. Methyl cobalamin
   b. Deoxyadenosylcobalamin
   c. Both of the above
   d. None of the above

132. All are one carbon donors *except*
   a. Serine
   b. S-adenosyl methionine
   c. Choline   d. Thiamine

133. All are needed as coenzyme for alpha ketoglutarate dehydrogenase complex *except*
   a. Niacin   b. Folic acid
   c. Riboflavin   d. Lipoic acid

134. Which of the following vitamins can act without phosphorylation?
   a. Pyridoxine   b. Lipoamide
   c. Niacin   d. Thiamine

135. Impaired thymidylate formation is due to the deficiency of
   a. Pantothenic acid
   b. Niacin
   c. Folic acid   d. B_{12}

136. Scurvy is due to impaired____synthesis.
   a. Collagen   b. Prothrombin
   c. Hemoglobin   d. Elastin

137. Epileptiform convulsions in infants are found in the deficiency of
   a. Riboflavin   b. Thiamine
   c. Niacin   d. Pyridoxine

138. Pantothenic acid is important for which of the following steps or pathways?
   a. Pyruvate carboxylase
   b. Fatty acid synthesis
   c. Gluconeogenesis
   d. Glycolysis

139. The yellow color of egg yolk is due to the presence of
   a. Riboflavin   b. Thiamine
   c. Niacin   d. Pyridoxine

140. Neurological manifestations are present in
   a. Dry beriberi   b. B_6 deficiency
   c. B_{12} deficiency   d. All of the above

141. Transketolase activity is measured for the detection of _____ deficiency.
   a. Riboflavin   b. Thiamine
   c. Niacin   d. Ascorbic acid

142. All are the synonyms of folic acid *except*
   a. Vitamin M   b. Vitamin B
   c. PGA   d. Vitamin S

143. Schilling test is done to detect the deficiency of
   a. Riboflavin   b. B_{12}
   c. Niacin   d. Biotin

144. Subacute combined degeneration of the spinal cord is found in the deficiency of
   a. B_{12} b. B_6
   c. Niacin   d. Pyridoxine

145. The transaminases require the presence of
    a. Inositol
    b. B_6
    c. B_{12}
    d. B_2

146. The active coenzyme form of vitamin D is
    a. Calcidiol
    b. Calcitriol
    c. Calcitetrol
    d. None of the above

147. All are one carbon compounds *except*
    a. Formyl
    b. Methyl
    c. Methylene

148. If the mitochondria were blocked at the site of NADH oxidation and were treated with succinate as substrate, what would the P : O ratio is?
    a. Zero
    b. One less than normally produced by succinate
    c. Same as that normally produced by succinate
    d. One more than normally produced by succinate
    e. Higher than normal because of the excessive heat produced from uncoupling

149. If the oxidative phosphorylation was uncoupled in the mitochondria, what would one expect?
    a. A decreased concentration of ADP in the mitochondria
    b. Increased inorganic phosphate in the mitochondria
    c. A decreased oxidative rate
    d. A decreased production of heat
    e. Increased transport of ADP from the cytosol to the mitochondrial matrix

150. If the rotenone is added to the mitochondrial electron transport chain
    a. P : O ratio of NADH is reduced from 3 : 1 to 2 : 1
    b. Rate of NADH oxidation is diminished to two-thirds of its initial value
    c. Succinate oxidation remains normal
    d. Oxidative phosphorylation is uncoupled at site I
    e. Electron flow is inhibited at site II

151. If 2, 4-dinitrophenol is added to tightly coupled mitochondria that are actively oxidizing succinate
    a. Electron flow will continue but ATP synthesis will not occur
    b. Electron flow will continue but ATP synthesis will be increased
    c. Electron flow will cease, but ATP synthesis will continue
    d. Both electron flow and ATP synthesis will be ceased
    e. Subsequent addition of oligomycin will cause ATP hydrolysis

152. The prosthetic group of NADH dehydrogenase
    a. FMN
    b. NADH
    c. FAD
    d. NADPH
    e. Iron

153. In substrate level phosphorylation
    a. The substrate reacts to form a product containing a high energy bond
    b. ATP synthesis is linked to dissipation of proton gradient
    c. High energy intermediate compounds cannot be isolated
    d. Oxidation of one molecule of substrate is linked to synthesis of more than one ATP molecule
    e. Only mitochondrial reactions participate in ATP formation

154. The chemiosmotic hypothesis involves all of the following *except*
    a. A membrane impermeable to protons
    b. Electron transport by the respiratory chain pumps protons out of the mitochondria
    c. Proton flow into the mitochondria depends on the presence of ADP and Pi
    d. ATPase activity is reversible
    e. Only proton transport is strictly regulated, other positively charged ions

can diffuse freely across the mitochondrial membrane

155. **The effect of valinomycin on oxidative phosphorylation involves all of the following** *except*
    a. The net yield of ATP decreases
    b. Rate of oxygen consumption increases
    c. Excessive heat is released
    d. pH gradient across the inner mitochondrial membrane decreases
    e. The rate of flow of electrons increases

156. **Which of the following ETC components accept only one electron?**
    a. Coenzyme Q
    b. Cytochrome b
    c. FAD
    d. FMN
    e. O_2

157. **Which of the following has highest redox potential in the respiratory chain?**
    a. O_2
    b. Ubiquinone
    c. NAD
    d. FMN
    e. FAD

158. **Biotin is a coenzyme for reactions involving**
    a. Decarboxylation
    b. Carboxylation
    c. Transamination
    d. Deamination
    e. Transmethylation

159. **Folic acid is important for which of the following processes?**
    a. **Fatty acid oxidation**
    b. Fatty acid synthesis
    c. Gluconeogenesis
    d. One carbon metabolism
    e. Glycogenesis

160. **Sideroblastic anemia is observed in the deficiency of which of the following?**
    a. Thiamine   b. B_6
    c. B_{12} d. Niacin
    e. Vitamin K

161. **Xanthurenic acid excretion (tryptophan loading) test is carried out to determine the deficiency of**
    a. Riboflavin   b. B_6
    c. Niacin   d. Biotin
    e. B_{12}

162. **A 45-year-old chronic alcoholic male has been brought to medical emergency in a semi-conscious state. Blood lactate level is high. Which of the following vitamins can be used as a part of the treatment?**
    a. Vitamin C
    b. Vitamin B_{12}
    c. Thiamine
    d. Folic acid
    e. Pantothenic acid

163. **Which of the following is the coenzyme form of thiamine?**
    a. TPP (thiamine pyrophosphate)
    b. TMP (thiamine monophosphate)
    c. TTP (thiamine triphosphate)
    d. Free thiamine
    e. TAD (thiamine adenine dinucleo-tide)

164. **A 20-year-old male presents with hypertension. He has been prescribed a drug that work by inhibiting the synthesis of catecholamines. Which of the following vitamins participates in the synthesis of catecholamines?**
    a. Vitamin C   b. Vitamin B_{12}
    c. Niacin   d. Folic acid
    e. Biotin

165. **Which of the following is aTPP dependent enzyme?**
    a. Lactate dehydrogenase
    b. Glucokinase
    c. Transketolase
    d. Glutathione reductase
    e. Glutamate dehydrogenase

166. **A 30-year-old pregnant female presents to her obstetrician for a prenatal visit. She has been conscious of her weight gain and has not been taking a multivitamin. Her red blood cells are found to**

have decreased glutathione reductase function. Glutathione reductase requires

a. TPP
b. Pyridoxine
c. Riboflavin
d. B_{12}
e. Pantothenic acid

167. Which of the following is required as a coenzymes in the conversion of histidine to histamine?

a. TPP
b. NAD^+
c. Vitamin C
d. Pyridoxal phosphate
e. Folic acid

168. Which of the following cofactors is correctly matched with the vitamins, it is derived from?

a. NADH: Vitamin B_2
b. FADH2: Vitamin B_3
c. Pyridoxal phosphate: B_1
d. TPP: Vitamin B_1
e. Pantothenic acid: vitamin B_6

169. Which of the following coenzymes is required during the conversion of Glutamic acid to gamma aminobutyric acid (GABA)?

a. TPP
b. NAD^+
c. Vitamin C
d. Pyridoxal phosphate
e. FMN

170. Which of the following compounds is a recipient of the one carbon fragments that tetrahydrofolate receives and transfers?

a. Serine
b. Formaldehyde
c. Glycine
d. Formiminoglutamate (FIGLU)
e. Tryptophan

171. Which of the following is a compound formed from hydroxylation requiring vitamin C and subsequent methylation?

a. Histamine
b. GABA
c. Epinephrine
d. Carnitine
e. Serotonin

172. Which amino acid can be converted to non-adenine portion of NAD^+?

a. Histidine
b. Tyrosine
c. Tryptophan
d. Arginine
e. Phenyl alanine

173. A 25-year-old female who is 10 weeks pregnant presents with intractable vomiting from morning sickness. She is admitted for intravenous glucose administration and hydration. Which of the following vitamins can also be tried for treating the morning sickness?

a. Vitamin C
b. Vitamin B_{12}
c. Pyridoxal-P
d. Folic acid
e. Vitamin B_{12}

174. A 60-year-old female presents with severe back pain for the past week, she is diagnosed with osteoporosis, a condition resulting from calcium depletion in bones. As treatment which of the following vitamins can be prescribed?

a. Vitamin A
b. Vitamin D
c. Vitamin E
d. Vitamin K
e. Vitamin C

175. A 30-year-old pregnant female presents to her obstetrician for a prenatal visit. She has been conscious of her weight gain and has not been taking a multivitamin. Her red blood cells are found to have decreased transketolase function. Transketolase requires

a. TPP
b. Pyridoxine
c. Folate
d. B_{12}
e. FAD

176. A 20-year-old male presents with muscle weakness, and extreme fatigue. After an extensive work up he is diagnosed with carnitine deficiency. Which of the following vitamins participates in the endogenous synthesis of carnitine?

a. Vitamin C
b. Vitamin B_{12}
c. Pyridoxal-P
d. Folic acid
e. Biotin

177. **Which of the following is not a clinical outcome of niacin deficiency?**
    a. Diarrhea
    b. Night blindness
    c. Dermatitis
    d. Dementia
    e. Death

178. **Which out of the following is not a TPP dependent enzyme?**
    a. PDH complex
    b. Glutathione reductase
    c. α-Ketoglutarate dehydrogenase complex
    d. α-Keto acid dehydrogenase complex
    e. Transketolase

179. **Methyl malonic aciduria is a disorder associated with impaired metabolism of methyl malonic acid. Which of the following vitamins participates in its metabolism to form succinyl CoA?**
    a. Vitamin C
    b. Vitamin B_{12}
    c. Pyridoxal-P
    d. Folic acid
    e. Niacin

180. **Which of the following vitamins is required as a coenzyme for the activity of dihydrofolate reductase?**
    a. Vitamin C
    b. Vitamin B_{12}
    c. Pyridoxal-P
    d. Folic acid
    e. Niacin

181. **Which of the following set of vitamins participates in the synthesis of catecholamines?**
    a. Vitamin B_6 and C
    b. Vitamin B_{12} and folic acid
    c. Pyridoxal-P and niacin
    d. Folic acid and riboflavin
    e. Vitamin B_6 and B_{12}

182. **The conversion of pyruvate to oxaloacetate requires the presence of**
    a. Biotin
    b. Vitamin B_{12}
    c. Pyridoxal-P
    d. Folic acid
    e. Niacin

183. **Which of the following forms of vitamin A is required for vision?**
    a. All *cis* retinal
    b. All *trans* retinal

    c. 11-*cis* retinal
    d. 11-*cis* retinol
    e. Any of the above

184. **Which of the followings is a FAD dependent enzyme?**
    a. Lactate dehydrogenase
    b. PDH complex
    c. Transketolase
    d. Glutathione reductase
    e. Dihydrofolate reductase

185. **Which vitamin deficiency is associated with neural tube defects?**
    a. Vitamin C
    b. Vitamin B_{12}
    c. Pyridoxal-P
    d. Folic acid
    e. Niacin

186. **Hyperhomocysteinemia can be treated by supplementation with**
    a. Folic acid
    b. Vitamin B_{12}
    c. Vitamin B_6-P
    d. All of the above
    e. None of the above

187. **"Tryptophan load test" is carried out to determine the underlying deficiency of**
    a. Vitamin B_6
    b. Biotin
    c. Niacin
    d. Vitamin B_{12}
    e. Folic acid

188. **What is the link between intake of polished rice and sudden cardiac failure?**
    a. Riboflavin deficiency
    b. Thiamine deficiency
    c. Folic acid deficiency induced hyperhomocysteinemia
    d. Vitamin C deficiency
    e. Niacin deficiency

189. **"Histidine load test" is carried out to determine the deficiency of which of the following vitamins?**
    a. Folic acid
    b. Vitamin B_{12}
    c. Pyridoxal-P
    d. Vitamin D
    e. Riboflavin

190. **'Burning feet syndrome' is associated with a deficiency of**
    a. Lipoic acid
    b. Pyridoxal-P

c. Pantothenic acid
d. Niacin
e. Vitamin C

191. Sideroblastic anemia is observed in the deficiency of

a. Vitamin C   b. Folic acid
c. Vitamin B_{12} d. Pyridoxal-P
e. Vitamin K

192. As a hormone, vitamin D has three target tissues. Which are they?

a. Kidney, small intestine, bone
b. Heart, blood, bone marrow
c. Kidney, liver, brain
d. Small intestine, liver, fat cells
e. Liver, spleen and bone marrow

193. Epileptiform convulsions in infants are found in the deficiency of

a. Riboflavin   b. Thiamine
c. Niacin   d. Pyridoxine
e. Thiamine

194. Which of the following vitamins is required for the transfer of one carbon fragments?

a. Vitamin C   b. Folic acid
c. Biotin   d. Niacin
e. Riboflavin

195. Which of the following vitamins is used therapeutically as a lipid lowering drug?

a. Vitamin C   b. Folic acid
c. Biotin   d. Niacin
e. Riboflavin

196. The deficiency of which of the following vitamins, is responsible for the clinical manifestations of egg white injury?

a. Vitamin C   b. Folic acid
c. Biotin   d. Niacin
e. Riboflavin

197. Which vitamin deficiency leads to impaired coagulation of blood?

a. Vitamin C   b. Vitamin D
c. Biotin   d. Niacin
e. Vitamin K

198. Transamination is a process of transfer of α-amino group from a donor amino acid to an acceptor α-keto acid for the formation of a new amino acid and a new keto acid. This process is a reversible process catalyzed by transaminases that require as a coenzyme

a. Vitamin C
b. Folic acid
c. Vitamin B_{12}
d. Pyridoxal-P
e. Vitamin K

199. The inner mitochondrial membrane is impermeable to fatty acids. Carnitine acts as a transporter for internalization of fatty acids into the matrix where the beta oxidation of fatty acids takes place to provide energy to the body. Which of the following vitamins is required as a coenzyme for the synthesis of carnitine?

a. Vitamin C   b. Folic acid
c. Vitamin B_{12} d. Pyridoxal-P
e. Vitamin K

Model Test Paper 2

1. **Which among the following is not a member of ASEAN?**
   a. India
   b. Thailand
   c. Singapore
   d. Malaysia

2. **"Operation flood" refers to**
   a. Dairy development
   b. Flood control
   c. Prime Minister
   d. Planning commission

3. **Lira is the currency of**
   a. Bulgaria
   b. Italy
   c. Spain
   d. France

4. **What is cause of night blindnss?**
   a. Cataract, disease of the eyes
   b. Damaging of retina
   c. Deficiency of vitamin A
   d. Dilation of cornea

5. **Who announced the introduction of National Food security Act?**
   a. Pranab Mukherjee
   b. Manmohan Singh
   c. P. Chidambaram
   d. Arun Jaitley

6. **Allergy is caused due to**
   a. Inflammation of upper respiratory tract
   b. Inhaling pollens
   c. Introduction of foreign material in the body
   d. Antigen-antibody reaction

7. **At what temperature, reading in both the centigrade and the fahrenheit thermoeters are the same?**
   a. 40°C
   b. 60°C
   c. −40°C
   d. −60°C

8. **Richter scale is used to measure**
   a. Ocean depth
   b. Intensity of wind
   c. Intensity of volcanity
   d. Magnitude of earthquakes

9. **Who composed "Sare jahan se achha"?**
   a. Rabindranath tagore
   b. Krishna Rao
   c. Bankim Chandra Chatterjee
   d. Mohammad Iqbal

10. **The famous Indian astronomer Aryabhatta lived during the reing of**
    a. Ashoka
    b. Harsh Vardhana
    c. Chandragupta Vikramaditya
    d. Kanishka

11. **Redcliffe line demarcates the boundary between**
    a. India and China
    b. India and Pakistan
    c. Germany and France
    d. Poland and Germany

12. **Which of the following places is treated as the place of reference for determining the Indian standard time?**
    a. Delhi
    b. Allahabad
    c. Kolkata
    d. Mumbai

13. **Rubber is cultivated largely in the region of**
    a. Low temperature and heavy rainfall
    b. High temperature
    c. Low temperature and low rainfall
    d. High temperature and hearvy to low rainfull

14. **The first Indira Gandhi award for national integration was awarded to**
    a. Mothere Teresa
    b. Rajiv Ghandi
    c. Swami Ranganathananda
    d. Sunil Dutt

15. **The next Asian games (eleventh) was held at**
    a. Seoul
    b. India
    c. Beijing
    d. Jakarta

16. **"Pulitzet" award is given for the outstanding performance in the field of**
    a. Literature
    b. Music
    c. Journalism
    d. Sports

17. **Indian population as per 1981 census was**
    a. 64.5 million
    b. 68.4 million
    c. 73.5 million
    d. 58.5 million

18. **Who won the world Billiards championship in 1985?**
    a. Bob Marshalla
    b. Geet Sethi
    c. Michal Gerreira
    d. Subhash Agarwal

19. **The total oilseeds production in 1983–84 in**
    a. 11.3 million tonnes
    b. 8.5 million tonnes
    c. 13.5 million tonnes
    d. 16.9 million tonnes

20. **The first Indian who won the Utant award for cultural understanding was**
    a. S Radhakrishnan
    b. Jawaharlal Nehru
    c. Vinoba Bhave
    d. Indira Ghandi

21. **Polio vaccine was developed in USA by**
    a. John Enders
    b. Jonas Salk
    c. Louis Pasteur
    d. Thomas Wheeler

22. **Which among the following four words is a misfit**
    a. Fortron
    b. Cobol
    c. Robot
    d. Pascal

23. **"Kuchipudi" refers to**
    a. A cottan-jute fibre product manufactured for export
    b. A fermened liquor brewed by the tribals in Madhaya Pradesh
    c. An ancient dance form of Andhra pradesh
    d. A warrior dance of Kerala

24. **Which mirror is used as rear view mirror in vehicles?**
    a. Canvex
    b. Concave
    c. Plain
    d. Inverred

25. **The name of the surface to surface missile developed by India indigenously is**
    a. Akash
    b. Prithvi
    c. Agni
    d. Trishula

26. **The book "voice of conscience" was written by**
    a. Jayaprakash Narayan
    b. Sarojini Naidu
    c. VV Giri
    d. Mulka Raj Anand

27. **Which is the fifth international airport of the county?**
    a. Bangalore
    b. Trivandrum
    c. Nagpur
    d. Ahamadabad

28. **The recipient of "Shanti Swarup Bhatnagar" award for 1990 in the field of biological science is**
    a. Dr SK Brahmachari
    b. Dr B Bhattacharya
    c. Dr MS Rao
    d. Dr MA Vishwamitra

29. According to 1991 census the density of population is the highest in
    a. Kerala
    b. West Bengal
    c. Karnataka
    d. Uttar Pradesh

30. One rupee note bears the signature of
    a. Finance Minister
    b. Secretary, Ministry of finance
    c. RBI Governor
    d. None of these

31. "Hirakud" is the world's longest dam and is located on the river
    a. Ganga   b. Mahandi
    c. Godavari   d. Krishna

32. The word "Ornithology" is used in the study of
    a. Insects   b. Reptiles
    c. Birds   d. Fossils

33. The Roman numeral MCDLVI means
    a. 1156   b. 1456
    c. 1146   d. 1246

34. "Jnanpith" award is given in the field of
    a. Science   b. Medicine
    c. Literature   d. Technology

35. Number of primes between 1 and 30 is
    a. 15   b. 12
    c. 10   d. 8

36. The term "pawn" is used in
    a. Bridge   b. Billiards
    c. Chess   d. Baseball

37. The sides of two squares are in the ratio of 3:4. The ratio of their areas is
    a. 3:4   b. 8:6
    c. 9:16   d. 16:9

38. Which of the following countries has won the World Cup soccer championship thrice since inception in 1990?
    a. West Germany   b. Uruguay
    c. Brazil   d. Italy

39. Priyadarshini academy's best sportsman award for 1991 was given to
    a. Leander Paes
    b. Sachin Tendulkar
    c. Vishwanathan Anand
    d. Pargat Singh

40. Animals that live both on land and water are
    a. Reptiles   b. Insects
    c. Amphibians   d. Mammals

41. Indira Gandhi prize for peace, disarmament and development for 1990 was given by
    a. Dr Sam Nujoma, Nambia
    b. Mr Mikhail Gorbachev, Soviet Union
    c. Ms Groharlem Bruntdland, Norway
    d. Mr Robert Mugabe, Zimbabwe

42. Aryabhatta was a famous
    a. Physician
    b. Painter
    c. Astronomer
    d. Scientist

43. Dialysis is used when a patient has serious trouble with
    a. Liver   b. Lungs
    c. Heart   d. Kidney

44. Mutation means
    a. Exchange of genes
    b. A change in the chromosomes or genes of a cell
    c. A change in the cell structure
    d. Hydrazine

45. "Operation flood" refers to
    a. Dairy development
    b. Flood control
    c. Prevention of soil erosion
    d. Generating

46. Sarkaria commission was set up to
    a. Study center-state relation
    b. Uplift rural community
    c. Look after the functioning of universities
    d. Uplift scheduled castes/tribes

47. The Indian king who ruled over the entire southern India, Maldives and parts of Sri Lanka was
    a. Samudragupta
    b. Rajaraja the great
    c. Vikramaditya
    d. None of these

48. Which is the oldest dynasty?
    a. Cholas
    b. Pallavas
    c. Chalukyas
    d. Satavahanas
    e. None of the above

49. Nalanda university was associated with
    a. Ashoka
    b. Kanishka
    c. Harshavardhana
    d. Chandragupta Vikramaditya

50. Quit-India movement was during
    a. 1935
    b. 1940
    c. 1942
    d. 1944

51. On which of the following rivers is the world's largest dam built?
    a. Krishna
    b. Mahanadi
    c. Sutlej
    d. Damodar

52. The birth anniversary of which Indian leader is celebrated as" Teacher's day" in India
    a. Dr S Radhakrishnan
    b. Dr Zakir Hussain
    c. Lal Bahadur Shastri
    d. Lala Har Dayal

53. How many hours India is ahead of GMT?
    a. 3 hours
    b. 3½ hours
    c. 5 hours
    d. 5½ hours

54. "My presidential years" is written by
    a. George Bush
    b. Gyani Zail Singh
    c. R Venkataraman
    d. Nikhilov Gorbacher

55. The gas used in fire extinguisher is
    a. Carbon monoxide
    b. Sulphur dioxide
    c. Carbon dioxide
    d. Hydrogen

56. Who is the father of Library Science in India?
    a. A Kent
    b. SR Ranganathan
    c. PN Kaul
    d. Mangla

57. The Nobel prize to Noman Borlaug was given in the field of
    a. Chemistry
    b. Physics
    c. Economics
    d. Agriculture

58. The 1996 Olympic games were scheduled to be held at
    a. Tokyo
    b. Berlin
    c. Atlanta
    d. Stockholm

59. The movie "jurassic park" has been widely talked about. What does "jurassic" mean?
    a. An imaginary dinosaur
    b. A period in the history of the Earth
    c. A famous zoological park
    d. A species of dinosaur

60. Dr Salim Ali was associated with the study of
    a. Birds
    b. Insects
    c. Reptiles
    d. Rodents

61. The TV serial "Malgudi Days" was based on the novel written by
    a. Manohar Malgaonkar
    b. RK Narayan
    c. Mulk Raj Anand
    d. Kamala Markandeya

62. Who is the recipient of 1993 Nehru Award for International Understanding, awarded on 08–05–1995?
    a. Ms Margaret Thatcher
    b. Ms Hillary Clinton
    c. Ms Aung san suu Kyi
    d. Ms Maurice F Strong

63. Bomsai is the art of
    a. Growing trees in small pots
    b. Doing embroidery on the clothes
    c. Flower arrangement
    d. None of these

64. **Breeding and management of been is called**
    a. Apiculture
    b. Sericulture
    c. Siliviculture
    d. Pisciculture

65. **Shifting cultivation is commonly used in which of the following states?**
    a. Tamil Nadu
    b. Maharashtra
    c. Jammu and Kashmir
    d. Nagaland

66. **Which of the following is the main cash crop in Kerala?**
    a. Tobacco
    b. Rubber
    c. Sugar
    d. Jute

67. **Which state in India is called the "Garden of Spices"?**
    a. Karnataka
    b. Kerala
    c. Assam
    d. Tamil Nadu

68. **Which of the following regions get most of the rainfall due to cyclonic disturbances?**
    a. Andhra coast
    b. Kerala coast
    c. Punjab region
    d. Phenazopyridines

69. **Parthenocarpic fruits are**
    a. False fruits
    b. Composite fruits
    c. Seedless fruits
    d. None of these

70. **The gross cropped area (million hectares) in India is approximately**
    a. 151
    b. 162
    c. 175
    d. 185

71. **Which one of the following nitrogenous fertilizers is NOT very effective in acidic soils?**
    a. Nitrolin
    b. Ammonium sulphate
    c. Urea
    d. Di-nitro-anilliness

72. **Which one of the following crop enriches nitrogen content is soil?**
    a. Solghum
    b. Pea
    c. Sunflower
    d. Potato

73. **The greatest diversity of animal and plant species occurs in**
    a. Temperate deciduous forests
    b. Tropical moist forests
    c. Heavily polluted rivers
    d. Deserts and Savannas

74. **Onion is the modification of**
    a. Stem
    b. Root
    c. Leaves
    d. Petiole

75. **Which is the first agriculture university established in India on Land Grant pattern?**
    a. Tamil Nadu Agriculture University
    b. Punjabrao Krishi Vidyapeeth
    c. GB Pant University of Agriculture and Technology
    d. Odisha University of Agriculture and Technology

76. **Mixed farming involves**
    a. Both crop and livestock
    b. Growing a series of different crops
    c. Specialized cultivation of vegetables and fruits
    d. Pooling land voluntarily and managing by jointly

77. **What is the chief constituent of DDT?**
    a. Phenol
    b. Bromine
    c. Chlorine
    d. Benzene

78. **Which one of the following is the fastest growing tree?**
    a. Eucalyptus
    b. Coconut
    c. Deodar
    d. Banyan

79. **Black soil is most favorable for the cultivation of which crop**
    a. Jute
    b. Rice
    c. Cotton
    d. Wheat

80. **Which of the following needs a well aerated sand for its growth?**
    a. Potato
    b. Ginger
    c. Paddy
    d. Onion

81. **"Operation flood" is**
    a. A project to control flood
    b. A project to check deforestation
    c. A project to promote dairying in India
    d. None of these

82. **Ornithology is the science of**
    a. Birds   b. Reptiles
    c. Fossils   d. Silkworms

83. **Limnology is the study of**
    a. Marine water   b. Aquatic biology
    c. Fresh water   d. All of the above

84. **Cow's milk appears yellow because it contains**
    a. Fat   b. Lipids
    c. Protein   d. Riboflavin

85. **Which of the following states accounts for highest percentage of silk production in India?**
    a. Andhra Pradesh
    b. Karnataka   c. Tamil Nadu
    d. Jammu and Kashmir

86. **Beriberi, a vitamin deficiency disease, is due to the lack of**
    a. Vitamin A   b. Vitamin B
    c. Vitamin D   d. Vitamin K

87. **Which one of these contains maximum energy?**
    a. Proteins   b. Fats
    c. Sugar   d. Vitamins

88. **The best source of vitamin A is**
    a. Lima bean   b. Carrot
    c. Tomato   d. Orange

89. **According to the Planning Commission, how many average daily calories per person define the poverty line in rural areas in India?**
    a. 2100   b. 2400
    c. 2700   d. 3000

90. **Cod liver oil is a rich source of**
    a. Vitamin D and A
    b. Iron

    c. Calcium
    d. Protein

91. **The Eighth Five-Year Plan is operative during the years**
    a. 1992–97   b. 1991–96
    c. 1990–95   d. 1993–93

92. **Jawahar Rozgar Yojana has been renamed as**
    a. Self-employment to educated unemployed
    b. Prime Minister Rozgar Yojana
    c. Rajiv Ganadhi Rozgar Yojana
    d. None of the above

93. **Which one is the apex bank for rural credit?**
    a. Rural Co-operative Credit Societies
    b. State Bank of India
    c. National Bank for Agriculture and Rural Development
    d. Regional Rural Banks

94. **The system of Panchayat Raj was first introduced in the state of**
    a. Maharashtra   b. Gujrat
    c. Rajasthan   d. Andhra Pradesh

95. **The"Chipko andolan" is**
    a. A Movement to end untouchability
    b. A save-the-tress movement
    c. A campaign to increase milk production
    d. A movement to produce vegetable gum

96. **The Swaminathan Committee is associated with**
    a. Population policy
    b. Agricultural sector reforms
    c. Insurance policy
    d. Telecom policy

97. **World Development Report (1995) is published by**
    a. Food and Agricultural Organization
    b. International Food Policy Research Institute

c. World Bank

d. World Watch Institute

98. **Which of the following places is associated with the "Earth Summit" held a few years ago?**

a. Geneva

b. Stockholm

c. Rio de Janeiro

d. Burenos Aires

99. **Granite and basalt are**

a. Sedimentary rocks

b. Igneous rocks

c. Metamorphic rocks

d. None of these

100. **Khaire disease of rice is caused by**

a. Boron toxicity

b. Magnesium deficiency

c. Zinc deficiency

d. Copper deficiency

101. **If the solution pH increases from 4 to 6, the H^+ concentration decreases by**

a. 1/2

b. 1/5

c. 1/10

d. 1/100

102. **Black color of vertisols is due to presence of**

a. Titanium

b. Selenium

c. Organic matter

d. Montmorillonite clay

103. **Numerical value of correlation coefficient (r) can range from**

a. −1 to +1

b. 0 and 1

c. 0 to 0.99

d. −0.99 to +0.99

104. **Soils having kaolinite as dominant clay mineral have the problem of**

a. P fixation

b. K fixation

c. NH_4^+ fixation

d. None of these

105. **SAR of a normal soil is**

a. Less than 13

b. More than 13

c. More than 15

d. Less 15

106. **Acid sulphate soils are found in**

a. Punjab

b. Bihar

c. MP

d. Kerala

107. **Micronutrient involved in molybdenum in plants is**

a. B

b. Zn

c. Mo

d. Fe

108. **Saline soils show pH less than 8.5 due to dominance of**

a. Exchangeable sodium

b. Carbonates

c. Bicarbonates

d. Neutrale

109. **Hydraulic conductivity of soils is determined by using**

a. Fick's law

b. Stoke's law

c. Boltzman's law

d. Darcy's law

110. **Optimum pH for nitrification is**

a. 6.5

b. 7.0

c. 7.5

d. 8.5

111. **Water logging of soil increases the availability of**

a. Boron

b. Zinc

c. Iron and manganese

d. Copper

112. **Terai forests are**

a. Tropical forests

b. Coniferous forests

c. Deciduous forests

d. Temperate forests

113. **The most widely used source of N in agriculture in India is**

a. Farm yard manure

b. DAP

c. Urea

d. Calcium ammonium

114. **The most widely used source of organic manures in agriculture in India is**

a. Farm yard manure

b. Vermicompost

c. City waste

d. Sugar industry waste

115. **The electrical conductivity of soil solution is a direct measure of**

a. Total number of ionic charges in solution

b. Osmotic potential

c. Freezing point depression

d. Rise in boiling point

116. The adverse effect of high ESP of soil on plant is mainly due to

a. Decrease in water availability

b. Increase in osmotic pressure of soil solution

c. Deterioration of soil physical conditions

d. Reduced nutrient availability

117. The adverse effect of high B in soil solution on plant is mainly due to

a. Decrease in water availability

b. Increase in osmotic pressure of soil solution

c. Deterioration of soil physical conditions

d. Specific ion effect

118. The relative electron activity is denoted by

a. The logarithmic value of e

b. The square root of e

c. The natural log of e

d. None of the above

119. In a dried plant, essential element that constitutes bulk of its weight is

a. Carbon   b. Nitrogen

c. Oxygen   d. Hydrogen

120. In a living plant, essential element that constitutes bulk of its weight is

a. Carbon   b. Nitrogen

c. Oxygen   d. Hydrogen

121. The major ultimate product of microbial decomposition of organic matter (OM) is

a. Methane   b. Carbonic acid

c. Carbon dioxide

d. Carbon bisulphate

122. "Humus" is made up of

a. Humic materials only

b. Non-humic materials only

c. Both humic and non-humic materials

d. Polyphenols and polyquinones only

123. In tropical arable soils, the CEC of non-humus ranges between

a. 75% of soil organic matter

b. 25% of soil organic matter

c. 100% of soil organic matter

d. Always <50% of soil organic matter

124. The C–N ratio in undecomposed straw residues of cereal plants generally ranges between

a. 25:1   b. 10:1

c. 50:1   d. 100:1

125. The C–N ratio in unrecomposed leguminous plants generally ranges between

a. 25:1   b. 10:1

c. 50:1   d. 100:1

126. From plant nutrient supply point of view, humus is

a. Only a direct source of plant nutrients

b. Direct as well as indirect source of nutrients

c. Only an indirect source of plant nutrients

d. Not an important direct source of nutrients

127. Most common method of determining soluble K in soil is

a. Colorimetric

b. Flame photometric

c. Potentiometric

d. Titrimetric

128. Most common method of determining soluble P in soil is

a. Colorimetric

b. Flame photometric

c. Potentiometric

d. Titrimetric

129. Most common method of determining ammoniacal N in soil is

a. AA-spectrophotometric

b. Flame photometric

c. Potentiometric

d. Titrimetric

130. **High soil acidity is mainly due to**

a. Excess of soluble H^- ions

b. Excess of exchangeable H^- ions

c. Excess of exchangeable soluble H^- ions

d. Excess of exchangeable

131. **High acidity soils are normally rich in**

a. Sometimes

b. Vermiculits

c. Kaolinites and oxides of Fe and Al

d. Fine-grained mica

132. **The lime requirement of a high acidic soil (pH = 4) mainly depends upon**

a. pH

b. Contents of Fe and Al oxides

c. Cation exchange capacity

d. Exchangeable and soluble H

133. **The removal of bases is much faster than their accumulation on**

a. Arid, calcareous soils

b. Humid, acid soils

c. Temperate soils

d. Laterite soils

134. **The arrangement of the sand silt and clay particles within the soil is termed as**

a. Soil texture   b. Soil separate

c. Soil structure   d. None of these

135. **The height of rise in a capillary tube _____proportional to the tube diameter.**

a. Directly   b. Inversely

c. Some time inversely and some time directly

d. None of these

136. **The diameter of most erodible soil particle is**

a. 0.2mm   b. 0.4 mm

c. 0.3 mm   d. 0.1 mm

137. **Weathering, leaching and erosion are more intense and of longer duration in which one of the following regions?**

a. Temperate   b. Warm

c. Humid   d. Warm and humid

138. **Blosson-end rot in tomato has been found to be caused by the deficiency of**

a. Nitrogen   b. Phosphorus

c. Calcium   d. Sulphur

139. **Which type of oxidation of ammonia has been termed as nitrification?**

a. Chemical   b. Physical

c. Biological   d. Physicochemical

140. **"Reclamation" due to copper deficiency occurs in plants grown on newly reclaimed acid**

a. Histosols   b. Alfisols

c. Aridisols   d. Ultisols

141. **There can actually be a build-up of toxic concentration of Fe^{2+} in the soil solution of**

a. Aridisol   b. Histosol

c. Latosol   d. Vertisol

142. **In the fertilized soil with soil solution concentration of ppm of phosphorus, mass flow contribution to phosphorus nutrition of crop could approach**

a. 0%   b. 20%

c. 30%   d. 40%

143. **The physical condition of soil in relation to plant growth is called**

a. Soil consistency   b. Soil texture

c. Soil structure   d. Tilth

144. **An alluvial horizon formed below the plough layer in cultivated soil by the formed by tillage is known as**

a. Argillic   b. Agric

c. Oxic   d. Spodic

145. **Carbon dioxide at what per cent depresses the process of nodulation in legumes?**

a. 1% (V/V)   b. 2% (V/V)

c. 3% (V/V)   d. 4% (V/V)

146. **High concentration of substrate iron can microorganisms may produce toxins**

a. Nitrogen   b. Phosphorus

c. Potash   d. Sulphur

147. The most conspicuous chemical change that takes place when soil is flooded in reduction of
   a. Iron
   b. Manganese
   c. Denitrification
   d. Immobilization

148. High levels of ammonium can retard plant growth and restrict the uptake of
   a. Phosphorus
   b. Potassium
   c. Calcium
   d. Sulphur

149. The low pH tolerance of which is especially important in decomposing the organic residues in acid forest soil
   a. Actinomycetes
   b. Bacteria
   c. Fungi
   d. Molds

150. The optimum soil temperature for microbial oxidation of ammonium ions to nitrate ions is
   a. 27–32°C
   b. 10–13°C
   c. 37–42°C
   d. 45–52°C

151. The structural stability of earthworm casts is several times as compared to that of soil. It is
   a. 2–3 times
   b. 5–7 times
   c. 8–10 times
   d. 12–13 times

152. In Russian terminology "solonet" is used to designate
   a. Saline soil
   b. Alkali soil
   c. Degraded alkali soil
   d. Acid soil

153. Which is called as white alkali soil?
   a. Saline soil
   b. Sodic soil
   c. Saline sodic
   d. Degraded alkali soil

154. In soil taxonomy 'udolls' is a suborder of
   a. Entisols
   b. Inceptisols
   c. Mollisols
   d. Alfisols

155. The C-N ration in saw dust is
   a. 25:1
   b. 55:1
   c. 125:1
   d. 225:1

156. A vertical section cut down through the soil is known as
   a. Soil column
   b. Soil profile
   c. Soil horizon
   d. Soil sample

157. Microorganisms which feed upon living organic matter are known as
   a. Autotrophic
   b. Heterotrophic
   c. Paratrophic
   d. None of these

158. Nitrogen fixing bacterium called Azotobacter flourishes in soil development under
   a. Pine forests
   b. Legumes
   c. Teak plantation
   d. Grasslands

159. Weathering of base-rich minerals high in calcium and magnesium favours the formation of
   a. Illite
   b. Montmorillonite
   c. Kaolinite
   d. Vermiculite

160. Occurrence of quartz in amount makes a rock
   a. Alkaline
   b. Acidic
   c. Hard
   d. Soft

161. Dry and coarse-grained soils generally occur in
   a. River basins
   b. High lands
   c. Low lands
   d. Lakes

162. Ectotrophic mycorrhiza is common on
   a. Cultivated crops
   b. Forest trees
   c. Ornamental plants
   d. Carnivorous plants

163. Gneiss is a metamorphic rocks derived from
   a. Granite
   b. Limestone
   c. Slate
   d. Quartz

164. Arrangement of soil particles is referred to as
   a. Soil texture
   b. Soil structure
   c. Soil organization
   d. Soil consistency

165. Gravitational water is held in soil at a tension of
    a. 5.0 atmosphere
    b. Less than 1/3 atmosphere
    c. 15 atmosphere
    d. 1.3 atmosphere

166. The most proper tool meant for collecting soil sample from field is a
    a. Sickle
    b. Harrow
    c. Khurpi
    d. Soil auger

167. Diameter of a silt particle is
    a. Less than 0.002 mm
    b. 0.002–0.05 mm
    c. 0.05–0.50 mm
    d. More than 2 mm

168. Which of the following is a biofertilizer?
    a. Green manure
    b. Green algae
    c. Farm yard manure
    d. Compost

169. In degraded acid soils root extension into anaerobic and highly reduced layer is restricted due to harmful concentrations of
    a. Nitrogen
    b. Phosphorus
    c. Iron
    d. None of these

170. Rice plants show no manganese induced toxicity symptoms up to its tissue lever of
    a. 3000 ppm
    b. 4000 ppm
    c. 5000 ppm
    d. 6000 ppm

171. Clubfoot disease of cabbage may be controlled by raising the soil pH to
    a. 5 and above
    b. 6 and above
    c. 7 and above
    d. 8 and above

172. Primary minerals are found at
    a. High temperature and low pressure
    b. Low temperature and high pressure
    c. High temperature high pressure
    d. None of the above

173. Soil air in well drained soils contains CO_2
    a. 5%
    b. <1%
    c. <0.1%
    d. <0.05%

174. Soil color may not predict relative amount(s) of
    a. Organic matter
    b. Quartz
    c. Fe and Mn
    d. Oxygen

175. Normal aeration in the soil takes place by the process of
    a. Mass flow
    b. Diffusion
    c. Gravitational force
    d. Adsorption

176. The best C–N ratio for release of soil organic matter N is
    a. 35:1
    b. 10:1
    c. 20:1
    d. 17:1

177. The relationship of Mg and P in plant nutrition may be described as
    a. Synergistic
    b. Antagonistic
    c. No relationship
    d. Redox

178. The chemical composition of hematite is
    a. FeO
    b. Fe_3O_4
    c. Fe_2O_4
    d. FeO_2

179. The example of mineral that supply magnesium upon weathering is
    a. Turmline
    b. Apatite
    c. Pyrite
    d. None of these

180. Which nutrient is responsible for the dieaback of tictus?
    a. K
    b. Mg
    c. Cu
    d. Zn

181. The EC of sea water is
    a. 48.5
    b. 46.0
    c. 24.0
    d. 58.0

182. It is used as a desiccating agent
    a. $CaCO_3$
    b. $CaSO_4$
    c. $CaCl_2$
    d. $CaHCO_3$

183. Hysteris is common in soil, which is
    a. Wetted and dried
    b. Light textured
    c. Organic   d. Heavy

184. CEC of kaolinite [(C mol/kg) (P$^+$) kg^{-1}]
    a. 15   b. 20
    c. 100   d. 30

185. Rhizobium of alfalfa group is
    a. Trifoli   b. Lupini
    c. Meliloti   d. Japonicum

186. A redox indicator in organic carbon estimation is
    a. Ethylene blue   b. Diphenylamine
    c. Ferochrome black T
    d. None of these

187. Ammonia fixation is more in
    a. Allophane   b. Illite
    c. Gibbsite   d. Kaolinite

188. During phosphorus detrimental, a blue color is development with
    a. BaCl$_2$ b. K2CrO$_2$
    c. NaCl   d. SnCl$_2$

189. The crystallization sequence was given by
    a. Jenny   b. Bowen
    c. Dockuchiev   d. Marbut

190. Amongst humic substance in soil, the solubility follows the order
    a. Fulvic acid > Humic acid > Humin
    b. Humic acid > Humin > Fulvic acid
    c. Humic acid = Humic > Fulvic acid
    d. Humin > Humic acid = Fulvic acid

191. The unconsolidated material above the bed rock is known as
    a. Soil solum   b. Bed rock
    c. Regolith   d. A-horizon

192. Phenolphthalein is an indicator, which is used in titration for the determination of
    a. P$_2$O$_5$
    b. K$_2$O

193. c. Organic carbon
    d. CaCO$_3$ equivalent

193. If the scope of the land is 3–5%, than it will be called
    a. Moderately sloped land
    b. Sloping land
    c. Level land
    d. None of the these

194. A process in which organic form of nitrogen is changed into organic form is called
    a. Nitrification   b. Immobilization
    c. Ammonification
    d. None of the above

195. The population of bacteria is _____ by inoculation process.
    a. Decrease   b. Remain same
    c. Increase   d. None of them

196. *Rhizobium melitoli* can fix N in the roots of
    a. Alfalfa   b. Pea
    c. Lentil   d. Beans

197. *Rhizobium japonicum* can fix the N in the roots of
    a. Cucurbita   b. Soybean
    c. Pea   d. Maize

198. Nutrient index is used to prepare the
    a. Map of soil fertility
    b. Soil productivity map
    c. Nutrient cycle map
    d. All is correct

199. The acidity of H$^+$ in aqueous phase of soil is called
    a. Active acidity
    b. Reserve acidity
    c. Permanent charge
    d. None of the above

200. Per cent N is equal to
    a. % organic matter × 5
    b. % organic matter × 1.5
    c. Per cent organic matter × 0.05
    d. None of the above

Model Test Paper 3

1. The repeating units of proteins are
  a. Glucose units   b. Amino acids
  c. Fatty acids   d. Peptides

2. Amino acids are joined by
  a. Peptide bond   b. Hydrogen bond
  c. Ionic bond   d. Glycosidic bond

3. The primary structure of protein represents
  a. Linear sequence of amino acids joined by peptide bond
  b. 3-dimensional structure of protein
  c. Helical structure of protein
  d. Subunit structure of protein

4. Peptide bond is
  a. Rigid with partial double bond character
  b. Planar, covalent
  c. Covalent
  d. All of the above

5. Enzymes are
  a. Proteins   b. Carbohydrates
  c. Nucleic acids   d. DNA molecule

6. The first protein sequenced by Frederick Sanger is
  a. Haemoglobin   b. Myoglobin
  c. Insulin   d. Myosin

7. A dipeptide has
  a. 2 amino acids and 1 peptide bond
  b. 2 amino acids and 2 peptide bonds
  c. 2 amino acids and 3 peptide bonds
  d. 2 amino acids and 4 peptide bonds

8. The most common secondary structure is
  a. α-helix
  b. β-pleated sheet
  c. β-pleated sheet parallel
  d. β-pleated sheet non-parallel

9. Myoglobin is a
  a. Protein with primary structure
  b. Protein with secondary structure
  c. Protein with tertiary structure
  d. Protein with quaternary structure

10. Fibrous protein such as silk fibroin consists of polypeptide chains arranged in
  a. α-helix
  b. β-pleated sheet
  c. β-helix
  d. None of these

11. α-helix has
  a. 3.4 amino acid residues/turn
  b. 3.6 amino acid residues/turn
  c. 3.8 amino acid residues/turn
  d. 3.0 amino acid residues/turn

12. Tertiary structure is maintained by
  a. Peptide bond
  b. Hydrogen bond
  c. Disulphide bond
  d. All of the above

13. **Haemoglobin has**
    a. Primary structure
    b. Secondary structure
    c. Tertiary structure
    d. Quaternry structure

14. **Disulphide bonds are formed between**
    a. Cysteine residues that are close together
    b. Cystine residues that are close together
    c. Proline residues that are close together
    d. Histidine residues that are close together

15. **The 3-D structure of protein can be determined by**
    a. Nuclear magnetic resonance
    b. X-ray crystallography
    c. Both a and b
    d. Spectroscopy

16. **The most important interaction that contribute to polysaccharide folding**
    a. Ionic bond
    b. Hydrophobic interaction
    c. van der Walls interaction
    d. Hydrogen bond

17. **All of the following are extracellular heteropolysccaharides *except***
    a. Dextran   b. Chondroitin
    c. Hyaluronate
    d. Dermatan sulpahte

18. **Functions of carbohydrates include**
    a. Cell recognition
    b. Cell to cell interaction
    c. Imparting structure and store energy
    d. All of the above

19. **Lipopolysaccharide in the outer membrane is responsible for the antigenic property in**
    a. Gram-positive bacteria
    b. Gram-positive and gram-negative bacteria
    c. Gram-negative bacteria
    d. Actinomycetes

20. **Many plasma glycoproteins have a terminal sialic acid residue that helps in**
    a. Cell to cell recognition
    b. Cells interaction with extracellular matrix
    c. Protection form degradation by liver
    d. Generating signals that favours degradation by liver

21. **Lectins are**
    a. Carbohydrate degrading proteins
    b. Proteins that binds to carbohydrates with high affinity and specificity
    c. Glycoproteins that binds to carbohydrates
    d. Glycoproteins present in bacteria

22. **Selectins are**
    a. Plasma membrane lectins involved in cell to cell recognition
    b. Cytosolic lectins involved in intracellular signalling
    c. Plasma membrane glycoproteins involved in cell to cell interaction
    d. Plasma membrane glycoproteins that functions as second messengers

23. **Lectins binds preferentially to**
    a. More polar region of the carbohydrate residue
    b. Less polar region of the carbohydrate residue
    c. Both polar and non-polar region of the carbohydrate residue
    d. All of the above

24. **Glycosylation takes place in**
    a. SER and Golgi
    b. RER and Golgi
    c. SER, RER and Golgi
    d. RER, Golgi and mitochondria

25. **O-linked oligosaccharides are attached to the protein via**
    a. OH group of serine or tyrosine
    b. OH group of serine or threonine
    c. OH group of tyrosine or threonine
    d. OH group of threonine only

26. N-linked oligosaccharides are linked to protein via NH$_2$ groups of asparagine. The sequence containing asparagine is usually asp-X-ser/thr. X can be any amino acid *except*
    a. Glycine   b. Histidine
    c. Proline   d. Glycine

27. Agar-agar is obtained from
    a. Gelidium   b. Polysiphonia
    c. Fucus   d. Laminaria

28. Plants, which are not differentiated into roots, stem and leaves are grouped under
    a. Gymnosperms   b. Pteridophytes
    c. Thallophytes   d. Spermatophytes

29. Which is the most primitive group of algae
    a. Blue green algae b. Red algae
    c. Brown algae   d. Green algae

30. Iodine is obtained from
    a. Ulothrix   b. Ectocarpus
    c. Laminaria   d. Oedogonium

31. Which of the following is the most advanced group of algae?
    a. Cyanophyta   b. Rhodophyta
    c. Phaeophyta   d. Chlorophyta

32. Which of the algae is responsible for red colour of red sea?
    a. *Chlamydomonas brauii*
    b. *Trichodesmium erythrium*
    c. *Ulothrix zonata*
    d. None of the above

33. One of the following is present in blue green algae
    a. Starch
    b. Cyanophacean granule
    c. Any polysaccharide
    d. Floridian starch

34. Ability to fix atmospheric nitrogen is found in
    a. Leaves of some crop plants
    b. Chlorella

    c. Some marine red algae
    d. Some blue green algae

35. Origin and evolution of sex in algae is best seen in
    a. Blue green algae b. Green algae
    c. Red algae   d. Brown algae

36. Kelps is obtained from
    a. Algae   b. Marine algae
    c. Aquatic algae d. Lichens

37. Algae differ from Riccia and Marchantia in having
    a. Multicellular body
    b. Multicellular sex organs
    c. Pyrenoids in the cell
    d. Thalloid body

38. Heterocysts are heterocystin Anaebaena
    a. Green and thin-walled
    b. Green and thick-walled
    c. Colourless and thin-walled
    d. Colourless and thick-walled

39. Zygotic meiosis is a characteristic feature of
    a. Algae   b. Bryophytes
    c. Pteridophytes d. Gymnosperms

40. Cephaleoures is
    a. An epiphytic green algae
    b. A parasitic green algae
    c. A fresh water green algae
    d. A colourless red algae

41. Sargasso sea is named after an algae Sargassum which is a
    c. Red algae   d. Blue greeen
    c. Green algae   d. Red green algae

42. Photosynthetic pigments are located in
    a. Stroma   b. Grana
    c. Cytoplasm   d. Thylakoids

43. The dark reaction of photosynthesis was worked out by
    a. Hatch and Slack
    b. Melvin Clavin
    c. Arnold   d. Emerson

44. During photosynthesis oxygen is evolved from
    a. Carbohydrates   b. Proteins
    c. Sunlight   d. Water

45. Light reaction occurs in chloroplast: Photosynthetic apparatus
    a. Grana   b. Stroma
    c. Thylakoids   d. Mitochondria

46. Photosynthetic pigments absorb
    a. UV radiation
    b. IR radiation
    c. Visible radiation
    d. Gama radiation

47. In cyclic photophosphorylation, the high energy electrons are driven out from
    a. Chlorophyll a 683
    b. P 700
    c. Chlorophyll a 673
    d. P 870

48. One among the following elements is very important for photolysis of water
    a. Mg   b. Mn
    c. Fe   d. Zn

49. The hypothesis that all photosynthesis organisms require a source of hydrogen was first proposed by
    a. Van Niel   b. Hatch and Slack
    c. Hill
    d. Ruber and Kamen

50. In the photosynthesis process, PS II absorbs energy at or just below
    a. 700 nm   b. 870 nm
    c. 680 nm   d. 780 nm

51. The amount of ATP required for the synthesis of one glucose molecule in C4 pathway is
    a. 18 ATP   b. 30 ATP
    c. 12 ATP   d. 24 ATP

52. In bacterial photosynthesis comes from
    a. H_2S b. H_2O
    c. H_2SO_4 d. NH_3

53. Isotopes popularly known to have been used in study of photosynthesis
    a. C_{16} and N_{15} b. C_{14} and O_{16}
    c. P_{32} and C_{12} d. C_{11} and P_{32}

54. Dark reaction is traced by
    a. O_{19} b. P_{32}
    c. X-rays   d. $_{14}CO_2$

55. Photosynthesis is maximum in
    a. Blue light
    b. Red light
    c. Blue and green light
    d. Blue and red light

56. Law of limiting factor was proposed by
    a. Blackman   b. Hill
    c. Arnold   d. Engle man

57. The process of photosynthesis is
    a. Reductive, exergonic and catabolic
    b. Reductive, endergonic and catabolic
    c. Reductive, endergonic and anabolic
    d. Reductive, exergonic and anabolic

58. A photosynthetic organism which does not release oxygen is
    a. Blue green algae
    b. Green alga
    c. Green sulphur bacterium
    d. Lichen

59. Who was the first to study the influence of light during photosynthesis?
    a. Van Niel   b. Blackmann
    c. Warburg   d. J. Ingenhouz

60. 90% of the total photosynthesis is carried out by
    a. Algae
    b. Mesophytes
    c. Pteridophytes
    d. Xerophytes

61. An essential process connected with photosynthesis is
    a. Synthesis of glucose
    b. Photolysis of water
    c. Photophosphorylation
    d. Breakdown of glucose

62. The site of dark reaction of photosynthesis is
   a. Grana
   b. stroma
   c. thaylakoids
   d. Both a and b

63. Which of the following is least effective in photosynthesis?
   a. Blue light
   b. Green light
   c. Red light
   d. Sunlight

64. The hydrogen donor in bacterial photosynthesis is usually
   a. Water
   b. Ammonia
   c. Sulphur
   d. Hydrogen sulphide

65. The per centage of light energy fixed in photosynthesis is generally around
   a. 0.1%
   b. 1%
   c. 10%
   d. 100%

66. Light is necessary in the process of photosynthesis to
   a. Split carbon dioxide
   b. Produce ATP and a reducing substance
   c. Release energy
   d. Combine carbon dioxide and water

67. Annelids show advancement over the nematode in having
   a. Metameric segmentation
   b. True coelom
   c. Closed circulatory ststem
   d. All of the above

68. Anticoagulant secreted by leech is
   a. Heparin
   b. Hirudin
   c. Haematin
   d. Haemoglobin

69. Leech belongs to the class
   a. Oligochaeta
   b. Hirudinea
   c. Polycheta
   d. Chaetopoda

70. Total marine annelids belong to the class
   a. Oligochaeta
   b. Hirudinea
   c. Polycheta
   d. Chaetopoda

71. The mode of respiration in earthworm is
   a. Cutaneous
   b. Gills
   c. Pulmonary
   d. Subcutaneous

72. The excretory units of annelids are
   a. Uriniferous tubules
   b. Flame cells
   c. Nephiridia
   d. Nephrostomes

73. The first body segment of earthworm is
   a. Peristome
   b. Peristomium
   c. Protostomium
   d. Protostome

74. The nephridia of earthworm without nephrostomes are
   a. Integumentary
   b. Pharyngeal
   c. Septal
   d. Both a and c

75. The mode of feeding in leech is
   a. Herbivorous
   b. Carnivorous
   c. Omnivorous
   d. Sanguinivorous

76. Which one is known as nature's plough man?
   a. Nereis
   b. Cattle leech
   c. Earhworm
   d. Polygordius

77. In earthworm fertilization occurs in
   a. Oviduct
   b. Water
   c. Coon
   d. Ootheca

78. Chromophil cells in earthworm are concerned with the secretion of
   a. Amylase
   b. Protease
   c. Lipases
   d. Coccon

79. Nereis is commonly called
   a. Earthworm
   b. Calm worm
   c. Ringworm
   d. Roundworm

80. Role of typhlosole in the intestine of earthworm is
   a. To increase absorptive surface
   b. To control flow of blood
   c. To produce digestive enzymes
   d. To kill bacteria

81. Hemoglobin is dissolved in plasma in
   a. Earthworm
   b. Ascaris
   c. Tapeworm
   d. Insects

82. **Differential staining of bacteria on Gram staining is due to**
    a. Difference in the cell wall layer components of gram-positive and gram-negative bacteria
    b. Difference in the cell structure of gram-positive and gram-negative bacteria
    c. Difference in the mode of nutrition of gram-positive and gram-negative bacteria
    d. None of the above

83. **The iodine used in Gram staining serves as a**
    a. Chelator   b. Catalyst
    c. Mordant   d. Cofactor

84. **Which among the following is called as filamentous bacteria?**
    a. Mycoplasmas   b. Spirochetes
    c. Actinomycetes   d. Vibrios

85. **Which of the following groups of bacteria is considered as a link between bacteria and virus?**
    a. Mycoplasmas   b. Spirochaetes
    c. Actinomycetes   d. Vibrios

86. **Cork-screw shaped forms of bacteria are**
    a. Bacilli   b. Stalked bacteria
    c. Spirochaetes   d. Actinomycetes

87. **The ability of bacteria to change their morphological form frequently is termed as**
    a. Lysogeny
    b. Pleomorphism
    c. Alteromorphism
    d. None of these

88. **Bacterial cell wall is made up of**
    a. Chitin
    b. Cellulose
    c. Dextran
    d. Peptidoglycan

89. **Bacterial flagella is made up of**
    a. Microtubules   b. Tubulin
    c. Flagellin   d. Spinin

90. **Surface appendage of bacteria meant for cell to cell attachment during conjugation is**
    a. Pili   b. Flagella
    c. Spinae   d. Cilia

91. **Spinae is rigid tubular appendages in**
    a. Gram-positive bacteria
    b. Gram-negative bacteria
    c. Both a and b
    d. Actinomycetes

92. **The region where bacterial genome resides is termed as**
    a. Nucleus
    b. Cytoplasm
    c. Nucleoid
    d. Ribosome free region

93. **Bacterial chromosome is**
    a. Single-stranded and circular
    b. Double-stranded and circular
    c. Single-stranded and linear
    d. Double-stranded and linear

94. **Extrachromosomal, circular, double-stranded, self-replicating DNA molecule in bacteria is called**
    a. Cosmid   b. Plasmid
    c. Phagemid   d. Phasmid

95. **Membraneous infolding in bacteria that initiate DNA replication is**
    a. Mesosomes   b. Carboxysome
    c. Magnetosome   d. Nulcleosome

96. **The matrix of blood is known as**
    a. Plasma
    b. Serum
    c. RBC and WBC
    d. WBC and platelets

97. **The per centage of formed elements in the blood is**
    a. 45%   b. 50%
    c. 55%   d. 65%

98. **The lifespan of RBC**
    a. 100 days   b. 110 days
    c. 120 days   d. 130 days

99. The ratio of WBC and RBC is
    a. 1 : 60
    b. 1 : 600
    c. 1 : 6000
    d. 1 : 60000

100. During blood coagulation, thrombo-plastin is released by
    a. RBC
    b. Blood plasma
    c. Leucocytes
    d. Clumped platelets and damaged tissues

101. The lifespan of WBC is approximately
    a. Less than 10 days
    b. Between 20–30 days
    c. Between 2–3 months
    d. More than three months

102. The normal level of Hb per 100 ml of blood in women is
    a. 14g
    b. 18 g
    c. 20 g
    d. 10 g

103. Blood circulation was first explained by
    a. Jenner
    b. William Harvey
    c. Mendel
    d. Pasteur

104. Normal blood pressure of a healthy person is
    a. 120/100
    b. 110/90
    c. 120/80
    d. 120/90

105. What is the name of the iron-containing protein that gives red blood vessels and their colour?
    a. Hemocyanin
    b. Pyrite
    c. Hemoglobin
    d. Myoglobin

106. Which of the following in the body's largest blood vessel?
    a. Aorta
    b. Capillaries
    c. Pulmonary vein
    d. Heart

107. Which of the following is not the component of blood?
    a. Plasma
    b. Blood cells and platelets
    c. Gases and other dissolved substances
    d. All of the above

108. The ___ produces red blood cells, which transport ___ and some ___ .
    a. Liver; oxygen; mineral ions
    b. Liver; oxygen; carbon dioxide
    c. Bone marrow; oxygen; hormones
    d. Bone marrow; oxygen; carbon dioxide

109. Which of the following cations is required for the conversion of prothrombin into active thrombin by thromboplastin (blood coagulation step)?
    a. Ca^{2+}
    b. Fe^{2+}
    c. Mg^{2+}
    d. Mn^{2+}

110. A rise in blood cholesterol may lead to a deposition of cholesterol on the walls of blood vessels. This causes the arteries to lose their elasticity and get stiffened. This is called
    a. Hypertension
    b. Hypotension
    c. Arteriosclerosis
    d. Systolic pressure

111. Environmental biotechnology involves
    a. The use of microbes to clean up the environment
    b. Bioremediation
    c. The study of benefits and hazards associated with GMMs
    d. All of these

112. The use of living microorganism to degrade environmental pollutants is called
    a. Microremediation
    b. Nanoremediation
    c. Bioremediation
    d. All of these

113. Which of the following bacterium is called the superbug that could clean up oil spills?
    a. *Bacillus subtilis*
    b. *Pseudomonas putida*
    c. *Pseudomonas denitrificans*
    d. *Bacillus denitrificans*

114. **The process of extracting metals from ore bearing rocks is called**
    a. Bioextraction
    b. Microbial extraction
    c. Biofiltration
    d. Bioleaching

115. **The process of converting environmental pollutants into harmless products by naturally occurring microbes is called**
    a. *Ex situ* bioremediation
    b. Intrinsic bioremediation
    c. Extrinsic bioremediation
    d. None of these

116. ***Ex situ* bioremediation involves the**
    a. Degradation of pollutants by microbes directly
    b. Removal of pollutants and collection at a place to facilitate microbial degradation
    c. Degradation of pollutants by genetically engineered microbes
    d. None of these

117. **Which of the following microbes is widely used in the removal of industrial wastes**
    a. Trichoderma sp
    b. *Aspergillus niger*
    c. *Pseudomonas putida*
    d. All of these

118. **Microorganisms remove metals by**
    a. Adsorption and complexation
    b. Adsorption and precipitation
    c. Adsorption and volatilization
    d. All of these

119. **Chlorella spp are widely used in the removal of**
    a. Organic wastes   b. Hydrocarbons
    c. Heavy metals   d. All of these

120. **A non-directed physicochemical interaction between heavy metal ions and microbial surface is called**
    a. Biotransformation
    b. Bioconversion

    c. Biosorption
    d. Biomining

121. **Animal biotechnology involves**
    a. Production of valuable products in animals using rDNA technology
    b. Rapid multiplication of animals of desired genotypes
    c. Alteration of genes to make it more desirable
    d. All of these

122. **Animal cell cultures are used widely for the production of**
    a. Insulin   b. Somatostatin
    c. Mabs   d. Thyroxine

123. **The first vaccine developed from animal cell culture was**
    a. Hepatitis B vaccine
    b. Influenza vaccine
    c. Smallpox vaccine
    d. Polio vaccine

124. **Which of the following is commonly produced in animal cell cultures?**
    a. Interferon   b. Mab
    c. Vaccines   d. All of these

125. **The cell line used for the production of polio vaccine was**
    a. Primate kidney cell line
    b. CHO cell line
    c. Dog kidney cell line
    d. Mouse fibroblast cell line

126. **Recombinant proteins are**
    a. Proteins synthesized in animals
    b. Proteins synthesized by transgene in host cell by rDNA technology
    c. Proteins synthesized in cells that are produced by protoplast fusion
    d. Proteins synthesized in mutated cell lines

127. **Interferons are**
    a. Antibacterial proteins
    b. Antiviral proteins
    c. Bacteriostatic proteins
    d. All of these

128. The virus commonly used to infect cell cultures for the production of interferon is
    a. Coronavirus   b. Sendaivirus
    c. Poliovirus   d. Smallpox virus

129. Hybrid antibodies are
    a. Antibodies produced in cell cultures
    b. Antibodies designed using rDNA technology produced in cell cultures
    c. antibodies produced in *in vivo*
    d. Both a and b

130. The technique used in animal biotechnology for the rapid multiplication and production of animals with a desirable genotype is
    a. Protoplast fusion and embryo transfer
    b. Hybrid selection and embryo transfer
    c. *In vitro* fertilization and embryo transfer
    d. All of these

131. The production of complete animals from somatic cells of an animal is called
    a. Gene cloning
    b. Animal cloning
    c. Cell cloning
    d. All of these

132. The first successfully cloned animal was
    a. Monkey   b. Gibbon
    c. Sheep   d. Rabbit

133. In humans, the babies produced by *in vitro* fertilization and embryo transfer was popularly called
    a. *In vitro* babies
    b. Test tube babies
    c. *In vitro-in vivo* babies
    d. All of these

134. Who is the father of tissue culture?
    a. Bonner   b. Haberlandt
    c. Laibach   d. Gautheret

135. The production of secondary metabolites require the use of
    a. Protoplast   b. Cell suspension
    c. Meristem   d. Auxillary buds

136. Synthetic seed is produced by encapsulating somatic embryo with
    a. Sodium chloride
    b. Sodium alginate
    c. Sodium acetate
    d. Sodium nitrate

137. Hormone pairs required for a callus to differentiate are
    a. Auxin and cytokinin
    b. Auxin and ethylene
    c. Auxin and abscissic acid
    d. Cytokinins and gibberellin

138. DMSO (dimethyl sulfoxide) is used as
    a. Gelling agent
    b. Alkylating agent
    c. Chelating agent
    d. Cryoprotectant

139. The most widely used chemical for protoplast fusion, as fusogens, is
    a. Manitol   b. Sorbitol
    c. Mannol
    d. Polyethylene glycol (PEG)

140. Cybrids are produced by
    a. Fusion of two different nuclei from two different species
    b. Fusion of two same nuclei from same species
    c. Nucleus of one species but cytoplasm from both the parent species
    d. None of the above

141. Callus is
    a. Tissue that forms embryo
    b. An insoluble carbohydrate
    c. Tissue that grows to form embryoid
    d. Un organised actively dividing mass of cells maintained in cultured

142. Part of plant used for culturing is called
    a. Scion   b. Explant
    c. Stock   d. Callus

143. Growth hormone producing apical dominance is
    a. Auxin   b. Gibberellin
    c. Ethylene   d. Cytokinin

144. A medium which is composed of chemically defined compound is called
    a. Natural media   b. Synthetic media
    c. Artificial media   d. None of these

145. To obtain haploid plant, we culture
    a. Entire anther   b. Nucleus
    c. Embryo   d. Apical bud

146. Somaclonal variations are the ones
    a. Caused by mutagens
    b. Produce during tissue culture
    c. Caused by gamma rays
    d. Induced during sexual embryogeny

147. Which of the following plant cells will show totipotency?
    a. Xylem vessels   b. Sieve tube
    c. Meristem   d. Cork cells

148. Which vector is mostly used in crop improvement?
    a. Plasmid   b. Cosmid
    c. Phasmid   d. Agrobacterium

149. The major pollutant from automobile exhaust is
    a. NO   b. CO
    c. SO_2 d. Soot

150. The greenhouse gases, otherwise called radioactively active gases includes
    a. Carbon dioxide
    b. CH_4
    c. N_2O
    d. All of these

151. Algal bloom results in
    a. Global warming
    b. Salination
    c. Eutrophication
    d. Biomagnification

152. A high biological oxygen demand (BOD) indicates that
    a. Water is pure
    b. Absence of microbial action
    c. Low level of microbial pollution
    d. High level of microbial pollution

153. The effects of radioactive pollutants depend upon
    a. Rate of diffusion
    b. Energy releasing capacity
    c. Rate of deposition of the contaminant
    d. All of these

154. The range of normal human hearing is in the range of
    a. 10 Hz to 80 Hz
    b. 50 Hz to 80 Hz
    c. 50 Hz to 15000 Hz
    d. 15000 Hz and above

155. The pollution which does not persistent harm to life supporting system is
    a. Noise pollution
    b. Radiation pollution
    c. Organochlorine pollution
    d. All of these

156. Soap and detergents are the source of organic pollutants like
    a. Glycerol
    b. Polyphosphates
    c. Sulphonated hydrocarbons
    d. All of these

157. Growing agricultural crops between rows of planted trees are known as
    a. Social forestry
    b. Jhum
    c. Taungya system
    d. Agroforestry

158. The main atmospheric layer near the surface of earth is
    a. Troposphere   b. Mesophere
    c. Ionosphere   d. Stratospere

159. Observable characters of an organism is called
    a. Trait   b. Phenotype
    c. Genotype   d. Character

160. The unit of recombination is called
    a. Muton   b. Recon
    c. Cistron   d. All of these

161. A segment of DNA that codes for a functional polypeptide or an RNA molecule is called
    a. Allele
    b. Gene
    c. Recon
    d. Muton

162. Haploid refers to
    a. The number of chromosomes in the somatic cell of an adult organism
    b. The number of chromosomes in the gamete of an organism
    c. More than one set of chromosomes
    d. Sets of chromosome

163. Alternate forms of a gene is called
    a. Phenotype
    b. Allele
    c. Genotype
    d. Genome

164. The genetic constitution of an organism is called
    a. Genotype
    b. Trait
    c. Phenotype
    d. Genome

165. The character which is expressed in the F1 generation is called
    a. Co-dominant
    b. Dominant
    c. Recessive
    d. Hemizygous

166. An individual having two different alleles for one or more genes is referred as
    a. Homozygous
    b. Heterozygous
    c. Hemizygous
    d. Heterochromatic

167. Holandric genes are
    a. Genes carried on autosomes
    b. Genes carried on X chromosomes
    c. Genes carried on Y chromosomes
    d. Genes carried on any chromosomes

168. The crossing of F1 hybrid to one of its parents is called
    a. Test cross
    b. Back cross
    c. Reciprocal cross
    d. Monohybrid cross

169. The crossing of F1 hybrid to recessive parent is called
    a. Test cross
    b. Back cross
    c. Reciprocal cross
    d. Monohybrid cross

170. The phenotype found normally in a species is called
    a. Dominant type
    b. Mutant type
    c. Wild type
    d. None of these

171. Who coined the term linkage?
    a. Correns
    b. Mendel
    c. Morgan
    d. de Vries

172. Mendel did not observe linkage due to
    a. Mutation
    b. Synapsis
    c. Crossing over
    d. Independent assortment

173. The phenomenon of linkage was first observed in the plant
    a. *Lathyrus odoratus*
    b. *Pisum sativum*
    c. Datura
    d. *Mirabilus jalapa*

174. How many linkage groups of chromosomes will be present in case of maize, if all its genes are mapped?
    a. 5
    b. 10
    c. 15
    d. 100

175. Crossing over occurs during
    a. Pachytene
    b. Diplotene
    c. Diakinesis
    d. Pachytene

176. Crossing over is more frequent in
    a. Males
    b. Females
    c. Both
    d. None of these

177. Crossing over in diploid organism is responsible for
    a. Dominance of genes
    b. Segregation of alleles
    c. Recombination of linked genes
    d. Linkage between genes

178. Complete linkage has been reported in
    a. Maize
    b. Human female
    c. Male Drosophila
    d. Female Drosophila

179. **Coupling and repulsion phenomenon was concerned with**
    a. Crossing over   b. Mutation
    c. Linkage   d. All of these

180. **Linkage prevents**
    a. Homozygous condition
    b. Segregation of alleles
    c. Hybrid formation
    d. Heterozygous condition

181. **Observable characters of an organism is called**
    a. Trait   b. Phenotype
    c. Genotype   d. Character

182. **The unit of recombination is called**
    a. Muton   b. Recon
    c. Cistron   d. All of these

183. **A segment of DNA that codes for a functional polypeptide or an RNA molecule is called**
    a. Allele   b. Gene
    c. Recon   d. Muton

184. **Haploid refers to**
    a. The number of chromosomes in the somatic cell of an adult organism
    b. The number of chromosomes in the gamete of an organism
    c. More than one set of chromosomes
    d. Sets of chromosome

185. **Alternate forms of a gene are called**
    a. Phenotype   b. Allele
    c. Genotype   d. Genome

186. **The genetic constitution of an organism is called**
    a. Genotype   b. Trait
    c. Phenotype   d. Genome

187. **The character which is expressed in the F1 generation is called**
    a. Co-dominant
    b. Dominant
    c. Recessive
    d. Hemizygous

188. **An individual having two different alleles for one or more genes is referred as**
    a. Homozygous
    b. Heterozygous
    c. Hemizygous
    d. Heterochromatic

189. **Holandric genes are**
    a. Genes carried on autosomes
    b. Genes carried on X chromosomes
    c. Genes carried on Y chromosomes
    d. Genes carried on any chromosomes

190. **The crossing of F1 hybrid to one of its parents is called**
    a. Test cross
    b. Back cross
    c. Reciprocal cross
    d. Monohybrid cross

191. **The crossing of F1 hybrid to recessive parent is called**
    a. Test cross
    b. Back cross
    c. Reciprocal cross
    d. Monohybrid cross

192. **The phenotype found normally in a species is called**
    a. Dominant type   b. Mutant type
    c. Wild type   d. None of these

193. **Breeding for disease resistance requires**
    a. A good source of resistance
    b. Planned hybridization
    c. Diseases test
    d. All of these

194. **Polyploidy is induced through**
    a. Irradiation
    b. Mutagenic chemicals
    c. Ethylene
    d. Colchicine

195. **Heterosis is**
    a. Appearance of spontaneous mutations
    b. Induction of mutations

c. Mixture of two or more traits

d. Superiority of hybrids over their parents

196. The quickest method of plant breeding is

a. Introduction

b. Selection

c. Hybridisation

d. Mutation breeding

197. The new varieties of plants are produced by

a. Introduction and mutation

b. Selection and hybridisation

c. Mutation and selection

d. Selection and introduction

198. Pure line breed refers to

a. Heterozygosity only

b. Homozygosity only

c. Homozygosity and self assortment

d. Heterozygosity and linkage

199. A scientist wants to study the viral effects on plants. Which of the following part of the plant should be excluded?

a. Pith   b. Shoot apex

c. Phloem   d. Cortex

200. Somatic hybridization is achieved through

a. Grafting   b. Conjugation

c. Protoplast fusion

d. Recombinant DNA technology

Model Test Paper 4

1. Which weeds are indigenous?
a. *Acalypha indica*
b. *Abutilon indicum*
c. *Sorghum halepanse*
d. All

2. Which weeds are exotic weeds
a. *Parthenium hysterophorus*
b. *Acanthospermum hispidum*
c. *Lantana camera*
d. All

3. Season bound weeds are
a. *Sorghum halepans*
b. *Circium orvense*
c. *Phalaris minor*   d. All

4. Which weeds are summer annuals?
a. *Sorghum halepans*
b. *Avena fatua*
c. *Phalaris minor*   d. All

5. Weeds which usually parasite the host crop partially or fully for their nourishment are called as
a. Season bound weed
b. Crop bound weeds
c. Crop associated weed
d. None of these

6. Orbanche is
a. Complete root parasite
b. Complete stem parasite
c. Partial root parasite
d. Partial stem parasite

7. Trade name of Metaxuron is
a. Argold   b. Tip top
c. Dosanex   d. Stam F 34

8. Loranthus is
a. Complete root parasite
b. Complete stem parasite
c. Partial root parasite
d. Partial stem parasite

9. Critical period of crop-weed competition in jowar anigsesame is
a. 2–8 WAS   b. 2–5 WAS
c. 3–6 WAS   d. Up to 12 WAS

10. Orbanche is also known as
a. Broom rape   b. Witch weed
c. Dodder   d. None of these

11. Trade name of Isoproturon is
a. Arelon   b. Isoguard
c. Graminon   d. All

12. Cuscuta is also known as
a. Witch weed   b. Dodder
c. Both a and b   d. Broom rape

13. Cuscuta is mostly associated with
a. Lucerne   b. Berseem
c. Both a and b   d. Tobacco

14. Striga spp is mostly associated with
a. Vegetables   b. Fruit crops
c. Millest   d. Berseem

242

15. **Echinochloa colonum is mimic the crop of**
    a. Sorghum   b. Wheat
    c. Both a and b   d. Rice

16. **Trade name of Metsulfuron methyl is**
    a. Kloben   b. Almix
    c. Dosanex   d. Algrip

17. **Which weeds are contaminations with the crops?**
    a. *Echinochloa colonum*
    b. Allium spp
    c. *Phalaris minor*
    d. Both a and b

18. **Weeds habitat acid soils are called as**
    a. Neutrophile
    b. Basophile
    c. Herbaceous weeds
    d. Acidophile

19. **Weeds dominate saline/alkaline soil is called as**
    a. Neutrophile   b. Basophile
    c. Both a and b   d. Acidophile

20. **Simazine herbicide is**
    a. Soil-active herbicide
    b. Foliage-active herbicide
    c. Both a and b
    d. None of these

21. **Summer and kharif annuals weeds are**
    a. Trianthema sp.   b. *Digera arvensis*
    c. *Setaria glauca*   d. All

22. **Facultative weeds are also called**
    a. Mimicry
    b. Seasonal bond weeds
    c. Apophytes
    d. Anopheles

23. **Trade name of Chlorimuron ethyl is**
    a. Kloben   b. Almix
    c. Dosanex   d. Algrip

24. **Modes of propagation in weeds are**
    a. Sexual   b. Asexual
    c. Vegetative   d. All

25. **Vegetative propagation is primarily a feature of**
    a. Perennial weeds b. Annual weeds
    c. Both a and b   d. None of these

26. **Runners of floating weeds like water hyacinth and water lettuce (pistia lanceolata are called as**
    a. Stolon   b. Runners
    c. Suckers   d. Offset

27. **Swollen ends of its wiry rhizomes and suckers are called**
    a. Tubers   b. Bulbs
    c. Suckers   d. Runners

28. **Seed production of Amaranthus spp is**
    a. 170   b. 16,000
    c. 72,000   d. 1,96,000

29. **Trade name of Atrazine is**
    a. Aniloguard   b. Atrataf
    c. Machete   d. Graminon

30. **Alchlor, Butachlor and Propachlor belong to group of herbicide**
    a. Amides   b. Phenols
    c. Phynoxy acids d. Aliphatic acids

31. **Which herbicide belongs to group of aliphatic acids?**
    a. Alchlor   b. Butachlor
    c. Glyphosate   d. Propachlor

32. **Seed production of *Chenopodium album* is**
    a. 1345   b. 129
    c. 72000   d. 400

33. **Seed production of *Cyperus rotundus* is**
    a. 100   b. 40
    c. 300   d. 140

34. **Weeds are**
    a. Persistent   b. Hardy
    c. Both a and b   d. Tap root system

35. **Principles of crop weed competition are**
    a. Competition for nutrients
    b. Competition for moisture

c. Competition for light

d. Competition for co

36. Herbicide group of TCA is

a. Amides

b. Aliphatic acids

c. Phenols

d. Phynoxy acids

37. Glyphosate belongs to group of herbicide is

a. Amides

b. Phenols

c. Aliphatic acids

d. Phynoxy acids

38. Weed competition for

a. Water

b. Space

c. Light

d. All

39. Weed seeds are classified as

a. Deep germinating

b. Shallow germination

c. Shallow germination

d. All

40. Critical period of crop-weed competition in rice crop is

a. Up to 6 WAT

b. Up to 9 WAT

c. Up to 5 WAT

d. Up to 12 WAT

41. MCPB, amitrole, and herbicidal oils are

a. Soil-active herbicide

b. Foliage-active herbicide

c. Both a and b

d. None of these

42. Critical period of crop-weed competition in cotton is

a. 4–6 WAS

b. 2–3 WAS

c. 3–9 WAS

d. 4–6 WAS

43. The term allelopathy was introduced by

a. Molisch (1937)

b. Donald (1945)

c. Bain (1920)

d. None of these

44. Chemical group of MCPB, 2, 4-DB and Dichlorprop is

a. Phynoxy acids

b. Indole

c. Phenols

d. Traizines

45. EPTC herbicide is

a. Soil-active herbicide

b. Foliage-active herbicide

c. Both a and b

d. None of these

46. The word allelopathy is derived from

a. Greek

b. Latin

c. American

d. None of these

47. Trade name of Imazethypr is

a. Machete

b. Graminon

c. Persuit

d. Lasso

48. Allele chemicals released in the form of

a. Vapour

b. Leachates

c. Exudates from roots

d. All

49. Principles of weed management are

a. Prevention

b. Eradication

c. Control

d. All

50. Chemical group of Cycloxidimis

a. Imidazolines

b. Aryloxphenoxy propionate

c. Phynoxy acids

d. Cyclohexanedione

51. The hand hoe first animal drawn implement invented by

a. Jethro Tull

b. S.S. Bain

c. Thronwait

d. Condole

52. The mechanical methods include

a. Hand weeding

b. Hand hoeing

c. Supdding

d. Digging

53. Tillage and summer ploughing are method of

a. Physical and mechanical methods

b. Biological method

c. Chemical method

d. Cultural method

54. 2, 4-D was first time tested in India in

a. 1946

b. 1950

c. 1968

d. 1900

55. *Chondrilla juncea* is controlled by bioagent of

a. *Puccina chondrilla*

b. *Septoria cirsii*

c. *Bactra verutana*
d. Emmalocera spp.

56. *Cirsium arvensis* **is controlled by bio-agent of**

a. *Puccina chondrilla*
b. *Septoria cirsii*
c. *Bactra verutana*
d. *Emmalocera* spp.

57. Echinochloa spp is controlled by bio-agent of

a. *Puccina chodrillina*
b. *Septoria cirsii*
c. *Bactra verutana*
d. *Emmalocera* spp.

58. *Hydrilla verticillata* **is controlled by bioagent of**

a. *Chenopodium album*
b. Vicia spp
c. *Avena fatua*
d. *Hydrellia pakistanae*

59. Trade name of Clomozone is

a. Command   b. Atrataf
c. Machete   d. Lasso

60. Trade name of Ethoxysulfuron is

a. Sunrise   b. Atrataf
c. Machete   d. Graminon

61. Alchlor herbicide is

a. Soil-active herbicide
b. Foliage-active herbicide
c. Both a and b
d. None of these

62. Which herbicide belongs to group of benzoics?

a. 2, 3, 6 TBA   b. Dicamba
c. Both a and b   d. Paraquat

63. Tricamba and Chloramben both are belong to group of

a. Sylfonylureas
b. Benzoics
c. Imidazolines
d. Amides

64. Propham, Chlorpropham and Barban are belong to the group of

a. Amides   b. Aliphatic acids
c. Carbamates   d. Phynoxy acids

65. Butylate and Diallate both belonged to the herbicide group of

a. Amides   b. Thiocarbamates
c. Phynoxy acids   d. Aliphatic acids

66. CDEC and Metham are included herbicide group of

a. Aliphatic acids
b. Amides
c. Phenols
d. Dithiocarbamates

67. Chemical group of Fluchloralin is

a. Dintroanilins   b. Benzoics
c. Imidazolines   d. By Pyridillums

68. Chemical group of Isoproturon is

a. Thiocarbamates   b. Dintroanilins
c. Imidazolines   d. By Pyridillums

69. Chemical group of Dinoseb, DNOC and PCP is

a. Phynoxy acids   b. Traizines
c. Phenols   d. Dintroanilins

70. Chemical group of 2, 4-D, 2, 4, 5-T and MCPA is

a. Phynoxy acids   b. Traizines
c. Phenols   d. Dintroanilins

71. Chemical group of Metribuzine, Amytrin, Terbutrin is

a. Phynoxy acids   b. Ureas
c. Traizines   d. Uracils

72. Chemical group of Monuron, Diuron and Linuronis is

a. Phynoxy acids   b. Ureas
c. Traizines   d. Uracils

73. Chemical group of Bromacil, Terbacil and Lenacil is

a. Dintroanilins   b. Benzoics
c. Ureas   d. Uracils

74. **Chemical group of Nitrofen and Oxy-fluorfen is**
    a. Diphenly ethers
    b. Ureas
    c. Traizines
    d. Uracils

75. **Chemical group of Nitrofluorfen is**
    a. Thiocarbamates
    b. Dintroanilins
    c. Diphenly ethers
    d. By Pyridillums

76. **Trade name of Oxadiargyl is**
    a. Raft SC   b. Topstar WG
    c. Both a and b   d. Whipsuper

77. **Trade name of Paraquat is**
    a. Gramoxone   b. Stomp
    c. Both a and b   d. Rifit

78. **Chemical group of Clomozone is**
    a. Isoxazolidinones
    b. Ureas
    c. Traizines   d. Uracils

79. **Chemical group of Oxadiazon is**
    a. Isoxazolidinones
    b. Oxadiazoles
    c. Traizines   d. Uracils

80. **Chemical group of Methazole is**
    a. Diphenly ethers b. Oxadiazoles
    c. Traizines   d. Oxadiazolides

81. **Trade name of Pendimethalin is**
    a. Turgasyper   b. Topstar WG
    c. Stomp   d. Whipsuper

82. **Chemical group of Sulfentrazone is**
    a. Phenylpyridazones
    b. Dintroanilins
    c. Diphenly ethers
    d. By Pyridillums

83. **Chemical group of Pyridates is**
    a. T Aryloxphenoxy propionate
    b. Dintroanilins
    c. Triazolinones
    d. By Pyridillums

84. **Trade name of Pretilachalor is**
    a. Turgasuper   b. Rifit
    c. Stomp   d. Sofit

85. **Paraquat and diquat herbicide are**
    a. Soil-active herbicide
    b. Foliage-active herbicide
    c. Both a and b
    d. None of these

86. **Method of treating brush and trees is**
    a. Foliage treatment
    b. Basal bark treatment
    c. Cut stump treatment
    d. All

87. **Trade name of Pretilachalor-S is**
    a. Turgasuper   b. Rifit
    c. Stomp   d. Sofit

88. **2, 4-D is as**
    a. Translocated herbicide
    b. Contact
    c. Mobile in plant
    d. Non-mobile in plants

89. **Which herbicides are selective herbicides?**
    a. 2, 4-D   b. Alachlor
    c. Both a and b   d. None of these

90. **Trade name of Pyrazosulfuron ethyl is**
    a. Saathi   b. Turgasuper
    c. Fernoxone   d. Agrodon

91. **Contact herbicides are**
    a. Paraquat   b. Diquat
    c. Propanil   d. All

92. **Trade name of Quizalofopethyl is**
    a. Saathi   b. Turgasuper
    c. Fernoxone   d. Agrodon

93. **A residual herbicide is**
    a. 2, 4-D   b. EPTC
    c. Both a and b   d. Atrazine

94. **A non-residual herbicide is**
    a. Paraquat   b. Diquat
    c. Amitrole   d. All

95. **Narrow spectrum herbicide is**
    a. Metaxuron   b. Difenzoquat
    c. Diclofop   d. All

96. **Trade name of 2, 4-D is**
    a. Saathi   b. Turgasuper
    c. Fernoxone   d. Agrodon

97. **The temporary soil sterilants sterilize the soil for up to**
    a. 16 weeks   b. 23 weeks
    c. 5 weeks   d. 9 weeks

98. **Soil sterilants are also called as**
    a. Soil fumigants
    b. Adjuvant
    c. Contact herbicide
    d. None of these

99. **Form of herbicide formulation is**
    a. Water soluble concentrate (SC)
    b. Wettable powders (WP)
    c. Dry flowables (DF)
    d. All

100. **Trade name of Glufosinate is**
    a. Basta   b. Turgasuper
    c. Fernoxone   d. Arelon

101. **Form of sprayable concentrate is**
    a. Soluble concentrate
    b. Emulsifiable concentrate
    c. Wettable powder
    d. All

102. **Which herbicide is water soluble?**
    a. 2, 4-D   b. Diquat
    c. Glyphosate d. All

103. **Trade name of Isoproturon is**
    a. Basta   b. Turgasuper
    c. Fernoxone   d. Arelon

104. **Diameter of granular herbicides is**
    a. 0.04 to 1.0 mm   b. 1.0 to 1.5 mm
    c. 0.3 to 1.0 mm   d. 0.7 to 2.0 mm

105. **Granular herbicides are**
    a. 2, 4-D   b. Butachlor
    c. Glyphosate d. Both a and b

106. **Any approved herbicide is known as**
    a. Common name   b. Chemical name
    c. Trade name   d. All

107. **Trade name of Fenoxaprop-p-ethyl is**
    a. Machete   b. Graminon
    c. Whipsuper   d. Atrataf

108. **Trade name of Glyphosate is**
    a. Roundup   b. Glycel
    c. Both a and b   d. Whipsuper

109. **The weeds introduced from other countries are called as**
    a. Alein weeds
    b. Exotic weeds
    c. Both a and b
    d. Indigenous weeds

110. **When man aids in its introduction, such weeds are called**
    a. Anthrophytes
    b. Xanthrophytes
    c. Both a and b
    d. Indigenous weeds

111. **Trade name of Thiobencarb is**
    a. Roundup   b. Glycel
    c. Saturn   d. Stam F 34

112. **Weeds are classified based on association**
    a. Season bound weed
    b. Season unbound weeds
    c. Crop associated weed
    d. All

113. **Season bound weeds are**
    a. *Sorghum halepans*
    b. *Circium arvense*
    c. *Phalaris minor*
    d. All

114. **Which weeds are summer annuals**
    a. *Sorghum halepans*
    b. *Avena fatua*
    c. *Phalaris minor*
    d. Both a and b

115. **Trade name of Trifluralin is**
    a. Argold
    b. Tip top
    c. Dosanex
    d. Stam F 34

116. **Parasitism also called as**
    a. Stem parasitic
    b. Root parasitic
    c. Parasitic weeds
    d. None of these

117. **Orbanche is**
    a. Complete root parasite
    b. Complete stem parasite
    c. Partial root parasite
    d. Partial stem parasite

118. **Critical period of crop-weed competition in sugarcane is**
    a. 1 2–14 WAS
    b. 8–9 WAS
    c. 3–6 WAS
    d. 8–12 WAS

119. **Striga spp is**
    a. Complete root parasite
    b. Complete stem parasite
    c. Partial root parasite
    d. Partial stem parasite

120. **Trade name of Metaxuron is**
    a. Argold
    b. Tip top
    c. Dosanex
    d. Stam F 34

121. **Cuscuta is**
    a. Complete root parasite
    b. Complete stem parasite
    c. Partial root parasite
    d. Partial stem parasite

122. **Loranthus is**
    a. Complete root parasite
    b. Complete stem parasite
    c. Partial root parasite
    d. Partial stem parasite

123. **Orobanche is also known as**
    a. Broom rape
    b. Witch weed
    c. Dodder
    d. None of these

124. **Striga spp is also known as**
    a. Broom rape
    b. Witch weed
    c. Dodder
    d. All

125. **Trade name of Isoproturon is**
    a. Arelon
    b. Isoguard
    c. Graminon
    d. All

126. **Trade name of Alachlor is**
    a. Arelon
    b. Isoguard
    c. Graminon
    d. Lasso

127. **Loranthus is mostly associated with**
    a. Vegetables
    b. Fruit crops
    c. Cereals crop
    d. None of these

128. **Trade name of Cinmethylin is**
    a. Argold
    b. Tip top
    c. Dosanex
    d. Stam F 34

129. **Striga spp is mostly associated with**
    a. Vegetables
    b. Fruit crops
    c. Millest
    d. Berseem

130. **Orobanche is mostly associated with**
    a. Berseem
    b. Solanease family crops
    c. Cereals crops
    d. None of these

131. **Echinochloa colonum is mimic the crop of**
    a. Sugarcane
    b. Wheat
    c. Both a and b
    d. Rice

132. **Halaris minor is mimic of crops**
    a. Wheat
    b. Tea plantation
    c. Both a and b
    d. Bajra

133. **Trade name of Metsulfuron methyl is**
    a. Kloben
    b. Almix
    c. Dosanex
    d. Algrip

134. **Chicory is common name of**
    a. Cichorium intybus
    b. Coronopus didymus
    c. Phalaris minor
    d. All is correct

135. **Which weeds are contaminations with the crops?**
    a. Echinochloa colonum
    b. Allium spp
    c. Phalaris minor
    d. Both a and b

136. Lantana camera is
a. Non-woody weeds
b. Woody weeds
c. Herbaceous weeds
d. None of these

137. Weeds habitat acid soils are called
a. Neutrophile
b. Basophile
c. Herbaceous weeds
d. Acidophile

138. Weeds dominate saline /alkaline soil is called
a. Neutrophile   b. Basophile
c. Both a and b   d. Acidophile

139. Weeds of natural soils are called
a. Neutrophile   b. Basophile
c. Both a and b   d. Acidophile

140. Simazine herbicide is
a. Soil-active herbicide
b. Foliage-active herbicide
c. Both a and b
d. None of these

141. Trifluralin herbicide is
a. Soil-active herbicide
b. Foliage-active herbicide
c. Both a and b
d. None of these

142. Summer and kharif annuals weeds are
a. Trianthema sp.   b. Digera arvensis
c. Setaria glauca   d. All

143. Winter annuals weeds are
a. Chenopodium album
b. Vicia spp
c. Avena fatua   d. All

144. Facultative weeds are also called
a. Mimicry
b. Seasonal bond weeds
c. Apophytes   d. Anopheles

145. Trade name of Chlorimuron ethyl is
a. Kloben   b. Almix
c. Dosanex   d. Algrip

146. Trade name of Chlorimuron + Metsul-furon methyl is
a. Kloben   b. Almix
c. Dosanex   d. Algrip

147. Modes of propagation in weeds are
a. Sexual   b. Asexual
c. Vegetative   d. All

148. Vegetative propagation is primarily a feature of
a. Perennial weeds
b. Annual weeds
c. Both a and b   d. None of these

149. Aerial shoots coming from axils of lower leaves are called
a. Rhizomes   b. Runners
c. Bulbs   d. None of these

150. Swollen ends of its wiry rhizomes and suckers are called
a. Tubers   b. Bulbs
c. Suckers   d. Runners

151. Seed production of Amaranthus spp is
a. 170   b. 16,000
c. 72,000   d. 1,96,000

152. Trade name of Anilofos is
a. Aniloguard   b. Atrataf
c. Graminon   d. Lasso

153. Trade name of Atrazine is
a. Aniloguard   b. Atrataf
c. Machete   d. Graminon

154. Trade name of Butachlor is
a. Command   b. Atrataf
c. Machete   d. Lasso

155. Alchlor, Butachlor and Propachlor belong to group of herbicide
a. Amides   b. Phenols
c. Phynoxy acids   d. Aliphatic acids

156. Which herbicide belongs to group of aliphatic acids?
a. Alchlor   b. Butachlor
c. Glyphosate   d. Propachlor

157. Trade name of Thiobencarb is
    a. Roundup
    b. Glycel
    c. Saturn
    d. Stam F 34

158. Which weeds are winter annuals?
    a. Sorghum halepans
    b. Circium orvense
    c. Phalaris minor   d. All

159. Trade name of Trifluralin is
    a. Argold
    b. Tip top
    c. Dosanex
    d. Stam F 34

160. Cuscuta is
    a. Complete root parasite
    b. Complete stem parasite
    c. Partial root parasite
    d. Partial stem parasite

161. Striga spp is also known as
    a. Broom rape
    b. Witch weed
    c. Dodder
    d. All

162. Trade name of Alachlor is
    a. Arelon
    b. Isoguard
    c. Graminon
    d. Lasso

163. Loranthus is mostly associated with
    a. Vegetables
    b. Fruit crops
    c. Cereals crops
    d. None of these

164. Trade name of Cinmethylin is
    a. Argold
    b. Tip top
    c. Dosanex
    d. Stam F 34

165. Halaris minor is mimic of crops
    a. Wheat
    b. Tea plantation
    c. Both a and b
    d. Bajra

166. Striga spp is
    a. Complete root parasite
    b. Complete stem parasite
    c. Partial root parasite
    d. Partial stem parasite

167. Who announced the launch the Rashtriya Krishi Vikas Yojana?
    a. Narendra Modi
    b. De. Manmohan Singh
    c. Atal Bihari Vajpayee
    d. I.K. Gujral

168. Trade name of Chlorimuron-metsulfuron methyl is
    a. Kloben
    b. Almix
    c. Dosanex
    d. Algrip

169. Weeds of natural soils are called
    a. Neutrophile
    b. Basophile
    c. Both a and b
    d. Acidophile

170. Trifluralin herbicide is
    a. Soil-active herbicide
    b. Foliage-active herbicide
    c. Both a and b
    d. None of these

171. Winter annuals weeds are
    a. *Chenopodium album*
    b. Vicia spp
    c. *Avena fatua*
    d. All

172. Trade name of Chlorimuron-metsulfuron methyl is
    a. Kloben
    b. Almix
    c. Dosanex
    d. Algrip

173. Trade name of Butachlor is
    a. Command
    b. Atrataf
    c. Machete
    d. Lasso

174. Trade name of Anilofos is
    a. Aniloguard
    b. Atrataf
    c. Graminon
    d. Lasso

175. Dalapon belongs to the herbicide group of
    a. Aliphatic acids
    b. Amides
    c. Phenols
    d. Phynoxy acids

176. Trade name of Metolachlor is
    a. Command
    b. Atrataf
    c. Whipsuper
    d. Dual

177. Weed control includes
    a. Cultural
    b. Biological
    c. Chemical
    d. All

178. Chemical group of Naptalamis
    a. Phenylpyridazones
    b. Dintroanilins

c. Diphenly ethers

d. Phthalamates

179. 2, 4, 5-T herbicide is

a. Soil-active herbicide

b. Foliage-active herbicide

c. Both a and b

d. None of these

180. Which weeds are winter annuals?

a. Sorghum halepans

b. Avena fatua

c. Phalaris minor

d. All

181. Cuscuta is also known as

a. Witch weed   b. Dodder

c. Both a and b   d. Broom rape

182. Cuscuta is mostly associated with

a. Lucerne   b. Berseem

c. Both a and b   d. Tobacco

183. Trade name of Chlorimuron + metsulfuron methyl is

a. Kloben   b. Almix

c. Dosanex   d. Algrip

184. The herbicide may exhibit both, contact and transportation activities is

a. Paraquat   b. Diquat

c. Propanil   d. Atrazine

185. Narrow spectrum herbicide is widely used against specific weeds like

a. Phalaris minor

b. Avena fatua

c. Both a and b

d. Chenopodium album

186. The herbicide that kills plants without regard to species is called

a. Selective herbicide

b. Nonselective herbicide

c. Both a and b

d. None of these

187. Chemical group of Flumiclorac is

a. Phenoxy acids

b. Traizines

c. N-phenylphthalamides

d. Dintroanilins

188. Chemical group of Atrazine, Simazine and Metribuzine is

a. Aldehydes   b. Traizines

c. Phenols   d. Dintroanilins

189. Dichlormate and Asulam belong to group of herbicide

a. Carbamates   b. Benzoics

c. Imidazolines   d. Amides

190. Bromoxynil, Loxynil and Dichlobenil belonged to the group of

a. Amides   b. Phenols

c. Phynoxy acids   d. Nitrites

191. Insects, herbivorous fish, other animals, disease organisms are come under

a. Cultural control

b. Biological control

c. Chemical control

d. None of these

192. Chemical group of Haloxyfop-p and Fluazifop is

a. Phynoxy acids

b. T aryloxphenoxy propionate

c. Phenols

d. Dintroanilins

193. Cacodylic acid, MSMA and DSMA belong to group of herbicide

a. Amides   b. Phenols

c. Phynoxy acids   d. Aliphatic acids

194. Orobanche cernua is controlled by bio-agent of

a. *Bactra verutana*

b. *Septoria cirsii*

c. *Hydrellia pakistanae*

d. Sclerotinia spp.

195. Critical period of crop-weed competition in tobacco is

a. Up to 9 WAT

b. Up to 4 WAT

c. Up to 5 WAT

d. Up to 12 WAS

196. Seed production of Cuscuta spp is

    a. 1345   b. 16,000

    c. 129   d. 1,96,000

197. Chemical group of sethoxydim, Cletho-dim and Tralkoxydim

    a. Imidazolines

    b. T aryloxphenoxy propionate

    c. Phynoxy acids

    d. Cyclohexanedione

198. Different soil application methods are

    a. Surface application

    b. Band application

    c. Soil fumigation

    d. All

199. MB, metham, and dazomet are good examples of

    a. Soil fumigants   b. Adjuvant

    c. Contact herbicide

    d. None of these

200. Paraquat, diquat, sodium chlorate, weed oils, and acrolein are

    a. Selective herbicide

    b. Non selective herbicide

    c. Both a and b

    d. None of these

Model Test Paper 5

1. **Cultivation of viruses in the labotory using which method?**
   a. Chick embryo
   b. Animal cell line
   c. Bacterial culture
   d. All

2. **Antibiotic is not effective against which disease?**
   a. Bacterial infection
   b. Fungal infection
   c. Influenza
   d. None

3. **Similarities between the archaea and eukarya include**
   a. Same ribosomal proteins
   b. Archaea are more phylogenetically similar to eukarya
   c. They both lack peptidoglycan in their cell walls
   d. All

4. **Which of these is true for viruses?**
   a. Connective link between living and nonliving organism
   b. Having both DNA and RNA as the genetic material
   c. Genetic material is surrounded by protein capsid
   d. All

5. **Pasteur use word virus meaning**
   a. Nonliving
   b. Having only membranes envelope

   c. Poison
   d. Infectious

6. **In the case of both enveloped and non-enveloped virus genetic is surrounded by**
   a. Membranous envelope
   b. Host DNA
   c. Capsomers assembly
   d. Pantones and hexones

7. **Virus is said to be episomal latent this means**
   a. It can infect in each type of hast cell
   b. It cannot entered a lytic cycle
   c. It can produce persistent infection not chronic
   d. Both B and C

8. **Some viruses contain _____ which gives the outer boundary and it is mostly same as host PM.**
   a. Envelope   b. Capsid protein
   c. Spikes   d. Genetic material

9. **During virus infection to a cell**
   a. Its protein comes into the cell while the nucleic acid remains attached to the host cell surface
   b. Its genetic material comes inside through the pore made by receptor protein on the surface
   c. Only envelope interacts with plasma membrane of host and from endosome

253

d. There are always protections of pillus like extension appears which helps in DNA transfer

10. The viral infection cycle in which the infected host cell undergoes cell destruction is called

a. Lysogenic cycle
b. Lysozyme cycle
c. Lytic cycle
d. Template phage cycle

11. The viral infection cycle in which the viral DNA integrated into the bacterial DNA is called

a. Lysogenic cycle
b. Lysozyme cycle
c. Lytic cycle
d. Temperate

12. Retrovirus is

a. Causative agent of cancer or AIDS
b. Possesses the unique enzyme reverse transcription
c. It has the capacity to produce cDNA from RNA
d. All

13. Adenovirus has

a. ds linear DNA genome
b. ss linear DNA genome
c. ds circular DNA genome
d. None of these

14. What is true about viruses?

a. They have their own genetic material which is material as host
b. Outside the host they can survive
c. They got their capsid proteins from host protein
d. All are false

15. What is true about prions?

a. Prions are infectious protein presents in its misfolded form
b. Cause BSE in cattle and Cruetzfeld-Jakob disease in human
c. All known diseases affect the structure of the brain or other natural tissue
d. All

16. The route of transmission of measles virus is

a. Respiratory tract
b. Intestinal tract
c. Genital tract
d. None

17. Vector for yellow fever virus transmission is

a. Mosquitoes   b. Midges
c. Ticks   d. Syringes

18. Parvoviruses enter in host cell at what phase of cell cycle?

a. G1   b. G2
c. S   d. M

19. Cell receptor of poliovirus and the protein involved is

a. CO_4 and gp 120   b. CD155 and vp 1
c. LDP and vp 1   d. None

20. The force that not bind virus attachments site to receptor is

a. H bonds
b. Ionic interactions
c. van der Waals forces
d. Covalent bonds

21. Which virus uses –OH group of amino acid for next nucleotide?

a. Poliovirus   b. Adenovirus
c. Rotavirus   d. HIV

22. Virus having (–) RNA segmented genome is replicated in

a. Cytoplasm   b. Nucleus
c. Both   d. None

23. Okazaki fragments are synthesized on which strand of DNA?

a. Leading strand b. Lagging strand
c. Both   d. None

24. Which of the following is not involved in replication of DNA?

a. DNA polymerase
b. DNA ligase
c. Helicase
d. Rho factor

25. TATA box is the site of initiation of
    a. Replication   b. Transcription
    c. Translation   d. All

26. In T4 phase genome which nucleic acid is absent?
    a. T   b. C
    c. G   d. A

27. Potato X virus causes necrotic spotting in
    a. Potato   b. Tomato
    c. Tobacco   d. All

28. Gemini virus belongs to class
    a. Class II   b. Class I
    c. Class IV   d. Class V

29. CMV movement protein is produced by
    a. ORF I   b. ORF I
    c. IORF VI   d. ORF VII

30. Viroids are plant pathogen having
    a. ssRNA
    b. ssRNA + envelope
    c. ssDNA
    d. Only envelope

31. Which virus carries important enzymes from last infected host?
    a. Poliovirus   b. Adenovirus
    c. Rotavirus   d. Poxvirus

32. Which virus has CD150 and haemaglutinine as cell receptor and attachment protein?
    a. Polivoirus
    b. Measles virus
    c. Rotavirus
    d. HIV

33. Virus having (+) RNA segmented genome is replicated in
    a. Cytoplasm
    b. Nucleus
    c. Both   d. None

34. The genome of poxvirus is
    a. dsDNA   b. ssDNA
    c. dsRNA   d. ssRNA

35. According to Baltimore classification of RT virus belongs to
    a. Class I   b. Class II
    c. Class IV   d. Class VI

36. The protein constituent having capacity to cause disease is
    a. class 1   b. class II
    c. class IV   d. class VI

37. What is the biochemical nature of viruses?
    a. Protein   b. Nucleoprotein
    c. Virions   d. All

38. According to ICTV classification virus is divided in how many order?
    a. 8   b. 7
    c. 6   d. 9

39. Which of the following is the major function of viruses enveloped?
    a. Antigenicity   b. Infectivity
    c. Resistant   d. All

40. Which of the following is not a component of icosahedrons structure?
    a. 20 faces   b. Faces 12
    c. 40 edges   d. 60 protein

41. How many capsomers are present in capsids of papillomavirus?
    a. 45   b. 72
    c. 67   d. 80

42. Viroids are plant pathogen having
    a. ssRNA   b. ssRNA
    c. ssDNA   d. Only envelope

43. Hepatitis D virus resembles with
    a. Virions   b. Prions
    c. Viriods   d. Virus capsids

44. The bacteriophage having tail is usually
    a. Motile   b. Nonmotile
    c. Metabolically high active
    d. None

45. Which of the following waterborne diseases is caused by virus?
    a. Typhoid fever   b. Poliomyelitis
    c. Shigellosis   d. None

46. **Which one of the following conditions leads to death in a case of cholera?**
    a. Toxic dilation of the colon
    b. Rapid dehydration causing shock
    c. Toxic substance produced by *Vibrio cholerae*
    d. All

47. **Which one of the following waterborne diseases can be prevented by vaccination?**
    a. Poliomyelitis   b. Typhoid fever
    c. Both   d. None

48. **Which of the following is true about hepatitis A?**
    a. Transmission is mainly fecal oral route
    b. Transmission is the caused by hepatitis A virus
    c. Liver cell is mainly attached by virus
    d. All of the above

49. **Which of the following microorganisms causes diarrhea?**
    a. Cyanobacteria   b. Salmonella
    c. Shigella   d. All

50. **Which of the following is not a water borne disease?**
    a. Botulism   b. Shigellosis
    c. Poliomyelitis   d. Hepatitis

51. **The group having maximum risk of waterborne diseases are**
    a. Oil age people
    b. Age group 20 to 40
    c. Childrens under five years of age
    d. Child of 10 to 15 years

52. **Ceftriaxone is used against which disease**
    a. Botulism   b. Shigellosis
    c. Dracunculiasis   d. Typhoid fever

53. **A large scale water treatment is**
    a. Boiling
    b. Home made sand filter
    c. Municipal treatment using sand filter
    d. None

54. **To prevent waterborne diseases, more attention should be given to**
    a. Protecting water sources
    b. Cleanliness of water containers
    c. Hygienic behavior of users
    d. All

55. **The diagnosis of intestinal amoebiasis can be made by identifying the**
    a. Cyst stage
    b. Trophozoite stage
    c. Larvae
    d. Only a and b

56. **Mild diarrhea to severe dysentery with blood and mucus is the symptoms of**
    a. Botulism
    b. Shigellosis
    c. Amoebiasis
    d. Typhoid fever

57. **Which of the following specimens is not used for the diagnosis of giardiasis?**
    a. Stood   b. Shigellosis
    c. Serum   d. None

58. **The most serious foodborne disease is**
    a. Dysentery   b. Tetanus
    c. Botulism   d. Gas gangrene

59. **_____ disease is caused by the amoeba *Entamoeba histolytica*.**
    a. Botulism   b. Shigellosis
    c. Amoebiasis   d. Typhoid fever

60. ***Entamoeba histoltyica* is spread through**
    a. Bite of Anopheles mosquito
    b. Intake of contaminated food or water
    c. Virus
    d. Pigs

61. **____ organism causes sleeping sickness.**
    a. Trypanosoma   b. Leishmania
    c. Virus   d. None

62. **Which of the following diseases is caused by DNA virus?**
    a. Smallpox   b. Shigellosis
    c. Measles   d. Typhoid fever

63. Which among the following factors protect eye and the respiratory tract against infection?
    a. The B cells produced by plasma cell
    b. The acidic secretions by the local tissue
    c. The lysozyme secreted onto their surface
    d. All

64. What is not true about complement system?
    a. Is a part of individual's innat immunity not acquired immunity
    b. There are 3 basic pathways—classical complement pathway, the alternative complement pathway and the lectin pathway
    c. They do not form MAC
    d. Main function is opsonization and chemotaxis

65. The antibody having capacity to cross the placenta is
    a. IgA
    b. IgG
    c. IgE
    d. IgM

66. Mostly the concentration of self reactive antibodies is very low in normal serum. It is due to
    a. Self-reactive antibody is not generated in normal condition
    b. Once it is formed, it is immediately killed by effector cell
    c. B cells that are stimulated via their surface bound antibody in the absence of T cell help to commit suicide
    d. Self reactive B cells are converted to effector B cells and participate in immunological response

67. Which among them is the first antibody to be appeared due to an antigen response?
    a. IgM
    b. IgA
    c. IgD
    d. IgG

68. Which of the following part of antibody is act as site where antigen binding domain is present?
    a. V and C regions of heavy chain
    b. V and C regions of light chain
    c. Fab regions of the antibody
    d. All

69. Antibody which mediates Type I hypersensitivity reaction is
    a. IgA   b. IgD
    c. IgE   d. IgD

70. Which of the following theories of antibody production is most appropriate?
    a. Class switching theory
    b. Clonal selection theory
    c. P-K reaction
    d. All

71. Antibody involved in complement fixation is
    a. IgD   b. IgG
    c. IgM   d. IgA

72. The class of immunoglobulin having longest help life
    a. IgD   b. IgE
    c. IgG   d. IgM

73. The class of immunoglobulin having largest molecular weight
    a. IgD   b. IgE
    c. IgG   d. IgM

74. The class of immunoglobulin able to bind with mast cell
    a. IgD
    b. IgE
    c. IgG
    d. IgM

75. What is true abut IgG?
    a. Most abundant antibody (80%) in serum
    b. Ability to cross placenta
    c. Capacity of activates or fixes complement system
    d. All

76. **Which of the following antibodies has J chain?**
    a. IgA and IgM   b. IgM and IgD
    c. IgA and IgE   d. IgM only

77. **Which immunoglobulin is heat-labile?**
    a. IgA   b. IgE
    c. IgG   d. All

78. **Fc fragment of IgG is involved in**
    a. It determines catabolic rate
    b. It binds complement
    c. It is related to passage of IgG across the placental barrier
    d. All

79. **The IgA possesses the secretory component, which is formed by**
    a. Secretory gland which has receptor for IgA
    b. IgG
    c. Gleavage of an epithelial cell receptor used to transport the dimeric IgA across the epithelial cell
    d. Mucous secretion

80. **Which of the following is Anti-Rh antibody?**
    a. IgG   b. IgA
    c. IgM   d. IgD

81. **Immonoglobulin A can perform following functions *except***
    a. It is predominant in external secretion
    b. Crosses placenta
    c. Precept in colostrums of milk
    d. Agglutinate antigen

82. **For the detection of antigen antibody complexes which method is more sensitive?**
    a. Agglutination reaction
    b. Precipitation reaction
    c. Radial immunodiffusion
    d. Ouchterlony method

83. **Antigenic drift is caused due to _____ in the genes encoding epitopes.**
    a. Point mutation   b. Rearrangement
    c. Deletion   d. Duplication

84. **DiGeorge syndrome is caused due to**
    a. Deletion of chromosome 18
    b. Deletion of chromosome 22
    c. Duplication of chromosomes 18
    d. Duplication of chromosomes 22

85. **Zone of equivalence is formed when**
    a. Antibody is in excess
    b. Antigens and antibodies are in optimal proportion
    c. Antigen is in excess
    d. None of these

86. **SCID is the genetic disorder which is characterized by**
    a. Non-functional B cell
    b. Non-functional T cells
    c. Both a and b
    d. None of these

87. **When was NFSM launched?**
    a. Mid of 9th Five-Year Plan
    b. End of 10th Five-Year Plan
    c. Mid of 11th Five-Year plan
    d. End of 11th Five-Year plan

88. **Slide agglutination reaction is used for the diadnosis of**
    a. Typhoid
    b. Rheumatoid factor
    c. Salmonella   d. All

89. **The phenomena of antigens and antibodies cross-linkage is known as**
    a. Agglutination   b. Precipitation
    c. Immunodiffusion
    d. Immunodetection

90. **In the technique used for protection of monoclonal antibody myeloma cell is combined with lymphoma cell combination produces_____cells which is selected on HAT media.**
    a. Hybridoma
    b. Unfused myeloma cell
    c. Unfued lymphoma cell
    d. All of above

91. The site of maturation of B cells and T cells is
    a. Bone marrow and thymus respectively
    b. Lymph nodes and spleen respectively
    c. Thymus only
    d. Bursa of fabricus

92. Which of them is also called mosaic antigen?
    a. Virus
    b. Mycoplasma
    c. An adjuvant
    d. Fungas

93. T cells can produce
    a. Cytokines   b. Interferon
    c. TNF   d. All

94. Which of them is primary B cell receptor?
    a. IgD   b. CD 34
    c. CD4   d. IgE

95. To become immunogenic which of the following characters is important?
    a. Foreign to the host
    b. Molecular wt >1000 Da
    c. Chemical complexity
    d. All

96. What is the function of TH cells?
    a. Activate effector mechanism
    b. Activate to cells
    c. Activate both B cells and to cells
    d. Complement fixation

97. A person is suffering from immuno-inflammatory diseases such as hemolytic anaemia, eczema, etc. they may have
    a. Tc cells are greatly reduced
    b. Tc cells are greatly increased
    c. TH cells are greatly reduced
    d. TH cells are greatly increased

98. A person is suffering from hemolytic anaemia he has chances to develope
    a. Jaundice   b. Influenza
    c. HIV   d. Cancer

99. Hemolytic anaemia is different to other anemia with respect to
    a. Abnormal breakdown of red blood cells and bilirubin a breakdown product of hemoglobin can accumulate in the blood causing jaundice
    b. Erythrocytes become comma shaped
    c. Blood glucose level is low down
    d. None

100. Hybridoma technique was given by
    a. Niels Jurne
    b. Koehler and Milstein
    c. Hodgkin
    d. All of above

101. Monoclonal antibodies are used in
    a. Diagnose and treat diseases
    b. Immunpuification
    c. Cancer diagnosis
    d. All

102. Network theory was given by
    a. Niels Jurne
    b. Koehler and Milstein
    c. Hodgkin
    d. All of the above

103. Which of the following stimulates the activity of B cells?
    a. Cytokines   b. Interlukin-2
    c. INF   d. Histamine

104. Antibodies are secreted by
    a. Plasma cells
    b. Haematopoietic cells
    c. Complement cell
    d. NK cells

105. Tc cells can effect against
    a. Virus infections b. Allergy
    c. Autoimmunity   d. All of these

106. Haptens are
    a. Antigenic   b. Immunogenic
    c. Both   d. None

107. Haptens become immunogenic when complex with
    a. Polysaccharide   b. Carrier protein
    c. Epitopes   d. Paratypes

108. The overall binding between antibodies and multivalent antigen is called as

    a. Affinity
    b. Avidity
    c. Interaction
    d. Immunogenicity

109. What is true for an epitope?

    a. Epitopes are usually nonproteins sequences derived from the host
    b. Known as antigenic determinant
    c. Epitopes interact with the paratope based on the 3-D surface features and shape or tertiary structure of the antigen
    d. All

110. Homopolymer of poly-γ-D glutamic acid (mol. wt −50, 000 Da) is not immunogenic due to

    a. Foreignness
    b. Route of administration
    c. Less chemical complexity
    d. Size

111. Adjuvants can enhance immunological reaction by which of the following meachanisms?

    a. May help in the translocation of antigens to the lymph nodes where they can be recognized by T cells
    b. May provide physical protection to antigens which grants the antigen of a prolonged delivery
    c. Adjuvants are believed to increase the innate immune response to antigen by interacting with pattern recognition receptors
    d. All

112. Once an antigen attack on the host take time to respond and activate adaptive immunity during this gap period which among is effective against antigen

    a. Macrophages
    b. Innate immune effectors
    c. Old plasma cell
    d. New B and T cells

113. Site of lymphocytes activation is

    a. Thymus
    b. Bone marrow
    c. MALT
    d. Lymph nodes

114. Which among them is capable to activate immunological reaction?

    a. Haptens
    b. Carrier
    c. Bacteria
    d. All

115. IgM antibodies are involved in following processes *except*

    a. Fix complement system
    b. Present on the membrane of mature B cell
    c. Thy predominant in the primary response to antigen
    d. Cross placenta

116. IgM contains an additional Fc linked polypeptide required for polymerization of monomers to forn pentamers is known as

    a. Hinge region
    b. J chain
    c. Heavy chain
    d. Light chain

117. Class I and Class II major histocompatability complex (MHC) proteins are associated with

    a. Cytosolic pathway and endocytic pathway respectively
    b. Endocytic and cytosolic pathway respectively
    c. Only cytosolic pathway
    d. Only endocytic pathway

118. A large protein complex proteasome is formed during which pathway

    a. Cytosolic pathway and endocytic pathway respectively
    b. Endocytic and cytosolic pathway respectively
    c. Only cytosolic pathway
    d. Only endocytic pathway

119. TAP (transporters associated with antigen processing) is occurs during which pathway?

    a. Cytosolic pathway and endocytic pathway respectively
    b. Endocytic and cytosolic pathway respectively
    c. Only cytosolic pathway
    d. Only endocytic pathway

120. Invariant chain blocks the antigen binding domain of newly synthesized MHC II in
    a. Cytosolic pathway and endocytic pathway respectively
    b. Endocytic and cytosolic pathway respectively
    c. Only cytosolic pathway
    d. Only endocytic pathway

121. Invariant chain blocks the antigen binding domain of newly synthesized MHC II. What is the reason behind it?
    a. Inhibit the binding of endogenous protein with MHC II
    b. Reduce the effect of CLIP
    c. Both   d. None

122. Which of the following is less effective towards immune response generation?
    a. Polypeptide   b. Lipid
    c. DNA/RNA   d. Carbohydrate

123. Immunoglobulin presents at the highest concentration in plasma is
    a. IgG   b. IgD
    c. IgA   d. IgE

124. A person was suffering from excessive internal bleeding after diagnosis it was found that number of ____ in circulation is very less.
    a. T cell   b. B-lymphocyte
    c. Platelets   d. NK cells

125. MHC locus in human is reffered as
    a. HLA complex   b. H-2 complex
    c. Both   d. None

126. Which of following is the first recombinant antigen vaccine approved for human use
    a. Hepatitis B vaccine
    b. Hib vaccine   c. DPT vaccine
    d. None

127. The immunoglobulin presents predominantly in secretions such as milk is
    a. IgG   b. IgA
    c. IgD   d. IgE

128. Individuals unable to make the J protein found in certain immunoglobulins would be expected to have frequent infections of the
    a. Brain   b. Blood
    c. Liver   d. Intestinal tract

129. MHC complex is located on _____ chromosome in human and ____ in mice.
    a. 6 and 17   b. 16 and 7
    c. 7 and 16   d. 17 and 6

130. Class II MHC molecule in human is encoded by which region?
    a. D, DQ, DR   b. B, C, A
    c. CD4, C2, BF   d. D, IA, IE

131. Transmembrane molecules IgA and IgB which are disulphide linked to each other forms
    a. TCR   b. BCR
    c. Pro B cell   d. All

132. Class I MHC molecule in human is encoded by which region?
    a. DS, DQ, DR   b. B, C, A
    c. C4, C2, BF   d. K, IA, IE

133. Class III MHC molecule in human is encoded by which region?
    a. DS, DQ, DR   b. B, C, A
    c. C4, C2, BF   d. K, IA, IE

134. Class II MHC molecule in mice is encoded by which region?
    a. DS, DQ, DR   b. B, C, A
    c. C4, C2, BF   d. IA, IE

135. Light chain
    a. Same for each class of antibody
    b. Different for each class of antibody
    c. Both
    d. None

136. Which of the following is known as B cell co-receptor?
    a. TAPA-1 (CD81)
    b. CD 19
    c. CD 21
    d. Combination of all

137. **Which of the following is the ligand for the T cell receptor?**
    a. MHC antigen
    b. Phospholipid antigen
    c. Proteins
    d. Carbohydrate antigen

138. **MHC restriction is absent in**
    a. T cells   b. WBCs
    c. Both   d. None

139. **Example of thymus independent antigen is**
    a. Bacterial cell membrane component example lipopolysaccharides
    b. Polymorphic protein
    c. Capsular polysaccharide
    d. All

140. **Mancini method is**
    a. Radial immunodiffusion
    b. Used in immunology to determine the quantity of an antigen by measuring the diameters of circles
    c. Diameters of the circles increase with time as antigen diffuses into the medium
    d. All

141. **Which among them is true?**
    a. IgM and IgG can fix complement
    b. IgA is a secretory immunoglobulin
    c. IgE mediates immediate hypersensitivity
    d. All

142. **Ouchterlony method is**
    a. Passive double immune diffusion
    b. Used in the detection identification and quantification of antibodies and antigens
    c. Pattern of precipitin line is identity, nonidentity and partial identity
    d. All

143. **Class I and Class II major histocompatibility complex (MHC) proteins are associated with**
    a. Cytosolic pathway and endocytic pathway respectively
    b. Endocytic and cytosolic pathway respectively
    c. Only cytosolic pathway
    d. Only endocytic pathway

144. **A large protein complex proteasome is formed during which pathway?**
    a. Cytosolic pathway and endocytic pathway both
    b. Neither endocytic nor cytosolic pathway
    c. Only cytosolic pathway
    d. Only endocytic pathway

145. **TAP (transporters associated with antigen processing) is occurs during which pathway?**
    a. Cytosolic pathway and endocytic pathway respectively
    b. Endocytic and cytosolic pathway respectively
    c. Only cytosolic pathway
    d. Only endocytic pathway

146. **Invariant chain blocks the antigen binding domain of newly synthesized MHC II in**
    a. Cytosolic pathway and endocytic pathway respectively
    b. Endocytic and cytosolic pathway respectively
    c. Only cytosolic pathway
    d. Only endocytic pathway

147. **Invariant chain blocks the antigen binding domain of newly synthesized MHC II. What is the reason behind it**
    a. Inhibit the binding of endogenous protein with MHC II
    b. Reduce the effect of CLIP
    c. Both
    d. None

148. **MHC locus in mouse known as**
    a. HLA complex   b. H-2 complex
    c. Both   d. None

149. **MHC locus in human is reffered as**
    a. HLA complex   b. H-2 complex
    c. Both   d. None

150. The immunoglobulin presents predominantly in secretions such as milk is
    a. IgG
    b. IgA
    c. IgD
    d. IgE

151. Individuals unable to make the J protein found in certain immunoglobulins would be expected to have frequent infections of the
    a. Brain
    b. Blood
    c. Liver
    d. Intestinal tract

152. MHC complex is located on _____ chromosome in human and _____ in mice.
    a. 6 and 17
    b. 16 and 7
    c. 7 and 16
    d. 17 and 6

153. Class II MHC molecule in human is encoded by which region?
    a. DP, DQ, DR
    b. B, C, A
    c. C4, C2, BF
    d. K, IA, IE

154. Class I MHC molecule in human is encoded by which region?
    a. DP, DQ, DR
    b. B, C, A
    c. C4, C2, BF
    d. K, IA, IE

155. Class III MHC molecule in human is encoded by which region?
    a. DP, DQ, DR
    b. B, C, A
    c. C4, C2, BF
    d. K, IA, IE

156. Class II MHC molecule in mice is encoded by which region?
    a. DP, DQ, DR
    b. B, C, A
    c. C4, C2, BF
    d. IA, IE

157. Which of the following is known as B cell co-receptor?
    a. TAPA-1 (CD81)
    b. C D 19
    c. C D 21
    d. Combination of all

158. Which of the following is the ligand for the T cell receptor?
    a. MHC antigen
    b. Phospholipid antigen
    c. Proteins
    d. Carbohydrate antigen

159. Excess of antibody inhibits precipitation reaction and agglutination reaction, this effect is known as
    a. DiGeorge syndrome
    b. P-K reaction
    c. Prozone effect
    d. None

160. A child born without a thymus or lacking thymus is having
    a. DiGeorge syndrome
    b. P-K reaction
    c. Prozone effect
    d. None

161. Complement system
    a. Consists of 20 serum proteins
    b. Serum proteins acts as biological cascade
    c. Having two pathways—classical and alternate
    d. All

162. Component system is involved in
    a. Specific defense mechanism
    b. Nonspecific defense mechanism
    c. Both
    d. None

163. What is true about complement activation?
    a. Lysis of pathogen
    b. Activation of cytokines
    c. Phagocytosis
    d. All

164. In complement system classical pathway is activated by
    a. Ag-Ab complexes
    b. Only Ag
    c. Small foreign peptides
    d. MHC bound processed peptide

165. In complement system alternate pathway is activated by
    a. Ag-Ab complexes
    b. Only antigen
    c. MHC bound processed peptide
    d. Microorganisms or its toxins

166. Classical pathway of complement system is involved in
    a. Innate immunity
    b. Adaptive immunity
    c. Nonspecific defence
    d. All

167. Classical pathway of complement system C3 convertase is
    a. C4b2a3b
    b. C4b2a
    c. C3Bb
    d. C3Bb 3b

168. Alternate pathway of complement system C3 convertase is
    a. C4b2a3b
    b. C4b2a
    c. C3bBb
    d. C3bBb 3b

169. Alternate pathway of complement system C5 convertase is
    a. C4b2a3b
    b. C4b2a
    c. C3bBb
    d. C3bBb 3b

170. Classical pathway of complement system C5 convertase is
    a. C4b2a3b
    b. C4b2a
    c. C3bBb
    d. C3bBb 3b

171. Which of the following is the central molecule in complement pathway?
    a. C2a
    b. C4b
    c. C3b
    d. C5

172. Alternate pathway of complement system C3 convertase is stabilized by
    a. Fector B
    b. Fector D
    c. Properdine
    d. None

173. Cell lysis in complement pathway is initiated by
    a. Membrane arrested complex
    b. Membrane around complex
    c. Membrane attacking complex
    d. All

174. MHC (membrane attacking complex) is
    a. C5b689 complex
    b. C4b578 complex
    c. C4a5b789 complex
    d. None

175. Which element is required for activation of C1?
    a. Ca
    b. Mg
    c. Mn
    d. Zn

176. Which of the following is the anaphylotoxins?
    a. C3
    b. C4a
    c. C5b
    d. C4b

177. Which of the following is the most patent chemotactic?
    a. C3a
    b. C4a
    c. C5a
    d. C1

178. Which factor is involved in alternate pathway?
    a. Fector B
    b. Fector D
    c. Both a and b
    d. None

179. Which among the following is the function of complement system?
    a. Cell lysis
    b. Opsonisation
    c. Anaphylotoxin and chemotactics
    d. All

180. Body own cells are protected from MAC by a surface glycoprotein called
    a. MHC (major histocompatibility complex)
    b. DAF (decay accelerating factor)
    c. TCR (T cell receptor)
    d. BCR (B cell receptor)

181. DAF prevents the formation of membrane attack complex by
    a. Destabilizing C3 and C5 convertase
    b. Inactivate MAC
    c. Disturbing the attachment of C2 with Ig
    d. None

182. In alternate pathway complement component C3 is cleaved by
    a. C3b
    b. C3bBb
    c. Factor B
    d. Factor D

183. **Complement component C3b is**
    a. Phagocytosed microorganism
    b. An anaphylotoxin
    c. Chemotactic
    d. Do not harm bacteria

184. **A complement component which is strongly chemotactic**
    a. C3a
    b. C3b
    c. C5a
    d. C5b

185. **The starting complement component bound by IgG is**
    a. Clq
    b. Cls
    c. Clr
    d. All

186. **Most of the complement components having the basic nature of**
    a. Antibodies
    b. Cytokines
    c. Enzymes
    d. Glycolipids

187. **The common component of classical and alternative pathways**
    a. C3
    b. C4
    c. C4b
    d. C5

188. **_____ pathway is activated by binding of mannose binding lectin (MBL) to mannose residues on glycoproteins.**
    a. Classical pathway
    b. Alternate pathway
    c. Lectin pathway
    d. All

189. **The steps of activation of lectin pathway is same as**
    a. Classical pathway
    b. Alternate pathway
    c. Both
    d. None

190. **The mechanism of administration of weakened pathogen into human body is called**
    a. Immunization
    b. Attenuation
    c. Vaccination
    d. All

191. **Who developed the first vaccine?**
    a. Louis Pasteur
    b. Chain
    c. Edward Jenner
    d. None

192. **The concept of vaccination was first developed by**
    a. Louis Pasteur
    b. Chain et al
    c. Edward Jenner
    d. None

193. **The process of weakening a pathogen is called**
    a. Vaccination
    b. Attenuation
    c. Immunization
    d. All

194. **The first vaccine developed by Louis Pasteur acts against**
    a. Poliovirus
    b. HIV
    c. Rabies virus
    d. Done of these

195. **A vaccine is**
    a. An antigenic peptide
    b. Weakened pathogen
    c. Live attenuated pathogen
    d. All

196. **What is true for passive immunization?**
    a. Introduction of antibodies directly
    b. Transfer of lymphocyte directly
    c. Transfer of maternal antibodies across placenta
    d. All

197. **What is true about vaccination?**
    a. Method of active immunisation
    b. Method of passive immunisation
    c. Method of attenuation
    d. None

198. **Which of the following introduce active immunity?**
    a. Natural infection
    b. Vaccines
    c. Toxoids
    d. All of these

199. **A conjugate vaccine is**
    a. Hepatitis B vaccine
    b. Hib vaccine
    c. DPT vaccine
    d. None

Model Test Paper 6

1. **Crop weather calendar is launched by**
   a. ICAR
   b. IARI
   c. WMO
   d. IMD

2. **CO_2 concentration (%) on volume basis in atmosphere is**
   a. 78%
   b. 20%
   c. 0.930%
   d. 0.033%

3. **Argon concentration (%) on volume basis in atmosphere is**
   a. 78%
   b. 20%
   c. 0.93 %
   d. 0.033%

4. **Water vapor in atmosphere is almost absent above**
   a. 10–12 km
   b. 20 km
   c. 15–17 km
   d. None of these

5. **In troposphere, general decrease in temperature with height at a mean rate of about**
   a. 10.5
   b. 13
   c. 14
   d. 35

6. **The variations in the altitude of the tropopause as different latitudes at the poles are**
   a. 18 km
   b. 16 km
   c. 20 km
   d. 8 km

7. **Temperature decreases with increase in altitude, this character of**
   a. Troposphere
   b. Stratosphere
   c. Mesosphere
   d. Both a and c

8. **The stratosphere which extend up to height of**
   a. 35 km
   b. 75 km
   c. 50 km
   d. 100 km

9. **The maximum temperatures associated with the absorption of sun's ultraviolet radiation by ozone occur at**
   a. Troposphere
   b. Stratosphere
   c. Mesosphere
   d. Thermosphere

10. **Temperature increases with increase in altitude, these characters of**
    a. Thermosphere
    b. Stratosphere
    c. Mesosphere
    d. Both a and b

11. **The mesosphere average temperatures decrease to a minimun of about**
    a. –80°C around 80 km
    b. –75°C around 100 km
    c. –90°C around 8 km
    d. –40°C around 80 km

12. **The atmosphere is increasingly affected by X-rays and ultraviolet radiation causes**
    a. Ionization
    b. Radiation
    c. Both a and b
    d. None of these

13. **The pressure exerted by the atmosphere on the earth's surface is called**
    a. Atmosphere pressure
    b. Hydrological pressure
    c. Both a and b
    d. None of these

14. **Airpressure always decreases with an increase in**
    - a. Altitude
    - b. Latitude
    - c. Both a and b
    - d. All

15. **The actual density of air depends upon**
    - a. Temperature
    - b. Humidity
    - c. Amount of water vapour
    - d. Both a and b

16. **Pressure is measured as**
    - a. Force/cm
    - b. Force per unit area
    - c. Force per unit km
    - d. None of these

17. **Pesssure at sea level is around**
    - a. 1030 mb
    - b. 1013.25 mb
    - c. 1245.50 mb
    - d. 1232 mb

18. **A line of equal wind speed is called**
    - a. Isotach
    - b. Isopleths
    - c. Isohyets
    - d. Isonephs

19. **A line of equal water table is called**
    - a. Isotach
    - b. Isopleths
    - c. Isohels
    - d. Isonephs

20. **A line of equal number of neutrons is called**
    - a. Isotach
    - b. Isopleths
    - c. Isohels
    - d. Isonephs

21. **Farmer weather bulletins started in**
    - a. Isotach
    - b. Isopleths
    - c. Isohels
    - d. Isonephs

22. **Polar altitude with persistent higher pressure areas are called as**
    - a. Equatorial low
    - b. Doldrums
    - c. Polar highs
    - d. All

23. **Central at about 25′ to 35′north and south latitude are called**
    - a. Subtropic high pressure belts
    - b. Subpolar high pressure belts
    - c. Subpolar low pressure belts
    - d. None of these

24. **Atmospheric pressure is measured by**
    - a. Altimeter
    - b. Aneroid barometer
    - c. Anemometer
    - d. Atmometer

25. **Growth of plant is measured by**
    - a. Altimeter
    - b. Auxanometer
    - c. Anemometer
    - d. Atmometer

26. **Continuous atmospheric pressure is measured by**
    - a. Altimeter
    - b. Aneroid barometer
    - c. Barograph
    - d. Atmometer

27. **Continuous temperature is measured by**
    - a. Thermograph
    - b. Tensiometer
    - c. Barograph
    - d. Anemometer

28. **Long wave radiation is measured by**
    - a. Altimeter
    - b. Aneriod barometer
    - c. Pyrgeometer
    - d. Atmometer

29. **Rainfall is measured by**
    - a. Pulvimeter
    - b. Pressuer chamber
    - c. Anemometer pressure membrane apparatus
    - d. Anemometer

30. **Total incoming solar radiation is measured by**
    - a. Altimeter
    - b. Pyranometer
    - c. Anemometer
    - d. Atmometer

31. **Transpiration rate is measured by**
    - a. Altimeter
    - b. Aneroid barometer
    - c. Porometer
    - d. Atmometer

32. **PAR is measured by**
    - a. Pulvimeter
    - b. Pressure chamber
    - c. Anemometer
    - d. Quantum sensor

33. Both long and short wave radiations are measured by
   a. Pyradiometer
   b. Aneroid barometer
   c. Anemometer
   d. Atmometer

34. Soil specific gravity is measured by
   a. Altimeter   b. Pycnometer
   c. Anemometer   d. Atmometer

35. Evapotranspiration is measured by
   a. Lysimeter
   b. Aneroid barometer
   c. Anemometer
   d. Atmometer

36. Duration of bright sunshine hours is measured by
   a. Heliograph
   b. Aneroid barometer
   c. Anemometer
   d. Atmometer

37. Relative humidity is measured by
   a. Hygrometer   b. Psychomotor
   c. Both a and b   d. Atmometer

38. Sunshine duration is measured by
   a. Cambel stokes recoder
   b. Aneroid barometer
   c. Anemometer
   d. Atmometer

39. The oceans are associated with low pressure in
   a. Winter   b. Summer
   c. Both a and b   d. None of these

40. The oceans are associated with high pressure in
   a. Winter   b. Summer
   c. Both a and b   d. None of these

41. Where winds are converging and rise?
   a. Where pressures are low
   b. Where pressures are high
   c. Both a and b
   d. None of these

42. The tropical rains come about when moisture laden air from south meets falling cooler air from north in a area called
   a. Intertropical unconvergence zone
   b. Tropical zone
   c. Subtropixal zone
   d. Intertropical convergence

43. Wind creates moist conditions in the
   a. Leeward side
   b. Windward side
   c. According to wind direction
   d. All

44. Sources of all water are
   a. Runoff
   b. Precipitation
   c. Water harvesting
   d. All

45. One of the rainiest areas of the world with an annual rainfall average of 10000–10500 mm
   a. Cambel stokes recorder
   b. Aneroid barometer
   c. Anemometer
   d. Atmometer

46. The sun radiates its energy in the form of
   a. Wavelengths   b. Quantum
   c. Radiation   d. None of these

47. After absorption of solar energy, earth emits its energy between
   a. 4 to 10 u   b. 4. to 200 u
   c. 4 to 100 u   d. None of these

48. 4 to 100 u is the
   a. Short wavelengths
   b. Long wavelengths
   c. Both a and b
   d. All

49. Radiation takes place in the form of electromagnetic waves
   a. Electromagnetic waves
   b. Magnetic waves

c. Electrogenetic waves

d. All

50. The transfer of heat energy in the form of electromagnetic waves with the speed of light is known as

a. Radiation

b. Light

c. Solar constant

d. Both a and c

51. A line of equal number of electrons is called

a. Isotach

b. Isopleths

c. Isotope

d. Isonephs

52. In which of the following is a aromatic acid?

a. Tyrosine

b. Glycine

c. Leucine

d. Isoleucine

53. The ratio of the radiant energy reflected to the total that is incident upon the surface permeameter

a. Reflectivity

b. Transmissivity

c. Absorptive

d. None of these

54. In which of the following is a S-containing amino acid?

a. Glycine

b. Cysteine

c. Phenylalanine

d. Tyrosine

55. The radiation reaching to the earth surface from the sun atmosphere and from earth to atmosphere space follows certain physical laws known as radiation laws permeameter

a. Radiation law

b. Radiation rules

c. Infiltrate law

d. None of these

56. Which is a measure of the rate at which solar wave radiation is received at the top of the atmosphere on a unit surface unit time?

a. Solar constant

b. Radiation

c. Conduction

d. Both a and b

57. The rate of change of atmospheric pressure per unit horizontal distance between two points at the same elevation is known as pressure grdient or isobaric slope

a. Pressure gradient

b. Isobaric slope

c. Both a and b

d. Albedo

58. The rising of air from equtor causes increase unpressure at 350 N 350S which is known as

a. Horse latitude belt

b. Sub-tropical high

c. Calm

d. Both a and b

59. The blow os air from equtor and accumulation of air over 24–35 latitudes giving rise to high pressure belt region of descending air is known as

a. Hadley cell

b. Feral cell

c. Both a and b

d. Pressure belt

60. In the upper atmosphere the reverse air movement takes place. This circulation is known as

a. Hadley cell

b. Feral cell

c. Both a and b

d. Pressure belt

61. In the Northern hemisphere the direction of rotation of cyclone is

a. Anticlockwise

b. Clockwise

c. Both a and b

d. Wind direction

62. In the Southern hemisphere the direction of rotation of cyclone is

a. Anticlockwise

b. Clockwise

c. Both a and b

d. Wind direction

63. When air contains all the moisture that can hold to its maximum limit it is called saturated air and the vapour pressure excreted by this air is called saturated vapour pressure

a. Low pressure

b. High pressure

c. Vapour pressure

d. Saturated

64. The amount of water vapour actually presents in air campared with the maximum amount of vapour can be held by same air at a given temperature is known as

a. Relative humidity

b. Specific humidity

c. Absolute humidity

d. Saturated vapour

65. The ratio of actual mass of water vapour presents to the total volume of moist air is known as
    a. Relative humidity
    b. Specific humidity
    c. Absolute humidity
    d. Saturated vapour

66. All the three dimensions are about the same size and the peds are cube-like with flat or rounded faces is called
    a. Prism structure   b. Platy structure
    c. Block structure   d. None of these

67. The ratio of mass of water vapour to the given mass of air containing the moisture is called
    a. Relative humidity
    b. Specific humidity
    c. Absolute humidity
    d. Saturated vapour

68. Nucleic acids have multiple negative charges due to
    a. Sugars
    b. Phosphoryl groups
    c. Associated proteins
    d. Purines and pyrimidines

69. RH reaches maximum in
    a. Summer
    b. Winter
    c. Both a and b
    d. None of these

70. Clouds and fogs are composed of water droplets or ice crystals or both of the order of size
    a. 20 to 30 microns
    b. 10 to 20 microns
    c. 5 to 10 microns
    d. 2 to 6 microns

71. When the temperature of air falls below 0°C before the dew point is reached, the water vapour is directly converted into crystals of ice and this is called as
    a. Dew   b. Frost
    c. Fog   d. All

72. Extermely small water droplets suspending in the atmosphere and reducing the horizontal visibility is
    a. Dew   b. Frost
    c. Fog   d. All

73. Classification of fog is
    a. Thick fog: Restricts visibility up to 45 meters
    b. Moderate fog: Restricts visibility up to 450 meters
    c. Thin fog: Restricts visibility up to 900 meters
    d. All

74. The suspended water droplets visibility between 1000 to 2000 meters or 4 on the coded scale (IMD), the obscurity is known as
    a. Mist   b. Rime
    c. Smog   d. Haze

75. The combined effect of smoke and fog droplets may reduce visibility and this phenomenon is called
    a. Mist   b. Rime
    c. Smog   d. Haze

76. Forms of precipitation are
    a. Liquid form   b. Solid form
    c. Mixed form   d. All

77. Types of rain are
    a. Convectional
    b. Graphic or relief rain
    c. Cyclic/frontal and convergent rains
    d. All

78. Precipitation of water in the solid form of small or large ice crystals. It occurs only when the condensing medium has a pemperature below freezing temperature is
    a. Precipitation   b. Hail
    c. Snow   d. Rime

79. Mechanisms of precipitation are
    a. Bergeron mechanism
    b. Collision and coalescence mechanism

c. Both a and b

d. None of these

80. Meteorological droughts are classified into

a. Slight drought: When rainfall is 11 to 25% less from the normal rainfall.

b. Moderate drought: When rainfall is 26 to 50 % less than the normal rainfall

c. Severe drought: When rainfall is more than 50% less than the normal rainfall

d. All

81. The irregular and variability in rainfall, especially in humid and subhumid regions are

a. Agriculture drought

b. Contingent drought

c. Permanent drought

d. Seasonal drought

82. The condition when soil moisture depletes and falls short to meet potential evapotranspiration of the crop is called

a. Atmosphere drought

b. Contingent drought

c. Permanent drought

d. Soil drought

83. Classification of weather forecasting based on

a. Validity of period

b. Time of scale

c. Both a and b

d. None of these

84. Which crop is knwon as king of pulses?

a. Red gram   b. Mung

c. Soya bean   d. Chick pea

85. Which crop is known as queen of pulse?

a. Red gram   b. Mung

c. Pea   d. Chick pea

86. The based on synaptic situation prevailing at the time of forecasting and is valid up to 3 days or 72 hrs is called

a. Short range forecasting

b. Medium range forecasting

c. Long range forecasting

d. None of these

87. The forecast valid for more than 10 days (i.e. a month or a season) is known as

a. Short range forecasting

b. Medium range forecasting

c. Long range forecasting

d. None of these

88. Bar (1979) has tried to classify the basic type of crop weather models is

a. Crop growth stimulating models

b. Crop weather analysis model

c. Empirical statistical model

d. All

89. Which crop is known as king of oilseed?

a. Groundnut   b. Sesame

c. Mustard   d. Sunflower

90. Which weed is known as king of weeds?

a. Parthenium hysterophours

b. Cyanodon dactylon

c. Fatua   d. Pistia spp

91. Which crop is known as wonder crop?

a. Red gram   b. Mung

c. Soybean   d. Groundnut

92. Which crop is known as king of fodder crops?

a. Berseem   b. Lucerne

c. Sorghum   d. Napier grass

93. Which crop is known as yellow jewel of America?

a. Red gram   b. Groundnut

c. Soybean   d. Chick pea

94. The processes of exchange of heat and moisture between earth and atmosphere over a longer period is known as

a. Weather   b. Climate

c. Microclimate   d. None of these

95. The processes of exchange of heat and moisture between earth and atmosphere over a short period is known as

a. Weather   b. Climate

c. Microclimate   d. None of these

96. The science dealing with the factors which determine and control the distribution of climate over the earth surface is called
    a. Meteorology
    b. Agriculture meteorology
    c. Climatology
    d. None of these

97. The word "Meteorology" is derived from
    a. Greek   b. Latin
    c. Both a and b   d. None of these

98. Who was discovered the thermometer?
    a. Galileo   b. Toricelli
    c. De condole   d. Koppen

99. World Meteorological Organization (WMO) is situated at
    a. Geneva, Switzerland
    b. Pune
    c. Mexico
    d. Peru

100. Indian meteorology department was started in
    a. 1934   b. 1932
    c. 1878   d. 1900

101. Net return per hectare is
    a. Overall efficiency
    b. Partial efficiency measure
    c. Specific efficiency measure
    d. None of the above

102. Farmer weather bulletins started in
    a. 1950   b. 1975
    c. 1945   d. 1923

103. The period of medium weather forecasting is
    a. 10–15 days   b. 3–10 days
    c. 20 days   d. None of these

104. The ICAR launched AICRPAM at CRIDA in
    a. 1980   b. 1975
    c. 1983   d. 1950

105. Argon concentration (%) on volume basis in atmosphere is
    a. 78%   b. 20%
    c. 0.930%   d. 0.033%

106. Farmer weather bulletins started in
    a. 1950   b. 1975
    c. 1945   d. 1923

107. Water vapor in atmosphere is almost absent above
    a. 10–12 km   b. 20km
    c. 15–17 km   d. None of these

108. The variation in the altitude of the tropopause at the equator is
    a. 18 km   b. 17 km
    c. 20 km   d. 80 km

109. The variation in the altitude of the tropopause as different latitudes at the poles is
    a. 18 km   b. 16 km
    c. 20 km   d. 8 km

110. The stratosphere which extend up to height of
    a. 35 km   b. 75 km
    c. 50 km   d. 100 km

111. The stratosphere and mesosphere are separated by narrow layer is called
    a. Stratopause
    b. Tropopause
    c. Mesosphere
    d. Both a and b

112. Mesosphere is above the
    a. Stratopause
    b. Tropopause
    c. Mesopause
    d. Thermopause

113. The mesosphere average temperatures decrease to a minimum of about
    a. –80°C around 80 km
    b. –75°C around 100km
    c. –90°C around 80 km
    d. –40°C around 80 km

114. **Agrometeorology mainly deals with**
    a. Atmosphere pressure, clouds
    b. Solar radiation, temperature
    c. Wind, relative humidity and precipitation
    d. All

115. **Fifty per cent of the total mass of air is found below**
    a. 10 km
    b. 16 km
    c. 5 km
    d. 8 km

116. **The actual density of air depends upon**
    a. Temperature
    b. Humidity
    c. Amount of water vapour
    d. Both a and b

117. **Pressure in measured as**
    a. Force/cm
    b. Force per unit area
    c. Force per unit km
    d. None of these

118. **Pressure at sea level is around**
    a. 1030 mb
    b. 1013.25 mb
    c. 1245.50 mb
    d. 1232 mb

119. **Isother are used to show**
    a. Humidity distribution
    b. Rain distribution
    c. Temperature distribution
    d. All

120. **A line of equal wind speed is called**
    a. Isotach
    b. Isopleths
    c. Isohyets
    d. Isonephs

121. **A line of equal depth of rain falls is called**
    a. Isotach
    b. Isopleths
    c. Isohels
    d. Isobaths

122. **Farmer weather bulletins started in**
    a. Isotach
    b. Isopleths
    c. Isohels
    d. Isonephs

123. **Polar altitudes with persistent higher pressure areas are called**
    a. Equatorial low
    b. Doldrums
    c. Polar highs
    d. All

124. **Central at about 25′ to 35′ north and south latitude are called**
    a. Subtropic high pressure belts
    b. Subpolar high pressure belts
    c. Subpolar low pressure belts
    d. None of these

125. **Wind velocity is measured by**
    a. Altimeter
    b. Aneroid barometer
    c. Anemometer
    d. Atmometer

126. **Growth of plant is measured by**
    a. Altimeter
    b. Auxanometer
    c. Anemometer
    d. Atmometer

127. **Growth of plant is also measures by**
    a. Altimeter
    b. Crescograph
    c. Anemometer
    d. Atmometer

128. **Wind direction is measured by**
    a. Altimeter
    b. Tensiometer
    c. Anemometer
    d. Wind vane

129. **Wavelength of light is measured by**
    a. Altimeter
    b. Spectrophotometer
    c. Anemometer
    d. Atmometer

130. **Long wave radiation is measured by**
    a. Altimeter
    b. Aneroid barometer
    c. Pyrgeometer
    d. Atmometer

131. **Rainfall is measured by**
    a. Pulvimeter
    b. Pressure chamber
    c. Anemometer
    d. Pressured membrane apparatus

132. Leaf water potential is measured by
   a. Sychrometer
   b. Aneroid barometer
   c. Porometer   d. Atmometer

133. Both long and short wave radiation is measured by
   a. Pyradiometer
   b. Aneroid barometer
   c. Anemometer
   d. Atmometer

134. Hybraulic conductivity is measured by
   a. Permeameter
   b. Aneroid barometer
   c. Anemometer
   d. Atmometer

135. Infiltration is measured by
   a. Permeameter
   b. Aneroid barometer
   c. Infiltrometer
   d. Atmometer

136. Canopy temperature is measured by
   a. Permeameter
   b. Infrared thermometer
   c. Anemometer
   d. Atmometer

137. Relative humidity is measured
   a. Hygrometer   b. Psychrometer
   c. Both a and b   d. Atmometer

138. Manipulation of the soil for crop production modifies the natural state of upper
   a. 10–20 cm   b. 12–30 cm
   c. 30–40 cm   d. 40–50 cm

139. Soil with relatively low organic content ranging from 1 to 6 per cent in surface layer usually called
   a. Organic soil   b. Mineral soil
   c. Inorganic soil   d. Both b and c

140. The organic matter content in organic soil by volume basis is
   a. More than 50%   b. Less than 50%
   c. 30%   d. 20%

141. The organic matter content in organic soil by weight basis is
   a. 40%   b. 80%
   c. 20%   d. 30%

142. Quartzite formed from
   a. Granite   b. Sandstone
   c. Limestone   d. None of these

143. Organic matter presents in soil by volume basis is
   a. 10%   b. 20%
   c. 5%   d. 25%

144. Air presents in soil by volume basis is
   a. 25%   b. 30%
   c. 0.94%   d. 78%

145. The total pore space of the soil occupied by air and water by about is
   a. 25 and 25%
   b. 30% and 40%
   c. 10% and 20%
   d. 45% and 60%

146. Solidification is takes place at moderate depths is called
   a. Plutonic rock
   b. Valcanic rock
   c. Sedimentary rock
   d. All

147. Surface soil is also called
   a. Furrow slice soil layer
   b. Surface soil
   c. Fertile soil
   d. Top soil

148. The formula of gypsum is
   a. SiO_2 b. $KAISi_3O_8$
   c. $CaCO_3$ d. $CaSO_2.H_2O$

149. Optimum soil reaction (pH range) of cereals is
   a. 6.0–7.5   b. 5.0–6.5
   c. 4.0–6.0   d. 4.0–6.5

150. The formula of calcite is
   a. SiO_2 b. $KAISi_3O_8$
   c. $CaCO_3$ d. $CaSO_2.H_2O$

151. Eluvial horizon is
    a. O horizon
    b. A horizon
    c. C horizon
    d. Regolith

152. Which horizon is the zone washing in and accumulation of iron and aluminium?
    a. A horizon
    b. B horizon
    c. C horizon
    d. Regolith

153. Magnesium mica is also known as
    a. White mica
    b. Muscovite mica
    c. Black mica
    d. Both b and c

154. The unconsolidated material the solum (a plus B horizon) is called
    a. B horizon
    b. A horizon
    c. C horizon
    d. Regolith

155. Underlying soil is
    a. A horizon
    b. B horizon
    c. C horizon
    d. Regolith

156. The element which ionizes readily or form stable oxyanions is
    a. Lithophile elements
    b. Chalcophile elements
    c. Atmosphile elements
    d. Biophile element

157. Diameter of coarse sand is
    a. 0.02–0.2
    b. 0.2–2
    c. <0.002
    d. < 20

158. The formula of quartz is
    a. SiO_2
    b. $KAISi_3O_8$
    c. $CaCO_3$
    d. $CaSO_2.2H_2O$

159. The used for a coherent mass of soil broken into any shape by artifical means such as by tillage is called
    a. Clod
    b. Peda
    c. Fragment
    d. Aggregates

160. Who was given the concept of carbon uptake of plant by roots?
    a. Sir Humphry Devy
    b. John Woodward
    c. Jethro Tull
    d. Glauber

161. The formed by solidification of molten material magma on or beneath the surface of earth is called
    a. Igneous rock
    b. Sedimentary rock
    c. Metamorphic rock
    d. None of these

162. Diameter of fine earth is
    a. 0.02–0.2
    b. 0.002–0.02
    c. <0.002
    d. <2

163. The consolidation of sediments derived from the breaking down of pre-existing rocks is called
    a. Igneous rock
    b. Sedimentary
    c. Metamorphic
    d. All

164. Gneiss and marble are type of rocks
    a. Igneous rocks
    b. Sedimentary rocks
    c. Metamorphic rocks
    d. None of these

165. Gneiss formed from
    a. Granite
    b. Sandstone
    c. Limestone
    d. None of these

166. Feldspars constitute of the earth crust is
    a. 48%
    b. 39%
    c. 4%
    d. 10%

167. Quartz constitute of the earth crust is
    a. 50%
    b. 78%
    c. 36%
    d. 10%

168. Which mica is also known as white micas?
    a. Potash mica
    b. Magnesium mica
    c. Both a and b
    d. None of these

169. Diameter of gravel is
    a. 2–20
    b. 0.002–0.02
    c. <0.002
    d. <20

170. The basic processes of weathering is
    a. Physical   b. Mechanical
    c. Chemical   d. All

171. Diameter of clay is
    a. 0.02–0.2   b. 0.002–0.02
    c. <0.002   d. None of these

172. Mica is a type of mineral
    a. 1 : 1 type mineral
    b. 2 : 1 type mineral
    c. 2 : 2 type mineral
    d. None of these

173. Which property of soil is basic property?
    a. Soil structure   b. Soil texture
    c. Particle density d. None of these

174. The bulk density (gm/cc) in very compact sub-soil is
    a. 1   b. 4
    c. 2   d. 5

175. The biological process in weathering is designated as
    a. Decomposition b. Disintegration
    c. Both a and b   d. All

176. Natural aggregates are called
    a. Clod   b. Peds
    c. Fragment   d. Aggregates

177. Nitrite (NO_2^-) oxidized to nitrate (NO_3^-) by
    a. Nitrosomonas
    b. Nitrobacter
    c. Thiobacillus
    d. Ferrobacillus

178. Which soil has leachable characters?
    a. White alkali soil
    b. Black alkali soil
    c. Reclamation
    d. All

179. In prism structure, when the top of prisms are still plane level and clean called
    a. Columnar   b. Platy
    c. Blocky   d. Prismatic

180. Generally in normal soils the bulk density (gm/cc) ranges from
    a. 1.67–3.12   b. 1.2–2.65
    c. 1–1.65   d. 1.00

181. Yellowing in upper leaves is a deficiency of
    a. Phosphorus b. Sulphur
    c. Copper   d. Nitrogen

182. The bulk density (gm/cc) of organic peat soils is
    a. 1.12   b. 0.5
    c. 1.65   d. 1.5

183. The analytical procedure by which the particles are separated into varies fraction of soils is called
    a. Mechanical analysis
    b. Chemical analysis
    c. Biological analysis
    d. All

184. Stoken's law was given by
    a. Stokes   b. Buoyance
    c. Donal   d. None of these

185. Particle density is expressed in CGS system
    a. gm/cc   b. Ib/cft
    c. mgm–3   d. None of these

186. Diameter of fine sand is
    a. 0.02–0.2
    b. 0.002–0.02
    c. <0.002
    d. None of these

187. The weight per unit volume of the solid portion of soil is called
    a. Bulk density
    b. Particle density
    c. Both a and b
    d. None of these

188. The vertical axis is more developed than other soil structure in
    a. Prism   b. Platy
    c. Block   d. Spheroidal

189. The deflocculating effect of ___ ion is the contributing factor for stable granulation of soil particles.
   a. Ca
   b. Al
   c. Both a and b
   d. Na

190. In block structure of the soil, when the faces and edges are mainly rounded is called
   a. Subangular blocky
   b. Columnar
   c. Angular blocky
   d. None of these

191. Ammonium (NH_4^+) oxidized to nitrite NO_2^- by
   a. Nitrosomonas
   b. Nitrobacter
   c. Thiobacillus
   d. Ferrobacillus

192. The percentage of soil volume occupied by pore spaces is called
   a. Density
   b. Porosit
   c. True density
   d. None of these

193. Which soil has deflocculating and poor physical properties?
   a. White alkali soil
   b. Black alkali soil
   c. Reclamation of alkali soil
   d. All

194. The arrangement of primary particles and their aggregated into a certain definite pattern is called
   a. Soil texture
   b. Peds
   c. Soil structure
   d. Aggregates

195. Types of structure are
   a. Plate
   b. Prism
   c. Block
   d. All

196. Montmorillonite is a type of mineral
   a. 1 : 1 type mineral
   b. 2 : 1 type mineral
   c. 2 : 2 type mineral
   d. None of these

197. The aggregates of granular type are usually termed as
   a. Granular
   b. Less porous
   c. Both a and b
   d. Crumb

198. Gredes of soil structure are
   a. Structureless
   b. Weak
   c. Moderate
   d. Strong
   e. All

199. Potassium concentration in plant on dry weight basis is
   a. 1–4%
   b. 0.02–1%
   c. 0.1–0.4
   d. None of these

Model Test Paper 7

1. "Heart of Garden" is known as
   - a. Hedge
   - b. Edge
   - c. Lawn
   - d. Rose

2. Concept of lawn is developed from
   - a. USA
   - b. Japan
   - c. India
   - d. England

3. The ideal soil pH for lawn is
   - a. 5.0–5.5
   - b. 4–4.5
   - c. 7–8
   - d. 9–10

4. ___ and nitrogen can be applied to make grass green.
   - a. Magnesium
   - b. Calcium
   - c. Iron
   - d. Sulphur

5. Most turf grass diseases are caused by
   - a. Fungus
   - b. Bacteria
   - c. Virus
   - d. All of the above

6. The green carpet for the landscape maintained by growing and mowing grasses is
   - a. Ground cover
   - b. Lawn
   - c. Hedge
   - d. Herbarium

7. Which of the following is not important characteristics of lawn grass?
   - a. Quick growing
   - b. Soft to touch
   - c. Bad odour
   - d. Look fresh

8. Which of the following is cultivar of *Cynodon dactylon*?
   - a. Hariyalli
   - b. Calcuttia
   - c. Selection-1
   - d. All of the above

9. Mowing of lawn is done to
   - a. Levelling of ground
   - b. Aeration
   - c. To prevent excessive growth
   - d. Touch nodes with ground

10. The remove of cut over grasses from lawn is termed as
    - a. Scrapping
    - b. Raking
    - c. Sweeping
    - d. Mowing

11. Doob or Haryali is common name of
    - a. *Axonopus affinis*
    - b. *Zoysia japonica*
    - c. *Cynodon dactylon*
    - d. None of the above

12. Pale or yellow lawn is due to deficiency of
    - a. Calcium
    - b. Boron
    - c. Magazine
    - d. Nitrogen

13. Carpet grass is common name of
    - a. *Cynodon dactylon*
    - b. *Axonopus affinis*
    - c. *Zoysia tenuifolia*
    - d. *Poa trivailis*

14. Which of the following grasses is not fine texture?
    - a. *Zoysia tenuifolia*
    - b. *Zoysia japonica*
    - c. *Stenotaphrum secundatum*
    - d. *Festuca avina*

15. Which of the following is highly drought resistant?
    a. Tall fescue
    b. Carpet grass
    c. Bahia grass
    d. Manilla grass

16. For large area which species of doob grass is suitable?
    a. *Zoysia japonica*
    b. *Cynodon dactylon*
    c. *Agrostis alba*
    d. *Agrostis canina*

17. *Cassia fistula* belongs to family_____.
    a. Leguminoceae
    b. Casuarinaceae
    c. Moraceae
    d. Rubiaceae

18. Delonix regia belongs to family_____.
    a. Fabaceae
    b. Bignoniaceae
    c. Anonaceae
    d. Rubiaceae

19. Which of the following flowering trees is bears blue-coloured flowers?
    a. *Jacaranda acutifolia*
    b. *Guaicum officinale*
    c. *Jacaranda mimosifolia*
    d. All of these

20. Tree suitable for screening purpose is/are ____ .
    a. *Grevillea robusta*
    b. *Polyalthia longifolia*
    c. *Polyalthia pendula*
    d. All of these

21. Tree suitable for alkaline and saline soil is /are ____.
    a. *Cassia fistula*
    b. *Parkinsonia aculeata*
    c. *Casuarina equisetifolia*
    d. All of these

22. Which of the following trees is not bears red colour flowers?
    a. *Callistemon lanceolatus*
    b. *Bassia latifolia*
    c. *Spathodea camponulata*
    d. *Grevillea robusta*

23. Which of the following flowering trees is not of Indian origin?
    a. *Cassia fistula*
    b. *Butea monosperma*
    c. *Michelia champaca*
    d. *Grevillea robusta*

24. The flowering time of *Grevillea robusta* and *Jacaranda acutifolia* is
    a. July–August
    b. January–February
    c. April–May
    d. Throughout the year

25. *Cassia fistula* bears___of golden yellow flower during hot weather.
    a. Spike
    b. Raceme
    c. Panicle
    d. Cyme

26. Kigelia pinnata is mostly used for
    a. Screening purpose
    b. Avenue tree
    c. Flowering tree
    d. Checking air pollution

27. Botanical name of Maulsari is____.
    a. *Mimusops elengi*
    b. *Salix babylonica*
    c. *Magnolia grandiflora*
    d. *Kigelia pinnata*

28. Maulsari belongs to _____ family.
    a. Caesalpiniaceae
    b. Sterculiaceae
    c. Sapotaceae
    d. Bignoniaceae

29. Temple tree or Pagoda tree is common name of
    a. *Cassia fistula*
    b. *Delonix regia*
    c. *Poinciana regia*
    d. *Plumeria alba*

30. Which of the following ornamental trees is planted in saline soil?
    a. *Cassia fistula*
    b. *Azadirachta indica*
    c. *Bombax ceiba*
    d. All of the above

31. A perennial plant having distinct trunk and crown at the top is known as
    a. Shrub
    b. Climber
    c. Tree
    d. Creeper

32. *Jacaranda mimosifolia* flowers are____ in colour.

    a. Red   b. Yellow
    c. Orange   d. Blue

33. The silk floss tree (*Ceiba speciosa*) blooms best during the month of

    a. October   b. February
    c. May   d. August

34. *Jacaranda acutifolia* belongs to family

    a. Fabaceae   b. Bignoniaceae
    c. Myrtaceae   d. None of these

35. Parrot flower is name of ____.

    a. *Impatiens psittacina*
    b. *Delonix regia*
    c. *Alianthus excelsa*
    d. None of the above

36. The great emperor Ashoka adopted

    a. Agriculture
    b. Sericulture
    c. Arboriculture
    d. Bioaesthetic planning

37. *Michelia champaca* bears_____colour flowers.

    a. Light-yellow   b. Light-bule
    c. White   d. Dark-red

38. Trees are used as a ____.

    a. Specimen plant
    b. Ornamental plant
    c. For screening purpose
    d. All of these

39. Mostly deciduous plants are planted in month of ____.

    a. June–July
    b. April–May
    c. September–October
    d. December–January

40. Which of the following ornamental plants is planted for fragrant flowers?

    a. *Magnolia grandiflora*
    b. *Plumeria alba*
    c. *Gardenia latifolia*
    d. All of these

41. *Cryptomeria japonica* has_____foliage texture.

    a. Coarse   b. Fine
    c. Medium   d. Rough

42. *Amherstia nobilis* (pride of Burma) is a tropical flowering tree bears_____colour flowers.

    a. Violet   b. Red
    c. Blue   d. Pink

43. For checking air pollination foliage should be

    a. Fine   b. Thick and shining
    c. Pubescent   d. Both a and b

44. Which of the following trees has medicinal value?

    a. *Ficus religiosa*
    b. *Tecomella undulata*
    c. *Terminalia cattapa*
    d. *Terminalia arjuna*

45. "Flowering trees in India" book written by

    a. M.S. Randhwa   b. G.S. Randhwa
    c. V. Swaroop   d. J.S. Arora

46. Which of the following trees is associated with life of Lord Budha?

    a. *Butea monosperma*
    b. *Saraca indica*
    c. *Shorea robusta*
    d. All of the above

47. Goddess Sita is associated with

    a. *Saraca indica*
    b. *Michelia champaca*
    c. *Polyalthia longifolia*
    d. *Shorea robusta*

48. The birth of Lord Budha took under____ tree in 563 BC.

    a. *Butea monosperma*
    b. *Saraca indica*
    c. *Shorea robusta*
    d. *Bauhinia variegata*

49. A shade tree should have____canopy.

    a. Wild oval or dome-like
    b. Columnar

c. Conical

d. Globular or round

50. **Which of the following produces beautiful fruits?**

   a. Cassia   b. Jacaranda

   c. Delonix   d. Kigelia

51. **Which of the following is not a part of texture?**

   a. Fine   b. Medium

   c. Large   d. Coarse

52. **In North and Eastern India, the time of pruning in bougainvillea is**

   a. May–june   b. July–August

   c. December–February

   d. October–December

53. **Kamini (*Murraya paniculata*) belongs to family Rutaceae and comes under category**

   a. Small shrup   b. Medium shrup

   c. Tall shrup   d. None of these

54. **Shrup which not bears yellow colour flowers is**

   a. *Hamelia patens*

   b. *Mussaenda luteola*

   c. *Abutilon indicum*

   d. *Cassia glauca*

55. **Which of the following is used for rooting in cuttings?**

   a. IAA   b. IBA

   c. NAA   d. GA

56. **Which of the following is not a dwarf ornamental hedge?**

   a. *Ligustrum ovalifolium*

   b. *Codiaeum variegatum*

   c. *Lantana sellowiana*

   d. *Acacia fernesiana*

57. **Which of the following shrubs is valued for its ornamental fruits?**

   a. *Carissa opaca*

   b. *Duranta plumeri*

   c. *Solanum pseudocapsicum*

   d. All of these

58. **Which of the following is not suitable for hedge?**

   a. Eupatorium

   b. Bougainvillea

   c. Lawsonia

   d. *Carisaa carandus*

59. **Formal or mechanical edging is made from**

   a. Grass verge

   b. Low growing plants

   c. Stones   d. Annuals

60. **Which of the following is not flowering shrubs?**

   a. *Rosa indica*   b. *Cassia biflora*

   c. *Hibiscus rosasinensis*

   d. Acalypha

61. **Tecoma stans belongs to family____.**

   a. Oleaceae   b. Apocynaceae

   c. Fabaceae   d. Bignoniaceae

62. **Which bougainvillea cultivar is suitable for pot culture**

   a. Begma Sikandar b. Shweta

   c. Surekha   d. Archana

63. **Bottom heating in cuttings enhances rooting percentage in which flower crop?**

   a. Rose   b. Chrysanthemum

   c. Bougainvillea d. Hibiscus

64. **Spectacular display of shrubs is done through**

   a. Edging

   b. Shrubbery

   c. Hedging

   d. Herbaceous border

65. **Which of the following is not a member of family Malvaceae?**

   a. Hibiscus   b. Achania

   c. Abutilon   d. Duranta

66. **The most suitable time of planting hedge is**

   a. Summer season b. Rainy season

   c. Winter season d. None of the above

67. **"Crown of Thorns" is a common name of**
    a. *Euphorbia splendens*
    b. *Cassia allata*
    c. *Lantana camera*
    d. *Reinwardtia indica*

68. **Which of the following plants is used as an edge?**
    a. *Hibiscus mutabilis*
    b. *Doembya spectabilis*
    c. *Iresine herbstii*
    d. *Stenolobium stans*

69. **Which of the following plants is used as an ornamental hedge?**
    a. *Carrisa carandas*
    b. *Acacia fernesiana*
    c. *Poinsettia pulcherima*
    d. *Lawsonia alba*

70. **Which of the following plants is used as topiary?**
    a. *Duranta plumeri*
    b. *Clerodendron inerme*
    c. Both a and b
    d. None of the above

71. **Informal edging is made from**
    a. Low growing plants
    b. Stones
    c. Grass verge
    d. Both a and c

72. **Changeable rose is common name of**
    a. *Hibiscus mutabilis*
    b. *Hibiscus rosa sinensis*
    c. *Hibiscus syriacus*
    d. *Hibiscus schizopetalus*

73. ***Quisqualis indica* is a _____ type of ornamental plant.**
    a. Rambler   b. Shrub
    c. Climber   d. Creeper

74. **Which of the following climb by means of thorns?**
    a. *Ficus repens*
    b. *Campsis grandiflora*
    c. *Antigonon leptopus*
    d. Bougainvillea

75. **Which of the following climbs by means of tendrils?**
    a. *Antigonon leptopus*
    b. *Pyrostegia venusta*
    c. *Bignonia gracilis*
    d. All of these

76. **Extranuclear DNA is found in**
    a. Chloroplast
    b. Endoplasmic reticulum
    c. Ribosomes
    d. Nucleus

77. **Cell theory states that**
    a. All cells have nuclei
    b. All cells are living
    c. Cell reproduces by mitosis and meiosis
    d. Cells are fundamental structural units of plants and animals

78. **Mitochondria have first seen by**
    a. Robert Hooke   b. Robert Brown
    c. Lipmann   d. Altman

79. **Prokaryotic cell does not possess**
    a. Cell wall
    b. Nuclear membrane
    c. Cytoplasm
    d. Plasma membrane

80. **Plasma membrane is composed of**
    a. Protein
    b. Lipids   c. Cellulose
    d. Protein and lipids

81. **Cellular organelles containing hydrolytic enzymes are called**
    a. Peroxisomes   b. Lysosome
    c. Ribosomes   d. Mesosomes

82. **The sedimentation constant of ribosome is generally 70S. Its breaks up into two subunits whose sedimentation constants are**
    a. 50S and 20S   b. 40 S and 30S
    c. 60S and 10S   d. 50 S and 30S

83. **Ribosomes help in**
    a. Photosynthesis
    b. Protein synthesis
    c. Lipid synthesis
    d. Respiration

84. **Food is converted to energy in**
    a. Nucleus
    b. Nucleolus
    c. Chloroplast
    d. Mitochondria

85. **Pollination by snail and slug is known as**
    a. Entomophilus
    b. Ornithophilus
    c. Hydrophilus
    d. Malacophilus

86. **Which is the example of conditioned reflex?**
    a. Eye closed when anything enter into it
    b. Your kneeing took up a stone than dog run away
    c. Hand took up when piercing with needle
    d. Digestive food goes forward in alimentary canal
    e. None of these

87. **Colchicine prevents the mitosis of cells at which of the following stage?**
    a. Anaphase
    b. Leptotene
    c. Zygotene
    d. Interphase
    e. Metaphase

88. **Hydrolytic enzymes are found in**
    a. Lysosomes
    b. Peroxisomes
    c. Ribosomes
    d. Centrosomes
    e. Nucleus

89. **The binomial name was accepted by all after the publication of the work by**
    a. Darwin
    b. Bentham
    c. Darwin
    d. Lamarck
    e. Linnaeus

90. **The pair of disease caused by virus is**
    a. Typhoid, tetanus
    b. Cholera, tuberculosis
    c. Rabies, mumps
    d. AID, syphilis
    e. Typhoid, TB

91. **An angiosperm leaf carries 16 chromosomes. The number of chromosomes in its endosperm will be**
    a. 16
    b. 24
    c. 12
    d. 8
    e. 32

92. **A chemical fertilizing is produced from**
    a. Polar bodies
    b. Middle piece of sperm
    c. Mature eggs
    d. Sertoli cells
    e. Acrosome

93. **Free living, aerobic, non photosynthetic nitrogen fixing bacterium is**
    a. Azotobacter
    b. *E. coli*
    c. Nostoc
    d. Clostridium
    e. Salmonella

94. **Which of the following hormones stimulates the stomach to secrete gastric juice?**
    a. Gastrin
    b. Enterokinase
    c. Renin
    d. Zymase
    e. Secretin

95. **The host bacterium follows the instruction of the**
    a. DNA ligase
    b. Foreign rDNA
    c. Plasmid
    d. Auxin

96. ***Bacillus subtilis* and Streptomyces spp are prokaryotes which are used as hosts for introducing**
    a. Plasmid
    b. Replicon
    c. Auxin
    d. rDNA

97. **The most suitable vectors are**
    a. Yeast
    b. Bacteriophages
    c. Moulds
    d. Algae

98. **Replicons are also known as**
    a. Ligase
    b. Plasmids
    c. Auxin
    d. Vectors

99. **The following is not a branch of biotechnology**
    a. Genetic engineering
    b. Tissue culture

c. Physiology

d. Protoplast fusion

100. Molecular cloning is also known as

a. Splicing

b. Gene cloning

c. Gene manipulation

d. Hardening

101. The rDNA is introduced into this host

a. *E. coli*   b. Yeast

c. Mould   d. Algae

102. Industrial production of enzymes, vitamins, vaccines and biofertilizers are the products of

a. Ploidy   b. Genetics

c. Physiology   d. Biotechnology

103. Each colony is a collection of bacteria having many copies of

a. rDNA fragments called

b. Molecular cloning

c. Splicing

d. Cloning vehicles vectors

104. DNA recombinant technology is also known as

a. Gene manipulation

b. Totipotency

c. Splicing

d. Gene cloning

105. Restriction endonucleases are discovered in

a. 1910   b. 1906

c. 1966   d. 1970

106. Genetic engineering started with flying colours in the early

a. 1900   b. 1950

c. 1960   d. 1970

107. Yoghurt is a food product produced by employing

a. Hybridization

b. Tissue culture

c. Protoplast fusion

d. Biotechnology

108. The donor DNA fragments and vector DNA fragments are joined together by

a. DNA ligase   b. Plasmid

c. Auxin   d. Cytokinin

109. The following is used in industrial fermentation to produce food and drinks

a. Yeast   b. Algae

c. Vitamins   d. Vaccine

110. The enzyme which acts like a paste molecule to join DNA fragments

a. Plasmid   b. Clone

c. DNA ligase   d. Protease

111. The number of segments in leech is

a. 26   b. 33

c. 36   d. 40

112. To make half a kilogram of honey, the nectar from how many flowers is collected by the honeybees?

a. 10 lakhs   b. 20 lakhs

c. One thousand   d. 5 thousands

113. Which of the following is a rich source of protein?

a. Wheat   b. Rice

c. Gram   d. Soya bean

114. Vitamin soluble in water is

a. Vitamin A   b. Vitamin C

c. Vitamin D   d. Vitamin K

115. All genes are made up of

a. Ribonucleic acid

b. Deoxyribonucleic acid

c. Nucleic acids

d. Amino acids

116. DNA ligase was discovered in

a. 1906   b. 1910

c. 1966   d. 1970

117. The mechanism which has the ability to engineer new organisms is known as

a. Totipotency

b. Molecular cloning

c. Genetic engineering

d. Splicing

118. **The production of new characteristics by introducing new genes and altering the genome is known as**
    a. DNA recombinant technology
    b. Protoplast fusion
    c. Totipotency
    d. Splicing

119. **The molecular scissors which cut DNA at specific sites are**
    a. Plasmids
    b. Fusogenic agents
    c. Inoculum
    d. Restriction enzymes

120. **The extrachromosomal circular DNA found in the *E. coli* is**
    a. Plasmid   b. DNA ligase
    c. Vector   d. Cytokinin

121. **If the DNA fragments of donor do not replicate in the host they are attached to a suitable**
    a. DNA ligase   b. Plasmid
    c. Splicing   d. Replicon

122. **The other name for hybrid DNA is**
    a. Recombinant DNA (rDNA)
    b. DNA ligase
    c. Plasmid
    d. Replicon

123. **Joining of donor DNA fragments and vector DNA fragments with the help of DNA ligase enzyme is known as**
    a. Gene cloning
    b. Splicing
    c. Gene manipulation
    d. Molecular cloning

124. **Vectors are also known as**
    a. DNA ligase
    b. Plasmid
    c. Cloning vehicles
    d. Inoculum

125. **The recent and fascinating branch of biology is**
    a. Physiology
    b. Genetics

c. Genetic engineering
    d. Ecology

126. **Suitable host in genetic engineering to introduce DNA fragments of donor is**
    a. Yeast   b. *Bacillus subtilis*
    c. *Escherichia coli* d. Bacteriophages

127. **The DNA of vector is cut into fragments by**
    a. Plasmid
    b. Auxin
    c. Restriction endonucleases
    d. Cytokinin

128. **DNA ligase and restriction endonucleases are the basic tools required for**
    a. Genetic engineering
    b. Physiology
    c. Genetics
    d. Totipotency

129. **Genetic engineering is possible, because**
    a. We can cut DNA at specific sites by endonucleases like DNAase-I
    b. Restriction endonucleases purified from bacteria can be used *in vitro*
    c. The phenomenon of transduction in bacteria is well understood
    d. We can see DNA by electron microscope

130. **Restriction endonucleases (restriction enzymes) are used for**
    a. Used to *in vitro* DNA synthesis
    b. Used in genetic engineering
    c. Synthesized by bacteria
    d. Present in mammalian cells for degradation of DNA

131. **Transgenic animals are those which are**
    a. Foreign RNA in all its cells
    b. Foreign DNA in some of its cells
    c. Foreign DNA in all its cells
    d. Both a and b

132. **The first transgenic plant was**
    a. Tobacco   b. Pea
    c. Flax   d. Cotton

133. Which of the following is related to genetic engineering?
    a. Plastid
    b. Plasmid
    c. Heterosis
    d. Mutation

134. First cloned animal
    a. Dolly sheep
    b. Dog
    c. Mule
    d. Cat

135. Which of the following bases in plasmids discovered so far
    a. 50 kilo base
    b. 500 kilo base
    c. 5 kilo base
    d. 500 kilo base

136. Plasmid has been used as vector because
    a. It has antibiotic resistance gene
    b. It is circular DNA which have capacity to join to eukaryotic DNA
    c. Both ends show replication
    d. It can move between prokaryotic and eukaryotic cells

137. The bacteria generally used for genetic engineering is
    a. Bacillus
    b. Pseudomonas
    c. Clostridium
    d. Agrobacterium

138. Which of the following cut the DNA from specific places
    a. *E. coli* restriction endonuclease II
    b. Ligase
    c. Exonuclease
    d. Alkaline phosphatase

139. Golden rice is a transgenic crop of the future with the following improved trait
    a. Insect resistance
    b. High protein content
    c. High vitamin A content
    d. High lysine content

140. DNA fingerprinting refers to
    a. Techniques used for identification of fingerprints of individuals
    b. Molecular analysis of profiles of DNA samples
    c. Analysis of DNA samples using imprinting devices
    d. Techniques used for molecular analysis of different specimens of DNA

141. The technique of obtaining large number of plantlet by tissue culture method is called
    a. Plantlet culture
    b. Plant biotechnology
    c. Organ culture
    d. Macropropagation

142. Maximum application of animal cell culture technology today is in the production of
    a. Insulin
    b. Interferons
    c. Edible proteins
    d. Vaccines

143. In tissue culture medium, the embryoids formed from pollen grains is due to
    a. Organogenesis
    b. Cellular totipotency
    c. Double fertilization
    d. Test tube culture

144. What is true for monoclonal antibodies?
    a. These antibodies obtained from one parent and for one antigen
    b. These obtained from many parents and for many antigens
    c. These obtained from different parents and for one antigen
    d. These obtained from one parent and for many antigens

145. Two bacteria found to be very useful in genetic engineering experiments are
    a. Nitrobacter and Azotobacter
    b. Rhizobium and diplococci
    c. Nitrosomonas and Klebsiella
    d. Escherichia and Agrobacterium

146. A genetically engineered microorganism used successfully in bioremediation of oil spills is a species of
    a. Trichoderma
    b. Bacillus
    c. Xanthomonas
    d. Pseudomonas

147. Probiotics are
    a. Cancer inducing microbes
    b. Safe antibiotics
    c. New kind of food allergens
    d. Live microbial food supplement

148. In order to obtain virus free plants through tissue culture the best method is
    a. Meristems culture
    b. Protoplast culture
    c. Anther culture
    d. Embryo rescue

149. Which of the following is the lower most category of classification?
    a. Class
    b. Order
    c. Genus
    d. Species

150. A group of individuals of a plant or animal species, inhabiting a given area is called
    a. Biome
    b. Population
    c. Ecosystem
    d. Community

151. Climate includes
    a. Seasonal variation
    b. General patterns of atmosphere conditions
    c. Average weather of an area
    d. All of these

152. The maintenance of relatively constant internal environment is called
    a. Homeostasis
    b. Exotherms
    c. Homeobox
    d. Endotherms

153. Ultraviolet radiation which is not lethal but harm to the organism is
    a. 0.1 to 0.28 μm
    b. 0.28–0.32 μm
    c. 0.32–0.4 μm
    d. 0.4–0.5 μm

154. Ecological niche of an organism represents
    a. The resource it utilizes
    b. Functional role in the ecological system
    c. The range of conditions that it can tolerate
    d. All of these

155. Respiratory roots are known as
    a. Velamen
    b. Pneumatophores
    c. Hydathodes
    d. Prop roots

156. The gradual physiological adjustment to slowly changing new environmental conditions is known as
    a. Selection
    b. Introduction
    c. Acclimatization
    d. Quarantine

157. Upper layer of water in a single body of water is known as
    a. Hypolimnion
    b. Epilimnion
    c. Thermocline
    d. Hydroline

158. The lower limit of water availability in soil is known as
    a. Field capacity
    b. Hypolimnion
    c. Thermocline
    d. Wilting point

159. Example for a natural ecosystem
    a. Agricultural crop
    b. Forest
    c. Prairies
    d. Both b and c

160. The food relation from grass—> deer—>tiger >decomposer is called
    a. Food web
    b. Food chain
    c. Trophic level
    d. Energy flow

161. Each step of food chain represents
    a. Food web
    b. Sere
    c. Trophic level
    d. Consumers

162. The energy transferred to the next higher level
    a. Increases
    b. Decreases
    c. Remains the same
    d. None

163. The first order consumers are called
    a. Autotrophs
    b. Producers
    c. Chemotrophs
    d. Herbivores

164. The study of the relation between agricultural crops and environment is called
    a. Agriculture
    b. Agronomy
    c. Agroecology
    d. Agroforestry

165. The pyramid of energy in a food chain is
    a. Inverted
    b. Remains unchanged
    c. Vertical
    d. Variable

166. The rate of storage of organic matter in producers in excess of their metabolic consumption is
    a. Biomass
    b. Community productivity
    c. Gross primary productivity
    d. Net primary productivity

167. In biogeochemical cycles, mineral cycles are
    a. Gaseous cycle
    b. Hydrocycle
    c. Carbon cycle
    d. Sedimentary cycle

168. More than half of the Earth's flora and fauna are found in
    a. Tundra
    b. Tropical rain forests
    c. Grasslands
    d. Chappara

169. Conservation of grasslands is done by
    a. Protection from grazing of severely damaged vegetation
    b. Rotational grazing
    c. Conservation of soil and water
    d. All of these

170. Grasslands in India include
    a. 12% total land area
    b. 14% total land area
    c. 18% total land area
    d. 20% total land area

171. Biogas is a mixture of
    a. 40% methane and 60% CO_2
    b. 40% methane and 60% ethane
    c. 40% CO_2 and 60% methane
    d. 60% methane and 40% CO_2

172. The law which ensure environmental stability and maintenance of ecological balance is
    a. Forest Act 1927
    b. National Forest Policy 1988
    c. Wildlife Act 1972
    d. Wild Life Protection Act 1991

173. Example for a renewable resource
    a. Soil fertility
    b. Water
    c. Living organisms
    d. All of the above

174. The total energy required by one man approximately per day
    a. 10000–20000 kcal
    b. 1000–2000 kcal
    c. 2000–4000 kcal
    d. 3000–5000 kcal

175. Which is an extinct species?
    a. Dodo of Mauritius
    b. Kiwi from New Zealand
    c. Cheetah from India
    d. Both b and c

176. The key objective of convention at Rio de Janeiro of Earth Summit in 1992
    a. Conservation of biological diversity
    b. Sustainable use of biodiversity
    c. Fair and equitable sharing of benefits arising out of the utilization of genetic resources
    d. All of these

177. Objective Forest Act 1927 is
    a. Setting up and managing reserved forests, protected forests and village forests
    b. Control of movement of forest product
    c. Protection of non-government forests and forest land
    d. All of the above

178. Causes of extinction of species
    a. Introduction of exotic species
    b. Habitat destruction
    c. Over exploitation
    d. All of these

179. Surface area of micaceous clay is
    a. 300–500 m^2/g
    b. 700–800 m^2/g
    c. 100–300 m^2/g
    d. 5–100 m^2/g

180. **Magnesium concentration in plant on dry weight basis is**
    a. Less than 0.4%   b. 0.2–1%
    c. 0.2–0.4   d. None of these

181. **Optimum soil reaction (pH range) of sugar beet is**
    a. 6.0–7.5   b. 5.0–7.5
    c. 5.0–6.0   d. 6.5–8.0

182. **The sizes of the particles in true solutions and in colloidal suspension are**
    a. 0.2–1 ms´   b. 1–3 ms
    c. 0.1–2 ms´   d. 3–4 ms´

183. **Optimum soil reaction (pH range) of cotton is**
    a. 6.0–7.5   b. 5.0–5.5
    c. 4.0–6.0   d. 4.0–6.5

184. **Surface area of vermiculites is**
    a. 300–500 m^2/g   b. 700–800 m^2/g
    c. 100–300 m^2/g   d. 5–100 m^2/g

185. **Silicate clays are dominant in**
    a. Temperature region
    b. Tropical region
    c. Subtropical
    d. All

186. **Sulphur concentration in plant on dry weight basis is**
    a. 1.4%   b. 0.1–0.4%
    c. 0.1–1%   d. 1–2 %

187. **Which soil is known as young soils?**
    a. Histosols   b. Inceptiosols
    c. Mollisols   d. Oxysols

188. **The role of phosphorus in plant is**
    a. Protein formation
    b. Nucleic
    c. Pollen formation
    d. None of these

189. **How many bones are there in a human body?**
    a. 206   b. 205
    c. 150   d. 300

190. **Which of the following is a flightless bird?**
    a. Peacock   b. Duck
    c. Emu   d. Swan

191. **Which of the following is the best source of vitamin 'A'?**
    a. Apple   b. Honey
    c. Carrot   d. Peanut

192. **The genetic unit of a cell is**
    a. Chromosome   b. Ribonucleic acid
    c. Lysosome   d. Genes

193. **Who is called the Father of Genetics?**
    a. Fleming   b. Lamarck
    c. Darwin   d. Mendel

194. **House fly spreads**
    a. Filaria   b. Jaundice
    c. Cholera   d. TB

195. **Number of eyes in leech is**
    a. One pair
    b. Two pairs
    c. Three pairs
    d. Five pairs

Model Test Paper 8

1. **Which is distributed more widely in a cell?**
   a. DNA
   b. RNA
   c. Chloroplast
   d. Spherosomes

2. **What are the most diverse molecules in the cell?**
   a. Lipids
   b. Proteins
   c. Carbohydrates
   d. Mineral salts

3. **Which of the following is a reducing sugar?**
   a. Sucrose
   b. Galactose
   c. β-Methyl galactocidase
   d. Gluconic acid

4. **The four elements that make up 99% of all elements found in a living system are**
   a. C, H, O and P
   b. C, H, O and S
   c. C, H, O and N
   d. C, N, O and P

5. **Transgenic animals are those which are**
   a. Foreign RNA in all its cells
   b. Foreign DNA in some of its cells
   c. Foreign DNA in all its cells
   d. Both a and b

6. **The first transgenic plant was**
   a. Tobacco
   b. Pea
   c. Flax
   d. Cotton

7. **Which of the following is related to genetic engineering?**
   a. Plastid
   b. Plasmid
   c. Heterosis
   d. Mutation

8. **First cloned animal**
   a. Dolly sheep
   b. Dog
   c. Mule
   d. Cat

9. **Which of the following bases in plasmids discovered so far**
   a. 50 kilo base
   b. 500 kilo base
   c. 5 kilo base
   d. 5000 kilo base

10. **Plasmid has been used as vector because**
    a. It has antibiotic resistance gene
    b. It is circular DNA which has capacity to join to eukaryotic DNA
    c. Both ends show replication
    d. It can move between prokaryotic and eukaryotic cells

11. **The bacteria generally used for genetic engineering are**
    a. Bacillus
    b. Pseudomonas
    c. Clostridium
    d. Agrobacterium

12. **Which of the following cut the DNA from specific places?**
    a. *E.coli* restriction endonuclease II
    b. Ligase
    c. Exonuclease
    d. Alkaline phosphatase

13. **Carbohydrates, the most abundant biomolecules on earth, are produced by**
    a. All bacteria, fungi and algae
    b. Viruses, fungi and bacteria
    c. Some bacteria, algae and green plant cells
    d. Fungi, algae and green plant cells

14. **Which of the following is the simplest amino acid?**
    a. Alanine
    b. Glycine
    c. Asparagine
    d. Tyrosine

15. **Which is wrong about nucleic acids?**
    a. DNA is single-stranded in some viruses
    b. One turn of Z DNA has 12 bases
    c. RNA is double-stranded occasionally
    d. Length of one helix is 45A in B-DNA

16. **A segment of DNA has 120 adenine and 120 cytosine bases. The total number of nucleotides present in the segment is**
    a. 480
    b. 240
    c. 120
    d. 60

17. **Mineral associated with cytochrome is**
    a. Cu
    b. Mg
    c. Fe
    d. Cu and Ag

18. **Photosynthesis involves**
    a. Sugar and oxygen
    b. Carbon dioxide, water, and energy
    c. Carbon dioxide and energy
    d. Water and energy

19. **Oxidative phosphorylation is production of**
    a. ATP in photosynthesis
    b. ATP in respiration
    c. NADPH in photosynthesis
    d. NADPH in respiration

20. **End product of glycolysis**
    a. Acetyl CoA
    b. Pyruvic acid
    c. Glucose-1-phosphate
    d. Fructose-1-phosphate

21. **In alcohol fermentation**
    a. Triose phosphate is the electron donor while acetaldehyde is the electron acceptor
    b. There is no electron donor
    c. Oxygen is the electron acceptor
    d. Triose phosphate is the electron donor while pyruvic acid is the electron acceptor

22. **EMP can produce a total of**
    a. 6 ATP
    b. 8 ATP
    c. 24 ATP
    d. 38 ATP

23. **The overall goal of glycolysis, Krebs cycle and the electron transport system is the formation of**
    a. ATP
    b. DNA
    c. Fat
    d. Lipids

24. **What are the most diverse molecules in the cell?**
    a. Lipids
    b. Proteins
    c. Carbohydrates
    d. Mineral salts

25. **Which of the following is a reducing sugar?**
    a. Sucrose
    b. Galactose
    c. β-Methyl galactocidase
    d. Gluconic acid

26. **The four elements that make up 99% of all elements found in a living system are**
    a. C, H, O and P
    b. C, H, O and S
    c. C, H, O and N
    d. C, N, O and P

27. **Glycogen is a polymer of**
    a. Galactose
    b. Glucose
    c. Fructose
    d. Sucrose

28. **During meiosis crossing over occurs at**
    a. Diplotene
    b. Leptotene
    c. Pachytene
    d. Diakinesis

29. **How many generations of mitotic division must occur in a cell of root tip to form 256 cells?**
    a. 8
    b. 32
    c. 64
    d. 128

30. **The main difference between animal and plant cell is that**
    a. Animal cell lack rigid cell wall
    b. Animal cells have vacuoles
    c. Plant cell lack rigid cell wall
    d. Plant cells have small vacuoles

31. **A segment of DNA has 120 adenine and 120 cytosine bases**
    a. Cu
    b. Mg
    c. Fe
    d. Cu and Ag

32. The host bacterium follows the instruction of the
    a. DNA ligase
    b. Foreign rDNA
    c. Plasmid
    d. Auxin

33. *Bacillus subtilis* and Streptomyces spp. are prokaryotes which are used as hosts for introducing
    a. Plasmid
    b. Replicon
    c. Auxin
    d. r DNA

34. The most suitable vectors are
    a. Yeast
    b. Bacteriophages
    c. Moulds
    d. Algae

35. Replicons are also known as
    a. Ligase
    b. Plasmids
    c. Auxin
    d. Vectors

36. The following is not a branch of biotechnology
    a. Genetic engineering
    b. Tissue culture   c. Physiology
    d. Protoplast fusion

37. Molecular cloning is also known as
    a. Splicing
    b. Gene cloning
    c. Gene manipulation
    d. Hardening

38. The rDNA is introduced into the host
    a. *E. coli*
    b. Yeast
    c. Mould
    d. Algae

39. Industrial production of enzymes, vitamins, vaccines and biofertilizers are the products of
    a. Ploidy
    b. Genetics
    c. Physiology
    d. Biotechnology

40. Each colony is a collection of bacteria having many copies of
    a. rDNA fragments
    b. Molecular cloning
    c. Splicing
    d. Cloning vehicles

41. DNA recombinant technology is also known as
    a. Gene manipulation
    b. Totipotency

    c. Splicing
    d. Gene cloning

42. Restriction endonucleases are discovered in
    a. 1910
    b. 1906
    c. 1966
    d. 1970

43. Genetic engineering started with flying colours in the early
    a. 1900
    b. 1950
    c. 1960
    d. 1970

44. Yoghurt is a food product produced by employing
    a. Hybridization
    b. Tissue culture
    c. Protoplast fusion
    d. Biotechnology

45. The donor DNA fragments and vector DNA fragments are joined together by
    a. DNA ligase
    b. Plasmid
    c. Auxin
    d. Cytokinin

46. The following is used in industrial fermentation to produce
    a. Food and drinks
    b. Yeast
    c. Algae
    d. Vitamins

47. The enzyme which acts like a paste molecule to join DNA fragments
    a. Plasmid
    b. Clone
    c. DNA ligase
    d. Protease

48. DNA ligase was discovered in
    a. 1906
    b. 1910
    c. 1966
    d. 1970

49. The mechanism which has the ability to engineer, new organisms is known as
    a. Totipotency
    b. Molecular cloning
    c. Genetic engineering
    d. Splicing

50. The production of new characteristics by introducing new genes and altering the genome is known as
    a. DNA recombinant technology
    b. Protoplast fusion

c. Totipotency

d. Splicing

51. The molecular scissors which cut DNA at specific sites are

a. Plasmids

b. Fusogenic agents

c. Inoculum

d. Restriction enzymes

52. The extrachromosomal circular DNA found in the *E. coli* is

a. Plasmid   b. DNA ligase

c. Vector   d. Cytokinin

53. If the DNA fragments of donor do not replicate in the host they are attached to a suitable

a. DNA ligase   b. Plasmid

c. Splicing   d. Replicon

54. The other name for hybrid DNA is

a. Recombinant DNA (rDNA)

b. DNA ligase

c. Plasmid

d. Replicon

55. Joining of donor DNA fragments and vector DNA fragments with the help of DNA ligase enzyme is known as

a. Gene cloning

b. Splicing

c. Gene manipulation

d. Molecular cloning

56. Vectors are also known as

a. DNA ligase   b. Plasmid

c. Cloning vehicles

d. Inoculum

57. The recent and fascinating branch of biology is

a. Physiology   b. Genetics

c. Genetic engineering

d. Ecology

58. Suitable host in genetic engineering to introduce DNA fragments of donor is

a. Yeast   b. *Bacillus subtilis*

c. *Escherichia coli*   d. Bacteriophages

59. The DNA of vector is cut into fragments by

a. Plasmid

b. Auxin

c. Restriction endonucleases

d. Cytokinin

60. DNA ligase and restriction endo-nucleases are the basic tools required for

a. Genetic engineering

b. Physiology

c. Genetics

d. Totipotency

61. The work on GFP, widely used as a reporter gene, won the Nobel Prize in

a. Medicine/Physiology, 2000

b. Chemistry, 2008

c. Physics, 2008

d. Biochemistry, 2007

62. The method of plasmid isolation by alkaline lysis was published by

a. Mandel and Higa

b. Sharp and Lederberg

c. Temin and Baltimore

d. Birnboim and Doly

63. Alec Jeffery's name is associated with

a. DNA sequencing

b. DNA fingerprinting

c. RNA sequencing

d. Site directed mutagenesis

64. The name Kary Mullis is associated with

a. RFLP   b. PCR

c. Chain termination reaction

d. RAPD

65. The group associated with first man-made recombinant DNA molecules

a. Daniel Nathans, Arber, Kary Mullis

b. Paul Berg, Annie Chang, Boyer, Stanley Cohen

c. Howard Temin, Sydney Brenner, Philip Sharp

d. Tim Hunt, Paul Nurse, Leyland Hartwell

66. In 2006, Nobel Prize for RNA interference phenomenon was won for the work carried out on
    a. *D. melanogaster*   b. *A. thalliana*
    c. *C. elegans*   d. *S. pombe*

67. GFP protein was originally isolated from
    a. *Arabidopsis thaliana*
    b. *Aequoria victoria*
    c. *C. elegans*
    d. *Drosophila melanogaster*

68. The first crop plant genome sequenced
    a. Maize   b. Wheat
    c. Rice   d. Barley

69. The first transgenic plant to be produced
    a. Rice   b. Maize
    c. Cotton   d. Tobacco

70. The year of launching of Human Genome Project and completion of rough draft of the sequence was in
    a. 1992–2000   b. 1990–2000
    c. 1990–2001   d. 1991–2001

71. The unique properties of each amino acid are determined by its particular
    a. Amino group
    b. R group
    c. Kinds of peptide bonds
    d. Presence of hydrogen
    e. Number of bonds to other amino acids

72. Which of the following amino acids is most compatible with the helical structure?
    a. Proline   b. Alanine
    c. Lysine   d. Cysteine
    e. Glycine

73. The greatest buffering capacity at physiological pH would be provided by a protein-rich in which of the following amino acids?
    a. Lysine   b. Valine
    c. Leucine   d. Histidine
    e. Histamine

74. The highest concentration of cystine can be found in
    a. Melanin
    b. Chondroitin sulphate
    c. Myosin
    d. Keratin
    e. Collagen

75. A peptide bond
    a. has a partial double bond character
    b. is ionized at physiological pH
    c. is cleaved by agents that denature proteins, such as organic solvents and high concentration of urea
    d. it is found in fatty acids
    e. is stable to heating in strong acids

76. Which one of the following statements is correct?
    a. The α helix can be composed of more than one polypeptide chain
    b. β-sheets exists only in the anti-parallel form
    c. β-bends often contain proline
    d. Motifs are a type of secondary structure
    e. The alpha helix is stabilized primarily by ionic interactions between the side chains of amino acids

77. Amino acids are mostly synthesized from
    a. Minerals salts   b. Fatty acids
    c. Volatile acids   d. Monosaccharides
    e. α-ketoglutaric acid

78. What are the most diverse molecules in the cell?
    a. Lipids   b. Carbohydrates
    c. Proteins   d. Mineral salts
    e. Vitamins

79. The structure of a protein can be denatured by
    a. Heat
    b. The presence of oxygen gas
    c. The presence of carbon dioxide gas
    d. The polar bonds of water molecules
    e. All of these

80. **Which one of the following statements about protein structure is correct?**
    a. Proteins consisting of one polypeptide can have quaternary structure
    b. The formation of a disulphide bond in a protein requires that the two participating cysteine residues be adjacent to each other in the primary sequence of the protein
    c. The stability of quaternary structure in proteins is mainly due to covalent bonds among the subunits
    d. The information required for the correct folding of a protein is contained in the specific sequences of amino acids along the polypeptide chain

81. **Genetic engineering is possible, because**
    a. We can cut DNA at specific sites by endonucleases like DNAase I
    b. Restriction endonucleases purified from bacteria can be used *in vitro*
    c. The phenomenon of transduction in bacteria is well understood
    d. We can see DNA by electron microscope

82. **Restriction endonucleases (restriction enzymes) are used for**
    a. Used to *in vitro* DNA synthesis
    b. Used in genetic engineering
    c. Synthesized by bacteria
    d. Present in mammalian cells for degradation of DNA

83. **Transgenic animals are those which are**
    a. Foreign RNA in all its cells
    b. Foreign DNA in some of its cells
    c. Foreign DNA in all its cells
    d. Both a and b

84. **The first transgenic plant was**
    a. Tobacco   b. Pea
    c. Flax   d. Cotton

85. **Which of the following is related to genetic engineering?**
    a. Plastid   b. Plasmid
    c. Heterosis   d. Mutation

86. **First cloned animal**
    a. Dolly sheep   b. Dog
    c. Mule   d. Cat

87. **When a cross is made between offspring and its parent, it is called**
    a. Back cross
    b. Intergeneric cross
    c. Interspecific cross
    d. Back cross

88. **When a heterozygous offspring is crossed with homozygous recessive parent, it is called**
    a. Test cross   b. Reciprocal cross
    c. Monohybrid cross
    d. Dihybrid cross

89. **The term genome is used for**
    a. Haploid set of a chromosome
    b. Diploid set of chromosome
    c. Polyploid set of chromosome
    d. Triploid set of chromosome

90. **The process of removing stamens from the flower during hybridization is called**
    a. Caping   b. Selfing
    c. Crossing   d. Emasculation

91. **Mendel choose pea plants for his experiments because**
    a. They were having contrasting characters
    b. They were cheap
    c. They were easily available
    d. All of the above

92. **The main reason for the success of Mendel was that**
    a. He selected pea plant
    b. He kept pedigree record
    c. He made statistical analysis of the offspring
    d. He first took only one character at a time in his crosses

93. **Meiosis takes place**
    a. Only in haploid individuals
    b. Only in diploid individuals

c. Both in haploid and diploid individuals

d. None of these

94. In one of the following stages of cell division, the DNA content is doubled. It is

a. G1 phase   b. G2 phase

c. Metaphase   d. S phase

95. A mitosis is the usual process of cell division in

a. Meristematic cells

b. Prokaryotic cells

c. Eukaryotic cells

d. Spore mother cells

96. During synapsis the number of thread (Chromonemata) in each chromosome is

a. 2   b. 4

c. 8   d. Many

97. Homologous chromosomes are

a. Morphologically and genetically similar

b. Morphologically similar

c. Those which pair during synapsis

d. None of these

98. Cell division of mitosis is a normal process in a living cell but sudden and abnormal mitosis in an organ will some time results in

a. Cancer   b. New organ

c. Zygote   d. Gastrula

99. Synapsis is characteristic of

a. Leptotene   b. Diplotene

c. Zygotene   d. Pachytene

100. The mechanism ensuring genetic continuity in mitosis is

a. Having of chromosome number between the two new cells

b. Formation of cells with 8 chromosomes

c. Formation of two daughter cells

d. Formation of two cells with identical kind of DNA

101. Product of aerobic respiration are

a. Sugar and oxygen

b. Carbon dioxide, water, and energy

c. Carbon dioxide and energy

d. Water and energy

102. Oxidative phosphorylation is production of

a. ATP in photosynthesis

b. ATP in respiration

c. NADPH in photosynthesis

d. NADPH in respiration

103. End product of glycolysis

a. Acetyl CoA

b. Pyruvic acid

c. Glucose-1-phosphate

d. Fructose-1-phosphate

104. In alcohol fermentation

a. Triosephosphate is the electron donor while acetaldehyde is the electron acceptor

b. There is no electron donor

c. Oxygen is the electron acceptor

d. Triose phosphate is the electron donor while pyruvic acid is the electron acceptor

105. EMP can produce a total of

a. 6 ATP   b. 8 ATP

c. 24 ATP   d. 38 ATP

106. The overall goal of glycolysis, Krebs cycle and the electron transport system is the formation of

a. ATP in one large oxidation reaction

b. Sugars

c. ATP in small stepwise units

d. Nucleic acids

107. During which stage in the complete oxidation of glucose is the greatest number of ATP molecules formed from ADP?

a. Krebs cycle   b. Glycolysis

c. Electron transport chain

d. Conversion of pyruvic acid to acetyl CoA

108. Which of the following is the key intermediate compound linking glycolysis to the Krebs cycle?
    a. Malic acid
    b. Pyruvic acid
    c. Acetyl CoA
    d. ATP

109. How many ATP molecules are produced by the aerobic oxidation of one molecule of glucose?
    a. 8
    b. 30
    c. 36
    d. 38

110. Rickettsiae form a group under
    a. Fungi
    b. Bacteria
    c. Virus
    d. A category between viruses and bacteria

111. Give the correct matching of causative agent/germ and disease
    a. Glossina: Kala-azar
    b. Anopheles: Malaria
    c. Wuchereria: Filariasis
    d. Leishmania: Sleeping sickness

112. The blood cancer is known as
    a. Haemolysis
    b. Leukaemia
    c. Haemophilia
    d. Thrombosis

113. Which one of the following diseases is due to an allergic reaction?
    a. Skin cancer
    b. Goitre
    c. Hay fever
    d. Enteric fever

114. Which of the following pair of diseases is caused by virus?
    a. Rabies, mumps
    b. Typhoid, tetanus
    c. AIDS, syphilis
    d. Cholera, tuberculosis

115. Botulism caused by *Clostridium botulinum* affects the
    a. Lymph glands
    b. Spleen
    c. Intestine
    d. Central nervous system

116. Diphtheria is caused by
    a. Nematodes
    b. Virus
    c. Bacteria
    d. None of these

117. Which of the following causes plague?
    a. *Trichinella spiralis*
    b. *Yersinia pestis*
    c. *Salmonella typhimurium*
    d. *Leishmania donovani*

118. Which one of the following does correctly match sexually transmitted diseases (STDs) with its pathogen?
    a. Syphilis: *Treponema pallidium*
    b. Softsore: *Bacillus brevis*
    c. Gonorrhoea: *Entamoeba histolytica*
    d. Urethritis: *Bacillus anthracis*

119. The causative agent of mad cow disease is a
    a. Virus
    b. Prion
    c. Worm
    d. Bacterium

120. Evolution is
    a. Progressive development of race
    b. History and development of race along with variations
    c. History of race
    d. Development of race

121. The first organisms were
    a. Chemoautotrophs
    b. Autotrophs
    c. Eukaryotes
    d. Chemoheterotrophs

122. Theory of inheritance of acquired characters was given by
    a. Wallace
    b. Darwin
    c. de Vries
    d. Lamarck

123. Which one of the following is a living fossil?
    a. Cycas
    b. Moss
    c. Saccharomycetes
    d. Spirogyra

124. Basic principles of embryonic development were pronounced by
    a. Von Baer
    b. Haeckel
    c. Morgan
    d. Weismann

125. Which of the following amino acids was not found to be synthesized in Miller's experiment?
    a. Alanine
    b. Glycine
    c. Asparatic acid
    d. Glutamic acid

126. Two zoo geographical regions, separated by high mountain ranges, are
    a. Oriental and Australian
    b. Nearctic and Palaearctic
    c. Palaearctic and Oriental
    d. Neotrophical and Ethiopian

127. Origin of species was written by
    a. Oparin
    b. Lamarck
    c. Weismann
    d. Darwin

128. Praying mantis is a good example of
    a. Camouflage
    b. Müllerian mimicry
    c. Warning colouration
    d. Social insects

129. Continuity of germplasm theory was given by
    a. de Vries
    b. Darwin
    c. Weismann
    d. Lamarck

130. Rickettsiae form a group under
    a. Fungi
    b. Bacteria
    c. Virus
    d. A category between viruses and bacteria

131. There are approximately ____ muscles in human body.
    a. 206
    b. 360
    c. 500
    d. 700

132. Wisdom teeth normally grow during the age of
    a. 12–15 years
    b. 15–30 years
    c. 17–30 years
    d. 30–40 years

133. Inside the body, blood does not coagulate due to the presence of
    a. Fibrin
    b. Heparin
    c. Haemoglobin
    d. Thromboplastin

134. The saliva helps in the digestion of
    a. Proteins
    b. Fats
    c. Fibres
    d. Starch

135. The normal temperature of human body on the Kelvin scale is
    a. 280
    b. 290
    c. 300
    d. 310

136. The smallest unit of genetic material which when mutated produces a phenotypic effect is
    a. Recon
    b. Muton
    c. Gene
    d. Nucleic acid

137. Alleles are
    a. Linked genes
    b. Alternative forms of a gene
    c. Homologous chromosomes
    d. Chromosome that have crossed over

138. An organism with two identical alleles of a gene in a cell is called
    a. Homozygous
    b. Heterogeneous
    c. Hybrid
    d. Dominant

139. Genes do not occur in pairs in
    a. Body cells
    b. Gametes
    c. Fertilized egg
    d. Zygote

140. What is true of ecosystem?
    a. Primary consumers are least dependent upon producers
    b. Primary consumers out number producers
    c. Producers are more than primary consumers
    d. Secondary consumers are the largest and most powerful

141. In an ecosystem, which one shows one way passage
    a. Nitrogen
    b. Carbon
    c. Potassium
    d. Free energy

142. Upper part of sea/ aquatic ecosystem contains
    a. Plankton
    b. Nekton
    c. Benthos
    d. Plankton and nekton

143. **Pyramid of numbers in a grassland/ tree ecosystem is**
    a. Always inverted b. Always upright
    c. Both a and b d. Spindle shaped

144. **Food chain in which microorganisms breakdown the food formed by primary producers is**
    a. Parasitic food chain
    b. Detritus food chain
    c. Consumer food chain
    d. Predator food chain

145. **Pick up the correct food chain**
    a. Grass → chameleon → insect → bird
    b. Grass → fox → rabbit → bird
    c. Phytoplankton → zooplankton → fish
    d. Fallen leaves → bacteria → insect larvae

146. **Association of animals when both partners is benefitted**
    a. Colony   b. Mutualism
    c. Commensalism d. Ammensalism

147. **Pyramid of numbers deals with the number of**
    a. Species in area
    b. Subspecies in a community
    c. Individuals in a community
    d. Individuals in a tropic level

148. **The sum total of the populations of the same kind of organisms constitute**
    a. Colony   b. Genus
    c. Species   d. Community

149. **The dominant second trophic level, in a lake ecosystem, is**
    a. Benthos   b. Plankton
    c. Zooplankton   d. Phytoplankton

150. **Who introduced the term 'Nucleic Acid?'**
    a. Meisher   b. Robert Brown
    c. Lipmann   d. Altmann

151. **Hereditary information is indicated by**
    a. Sequence of nucleic acids
    b. Position of nucleic acid

    c. Number of nucleic acid
    d. All of these

152. **The strongest evidence that DNA is the genetic material comes from**
    a. The finding DNA is not present in the cytoplasm
    b. The fact that chromosomes are made up of DNA
    c. Studies of bacterial transformation
    d. The knowledge that DNA is present in the nucleus

153. **Who among the following scientists developed cytochemical technique for the detection of DNA?**
    a. Feulgen and Rossenbeck
    b. Watson and Crick
    c. Beadle and Tatum
    d. Knoll and Ruska

154. **Which of the following scientists demonstrated that DNA A=T and G=C?**
    a. Griffith
    b. Meselson and Stahl
    c. Hershey and Chase
    d. Chargaff

155. **Which ratio is constant for DNA?**
    a. A+G / T+C   b. A + T / G+ C
    c. A+ C/ U+G   d. A+ U/ C+G

156. **The dye involved in Feulgen reaction to stain DNA is**
    a. Janus green B   b. Basic Fuchsin
    c. Neutral Red   d. Haemoxylin

157. **If 30% of an organism's DNA is thymine, then**
    a. 70% guanine   b. 20% is guanine
    c. 30% adenine   d. Both b and c

158. **Hydrogen bonds between cytosine and guanine are**
    a. 1   b. 2
    c. 3   d. 4

159. **Nucleotide arrangement in DNA can be seen by**
    a. Light microscope
    b. Electron microscope

c. X-Ray crystallography

d. Ultracentrifuge

160. Photosynthesis, a process of manufacture of organic compound is

a. Catabolic process

b. Anabolic process

c. Both   d. None of these

161. Land plants utilize for photosynthesis

a. 1% of water absorbed

b. 10% of water absorbed

c. 0.1% of water absorbed

d. 100% of water absorbed

162. Who proved that oxygen evolved in photosynthesis comes from water?

a. Mayer   b. Melvin Calvin

c. Hatch

d. Ruben and Kamen

163. The first product of photosynthesis is sugar and it is converted

a. Into starch in all plants

b. Into proteins

c. Rarely into anything else

d. Glycogen

164. The site of light reactions of photosynthesis is

a. Grana   b. Stroma

c. Thylakoids   d. Both a and b

165. The dark reaction in photosynthesis is called so because it

a. Cannot occur during day time

b. It is light dependent

c. It is light independent

d. Occurs rapidly at night

166. Which is the most effective wavelength of light for photosynthesis?

a. Green   b. Violet

c. Red   d. Yellow

167. Q 10 is

a. The respiratory coefficient

b. A temperature coefficient

c. A scale of quality

d. A constant in quantum equation

168. The bacterial photosynthesis differs from the green plant photosynthesis in

a. Photolysis of water

b. Evolution of oxygen

c. Obtaining energy from sunlight

d. The obtaining energy from chemical compounds

169. During photochemical reaction of photosynthesis

a. Liberation of oxygen

b. Liberation of ATP and NADPH

c. Assimilation of CO_2

d. Liberation of oxygen, formation of ATP and $NADPH_2$ takes place

170. Which of the following is essential for blood clotting?

a. RBC   b. WBC

c. Blood platelets   d. Lymph

171. Short sightedness is due to

a. Weaker muscles

b. Shifting of the iris

c. Elongation of eyeballs

d. Weakening of the retina

172. A person will have brown eyes, blue eyes or black eyes depending upon the particular pigment presents in the

a. Pupil   b. Cornea

c. Iris   d. Choroid

173. A colour blind person has difficulty in distinguishing between which colours?

a. Black and blue   b. Green and red

c. Green and violet

d. White and yellow

174. What is the maximum limit of sound intensity in decibel units, which a person cannot hear?

a. 65   b. 75

c. 85   d. 95

Model Test Paper 9

1. **Total duration from the harvest to the wilting of cut flowers called as**
   a. Longevity
   b. Vase life
   c. Both a and b
   d. Duration of flowering

2. **The factors which are major determinates of vase life are**
   a. Pre-harvest factors
   b. Harvesting factors
   c. Post-harvest factors
   d. All of these

3. **Precooling is done to**
   a. Remove field heat
   b. Flower opening
   c. Increase transpiration
   d. Reduce microbial activity

4. **Harvesting of cut flowers at tight bud stage is always preferred because**
   a. Long vase life
   b. Easy to handling
   c. Less sensitive to ethylene
   d. All of these

5. **Most effective method of removing the field heat from the flowers is**
   a. Vacuum cooling
   b. Forced air cooling
   c. Hydro cooling
   d. Room cooling

6. **Most of the cut flowers are stored at ____°C**
   a. 0–4   b. 5–9
   c. 10–13   d. 20–24

7. **Tropical orchids and Anthurium should be stored at ____°C**
   a. 2–4   b. 5–8
   c. 10–13   d. 18–20

8. **Which of the following factors determines the potential longevity of cut flowers?**
   a. Time of harvesting
   b. Method of harvesting
   c. Stage of harvesting
   d. All of these

9. **Which of the following flowers is highly sensitive to chilling injury?**
   a. Rose   b. Gladiolus
   c. Anthurium   d. Carnation

10. **Hypobaric storage is mostly used for __**
    a. Vegetable   b. Fruits
    c. Spices   d. Flowers

11. **Which of the following is used to increase vase life of flowers?**
    a. Glucose   b. Salt
    c. Sucrose   d. Any of them

12. **Which of the following agrochemicals used as flower preservative?**
    a. STS   b. 1-MCP
    c. 8-HQC   d. ALL of these

13. Stem break is the main problem of
    a. Rose   b. Carnation
    c. Anthurium   d. Gerbera

14. Bent neck is the disorder of____.
    a. Gerbera   b. Rose
    c. Camation   d. Gladiolus

15. "Sleepiness" disorder is associated with____.
    a. Rose   b. Carnation
    c. Gladiolus   d. Gerbera

16. A material that is added to the water to extend the life of flower is known as
    a. Floral preservative
    b. Preservative   c. Pasteurization
    d. None of these

17. A disease that causes brown spots on the petals of flower is____.
    a. Powdery mildew
    b. Botrytis   c. Downy mildew
    d. Rust

18. Flower senescence is often associated with increased
    a. Gibberellins   b. Auxin
    c. Abscissic acid   d. Ethylene

19. Tropical flowers are best stored at____°F.
    a. 30–35   b. 35–40
    c. 45–50   d. 60–70

20. Which of the following is a rapid pre-cooling method?
    a. Vacuum cooling
    b. Hydro cooling   c. Room cooling
    d. Forced air cooling

21. Generally loose flowers are packed in
    a. Gunny bags
    b. Bamboo baskets
    c. Corrugated fiber board
    d. Both a and b

22. In normal air how much ethylene is present?
    a. 2–3 ppm   b. 5–10 ppb
    c. 3–5 ppb   d. 3–5 ppm

23. Bent neck in rose is very common where light intensity is____.
    a. Low   b. Medium
    c. High   d. Extreme high

24. Ideal packaging of cut flowers should be
    a. Air tight
    b. Waterproof
    c. Strong enough to withstand handling
    d. All of the above

25. Pulsing is related to____.
    a. Fruits   b. Transportation
    c. Cut flowers   d. Harvesting

26. Red color of rose flower is due to
    a. Anthocyanin   b. Carotene
    c. Xanthophyll   d. None of the above

27. Paint brush stage of flower harvesting is related to
    a. Gladiolus   b. Rose
    c. Carnation   d. Dahlia

28. Leaf scorch and bud blast is disorder of
    a. Anthurium   b. Orchids
    c. Gladiolus   d. Lilium

29. Calyx splitting is major problem in
    a. Carnation   b. Orchids
    c. Lily   d. Rose

30. Phyllody is common disorder in
    a. Marigold   b. Rose
    c. Lily   d. Gerbera

31. Leaf scorching in lily is due to high____.
    a. Phosphorus   b. Potassium
    c. Fluorine   d. Nitrogen

32. Quilling of florets is common disorder in
    a. Marigold   b. Chrysanthemum
    c. Carnation   d. China aster

33. Which of the following is most sensitive to ethylene?
    a. Freesia   b. Asparagus
    c. Anthurium   d. Gerbera

34. **Chemical which is used as germicide**
    a. HQC   b. Sucrose
    c. Urea   d. Ammonia

35. **Abscissic acid promotes**
    a. Shoot elongation
    b. Cell division
    c. Leaf senescence
    d. Seed germination

36. **Sorting of the flowers done according to**
    a. Cultivar
    b. Stage of maturity
    c. Extent of damage
    d. All of the above

37. **Pre-cooling temperature of Anthurium is____°C.**
    a. 7   b. 13
    c. 3   d. 6

38. **Shattering of snapdragon florets is due to**
    a. Ethylene
    b. High light intensity
    c. Genetically factor
    d. High temperature

39. **Which of the following is less sensitive to ethylene?**
    a. Carnation   b. Gerbera
    c. Lilium   d. Alstroemeria

40. **Bluing of rose petals is due to**
    a. Accumulation of ammonia
    b. Methane   c. Ethylene
    d. Carbon dioxide

41. **Who has contributed the modern theory of interest?**
    a. Knut Wicksell
    b. Gunnar Myrdal
    c. J.R. Hicks
    d. R.G. Hawtrey

42. **Which of the following is most important ethylene inhibitor?**
    a. $ZnSO_4$ b. STS
    c. $AgNO_3$ d. BA

43. **Purpose of "preservatives" is /are**
    a. Keep water acid
    b. Counteract ethylene effect
    c. Provide sugars
    d. All of the above

44. **Hard wood stems of cut flowers should always be given**
    a. Horizontal cut   b. Vertical cut
    c. Slanting cut   d. Any of the above

45. **Ethylene commonly known as**
    a. Maturity hormone
    b. Ripening hormone
    c. Growth hormone
    d. Abscission hormone

46. **A short-term treatment given to the cut flower before packaging is**
    a. Pulsing   b. Conditioning
    c. Pre-cooling   d. Hardening

47. **Bull head physiological disorder of rose is due to**
    a. Low temperature
    b. High temperature
    c. Thrips
    d. Light intensity

48. **Which cut flower is suitable for wet packaging?**
    a. Rose   b. Orchid
    c. Anthurium   d. Both b and c

49. **Which cut flower is not sensitive to geotropic bending?**
    a. Larkspur   b. Gerbera
    c. Snapdragon   d. Gladiolus

50. **AVG is inhibitor of**
    a. GA3   b. Auxins
    c. Ethylene   d. Cytokinins

51. **The term "Pulsing" is related to**
    a. Preservation   b. Cut flowers
    c. Freezing   d. Storage

52. **Red colour of rose flower is due to**
    a. Carotene   b. Anthocyanin
    c. Globulin   d. Xanthophyll

53. **Main aim of pre-cooling is**
    a. Removal of field heat
    b. Reduced microbial growth
    c. Improve quality
    d. None of these

54. **Among the following, pre-cooling is related**
    a. Cut flowers
    b. Dry flowers
    c. Fruit preservation
    d. Freezing

55. **Which of the following is a flower preservative?**
    a. $HgCl_2$
    b. $C_{12} H_{22} O_{11}$
    c. $KMnO_3$
    d. KNO_3

56. **For cut flower production, rose is harvested at**
    a. Tight bud stage
    b. Half opened stage
    c. Fully open
    d. All of these

57. **Harvesting stage of rose for loose flower purpose is**
    a. Tight bud stage
    b. Half opened stage
    c. Fully open
    d. All of these

58. **Controlled atmosphere storage was invented by**
    a. Kidd and wert
    b. Gane
    c. Wade
    d. James

59. **"Queen Elizabeth" variety of rose belongs to group**
    a. Hybrid tea
    b. Tea rose
    c. Floribunda
    d. Grandiflora

60. **Pseudobulb is commercially propagation method of**
    a. Tulip
    b. Orchids
    c. Gladiolus
    d. Tuberose

61. **The term "Ikebana " is related to**
    a. Flower drying
    b. Flower arrangement

    c. Flower storage
    d. Flower package

62. **Maximum rose oil producing country is**
    a. China
    b. Turkey
    c. Bulgaria
    d. India

63. **Essential oil from the flowers is mostly obtained by**
    a. Liquidification
    b. Distillation
    c. Solvent extraction
    d. Crystallization

64. **Which of the following is a free flower arrangement?**
    a. Jiyubana
    b. Morimana
    c. Moribana
    d. Zenika

65. **Which of the following flower crops is grown for lutein extraction?**
    a. Rose
    b. Gaillardia
    c. Marigold
    d. Dahlia

66. **Most commonly used material for holding the stems of flowers**
    a. Floral foam
    b. Pin point holders
    c. Frogs
    d. Copper wire

67. **Generally in hanging method flowers dry in____.**
    a. 1–3 weeks
    b. 1–3 days
    c. 2–4 months
    d. 5–8 months

68. **Which of the following is probably the best drying agent for preserving flowers?**
    a. Silica gel
    b. Kitty litter
    c. Borax
    d. Saw dust

69. **Which species of Marigold is commercially grown for oil extraction?**
    a. *T. Patula*
    b. *T. erecta*
    c. *T. minuta*
    d. *T. tenuifolia*

70. **Rose hip is good source of**
    a. Vitamin A
    b. Vitamin D
    c. Vitamin C
    d. Vitamin E

71. **Which is the major flower crop grown for fragrance in India?**
    a. Rose
    b. Jasmine
    c. Carnation
    d. Tuberose

72. **Which of the following is an example of value added product of flowers?**
    a. Fresh flower arrangement
    b. Flower wreaths
    c. Pot pourri
    d. All of these

73. **Which of the following is not associated with loose flowers?**
    a. Garlands
    b. Veni
    c. Bouquets
    d. Essential oil

74. **Dry flowers are also known as**
    a. Everlasting flowers
    b. Dehydrated flowers
    c. Both a and b
    d. None of these

75. **Which of the following plant parts can be used for drying or dehydration purpose?**
    a. Flowers
    b. Seeds
    c. Shoots
    d. Any plant parts

76. **A mixture of dried, sweet-scented plant parts is known as**
    a. Perfume
    b. Pot pourri
    c. Flower ball
    d. Pomanders

77. **Suitable plant for air drying is/are**
    a. Acroclinum
    b. Helichrysum
    c. Gypsophila
    d. All of these

78. **In microwave oven, flowers are dehydrated within___minutes.**
    a. 20–25
    b. 10–15
    c. 2–5
    d. 40–50

79. **Ideal temperature for flower drying in hot air oven is____°C.**
    a. 45–65
    b. 66–85
    c. 3–15
    d. >85

80. **Which of the following is correct?**
    a. Shin-Heaven
    b. Hikae-Earth
    c. Soe-Man
    d. All of the above

81. **In Japanese flower arrangement Moribana means**
    a. Piled-up flowers
    b. Throw-in
    c. Free flowers
    d. Abstract

82. **Which of the following flowers has fragrance?**
    a. Tuberose
    b. Lilium
    c. Gerbera
    d. Gladiolus

83. **Which of the following types of ikebana resembles English flower arrangement?**
    a. Nageire
    b. Zeneibana
    c. Jiyubana
    d. Morimono

84. **One kg of rose oil extracted from____ tonnes flowers.**
    a. 1.5
    b. 5.5
    c. 3.5
    d. 10

85. **Vanilla is harvested at____stage.**
    a. Ripe
    b. Fully ripe
    c. Tender
    d. Immature

86. **The principle followed in freezing is**
    a. Condensation
    b. Drying
    c. Crystallization
    d. None of the above

87. **A process of increasing the economic value of any commodity is known as**
    a. Flower processing
    b. Value addition
    c. Genetic engineering
    d. Floriculture diversification

88. **Rose damascena is commercially cultivated for**
    a. Loose flowers
    b. Cut flowers
    c. Oil extraction
    d. All of these

89. **Flower used by woman for decorating hair is**
    a. Marigold
    b. Gladiolus
    c. Crossendra
    d. Rose

90. **The famous city for extracting rose perfume in India is**
    a. Aligarh
    b. Agra
    c. Ajmer
    d. Allahabad

91. The first school of ikebana called as lekenobo was started by Buddhist monk semmu in ___ century.
    a. 7th   b. 8th
    c. 6th   d. 10th

92. Pyrethrum obtained from which species of Chrysanthemum
    a. *C. morifolium*   b. *C. cinerifolium*
    c. *C. coronarium*   d. *C. sinense*

93. In ikebana arrangement which is used as an filler
    a. Shin   b. Soe
    c. Hikae   d. Jushi

94. Maximum economic life of vanilla is ____ years.
    a. 5   b. 10
    c. 15   d. 20

95. Saffron is expected from
    a. Fruit   b. Seed
    c. Dried stigma   d. Flowers

96. Commonly used method for extraction of flower perfume is
    a. Maceration
    b. Enfleurage
    c. Solvent extraction
    d. Distillation

97. Source of essential oil in rose is____.
    a. Sepals   b. Petals
    c. Stigma   d. Style

98. Which country is largest producer of jasmine perfume?
    a. Brazil   b. Bulgaria
    c. France   d. Egypt

99. Which alkaloid is used as artificial vanilla?
    a. Linalool   b. Terpenop
    c. Gernanol   d. Camphor

100. Who is credited for the discovery of rose oil?
    a. Mumtaj   b. Shahjahan
    c. Akbar   d. Noorjahan

101. Costliest oil in the world is
    a. Rose   b. Jasmine
    c. Tuberose   d. Carnation

102. Himroz cultivar of *R. damascena* is suitable for which climatic region?
    a. Temperate   b. Tropical
    c. Subtropical   d. Arid

103. The word jasmine derived from _____ word 'yasmine'.
    a. Arabian   b. Italian
    c. Greek   d. English

104. Which technique is used for coloring of flowers?
    a. Tinting   b. Chromatization
    c. Sulphuring   d. Dyeing

105. "Noorjahan" cultivar belongs to
    a. *R. centifolia*   b. *R. damascena*
    c. *R. borboniana*   d. *R. gallica*

106. Vanillin was first isolated from vanilla pods by Gobley in
    a. 1858   b. 1814
    c. 1921   d. 1957

107. Which of the following is not a value-added product?
    a. Gulkand   b. Vanilla
    c. Corm   d. Natural dye

108. Which of the following is not a value added product of rose?
    a. Gulkand   b. Pankhuri
    c. Rose water   d. Vanilla

109. Gulkand is prepared by mixing rose petals and sugar in the ratio of
    a. 2:1   b. 3:1
    c. 1:1   d. 1:2

110. Which of the following is not a single-flowered variety of tuberose?
    a. Rajat Rekha
    b. Shringar
    c. Single Mexican
    d. Svarna Rekha

111. Which chemical is responsible for fragrance in rose?
    a. Eugenol
    b. Rhodinol
    c. Magnolia
    d. Geraniol

112. Which pigment presents in bracts of bougainvillea?
    a. Cyanidin
    b. Lutein
    c. Malvidin
    d. Betain

113. Rhizomes of which are edible?
    a. Lotus
    b. Dahlia
    c. Canna
    d. Calla lily

114. 100 gm rose fruit syrup will contain _____ mg ascorbic acid
    a. 150
    b. 500
    c. 50
    d. 75

115. Annual which is suitable for dry flower
    a. Helichrysum
    b. Corn flower
    c. Ice plant
    d. Hollyhock

116. Leading dry flower producing state of India is
    a. Tamil Nadu
    b. Karnataka
    c. Maharashtra
    d. Andhra Pradesh

117. Leading dry flower exporting country is
    a. Australia
    b. USA
    c. Canada
    d. India

118. Which of the following commodities has maximum share in floriculture export from India?
    a. Loose flower
    b. Cut flower
    c. Dry flower
    d. Cut greens

119. Which part of lotus plant is edible?
    a. Seeds
    b. Carpels
    c. Leaves
    d. Stem

120. Makhana is obtained from
    a. Trapa natans
    b. Eichhornia crassipes
    c. Euryale ferox
    d. Najas marina

121. Kewda perfume is produced from
    a. Male spadix
    b. Female spadix
    c. Leaves
    d. Roots

122. The extracted from Marigold petals are added to poultry feed for intensification of yellow color of egg yolk
    a. Carotene
    b. Lutein
    c. Chlorophyll
    d. Anthocyanins

123. The rhizomes of _____ are utilized for production of resinoids and perfume.
    a. *Iris germanica*
    b. *Iris pallida*
    c. *Nelumbo nucifera*
    d. Both a and b

124. Which variety of *Rosea damascena* gives the best quality rose oil in the world?
    a. Gruss an teplitz
    b. Himroz
    c. Jwala
    d. Triginipetala

125. About _____ kg tuberose flowers are required to produce one kg of a brown semi-solid absolute of effleurage.
    a. 50
    b. 100
    c. 150
    d. 200

126. Species of Chrysanthemum which is cultivated as a source of pyrethrum
    a. *C. coccineus*
    b. *C. cinerariifolium*
    c. *C. indicum*
    d. Both a and b

127. Rock garden is located at
    a. Chandigarh
    b. New Delhi
    c. Kolkata
    d. Karnataka

128. Which of the following is known as city of gardens?
    a. Chandigarh
    b. Bangalore
    c. Jaipur
    d. Lucknow

129. Which of the following is a formal type garden?
    a. Italian
    b. Persian
    c. Mughal
    d. All of these

130. Mughal style of gardening in India developed by
    a. Babar
    b. Akbar
    c. Shahjahan
    d. Noorjahan

131. Baradari garden of Patiala was built by _____ in 1876.
    a. Rajinder Singh
    b. Raja Jai Singh
    c. Akbar
    d. Babar

132. **Baradari garden of Patiala was built in a ___ style.**
    a. Formal
    b. Informal
    c. Free
    d. Wild

133. **Japanese styles of garden are**
    a. Formal
    b. Informal
    c. Free style
    d. Wild style

134. **Mughal gardens are ___ in garden style.**
    a. Formal
    b. Informal
    c. Free style
    d. Wild style

135. **Which gardening style expounded by William Robinson**
    a. Formal style
    b. Informal style
    c. Free style
    d. Wild style

136. **Brindavan gardens is famous for**
    a. Topiary
    b. IIluminated dancing fountains
    c. Rose varieties
    d. Rockery

137. **Main feature of English garden is**
    a. Herbarium
    b. Lawn
    c. Rockery
    d. All of the above

138. **Sand gardens are of which style?**
    a. Persian style
    b. Mughal style
    c. Italian style
    d. Japanese style

139. **Lioyd's botanical garden is situated at**
    a. Calcutta
    b. Bangalore
    c. Coimbatore
    d. Darjeeling

140. **Pinjore garden was laid out by**
    a. Fidia khan
    b. Akbar
    c. Babar
    d. Shahjahan

141. **"Verinag garden" is situated in**
    a. Lucknow
    b. Kashmir
    c. New Delhi
    d. Kolkata

142. **"Hilocks" are the characteristic features of**
    a. Mughal garden
    b. Persian garden
    c. Italian garden
    d. Japanese garden

143. **Garden pagoda, lanterns, bridges, etc. are the unique feature of**
    a. Persian garden
    b. Mughal garden
    c. Japanese garden
    d. English garden

144. **Mughal style of gardening was developed by**
    a. Akbar
    b. Babar
    c. Shahjahan
    d. None of these

145. **Axis is powerful in which type of garden?**
    a. Mughal
    b. English
    c. Japanese
    d. Italian

146. **Island is an important feature of ___ style of gardening.**
    a. Formal
    b. Informal
    c. Wild
    d. Free

147. **Shalimar Bag garden was built by**
    a. Jahangir
    b. Shahjahan
    c. Akbar
    d. Hyder Ali

148. **Baradari is a canopied structure with doors**
    a. 6
    b. 8
    c. 12
    d. 14

149. **Trimmed hedges and topiary are typical features of which type of garden?**
    a. Mughal
    b. Persian
    c. English
    d. Italian

150. **Japanese garden is also called ___ garden.**
    a. Formal
    b. Japanese
    c. Informal
    d. Italian

151. **Repetition of same object at equidistance is called**
    a. Rhythm
    b. Balance
    c. Proportion
    d. Scale

152. **Hills and lakes are main feature of ___.**
    a. Japanese garden
    b. Italian
    c. Persian
    d. Mughal

153. **The presence of running water is the main feature of ___ garden.**
    a. Mughal
    b. English
    c. Japanese
    d. Italian

154. The distribution of visual weight on either side of a vertical axis is known as
    a. Unity
    b. Hormony
    c. Focal point
    d. Balance

155. Informal garden has ____ design.
    a. Non-symmetrical
    b. Symmetrical
    c. Irregular
    d. Parallel

156. Pagoda is common feature in ____ type of garden.
    a. Mughal
    b. Persian
    c. English
    d. Japanese

157. Royal botanic garden of Kew is located in
    a. Germany
    b. China
    c. France
    d. England

158. Zakir Hussain rose garden is located at
    a. Chandigarh
    b. Ludhiana
    c. Delhi
    d. Pinjore

159. Pinjore garden is a _____ style of gardening.
    a. Free
    b. Mughal
    c. Japanese
    d. Italian

160. Rock garden is located in which city?
    a. Jodhpur
    b. Jaipur
    c. Chandigarh
    d. Delhi

161. Which plant is grown to symbolize death and eternity by Mughals?
    a. Chenar
    b. Cypress
    c. Cassia
    d. Bauhinia

162. Pinjore garden also known as
    a. Yadavindra garden
    b. Ramniwas garden
    c. Buddha Jayanti park
    d. None of the above

163. Where cooling water flower is paradise in associated with the gardening style?
    a. Persian style
    b. Japanese style
    c. English style
    d. Mughal style

164. Buddha Jayanti smarak park is located at
    a. Jaipur
    b. Kolkata
    c. Bengaluru
    d. New Delhi

165. The Bryant park is situated at
    a. Jaipur
    b. Chandigarh
    c. Kodaikanal (TN)
    d. Pinjore (Haryana)

166. Taj garden of Agra (Tajmahal) is the typical example of
    a. Japanese style of gardening
    b. Italian style of gardening
    c. Mughal style of gardening
    d. English style of gardening

167. Rashtrapati Bhavan garden, New Delhi, was completed in
    a. 1921
    b. 1929
    c. 1932
    d. 1948

168. Which garden is regarded as "genesis of gardening"?
    a. Osaka
    b. Botanical garden
    c. Eden
    d. Lalbagh

169. Chasma-e-shahi garden was built by
    a. Nurjaha
    b. Alimarden Khan
    c. Prof K Mori
    d. Le Notre

170. Sikandar Bagh, Lucknow, was developed by
    a. Robinson
    b. Firoz Shah
    c. Shahjahan
    d. Nawab Wajid Ali Shah

171. Stone lanterns are important feature in
    a. Japanese garden
    b. Persian garden
    c. English garden
    d. Mughal garden

172. Cottage gardens in England were developed by
    a. W Kent
    b. G Jekyell
    c. C Lorraine
    d. L Brown

173. Tulip garden is located at
    a. New Delhi
    b. Bengaluru
    c. Kashmir
    d. Tamil Nadu

174. Tulip garden is also known as
    a. Jawaharlal Nehru Tulip garden
    b. Indira Gandhi Tulip garden
    c. Ferozshah Tulip garden
    d. None of the above

175. Roshnara park, New Delhi, was laid out by
    a. Let Notre   b. J D Singh
    c. Willim Sim   d. Prof K Mori

176. Budha Jayanti park, New Delhi, is _____ style garden.
    a. Japanese   b. Mughal
    c. Italian   d. Wild

177. An art of training plants into different shapes is known as
    a. Bonsai   b. Hedges
    c. Topiary   d. Baradari

178. Which of the following plants is not suitable for making bonsai?
    a. Amaltas   b. Bougainvillea
    c. Chinese orange d. Rubber plants

179. Which of the following wires is most suitable for making bonsai?
    a. Iron   b. Plastic
    c. Copper   d. All of these

180. Bonsai art was originate from
    a. Japan   b. China
    c. India   d. Brazil

181. Bonsai culture actually popularize by _____ in the world.
    a. Chinese   b. Japanese
    c. India   d. Korean

182. The word "Bonsai" is _____ term.
    a. Japanese   b. Greek
    c. French   d. Italian

183. Which of the following is not a bonsai style?
    a. Formal upright
    b. Wind swept
    c. Oval
    d. Broom

184. A structure in which plants are conserved or displayed during difficult season?
    a. Polyhouse   b. Conservatory
    c. Xeriscaping   d. Lath-house

185. The idea of vertical gardening was conceived by
    a. Jared Aller   b. Patrick Blac
    c. Beau Oyler   d. Le Corbusier

186. Lioyd botanical garden was laid down by ____ in 1878.
    a. Sir George King
    b. Sir Edwin Lutyens
    c. Mr JD Sim
    d. Raja Abhai Singh

187. Garden created in wetlands or marshy land is known as
    a. Rock garden   b. Water garden
    c. Paved garden   d. Bog garden

188. Which of the following is example of soft scape in garden
    a. Masonry work   b. Tile work
    c. Plants   d. Statue

189. Topiary is a typical example of
    a. Japanese   b. Mughal
    c. Persian   d. Italian

190. The tallest topiary of the world 'Samban-Lei Sekpil' is in
    a. Manipur   b. West Bengal
    c. Srinagar   d. Pune

191. Gladiolus spike should be held in _____ position during transportation.
    a. Horizontal   b. Vertical
    c. Slanting   d. None of these

192. The flowers of rose and tulip should be harvested at ____ for distinct market.
    a. Fully open   b. Tight bud stage
    c. Partially open d. Any stage

193. In pre-cooling, water is mostly removed by _____.
    a. Radiation   b. Convection
    c. Both a and b   d. Conduction

194. Pre-cooling should be done____.
    a. Immediately after harvesting
    b. After storage
    c. Before storage
    d. After packaging

195. The purpose of conditioning is____.
    a. To remove field heat
    b. To restore the turbidity
    c. To open the bud
    d. All of these

196. Which of the following factors determine the correct harvesting stage of cut flowers?
    a. Market distance
    b. Cultivar
    c. Purpose
    d. All of the above

197. Which is a productive form of aging leading to organ/plant death?
    a. Abscission
    b. Senescence
    c. Germination
    d. Wilting

198. Which of the following is not associated with improving vase life of cut flowers?
    a. Tinting
    b. Conditioning
    c. Pre-cooling
    d. Pulsing

199. Which sugar is used to enhance the shelf life of cut flowers?
    a. Sucrose
    b. Glucose
    c. Fructose
    d. Lactose

200. Rose water is an important commercial product obtained from
    a. Fruits
    b. Leaves
    c. Petals
    d. Stem

Model Test Paper 10

1. **According to Pasteur statements which one of the following is true?**
   a. Living organisms discriminate between stereoisomer
   b. Fermentation is a aerobic process
   c. Living organisms doesn't discriminate between stereoisomer
   d. Both a and b

2. **"I found floating therein earthly particles, some green streaks, spirally wound serpent-wise, and orderly arranged, the whole circumstance of each of these streaks was about the thickness of a hair on one's head". These words are of**
   a. Leeuwenhoek   b. Jenner
   c. Pasteur   d. Koch

3. **The principle light-trapping pigment molecule in plants, Algae, and Cyanobacteria is**
   a. Chlorophyll a
   b. Chlorophyll b
   c. Porphyrin
   d. Rhodopsin

4. **During bio- and geochemical cycles some amount of elemental carbon was utilized by the microorganisms. The phenomenon is called**
   a. Dissimilation
   b. Immobilization
   c. Decomposition
   d. Neutralization

5. **Who demonstrated that open tubes of broth remained free of bacteria when air was free of dust?**
   a. A. Spallanzani
   b. John Tyndall
   c. Francisco Redi
   d. Pasteur

6. **Reverse isolation would be appropriate for**
   a. A patient with tuberculosis
   b. A patient who has had minor surgery
   c. A patient with glaucoma
   d. A patient with leukemia

7. **The symptom "general feeling of illness and discomfort " is called**
   a. Cystitis
   b. Malaise
   c. Anaphylactic shock
   d. Arthritis

8. **On soybean which of the following forms symbiotism?**
   a. *Azotobacter paspali*
   b. Rhizobium
   c. Noctoc
   d. Bradyrhizobium

9. **Who provide the evidence that bacteriophage nucleic acid but not protein enters the host cell during infection?**
   a. Alfred (d) Hershey and Leonard Tatum in 1951

b. Alfred (d) Hershey and Zindar Lederberg in 1951

c. Alfred (d) Hershey and Martha Chase in 1952

d. Alfred (d) Hershey and Macleod in 1952

10. Spirulina belongs to

a. Xanthophyceae   b. Cyanophyceae
c. Rhodophyceae   d. Pheophyceae

11. The first antibody to contact invading microorganisms was

a. IgG   b. IgM
c. IgA   d. IgD

12. The light emitted by luminescent bacteria is mediated by the enzyme

a. Coenzyme Q
b. Luciferase
c. Lactose dehydrogenase
d. Carboxylase reductase

13. Pick out the vector using in human genome project

a. Phagemid vector
b. Yeast artificial chromosomes
c. Cosmid vectors
d. Yeast episomal plasmids

14. Salt and sugar preserve foods because they

a. Make them acid
b. Produce a hypotonic environment
c. Deplete nutrients
d. Produce a hypertonic environment

15. In a fluorescent microscope the objective lens is made of

a. Glass
b. Quartz
c. Polythene
d. None of these

16. Fixation of atmospheric nitrogen is by means of

a. Biological process
b. Lightening
c. Ultraviolet light
d. All of the above

17. Which one of the following fungi is the most serious threat in a bone marrow transplant unit?

a. *Candida albicans*
b. Aspergillus
c. Blastomyces
d. Cryptococcus

18. Direct microscopic count can be done with the aid of

a. Neuberg chamber
b. Anaerobic chamber
c. Mineral oil   d. Olive oil

19. The image obtained in a compound microscope is

a. Real   b. Virtual
c. Real inverted   d. Virtual inverted

20. Enzymes responsible for alcohol in fermentation

a. Ketolase   b. Zymase
c. Peroxidase   d. Oxidase

21. Which type of spores is produced sexually?

a. Conidia   b. Sporangiospores
c. Ascospores   d. None of these

22. Bacterial transformation was discovered by

a. Lederberg and Tatum
b. Beadle and Tatum
c. Griffith   d. None of these

23. Father of microbiology is

a. Louis Pasteur   b. Lister
c. V. Leeuwenhoek
d. Robert Koch

24. The antiseptic method was first demonstrated by

a. Lwanowski   b. Lord Lister
c. Edward Jenner   d. Beijerinck

25. Smallpox vaccine was first discovered by

a. Robert Koch
b. Louis Pasteur
c. Lister   d. Edward Jenner

26. The term mutation was coined by
    a. Pasteur
    b. Darwin
    c. Hugo de Vries
    d. Lamarck

27. Compound microscope was discovered by
    a. Antony von
    b. Pasteur
    c. Johnson and Hans
    d. None of these

28. Father of Medical Microbiology is
    a. Pasteur
    b. Jenner
    c. Koch
    d. L. Hock

29. Disease that affects many people at different countries is termed as
    a. Sporadic
    b. Pandemic
    c. Epidemic
    d. Endemic

30. Prophylaxis of cholera is
    a. Protected water supply
    b. Environmental sanitation
    c. Immunization with killed vaccines
    d. All of these

31. In electron microscope, what material is used as an objective lens?
    a. Magnetic coils
    b. Superfine glass
    c. Aluminum foils
    d. Electrons

32. The main feature of prokaryotic organism is
    a. Absence of locomotion
    b. Absence of nuclear envelope
    c. Absence of nuclear material
    d. Absence of protein synthesis

33. The stalked particles on the cristae of mitochondria are called
    a. Glyoxysomes
    b. Peroxisomes
    c. Oxysomes
    d. Spherosomes

34. Antiseptic methods were first introduced by
    a. Lord Lister
    b. Lwanowski
    c. Beijerinck
    d. Edward Jenner

35. Kuru disease in humans is caused by
    a. Bacteria
    b. Viroides
    c. Prions
    d. Mycoplasma

36. A mutation that produces termination codon is
    a. Missense mutation
    b. Neutral mutation
    c. Nonsense mutation
    d. Reverse mutation

37. During conjunction the genetic material will be transferred through
    a. Cell wall
    b. Medium
    c. Pili
    d. Capsule

38. Antiseptic surgery was discovered by
    a. Joseph Lister
    b. Ernest Abbe
    c. Pasteur
    d. Beijerinck

39. Tuberculosis is a
    a. Waterborne disease
    b. Airborne disease
    c. Foodborne disease
    d. Arthropodborne disease

40. Phagocytic phenomenon was discovered by
    a. Louis Pasteur
    b. Alexander Fleming
    c. Metchnikoff
    d. Robert Koch

41. Meosomes are also known as
    a. Mitochondria
    b. Endoplasmic reticulum
    c. Plasmids
    d. Chondroids

42. Hybridoma technique was first discovered by
    a. Kohler and Milstein
    b. Robert Koch
    c. 'D' Herelle
    d. Land Steiner

43. The minimum number of bacteria is required to produce clinical evidence of death in a susceptible animal under standard condition is called
    a. LD50
    b. ID
    c. MLD
    d. All of these

44. In electron microscope source of electrons is from
    a. Mercury lamp   b. Tungsten metal
    c. Both a and b   d. None of these

45. Griffith (1928) reported the phenomenon of transformation first in
    a. *H. influenzae*   b. Bacillus species
    c. Pneumococci   d. *E. coli*

46. The resolution power of the compound microscope is
    a. 0.2 micron
    b. 0.2 millimeter
    c. 0.2 Angstrom units
    d. 0.2 centimeter

47. The capacity of a given strain of microbial species to produce disease is known as
    a. Pathogen   b. Virulence
    c. Infection   d. None of these

48. Monoclonal antibodies are associated with the name of
    a. Burnet   b. Medawar
    c. Milstein Kohler   d. Owen

49. Lederberg and Tatum (1946) described the phenomena of
    a. Conjunction   b. Transformation
    c. Mutation   d. Plasmids

50. Hanging drop method for motility study was first introduced by
    a. Robert Koch   b. Louis Pasteur
    c. Jenner   d. Leeuwenhoek

51. Electron microscope gives magnification up to
    a. 100X   b. 2000X
    c. 50,000X   d. 2,00,000X

52. Term vaccine was coined by
    a. Robert Koch   b. Pasteur
    c. Needham   d. None of these

53. The inventor of microscope is
    a. Galileo   b. Antony von
    c. Pasteur   d. Koch

54. First Pasteur conducted fermentation experiments in
    a. Milk   b. Food material
    c. Fruit juices   d. Both a and c

55. Modern concepts of chemotherapy was proposed by
    a. Paul Ehrlich
    b. Joseph Lister
    c. Elie Metchnikoff
    d. None of these

56. The role of phagocytosis was discovered by
    a. Paul Ehrlich   b. Joseph Lister
    c. Elie Metchikoff   d. Pasteur

57. L-forms are discovered by
    a. Klein Berger
    b. Louis Pasteur
    c. Robert Koch
    d. Antony von Leeuwenhoek

58. The causative organism of Rocky Mountain spotted fever was first described by
    a. Howard Ricketts
    b. da Rochalima
    c. Both a and b
    d. Robert Koch

59. The term bacteriophage was coined by
    a. De'Herelle
    b. FW Twort
    c. Beijerinck   d. Jwanosky

60. Viral infection of bacteria was discovered by
    a. De'Herelle   b. FW Twort
    c. Beijernick   d. Jwanoksy

61. Eye cannot resolve any image less than
    a. 1 μm   b. 2 μm
    c. 7 μm   d. 5 μm

62. Compound microscope was discovered by
    a. V Leeuwenhoek
    b. Pasteur
    c. Janssen and Hans
    d. None of these

63. Electron microscope was discovered by
    a. Prof Fritz
    b. Janssen and Hans
    c. Knoll and Ruska
    d. None of these

64. Magnification range of light microscope is
    a. 1000X–5000X   b. 1000X–2000X
    c. 500X–1000X   d. None of these

65. Condensation of light in light microscope is by
    a. Objective   b. Condenser
    c. Ocular   d. All of these

66. Light gathering capacity of microscope is called
    a. Numerical aperture
    b. Angular aperture
    c. Both a and b
    d. None of these

67. If 10X and 40X objectives are used (air is the medium), the numerical aperture is
    a. 1.5   b. 2.0
    c. 1.0   d. 1.8

68. The ability of microscope to distinguish two objects into two separate objects, is called
    a. Resolving power
    b. Wavelength
    c. Both a and b
    d. None of these

69. Limit of resolution of compound microscope is
    a. 0.018 A   b. 0.1 mm
    c. 5 mm   d. 1 mm

70. Source of light in fluorescence microscopy is from
    a. Mercury lamp   b. Sunlight
    c. Both a and b   d. None of these

71. Who perfected a magnetic lens in 1927?
    a. Gabor   b. Broglie
    c. Busch   d. None of these

72. The magnification power of electron microscope developed by Knell and Ruska is
    a. 10,000X   b. 12,000X
    c. 15,000X   d. 20,000X

73. In electron microscope source of electrons is from
    a. Mercury lamp   b. Tungsten metal
    c. Both a and b   d. None of these

74. The electron passed out from the specimen are called
    a. Primary electrons
    b. Secondary electrons
    c. Tertiary electrons
    d. None of these

75. Mycorrihzza was first observed by
    a. Funk   b. Frank
    c. Fisher   d. Crick

76. The transfer of genetic material during transformation is proved basing on Griffith's experiment by
    a. Avery Macleod and McCarthy
    b. Lederberg and Tautaum
    c. Zinder and Lederberg
    d. Watson and Crick

77. Phagocytic theory was proposed by
    a. Louis Pasteur
    b. Elie Metchnikoff
    c. Behring
    d. Widal

78. Anaphylaxis was first observed by
    a. Parter and Richet
    b. Coombs
    c. Gell
    d. None of these

79. Primary mediators in anaphylaxis
    a. Histamine   b. Seratonin
    c. Heparin   d. All of these

80. Arthus reaction was discovered by
    a. Marrice Arthus b. von Perquit
    c. Richet   d. Porter

81. **Serum sickness reaction was discovered by**
    a. Marrice Arthus   b. von Perquit
    c. Richet   d. Porter

82. **Hybridoma technique was developed by**
    a. Kochler and Milston
    b. Niel's Jerne
    c. Both a and b
    d. None of these

83. **Disease that affects many people at different countries is termed as**
    a. Sporadic   b. Pandemic
    c. Epidemic   d. Endemic

84. **If the vectors transmit the infection mechanically they are called**
    a. Biological vectors
    b. Mechanical vectors
    c. Biological reservoir
    d. Both a and c

85. **If a person can be infected by direct contact with infected tissue of another person, it is termed as**
    a. Indirect contact transmission
    b. Attachment
    c. Direct contact transmission
    d. None of these

86. **Reduction of virulence is known as**
    a. Exaltation   b. Attenuation
    c. Both a and b d. None of these

87. **Enhancement of virulence is known as**
    a. Exaltation   b. Attenuation
    c. Both a and b d. None of these

88. **The virulence of a pathogen is usually measured by**
    a. LD   b. MLD
    c. ID   d. All of the above

89. **The lethal dose required to kill 50% of the lab animals tested under standard called**
    a. ID   b. LD50
    c. ID50   d. MLD

90. **The most important virulence factors are**
    a. Adhesions   b. Invasiveness
    c. Toxigenicity   d. Enzymes
    e. All of the above

91. **The ability of a pathogen to spread in the host tissues after establishing the infection is known as**
    a. Adhesion   b. Invasiveness
    c. Toxigenicity   d. None of these

92. **Which of the following enzymes acts as a spreading factor?**
    a. Hyaluronidase   b. Coagulase
    c. Catalase   d. DNase

93. *Vibrio cholerae* **was discovered by**
    a. Koch   b. Metchnikoff
    c. John Snow   d. Virchow

94. *E. coli* **was first isolated by**
    a. Louis Pasteur   b. Escherich
    c. Shiga   d. Robert Koch

95. *Mycobacterium tuberculosis* **was first discovered by**
    a. Robert Koch
    b. Edward Jenner
    c. Louis Pasteur
    d. None of these

96. *Mycobacterium leprae* **was discovered by**
    a. Robert Koch   b. Hansen
    c. Edward Jenner   d. Louis Pasteur

97. *Streptococcus pneumoniae* **was isolated by**
    a. Robert Koch
    b. Edward Jenner
    c. Antony von Leuwenhoek
    d. Louis Pasteur

98. **Anthracis bacteria was isolated by**
    a. Louis Pasteur
    b. Robert Koch
    c. Antony von Leeuwenhoek
    d. None of these

99. *Staphylococcus aureus* was isolated by
    a. Rosenbach
    b. Louis Pasteur
    c. Passet
    d. Sir Alexander Ogston

100. *Pseudomonas aeruginosa* was first named
    a. Schroeter and Gessard
    b. Robert Koch
    c. Louis Pasteur
    d. Edward Jenner

101. *T. pallidum* was discovered by
    a. Robert Koch
    b. Schaudinn and Hoffman
    c. Louis Pasteur
    d. Edward Jenner

102. Enzyme active site is made up of
    a. Catalytic site
    b. Substrate binding site
    c. Both
    d. None

103. In the following plants in which a part of leaf gives rise to a new plant?
    a. Rose
    b. Mango
    c. Bryophylum
    d. Banana

104. Which is called the 'Powerhouse' of cell?
    a. Mitochondria
    b. Lysosome
    c. Ribosome
    d. Golgi body

105. Which would do maximum harm to a tree?
    a. The loss of its bark
    b. The loss of half of its leave
    c. The loss of all its leaves
    d. The loss of half of its branches

106. Which of the following is not a fish?
    a. Hippocampus   b. Eel
    c. Shark   d. Whale

107. Which is an edible fungus?
    a. Penicillium   b. Rhizopus
    c. Mucor   d. Agaricus

108. Agar-agar is obtained from
    a. Fungus   b. Gymnosperm
    c. Pteridophyte   d. An algae

109. 'Little leaf disease' develops due to the deficiency of
    a. Copper   b. Sodium
    c. Zinc   d. Molybdenum

110. RNA is found in
    a. Animal cell   b. Plant cell
    c. Virus   d. All of the above

111. Mitochondrial membrane is a double-layered structure composed of
    a. Lipids and proteins
    b. Lipids and carbohydrates
    c. Proteins and carbohydrates
    d. Proteins and ribonucleic acid

112. In leech, the male and female genital apertures are located respectively in the
    a. 7th and 8th segment
    b. 10th and 11th segment
    c. 13th and 14th segment
    d. 18th and 21st segment

113. Dental formula of rabbit is
    a. 2, 0, 3, 3/1, 0, 2, 3
    b. 1, 0, 2, 3/2, 2, 0, 3
    c. 1, 0, 3, 3/2, 2, 0, 3
    d. 2, 1, 3, 2/2, 1, 2, 3

114. The gestation period of rabbit is
    a. 20–25 days
    b. 25–28 days
    c. 28–32 days
    d. 32–38 days

Important Text Questions for Various Job-oriented Examinations

Q1. What do you mean by pulses and their significance?

The world food supplies are usually debated in terms of cereals being the dominant commodities, but there exists a second group of crops, the pulses (legume grains). The pulses by virtue of having almost twice the amount of protein in comparison with cereals, make a major contribution to human diet in developing countries of tropical and subtropical areas where their nutritional contribution is of paramount importance as a large segment of the population in these areas has limited access to food of animal origin. As far as our country is concerned, 12 different pulse crops, namely chick pea, pigeon pea, lentil, black gram, green gram, lablab, moth bean, horse gram (*Dolichos uniflorus* Lam.), pea (*Pisum sativum* L.), grass pea (*Lathyrus sativus* L.), cowpea (*Vigna unguiculata* L. Walp.) and faba bean (*Vicia faba* L.), are cultivated. Among pulses, for production, chick pea occupies the first position in India and third position at global level. Chick pea is of two types 'Desi' and 'Kabuli'.

Desi type is generally small, dark-yellow brown seeded, while Kabuli is larger cream colour seeded. The desi type contributes to around 80 per cent and Kabuli type around 20 per cent of the total production. Eleven primary pulses have been recognized by the Food and Agriculture Organization (FAO) of the United Nations at global level. These pulses include dry beans (common bean, *Phaseolus vulgaris* L.; lima bean, *Phaseolus lunatus* L.; tepary bean, *Phaseolus acutifolius* A. Gray; scarlet runner bean, *Phaseolus coccineus* L.; black gram, *Vigna mungo* L. Hepper; green gram, *Vigna radiata* L. Wilczek; moth bean, *Vigna aconitifolia* Jacq Marechal; rice bean, *Vigna umbellata* Thumb Ohwi and Ohashi and adzuki bean, *Vigna angularis* Willd Ohwi and Ohashi), dry broad bean (*Vicia faba* L.), dry peas (*Pisum* spp.) dry cowpea (*Vigna unguiculata* L. Walp), pigeon pea (*Cajanus cajan* L. Millspaugh), chick pea (*Cicer arietinum* L.), lentil (*Lens culinaris* Medik or *Lens esculenta* Moench), bambara groundnut (*Vigna subterranean* L. Verdc.), lupines (*Lupinus* spp.), common vetch (*Vicia sativa* L.) and minor pulses (lablab, *Lablab purpureus* L. Sweet; jack beans, *Canavalia ensiformis* L. DC.; sword bean, *Canavalia gladiata* Jacq. DC.; winged bean, *Psophocarpus teragonolobus* L.DC.; velvet bean, *Mucuna pruriens* L. DC. and yam bean, *Pachyrhizus erosus* L. Urb.).

Q2. What are the factors affecting pulse production in India?

The major producers of this crop include Algeria, Australia, Canada, Ethiopia, India, Iran, Kazakstan, Malawi, Mexico, Morocco, Myanmar, Pakistan, Russia, Spain, Sudan, Syria, Tanzania, Tunisia, Turkey, the United States of America (USA) and Yemen. India is the largest producer of chick pea followed by Australia, Pakistan and Turkey. This crop is grown on 8.21 million hectares of our country with the annual production of 7.48 million tonnes and average productivity of 911 kg/ha. There are several factors for low productivity of chick pea in our country. A few of these are described here (i) more than 75% of Indian farmers own small or marginal holdings of less than two hectares, (ii) severe drought results in sudden decline in chick pea area and ultimately productivity (iii) even, otherwise, the farmer does not give the same weightage to pulses (including chick pea) as to cereals, (iv) excessive cold conditions adversely affect productivity, (v) most of the area under chick pea is rain-fed (vi) use of poor quality seed diminishes productivity further, (vii) low or no use of fertilizers due to scarcity of funds, (viii) generally, farmers are ignorant of precise doses of fertilizers recommmended by the Agriculture Department for a particular cultivar and region, the techniques of cultivation of high yielding varieties, post-harvest technology and poor processing and storage facilities, (ix) about one-third of flowers produced do not develop into fruits, (x) pest and diseases cause considerable losses, (xi) sudden excessive rain soon after sowing or at flowering does great harm, (xii) an early hot summer shortens the growing period, hastens maturity and ultimately reduces yield and (xiii) hailstorms at ripening causes much damage.

Q3. Write a comment on chick pea crop.

Chick pea (*Cicer arietinum* L.) is one of the earliest pulse crops cultivated by humans. It is known as by different names in different languages of India and globe. For example, in Hindi, it is chana; in Gujarati, chania; in Sanskrit, chanaka; in Marathi, harbharaa; in Telgu, shanaga; in Bengali, chhola; in Tamil, kondakondalai; in Ayurveda, shimbykul; in English, chick pea; in Spanish, algarroba; in Portuguese, aravanco and in French, chiche. It belongs to family Fabaceae (Papilionaceae), tribe Cicereae and genus *Cicer*. The genus includes 43 species. Two major types of chick pea are 'Desi' (2n=14) and 'Kabuli' (2n=16).

The 'Desi' type is generally light seeded, i.e. less than 200 milligram (mg) per seed, and characterized by dark yellow-brown seeds with thicker husks and a rough surface while the 'Kabuli' seeds are heavier (more than 350 mg per seed), beige or cream in colour with a thin husk. The 'Desi' type chick pea is grown in semi-arid tropics while 'Kabuli' type in temperate regions. Various cultivars differ in flower and seed colour and size, growth duration, yield and disease resistance.

Q4. Define morphology of Bengal gram (*Cicer arietinum* L.).

It is an annual herb with robust root system and major portion up to 60 centimetre (cm) deep. The stem is erect up to 60 cm high and has small imparipinnately compound feathery leaves on either side of the stem. The stem is highly branched. The main stem is generally circular and branches may be quadrangular. The stem is covered by glandular hairs which secrete oxalic acid and maleic acid. Its leaves are alternately arranged and are pinnate having a length of 5 cm. It has about 10–20 leaflets. Leaflets are ovate to elliptical, 0.6–2.0 cm long, 0.3 to 1.4 cm wide; margin serrate, apex acuminate to aristae, base cuneate, stipules 2–5 toothed. Flowers solitory, sometimes 2 per inflorescence, axillary, peduncles 0.6–3 cm long, pedicels 0.5 to 1.3 cm long, bracts triangular or tripartite; calyx 7–10 millimetre (mm) long; corolla white, pink, purplish or blue, 0.8–1.2 cm long. The first flowers to appear may desiccate and abort at different stages before opening and so these are called pseudoflowers. They are greater in shorter photo-periods and cool temperature and where the moisture is ample. Flowers also abort after opening, especially if nights are cold. This feature is important for crop development in North India. It has a adaptive significance as it delays reproductive growth until the conditions are favourable for fruit development. They are monosexual. Fertilization takes place by self-pollination. Cross pollination is very rare; only 0–1 per cent. The staminal column is diadelphous

(9–1) and the ovary is sessile, inflated and pubescent. Pods are rhomboidal, ellipsoidal, 1–2 with three seeds as a maximum and inflated, glandular-pubescent. The pods are about 3 to 4 cm long and 1 to 2 cm in breadth. Seeds are spherical or angular having a diameter of about 0.5 to 1 cm. They have wrinkled appearance and colour varies from white to yellow to blackish. Seeds are laterally compressed with a median groove around two-thirds of the seed, anterior beaked. Cotyledons are thick and yellowish. Germination is cryptocotylar.

Q5. Write the classification of chick pea.

Based on the system of classification given by Cronquist (1981), chick pea could be classified as follows:

Division:	Magnoliophyta
Class:	Magnoliopsida
Subclass:	Rosidae
Order:	Fabales
Family:	Papilionaceae
Genus:	*Cicer*
Species:	*arietinum*

Q6. Write an assay on origin and distribution of chick pea crop.

Cicer echinospermum Davis and *Cicer reticulatum* Ladiz are morphologically, and by their seed protein profile, found close to the cultivated species and could be suspected as its wild progenitor/s. As these wild species are distributed in south-east Anatolia, chick pea is likely to have been domesticated in this region. This is supported by the distribution of early Neolithic chick pea (7260-6000 BC) which was confined to Fertile Crescent, particularly in modern Anatolia and the eastern Mediterranean. In the late Neolithic era (5450-3500 BC) chick pea spread westwards to modern Greece. By the Bronze age (2800-1300 BC) chick pea had been disseminated widely to Crete in the west, upper Egypt in the south, eastwards through present-day Iraq to the Indian subcontinent, where remains have been found in Harrapan settlements in Pakistan and a variety of sites in Uttar Pradesh and Maharashtra. By the Iron Age, chick pea consolidated its distribution in South and West Asia, and appeared in Ethiopia for the first time. The very large seeded Kabuli types appear to have evolved from the smaller seeded Desi types in the Mediterranean region.

The geographic distribution differs for these two types, with the Kabuli tending to be restricted to the Western Mediterranean where the Desi is mainly absent. The Desi ranges more widely from the Eastern Mediterranean to central Asia and Indian subcontinent. The Kabuli type is believed to have spread in India via Afghan capital about two century ago in the East and Chile in the West. Presently, the Desi type chick pea is cultivated on a large scale in India, Pakistan, Myanmar, Australia and Bangladesh and the "Kabuli" type chick pea in Turkey, Iran, Ethiopia, Mexico, Syria, Spain, Canada, USA, Algeria, Sudan, Tanzania, Tunisia, Malawi and Portugal. India produces mostly Desi type chick pea and not the Kabuli type. Chick pea is grown all over the India particularly Madhya Pradesh sharing of around 40%, Uttar Pradesh, 16%, Rajasthan, 14%, Maharashtra, 11% and Andhra Pradesh, 11% in the Indian production.

Q7. What is the approaches of cultivation of Bengal gram in India?

The crop is grown as a 'rabi' crop all over India. The crop could be grown from late September to mid-December or later, the most successful period being October. Third and fourth week of October is the best time for sowing in semi-arid and Northern plains whereas first forthnight of October for central India. The crop is grown alone or mixed with wheat, barley, linseed, safflower or mustard. The preparation of land is the same as for wheat, except that no fine tilth is attempted and the soil is not compacted but is left somewhat cloddy. Chick pea is propagated from seeds. Seed is broadcast or (more often) drilled in rows 20–30 cm apart, spaced at 10 cm between seeds at a depth of 7–10 cm with soil well pressed down. Seeding rates vary from 25–40 kg/ha to 80–120 kg/ha, depending on the area and seed type.

On poor soils, manure or compost is beneficial. Seed inoculation improves yield only for crops grown for the first time or after rice where *Rhizobium* populations are naturally low or absent. Fertilizers or manures have often failed to increase yields substantially because of fixation of P by soils and the accumulation of nutrients in the upper layer of the soil which are often dry. Therefore, the crop is rarely mannured, but the application of phosphatic fertilizers has been shown to increase the grain yields. Placing the phosphatic fertilizers a little below or to the side of the seed has been found beneficial. 25 to 45 kg phosphorus pentoxide (P_2O_5) (depending upon the P content of the soil) plus 15 kg N per hectare is recommended. The crop is rarely weeded or inter-cultivated, as it is thought that this crop suppresses weed growth. However, weed control during the first 4–6 weeks, either mechanically or with weedicides (applied immediately after sowing) has been found to result in a higher yield.

Irrigation around 45 days after sowing (DAS) and at the early pod filling stage (around 110 DAS) is useful. When winter rains fail or frost occurs one or two irrigations are very beneficial. However, the regular irrigated crop receives three to four watering. Chick pea matures in about 150 days or more in Punjab and Uttar Pradesh and 120 days or less in Deccan Plateau and South India. For dry seeds, the plants are harvested at maturity or slightly earlier by cutting them close to the ground or uprooting. The plants are stacked in the field for a few days to dry and later the crop is threshed by trampling or beating with wooden flails. The chaff is separated from the grain by winnowing. Tall cultivars are suitable for mechanized harvesting in which case combines can be used. Chick pea seeds are usually stored in bags, but are more subject to insect's damage than when stored in bulk. Proper cleaning, drying and aeration are necessary to control seed beetles.

Q8. What are the plant growth regulators?

These are organic compounds, either natural or synthetic which modify or control one or more specific physiological processes within a plant. They are also known as plant growth substances or PGRs. They are required in very low concentration ranging from 10^{-6} molar (M) to 10^{-5} M, with high application rates of the same compound often being herbicidal. Those substances elaborated by the plant are referred to as phytohormones (or simply hormones) whereas the others are called synthetic plant growth substances. There are five major endogenous plant growth substances. These include auxins, gibberellins, Cytokinins, abscissic acid (ABA) and ethylene. Moreover, plants contain numerous other molecules that are active in various aspects of growth and development. For example, among others, brassinolide (BS), cyclitols, phenolics, salicylic acid (SA), triacontanol (Tria) and vitamins. Phytohormones occur in free or conjugated with sugars, amino acids and possibly peptides. Free forms are considered to be biologically active, while conjugates are viewed as functioning in controlling levels of the more active free forms. There are no specific or specialized glands that produce hormones. These are synthesized anywhere in the plant and act on any part as their target. They are transported via xylem and/or phloem and by diffusion. They differ in their effects.

Q9. What do you mean by auxins?

The word 'auxin' was derived from the Greek word 'auxein' meaning to grow. These are organic compounds having a ring structure and a side chain. A number of auxins including indole 3-acetic acid (IAA), indole 3-butyric acid, phenyl acetic acid and 4-chloroindole acetic acid have been isolated from different parts of plants. IAA (Fig. 1) has been recognized as the principal auxin in higher plants and was discovered by Kogl *et al.* (1934).

They are generally produced by the growing apices of the stem and roots, from where they migrate polarly through phloem to the regions of their action. However, they may also be produced in young leaves, seeds and fruits of higher plants. Typical IAA concentration ranges from 0.01 to 3 mg per litre. Auxins enhance a number of physiological processes in plants, including abscission of older mature leaves and fruits, apical dominance, cell division, cell-enlargement, distribution of growth between primary and lateral root and shoot meristems, flowering and parthenocarpy, loosening of cell-wall, mediation of tropistic responses of shoot and roots to light and gravity, patterning of embryos, root initiation, synthesis of ribonucleic acid (RNA), deoxyribonucleic acid (DNA) and protein and vascular tissue differentiation.

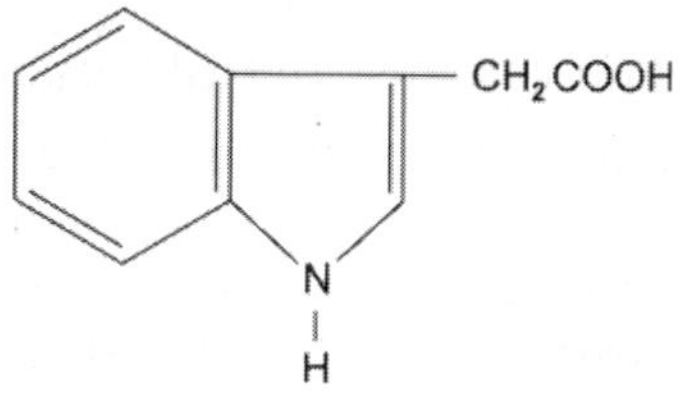

Fig. 1: Indole 3-acetic acid

Q10. What do you mean by cytokinins?

The word 'cytokinin' was derived from the Greek word 'kineein' meaning to move. These are the substances that regulate plant growth primarily by inducing cell division. All naturally occurring cytokinins are aminopurine derivatives while nearly all compounds active as cytokinins are N^6-substituted aminopurines. Zeatin, dihydrozeatin and isopentenyl adenine are the three most commonly detected and most physiologically active cytokinins in various plants. Kinetin (Kn) and benzyladenine are highly active but not formed by plants. Miller *et al.* (1955) for the first time isolated and identified kinetin as 6-furfurylaminopurine.

Cytokinins are produced by both lower and higher plants. In the latter, they are synthesized in growing areas such as roots and shoots, actively dividing tissues of seeds, fruits and leaves, root tips, germinating seeds as well as wounding tissues. Studies indicate

that root tips are most likely the location of cytokinins production. Cytokinins are transported from the root to the shoot in the xylem in a polar fashion. Kn is generally used at a concentration ranging from 0.01 to 10.0 mg/L enhance a number of physiological processes in plants, including activation of cell growth in leaves, apical-dominance, breaking of bud dormancy, cell-cycling, chloroplast differentiation, floral-development, leaf-senescence, nutrient mobilization, N-dependent regulation of gene expression in photosynthesis, P_N, seed germination and source-sink balance.

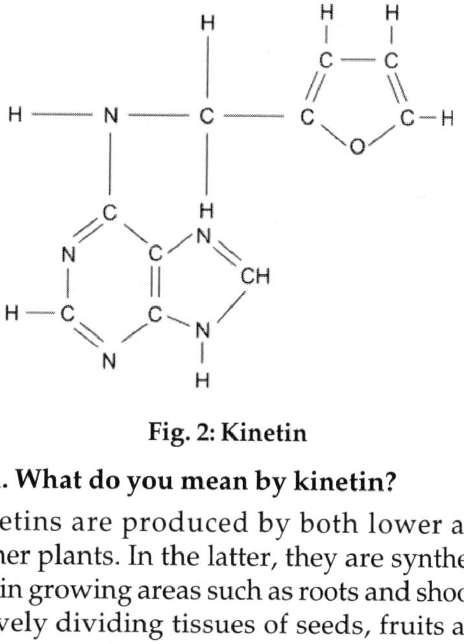

Fig. 2: Kinetin

Q11. What do you mean by kinetin?

Kinetins are produced by both lower and higher plants. In the latter, they are synthesized in growing areas such as roots and shoots, actively dividing tissues of seeds, fruits and leaves, root tips, germinating seeds as well as wounding tissues. Studies indicate that root tips are most likely the location of cytokinins production. Cytokinins are transported from the root to the shoot in the xylem in a polar fashion. Kn is generally used at a concentration ranging from 0.01 to 10.0 mg/L. They enhance a number of physiological processes in plants, including activation of cell growth in leaves, apical-dominance, breaking of bud dormancy, cell-cycling, chloroplast differentiation, floral-development, leaf-senescence, nutrient mobilization, N-dependent regulation of gene expression in photosynthesis, P_N, seed germination and source-sink balance.

Q12. What do you mean by salicylic acid as plant hormones?

The word 'salicylic acid' (salicylate) was coined by Raffaele Piria in 1838 from the Latin word *salix* meaning willow tree from bark of which he obtained the active principle, i.e. SA. Salicylates are a class of compounds having activity similar to SA (orthohydroxybenzoic acid) which is a plant phenolic compound. Green leaves and reproductive organs are the main site of SA biosynthesis. However, the highest level of SA synthesis was reported in the inflorescence of thermogenic plants and plants infected by necrotizing pathogens. SA could be readily transported throughout the plant with the help of vascular tissues. SA reduces ethylene biosynthesis and enhances a number of physiological processes, including defense mechanism against abiotic and biotic stress, membrane permeability, photosynthesis, and seed germination, specific changes in leaf anatomy and chloroplast structure, synthesis of auxin and cytokinin and transpiration rate.

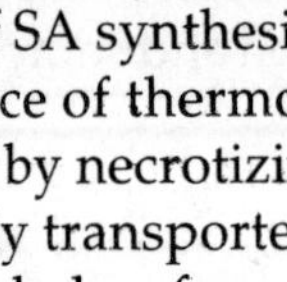

COOH

OH

Fig. 3: Salicylic acid

Q13. What do you mean by triacontanol?

It is a trivial name for a long, straight chain saturated primary alcohol, 1-hydroxytricontane. It is a constituent of beeswax and the cuticle of many leaves and also a synthetic PGR. Tria reduces the level of abscisic acid but enhances a number of physiological processes including activity of RuBPcase and nitrate reductase (NR), bunching of grapes, breaking of seed and bud dormancy, chlorophyll content, cell wall plasticity, CO_2 fixation, cell-elongation, dark-respiration, dry weight, flowering, growth and yield, Gibberellin-like activities, leaf-area ratio, nutrient uptake, photosynthesis and its related processes like

photorespiration, parthenocarpy, protein-synthesis, phloem-loading, RGR, reducing sugars and free amino acids, stomatal aperture, senescence, stem-elongation, seed-germination, shoot weight, synthesis and secretion of hydrolyzing enzymes particularly α-amylase for promoting hydrolysis of storage-reserves, tolerance against salinity and acidic mist, transpiration rate, transcription of mRNA and vernalization.

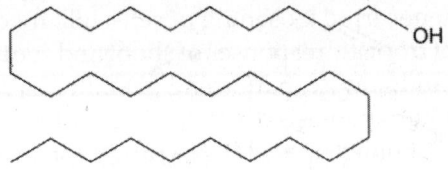

Fig. 4: Triacontanol

Q14. What do you mean by gibberellins?

The word 'gibberellin' was coined by Yabuta and Sumiki (1938) after the genus name of the fungus (Gibberella fujikuroii) from which the active factor was isolated. These are tetracyclic diterpenoid acids. Over 136 naturally occurring gibberellins have been isolated from plants, fungi and bacteria. These are abbreviated as GA with a subscript such as GA_1, GA_2, GA_3 and so on. These are numbered in order of their discovery. Of these, GA_3 also known as gibberellic acid (GA) is commonly available and most widely used in plant physiological research. It was isolated and characterized by two groups, one headed by Cross in England and one by Stodola in the USA.

In plants, they are synthesized in expanding leaves and shoot apex as also in other parts of shoot, including fruits and seeds and presumably in roots. In general, GA movement is non-polar and occurs through the conducting tissue. The typical GA concentration ranges from 0.01 to 5 mg/L. Gibberellins inhibit the adventitious root formation but enhance a number of physiological processes including activity of ribulose-1,5-bisphosphate carboxylase (RuBPcase), bunching of grapes, breaking of seed and bud dormancy, cell-wall plasticity, cell elongation, flowering, growth and yield of sugarcane, PN, parthenocarpy, protein synthesis, phloem-loading, relative growth rate (RGR), stomatal aperture, senescence, stem-elongation, seed-germination, synthesis and secretion of hydrolyzing enzymes particularly α-amylase for promoting hydrolysis of storage-reserves, transpiration rate, transcription of messenger (m) RNA and vernalization.

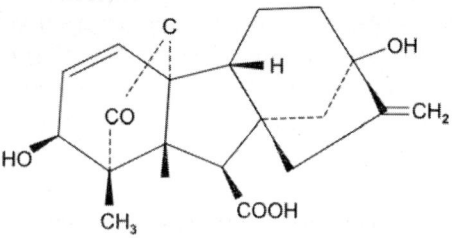

Fig. 5: Gibberellic acid

Q15. What do you mean by GA3 and give its significance?

Over 136 naturally occurring gibberellins have been isolated from plants, fungi and bacteria. These are abbreviated as GA with a subscript such as GA_1, GA_2, GA_3 and so on. These are numbered in order of their discovery. Of these, GA_3 also known as gibberellic acid (GA) is commonly available and most widely used in plant physiological research. It was isolated and characterized by two groups, one headed by Cross in England and one by Stodola in the USA.

Q16. What is the mechanism of PGRs application?

There are two general classes of hormones found in animal systems, steroid and peptide, both of which probably also occur in plant systems. The steroid class forms a hormone receptor complex in the cytoplasm, which is then transported into the nucleus where mRNA is synthesized, resulting in a given response. The peptide class binds to a receptor at the plasma membrane forming hormone-receptor complex, which causes the synthesis of secondary messenger for a given response. Each receptor is specific to one hormone.

Q17. Write an assay on "Mineral nutrition".

The history of plant nutrition can be traced back from the time of Democritus of Abdera (460-360 BC). He added "Mother earth when fructified by rain gives birth to crops for the nourishment of man and beast. But that which come from earth must return to earth and that which came from air to air. Death, however, does not destroy matter but only breaks up the union of its elements which are then recombined into other forms (Willis, 2007). Aristotle (384-322 BC) assumed "Plants assimilate organic matter from the roots", Pliny (23-79 BC) concluded "It is universally agreed by all writers that there is nothing more beneficial than to turn-up a crop of lupines, therefore that have podded, either with the plough or the fork, or else to cut them and bury them in heaps at the roots of trees and vines", Plissy (1510-1589) proposed the concept that manuring was to replace substances lost by crop removal and von Helmont (1580-1644) attributed plant growth to water. Woodward (1655-1662) analyzed salts such as wood ash, limestone and saltpetre (potassium nitrate) on plant growth and invented a chemical fertilizer called "flattening salt". Despite the ever-prevalent belief that humus (organic matter) was the entire source of plant nutrients, i.e. in the "Humus theory" of Aristotle, it was critically examined by de Saussure (1767-1845) who claimed the importance of N for plant growth and N is obtained wholly by absorption of soluble organic substances present in the soil, however, in the early 19th century, Liebig (1803-1873) assumed that N is absorbed from the air and not from humus. More meaningful developments in plant nutrition began in 1860s when Pfeffer, Sachs and Knop began the practice of growing plants in water culture to determine the elements essentially for the growth of plants. They showed conclusively that potassium (K), magnesium (Mg), calcium (Ca), iron, P, S, carbon (C), N, hydrogen (H), and oxygen (O) are necessary for plant life and at present known as macronutrients. The contribution of plant nutrition as a science bloomed in the 20th century. In due course of time, different researches using sophisticated analytical techniques were able to demonstrate the essentiality of seven more elements referred to as micronutrients.

Q18. What are the physiological roles of nitrogen (N) in crop growth and development?

N is one of the most widely distributed elements in nature. It is present in the atmosphere, lithosphere and hydrosphere. The soil accounts for only a minute fraction of lithospheric N, and of this soil N, only a very small proportion is directly available to plants. This occurs mainly in the form of nitrate (NO_3^-) or ammonium (NH_4^+) ions. N is absorbed by plants as NO_3^-, NH_4^+ and as urea (if applied). Of these, NO_3^- is often a preferential source for crop growth but much depends on plant species and other environmental factors. It is the fourth most abundant element in plants (2–4% on dry weight basis) after C, H and O. It is an elementary constituent of numerous orga-nic compounds of general importance, including amino acids, alkaloids, co-enzymes, chlorophyll, nucleosides, nucleotides, nucleic acids, proteins, porphyrins, purines, pyrimidines, PGRs, and some vitamins.

N evidently plays a central role in cellular metabolism. Hence, physiological maturity and yield of many crops has been governed by the N-supply to the crops. Plants suffering from N deficiency mature earlier, and the vegetative growth stage is often shortened. The plants remain small, the stems have a spindly appearance, the leaves are small and the older ones often fall prematurely. Root growth is affected and in particular, branching is restricted. The root-shoot ratio, however, is usually increased by N-deficiency. The early senescence probably relates to the effect of the N supply on the synthesis and translocation of cytokinins. Also, N-deficiency results in a disturbance of chloroplast development.

Q19. What are the physiological roles of phosphorus (P) in crop growth and development?

P in soils occurs almost exclusively in the form of orthophosphate. In soils, the amount of phosphate present in the soil solution is very low in comparison with adsorbed phos-phate. The most important P-containing ions are monovalent phosphate anion ($H_2PO_4^-$) and divalent anion ($H_2PO_4^-$). At neutral pH of soil solution, both ions are present in fairly equal proportions, however, below pH 7 favours high proportion of $H_2PO_4^-$ and above pH 7, $H_2PO_4^-$. Roots absorb phosphate from solution of very low phosphate concentrations.

P occurs in plants at 0.1–0.4 per cent on dry weight basis. It is an essential nutrient and an integral component of several important compounds, including adenosine triphosphate and other related high energy compounds, all sugar-phosphates in photosynthesis, co-enzymes, glycerol phosphatides, nucleic acids, nicotinamide adenine dinucleotide, nicotinamide adenine dinucleotide phosphate, phospholipids and phosphoglycerides. High amounts of P are found in the meristematic regions of actively growing plants where it is involved in the synthesis of nucleoproteins. Because of high mobility of P in the plant, the older leaves are usually the first to exhibit deficiency symptoms. The most characteristic manifestations of P deficiency are an intense green colouration of the leaves due to accumulation of anthocyanin and development of necrotic areas on the leaves, petioles or fruits. Most often, P deficiency leads to increased root: shoot ratio, changes in root morphology and architecture, increased root-hair proliferation, root-hair elongation, accumulation of anthocyanins, proteoid root formation, increased association with mycorrhizal fungi, shedding of premature leaves and delay in flowering and fruiting. It also causes a decrease in photosynthesis and resistance against pest.

Q20. What are the physiological roles of sulphur (S) in crop growth and development?

It occurs in the soil in inorganic and organic forms. The inorganic form of S in soil consists mainly of sulphate ion (SO_4^-). S is taken up by the plants from the soil as SO_4^-. After taken up, SO_4^- is enzymatically converted into an activated form before it can be incorporated into organic compounds. The activated sulphate is converted into reduced S compounds, a wide variety of sulphate esters and sulpholipids in plants. This element represents the ninth and least abundant essential macroelements in plants, preceded by C, O, H, N, K, Ca, Mg and P. The total S content in plant tissues is in the order of 0.2 to 0.5% S in the dry matter. S plays critical roles in the catalytic and/or electro-chemical functions of the biomolecules in cells and also as signaling molecules for fundamental cellular functions. S is a constituent of many organic compounds, including aliens, biotin, co-enzyme A, cysteine and methionine, ferredoxins, lipoic acid, glucosinolates, thiamine and thiamine pyrophosphate. In field crops, S deficiency is sometimes different to distinguish. As most soils contain enough SO_4^-.

Generally S deficiency symptoms include a general chlorosis throughout the entire leaf including veins appears first in younger leaves, accumulation of nitrate-N, inward rolling of leaf tips and margins, inhibition of terminal bud growth, increase in grana-stacking, inhibition of terminal bud growth, inhibition of protein synthesis, premature lateral bud development, poor photosynthetic activity and rapid leaf fall.

Q21. What are the physiological roles of potassium (K) in crop growth and development?

The average K content of the earth's crust is in the order of about 2.3%. By far the greatest part of this K is bound in primary minerals or is present in the secondary clay minerals which largely make up the clay fraction of the soil. Clay soils may often have in excess of 4% total K. The main source of K^+ for plants growing under natural conditions comes from the weathering of K containing minerals. In soils, it exists in non-exchangeable (fixed), exchangeable and soluble form.

K ions is the most abundant cation in cytoplasm of plants (up to 10% on dry weight basis) and make a major contribution to the osmotic potential of cells and tissues of glycophytic plants species. It plays a role in basic function, such as control of cell membrane polarization, electrical neutralization of anionic groups and osmoregulation. It enhances the ability of the plants to resist diseases, insect attacks, cold and adverse conditions and help in cell-extension, light-driven and seismonastic movements, opening and closing of stomata, photosynthesis, protein synthesis and respiration. Also, many enzymes including fructokinase, pyruvic kinase and transacetylase, are either completely dependent on or stimulated by K ions.

Q22. Write an article on N-P-K and S-containing fertilizers.

The increasing world population is now confronted by a major shortage of plant products, and there is a worldwide need to produce higher yielding quantity crops. One crop aspect of plant production is that of plant nutrition as high productivity can only be achieved if plants are probably fed. As crop plants require N, P, K and S in larger quantities, it is, therefore, highly desirable to have knowledge on their sources. Thus, for N, anhydrous ammonia, ammonium sulphate, ammonium chloride, ammonium nitrate-sulphate, ammonium nitrate with lime, ammonium phosphate-sulphate, ammonium polyphosphate solution, ammonium thio-sulphate solution, calcium nitrate, potassium nitrate (KNO_3), sodium nitrate, urea, urea-sulphate, urea-ammonium nitrate, urea-ammonium phosphate and urea phosphate are the chief sources. Single superphosphate, nitric phosphate, diammonium phosphate, apatite and calcium phosphate are dominant sources of P. inositol phosphate, phospholipids, nucleic acids, phosphate sugars are applied as organic P sources. Muriate of potash, potassium sulphate, potassium magnesium sulphate, potassium nitrate, potassium phosphate, potassium carbonate, potassium hydroxide, potassium thiosulphate and potassium polysulphate are the principal potassium fertilizers. The sources of S comprise phosphate sulphate, ammonium polysulphide, ammonium sulphate, ammonium thiosulphate, ferrous sulphate, gypsum, magnesium sulphate, potassium sulphate, pyrite, potassium magnesium sulphate, potassium thiosulphate, potassium polysulphide, sulphuric acid (100%), sulphur and sulphur dioxide, single-superphosphate, triple superphosphate, urea-sulphur, urea-sulphuric acid and zinc sulphate.

Q23. How do you estimate the values of leaf area (LA) and leaf area index (LAI)?

Leaf area (LA) of a plant was obtained by gravimetric method. The LA of four leaves selected randomly from each plant was determined by tracing on graph sheets and dry weight for these leaves was recorded. The LA per plant was computed by using total leaf dry weight per plant and dry weight of those leaves for which the area was obtained. The following formula was used:

$$\text{Leaf area per plant} = \frac{LA \times W_2}{W_1}$$

LA= Leaf area of four leaves tracing on graph sheet
W1= Dry weight of leaves for their the area was traced on graph sheet
W2= Total leaf dry weight per plant
Leaf area index (LAI) is the ratio of foliage area to ground area. It is determined by the following formula suggested by Watson (1958):

$$\text{LAI} = \frac{\text{Leaf area}}{\text{Ground area}}$$

Q24. Describe the methods of PGRs and nutrient application in detail.

In nature, PGRs required for growth and development are synthesized in plants themselves. However, they could be added exogenously to exploit the full genetic potential of crop plants. There are several methods of application of hormones depending on the plant material and the response for which these are used. These methods include lanolin pasting, dusting, seed-soaking and soil and foliar application. Plants grow in soil and obtain nutrients from it through their root system. However, continuous cultivation results in depletion of nutrients in the soil. To maintain proper fertility of such soils, application of fertilizers (nutrients) to soil becomes an essential to ensure good harvest. In this regard, farm scientists have developed several fertilizer application methods including solid application, gaseous application, application in irrigation water, banding, broadcasting, strip placement, side-dressing and top-dressing. It was, however, found that added fertilizers are rendered partly unavailable to the crops after their application owing to various reasons, including fixation, volatilization and leaching. Moreover, the escalating cost of these fertilizers possessesa great problem for farmers in developing countries. Under such circumstances, the novel technique of foliar application of nutrients seems to be a good alternative to obtain maximum nutrient use efficiency.

Q25. How do you estimate the value of leaf chlorophyll (Chl) content?

The chlorophyll content was estimated in fresh leaves collected randomly from each replicate by the method of Arnon (1949). The details are given below. 1 g finely cut leaves from each replicate was homogenized in a sufficient amount of 80% acetone using a mortar and pestle. The extract was filtered through Whatman No. 42 filter paper and the filtrate was collected into a 100 ml volumetric flask. Finally, the volume was made up to 100 ml using 80% acetone. 5 ml extract from the 100 ml volumetric flask was transferred into a 50 ml volumetric flask and the volume was made up to the mark using 80% acetone. From 50 ml volumetric flask, 5 ml chlorophyll extract was transferred into a cuvette and the optical density (OD) was read at 645 and 663 nano metre (nm) on a spectrophotometer (Spectronic 20 D, Milton Roy, USA). The total chlorophyll content was calculated using the following formula:

Chlorophyll content =

$$\frac{20.2 \times (OD\,645) + 8.02\,(OD\,663) \times V \times W}{1000}\,mg\,g^{-1}$$

(leaf fresh mass)

Where,

V = Volume of the extract in ml

W = Weight of the fresh leaves used for the extraction of the pigment in g.

Q26. How do you estimate the values of net photosynthetic rate (P_N) and stomatal conductance (gs)?

P_N is the total rate of photosynthetic CO_2 fixation minus the rate of loss of CO_2 during the respiration. The P_N was measured in fully expanded leaves of somewhat the same age in all replicates by using the infrared gas analizer (IRGA), LICOR-6400, nebraska, USA). Each observation was repeated thrice. All the measurements were made on cloudless clear days between 11.00 O' clock and 12.00 Noon. The P_N was expressed in terms of μ mol (CO_2) m^{-2} second $(s)^{-1}$. gs is a numerical measure of the maximum rate of passage of either water vapour or CO_2 through the stomata. It was also measured by the IRGA simultaneously with P_N. gs was expressed in terms of mol m^{-2} s^{-1}.

Q27. How do you estimate the values of photosynthetic enzymes, carbonic anhydrase (CA)?

Carbonic anhydrase (CA) activity was determined in fresh leaves collected randomly from each replicate. The enzyme CA catalyzes the reversible hydration of CO_2 to give the bicarbonate ion (HCO_3^-)

$$H_2O + CO_2 \underset{}{\overset{CA}{\rightleftharpoons}} H^+ + HCO_3^-$$

The activity of the enzyme was estimated by adopting the method of Dwivedi and Randhawa (1974). The collected leaves were cut into the small pieces (1 cm^2) at a temperature below 20° celsius (C). After mixing them, 200 mg leaf pieces were weighed and cut further into smaller pieces keeping them in

100 ml 0.2 M aqueous cysteine hydrochloride (Appendix) solution in a Petridish at 0 to 4°C for 20 minutes (min). The solution adhering on their surface was thin removed with the help of a blotting paper. This was followed by transfer immediately into a test tube having 4 ml phosphate buffer of pH 6.8 (Appendix). To this, 4 ml 0.2 M sodium bicarbonate in 0.2 M sodium hydroxide (NaOH) solution and 0.2 ml 0.002% bromothymol blue indicator (Appendix) were added. After shaking, the tubes were kept at 0–4°C for 20 min. CO_2 liberated during catalytic action of the enzyme on sodium bicarbonate was estimated by titrating the reaction mixture against 0.05 N hydrochloric acid (HCl) using methyl red as an indicator (Appendix). A control reaction mixture was also titrated against 0.05 N HCl. The difference of the sample reading and blank reading was noted for further calculations of enzyme activity. The activity of the enzyme was calculated by the following formula:

$$\frac{0.5 \times V \times N}{W \times T}\,mmol\,(CO_2)mg^{-1}$$

(leaf fresh mass)min^{-1}.

Where,

V = Difference in volume (ml) of HCl used in blank and test sample titration

N = Normality of HCl

W = Fresh weight of tissue in mg

T = Duration of the catalytic action of the enzyme (min)

Finally, the activity of the enzyme was expressed in terms of mol CO_2 kg^{-1}(leaf fresh mass)s^{-1}[1].

Q28. How do you estimate the values of N-fixation enzyme, nitrate reductase (NR)?

The enzyme, NR catalyses the reduction of NO_3^- to nitrite (NO_2^-).

$$NO_3^- + NADH + H^+ \xrightarrow{NR} NO_2^- + NAD + H_2O$$

The NR activity in fresh leaves was estimated by the method of Jaworski (1971). The leaves were cut into small pieces (1 cm^2). Two hundred mg of these chopped leaves were weighed and transferred into plastic vials. To each vial, 2.5 ml phosphatic buffer of pH 7.5 and 0.5 ml KNO$_3$ solution were added followed by the addition of 2.5 ml 5% isopropanol. These vials were incubated in a BOD incubator for 2 h at 30±2°C in the dark. 0.4 ml of incubated mixture was taken into test tube to which 0.3 ml each of sulphanilamide and nephthyl-ethylenediamine-dihydrochloride solutions were added. The test tube was left for 20 min. for maximum colour development. The mixture was diluted to 5 ml using DDW. The OD was recorded at 540 nm using the spectrophotometer.

The standard curve was plotted by using known graded concentration of nitrite solution versus OD of the solution. A blank was also run simultaneously. The activity of the enzyme was determined with the help of a standard curve and was expressed as nmol (NO$_2^-$) kg^{-1} (leaf fresh mass) s^{-1}.

Q29. How do you estimate the values of leaf nitrogen content (N)?

N, P and K were estimated in dried powder of leaves obtained from each replicate. The sampled plant leaves were dried in an oven at 80°C for 24 h. The dried leaves from each sample were finally powdered and then passed through a 72-mesh screen. For the estimation of these nutrients the leaf powder was first digested according to the standard technique described below.

100 mg oven dried powder of leaf material was transferred into a digestion tube to which 2 ml sulphuric acid (H$_2$SO$_4$) was added. The tube was then kept on a digestion assembly at 80°C for about 2 h to allow the complete reduction of NO$_3^-$ present in the plant material by the organic matter itself. Initially, dense white fumes were given off and then the content of the tube turned black. After cooling the tube for about 15 min, 0.5 ml 30% hydrogen peroxide (H$_2$O$_2$) was added drop by drop and the tube was heated again till the colour of the solution changed from black to light yellow. The digestion tube cooled for 10 min. and an additional amount (2–3 drops) of 30% H$_2$O$_2$ was added followed by gentle heating for about 15 min to get a clear and colourless solution. At this stage, care was taken in the addition of H$_2$O$_2$ because its excess might oxidize ammonia in the absence of organic matter. The H$_2$O$_2$ digested material was diluted with DDW and transferred with three washings into a 100 ml volumetric flask and finally the volume was made up to the mark with DDW. The details of methods employed for the estimation of N, P and K are given below.

Nitrogen

N was estimated according to the method of Lindner (1944). A 10 ml H$_2$SO$_4$-H$_2$O$_2$ digested material was taken into a 50 ml volumetric flask and the excess of the acid was neutralized by the addition of 2 ml 2.5 N NaOH. 1 ml 100% sodium silicate was added to prevent turbidity and finally, the volume was made up with DDW. Into a 10 ml graduated test tube, 5 ml this solution was taken and 0.5 ml Nessler's reagent was added. The content of the test tube were allowed to stand for 5 min for maximum colour developed. The solution was transferred into a calorimetric tube and OD was read at 525 nm, using a blank on the spectrophotometer. N content was determined with the help of the standard curve and was expressed in terms of percentage on dry weight basis.

50 mg ammonium sulphate was dissolved 100 ml DDW and the final volume was made 1l with DDW. From this stock solution, 0.1, 0.2, 0.3, 0.4, 0.5, 0.6, 0.7, 0.8, 0.9 and 1.0 ml aliquots were pipetted into ten different test tubes. The solution in each test tube was diluted to 5 ml with DDW. In each test tube, 0.5 ml Nessler's reagent was added. After 5 min, the solution was transferred into a calorimetric tube and OD was read on the spectrophotometer at 525 nm. A blank was run with each determination. A curve was plotted for various concentrations of ammonium sulphate solution versus OD.

Q30. How do you estimate the values of leaf phosphorus (P) content?

Leaf P content in the H_2SO_4-H_2O_2 digested material was estimated by the method of Fiske and Subbarow (1925). 5 ml H_2SO_4-H_2O_2 digested material was taken into a 10 ml graduated test tube and 1 ml molybdic acid was carefully added followed by the addition of 0.4 ml 1-amino-2-naphthol-4-sulphonic acid. The colour of the solution turned blue. The final volume in the tubes was made up to 10 ml with DDW. After mixing throughly, the contents of the tube were allowed to stand for 5 min. They were then transferred into a calorimetric tube and OD was read at 620 nm on the spectrophotometer. A blank was run simultaneously for each determination. P content was computed with the help of the standard curve and was expressed in terms of percentage on dry weight basis.

0.351 g potassium dihydrogen orthophosphate was dissolved in 100 ml DDW followed by the addition of 10 ml 10 N H_2SO_4. The final volume was made up to 1 l with DDW. From this stock solution, 0.1, 0.2, 0.3, 0.4, 0.5, 0.6, 0.7, 0.8, 0.9 and 1.0 ml aliquots were taken in separate test tubes. 1 ml molybdic acid and 0.4 ml 1-amino-2-naphthol-4-sulphonic acid were added in each test tube. The final volume in each test tube was made up to 10 ml with DDW. After 5 min, OD of the developed colour was read at 620 nm on the spectrophotometer. A blank was run with each set of determination. A curve was plotted for various concentrations of potassium dihydrogen orthophosphate solution versus OD.

Q31. How do you estimate the values of leaf potassium (K) content?

It was estimated flame photometrically. 10 ml H_2SO_4-H_2O_2 digested material was taken into a vial and was run into a flame-photometer (Model, C 150, AIMIL, India) using the filter for K. A blank was run side b y side. K content was computed with the help of a standard curve and was expressed in terms of percentage on dry weight basis.

1.91 g potassium chloride (KCl) was dissolved in 50 ml DDW followed by dilution to 100 ml. 1 ml of this solution was diluted to 1 l. The resultant stock solution would contain 10 ppm K, from which 1, 2, 3, 4, 5, 6, 7, 8, 9 and 10 ml aliquots were transferred into 10 different vials. The solution in each vial was diluted to 10 ml. The diluted solution of each vial was run separately. A blank was also run with each set of determination. Standard curve was prepared for different dilutions of KCl solution versus readings on the scale of the galvanometer.

Q32. How do you estimate the values of leaf leghaemoglobin (Lb) content?

Leghaemoglobin occurs in the infected cells of legume root nodules. It facilitates oxygen gas diffusion across the nodule into the N fixing bacteroids to support oxidation and at the same time ensures the oxygen gas sensitive nitrogenase activity without damage. The leghaemoglobin content in fresh nodules was estimated following the method described by Sadasivam and Manickam (2008).

200 mg fresh nodules were mixed with 3 ml phosphate buffer (pH 7.4) and macerated with the help of pestle and mortar followed by filtration through two layers of cheese cloth. The nodule debris was discarded. The turbid reddish brown filterate was centrifuged at 10, 000 revolutions per minute (rpm) for 15 min. The supernatant was diluted to 5 ml with DDW. The extract (5 ml) was taken into a test tube followed by the addition of the same volume of alkaline pyridine reagent. The solution became greenish yellow due to the formation of haemochrome. The haemochrome was divided equally into the two test tubes. To the first test tube, 50 mg potassium hexacyanoferrate was added to oxidize the haemochrome and read at 539 nm on the spectrophotometer against a reagent blank. To the second test tube, 50 mg of sodium dithionate was added to reduce the haemochrome. The absorbance was read after 5 min at 556 nm against a reagent blank. The leghaemoglobin content was calculated by the following formula:

Leghaemoglobin content =

$$\frac{A556 - A539 \times 2D}{23.4} \text{ mmol g}^{-1}$$

(nodule fresh mass)

Where,

D is the initial dilution

A556 and A539 are the absorbances at 556 and 539 nm, respectively. The calculation is based upon the equation $E = 23.4 \times 10^3 \text{ mol}^{-1} \text{cm}^{-1}$.

Q33. What do you mean by yield attributes?

The following yield characteristics were studied at harvest:

1. Pod number per plant
2. Seed number per pod
3. 100-seed weight
4. Seed yield per plant
5. Biological yield per plant
6. Harvest index

To assess the yield performance of the crop, the remaining two plants from each pot were harvested. The harvested plants were sun-dried in a net-house to prevent losses. After drying the crop, each sample was threshed individually. The seeds were utilized for assessing the other characteristics.

The weight of 100 seeds was determined with the help of an electronic balance.

Q34. How do you estimate the values of seed yield, biological yield?

The total seeds of two plants were threshed, cleaned and allowed to dry in the sun for some time and their weight was obtained with the help of an electronic balance, with expressing their weight on per plant basis. The biological yield was recorded before the threshing of plants. It was determined by weighing the dry mass of the two complete plants with the help of an electronic balance, with expressing the yield on per plant basis.

Q35. What is harvest index?

The proportions of the biological yield representing the economic yield are called HI. The HI was computed by dividing the seed yield (economic yield) of a plant by the biological yield of the plant and expressed on per cent basis. HI was calculated by the following formula:

$$HI = \frac{\text{Economic yield}}{\text{Biological yield}} \times 100$$

Q36. How do you estimate the values of seed protein content in any pulse crop-like chickpea?

The total protein content in the dry seeds was estimated by adopting the methodology of Lowry *et al* (1951). 50 mg oven dried seed powder was taken into a centrifuge tube and 5 ml of 5% trichloroacetic acid was added to it. The solution was shaken throughly and allowed to stand for 30 min at room temperature. The solution was centrifuged for 10 min at 4000 rpm and the supernatant was discarded. To the residue, 5 ml of 1N NaOH was added and mixed well. After 30 min, the solution was centrifuged and the supernatant was collected into a 50 ml volumetric flask. The residue was washed twice with 5 ml 1N NaOH and the washings were collected in the flask containing the supernatant. The volume of the flask was made up to the mark with 1N NaOH.

1 ml of this NaOH extract was transferred to a 10 ml test tube and 5 ml of reagent B was added to it. The solution was mixed well and allowed to stand for 10 min at room temperature. Reagent C at 0.5 ml was added rapidly with immediate mixing. After waiting for 30 min, the solution turned blue. The intensity of the bluecoloured solution was measured with the spectrophotometer at 660 nm. A blank was run with each sample.

50 mg egg albumin was dissolved in 100 ml 1N NaOH in a 100 ml volumetric flask by heating the content on a heating plate. Ten different concentrations, i.e. 0.1, 0.2, 0.3, 0.4, 0.5, 0.6, 0.7, 0.8, 0.9 and 1.0 ml from this solution were taken into different test tubes and the volume was maintained to 1 ml. Into each test tube, 5 ml of reagent B was added, was mixed well and was allowed to stand for 10 min at room temperature followed by the

addition of 0.5 ml reagent C rapidly with immediate mixing. After waiting for 30 min, the solution turned blue. The intensity of the colour was read at 660 nm using the spectrophotometer. A blank was used with each determination.

Q37. Write an article on effect of GA_3 and P, and S application on crop especially pulse crop.

PGRs are important control agents for growth and development of plants. Growth regulators like GA, IAA, Kn, SA and Tria have been found to have pronounced effect on the performance of plants. In view of their crucial roles in different facets of plant life and very small quantity involved (economic), it is reasonable to rope in these above mentioned PGRs in innovative farm cultural practices. Among PGRs, GA occupies a prominent position in mediating a variety of plant physiological processes including seed germination, leaf expansion, flower and fruit set, dry matter production, photosynthesis, translocation of food material and synthesis of mRNA coding for hydrolytic enzymes. The superiority of GA to the above mentioned PGRs has also been substantiated in the preliminary experiments. The vegetative and reproductive growth of plants depends mainly on their ability to fix C in organs having chloroplasts followed by the utilization of the photosynthates for sink organs. As the C fixing ability of plants is influenced by mineral elements among other factors, the availability of P and S to leguminous plants affects production of dry matter and partitioning of photosynthates.

It is, therefore, logical to include a very small quantity of P and S in scheme of GA treatments so that growth-cum-dilution effect may be compensated.

The experiments were so designed as to determine beyond doubt whether or not seed and foliar treatment of chick pea with GA combined with a small quantity of spray of P and S could be exploited to enhance the productivity of this important pulse crop. The performance of the crop has been assessed in terms of growth characters, physiological and biochemical characteristics as also yield as well as quality attributes. The results have been discussed parameter-wise in the light of the knowledge of the subject and research work undertaken by other pulse crop scientists below. Application of GA improves, among other processes, absorption and use efficiency of nutrients, activity of enzymes, cell division and cell enlargement, chlorophyll content, elongation of internode, membrane permeability, P_N, nucleic acid and protein synthesis, and transport of photosynthates. Foliar application of GA could have led to the observed improvement in plant height, leaf number per plant, and LA per plant of the treated plants.

Q38. Describe the methods of PGR and nutrient application.

In nature, PGRs required for growth and development are synthesized in plants themselves. However, they could be added exogenously to exploit the full genetic potential of crop plants. There are several methods of application of hormones depending on the plant material and the response for which these are used. These methods include lanolin pasting, dusting, seed-soaking and soil and foliar application. Plants grow in soil and obtain nutrients from it through their root system. However, continuous cultivation results in depletion of nutrients in the soil. To maintain proper fertility of such soils, application of fertilizers (nutrients) to soil becomes an essential to ensure good harvest. In this regard, farm scientists have developed several fertilizer application methods including solid application, gaseous application, application in irrigation water, banding, broadcasting, strip placement, side-dressing and top-dressing. It was, however, found that added fertilizers are rendered partly unavailable to the crops after their application owing to various reasons, including fixation, volatilization and leaching. Moreover, the escalating cost of these fertilizers possesses a great problem for farmers in developing countries.

Under such circumstances, the novel technique of foliar application of nutrients seems to be a good alternative to obtain maximum nutrient use efficiency.

Q39. What do you mean by ascorbic acid and its role in plant disease management?

L-ascorbic acid (AA, vitamin C) fulfils essential metabolic functions in the life of animals and plants. It is a small, water soluble, reductone sugar acid with antioxidant properties and acts as a primary substrate in the cyclic pathway for enzymatic detoxification of a number of reactive oxygen species (ROS). In a large number of studies associated with stress mitigation/tolerance in plants by adding the different natural and synthetic compounds such as PPGs (phenypropanoid glycosides), AA is used as a reference compound. It has been shown to have important functions in photosynthesis such as in the protection of the photosynthetic apparatus against the oxygen radicals and H_2O_2 that are formed during photosynthetic activity and against photoinactivation, since it is a factor of carotenoid deepoxidation. Indeed, AA plays an important role in resistance to abiotic stress such as heavy metal, saline and ultraviolet and biotic stresss. Rapidly increasing evidences indicate that AA is centrally involved in several physiological processes including photosynthesis, cell wall production and its extension by involving in a complex enigmatic array of phytohormone-mediated signalling networks. Due to its function as a co-factor for the biosynthesis of various plant hormones, AA appears to influence not only the endogenous level but also signaling of these plant hormones, and thus affect responses against the environmental stresses.

Q40. Describe the role of simbykul (chick pea) in Ayurveda system of medicine.

Chick pea (*Cicer arietinum* L.) is one of the earliest pulse crops cultivated by humans. It is known as by different names in different languages of India and globe. For example, in Hindi, it is chana; in Gujarati, chania; in Sanskrit, chanaka; in Marathi, harbharaa; in Telguu, shanaga; in Bengali, chhola; in Tamil, kondakondalai; in Ayurveda, shimbykul; in English, chick pea; in Spanish, algarroba; in Portuguese, aravanco and in French, chiche. It belongs to family Fabaceae (Papilionaceae), tribe Cicereae and genus *Cicer*. The genus includes 43 species. Medicinal plants play a significant role for human health care for wealth. About 70% of the world population relies on the application of traditional medicine, which is predominantly depending on plant material. A broad spectrum of scientific studies available on a good number of medicinal plants indicates that promising phytochemicals can be developed for various health problems. The plant kingdom offers a widely rich source of structural biodiversity in the form of a variety of natural products and produce. The demand for botanicals has increased worldwide and an unparalleled increase in the sector was observed on global scale. The demand is estimated to grow in the years to come fuelled by the growth of sales of herbal supplements and remedies according to a number of surveys. To compete with the growing market, there is urgency to expeditiously utilize and scientifically validate more number of medicinal herbs. But with increasing globalization, knowledge holders are associated about the erosion of traditional lifestyles and cultures through external pressures, including loss of their knowledge and reluctance of younger members of the community to maintain traditional practices. Since only 5 to 15% of the higher plants have been systematically investigated for the presence of bioactive compounds, nature's biodiversity still largely unexplored. In this article we emphasis the medicinal value of chick pea—a multipurpose pulse crop in India.

Q41. What do you mean by amino acid and its role in plant development?

Proline is a non-essential α-amino acid, one of the twenty DNA-encoded amino acids. It is unique among the 20 protein-forming amino acids in that the α-amino acid group is secondary. Biosynthetically, it is derived from the amino acid L-glutamate and its immediate precursor is the imino acid(s)-1-pyroline-5-carboxylate. Proline may function also as protein-compatible hydrotrope and as a hydroxyl radical scavenger. Proline considered under a class of small molecules, compatible osmolytes, also including other amino acids, quaternary ammonium compounds and the tertiary sulfinium compounds 3-dimethylsulfoniopropionate. It act as a signaling molecule to modulate mitochondrial functions, influence cell proliferation or cell death and trigger specific gene expression essential for plant recovery against various types of environmental stresses including drought, salinity, extreme temperatures, chemical toxicity and oxidative stress. In many plants, free proline accumulates in response to the imposition of a wide range of biotic and abiotic stresses. Proline is one of the most important compounds of plants defensive mixed action to environmental stresses. Although not all plants accumulate proline in sufficient amounts to help averting adverse effects of abiotic stresses. Further studies required to identification of multiple genes to enhance proline flux that could lead to new opportunities to improve plant tolerance.

Proline considered under a class of small molecules, compatible osmolytes, also including other amino acids, quaternary ammonium compounds (e.g., glycinebetaine, proline-betaine, β-alanine betaine, and choline-O-sulfate), and the tertiary sulfinium compounds 3-dimethylsulfoniopropionate (DMSP). Osmolytes or compatible solutes (e.g. proline) are groups of low molecular weight organic compounds that accumulate in organisms in response to osmotic stress. Abiotic stress evolves multiple responses that involve a series of physiological, biochemical and molecular events. In many plants, free proline accumulates in response to the imposition of a wide range of biotic and abiotic stresses. Efficiency of proline production considered as a major stress-induced diversion of N

metabolism. Although less proline accumulated in the oldest leaves, a significant amount transported from senescing to emerging leaves. Moreover, during rehydration, proline readily recycled. Proline plays a significant role in leaf N remobilization and in N use efficiency in oilseed rape also. The purpose of this chapter is to outline recent advances and new approaches to the investigation of proline biosynthesis, accumulation and function, which are not yet completely understood.

Q42. What is the significance of garlic role in human cardiovascular system?

Currently natural products are attaining more popularity to combat various physiological threats including oxidative stress, cardiovascular complexities, cancer insurgence and immune dysfunction. The use of traditional remedies may encounter more frequently due to a broad myriad of scientific evidence in their remedic favour. Spices are a dried seed, fruit, roots, bark or vegetable substance. Spices possess a variety of phytochemicals that gaining wide attention for their well-recognized potential health benefits against advanced physiological threats in present scenarios. Among the spices, garlic (*Allium sativum* L.) holds a unique position for its recognized therapeutic potential. The potent remedic role of garlic recognized particularly with respect to aged-garlic extract (AGE) has been the subjects of much research interest as well as emergent focus for a large number of reviews. This review investigates the cardiovascular related health potential of garlic, examining the role of their bioactive chemicals like thiosulfinate organosulphur volatiles, vinyldithiins, ajoenes, and water soluble organosulphur compounds. In this review, much emphasis given to evidences for health benefits is based on potentialities of bioactive constituents to ameliorate oxidative stress, active participation in cardiovascular cure and their prospective as immune boosters.

Globally, unhealthy diets and physical inactivity are two of the most leading causes of major chronic diseases. According to the

WHO, non-communicable chronic disorders, such as heart diseases, stroke, cancer, chronic respiratory diseases, diabetes, are by far the principle leading cause of mortality in the world reporting 60% of all death. In 2004, the 192 member states of the WHO endorsed the global strategy on diet, physical activity and health addressing two main risk factors. Diet is a central pivotal link with human health and food rich in phytochemicals often associated with proper functionality of immune system. Food levels are widely used to convey the health benefits of conventional foods or a component of food to the consumer. The increasing amount of health information available regarding the health benefits of food has resulted in consumer interest in the health issues and has become a leading factor in purchasing decisions. Many consumers try to eat healthier foods, use natural medicines, and make life style changes in the quest to feel good, maintain body weight, reduce the risk of chronic disease, and live healthier longer lives. Thus, it is now widely accepted that the ageing and age-related disease are in part caused by free radical reactions or free radical induced reactions. The arrest of ageing and stimulation of rejuvenation of the human body is also being sought.

Q43. Potential of pulse derived phytochemicals against advanced physiological threats.

Soya bean is an annual plant widely cultivated for both medicinal and culinary uses. The seeds of this herb have been known through the ages for their medicinal value. Presently natural herbal products are attracting attention against a number of metabolic and physiological complexities including cardiovascular disorders, cancer and immunity based dysfunctions as a herbal healer. The use of pulse derived phytomedicine may encounter rapidly due to a broad spectrum of scientific proofs in their remedic behaviour. Pulses are the seeds of legumes. Pulses possess a variety of phytochemicals that gaining wide attention for their well-recognized

potential health benefits against advanced physiological threats in present scenarios. Among pulses, the most studied pulse is soybean (*Glycine max* L.), traditionally recognized as an herbal medicinally used pulse rather than as an oil seed or an ordinary crop. The plant of soyabean is quite nutritious, being high in proteins, ascorbic acid, niacin, and potassium. Also, Soya bean is very rich in some amino acids, as its content of lysine and isoleucine is lower than fenugreek. It holds a unique and peculiar status for its recognized therapeutic capacity. The potent remedic roles recognized especially with respect to isoflavones amount and quality have been the subjects of more research value as well as emergent target for a number of research papers and review articles. Present article investigates the cardiovascular associated health potential of soy, observing the role of their bioactive products like isoflavones, phytosterols, resistant starch, carbohydrate, alkaloids, and saponins. Here, much emphasis given to evidences for health benefits is based on strong activities of bioactive constituents to combat oxidative stress, active participation in cardiovascular cure and their prospective as immune stimulators. These preliminary studies not only suggest alternative and cheaper remedies for the pharmaceutical industries also.

Q44. Describe the effective internal physiological approaches of natural plant derivatives against environmental stresses.

Although, under normal metabolic processes, the low amounts of ROS are metabolic by-products of plant cells, release of radicals in to the cytosol can be enhanced under certain stress conditions, producing oxidative stress in the cells. $O_2 \bullet -$ are immediately converted into O_2 and H_2O_2. Therefore, the production of these radicals results in an increase of H_2O_2 in the cell. Saumya and Basha stated that aqueous leaf extract of *Lagerstroemia speciosa* have the potential to inhibit lipid peroxidation and effectively neutralize ROS such as H_2O_2 and NO based free radicals. Plant cell wall expresses monoamine oxidases (MAOs) that catalyze oxidation of secreted amines enhanced generation of ROS in plants during abiotic stress and is referred to as oxidative stress because of their potential for cell damage. Similarly, Verma and Sharma propose that H_2O_2 generated within cell walls of seeds serves as a signaling molecule guiding germination events, including protein reserve mobilization. H_2O_2 and NO both function as stress signaling molecules in plants, mediating a range of defensive mechanisms in plants under stressful conditions.

Injury to plants exposed to stress is related to oxidative damage at the cellular level. Stress like heavy metal constitutes the most significant factor leading to substantial and unpredictable loss in yield. Various stresses limit CO_2 assimilation more than electron transport capacity leading to modulation of the latter by photosynthetic control. H_2O_2 and NO both function as stress signaling molecules in plants, mediating a spectrum of defensive mechanisms in plants under stressful conditions. Alternatively, it can initiate programmed cell death, particularly when NO is also produced depending on the intensity of the oxidative signal or oxidative load exerted by heavy metals toxicity on the tissues. In this review article, we targeted to examine the regulatory role of NO (naturally produced in damaged plant tissues) signaling against biotic environmental stresses induced oxidative stress in plants. In many recent researches, high levels of NO has the capacity to damage membranes and DNA fragmentation, and to reduce photosynthesis in oat and alfalfa, as well as regulating the multiple plant responses towards a variety of biotic stresses, for example, insect attack and grazing etc. Also, this article shade a small beam of light on recent advances about responses induced to heavy metal stress reported by a number of previous researches.

Q45. What do you mean by hydrogen peroxide and its role in abiotic stresses in crop plants?

H_2O_2 has been implicated as a key factor mediating programmed cell death. Plants exposed to abiotic stresses can produce a systemic signal, a component of which may be H_2O_2 which sets up an acclamatory response in unstressed regions of plants. Also H_2O_2 is an ancient signaling molecule that not only played a key role in inducing evolution of oxygenic photosynthesis but also modulates many physiological events, such as stomatal movement, hypersensitive responses, and programmed cell death. Increasing evidence now indicates that H_2O_2 acts as a local and systemic signal that directly regulates expression of numerous genes. During normal metabolism in a plant cell, H_2O_2 is generated in chloroplast, mitochondria and peroxisome and is kept in homeostasis by complicated and effective scavenging systems that have developed over the course of evolution. H_2O_2 has a long lifespan, is able to cross biological membranes, and rapidly diffuses from cell to cell or can be transported long distances from its sites of origin in plants. Also, its production quickly responds to various environment stimuli. Thus, H_2O_2 has all of the characteristic features of an intercellular signaling molecule and, for this reason, has received increasing attention in recent years. Several recent reviews have described the biological activities of ROS, placing special emphasis on the signaling role of H_2O_2. In particular, H_2O_2 that is produced by cytosolic membrane-bound NADPH oxidases has been implicated as a signal in a wide range of biotic and abiotic stress responses. These responses include defense reactions against pathogens and herbivores, the closure of stomata and the regulation of cell expansion and plant development.

Abiotic stresses are major constraint to agricultural production worldwide. The plants have an inbuilt mechanism to respond to fluctuations in circadian and seasonal environmental conditions. Abiotic stresses disrupt the cellular redox homeostasis which leads to the oxidative stress or generation of ROS. H_2O_2 is the two electron reduction product of

O_2. It is potentially reactive oxygen, but not a free radical, generated as a result of oxidative stress via superoxide ($O_2\bullet-$), presumably in a non-controlled manner during electron transport processes such as photosynthesis and mitochondrial respiration. H_2O_2 generation via electron transport is increased in response to environmental stresses such as excess excitation energy, drought and cold and also induced in plants following exposure to a wide variety of abiotic and biotic stimuli. Although, in the last two decades, the potential of H_2O_2 as a stress induced signal to abiotic stress in plants has positioned for much attention. H_2O_2 is produced in response to various stimuli and mediates cross-talk between signaling pathways and is an attractive signaling molecule contributing to the phenomenon of cross-tolerance in which exposure of plants to one stress offers protection towards another. As it is well cleared in present review, recent studies on H_2O_2 functionality to induce tolerance in plants to abiotic stresses has been unravelled and very impressive.

Q46. What do you mean by nitrogenase—a nitrogen fixing enzyme?

Nitrogenase is an enzyme widely distributed among bacteria and is key to the fixation of nitrogen (N) in the terrestrial nitrogen cycle with an estimated annual global ammonia production. Nitrogenase (EC: 1.18.6.1), an iron-Mo protein, represents a diverse group of bacteria and archea. It is a two-component enzyme that catalyzes the nucleotide-dependent reduction of N to $2NH_3$ and the key to the nitrogen fixation in the terrestrial nitrogen cycle with an estimated annual global ammonia production and also is able to reduce nitrogen to ammonia via using a relatively mild source of electrons a reduced ferredoxin in vivo and sodium dithionite in vitro together with protons from the medium. This process involves three redox-active metal-containing cofactors including a (4Fe-4S) cluster, an eight-Fe-P cluster and a seven-Fe plus molybdenum FeMo-cofactor, the site of substrate reduction. Biological nitrogen fixation (BNF) performed by microorganisms that have its accounts for roughly two-thirds of the nitrogen fixed globally. Most nitrogen fixation is carried out by the activity of Mo nitrogenase, widely distributed in nature. Some bacteria and blue green algae are able to reduce atmospheric N to ammonia also. Several of them do even live in symbiosis or in association with green plants. The nodule bacteria like Rhizobium of leguminosae are best known.

Q47. Role of organic and inorganic natural plant derivatives plant-stress mitigation and efficiency.

All kinds of abiotic stress factors are proba-bly the most limiting for crop quality and productivity, comprising economical output and human food supply. Plants constantly monitor their surroundings and make appropriate metabolic, structural and physiological adjustments to accommodate environmental changes. Within frame work of genetic background, plant productivity is dependent on this constant adjustment of gene expression in response to environmental cues. The genome-environment interaction is an essential focus for the elucidation of the nature of the phenotypic variations leading to successful stress tolerance responses. Today, the role of organic chemicals and inorganic chemicals are recently emerged and also, widely used approaches for stress mitigation in plant systems. All these molecules modify constitutively expressed transcription factors, leading to the expression of early response transcriptional activators, which then activate downstream stress tolerance effectors genes, responsible for stress mitigation. Organic derivatives include amino acids, vitamins, ascorbic acid, plant hormones and salicylic acid; inorganic chemicals include as hydrogen peroxide, nitric oxide and nutrients.

Q48. Write an article on nitrate reductase.

NR is the first enzyme in the NO_3 assimilation pathway and probably represents the rate-limiting step in this process and generates NO_2 in the cytoplasm of a plant cell, which is translocated into the plastids for further reduction and metabolization. Nitrate reductase (EC: 1.6.6.1–3, NR) catalyzes the NAD (P) H reduction of NO_3 to NO_2 to ascertain its role in nitrogen fixation. NR serves plants, algae and fungi as a central point for integration of metabolism by governing flux of reduced nitrogen (N) by several regulatory mechanisms. Assimilatory NR also provides useful magneto-structural correlations to characterize EPR-detected species in mononuclear molybdoenzymes. The development of new N fertilizers is necessary to optimize crop production whilst improving the environmental aspects arising from the use of nitrogenous fertilization as a cultural practice.

Q49. Describes the role of chick pea in environmental-friendly and sustainability of soil fertility.

Chick pea is a crop that is environment friendly and sustains soil productivity. The benefits of the crop thus extend beyond the increase to the farmers and the farming systems. Chick pea has been well recognized as a valuable source of proteins particularly in the developing countries where majority of the populations depends on the low proceeds food for meeting the dietary requirements. Its magnitude of significance is more among Indians due to their reliance on vegetarians diet besides limited buying capacity of more than 200–250 millions (27%) people living below the poverty line (BPL). Like other pulses, supplementation of chick pea with cereals based diets is considered to be one of the possible solutions to the problems associated with protein energy malnutrition (PEM). The daily per capita availability of the chick pea is a source of approximately 2.3 % (56 kcal) energy and 4.7 (27 g) proteins to Indian population besides being a major source of calcium and iron.

The area occupied by the crop is 16% of the total pulse area but in some countries, e.g. India and Pakistan, it is the most important pulse crop and the area occupied could well be around 50% of the total pulse area. The productivity of chick pea is much low as compared to cereals crops due to varied reasons. Two of these are described here (i) excessive cold conditions adversely affect productivity, (ii) farmers are ignorant of precise doses of fertilizers recommended by the Agriculture Department for a particular cultivar and region, the techniques of cultivation of high yielding cultivars.

Among the factors determining the desired yield of chick pea, use of quality seeds and yield stability of cultivars over varied environments are most critically important. The study of cultivar environment interaction provides useful information to identify stable cultivars over a range of environments. The growth and development of any individual plant species proceed at a speed and extent pre-determined by the genetic constitution. The eventual expression of the pattern, however, is modified by many interlocking environmental complexities which individual plant inhabitants. It is already have been stated that vigorous seed germinates rapidly and uniformly after planting and the emerged seedlings have the ability to grow vigorously under the wide range of environmental conditions.

Q50. What are peroxisomes?

Peroxisomes are compartments enclosed by a single membrane and filled with the enzymes that function in a variety of metabolic pathways, such as breaking down fatty acids to smaller molecules or detoxifying alcohol and other poisons. An enzyme Catalase that converts H_2O_2, a toxic product of these pathways, is also packed into Peroxisomes.

Specialized peroxisomes called glyoxisomes are found in the tissues of germinating seeds and contain enzymes that convert the fatty acids stored in the seeds to sugar for the developing seedlings. They have more enzymes of the glyoxylate cycle, a pathway unique to plants that converts stored fats to carbohydrates during seed germination.

Q51. What do you mean by the channel and carrier proteins?

Channel protein is a membrane protein that forms a channel completely through the membrane. These form permanent channels in the lipid bi-layer through which certain ions can cross the membrane. Most channel proteins have a specific interior diameter and distribution of electrical charges that allow only particular ions to pass through. Facilitated diffusion is achieved by the channel proteins, for example, nerve cells have separate channels for sodium ions, potassium ions and calcium ions.

Carrier protein is a membrane protein that facilitates the diffusion of specific substances such as some amino acids, sugars or small proteins from the cytoplasm or extracellular fluid across the membrane. The molecule to be transported binds to the surface of the carrier proteins. The protein then changes shape, allowing the molecule to move across the membrane through the protein. Active transport is achieved by the carrier proteins and facilitated diffusion also occurs through these proteins that do not use cellular energy. These carrier proteins move molecules only down the concentration gradients.

Q52. What do you mean by raphides and sphaeraphides?

Crystals of various chemical compounds occur in plant cells. Inorganic intracellular crystals, calcium salts of carbonates, oxalate or phosphates are common. Calcium oxalate forms a bundle of needle-shaped crystals known as raphides in leaves, roots fruits, etc. A common form of irregular calcium oxalate crystals of plants form druses or shperaphides are found in florets of haplopappus, papaya and pistia.

Q53. The living organisms' exhibit diversity in form and function, yet their cells have some common characteristics. What are those characteristics common to all cells?

The genetic materials in all cells consist of nucleic acids. During cell division, the hereditary characters are transmitted as nucleic acids.

The basic structure of the membrane and their properties are also common.

The mechanism of aerobic respiration is uniform.

Nucleic acid and proteins are synthesized on the same plan in all cells.

Q54. The main drawback of Schleiden and Schwann's cell theory was that it could not explain how new cells are formed. What is present status of cell theory?

The present status of cell theory is:

All living things are composed of cells and their products.

All cells arise from pre-existing cells.

All cells are basically alike in chemical composition and metabolic activities.

The function of an organism as a whole is the outcome of the activities and interactions of the constituent cells.

Q55. By which subunit ribosomes are attached to endoplasmic reticulum or nuclear envelope. Name the two proteins which bound ribosomes to ER.

Ribosomes are attached to ER or nuclear envelope by their 60S subunit. The proteins which bound ribosomes to Er are two glycolproteins: Ribophorin-I and Ribophorin-II.

Q56. Write the structure and functions of nucleolus.

Nucleolus is a dense, spherical and acidophilic body present in the nucleus. It remains attached to special type of chromosome nucleolar organizing chromosome at a specific place-secondary constrictiction. It consists of three parts, viz. granular region, fibrillar region and amorphous matrix.

Q57. In brief describe the main functions of Golgi complex.

Secretion is the main function of the GC. The secretory proteins and lipids are concentrated and packed into secretory vesicles or granules. These are pinched off from the dilated tips of cisternae and appear as dense secretory or zymogen granules in the cytoplasm. Ultimately the vesicles release their content by exocytosis.

Q58. Name the two micro-bodies found in plant cells. Also mention their functions.

Three micro-bodies found in plants cells are: peroxisomes, glyoxisomes and spherosomes. These are spherical or oval bodies enclosed by a membrane and are filled with a fluid matrix. Peroxisomes contain peroxide destroying enzymes (CAT) and peroxide producing enzymes. They prevent peroxide from acting on the cellular contents. Glyoxisomes are micro-bodies in the cells of germinating fatty acids such as groundnut and castor. These are associated with the breakdown of fats into carbohydrates.

Q59. Describe four organic cell inclusions.

Four organic cell inclusions are starch grains, glycogen, granules, fat droplets and aleurone grains. Starch grains only found in plant cells particularly in storage organs such as rhizomes and tubers. Hilum in each concentric ring is made up of protein. Glycogen granules are small, spherical particles occurring near the SER in liver and muscle cells. Fat droplets are found in adipocytes of animals. One or several large fat droplets fill up the cell, found in endosperm of castor and coconut and cotyledons of groundnut and mustard seeds. Aleurone grains contain stored proteins in plant cells. They found in outermost cells of endosperm in cereal grains.

Q60. What are xenobiotics?

They are synthetic chemicals which are naturally occurring substances. They include pesticides, polychlorinated biphenyls (PCBs, used in the electric generating and related industries), munitions, dyes and chlorinated solvents, among other things. Many xenobiotics are structurally related to natural compounds and can thus be slowly degraded by enzymes that already exist to degrade these natural compounds. However, some xenobiotics differ chemically in such a major way from anything organisms have naturally experienced that they degrade extremely slowly, if at all.

Q61. What are "X-ray diffraction patterns" and "Chargaff principles" in genetics?

In 1962, **Watson and Crick** together with **Maurice Wilkins,** were awarded the Nobel prize for medicine for elucidating the structure of DNA. **Rosalind Franklin,** whose evidence from X-ray crystallography played such as important part in the hypothesis, had died in 1958, aged only 37.

When X-rays are passed through crystallized DNA, they are scattered in a way that represents the arrangements of atoms within atoms. By analysis of the X-ray diffraction pattern obtained, details of the three-dimensional structure of DNA can be deduced. This evidence indicates that DNA is of 2 nm diameters, a complete of twist of every 3.4 nm, each twist has 10 base pairs, and consist of two strands.

Chargaff rule tells about base analysis ratio in nucleic acid. This rule is given by Czech-American Edwin Chargaff, who began working at Columbia University, N.Y, in 1935 and investigated the organic base composition of nucleic acid. He showed that a single organism contains many different kinds of RNA, but its DNA is essentially of one kind—the characteristic of the organism.

This rule's analysis of DNA established the following rule:

    i. $A + G = T + C$
    ii. Number of adenine bases = Number of thymine bases
    iii. Number of guanine bases = Number of cytosine bases

These observations are best interpreted as adenine being always paired with thymine (A=T), and guanine with cytosine (G=C).

These rules are a key clue to the structure of DNA.

Q62. What do you mean by DNA replication *in vitro*?

Replication of a single strand of DNA was carried out in a test tube (*in vitro*) within three years of publication of Watson and Crick paper, using components and an enzyme obtained from the bacterium *E. coli*. The enzyme was named as DNA polymerase. Later, it was discovered that this enzyme catalyses the addition of nucleotides to the strand running in the 5' to 3' direction. A second enzyme, DNA ligase, catalyses the final assembly of the strand running in the 3' to 5' direction.

Q63. Name the three types of RNA molecules? How is each related to the concept of information flow?

Three types of RNA molecules are mRNA, tRNA and rRNA. mRNA carries the information for the type of protein to be synthesized. tRNA with the help of anticodons reads the message written on mRNA and brings the amino acids to the site of protein synthesis. rRNA the site of protein synthesis, i.e. ribosomes are made up proteins and mRNA.

Q64. Who gave operon concept? Explain this concept with regard to Lac operon.

Francis Jacob and Jacques Monod (1961) gave the operon concept according to which metabolic pathways are regulated as unit, e.g. Lac operon.

When lactose sugar is added to the culture of *E. coli*, it induces three enzymes necessary for the breakdown of lactose into glucose and galactose. These are β-galactosidase, permease and transacetylase. The genes for these three genes occur adjacent to each other and are linked. These are called structural genes. These three genes are regulated as a unit by a single switch called operator. This entire unit consisting of structural genes and operator is called operon.

Q65. When CO_2 is opaque to infrared waves? How their entry is possible in our atmosphere sufficient to produce greenhouse effect? Is there any relation between greenhouse effect and depletion of ozone layer?

Greenhouse effect describe the roles of water vapour, CO_2 and other trace gases in keeping the earths surface warmer than it would be otherwise. These radiatively active gases are relatively transparent to incoming short-waves radiation (visible spectrum), but are relatively opaque to outgoing reradiating (infrared rays) longwave radiation. The later radiation, which would otherwise escape to space, is trapped by these gases within the lower levels of the energy back to te surface maintains surface temperature higher than thy would be if the gases were absent (without the green house effect the earth's average global temperature would be 18°C rather than the present 15°C). There is concern that increasing concentration of the greenhouse gases including CO_2, CH_4 and man-made CFCs may enhance the green house effect and cause global warming.

During middle 1990s a team lead by D. Schindell found that the GHE was responsible not only for heating the lower atmosphere but also for cooling the upper atmosphere (stratosphere). The cooling poses the problems for O_3 molecules, which are most unstable at low temperature. Based on the teams observations, the build up of green house gases could chill the higher atmosphere near the poles by as much as 8° to 10°C. Greenhouse gases warm the earth surface but cool the stratosphere radioactively and therefore affect ozone depletion. The colder the stratosphere, the greater the destruction of ozone by CFCs.

Q66. What is numerical taxonomy?

It involves exhaustive quantitative estimation of taxonomic characters from all parts of the plant as well as from all stages in the life cycle.

Application of numerical methods (data) in the classification of taxonomic units is called numerical taxonomy. Its main objective is to clarify and illustrative degrees of relationship or similarlity in an objective manner.

Systematic deals with identification, nomenclature and taxonomic classification of organisms.

Q67. What do you mean by Lamakism?

Lamark's theory of evolution asserts that all life forms have arisen by a continous process of gradual modification thrpuguout geological history. To explain this process, he cited the then generally accepted theory of acquired characteristics, which held that new traits in an organism develop because of a need created by the environment and that they are transmitted to its offsprings. Although, the latter hypothesis was disputed during Lamark's lifetime by Cuvier and others and was rejected altogether as the principles of heredity was established. lamark theory of evolution was an important forerunner of the work of Charles Darwin,who recognized a modified influence of environment in evoluationary processes.

Q68. What is EMP?

Glycolysis is a metabolic pathway found in all organisms.This pathway consists of 10 chemical reactions catalyzed by proteins and is responsible for the degradation and synthesis of carbohydrates. EMP doesnot depend on the presence of oxygen an d is able to provide the cell with the universal energy currency called ATP. This can generate glucose only partially and will produce waste products such as lactate (mammalian muscles under anaerobic excersize conditions) or ethanol in microorganisms (used for fermentation of wine or beer).

Q69. What is Ames test?

Ames test is a widely used screening test for the potentially carcinogenic effect of substances—their mutagenic effect on microorganisms, cells and tissue cultures. It relies on the observation that the most common cause of cancer is somatic mutations brought about by DNA damage. Chemicals that damage bacterial DNA, and induce mutations, are likely to cause mutatons in mammalian cells.

Ames used mutants of Salmonella enteric (*S. typhimurium*). Doing the assay in bacteria gives much faster and less expensive results than animal studies, with results usually being available in two days.With this method, it is possible to assay directly the mutagenic and teratogenic effect of the substances in tobacco smoke.

Positive results in an Ames test (i.e. an increase in mutations) is an indicator of the potential for the material to cause genetic damage and possibly cancer.

Q70. What is ecological community and give its characteristics?

An assemblage of living organisms that occur together in an area is termed as ecological community. The nature of forces that knit these assemblahes into organized systems and thse properties of assemblage that manifest this organization have been topics of intense debate among ecologists.

A description of an ecological community may include following key characteristics:

1. Its size as number of species
2. The productivity of species
3. The ability of species to reproduce
4. The spatial distribution patterns of species
5. The pattern of succession
6. The functional organization of species

Q71. Why plants have much lower levels of fats than animals?

Plants are generally placed at a advantage in using starch (carbohudrate) as a principle storage macromolecules because of their sedimentary life style. In such conditions, efficient storage of calories is advantageous in plants as triglycerides.

Often seeds are rich in fats and oils as a result of this style (adaptation, sedentary life style) they store a maximum of calories in a limited space.

Its opposite, because of their increased locomotion than plants, animals benefits from lighter weight source of energy (fats) and hence have evolved mechanism to produce and store higher levels of fats than plants.

Q72. What is terracing? Mention its importance in Agriculture.

Terracing is a method of shaping land to control erosion on slopes of rolling land used for cropping and other uses. It consists of the construction of low-graded channels (levels) to carry the excess rainfall from the land at non-erosive velocities.

Two major types of terraces:

1. The bench, and
2. Broad base

The first type is essentially a steep land terrace and consists of an almost vertical retaining wall (called Riser) or steep vegetative slope to hold the nearly level surface of the soil or cultivation.

The second type has the distinguishing characteristics of formability, i.e. crop can be grown on this terrace and worked with modern day machinery.

Q73. What do you mean by protogyny?

In hermapherodite (dioecious) animals and plants, protogyny is a condition in which female reproductive structures, e.g. carpels in plants, mature before the male (anthers) structures. It is of rare occurrence. Botanically, protogyny occurs in some plant species in which the female part stigma develops withers and dies before male part anthers mature. Thus, protogyny is a condition in which female parts develops first.

Q74. What do you mean by defoliants and desiccants?

Defoliants are chemicals that cause leaves to drop from plants. Defoliation facilitates harvesting. Desiccants are chemicals that kill leaves of plants, the leaves may either drop off or remain attached; in the harvesting process the leaves are usually shattered and blown away from the harvested material. Defoliants are desirable for use on cotton plants because dry leaves are difficult to remove from the cotton fibres. Desiccants are used on many seed crops to hasten harvest; the leaves are cleaned from the seed in harvesting.

Q75. What is nystatin?

Nystatin is an antifungal antibiotic. Chemically, it is polyene. It is useful in the therapy of a wide variety of non-systematic fungal infections and also as an ingredient in animal feeds for enhanced growth rates with poultry and swine. It is active against a wide range of yeasts and other fungi, but it is without activity against bacteria.

Q76. What do you mean by glutamine?

Glutamine is an amino acid. Glutamine with its amide group is important storage form of N in plants and animals. It also serves as the precursor of certain ring N atoms in purine's and histidine and of the amino group in glucosamine.

Q77. What is the reverse osmosis?

This is the method of desalination of saline water and purification of sewage water. In this method, the brine (sea-water) or sewage and pure water are separated by a semi-permeable membrane. The pressure on the brine side is raised to about 25 atmospheres which causes water from brine to pass through membrane into pure water. The high pressure makes the process difficult to apply on a large scale.

Q78. What is peat?

Peat is a kind of compost of dead plants, compressed over the years into a spongy mass. It is a kind of coal which is used to improve the soil in the gardens. When dried it is used as a fuel.

Q79. What is PCR?

PCR was discovered by Kary Mullis (1985). Taq DNA polymerase enzyme is used in PCR. The amplified DNA is obtained by repeating the reaction after initiation by primer strand. The de-naturation of DNA takes place at 90–98°C and renaturation at 40–60°C.

Q80. What is codon?

A codon is made up of three nucleotides for example initiation codon AUG, GUG and termination codons AUG, UGA, UAA, etc.

Q81. What is N-fixation?

The breaking of soil nitrates or nitrites to molecular nitrogen is called denitrification. It is brought about by denitriflying bacteria (e.g. *Bacillus subtilis, Thiobacillus denitrificans, Pseudomonas stutzeri,* etc.) while ammonification is the breaking of proteins to ammonia through amino acids. Nitrification is the oxidation of ammonia to nitrates through nitrites and to fix atmospheric molecular nitrogen (N_2) into soil nitrates is called N-fixation.

Q82. Mention the photosynthesis in BGA.

Oxygen does not evolved during the photosynthesis of bacteria (photosynthetic bacteria) while oxygen is evolved during the photosynthesis of red algae, green algae and BGA/Cyanobacteria. BGA used two photo systems as in green plants. The purple photosynthetic bacteria, *Rhodospirillium rubrum* has single PS centre. For example, electron donor is H_2S which generates S. Although, H_2 gas and several organic compounds can be used as electron donors (normally at place of H_2O) by certain photosynthetic bacteria. So, no O_2 is evolved.

Q83. What do you mean by soil profile?

Humus is present in horizon-A which is rich in mineral elements. A large amount of completely decomposed organic matter is present in this region. Fully decomposed organic matter which can be mixed with mineral matter is called humus, where litter is used decomposed matter. When it is partly decomposed it is called as duff.

Q84. Mention the role of autoradiography in cell studies?

Microscopy and autoradiography are techniques used for study of cell. The latter technique is useful for studying the synthesis of molecules, and to trace metabolic events in the cells with the help of radioactive isotopes called tracers.

Q85. What do you mean by endarch xylem?

A vascular bundle with centrifugal xylem is known as endarch. Both in dicot and monocot stems, the xylem is endarch because its development is centrifugal, i.e. protoxylem which is formed first, lies towards the centre of the stem while metaxylem, which is formed later on, lies towards the pheriphery.

Q86. Can agricultural biotechnology reduce our dependence on petroleum?

Some of it. Plants harvest the energy in sunlight, the ultimate renewable resource, and plants are being developed through biotechnology that will produce plastics, fuels and other valuable products. This has the potential to reduce our consumption of petroleum base products. Biotechnology may allow us to reduce our reliance on fossil based fuels.

Q87. How the transgenic GMO tomato Flavr Savr has been achieved?

The transgenic GMO tomato called Flavr Savr has a much longer and more flavourful shelf life than conventional tomatoes, because of delayed repening.This is achieved by reducing the amount of cell wall degrading enzyme **polygalacturonase** responsible for fruit softening.

Q88. Which colour of light is least important to a green plant during photosynthetic activity?

Plants reflect green colour because that wavelength of light is least usable for photosynthesis. Blue and red wavelength of light are the best for photosynthesis, and are therefore seen the least in plants.

Q89. Given below is the transcribed strand of the DNA duplex.

3'-TAC CGA TCC GAC CTG—5'

i. What would be the sequence of the opposite stand or complementary DNA strand.

ii. Construct the RNA molecule, which will be transcribed?

iii. Which molecule bear codons and which molecules anticodons.

Ans. (a) i. 5'—ATG GCT AGG CTG GAC—3'

ii. RNA molecule A<u>U</u>G GC<u>U</u> AGG AGG C<u>U</u>G GAC

iii. mRNA bears codons and tRNA anticodons.

Q90. What are the transposones (jumping genes/controlling elements/mobile genetic elements) and what are their significance?

Transposons are those DNA segments which can join with other DNA segment completely unrelated and thus causing illigimate pairing. These DNA segments are transposable and may be present on different places on main DNA. So, they called jumping genes. They have been reported in maize and bacteria. They have profound effect on embryonic development and tumor formation in animal cells. Oncogenes (genes that cause tumors) may be activated by the random reshuffling of transposons to a position adjacent to the oncogenes.

Uses

1. They useful in genetic enginerring with eukarytic cells, by spiclcing in transposones to activate certain genes.

2. They can change the pattern of restriction fragment analysis,so used as genetic markers to make linkage maps.

3. They used in humans for distinguishing the carriers from non-carriers of disease like sickle cell anemia.

4. A set of cloned DNA fragment containing copies of transposons, should also contain unique sequences from specific regions of the genome and can be used in such studies.

Q91. People living at sea level have around 5 million RBC per cubic millimeter of their blood whereas those living at an altitude to 5400 meteres have around 8 million. This is because at high altitude.

Atmospheric O_2 level is less and hence more RBCs are needed to absorb the required amount of O_2 to survive

At high altitude composition of air remains almost same as at sea level, but density (barometric pressure) of air gradually decreases due to which arterial pO_2 is also decreased (hypoxemia).High altitude presents with complex conditions to which human body has to acclimatize. Number of RBCs per unit volume of blood is likely to be higher in a person living at high altitudes. This an in response to the air being less dense at high altitude. More number of RBCs are needed to trap O_2 from rarefied air having low pO_2 (partial pressure of oxygen).

Q92. Which of the following statements regarding mitochondrial membrane is not correct?

1. the outer membrane similar to a sieve, 2. the outer membrane is permeable to all kinds of molecules, 3. the inner membrane is highly convoluted forming a series of in-foldings. All are correct about mitochondrial membrane.

Mitochondria are membrane-enclosed organelles distributed through the cytosol of most eukaryotic cells. Their main function is the conversion of the potential energy of food molecules into ATP. Mitochondria have an outer membrane which allows the passage of most small molecules and ions, and a highly folded inner membrane (cristae), which does not even allow the passage of small ions and so maintains a closed space within the cell. The electron transferring molecules of the respiratory chain (also called the electron transport chain) and the enzymes responsible for ATP synthesis are located in and on of this membrane, while the space inside (matrix) contains the enzymes of the TCA cycle. The enzyme systems primarily responsible for the release and subsequent oxidation of reducing equivalents are thus closely related so that the reduced coenzymes formed during catabolism (NADH and FADH) are available as substrates for respiration.

The electron transport chin is a sequence of complexes that accept electrons from electron donors such as NADH or succinate, shuttle these electrons across the mitochondrial membrane crating an electrical and chemical gradient, and through the proton driven chemistry of the ATP synthase, generate adenosine triphosphate (ATP).

Q93. What is co-enzyme?

An organic substance bound to an enzyme and essential for its activity is called coenzyme. A coenzyme (generally defined as cofactor) is an organic non-protein molecules thatis a functional part of an enzyme. It plays an accessory role in enzyme catalyzed processes often by acting as donor or acceptor of a substance involved in thereaction.ATP and NAD are common coenzymes.

Isozymes are isoforms (closely related variants) of enzymes. It forms the same function as another enzyme but having a different set of amino acids. Holoenzyme may refer either to the complete and operative form of an enzyme with multiple protein subunits to to the combination of an apoenzymes with its cofactor.

An apoenzyme is an enzyme without its cofactor, i.e. the protein molecules to which a coenzyme will bind to produce the holo-enzyme.

Q94. Role of mRNA in protein synthesis.

mRNA is a RNA molecule, usually 400 to 10,000 bases long, that serve as templates for protein synthesis (translation). In eukaryotes they have characteristics post-transcriptional modifications, the 5'-cap and poly A tail. The base sequence of mRNA transcript completely specifies the corresponding polypeptide amino acid sequence.

rRNA is a type of RNA that forms structural and functional components of ribosomes; binds to both mRNA and tRNA to ensure the correct order of amino a acids in a protein during translation.

tRNA is a class of RNA having structures with triplet nucleotide sequences that are complementary to the triplet nucleotide coding sequences of mRNA. The role of tRNA in protein synthesis is to bond with amino acids and transfer them to the ribosomes, where proteins are assembled according to the genetic code carried by mRNA.

cDNA is a single strand of DNA synthesized in the lab to complement the bases in a given stand of messenger RNA. Complementary DNA represents the parts of a gene that are expressed in a cell to produce a protein.

Q95. In a moss, the sporophyte, what is partially parasitic on the gametophyte?

Mosses are bryophytes, or non-vascular plants. Aside from lacking a vascular system, they have a gametophyte-dominant life cycle, i.e. the plant cells are haploid for most of its life cycle. Saprophytes (i.e., the diploid body) are short-lived and dependent on the gametophyte.

Q96. What is the difference between the conifers and grasses? Conifers differ from grasses in the formation of endosperms before fertilization.

Gymnosperm is a small group of plants which constitutes a subdivisions of spermatophyte (phanerogams). These are with naked seeds, no fruits or flowers, have two classes—cycadales (produce cones, e.g. cycads) and coniferales (e.g. conifers). In conifers the megaspores undergoes many free nuclear divisions to form a multi-cellular tissue which is termed as female prothallus or endosperm.

Q97. What is Plasmodium?

The thalloid body of a slime mould (Myxomycetes, fungi) is known as Plasmodium. Slime moulds are peculiar protists that normally take the form of amobae, but under certain conditions develop the sporangia of fungi. Slime moulds were originally considered fungi by mycologists and amobae by zoologists respectively classified as Myxomycetes (slime fungi) or mycetozoa (fungus animals).

The vegetative phase of the non-cellular slime moulds—the myxomycota has a plasmodial form.

Plasmodium is the cytoplasmic mass containing many nuclei but lacking interveining plasma membranes and therefore having no cellular subdivisions. The fusion of two haploid cells results in a diploid zygote which transforms into a developing Plasmodium. As the diploid nuclei divide, the Plasmodium grows larger and larger, slowly moving (creeping) along the forest floor and feeding like a giant amoeba.

Q98. Explain the marginal placentation in sweet pea.

Placentation refers to the pattern of attachment of ovules within the ovary on placenta. Placentation seen in sweet pea is marginal type in which ovary is unilocular and ovules are borne on margin.

AXILE—a separate locule for each carpel and the ovules attached to placentae in the middle where septa come together, e.g. solanum, citrus, etc.

Free-central: Ovules attached to a peg or stalk that arises from the ovary floor but which does not reach the roof; ovules usually few to many, e.g. in family Caryophyllaceae (Stellaria).

Basal: Ovary is unilocular and ovules a few or reduced to one and borne at the base of the ovary, e.g. compositae.

Q99. Explain cytoplasmic mode of inheritance (extrachromosomal inheritance).

In this mode of inheritance, we expect more maternal influence among the offspring. It is transmission of inherited characters via DNA of extranuclear organelles, viz. mitochondria and chloroplasts. Since in many species the cytoplasm of the fertilized egg contains no sperm cytoplasm, the genetics of cytoplasmic organelles is most often non-mendelian and often exclusively maternal. Thus, the mitochondrial of higher vertebrates are believed to be exclusively of maternal origin.

Q100. Comment on style of maize.

Long filamentous threads protruding at the end of a young cob of maize are called style.

In maize the male inflorescence occupies the terminal position on the main axis, whereas the female inflorescence (ear/cob) are borne on modified lateral branches in the axile of leaves. The ear producing branch, has short internodes and bears a female spike at its apex. Each spikelet has a pair of small membraneous glumes and two florets. The feathery styles of the female florets are long and emerge out of the cob. The tip of the style has two short unequal stigmas.

Q101. Explain the common structural feature of vessel elements and sieve tube elements.

Both these are enucleated in starting but disappears in the later stages. Sieve elements are anucleated living cells found in phloem. Nucleus is present in the beginning which disappears later. They are meant for the conduction of food materials and are of two types—sieve cells (with sieve plates on the latral wall and without companion cell) and sieve tubes (with sieve plates on tranverse or oblique wall and with companion cell). Xylem vessels (tracheae) are hollow, elongated cells with open ends and pitted walls. Cell walls are highly lignified. The vessels are formed by fusions arising through the dissolution of end walls. The vessels are characteristics of angiosperms and are water conducting in plants that possesses them. At maturity nucleus is absent in vessels.

Q102. What are diatoms/protists?

Diatoms are protists. Protista is a proposed kingdom of all unicellular organisms lacking a definite cellular arrangement. For example, algae, bacteria, fungi and diatoms. Diatoms are freshwater or marine unicellular golden brown algae.

Slime molds (e.g. physarum) are found on cool moist habitats on leaves or surface of soil, etc. The protists posses a membrane bound nucleus and typical eukaryotic characters. Trypanosoma, Noctulica, Monocystis and Giardia are all unicellular protists.

Protista is the kingdom of unicellular eukaryotes. The protists include hetrotrophs, autotrophs and some other organisms that can vary their nutritional mode depending on environmental conditions. Protists occur in fresh water, salt water, soil, and as symbionts within other organisms. They are complex and diverse group of organisms that are placed together simply because they all are single celled eukaryotes.

Q103. What are pneumatophores?

Pneumatophores are breathing or respiratory roots which are mainly found in mangroves or plants growing in saline swamps near the sea shore, for example, sonneratia.

Q104. Relation between the prokaryotes and history of life?

Most of the history of life concerns the evolution of prokaryotes. Prokaryotes existed alone on the surface of the earth for atleast 1.5 billion years ago. During this time all the metabolic cells developed.

Q105. What do you mean by Cleistogamous flowers?

Cleistogamous flowers are bisexual hyaline and self-fertilized plant's flowers which do not open at all. There is a group of plants which sets seeds without exposing sex organs. Such flowers are called cleistogamous. This is most efficient floral adaptation for promoting self-pollination.

Q106. What is FAD?

FAD derived from the vitamin riboflavin. FAD (flavin adenine dinucleotide) is prosthetic group of enzymes (generally flavoproteins). It is derived from vitamin riboflavin. FAD acts as a coenzyme in ETC.

Q107. Comment on "Little leaf or Brinzal".

It is disease caused by Mycoplasma like organisms (MLO). Mycoplasmas are very minute, unicellular, filterable and usually non-motile prokaryotic organisms.

Q108. What is concept of life form classes and biological spectrum?

Christen Raunkier in 1903 considered that it is the unfavorable environmental condition that really matters as it limits the growth form. On this basis he classified higher plants into five major life forms.

Q109. Describe the stomata in apophysis of capsule.

In apophysis of capsule, there are primitive type of stomata are found. In apophysis of capsule only stomatal pores (without guard cells) are reported. Such stomata are considered to be primitive because guard cells are absent or nor well developed.

Q110. Describe the Hill reaction (photolysis of water) in photosynthesis.

This process is used in reduction of NADP. I occurs in PS-II which release O_2. H^+ released in this process are used for reduction of NADP to $NADPH_2$, which in turn, helps in the formation of assimilatory power.

Q111. What is frameshift mutation?

It occurs when base is deleted or added and the result is non-functioning protein. It occurs when one or more nucleotides are either inserted or deleted from DNA. The result of such mutation can be a completely non-functional protein because the sequence of codons is altered.

Q112. What is calyptra?

A protective cap or hoodlike covering on the developing capsule in a mass or liverworts is known as calyptras. In liverworts, it covers the capsule very early in its development.

Q113. Describe the apiculture.

Apiculture or bee culture is the rearing of honey bees by culturists in different parts of the world to obtain honey and bees's bax on commercial scale. Both the products are used in medicines, cosmetics and various other industries. Now a days, bees venum is also collected on commercial scale for the treatment of snake bite, arthritis and many other diseases.

Q114. Describe the cleaning of marine oil slicks.

Pseudomonas putida is a bioengineered bacterium is utilized for cleaning of marine oil slicks. This bacterium is with many different plasmids to degrade the pollutants. If is developed by Dr. Anand Mohan Chakraborty and is known as superbug or oil eating bug or Chakraborty's superbug. Nowadays, this genetically engineered bacterium is utilized for cleaning of marine oil slicks.

Q115. Comment on solanin.

Solanin is a glycoalkaloids poison or natural nerve toxin produced in the green part of the potato. It is a bitter poisonous crystalline alkaloid, which helps the plant to defined against predators, insects, diseases, etc. Ingestion of it may cause vomiting, diarrhea, headache and even paralysis of central nervous system.

Q116. Describe the pollen grain of pinus.

In Pinus, the microspore nucleus divides by a preclinal wall and forms a very small prothallial cell and large central cell. The central cell cuts off a second protahllial cell and antheridial cell. The nucleus of the antheridial cell divides to form generative cell and tube cell. Thus, the pollen grain of Pinus is shed at *four cell stages* when it consists of two vegetative prothallial cells, a generative cell and a tube cell.

Q117. What is the basic difference between the fern and moss?

A fern (Pteridophytes) differs from a moss (bryophytes) in the independent of sporophyte while in moss the sporophyte is simpler than the gametophyte and remains attached to the parent gametophyte throughout its life. This sporophyte is dependent upon gametophyte partially or wholly for its nutrition.

Q118. Describe the two microbes useful in genetic engineering.

Microbes found to be very useful in genetic engineering are *E. coli* and *Agrobacterium tumifaciens. E. coli is a facultative gram negative, rod shaped, non-spore forming bacterium abundant in large intestine of man and other mammals.* Because of its simple growth requirements, ease of culture and non-pathogenicity, *E. coli* has become a favorite organism for research in biochemistry, molecular biology and genetics. Tens of thousands of distinct strains of *E. coli* are available for study. *A. tumifaciens* is the causative agent of crown gall, an important disease of many commercial crops such as raspberries. This disease has come to be recognized in recent years as being caused by a DNA plasmid (Ti plasmid) carried by bacterium and transferred to the plant cells. Following the discovery of the relationship between crown gall and Ti plasmid, this plasmid has come to be widely used in plant genetic engineering as a vector, novel plant genes being spliced into the plasmid sequence by gene manipulation and thus carried into the host plant cells. This offers the possibility of recombination between the novel sequence in the plasmid and the plant genomic DNA.

Q119. What you mean by ontogeny and phylogeny?

Evolutionary history of an organism is known as phylogeny. Or is the evolutionary relationship between organisms. The phylogeny of an organism reflects the evolutionary branch that lead to the organism. During the late 19th century, Ernest Haecal's recapitulation theory or biogenetic law was widely accepted. This theory was often expressed as ontogeny recapitulates phylogeny, i.e. the development of an organism exactly mirrors the evolutionary development of the species.

Ontogeny (also ontogenesis or morphogenesis) describes the origin and the development of an organism from the fertilized egg to its mature form. Ancestry refers to a person's ethnic origin or descent, roots' heritage or the place of birth of the person.

Paleontology is the study of the developing history of life on the earth, of ancient plants and animals based on the fossil record, evidence of their existence preserved in rocks. This includes the study of body fossils, tracks, burrows, cast off parts, fossilized faces (Caprolites) and chemical residues.

Q120. What do you mean by relation between the glutamic acid and Miller's experiment?

In Miller's experiment alanine, glycine and aspartic acid is formed. Glutamic acid was not found to be synthesized in Miller's experiment. The Miller-Urey experiment simulated hypothetical conditions present on the early earth and tested for the occurrence of chemical evolution (the Oparin and Haldane hypothesis stated that conditions on the primitive Earth favored chemical reactions tat synthesized organic compounds from inorganic precursors; the miller-Urey tested this hypothesis). The experiment is considered to be the classic experiment on the origin of life. It was conducted in 1953 at the University of Chicago.

The experiment used water methane, NH_3 and H_2. At the end of one week of continuous operation. Miller and Urey observed that as much as 10–15% of the carbon within the system was now in the form of organic compounds. As much as 10–15% of the carbon had formed amino acids like alanine and glycine (the most abundant).

Q121. What do you mean by hot spot?

The areas that are extremely rich n species diversity have high endemism and are under constant threat. Among the 25 hot spot in the world, two are found in India extending into neighboring countries (i) the Western Ghat-Sri Lanka, (ii) the Indo-Berman region (Eastern Himalayas).

These are particularly rich in floral wealth and endemism, not only in flowering plants but also in reptiles', amphibian's swallow-tailed butterflies and some animals.

Q122. What do you mean by endangered species?

An endangered species is a living organism in danger in danger of disappearing from the face of the earth if it is not protected and its situation is not improved. Red Panda and Bentinckia nicobarica are endangered organisms of India like the giant panda, Red panda (Ailurus fulgens) faces problems with human encroachment into its habitat. Bentinckia nicobarica is a fast growing, slender and elegant, pinnate palm from the Nicobar Islands in Andaman Sea North of Sumatra. One of its most distinctive features is it is very tall, pale green crownshaft. Bentinckia prefers a tropical climate and is a beautiful palm for parks and gardens.

Q123. What is the relation between the Mesozoic era, Gymnosperms and birds?

Jurassic period of Mesozoic era is characterized by gymnosperms as dominant plant and the appearance of first bird. Conifers, cycads and ferns were widespread. Angiosperms o appear for the first time. During the Jurassic, the highest life forms living in the seas were fish and marine reptiles (ichthyosaurs plesiosaurs and marine crocodiles). In the invertebrate world, several new groups appeared such as planktoinic foraminifera and calpionelids; rudists, belemnites; and branchiopods. On land, the archosaurian reptiles remain dominants.

During the late Jurassic the first birds evolved from small coelurosaur dinosaurs.

Q124. What do you mean by "Sickle cell anaemia" and malaria relation?

Sickle cell anaemia has not been eliminated from the African population because it provides immunity against malaria. It is characterized by the presence of large number of crescent or sickle shaped red blood cells in the blood. This anaemia is hereditary and chronic. The homozygous infants die immediately after birth. *Heterozygous persons suffer from anaemia because they have normal as well as sickle shaped erythrocytes.* These hetrozygous persons are not affected by malaria as the malaria parasite cannot survive on the sickle shaped erythrocytes.

Q125. What do you mean by living fossils?

Living fossils is a term for any living species (clade) of organism which closely similar species otherwise only known by its fossilized bones and has no close living relatives. These species have all survived major extinction events and gradually retain low taxonomic diversities. Archaeopteryx lithographica is widely accepted as the earliest and most primitive known bird. Archaeoptryx was a prehistoric reptile with limbs which similar the wings of today's birds. It is considered a primary link in the evolutionary process between the ancient reptiles and today's birds. Aracheoptyryx is a powerful piece of evidence that birds evolved from dinosaurs. Examples

1. Coelocanth
2. Coral (poly)
3. Crinoids
4. Crocodylia (crocodiles, gravials, alligators)
5. Horsehoe crab (Limulus polyphemus)
6. Laotian rock rat (Laonastes aenigmamus)
7. Lingula anatine (an inarticulate brachiopod)
8. Monotremes (the Platypus and Echidnas)
9. Neopilina galateae (Mollusca)
10. Nut clam (Ennucula superb)
11. Onychophorans (Peripatus)
12. Snout-nosed frog (Nasikabatrachus sahyadrensis)
13. Triops cancriformis (Crustacean)
14. Tuatara (Sphenodon)

Q126. What do you mean by α-amylase?

This enzyme stimulates germination of barley seeds. Barley seeds are associated with this enzyme bioassay of GA. During seed germination of barley, maize, etc. The aleurone layer of endosperm of seed produces enzymes like α amylase, protease ligase. Under the influence of phytohormone GA (through mRNA) these enzymes solubilizes the reserve foods present in the seeds.

Q127. What do you mean by Scutellum, coleoptiles and coleorhiza?

Most of the common monocotyledonous seeds are albuminous, e.g. maize, wheat, rice, etc. In all these plants, the pericarp and testa are fused and the grains of these plants are actually fruits. The bulk of the grain is filled with endosperm and the embryo occupies a comparatively small space on one side of the grain. On one side of the embryo is the shield-shaped structure called scutellum, the single cotyledons of monocots. Scutellum is in intimate contact with the endosperm and acting as an absorptive organ.

Coleoptiles is the first leaf of grass seedlings. It appears above the ground first as a sheath around the plumule and contains little chlorophyll. Coleorhizae is a protective layer of cells around the radical of grass seedlings.

Prophyll or bracteole is a leaf on a flower stalk.

Q128. What is P-protein?

The translocation of organic solutes in sieve tube members is supported by P-protein. P proteins (phloem proteins) are typical components found in large amounts in phloem sieve tubes. It appears as thin threads when seen in the electron microscope. They aggregate in fibrils, tubules, membrane-like or paracrystalline structures, lamellae, flakes and other structures. They have been isolated from the exudates

Q129. What do you mean by vernalization?

Treatment of seeds at low temperature under moist conditions to break its dormancy is called vernalization.

Stratification is a process where seeds are pretreated to stimulated winter conditions so that germination may occur. The degradation of the seed coat is called scarification, and this process permits water to pass through the seed coat so that the embryo can begin metabolism, elongate its radical, and germinate. Vernalization is the requirement of chilling period for initiation of floral reproductive growth. In most cereals optimum temperature for vernalization is 4°C. Receptive organs to chilling are the apical meristems. Some spring habit cereals may have their floral induction hastened by chilling. Chelation is a process by which certain micronutrients are treated to keep them readily available to a plant once they are introduced into the soil. Some of the micronutrients which would not remain available without chelation are copper, iron magnesium, manganese and zinc.

Q130. What is role of folic acid and cobalamin in alleviation of anaemia? Examination of blood of a person suspected of having anaemia, shows large, immature, nucleated erythrocytes without haemoglobin. Supplementing his diet with which of the following is likely to alleviate his symptoms?

Anaemia is a not a disease. It is symptoms of various diseases which may result from excessive blood loss, excessive blood destruction or decreased blood cell formation. In the anaemia due to decreased blood cell formation replacement therapy is done to combat the specific deficiency, e.g. iron vitamin B_{12}, folic acid, ascorbic acid. Folic acid is a water-soluble vitamin that is important in red blood cell formation protein metabolism growth and cell division. Folic acid has been shown to work together with vitamin B_6 and B_{12} to reduce blood levels of homocysteine, an amino cid that cobalamin or vitamin B_{12}, is a chemical compound that is needed for nerve cells and red blood cells and to make DNA. It is a water soluble organometallic compound with a trivalent cobalt ion bound inside a corrin ring.

Q131. What do you mean by oxygen consumption during photorespiration?

During the photorespiration, the oxygen consuming reactions occur in stroma of chloroplasts and peroxisomes. Photorespiration is an alternate pathway for Rubisco, the main enzyme of photosynthesis (specifically Calvin cycle). It is the energetically-wasteful substitution of oxygen for carbon dioxide in the dark reactions of photosynthesis, which occurs when plant stomata close and carbon dioxide concentration declines. It is light dependent respiration. It produces glycolic acid in chloroplasts in the light. The glycolic acid may be oxidized by enzyme of peroxisomes.

Q132. Farmers in a particular region were concerned that pre-mature yellowing of leaves of a pulse crop might cause decrease in the yield. Which treatment could be most beneficial to obtain maximum seed yield?

Among the minerals N is required by plants in maximum quantity. Pulse crop requires high doses of N. Its deficiency results in generalized chlorosis of older leaves along with other damages. The older leaves become yellow and fall down prematurely. These crops well respond to NPK fertilizers. Cytokinins are growth promoters. They play a major role in plan development and have been implicated in the control of apical dominance, fruit development, leaf development, root growth senescence stolon development cambial activity and dormancy.

Q133. Describe the role of secondary messengers in hormone action.

cGMP, cAMP and calcium are all second messengers.

Secondary messengers are low weight diffusible molecules that are used in signal transduction to relay signals within a cell. They are synthesized or released by specific enzymatic reactions usually as a result of an external signal that are received by a transmembrane receptor and processessed by other membrane associated proteins. These are three basic types of secondary messengers

1. Hydrophobic molecules: For example, diaaceyl glycerol (DAG), InsP3 (IP3), and phosphatidylinositols are membrane-associated and diffuse from the plasma membrane into the juxtamembrane space where they can reach and regulate membrane associated effectors proteins.

2. Hydrophilic molecules: They are water soluble molecules like cAMP, cGMP, and Ca^{+2}, that are located within the cytosol.

3. Gases: NO, CO, that can diffuse both through cytosol and across cellular membranes.

4. Mineral: Na is a mineral; an essential nutrient which helps to maintain blood volume regulates the balance of water in the cells and keeps nerves functioning.

Q134. Limit of BOD prescribed by Central Pollution Control Board for the discharge of industrial and municipal waste waters into natural surface waters, is <30 ppm.

The strength of organic waste materials of sewage is measured in terms of demand for dissolved oxygen required n oxidation of organic matter by microorganisms. This value is expressed in terms of mg of O_2 per litre of waste and termed as BOD. If the volume of BOD is below 1500 mg per litre, the sewage is termed as weak waste, if it is below 4000 mg per litre it is medium and above this value it is termed as strong waste.

Q135. What is exponential population growth?

Nearly all populations will tend to grow exponentially as long as there are resources available. Most populations have the potential to expand at an exponential rate, since reproduction is genrally a multiplicative process. The formula for exponential population growth is $dN/dt = rN$. In this equation d is the rate of change, N is the number of existing individuals, r is the intrinsic growth rate, t is the time, and dN/dt is the rate of change in population size.

Q136. What is monoculture?

Monoculture describes systems that have very low diversity. Monoculture is the destruction of a diverse ecosystem and replacement with a single species or crop. This is a common practice in modern agriculture where large acreage of crops are grown for sale to other regions or countries. This practice deplete the

soil and fruits and vegetables become more susceptible to pests and diseases than those grown in a diverse crop environ-ment, thus requiring larger amounts of chemical sprays.

It can lead to large scale crop failure as this single genetic variant or cultivar becomes susceptible to a disease. The Irish potato famine was caused by susceptibility to *phytophthora infestans*. The wine industry in Europe was devastated by susceptibility to Phylloxera. Each crop then had be replaced by a new cultivar imported from another country that had used a different genetic variant that was not susceptible to the pathogen.

Q137. What is the significance of ecological pyramid?

The tropic structure and function of an eco-system can be indicated by means of ecological pyramids. There are different types of ecological pyramids such as pyramid of (showing the number of individuals in producers and in different order of consumers in an ecosystem), pyramid of biomass (showing the weights or biomass of the members of the food chain) and pyramids of energy (showing the amount of total energy utilized by the organisms at each trophic level of the food chain). In each ecological pyramid, producer level forms the base and successive levels make up the apex. Fresh weight is not used in the ecological pyramids.

Q138. What do you mean by Montreal protocol?

Montreal protocol is an agreement signed in Montreal (Canada) by over 150 countries in 1987 in which signatory nations consented to limit production and consumption of ozone-damaging chemicals. The aim of the protocol was *to protect the ozone layer in the stratosphere* by decreasing and eventually eliminating the use of ozone-depleting substances like CFCs. It is regarded as on e of the most successful International treaties in modern history.

Q139. What do you mean by niche overlap?

Niche overlap indicates sharing of one or more resources between the two species. Any population (animals or plants) can survive and grow within a certain environmental limits which refer to its niche. The biological role played by a species in the environment is called a niche. Organisms/populations in the competition have a niche overlap of a scarce resource for which they compete. While owls and foxes may compete for a common food resource, there are alternate sources of food available. Niche overlap is said to be minimal.

Q140. What is neomycin?

It is an antibiotic drug. It is an aminoglucoside antibiotic isolated from Streptomyces and auctioned with a broad spectrum of bacteria. It acts against both gram positive and negative bacteria. It acts by *selective inhibition of protein synthesis on the 70S ribosome* (prokaryotic). In this respect it closely resembles *streptomycin which inhibits prokaryotic peptide chain initiation*, also induces *mRNA misreading* by interfering with the normal pairing between codon and anticodon.

Q141. What is photochemical smog?

Photochemical smog is a mixture of pollutants which includes particulates, nitrogen oxides, ozone, aldehydes. Peroxyetahnol nitrate (PAN), unreacted hydrocarbons, etc. The conditions needed for the formation of the smog included sunlight, hydrocarbons, nitrogen oxides and particulates which act as catalyst.

Photochemical smog can cause headaches, eye, nose and thorat irritations. It may cause the lung function impaired, coughing and wheezing. It can cause rubbers and fabrics to deteriorate. It can damage plants, leading to the lost of crops.

Q142. What do you mean by phenotype?

The phenotype of an individual organism is either its total physical appearance and constitution or a specific manifestation of a trait such as size, eye colour or behavior that varies between individuals. Phenotype is determined to some extent by genotype or by the identity of the alleles that an individual carries at one or more positions on the chromosomes. Many phenotypes are determined by multiple genes and influences by environmental factors. Thus, the identity of one or few known alleles does not always enable prediction of the phenotype.

Q143. What is hybrid vigour?

In maize, hybrid vigour is exploited by crossing of two inbred parental lines. The increase in the level of production traits due to crossing is called hybrid vigour. This term points at the vigour which is a real factor that can be seen by the naked eye, in comparison to pure breeding. Hybrid vigour is the occurrence where hybrid offspring perform better than the parents. It is also called as heterosis. Hybrid vigour has been commercially exploited in different commercial crops like maize, sorghum, bajra, tomato, sugar beet, petunia, zinnia and cucumbers. The hybrid vigours lost after few generations.

Q144. What is B-turn of DNA?

One turn of the helix in a B-form of DNA is approximately 3.4 nm. The DNA helix can assume one of three slightly different geometries, of which the B form described by James D. Watson and Francis Crick is believed to predominate in cells. **It is 2 nm wide** and extends 3.4 nm per 10 bp of sequence. This is also the approximate length of sequence in which the double helix makes one complete turn about its axis. This frequency of twist (helical) depends largely on stacking forces that each base exerts on its neighbors in the chain.

Q145. Describes the restriction endonuclease.

Restriction endonucleases are protein enzymes that recognize specific nucleotide sequences and cleave both strands of the DNA containing those sequences. Restrction endonucleases provide an anti-viral protection for bacteria by cleaving the DNA of invading bacteriophage. Restriction endonucleases were discovered during the experiments to determines the ability of a bacterio-phage (the name given to viruses that infect bacteria) to infect two different laboratory strains of *E. coli* called strain B and strain K. The enzyme makes two incisions, one through each of the phosphate backbones of the double helix without damaging the bases.

Q146. What do you mean by Clostridium?

Clostridium is a large genus of gram +ve bacteria, belonging to the firmicutes. They are obligate anaerobes capable of producing Endospores. Individual cells are rod shaped which gives them their name, from Greek Kloster or spindle.

Foodborne disease caused by *Clostridium botulinum* is referred to as botulism (a muscle paralyzing disease). It is caused by the inges-tion of a neurotoxin (botulin) produced by the micro-organisms in the food. Botulin is the most potent known toxin, blocking nerve function and leading to respiratory and musculoskeletal paralysis. The toxic can be destroyed by normal cooking procedures. Symptoms of botulism include weakness, fatigue and dizziness, followed by blurred vision and progressive difficulty in speaking and swallowing. Weaking of the respiratory muscles is also observed and death may occur due to respiratory failure.

There are four main species responsible for disease in humans:

C. botulinum—an organisms producing a toxin in food that cause botulisms.

C. difficile—which can overgrow other bacteria in the gut during antibiotic therapy causing pseudomembranous coitus?

C. perfringens—causing a wide range of symptoms from food poisoning to gas gan-grene.

C. teani—the causative agent of tetanus (lockjaw).

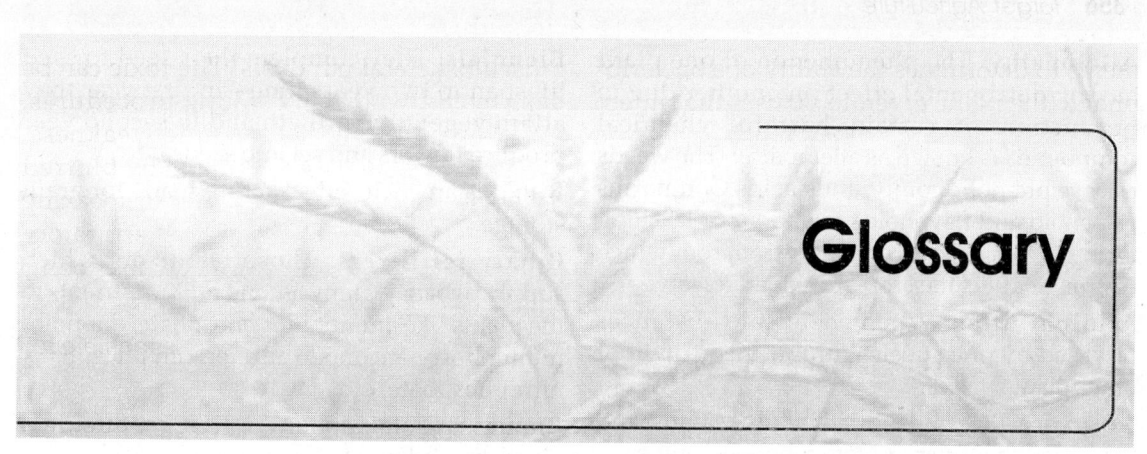

Glossary

"A" Line: This is a male sterile parent used for production of hybrid seeds as in case of maize.

Abnormal seedlings: It refers to those seedlings which fail to develop into healthy and normal plants even after providing all the ideal conditions needed for growth and development of plant.

Absorption: The attraction of compounds to surface of a solid.

Acedophiles: The weeds which grow well chracterically in acidic soils having a pH between 4.5 to 6.6 like *Cyanodon dactylon, Digitaria sanguinalis, Peridium spp.,* etc.

Achene: A small dry hard one-chambered and one-seeded indehiscent fruit-like buckwheat, lettuce, etc. is called an achene.

Acid equivalent: It is the active ingredient or the actual chemical in a commercial material which is responsible for required chemical reaction.

Acid forming fertilizers: Those commercial fertilizers which have acidic effect n soil like ammonium sulphate, urea, etc. are said to be acid forming fertilizers.

Acid soils: Soils having acidic reaction of pH below 7 due to leaching of soluble salts from the soil are called as acidic soils. The acidity increases with decrease in soil pH and becomes extremely acidic then pH falls below 4.5.

Active acidity: The activity of H ions in the aqueous phase of soil which is measured and expressed as a pH value.

Additive effect: It refers to the total effect of a combination which is equal to the sum of the effects of the components taken independently.

Additives: A materials technically called filler or conditioner which is added to fertilizers for making the bulk and improving the physical conditions of the fertilizers. These materials either have a negligible quantity or on nutrient at all.

Adhesion: It refers to molecular attraction which holds the surfaces of two substances in contact that is water and sand particle.

Aggressivity: It indicates the relationship between two or more intercrops grown together as whether they are non-competitive and if they are competitive then which of the two is dominant and which dominated species is. Thus a beneficial and most suitable combination can found out.

Agro forestry: It may be defined as a suitable land management system that increases overall yield of land. This includes yield of crop, forest plants and /or animals on the same unit of land.

Agronomy: A specialization of agriculture concerned with a theory and practice of field crop production and scientific management of soil fertility.

Alkali soils: The soils saturated with soluble salts due to salinization and akalinization processes which normally have a pH of more than 7 (except degraded alkali soils which have a pH of less than 7) and such soils need acid or acid forming substances for their reclamation.

Allelopathy: The phenomenon of one plant having detrimental effect on another due to production of certain harmful chemical compounds is known as allelopathy. The weeds release phenolic compounds acids Coumarins terpenoid and flavonoids as vapour or leaching form the foliage or as exudates from root which restrict or affect the crop growth adversely.

Alloinhibition: When chemical substances released by one species inhibit the growth of other plant species.

Aman rice. Rice transported in July–August and harvested in winter or November–December.

Annuals: Plants which complete their seed to seed life cycle within year.

Antagonistic effect: In this the total effect of a combination is smaller than the effect of that active component applied alone and the process is known as antagonism.

Ammonia volatilization: In soils with low cation exchange capacity and high pH associated with high concentration of ammonia and high temperature ammonia gets lost in vapour form which is technically called a ammonia volatilization.

"B" Line: It is the female fertile parent used for production of hybrid seeds which is also called maintainer line.

Backcross: It is a process of crossing a hybrid back to one of its parent whose characters are lacking in the hybrid.

Band application: refers to the application of chemical on only a narrow strip between the crops rows which is mostly done in case of total killer or non-selective herbicides.

Bar: A unit of pressure equal to one million dynes per square centimeter.

Basic slag: A byproduct of a steel industry obtained from phosphate iron ore which contains about 6–18% acid soluble phosphoric acid.

Basophiles: Weeds which grow well on alkali soils of pH between 7 to 8.5 are called as basophiles such as alkali grass (Puccinallia spp.) and quack grass (*Agropyron repens).*

Biennial: These are such plants which remain in vegetative growth phase in the first year and produce flowers fruits and seeds in the second year after they die.

Biennials: They complete their seed to seed lifespan in two years time—in first year they attain vegetative growth and in second year produce flowers and set into seeds.

Bin: It is an enclosed structure made for grain storage.

Binary fertilizers: Those fertilizers which supply two major (any among NPK) nutrients to the plants like ammonium phosphate, diammonium phosphate, mono ammonium phosphate, nitrophosphate, etc.

Biomasss: Total amount of living matter in a given area is known as biomass.

Biotype: A population of individual's identical genetic constitution which may be homo or heterozygous in nature.

Blanket application: refers to the application of herbicide over the entire soil surface of weed infested area which is done mostly in case of selecting herbicides.

Bolt: formation of an elongated floral stalk in biennial plants during second season of growth are termed as bolts.

Bone meal: Organic phosphatic fertilizers made up of powered bones either raw or steamed of animals. The raw bone meal contains small quantity of N about 2% but the steamed has only phosphate.

Border rows: These are outer a few crop rows that are used to isolate the main plot. In case of seed plots this are the rows of male sterile parents but in case of commercial crops the same seed materials is added for raising the border rows. In case of experimental plots the border rows are used to eliminate the effect of treatments applied in adjacent plots so that the main plot is not affected.

Boro rice: The rice crops planted in Nov–Dec and harvested in May–June is known as boro rice.

Breeder seed: It is genetically purest seed stock obtained from breeding devices where all the genetic characters are kept under full control and it becomes the source of multiplication for foundation and then certified seeds.

Buffer: A mixture of two solutions that is the solution of weak aid and its salts formed by a strong base or a weak base and its salt formed by a strong acid. For example, a mixed solution of acetic acid and sodium acetate. A buffer has a definite pH which remains more or less constant for a long time.

Bulbs: It is an enlarged fleshy thick underground part of the stem surrounded by a mass of scaly leaves and produces roots at the base as in case of onion, garlic, etc.

Capillary water: This is the water retained in the fine soil capillaries after seepage and percolation processes are over. It is available form of water for all biological activities and is held at 0.33 atmosphere, i.e. between field capacity and hygroscopic coefficient.

Carbon nitrogen ratio: It is zonal of arid regions which usually contain accumulations of lime at some point in the profile.

Caryopsis: The fruit which develops from a single carpel with pericarp united to seeds (in case of cereals and grasses) is called caryopsis.

Cash crops: These are such crops which may be sold directly from the field without processing like vegetables, potatoes, potato, maize, cobs, etc.

Catch crops: These are such crops which are grown to catch the season when a main crop of the season fails due to flood, frost drought, etc. The crops belonging to this group are quick growing and of short duration like Torai-9 (T-9), black gram, etc. The growing season of these crops is between last few weeks of preceding crop season and first few weeks of the succeeding season. Thus, they have practically no specific growing season.

Catena: A sequence of the soils of about the same age, derived from similar parent material, and occurring under similar climatic conditions but having different characteristics due to variations in drainage relief.

Cation exchange capacity (CEC): It refers to the amount of a cation species bound at pH 7.0 on a colloid or the exchange surface. Central Seed Laboratory: It is the seed testing laboratory established at IARI, New Delhi, under sub-Section (1) and Section 4 of Indian Seed Act, 1966.

Certified seed: It is the progeny of breeders/foundation or registered seed produced under strict supervision so as to maintain satisfactory genetic purity and identify to meet the minimum seed standard specifications of Indian Seed Act, 1966.

Check: These are local standard varities or strains used for comparison of newly evolved crop varities so that superior varieties may be identified and released for their commercial cultivations.

Chelating substances: Chelates are those microorganism complexes which are soluble and readily absorbed by plants. These compounds are not converted to insoluble forms when applied into the soil. The metallic ions, commercially cheated are iron copper, zinc and manganese. The most important and useful compounds are agriculture in cheated forms are: ethylene diaminetetra acetic acid (EDTA), diethylenetetra-amine pentetic acid (DTPA), cyclohexane diaminetetra-acetic acid (CDTA) and ethylene diaminedihydroxyphenoxy acetic acid (EDDHA).

Chemical fixation of nutrient: The fixation and / or reversion of available plant nutrient into unavailable forms due to the soil reaction are called as chemical fixation of plant nutrients.

Collurium: A deposit of rock fragments and soil material accumulated at the base of steep slopes as a result of gravitational action.

Competition coefficient: This indicates relative crowing in a mixed crop which not be harmful to each other.

Competitive crops: When production of one crop is increased at the cost of production of another crop then the cropping system is called competitive cropping. In this system the crop which gives higher yield is called as dominating and the other are called as dominated crop.

Compost: A mass of rotten organic matter made from farm wastes and the process of making compost is called as composting.

Cover crop: Close growing crops which covers the soil surface and protect it from erosion, weed growth and evaporation loss of water.

Consumptive use of water: It is the amount of water required by plants to meet their need for water in transpiration and growth. It is also referred as evapotranspiration.

Creeping perennials: They spread through their lateral extensions of the creeping above ground stems (rhizomes) either by roots or by seeds like *Convovulus arvensis*.

Cropping system: This shows the system in which various crops are grown together on a piece of land like mixed, inter or relay cropping etc.

Cropping Scheme: It is a theoretical chart showing different crop rotations to be included on a farm or plot during a given period of time.

Crop rotation: It is process of growing different types of crops one after the other with a view of getting maximum profit without losing soil fertility. It is always mentioned for a specific piece of land during a fixed period of time. This is also called sequential cropping.

Deflocculate: To separate the individual components of compound particles by chemical and /or physical means.

Defoliant: A chemical or any method of treatment causing falling of leave or abscise but fruits remain attached is technically called defoliant.

Desiccate: The process of drying of any object so as the moisture falls below and helps in determining the presence of caryopsis within the glumes of germanous seeds.

Diara lands: these are the areas which are located in river basins that get submerged during the rainy season and the soil is used for crop production only during rabi and/or and sometimes during zaid season. It is also known as Kachhar Lands. Dolomite: A naturally occurring material which is composed of calcium and Mg carbonate widely used as liming materials and fertilizers or soil conditioner.

Dry farming: It is a practice of raising successful and profitable rainfed crops in areas which receive an annual rainfall of 50 cm or less. Sometimes it is also called dry land agriculture.

Dry land agriculture: Scientific management of soil and crops under dry lands without irrigation is called dry land agriculture.

Dry land crop: It refers to all such crops which is drought resistant and can complete their life cycle without irrigation in areas which receive an annual rainfall of 50 cm or less.

Dry lands: These are areas which use to receive an annual rainfall of 50 cm or less and there is no irrigation facility from raising crops.

Duoculture: Practice of growing only two types of crops in a year.

Ear: An ear is large, dense or heavy spike or spike like inflorescence in gramineous plants especially in cereals like wheat barley rice, etc.

Ecofallow system: It is also called chemical fallow system which is a type of reduced tillage practice made possible by herbicides which kill weeds of fallow areas.

Eksali planting of sugarcane: It is a common in North India and takes about one year or 12 months for harvesting. The plating is done in January–February.

Eluviation: It is a part of the soil formation processes in which removal of materials in solution, colloidal solution, or even in suspension form in vertical direction forced by downward movement of water form one horizon to another.

Emulsifiable concentrates: These materials from stable emulsion when dilated with water, become suitable for spraying over the plant surfaces. Emulsifiable materials at the same active ingredient are better than suspensions. These are two types like concentrated emulsions which are prepared mechanically by dispersing an aqueous solution of the herbicides in a water-immiscible solvent by means of a colloid mill. Another type of emulsifiable material is miscible of which consists of herbicides solvents and emulsifier.

Enforced dormancy: Change in environment conditions especially temperature restrict germination of the polar nuclei of the enforced dormancy.

Epicotyl: A part of the embryo which produces shoot or the above ground part of the plant.

Epigeal: A type of germination in which the cotyledons appear above the soil surface.

Evaporation: Loss of water in vapour form either from soil or water surface subjected due to high atmospheric temperature associated with lower relative humidity. The evaporation loss of water is measured by open pan evaporimeter.

The evaporation can be checked by mulching or by use of anti-transpirants like plastic emulsion.

Farm forestry: Refers to the practice of growing forest trees on the wastelands of the farm like around the building, all along the fences or the roads with a view to utilize the wastelands in a purposeful manner.

Fertilizer legislation: This refers to the law and regulations formulated in 1957 by the GOI to be enforced with a view to regulate the quality of fertilizers sold to the consumers. According to the legislation each bag must be labeled with fertilizer grade and the material should have at least labeled quantity of nutrients in it.

Fertilizer application: It refers to the method in which fertilizers are applied to the soil for meeting the nutrient requirement of the crop plants.

Fertilizer placements: Application of commercial fertilizers at a specific place and depth in the soil is called as fertilizer placement. This method of fertilizer application reduces the loss of nutrients discourages weed growth and thereby a relatively lesser quantity of material is required.

Fertilizer requirement: It is the quantity of certain plant nutrient elements needed in addition to the amount supplied by the soil, to boost the growth and development to an optimum level.

Fallow: A cultivable land which is not cultivated during the year/season or cropland left idle during the growing season, sometimes called summer fallow. The practice of leaving land either uncropped or weed free.

Farming system: A combination of farm enterprises, viz. cropping system, livestock poultry fisheries, forestry and the means available to the farmer to raise them for increasing profitability.

Fauna and flora: Cousins to the Adams family......Oops wrong definition, fauna is the organism that live in and near the soil, from ants, snails and slugs to fungal mycelia, mycorhizae and algae. Flora is the plants living in soil.

Field capacity: The rate of downward movement of water has substantially decreased usually 1–3 days after rain or irrigation. It is expressed as a mass or volume fraction of soil water or a depth of water per metre of soil or mm m^{-1}.

Flame weeding: The practice of using heat to kill weeds. Typically a flame torch is used to sear weed species in a manner that does not affect the crop species or at a time or at a time when the crop species is not present.

FAO: A UNO founded in 1945 that collects and disseminates information about world agriculture. It also provides technical assistance to developing countries in agricultural production and distribution, food processessing, nutrition fisheries and forestry. The FAO global information early warning system monitors for famine conditions in regions of risk.

Food security: Access by all people at all times to enough food for an active healthy life. Food security at a minimum includes the ready availability of nutritionally adequate and safe food, and an assured ability to acquire acceptable foods in socially acceptable ways that is without aging to resort to emergency food supplies scavenging stealing or other coping strategies. The world Food Summit, convened in Rome in November 1996 by the Food and Agriculture Organization of the United Nations, estimated that 800 million people worldwide do not have enough food to maintain their basic nutritional needs. Representative of the more than 180 nations attending the summit pledged to work to reduce this number by half by number later than 2015. Causes of food insecurity may include poverty, civil conflict, governmental corruption, environmental degradation and natural disasters.

Forage: Vegetative matter, fresh or preserved that is gathered and fed to animals as roughage includes alfalfa hay corn silage and other hay crops.

Foundation seed: The second link in the certified seed chain produced from breeder seed and handled in such a way as to ensure genetic identity and varietal purity.

Furrow: A slot or depression created by the passage of planter tines into which the seed in placed. Furrows are also created by cultivation.

Furrow irrigation: A method of applying irrigation water to fields or orchards by small ditches or furrows which held drop the supply ditch.

Genome: The full set of chromosomes of an individual or all the genetic material in the chromosomes of a particular organism.

Genotype: The total of all genes/genetic structure of any gene.

Geographical Information System (GIS): Computerized systems used to compile retrieve analyze and display spatially referenced data. Farming activities that utilize GIS typically include harvesting fertilizing pest control seeding and irrigation. Use of GIS is called precision farming.

Ginning percentage: This refers to the lint percentage in seed cotton and higher percentage would be an indication of superior plant type.

Gleaning: Collection unharvested crops from fields or obtaining unused agricultural products from farmer's processor or retailers usually for distribution to food banks and charitable feeding organization.

Global Position System (GPS): A network of satellite that can be used by ground based units to precisely determine their location by latitude and longitude. GPS is part of the infrastructure required to operate geographic information systems that are used to practice precision farming.

Glyphosate: Translocated non-selective herbicide used in conservation farming systems.

Grasslands: it is the landscape dominated by grasses.

Gravitational water: Water that moves freely in response to gravity and drains out of the soil mainly through macrospores not available for plants.

Green leaf manure: Leaves twigs and plants collected from other fields and border rows and incorporated into the field, e. g. Glyricidia, Calotropis and Tephrosia.

Green manure: A cover crop grown to help maintain soil organic matter and increase N availability. Legumes often used because they have rhizobial bacteria living in their root nodules that are able to fix N from the air and add it to the soil, e.g. daincha and sun hemp.

Gross domestic product (GDP): The total final output of goods and services produced within a country in a year by resident and non-resident regardless of allocation of domestic and foreign claims.

Grow out test: Performed to determine the genuineness of seed as to species or variety of freedom from seedborne infection.

Guard crops: Growing secondary crops for protection, around the main crop in the field. For example, dhaincha around the sugarcane or safflower around the gram crop.

Gully erosion: The erosion process whereby water accumulates and often recurs in narrow channels and over short periods removes the soil from this narrow area to considerable depth often defined in terms of channel to deep to easily repair wit ordinary farm equipment.

Genetic shift: Changes n the genetic character of plant type when grown under unfavorable or non-adoptive conditions.

Glacial drift: Rock debris that has been transported by glaciers and subsequently deposited either from rice or from melting water.

Gley soil: Soil developed under conditions of poor drainage resulting into grew or mottle colour due to reduction in Fe and other elements.

Herbicidal selectivity: It refers to the phenomena wherein a chemical kills the target plant species in a mixed plant population without harming or only slightly affecting the companion plants.

Herbicidal carriers: These are the inert materials which have no herbicidal properties and do not react with active ingredient when mixed together. The most commonly used carriers are pearlite expanded vermiculites and diatomaceous earth clay mineral (bentonite, illite, kaolinite and attapulgite). Expanded shale, pyrophillite and finally ground parts have liquid retention capacities ranging from 1:10 to 1:20. Limestone, gypsum sand and fertilizers materials have also been used as carriers however their liquid retention capacities are less than 5%.

Herbicide drift: It is part of the herbicide which is carried away by the blowing wind.

Heterogeneity: It refers to the variation in seed; plant characters, etc. and the plants which are not truly bred for specific hereditary characters are termed as heterozygous.

High Yielding Variety Programmes (HYVP): Programme started for multiplication of seeds of high yielding varieties so that they may reach to the common growers and the yields can be increased.

Hybrid: Offspring's produced the result of controlled crossing between two parents only.

Hybrid vigour: When the offspring's become more vigorous than the parents then they are said to be hybrid vigour.

Hydraulic conductivity: The circuit of after movement from the atmosphere to the earth and returns to the atmosphere through various stages or processes as precipitation, interception, runoff infiltration percolation, storage and evaporation and transpiration.

Hay: A grass feed to cattle dry after green cut.

Inbred line: A relatively true breeding strain obtained from at least five successive generations of regulated self-fertilization or back crossing to a recurrent parent.

Inherent/Primary dormancy: It is due to the genetic background of plant species and is characterized by rudimentary embryos physiologically immature embryos resulting from inactive enzymes, hard coat which prevents embryo expansion, impermeable seed coat preventing entry of water and gases, and presence of excessive inhibitors.

Idiotype: Plan type in which morphological and physiological characteristics are ideally suited to achieve high production potential and yield reliability.

Illite: It is type of clay mineral having 2:1 silica: alumina layers—non-expanding type.

Immobilization: This occurs when inorganic ions are assimilated by soil organisms and are bound organically again or it is the conversion of element from inorganic to organic combination in microbial or plant tissues.

Immobilization of nitrogen: The conversion of N to an organic form in microbial or plant tissue which is unavailable for uptake or use by plants.

Indicator plant: A plant which reflects either by its presence or character of growth, specific growing conditions like deficiency of plant nutrient, soil moisture stress etc.

Integrated crop management: An agriculture management system that integrates all controllable agricultural production factors for long term sustained productivity, profitability and ecological soundness.

Integrated farming system: Integration of various agricultural enterprises like cropping, animal husbandry, fisheries, forestry, etc. A judicious mix of any one or more with cropping complements the cropping enterprises.

Integrated nutrient management: A nutrient management system which involves application of organic, inorganic and biofertilizers for maximum productivity and soil fertility.

Integrated pest management: Pest management systems which incorporate a range of practice to keep pests below economic injury levels. IPM includes chemical, cultural, biological, physical, and quarantine controls. A strategy of pest management that focuses on long-term prevention of pests or their damage through a combination of techniques such as biological control, habitat manipulation, modification of cultural practices and use of resistant varieties. Pesticides are used only after monitoring indicates they are needed according to established guidelines and treatments are made with the goal of removing on the target organism. Pest control material is selected and applied in a manner that minimizes risks to human health beneficial and non-target organism and the environment.

Integrated weed management: A weed management system that uses all suitable control methods like mechanical, chemical and biological methods in a compatible manner to reduce weed population and maintain at levels below those causing injury.

Intensive cropping: Growing of more number of crops in unit area in unit time so as to intensify the cropping intensity in a farm.

Intercropping: The growing of more than one species on the same pieces of land at the same time or it is growing of two or more crops simultaneously with definite row arrangements, e.g. groundnuts + red gram 6:1 ratio.

Intensive farming: A system of farming with the aim to produce the maximum number of crops in a year with a high yield from the land available and to maintain a high stocking rate of livestock.

Invasive species: A non-native species whose introduction causes, or is likely to cause economic or environmental harm or harm to human health. An invasive species can be a plant, animal or any other biologically viable species that enters an ecosystem beyond its native range.

Kaolinite: Hydrous, non-expanding clay mineral containing aluminosilicates and having 1:1 crystal structure. It is a type of clay mineral having 1:1 silica alumina layer present in red soil.

Kernel: Edible seed portion of rice, maize, sorghum, etc.

KVK—Krishi Vigyan Kendra: The scheme of KVK was launched by the ICAR during 1976 as an innovative institution for vocational training of agriculture and allied areas. The KVK aims at practical training to practicing farmers, farm women as well as school drop-outs who wish to acquire training for self-employment.

La Nin a: A cylindrical disruption in the ocean atmosphere system characteristically by unusually cold ocean temperatures in the equatorial pacific. These ocean conditions are just the opposite of El Nin o, in Latin La Nin a means temperature fall.

Laterite: An iron rich sub soil layer found in some highly weathered humid tropical soils formed by laterization process.

Lateritic soil: Soils of various textures containing (10–50%) ironstone gravel in the surface layers or within the profile.

Leaching: the process by which chemicals (fertilizers, pesticides, manure, etc.) are dissolved and transported through the soil by layer; the washing out or flushing of soluble substances from an insoluble one. Gardeners leach soil with water when they want to remove excess salts. In high rainfall rainwater leaches both and harmful substances from the soil .Or process of removing soluble material by the process of water through the soil.

Legume inoculation: Coating legume seed with a specific culture of Rhizobium bacteria to promote effective nodulation and enhances N fixing.

Light soil: A soil that is easy to work implements in or easy to cultivate as it lacks cohesive such as sandy and sandy loam soil.

Linters: The short fibres that remain on cottonseed after ginning. They are used mainly for biting matters stuffing and as a source of cellulose.

Liquid fertilizers: Commercial fertilizers in liquid form/Ex. Anhydrous ammonia, aqueous solution of N, they are applied to the soils through irrigation water known as fertigation.

Loam: Soil that is rich in organic material, does not compact easily and drains well after watering; an ideal garden soil; a mix of sand, silt and clay. A type of soil texture wit good water holding capacity and drainage suitable for cultivation of variety of loam contains 7–27% clay, 28–50% silt and less than 52% sand.

Low input sustainable agricultures (LISA): Alternative methods of farming that reduce the application of purchased inputs such as fertilizers, pesticides and herbicides. The goals of thse alternative practices are to diminish environmental hazards while maintain or increasing farm profits and productivity. Methods include crop rotations and mechanical cultivations to control weeds; integrated pets management strategies such as introducing harmless can use; application of livestock manures, municipal sludge and compost of fertilizers; and over seeding or legumes into maturing fields of grain crops or as post season cover crops to curtail soil erosion.

Lysimeter: A device for measuring percolation and leaching loses from a column of soil under controlled conditions.

Low land rice: Rice grown after wet land preparation of field or rice grown wit.

Maize Sheller: Equipment used to remove maize grain from cobs.

Malnutrition: A human condition that results from an excess, imbalance or deficit of nutrient.

Mariculture: The form of aquaculture where fish shellfish or aquatic plants are cultured in a salt water environment.

Manual: Pertaining to or performed with hand.

Meadow: An area covered with fine stemmed forage plants grown for hay.

Methane: A gas created by anaerobic decomposition of organic compounds, natural gas is composed mostly of methane. Methane is called a greenhouse gas, agricultural wastes, especially animal waste are a major source of methane release to the atmosphere.

Methanol: A liquid alcohol formed in the destructive distillation of wood or made synthetically and used especially as an alternative fuel, gasoline additive, solvent, an anti-freeze or a denaturant for ethyl alcohol. A is a gasoline additive it lowers the carbon monoxide emissions but increases hydrocarbon emission.

Mitscherlich law of diminishing returns (1909): This law states that increase in growth with each successive addition of the limiting element s progressively smaller and the response is curvilinear.

Monitoring: Regular inspection of crops to identify insect and disease activity in order to determine whether control measure are necessary, monitoring is an integral part of integrated pest management.

Mulch: Any plant residue, byproduct or other suitable material applied to the soil surface to conserve moisture, control erosion suppress weed growth, moderate soil temperatures improves soil condition or assist in establishing cover. Example includes bark wood chips, sawdust, straw or plastic.

Mulching: Practice of covering the soil surface with materials like plant residues straw leaves or plastic film of reduce evaporation, restrict weed growth and maintain the soil temperature.

Multi-tier cropping: Cultivation of two or more crops of different heights simultaneously.

Node: Slightly enlarged portion of the stem where leaves buds or root arise.

Nomadism: Continual movement of humans and animals with no fixed settlement generally in search of food and water.

Non-selective herbicide: An herbicide which is non-specific and controls most vegetation to which it is applied. Any plant which is deemed harmful, damaging or causes a loss in production or intrinsic values may be declared noxious. Its control will be determined by relevant legislation. Glyphosate is an example of a non-selective herbicide.

Noxious weed: Undersirable plants that infest either land or water resources and cause phycisally and economic damage or invasive plants that cause economic loss and harm the environment. Noxious weeds choke out crops, destroy range and pasture lands, clog waterways affect human and animal health, and/or threaten native plant communities.

Nutrient Management Plan: An assessment of how nutrient are utilized on a farm includes a determination of how much fertilizer is appropriate to apply on crops for a livestock operation, this includes an assessment of manure production collection storage and utilization.

Oasis effect: It is the exchange of heat between a growing crop and hot air whereby air over the crop is cooled.

Olericulture: A branch of horticulture which deals with the cultivation of vegetables.

Organic farming (organic agriculture): 1. A system of farming which excludes the use of synthetic fertilizers, pesticides, growth regulators and feed additives and relay upon crop rotation, crop residues, animal manures, legumes, green manures and biological pest and disease control, 2. referring to a type of agriculture that promotes the use of renewable resources and management of biological cycles to enhance biological diversity, without the use of genetically modified organisms, or synthetic pesticides, herbicides or fertilizers. organic livestock production promotes concern for animal welfare, without the use of synthetic foodstuffs, growth hormones or antibiotics.

Organic matter (SOM): Term used to identify the organic components in soil, including undecayed and undecaying plant and animal tissues. Sometimes, the word humus is used synonymously with regard to soil.

Over-story: the larger and taller trees that occupy a forest area and shade the young trees, brush, grass, forbs etc that grows below them.

Organophosphates: Insecticides that contain P, C and H. They are cholinesterase inhibitors; some are highly acutely toxic but they usually are not persistent in the environment, parathion is an important example.

Orthophotography: Aerial photographs that more precisely show the features of the landscape, including those that might be important for agriculture such as slope or size of gullies because they are corrected for distribution caused by tilt, curvature and ground relief.

Oxalate: Oxalic acid found in many plants casing gastroenteritis or hypocalcaemia of low blood calcium levels in livestock. Buffer grass and other pastures may contain oxalic acid. Horses are particularly susceptible to oxalic poisoning.

Ozone: It is important by two reasons (1) one as a naturally occurring screen of harmful radiation in the outer atmosphere (stratosphere), (2) as a component of polluting smog formed from emission resulting from human activities (urban smog). In the stratosphere 7 to 10 miles above the earth, naturally occurring ozone acts to shield the earth from harmful radiation. In the 1970 and 1980s, it was discovered that emissions of certain chemicals catalyze destruction of stratospheric ozone, allowing more radiation to reach the earth surface.

Pan: A pan is a well-defined layer forming in the soil, there are two common types; a plough pan, which builds up in field just below plough depth and an iron pan which forms naturally by iron oxide accumulations deposited in acid gley soils. Pan can impede the passage of water through the soil which in an agricultural context can lead to problems uncorrected.

Panicle: A group of flowers borne at unequal distance from the central system.

Papain: Latex exudates from unripe papaya fruit, having proteolytic activities.

ppm: It expresses weight units per million (10 lakh) weight units of solution or grams per million grams soil. 1 ppm = 1 milligram substance in one liter of water.

Pastureland: Land used mainly for the production of domesticated forage plants for livestock. Rotation pasture or cropland under winter cover crops is not included in this definition.

Peat: Peat is a type of soil formed in water-lodged conditions from incompletely decomposed plant material. Peat forms in wetlands or peat lands also commonly called bogs, moors, mires, swamps and fens.

Percolation: It is the downward movement of water through soil layers due to gravitational pull. It is also called infiltration or leaching of water.

Permaculture: a term coined in 1978 by bill Malison, Australian ecologist and one of his students, David Holmgren. It stands for permanent agriculture and it is a land use concept that refers to the design of ecological human habitat and food production system with goal of harmonious integration of human dwellings, annual and perennial plants, animals, soil and water, into stable, productive communities.

PF: The logarithm of the soil moisture tension expressed in centimeter height of a water column.

pH: An expression of the intensity of the basic or acidic condition of a liquid or of soil; the logarithmic scale ranges from 0 to 14, where 0 is the most acid, 7 is neutral, and above 7 is alkaline. Natural waters usually have a pH between 6.5 and 8.5. Plants have differing tolerance for acidity and alkalinity or it is negative of hydrogen concentration in the soil solution without units.

Physical dormancy: Dormancy due to impermeable seed coat.

Plough sole placement (fertilizers): In plugging process, placement of fertilizer in continuous band on the bottom of a furrow.

Plumule: In seed, the second part of axis covered inside by cotyledons.

Pomology: The science or study of growing fruits.

Precision farming: Farmers use global positioning technology (GPS) involving satellite and sensors on the ground and intensive information management tools to understand variations in resource conditions within fields. They use this information to more precisely apply fertilizers and other inputs and to more accuracy predict crop yields.

Pre-emergence: Herbicide; herbicides applied before the emergence of weeds, e.g. pendime-thalin etc.

Presswheel: Device used on plantars to assist in covering the furrow, improving seed to soil contact and enhancing emergence.

Productivity: The relationship between the quantity of inputs employed and the quantity of output produced. An increase in productivity means that more outputs can be produced from the same inputs or that the same outputs are produced with fewer inputs. Both single-factor and multifactor indexes are used to measure productivity. Single factor productivity indexes measure the output per unit of one input at the same time other inputs may be changing. Multifactor productivity indexes consider all productive resources as a whole, netting out the effects of substitution among inputs. Crop yield per acre output per work out, and livestock production per breeding animal are all single factor productivity indicators. The total output per unit of input index is multifactor measure.

Projected yield: The number of bushels (kg/quintal) per acre or ha that, based on current weather estimates and other factors.

Budding: It is the plugging operation carried out in stagnated water conditions to create an impervious layer below the plough pan.

Quarantine: A restraint on importation of certain animals or plants from areas where pests are endemic.

Rainbow revolution: Taking together all revolutions to go ahead came in agriculture is called rainbow revolution.

Rainfall: It is a form of precipitation and usually recorded with rain gauges in an interval of 24 hours and expressed in mm.

Rainfed farming: Growing of field crops entirely with rain water received during crop season usually more than 1150 mm.

Rainy day: The amount of rainfall received in a day is more than 2.5 mm and above.

Rationing: One of the important methods of intensive cropping, allowing the stubbles of the original crop to strike again after harvesting and to raise another crop.

Reclamation: The process of rehabilitation disturbed lands, or converting unproductive lands into the productive uses. The term is also used for the process of recycling or reusing water.

Rejuvenation of pasture: Renovation of rundown pasture by undertaking wed control, residing, fertilizing or other practice to improve productivity.

Remote sensing: The act of detecting objects when the sensor is not in direct contact; commonly refers to using aerial photographs to observe conditions on the earth surface. In agriculture, this technology can be used to determine what plants are being grown and their condition.

Residual herbicide: Herbicide which is soil acting and controls germinating weeds over an extended period.

Rhizome: Underground stems formed by many plants as a means of vegetative spread.

Rill erosion: An erosion process where numerous small channels, typically a few cm deep are formed.

Riparian zone: The transition area between an aquatic ecosystem and the adjacent upland area. These zones are identified by soil characteristics or plant communities and include the wet areas in and near streams, ponds, lakes, springs and other surface waters.

River basin: The total area or catchment drained by a river and its tributaries.

Rotational grazing: Pasturing system that allows short periods of heavy use, followed by recovery period, it allows the forage to be used more fully and effectively.

Rouging: Removing or cutting of individual plant from the seed plot which deviates in significant manner from the plants of the variety being multiplied. This is step in the maintenance of purity in an established variety.

Ruminant: Animal having a stomach with four compartments rumen, reticulum, stomch, and abo-smosum their digestive process is more complex than that of animals having a true stomach. Ruminant include cattle, sheep and goats as well as deer bison, buffalo, camels and giraffes.

Saturated zone: A portion of the profile in which all large pores are filled with water.

Sciophytes: Plants which are shade loving and requires less light intensity.

Sediment: Suspended soil particles which are carried away in runoff water and are deposited further down the slope, the soil material, both mineral and organic, that is in suspension, is being transported or has been moved from its site of origin by erosion.

Seed: Sexually or asexually propagated planting material which is used seedling or planting.

Seed bank: A facility used for the preservation and dissemination of seed, particularly varieties that are not in commercial use and that may be threatened with extinction.

Seed-firming wheel: A term given to a specific type of presswheel which presses the seed lightly into the bottom of the furrow rather than compacting soil on top of the seed.

Seed inoculation: Application of a specific Rhizobium culture to legume seeds to induce nodulation and n fixation.

Seepage: It is the lateral movement of water in the soil, water course, etc.

Selective herbicide: An herbicide which controls a specific group of plants but is inactive against others, i.e. grass herbicide.

Semiarid tropics: A term given to a tropical area in which there is a distinct dry period which severally limits plant growth.

Sheet erosion: The removal of a thin, relatively uniform layer of soil from the land surface caused by runoff or the removal of a relatively uniform thin layer of soil from the land surface by rainfall and largely un-channel surface runoff.

Sheltbelt: A plant barrier of trees, shrubs, or other approved perennial vegetating designed to reduce wind erosion, also called a windbreak.

Shifting cultivation: This is the old practice of cutting and clearing of forts for cultivation crops as long as the soils having fertility.

Silage: A mixture of raw chopped materials such as field corn, sorghum, grass or clover that is converted into winter feed for livestock through a process of fermentation.

Siliviculture: A branch of forestry dealing with the development and care of forests.

Soil colloids: The colloids fraction of soil primarily made up of inorganic material (clay) with varying amounts often organic colloids.

Soil compaction: Reduction in the specific volume of soil by means of mechanical manipulation.

Soil conditioners: An organic material like humus or compost that helps soil absorbs water, build a bacterial community and take up mineral nutrients or the chemicals which are added to maintain physical condition of the soil. For example, polyvinylites, polyacrylates, lignin derivatives, silicates, etc.

Sticker: These are corrosive salts which wash the wax coating from plant canopy and act as adhesive for nutrient solution, soap solution, surf, etc. are such materials.

Straight fertilizers: Commercial fertilizers containing only one nutrient as superphosphate, ammonium sulphate, calcium ammonium nitrate, etc.

Sucker: An off-shoot that develops from an underground adventitious but located on the juncture place of root and shoot.

Synergistic effect: When the total effect of a combination is greater or more prolonged than the sum of the effects of the two taken independently it is known as synergistic effect.

Tassel: The staminate inflorescence appearing on the apex of a maize plant.

Teast: Soils containing high proportion of Mo are said to become teast.

Tempering: It is a process of bringing grains or other products to desired moisture or temperature processing.

Terrace: A raised, more or less level or horizontal strip of earth usually constructed on or nearly on a contour and designed to make the land suitable for tillage and to prevent accelerated erosion.

Tile drain: Drains provided with pipe made of burnt clay, concrete or similar material, in shorter lengths, horizontally lay with open joints to collar and carry excess water from the soil.

Tillage: Mechanical manipulation of soil in order to bring about required physical conditions of the soil.

Tilth: It is the physical conditions of the soil which would be an ideal for tillage, sowing of seeds, seedling emergence and better root penetration.

Topography: The configuration of the soil surface including slope exposure position in the landscape and position from the surface is called as topography.

Truck gardening: Growing perishable crops at far of places from market and sending them every morning to the market through own transport like truck tractor etc.

Tz: A chemical (tetrozolium chloride) used to test viability of seeds.

Variety: An individual with distinctive differentiating characters, viz. physiological or morphological known for a specific purposes like agriculture, forestry or horticulture, etc.

Trace elements: Also called micronutrient. Elements required by plants in minute quantities but essential for healthy plant growth.

Transitional period: The period between the dry season and the onset of the wet season when sporadic storms cause spoilage of dry feed.

Trap crop: A crop that is planted to lure pest insects away from an economic crop. Trap cropping is the practice of growing a sacrifice crop to encourage insect pest which may later be chemically or physically controlled.

Tropics: Geographical regions between the tropics of capricon and cancer.

Truthful seed: Seeds free of physical purity and good germination.

Ultisols: Soils that are low in bases and have sub surface horizons of alluvial clay accumulations. They are usually moist, but during the warm season of the year some are dry part of the time.

Unit cost: The average cost to produce a single item. The total cost divided by the number of items produced.

Universal soil loss equation: A formula used to estimate erosion rates by considering climate soils and topographic conditions at a site, as well as nay degree to which the use and management of the soil reduce erosion.

Value added agriculture: A concept that has gained currency in the small farm policy debate in response to the concern that the farm value of the consumer food dollar continues to decrease.

Value-added product: In general, product that have increased in value because of processessing; such products include wheat flour and soyabean oil.

Virgin soil: A soil that has not been significantly disturbed from this natural environment.

Volunteer plants: Unwanted plants growing from seed that remains on the field from a previous crop.

Water holding capacity: Ability of a soil to retain water. The amount of water a soil can hold and make available for plant use. Sands and clays have low and high water holding capacities, respectively.

Water logging: Soil saturated with free water which may get accumulated on the ground surface or saturated with water. Conditions detrimental to plant growth.

Water meter: A device installed in a pipe under pressure for measuring and registering the quantity of water passing through it.

Water potential: The capability of soil water to do work compared with free water. The water potential at the surface of free water is taken as zero.

Water table: The upper level of a saturated zone in an aquifer below the soil surface. The surface at which tat which ground water has settled in the ground and below which fissures and pores in the rock strata or soil are saturated with water.

Water use efficiency: It is the amount of dry matter produced from a given quantum of water and expressed in kg/ha mm.

Weaning: Removal of young mammals from the source of milk.

Weed: Generally herbaceous plants or shrub not valued for use or plants growing where not wanted or unwanted plant hindering crop growth and yield.

Wetlands: Areas that are regularly wet or flood; areas with a water table within the root zone or standing at or above the land surface for at least part of the growing season. These areas are host to a prevalence of water loving plants.

Wind break: A living barrier that usually includes several rows of trees, and perhaps shrubs located upwind of a farm, field, feedlot or other area and intended to reduce wind velocities.

Winnower: A machine with one or two sieves and fan using air stream across falling grain to separate seed and chaff.

Winnowing: The process of separation of grains from the mixture of grain and chaff or straw or bhusa.

World Bank: A multilateral economic development institution established in 1945 to extend loans and technical assistance for development projects in developing countries. It is formally referred to as the international bank for reconstruction and development.

World Trade Organization (WTO): The international organization established by the uruguay round of multilateral trade negotiations to oversee implementation of the general agreement on tariffs and trade and agreements arising from the Uruguay round, including the Uruguay round agreement on agriculture.

Yield maximization: Agronomic practices adopted to get highest possible crop production per unit area per unit time without considering either the cost of production or net returns.

Zero grazing: Where forage is cut and transported to livestock.

Zero tillage: The extreme form of conservation tillage where opening the soil, placing seed and fertilizers and covering the soil is carried out in a single operation.

List of Research Institute

1. Central Arid Zone Research Institute (CAZRI) Jodhpur-Ber and Datepalm.
2. Central Institute for Arid Horticulture (CIAH), Beechwal, Sri Gangasagar Road, Bikaner (Rajasthan)-334006.
3. Central Institute for sub-tropical Horticulture (CISH), Rehman Dhera, Lucknow, U.P.
4. Central Research Institute for Dryland Agriculture (CRIDA), Hyderabad (AP).
5. Central Fruit Research Station, Hyderabad (AP).
6. Cashew Research Centre, Ratnagiri (Maharashtra).
7. Cashew Research Center, Mangalore.
8. Central Salt Research Institute for Jojobe (Gujarat).
9. Central Horticulture Experiment Station, Godhra (Gujarat).
10. Date palm Research Station, Kutch (Gujarat).
11. Date palm Research Center, Abohar (Punjab).
12. Fruit Research Station for Custard Apple and Fig (Pune).
13. Fruit Research Station (Chhattisgarh).
14. Fruit Research Station for Mango, Guava, Lichee (Saharanpur).
15. Custard Apple Research Station, Beed, Maharashtra.

Some Important Facts

Compression wood: Gymnosperms (monocotyledons) reaction wood develops on lower side of branches.

Tension wood: In angiosperms (dicotyledonous) it develops from the upper side of branches.

Cyanate carbamylate: It is an analog of CO_2 act as restrict O_2 affinity to Hb.

Polarity of hormones: Transport of GA-nonpolar, transport of auxins—polar, GA transported through phloem according to a flow pattern which is similar to those of carbohydrates and other organic solutes. GA found in both phloem and xylem. However, GA transport may also occur in xylem due to its lateral movement between two vascular tissues, i.e. xylem and phloem. GA is not translocated in plants as free molecules but probably in their bound form, i.e. Gibberellin-glucosides.

List of All Revolutions

Black revolution: Petroleum production.

Blue revolution: Fish production.

Brown revolution: Leather/non-conventional (India)/Cocoa production.

Golden fibre revolution: Jute production.

Golden revolution: Fruits and overall horti-culture development/honey production.

Green revolution: Grains production.

Grey revolution: Fertilizers production.

Pink revolution: Onion production/Pharma-ceutical (India)/Prawn production

Red revolution: Meat and tomato production.

Round revolution: Potato production.

Silver fibre revolution: Cotton production.

Silver revolution: Egg/poultry production.

White revolution (in India: Operation flood): Milky or dairy production.

Yellow revolution: Oil seed production.

Evergreen revolution: Overall development of agriculture.

Hindi names of most famous plants:

Hiptage: Madhavi lata

Moringa: Horseradish tree

Boerhaavia: Hog weed (Punarnava)

Ecballium: Mediterranean Vine

Alistonia: Shaitan Ki Jhar, Scholar tree, Devil tree, Blackboard tree (Apocyanaceae—Oleander family)

Antirrhinum: Dog flower family, Scrophula-riaceae

Vegetables and Crops of India

1. Solanaceous vegetables:

Common Names	Botanical Names
Potato	Solanum tuberosum
Tomato	Lycopersicon lycopersicum
Brinjal (egg plant)	Solanum melongena
Chillies	Capsicum frutescens
Sweet pepper	Capsicum annuna

2. Cole crops

Cauliflower	Brassica oleracea var. botrytis (phool gobi)
Cabbage	Brassica oleracea var. capitata (pata gobi)
Knol-khol	Brassica oleracea var. caulorapa (gat gobi)
Chinese cabbage	Brassica chinensis

3. Root crops

Radish	Raphanus sativus
Turnip	Brassica rapa
Beet rod	Beta vulgaris
Carrot	Daucus carota

4. Bulb crops

Onion	Allium cepa
Garlic	Allium sativum

5. Leguminous vegetables

Cowpea	Vigna unguiculata
French Bean	Phaseolus vulgaris
Broad bean	Vicia faba
Soybean	Glycine max
Pea	Pisum sativum

6. Cucurbitaceous vegetable fruits

Cucumber	Cucumis sativus (kera)
Muskmelon	Citrullus melo (Kerboza)
Water melon	Citrullus lunatus (Terboza)
Long melon	Cucumis melo var.utilissimus (Kakri)
Round melon	Praecitrullus fistulosus pang (Tinda)
Bottle gourd	Lengenoria siccraria (Loki)
Bittergourd	Momordlea charantia (Karela)
Spong gourd	Luffa cylindrical Roen (Torai)
Pointed gourd	Trichosanthes dioica Roxb (Perbal)
Snakegourd	Benincasa hispida
Red or pumpkin gourd	Cucurbita moschata poir (Kashipal)

7. Leafy vegetables

Spinach beet	Beta vulgaric var.bengalensis (Palak)
Spinach	Spincia oleracea (Bilayati palak)
Fenugreek	Trigonella foenumgraceum (Methi)
Coriander	Coriandrum sativum (Dhania)

Spearmint	*Mentha viridis (Pudina)*	**8. Tuber crops**	
Mustard	*Brassica napus (Sarso)*	Sweet potato	*Ipomea batatas (Sakerkand)*
Bathua	*Chenopodium album (Bathua)*	Calocasia	*Colocasia esculenta (Aruai)*
Lettuce	*Loctuca sativa (Salad)*	Gaint taro	*Alocasia spp (Banda)*
Purslane	*Portulaca oleracea (Kulfa)*	Elephant foot	*Amorphophallus campanulatus (jamikand)*
		Okra/Lady figner	*Abelmoschus esculentus (Bhindi)*

Common Weeds of the Locality

Scientific Name	English/ Common name	Family	Ontogeny	Season
Amaranthus viridis	Chaulai or Wilr amaranthus	Amaranthceae	Annual	Kharif
Abutilon indica	Vegetable chauli	Amaranthaceae	Annual	Kharif
Avena fatua	Wild oat	Poaceae	Annual	Rabi
Boerhavia diffusa	Biskhapra/Hog weed	Nyctaginaceae	Perennial	All
Cyperus rotundus/ esculentus	Yellow nut grass	Cyperaceae	Perennial	All
Calotropis procera	Aak	Caselpinaceae	Perennial	All
Catharanthus oxycantha	Kusum/wild safflower	Compositae	Annual	Rabi
C. murale	Goose grass/kurtua	Chenopodium	Annual	Rabi
Clitoria tematia	Butterfly pea	Leguminosae	Perennial	All
Commelina benghalensis	Tropical spiderwort	Commelinaceae	Annual	Kharif
Cyanodon dactylon	Stargrass/Bermuda grass	Poaceae	Perennial	All
Cyprus rotundus	Nut grass	Cyperaceae	Perennial	All
C. bulbosus	Bulb grass	Cyperaceae	Perennial	All
Dactylotenim aegyptium	Crowfoot grass	Poaceae	Perennial	All
Digitalis sanguinalis	Crab grass	Poaceae	Annual	Kharif
Echinocloa crusgalli	Barnyard grass	Poaceae	Annual	Kharif
Euphorbia macrophylla	Red spurage (Choti dudhi)	Euphorbiaceae	Perennial	All
Echhornia crasipes	Water hyacinth	Pontederiaceae	Perennial	All
E. colonum	Watergrass/Jungle rice	Poaceae	Annual	Kharif
Euphorbia hirta	Red spurage (Badi dudhi)	Euphorbiaceae	Perennial	All
Impmea pestigridis	Morning glory	Convolvulaceae	Perennial	All

Launia aesplanifolia	Wild gaubi	Compositae	Biennial	All
Melilotus alba	Sweet clover (Safed senji)	Leguminoceae	Annual	Rabi
M. indica	Sweet clover (senji)	Leguminoceae	Annual	Rabi
Ocimum canum	Hoary basil	Lablatae	Perennial	All
Opuntia dillenil	Prickl Pear (NAGPHANI)	Cactaceae	Perennial	All
Orobancahe aegyptiaca	Broom rape	Orobanchaceae	Annual	Rabi
Parthenium hysterophorous	Congress grass	Composiate	Perennial	All
Phalaria minor	Canary grass/ Gehunsa	Poaceae	Annual	Rabi
Phyllanthus niruri	Hazardana	Euphorbiaceae	Ephemeral	Kharif
Physalis minima	Groundcherry	Solanaceae	Annual	Kharif
Pluchea lanceolata	Arrow wood	Leguminosaceae	Perennial	All
Propis juliflora	Mesquite/Kikar babul	Leguminosaceae	Perennial	All
Rumex acetosella	Red/Sorrel	Polygonaceae	Annual	Rabi
Striga asiatica	Witch weed	Scrophularaceae	Annual	Kharif
Saccharum spontaneoum	Tiger grass	Poaceae	Perennial	All
Sesbania aculeata	Dhaincha	Leguminosae	Annual	Rabi
Solanum nigrum	Dreadly night shade	Solanaceae	Annual	Kharif
S. halepense	Johonsen grass	Poaceae	Perennial	All
Striga densiflora	Witch weed	Scrophulariaceae	Annual	Kharif
Trianthema monogyna	Carpet weed	Aizoaceae	Annual	Rabi
Tribulus terrestis	Puncture vine/ Gokhroo	Zygophyllaceae	Annual	Kharif
Vigna umbellata	Rice bean	Leguminosae	Perennial	All
Withania somnifera	Ashwagandha	Solanaceae	Perennial	All
Xanthemium strumarium	Cocklebur/Bur weed	Compositae	Annual	Kharif
Zizyphus nummularia	Jherberry	Rhamnaceae	Perennial	All
Zizyphus rotunudifolia	Wild ber	Rhamnaceae	Perennial	All
Azolla pinnata	Watervelvet/Azolla	Azollaceae	Perennial	All
Pistia stratiots	Waterlettuce	Araceae	Perennial	All
Nymphea stellata	Waterlily/ neelkamal	Nymphaceae	Perennial	All
Nelumbo nucifera	Sacred lotus/Kamal	Nymphaceae	Perennial	All
Ipomea aquitica	Water spinach	Convulaceae	Perennial	All
Hydrilla verticellata	Hydrilla	Hydrocharitaceae	Perennial	All
Utricularia vulgaris	Bladerwort	Lentibulariaceae	Perennial	All

Vallisnaria spiralis	Tapeweed/Eelgrass	Hydrochariataceae	Perennial	All
Phragmites karka	Common weed/ Marsh grass	Poaceae	Perennial	All
Salvinia molesta	Water fern	Salviniaceae	Poaceae	All
Anabaena spiroides	Waterbroom forming alage	Nostocaceae	Perennial	All
Rhizoclonium spp.	Kai	Chlorophyceae	Perennial	All
Char vulgaris	Stone wort/ Muskgrass	Chlorophyceae	Perennial	All

Chromosome Number (2n) in Some Plant Species

Plant Species	Chromosome Number	Animal Species	Chromosome Number (2n)
Arabidopsis thaliana	10	Common fruit fly	8
Maize	20	Dove	16
Durum wheat	28	Earthworm	36
Bread wheat	42	Domestic cat	38
Wild tobacco	24	Lab mouse	40
Cultivated tobacco	48	Rabbit	44
Barley	14	Hare	46
		Elephant	56
		Donkey	62
		Dog	78
		Guinea pig	64
		Snail	24
		Tibetan fox	36
		Domestic pig	38
		Cow	60
		Horse	64
		Chicken	39
		Silkworm	28
		Gorilla/Chimpanzee/ Cultivated Tobacco	4